W9-AQV-797

THE
ENDURING DEBATE

CLASSIC AND CONTEMPORARY READINGS
IN AMERICAN POLITICS

Fifth Edition

THE
ENDURING DEBATE

CLASSIC AND CONTEMPORARY READINGS
IN AMERICAN POLITICS

Fifth Edition

Edited by
David T. Canon
John J. Coleman
Kenneth R. Mayer

W. W. NORTON & COMPANY
NEW YORK   LONDON

W. W. Norton & Company has been independent since its founding in 1923, when William Warder Norton and Mary D. Herter Norton first published lectures delivered at the People's Institute, the adult education division of New York City's Cooper Union. The Nortons soon expanded their program beyond the Institute, publishing books by celebrated academics from America and abroad. By mid-century, the two major pillars of Norton's publishing program—trade books and college texts—were firmly established. In the 1950s, the Norton family transferred control of the company to its employees, and today—with a staff of four hundred and a comparable number of trade, college, and professional titles published each year—W. W. Norton & Company stands as the largest and oldest publishing house owned wholly by its employees.

Copyright © 2008, 2006, 2003, 2000, 1997 by W. W. Norton & Company, Inc.

All rights reserved
Printed in the United States of America
Fifth Edition

Editor: Aaron Javsicas
Managing Editor, College: Marian Johnson
Associate Managing Editor, College: Kim Yi
Director of Manufacturing, College: Roy Tedoff
Composition by PennSet
Manufacturing by Courier, Stoughton

The Acknowledgments pages serve as a continuation of the copyright page.

ISBN: 978-0-393-93217-1

W. W. Norton & Company, Inc., 500 Fifth Avenue, New York, N.Y. 10110
www.wwnorton.com

W. W. Norton & Company Ltd., Castle House,
75/76 Wells Street, London W1T 3QT

1 2 3 4 5 6 7 8 9 0

Contents

PART II   Institutions

PART III   Political Behavior: Participation

PART IV   Public Policy

APPENDIX

PART I

The Constitutional System

CHAPTER 1

Political Culture

1

From *The Liberal Tradition in America: An Interpretation of American Political Thought Since the Revolution*

Louis Hartz

Political culture refers to the orientation of citizens toward the political system and toward themselves as actors in it. This includes the basic values, beliefs, attitudes, predispositions, and expectations that citizens bring to political life. Given the great diversity of the American population, one might expect a similarly diverse array of thought within political culture, with rival sets of political values challenging each other. In his classic and influential work, Louis Hartz argues that in fact there is broad agreement in the United States around a set of political beliefs. Hartz refers to this as the "liberal tradition"; the terms "liberal consensus" and "American Creed" have also been used by other authors. "Liberal" here means a focus on the individual and minimizing government intervention in daily life. Within the liberal tradition, the values of equality, private property, liberty, individualism, protection of religious freedom, and democracy are especially powerful. There is certainly debate over what these terms mean or how much to emphasize one versus another, and these clashes drive party politics, but we do not see successful political movements in the United States that directly challenge these values. On the contrary, most movements seek to show how their beliefs and principles are highly consistent with these basic American values. Hartz argues that it is the nature of American history that led to this unusual uniformity. Not having had a feudal stage, Americans also did not witness the revolutionary stages and ideologies that challenged feudalism in Europe. As Hartz puts it, "no feudalism, no socialism." This historical path does present some problems, in Hartz's view. Americans view liberalism as natural, as obvious. Indeed, to some extent, we are hardly aware of it as an ideology because it has been unchallenged. To Hartz, writing in the 1950s, this sometimes blinds Americans to policy alternatives, heightens our fears of social disharmony and "foreign" ideas, and makes it hard for Americans to understand other societies where a liberal tradition is not so dominant.

1. America and Europe

The analysis which this book contains is based on what might be called the storybook truth about American history: that America was settled by men who fled from the feudal and clerical oppressions of the Old World. If there is anything in this view, as old as the national folklore itself, then the outstanding thing about the American community in Western history ought to be the non-existence of those oppressions, or since the reaction against them was in the broadest sense liberal, that the American community is a liberal community. We are confronted * * * with * * * America skipping the feudal stage of history * * *. "Feudalism" refers technically to the institutions of the medieval era, and it is well known that aspects of the decadent feudalism of the later period, such as primogeniture, entail, and quitrents, were present in America even in the eighteenth century. "Liberalism" is an even vaguer term, clouded as it is by all sorts of modern social reform connotations, and even when one insists on using it in the classic Lockian sense, as I shall insist here, there are aspects of our original life in the Puritan colonies and the South which hardly fit its meaning.[1] But these are the liabilities of any large generalization, danger points but not insuperable barriers. What in the end is more interesting is the curious failure of American historians, after repeating endlessly that America was grounded in escape from the European past, to interpret our history in the light of that fact. * * *

*   *   *

2. "Natural Liberalism": The Frame of Mind

One of the central characteristics of a nonfeudal society is that it lacks a genuine revolutionary tradition, the tradition which in Europe has been linked with the Puritan and French revolutions: that it is "born free," as Tocqueville said. And this being the case, it lacks also a tradition of reaction * * *. Its liberalism is * * * a "natural" phenomenon. But the matter is curiously broader than this, for a society which begins with Locke, and thus transforms him, stays with Locke, by virtue of an absolute and irrational attachment it develops for him, and becomes as indifferent to the challenge of socialism in the later era as it was unfamiliar with the heritage of feudalism in the earlier one. It has within it, as it were, a kind of self-completing mechanism, which insures the universality of the liberal idea. * * * It is not accidental that America which has uniquely lacked a feudal tradition has uniquely lacked also a socialist tradition. The hidden origin of socialist thought everywhere in the West is to be found in the feudal ethos. * * *

America has presented the world with the peculiar phenomenon, not of a frustrated middle class, but of a *"frustrated aristocracy"*—of men, Aristotelian-like, trying to break out of the egalitarian confines of middle-class life but suffering guilt and failure in the process. The South before the Civil War is the case par excellence of this, though New England of course exemplifies it also. * * * The Southerners were thrown into fantastic contradictions by their iconoclastic conservatism, by what I have called the "Reactionary Enlightenment," and after the Civil War for good historical reasons they fell quickly into oblivion. The South, as John Crowe Ransom has said, has been the part of America closest to Old World Europe, but it has never really been Europe. It has been an alien child in a liberal family, tortured and confused, driven to a fantasy life which, instead of disproving the power of Locke in America, portrays more poignantly than anything else the tyranny he has had.

* * * Here we have one of the great and neglected relationships in American history: the common fecklessness of the Southern "feudalists" and the modern socialists. It is not accidental, but something rooted in the logic of all of Western history, that they should fail alike to leave a dent in the American liberal intelligence. * * * Socialism arises not only to fight capitalism but remnants of feudalism itself, so that the failure of the Southern [feudalists], in addition to setting the pattern for the failure of the later Marxists, robbed them in the process of a normal ground for growth. * * *

Surely, then, it is a remarkable force: this fixed, dogmatic liberalism of a liberal way of life. It is the secret root from which have sprung many of the most puzzling of American cultural phenomena. Take the unusual power of the Supreme Court and the cult of constitution worship on which it rests. Federal factors apart, judicial review as it has worked in America would be inconceivable without the national acceptance of the Lockian creed, ultimately enshrined in the Constitution, since the removal of high policy to the realm of adjudication implies a prior recognition of the principles to be legally interpreted. * * * If in England a marvelous organic cohesion has held together the feudal, liberal, and socialist ideas, it would still be unthinkable there that the largest issues of public policy should be put before nine Talmudic judges examining a single text. But this is merely another way of saying that law has flourished on the corpse of philosophy in America, for the settlement of the ultimate moral question is the end of speculation upon it. Pragmatism, interestingly enough America's great contribution to the philosophic tradition, does not alter this, since it feeds itself on the Lockian settlement. It is only when you take your ethics for granted that all problems emerge as problems of technique. Not that this is a bar in America to institutional innovations of highly non-Lockian kind. Indeed, as the New Deal shows, when you simply "solve problems" on the basis of a submerged and absolute liberal faith, you can depart from Locke with a kind of inventive freedom that European Liberal reformers and even European socialists, dominated by ideological systems, cannot duplicate. * * *

Here is a Lockian doctrine which in the West as a whole is the symbol of rationalism, yet in America the devotion to it has been so irrational that it has not even been recognized for what it is: liberalism. There has never been a "liberal movement" or a real "liberal party" in America: we have only had the American Way of Life, a nationalist articulation of Locke which usually does not know that Locke himself is involved; and we did not even get that until after the Civil War when the Whigs of the nation, deserting the Hamiltonian tradition, saw the capital that could be made out of it. This is why even critics who have noticed America's moral unity have usually missed its substance. Ironically, "liberalism" is a stranger in the land of its greatest realization and fulfillment. But this is not all. Here is a doctrine which everywhere in the West has been a glorious symbol of individual liberty, yet in America its compulsive power has been so great that it has posed a threat to liberty itself. * * *

I believe that this is the basic ethical problem of a liberal society: not the danger of the majority which has been its conscious fear, but the danger of unanimity, which has slumbered unconsciously behind it: the "tyranny of opinion" that Tocqueville saw unfolding as even the pathetic social distinctions of the Federalist era collapsed before his eyes. But in recent times this manifestation of irrational Lockianism, or of "Americanism," to use a favorite term of the American Legion, * * * has neither slumbered nor been unconscious. It has been very much awake in a red scare hysteria which no other nation in the West has really been able to understand. And this suggests a very significant principle: that when a liberal community faces military and ideological pressure from without it transforms eccentricity into sin, and the irritating figure of the bourgeois gossip flowers into the frightening figure of an A. Mitchell Palmer or a Senator McCarthy. * * *

The decisive domestic issue of our time may well lie in the counter resources a liberal society can muster against this deep and unwritten tyrannical compulsion it contains. They exist. Given the individualist nature of the Lockian doctrine, there is always a logical impulse within it to transcend the very conformitarian spirit it breeds in a Lockian society * * *.

But the most powerful force working to shatter the American absolutism is, paradoxically enough, the very international involvement which tensifies it. This involvement is complex in its implications. If in the context of the Russian Revolution it elicits a domestic redscare, in the context of diplomacy it elicits an impulse to impose Locke everywhere. * * * Thus to say that world politics shatters "Americanism" at the moment it intensifies it is to say a lot: it is to say that the basic horizons of the nation both at home and abroad are drastically widened by it. * * * [W]hen has the nation appreciated more keenly the limits of its own cultural pattern as applied to the rest of the world? * * * [W]hen has the meaning of civil liberties been more ardently understood than now? * * * The outcome of the battle between intensified "Americanism" and new enlightenment is still an open question.

*   *   *

3. The Dynamics of a Liberal Society

So far I have spoken of natural liberalism as a psychological whole, embracing the nation and inspiring unanimous decisions. We must not assume, however, that this is to obscure or to minimize the nature of the internal conflicts which have characterized American political life. * * * What we learn from the concept of a liberal society, lacking feudalism and therefore socialism and governed by an irrational Lockianism, is that the domestic struggles of such a society have all been projected with the setting of Western liberal alignments. * * *

*   *   *

That society has been a triumph for the liberal idea, but we must not assume that this ideological victory was not helped forward by the magnificent material setting it found in the New World. The agrarian and proletarian strands of the American democratic personality, which in some sense typify the whole of American uniqueness, reveal a remarkable collusion between Locke and the New World. Had it been merely the liberal spirit alone which inspired the American farmer to become capitalistically oriented, to repudiate save for a few early remnants the village organization of Europe, to produce for a market and even to enter capitalist occupations on the side such as logging and railroad building, then the difficulties he encountered would have been greater than they were. But where land was abundant and the voyage to the New World itself a claim to independence, the spirit which repudiated peasantry and tenantry flourished with remarkable ease. Similarly, had it merely been an aspect of irrational Lockianism which inspired the American worker to think in terms of the capitalist setup, the task would have been harder than it was.

But social fluidity was peculiarly fortified by the riches of a rich land, so that there was no small amount of meaning to Lincoln's claim in 1861 that the American laborer, instead of "being fixed to that condition for life," works for "a while," then "saves," then "hires another beginner" as he himself becomes an entrepreneur. And even when factory industrialism gained sway after the Civil War, and the old artisan and cottage-and-mill mentality was definitely gone, it was still a Lockian idea fortified by material resources which inspired the triumph of the job mentality of Gompers rather than the class mentality of the European worker. The "petit-bourgeois" giant of America, though ultimately a triumph for the liberal idea, could hardly have chosen a better material setting in which to flourish.

* * *

One cannot say of the liberal society analysis that by concentrating on national unities it rules out the meaning of domestic conflict. Actually it discovers that meaning * * *. The argument over whether we should "stress" solidarity or conflict in American politics misleads us by advancing a false set of alternatives.

* * *

DISCUSSION QUESTIONS

1. Do you agree with Hartz that Americans have a hard time understanding other societies because of ideological uniformity in the United States?

2. Do you think Hartz is correct in saying that Americans are in agreement on the values of the liberal tradition? Are there parts of American history or society today that make you doubt his thesis?

3. Without limiting yourself to Hartz's observations, what do you think might be some of the advantages and disadvantages of a high degree of agreement on basic values for American society and politics?

NOTES

1. Ed. note: "Lockian" refers to John Locke, a British political theorist. Locke's ideas of individualism, liberty, property rights, and limited government were among those that influenced political leaders at the time of the American Revolution.

"Beyond Tocqueville, Myrdal, and Hartz: The Multiple Traditions in America"

Rogers M. Smith

Where liberalism points to notions of equality, Rogers Smith argues that there is another tradition in American political thought that has been influential. He does not deny the significance in American political history of liberalism or of republicanism, which argues for a more society-centered perspective on government than does liberalism. Smith, however, contends that an equally significant strand of thought, "ascriptive hierarchy," has been important across U.S. history. In this way of thinking, society is a hierarchy, where some groups are on top and others are below. Those on top are deserving of all the rights and benefits the liberal tradition can offer; those below are not. The most glaring examples of this throughout American history were the treatment of racial minorities, especially blacks, and the treatment of women. Smith notes that those holding these illiberal views were not on the fringes of society but, rather, were probably the majority view. We cannot, Smith argues, marginalize the impact of "ascriptive American" hierarchy or those who held these views. American public policy at the highest levels was influenced by its premises. Moreover, the same individuals often held these illiberal views in tandem with their liberal or republican views and expended great intellectual energy to make these views seem acceptable in the light of fundamental American beliefs.

Since the nation's inception, analysts have described American political culture as the preeminent example of modern liberal democracy, of government by popular consent with respect for the equal rights of all. They have portrayed American political development as the working out of liberal democratic or republican principles, via both "liberalizing" and "democratizing" socioeconomic changes and political efforts to cope with tensions inherent in these principles. Illiberal, undemocratic beliefs and practices have usually been seen only as expressions of ignorance and prejudice, destined to marginality by their lack of rational defenses. * * *

[Alexis de] Tocqueville's thesis—that America has been most shaped by the unusually free and egalitarian ideas and material conditions that prevailed at its founding—captures important truths. Nonetheless, the purpose of this essay is to challenge that thesis by showing that its adherents fail to give due weight to inegalitarian ideologies and conditions that have shaped the participants and the substance of American politics just as deeply. For over 80% of U.S. history, its laws declared most of the world's population to be ineligible for full American citizenship solely because of their race, original nationality, or gender. For at least two-thirds of American history, the majority of the domestic adult population was also ineligible for full citizenship for the same reasons. * * *

The Tocquevillian story is thus deceptive because it is too narrow. It is centered on relationships among a minority of Americans (white men, largely of northern European ancestry) analyzed via reference to categories derived from the hierarchy of political and economic statuses men have held in Europe: monarchs and aristocrats, commercial burghers, farmers, industrial and rural laborers, and indigents. Because most European observers and British American men have regarded these categories as politically fundamental, it is understandable that they have always found the most striking fact about the new nation to be its lack of one type of ascriptive hierarchy. There was no hereditary monarchy or nobility native to British America, and the revolutionaries rejected both the authority of the British king and aristocracy and the creation of any new American substitutes. Those features of American political life made the United States appear remarkably egalitarian by comparison with Europe.

But the comparative moral, material, and political egalitarianism that prevailed at the founding among moderately propertied white men was surrounded by an array of other fixed, ascriptive systems of unequal status, all largely unchallenged by the American revolutionaries. Men were thought naturally suited to rule over women, within both the family and the polity. White northern Europeans were thought superior culturally—and probably biologically—to black Africans, bronze Native Americans, and indeed all other races and civilizations. Many British Americans also treated religion as an inherited condition and regarded Protestants as created by God to be morally and politically, as well as theologically, superior to Catholics, Jews, Muslims, and others.

These beliefs were not merely emotional prejudices or "attitudes." Over time, American intellectual and political elites elaborated distinctive justifications for these ascriptive systems, including inegalitarian scriptural readings, the scientific racism of the "American school" of ethnology, racial and sexual Darwinism, and the romantic cult of Anglo-Saxonism in American historiography. All these discourses identified the true meaning of *Americanism* with particular forms of cultural, religious, ethnic, and especially racial and gender hierarchies. Many adherents of ascriptive Americanist outlooks insisted that the nation's political and economic structures should formally reflect natural and cultural inequalities, even at the cost of violating doctrines of universal rights. Although these views never entirely prevailed, their impact has been wide and deep.

Thus to approach a truer picture of America's political culture and its characteristic conflicts, we must consider more than the familiar categories of (absent) feudalism and socialism and (pervasive) bourgeois liberalism and republicanism. The nation has also been deeply constituted by the ideologies and practices that defined the relationships of the white male minority with subordinate groups, and the relationships of these groups with each other. When these elements are kept in view, the flat plain of American egalitarianism mapped by Tocqueville and others suddenly looks quite different. We instead perceive America's initial conditions as exhibiting only a rather small, recently leveled valley of relative equality nestled amid steep mountains of hierarchy. And though we can see forces working to erode those mountains over time, broadening the valley, many of the peaks also prove to be volcanic, frequently responding to seismic pressures with outbursts that harden into substantial peaks once again.

To be sure, America's ascriptive, unequal statuses, and the ideologies by which they have been defended have always been heavily conditioned and constrained by the presence of liberal democratic values and institutions. The reverse, however, is also true. Although liberal democratic ideas and practices have been more potent in America than elsewhere, American politics is best seen as expressing the interaction of multiple political traditions, including *liberalism, republicanism*, and *ascriptive forms of Americanism*, which have collectively comprised American political culture, without any constituting it as a whole. Though Americans have often struggled over contradictions among these traditions, almost all have tried to embrace what they saw as the best features of each.

Ascriptive outlooks have had such a hold in America because they have provided something that neither liberalism nor republicanism has done so well. They have offered creditable intellectual and psychological reasons for many Americans to believe that their social roles and personal characteristics express an identity that has inherent and transcendant worth, thanks to nature, history, and God. Those rationales have obviously aided those who sat atop the nation's political, economic, and social hierarchies. But many Americans besides elites have felt that they have gained meaning, as well as material and political benefits, from their nation's traditional structures of ascribed places and destinies.

Conventional narratives, preoccupied with the absence of aristocracy and socialism, usually stress the liberal and democratic elements in the rhetoric of even America's dissenters. These accounts fail to explain how and why liberalizing efforts have frequently lost to forces favoring new forms of racial and gender hierarchy. Those forces have sometimes negated major liberal victories, especially in the half-century following Reconstruction; and the fate of that era may be finding echoes today.

My chief aim here is to persuade readers that many leading accounts of American political culture are inadequate. * * * This argument is relevant to contemporary politics in two ways. First, it raises the possibility that novel intellectual, political, and legal systems reinforcing racial, ethnic, and gender inequalities might be rebuilt in America in the years ahead. That prospect does not seem plausible if the United States has always been essentially liberal democratic, with all exceptions marginal and steadily eliminated. It seems quite real, however, if liberal democratic traditions have been but contested parts of American culture, with inegalitarian ideologies and practices often resurging even after major enhancements of liberal democracy. Second, the political implications of the view that America has never been completely liberal, and that changes have come only through difficult struggles and then have often not been sustained, are very different from the complacency—sometimes despair—engendered by beliefs that liberal democracy has always been hegemonic.

* * *

The Multiple-Traditions Thesis of American Civic Identity

It seems prudent to stress what is not proposed here. This is not a call for analysts to minimize the significance of white male political actors or their conflicts with each other. Neither is it a call for accounts that assail "Eurocentric" white male oppressors on behalf of diverse but always heroic subjugated groups. The multiple-traditions thesis holds that Americans share a *common* culture but one more complexly and multiply constituted than is usually acknowledged. Most members of all groups have shared and often helped to shape all the ideologies and institutions that have structured American life, including ascriptive ones. A few have done so while resisting all subjugating practices. But members of every group have sometimes embraced "essentialist" ideologies valorizing their own ascriptive traits and denigrating those of others, to bleak effect. Cherokees enslaved blacks, champions of women's rights disparaged blacks and immigrants, and blacks have often been hostile toward Hispanics and other new immigrants. White men, in turn, have been prominent among those combating invidious exclusions, as well as those imposing them.

Above all, recognition of the strong attractions of restrictive Americanist ideas does not imply any denial that America's liberal and democratic traditions have had great normative and political potency, even if they have not been so hegemonic as some claim. Instead, it sheds a new—and, in some respects, more flattering—light on the constitutive role of liberal democratic values in American life. Although some Americans have been willing to repudiate notions of democracy and universal rights, most have not; and though many have tried to blend those commitments with exclusionary ascriptive views, the illogic of these mixes has repeatedly proven a major resource for successful reformers. But we obscure the difficulty of those reforms (and thereby diminish their significance) if we slight the ideological and political appeal of contrary ascriptive traditions by portraying them as merely the shadowy side of a hegemonic liberal republicanism.

At its heart, the multiple-traditions thesis holds that the definitive feature of American political culture has been not its liberal, republican, or "ascriptive Americanist" elements but, rather, this more complex pattern of apparently inconsistent combinations of the traditions, accompanied by recurring conflicts. Because standard accounts neglect this pattern, they do not explore how and why Americans have tried to uphold aspects of all three of these heterogeneous traditions in combinations that are longer on political and psychological appeal than on intellectual coherency.

A focus on these questions generates an understanding of American politics that differs from Tocquevillian ones in four major respects. First, on this view, purely liberal and republican conceptions of civic identity are seen as frequently unsatisfying to many Americans, because they contain elements that threaten, rather than affirm, sincere, reputable beliefs in the propriety of the privileged positions that whites, Christianity, Anglo-Saxon traditions, and patriarchy have had in the United States. At the same time, even Americans deeply attached to those inegalitarian arrangements have also had liberal democratic values. Second, it has therefore been typical, not aberrational, for Americans to embody strikingly opposed beliefs in their institutions, such as doctrines that blacks should and should not be full and equal citizens. But though American efforts to blend aspects of opposing views have often been remarkably stable, the resulting tensions have still been important sources of change. Third, when older types of ascriptive inequality, such as slavery, have been rejected as unduly illiberal, it has been normal, not anomalous, for many Americans to embrace new doctrines and institutions that reinvigorate the hierarchies they esteem in modified form. Changes toward greater inequality and exclusion, as well as toward greater equality and inclusiveness, thus can and do occur. Finally, the dynamics of American development cannot simply be seen as a rising tide of liberalizing forces progressively submerging contrary beliefs and practices. The national course has been more serpentine. The economic, political, and moral forces propelling the United States toward liberal democracy have often been heeded by American leaders, especially since World War II. But the currents pulling toward fuller expression of alleged natural and cultural inequalities have also always won victories. In some eras they have predominated, appearing to define not only the path of safety but that of progress. In all eras, including our own, many Americans have combined their allegiance to liberal democracy with beliefs that the presence of certain groups favored by history, nature, and God has made Americans an intrinsically "special" people. Their adherents have usually regarded such beliefs as benign and intellectually well founded; yet they also have always had more or less harsh discriminatory corollaries.

To test these multiple-traditions claims, consider the United States in 1870. By then the Civil War and Reconstruction had produced dramatic advances in the liberal and democratic character of America's laws. Slavery was abolished. All persons born in the United States and subject to its jurisdiction were deemed citizens of the United States and the states in which they resided, regardless of their race, creed or gender. None could be denied voting rights on racial grounds. The civil rights of all were newly protected through an array of national statutes. The 1790 ban on naturalizing Africans had been repealed, and expatriation declared a natural right. Over the past two decades women had become more politically engaged and had begun to gain respect as political actors.

*   *   *

[Neither liberal or republican analyses] would have had the intellectual resources to explain what in fact occurred. Over the next fifty years, Americans did not make blacks, women, and members of other races full and equal citizens, nor did racial and gender prejudices undergo major erosion. Neither, however, were minorities and women declared to be subhuman and outside the body politic. And although white Americans engaged in extensive violence against blacks and Native Americans, those groups grew in population, and no cataclysm loomed. Instead, intellectual and political elites worked out the most elaborate theories of racial and gender hierarchy in U.S. history and partially embodied them in a staggering array of new laws governing naturalization, immigration, deportation, voting rights, electoral institutions, judicial procedures, and economic rights—but only partially. The laws retained important liberal and democratic features, and some were strengthened. They had enough purchase on the moral and material interests of most Americans to compel advocates of inequality to adopt contrived, often clumsy means to achieve their ends.

The considerable success of the proponents of inegalitarian ideas reflects the power these traditions have long had in America. But after the Civil War, * * * evolutionary theories enormously strengthened the intellectual prestige of doctrines presenting the races and sexes as naturally arrayed into what historians have termed a "raciocultural hierarchy," as well as a "hierarchy of sex." Until the end of the nineteenth century, most evolutionists * * * thought acquired characteristics could be inherited. Thus beliefs in biological differences were easily merged with the * * * historians' views that peoples were the products of historical and cultural forces. Both outlooks usually presented the current traits of the races as fixed for the foreseeable future. Few intellectuals were shy about noting the implications of these views for public policy. Anthropologist Daniel G. Brinton made typical arguments in his 1895 presidential address to the

American Association for the Advancement of Science. He contended that the "black, brown and red races" each had "a peculiar mental temperament which has become hereditary," leaving them constitutionally "recreant to the codes of civilization." Brinton believed that this fact had not been adequately appreciated by American lawmakers. Henceforth, conceptions of "race, nations, tribes" had to "supply the only sure foundations for legislation; not *a priori* notions of the rights of man."

As Brinton knew, many politicians and judges had already begun to seize on such suggestions. In 1882, for example, California senator John Miller drew on the Darwinian "law of the 'survival of the fittest' " to explain that "forty centuries of Chinese life" had "ground into" the Chinese race characteristics that made them unbeatable competitors against the free white man. They were "automatic engines of flesh and blood," of "obtuse nerve," marked by degradation and demoralization, and thus far below the Anglo-Saxon, but were still a threat to the latter's livelihood in a market economy. Hence, Miller argued, the immigration of Chinese laborers must be banned. His bill prevailed, many expressing concern that these Chinese would otherwise become American citizens. The Chinese Exclusion Act was not a vestige of the past but something new, the first repudiation of America's long history of open immigration; and it was justified in terms of the postwar era's revivified racial theories.

Yet although men like Miller not only sustained but expanded Chinese exclusions until they were made virtually total in 1917 (and tight restrictions survived until 1965), they never managed to deny American citizenship to all of the "Chinese race." Until 1917 there were no restrictions on the immigration of upper-class Chinese, and in 1898 the Supreme Court declared that children born on U.S. soil to Chinese parents were American citizens (*United States* v. *Wong Kim Ark* 1898). Birthplace citizenship was a doctrine enshrined in common law, reinforced by the Fourteenth Amendment, and vital to citizenship for the children of *all* immigrant aliens. Hence it had enough legal and political support to override the Court's recognition of Congress's exclusionary desires. Even so, in other cases the Court sustained bans on Chinese immigration while admitting the racial animosities behind them, as in the "Chinese Exclusion Case" (*Chae Chan Ping* v. *United States* 1889); upheld requirements for Chinese-Americans to have certificates of citizenship not required of whites (*Fong Yue Ting* v. *United States* 1893); and permitted officials to deport even Chinese persons who had later been judged by courts to be native-born U.S. citizens (*United States* v. *Ju Toy* 1905).

The upshot, then, was the sort of none-too-coherent mix that the multiple-traditions thesis holds likely. Chinese were excluded on racial grounds, but race did not bar citizenship to those born in the United States; yet Chinese ancestry could subject some American citizens to burdens, including deportation, that others did not face. The mix was not perfect from any ideological viewpoint, but it was politically popular. It maintained a valued inclusive feature of American law (birthplace citizenship) while sharply reducing the resident Chinese population. And it most fully satisfied the increasingly powerful champions of Anglo-Saxon supremacy.

From 1887 on, academic reformers and politicians sought to restrict immigration more generally by a means that paid lip service to liberal norms even as it aimed at racist results—the literacy test. On its face, this measure expressed concern only for the intellectual merits of immigrants. But the test's true aims were spelled out in 1896 by its sponsor, Senator Henry Cabot Lodge, a Harvard Ph.D. in history and politics. Committee research, he reported, showed that the test would exclude "the Italians, Russians, Poles, Hungarians, Greeks, and Asiatics," thereby preserving "the quality of our race and citizenship." Citing "modern history" and "modern science," Thomas Carlyle and Gustave le Bon, Lodge contended that the need for racial exclusion arose from "something deeper and more fundamental than anything which concerns the intellect." Race was above all constituted by moral characteristics, the "stock of ideas, traditions, sentiments, modes of thought" that a people possessed as an "accumulation of centuries of toil and conflict." These mental and moral qualities constituted the "soul of a race," an inheritance in which its members "blindly believe," and upon which learning had no effect. But these qualities could be degraded if "a lower race mixes with a higher"; thus, exclusion by race, not reading ability, was the nation's proper goal.

When the literacy test finally passed in 1917 but proved ineffective in keeping out "lower races," Congress moved to versions of an explicitly racist national-origins quota system. It banned virtually all Asians and permitted European immigration only in ratios preserving the northern European cast of the American citizenry. Congressman Albert Johnson, chief author of the most important quota act in 1924, proclaimed that through it, "the day of indiscriminate acceptance of all races, has definitely ended." The quota system, repealed only in 1965, was a novel, elaborate monument to ideologies holding that access to American citizenship should be subject to racial and ethnic limits. It also served as the prime model for similar systems in Europe and Latin America.

*   *   *

But despite the new prevalence of such attitudes on the part of northern and western elites in the late nineteenth century, the Reconstruction amendments and statutes were still on the books, and surviving liberal sentiments made repealing them politically difficult. Believers in racial inequality were, moreover, undecided on just what to do about blacks. * * * "Radical" racists * * * argued that blacks, like other lower races, should be excluded from American society and looked hopefully for evidence that they were dying out. Their position was consistent with Hartz's claim that Americans could not tolerate permanent unequal statuses; persons must either be equal citizens or outsiders. But * * * "Conservatives" believed * * * that blacks and other people of color might instead have a permanent "place" in America, so long as "placeness included hierarchy." Some still thought that blacks, like the other "lower races," might one day be led by whites to fully civilized status, but no one expected progress in the near future. Thus blacks should instead be segregated, largely disfranchised, and confined to menial occupations via inferior education and discriminatory hiring practices—but not expelled, tortured, or killed. A few talented blacks might even be allowed somewhat higher stations.

* * * The result was a system closest to Conservative desires, one that kept blacks in their place, although that place was structured more repressively than most Conservatives favored. And unlike the ineffective literacy test, here racial inegalitarians achieved much of what they wanted without explicitly violating liberal legal requirements. Complex registration systems, poll taxes, and civics tests appeared race-neutral but were designed and administered to disfranchise blacks. This intent was little masked. * * * These efforts succeeded. Most dramatically, in Louisiana 95.6% of blacks were registered in 1896, and over half (130,000) voted. After disfranchising measures, black registration dropped by 90% and by 1904 totaled only 1,342. The Supreme Court found convoluted ways to close its eyes to these tactics.

By similar devices, blacks were virtually eliminated from juries in the south, where 90% of American blacks lived, sharply limiting their ability to have their personal and economic rights protected by the courts. "Separate but equal" educational and business laws and practices also stifled the capacities of blacks to participate in the nation's economy as equals, severely curtailed the occupations they could train for, and marked them—unofficially but clearly—as an inferior caste. Thus here, as elsewhere, it was evident that the nation's laws and institutions were not meant to confer the equal civic status they proclaimed for all Americans; but neither did they conform fully to doctrines favoring overt racial hierarchy. They represented another asymmetrical compromise among the multiple ideologies vying to define American political culture.

So, too, did the policies governing two groups whose civic status formally improved during these years: Native Americans and women. * * *

*   *   *

This period also highlights how the influence of inegalitarian doctrines has not been confined to white male intellectuals, legislators, and judges. The leading writer of the early twentieth-century women's movement, Charlotte Perkins Gilman, was a thoroughgoing Darwinian who accepted that evolution had made women inferior to men in certain respects, although she insisted that these differences were usually exaggerated and that altered social conditions could transform them. And even as he attacked Booker T. Washington for appearing to accept the "alleged inferiority of the Negro race," W. E. B. DuBois embraced the widespread Lamarckian view that racial characteristics were socially conditioned but then inherited as the "soul" of a race. He could thus accept that most blacks were "primitive folk" in need of tutelage. * * *

The acceptance of ascriptive inegalitarian beliefs by brilliant and politically dissident female and black male intellectuals strongly suggests that these ideas had broad appeal. Writers whose interests they did not easily serve still saw them as persuasive in light of contemporary scientific theories and empirical evidence of massive inequalities. It is likely, too, that for many the vision of a meaningful natural order that these doctrines provided had the psychological and philosophical appeal that such positions have always had for human beings, grounding their status and significance in something greater and more enduring than their own lives. * * *

In sum, if we accept that ideologies and institutions of ascriptive hierarchy have shaped America in interaction with its liberal and democratic features, we can make more sense of a wide range of inegalitarian policies newly contrived after 1870 and perpetuated through much of the twentieth century. Those policies were dismantled only through great struggles, aided by international pressures during World War II and the Cold War; and it is not clear that these struggles have ended. The novelties in the policies and scientific doctrines of the Gilded Age and Progressive Era should alert us to the possibility that new intellectual systems and political forces defending racial and gender inequalities may yet gain increased power in our own time.

* * *

The achievements of Americans in building a more inclusive democracy certainly provide reasons to believe that illiberal forces will not prevail. But just as we can better explain the nation's past by recognizing how and why liberal democratic principles have been contested with frequent success, we will better understand the present and future of American politics if we do not presume they are rooted in essentially liberal or democratic values and conditions. Instead, we must analyze America as the ongoing product of often conflicting multiple traditions.

DISCUSSION QUESTIONS

1. According to Smith, what are some examples of how Americans in the late nineteenth century simultaneously held liberal and ascriptive hierarchical views?

2. What are the key components of the classical republican outlook, as presented by Smith? How do they differ from the liberal tradition?

3. Do you believe that ascriptive hierarchy is still a powerful strain of thought in American political culture? If so, what are some examples?

4. How would you know if ascriptive hierarchy was as widespread as Smith contends? What kind of evidence would you look for?

5. How might an advocate of liberalism, republicanism, and ascriptive hierarchy define "the public good"?

"The Three Political Cultures"

Daniel J. Elazar

Both Hartz and Smith touch on the various regions in the United States, but Daniel Elazar makes regional differentiation the centerpiece of his analysis of American political culture. Elazar argues that political beliefs in the United States are unevenly distributed across the country. In large part, this has to do with migration patterns. Once certain ethnic groups and nationalities predominated in a particular area, the institutions they built and the practice of politics tended to become ingrained with their political cultural beliefs. Elazar sees three types of value systems across the United States: moralism, individualism, and traditionalism. Moralism is similar to republicanism in its focus on the community and engaging in politics to do good. Individualism is similar to liberalism in its focus on individual rights and tends to view governing as a set of transactions with individuals and groups. Traditionalism is similar to ascriptive hierarachy in its quest to use the power of government to preserve existing social arrangements. These three approaches vary in their prevalence across the country, and even within states there may be variation on which of the three predominates. Some areas have a mixture of two of these value systems, while other areas are more purely of one type. Elazar's formulation has been influential, with many studies using his assessment of political culture across the states as an explanatory factor when trying to understand differences in politics, public opinion, and policies across the country.

* * *

The United States is a single land of great diversity inhabited by what is now a single people of great diversity. The singleness of the country as a whole is expressed through political, cultural, and geographic unity. Conversely, the country's diversity is expressed through its states, subcultures, and sections. In this section, we will focus on the political dimensions of that diversity-in-unity—on the country's overall political culture and its subculture.

Political culture is the summation of persistent patterns of underlying political attitudes and characteristic responses to political concerns that is manifest in a particular political order. Its existence is generally unperceived by those who are part of that order, and its origins date back to the very beginnings of the particular people who share it. Political culture is an intrinsically political phenomenon. As such, it makes its own demands on the political system. For example, the definition of what is "fair" in the political arena—a direct manifestation of political culture—is likely to be different from the definition of what is fair in family or business relationships. Moreover, different political cultures will define fairness in politics differently. Political culture also affects all other questions confronting the political system. For example, many factors go into shaping public expectations regarding government services, and political culture will be significant among them. Political systems, in turn, are in some measure the products of the political cultures they serve and must remain in harmony with their political cultures if they are to maintain themselves.

*   *   *

Political-culture factors stand out as particularly influential in shaping the operations of the national, state, and local political systems in three ways: (1) by molding the perceptions of the political community (the citizens, the politicians, and the public officials) as to the nature and purposes of politics and its expectations of government and the political process; (2) by influencing the recruitment of specific kinds of people to become active in government and politics—as holders of elective offices, members of the bureaucracy, and active political workers; and (3) by subtly directing the actual way in which the art of government is practiced by citizens, politicians, and public officials in the light of their perceptions. In turn, the cultural components of individual and group behavior are manifested in civic behavior as dictated by conscience and internalized ethical standards, in the forms of law-abidingness (or laxity in such matters) adhered to by citizens and officials, and in the character of the positive actions of government.[1]

*   *   *

The national political culture of the United States is itself a synthesis of three major political subcultures. These subcultures jointly inhabit the country, existing side by side or sometimes overlapping one another. All three are of nationwide proportions, having spread, in the course of time, from coast to coast. Yet each subculture is strongly tied to specific sections of the country, reflecting the streams and currents of migration that have carried people of different origins and backgrounds across the continent in more or less orderly patterns.[2]

Given the central characteristics that define each of the subcultures and their centers of emphasis, the three political subcultures may be called individualistic, moralistic, and traditionalistic. Each reflects its own particular synthesis of the marketplace and the commonwealth.

It is important, however, not only to examine this description and the following ones very carefully but also to abandon the preconceptions associated with such idea-words as individualistic, moralistic, marketplace, and so on. Thus, for example, nineteenth-century individualistic concep-tions of minimum intervention were oriented toward *laissez-faire*, with the role of government conceived to be that of a policeman with powers to act in certain limited fields. And in the twentieth century, the notion of what constitutes minimum intervention has been drastically expanded to include such things as government regulation of utilities, unemployment compensation, and massive subventions to maintain a stable and grow-ing economy—all within the framework of the same political culture. The demands of manufacturers for high tariffs in 1865 and the demands of la-bor unions for worker's compensation in 1965 may well be based on the same theoretical justification that they are aids to the maintenance of a working marketplace. Culture is not static. It must be viewed dynami-cally and defined so as to include cultural change in its very nature.

The Individualistic Political Culture

The *individualistic political culture* emphasizes the conception of the demo-cratic order as a marketplace. It is rooted in the view that government is instituted for strictly utilitarian reasons, to handle those functions de-manded by the people it serves. According to this view, government need not have any direct concern with questions of the "good society" (except insofar as the government may be used to advance some common con-ception of the good society formulated outside the political arena, just as it serves other functions). Emphasizing the centrality of private con-cerns, the individualistic political culture places a premium on limiting community intervention—whether governmental or nongovernmental—into private activities, to the minimum degree necessary to keep the mar-ketplace in proper working order. In general, government action is to be restricted to those areas, primarily in the economic realm, that encourage private initiative and widespread access to the marketplace.

The character of political participation in systems dominated by the in-dividualistic political culture reflects the view that politics is just another means by which individuals may improve themselves socially and eco-nomically. In this sense politics is a "business," like any other that com-petes for talent and offers rewards to those who take it up as a career. Those individuals who choose political careers may rise by providing the governmental services demanded of them and, in return, may expect to be adequately compensated for their efforts.

Interpretation of officeholders' obligations under the individualistic political culture vary among political systems and even among individu-als within a single political system. Where the standards are high, such people are expected to provide high-quality government services for the general public in the best possible manner in return for the status and economic rewards considered their due. Some who choose political ca-reers clearly commit themselves to such norms; others believe that an office-holder's primary responsibility is to serve him- or herself and those who have supported him or her directly, favoring them at the expense of others. In some political systems, this view is accepted by the public as well as by politicians.

Political life within an individualistic political culture is based on a system of mutual obligations rooted in personal relationships. Whereas in a simple civil society those relationships can be direct ones, those with individualistic political cultures in the United States are usually too complex to maintain face-to-face ties. So the system of mutual obligation is harnessed through political parties, which serve as "business corporations" dedicated to providing the organization necessary to maintain that system. Party regularity is indispensable in the individualistic political culture because it is the means for coordinating individual enterprise in the political arena; it is also the one way of preventing individualism in politics from running wild.

In such a system, an individual can succeed politically, not by dealing with issues in some exceptional way or by accepting some concept of good government and then by striving to implement it, but by maintaining his or her place in the system of mutual obligations. A person can do this by operating according to the norms of his or her particular party, to the exclusion of other political considerations. Such a political culture encourages the maintenance of a party system that is competitive, but not overtly so, in the pursuit of office. Its politicians are interested in office as a means of controlling the distribution of the favors or rewards of government rather than as a means of exercising governmental power for programmatic ends; hence competition may prove less rewarding than accommodation in certain situations.

Since the individualistic political culture eschews ideological concerns in its "business-like" conception of politics, both politicians and citizens tend to look upon political activity as a specialized one—as essentially the province of professionals, of minimum and passing concern to laypersons, and with no place for amateurs to play an active role. Furthermore, there is a strong tendency among the public to believe that politics is a dirty—albeit necessary—business, better left to those who are willing to soil themselves by engaging in it. In practice, then, where the individualistic political culture is dominant, there is likely to be an easy attitude toward the limits of the professional's perquisites. Since a fair amount of corruption is expected in the normal course of things, there is relatively little popular excitement when any is found, unless it is of an extraordinary character. It is as if the public were willing to pay a surcharge for services rendered, rebelling only when the surcharge becomes too heavy. Of course, the judgments as to what is "normal" and what is "extraordinary" are themselves subjective and culturally conditioned.

Public officials, committed to "giving the public what it wants," are normally not willing to initiate new programs or open up new areas of government activity on their own initiative. They will do so when they perceive an overwhelming public demand for them to act, but only then. In a sense, their willingness to expand the functions of government is based on an extension of the *quid pro quo* "favors" system, which serves as the central core of their political relationships. New and better services are the reward they give the public for placing them in office. The value mix and legitimacy of change in the individualistic political culture are directly related to commercial concerns.

The individualistic political culture is ambivalent about the place of bureaucracy in the political order.[3] In one sense, the bureaucratic method of operation flies in the face of the favor system that is central to the individualistic political process. At the same time, the virtues of organizational efficiency appear substantial to those seeking to master the market. In the end, bureaucratic organization is introduced within the framework of the favor system; large segments of the bureaucracy may be insulated from it through the merit system, but the entire organization is pulled into the political environment at crucial points through political appointment at the upper echelons and, very frequently, also through the bending of the merit system to meet political demands.[4]

* * *

The Moralistic Political Culture

To the extent that American society is built on the principles of "commerce" (in the broadest sense) and that the marketplace provides the model for public relationships, all Americans share some of the attitudes that are of great importance in the individualistic political culture. At the same time, substantial segments of the American people operate politically within the framework of two political cultures—the moralistic and traditionalistic political cultures—whose theoretical structures and operational consequences depart significantly from the individualistic pattern at crucial points.

The *moralistic political culture* emphasizes the commonwealth conception as the basis for democratic government. Politics, to this political culture, is considered one of the great human activities: the search for the good society. True, it is a struggle for power, but it is also an effort to exercise power for the betterment of the commonwealth. Accordingly, in the moralistic political culture, both the general public and the politicians conceive of politics as a public activity centered on some notion of the public good and properly devoted to the advancement of the public interest. Good government, then, is measured by the degree to which it promotes the public good and in terms of the honestly, selflessness, and commitment to the public welfare of those who govern.

In the moralistic political culture, individualism is tempered by a general commitment to utilizing communal (preferably nongovernmental, but governmental if necessary) power to intervene in the sphere of "private" activities when it is considered necessary to do so for the public good or the well-being of the community. Accordingly, issues have an important place in the moralistic style of politics, functioning to set the tone for political concern. Government is considered a positive instrument with a responsibility to promote the general welfare, although definitions of what its positive role should be may vary considerably from era to era.

As in the case of the individualistic political culture, the change from nineteenth- to twentieth-century conceptions of what government's positive role should be has been great; for example, support for Prohibition has given way to support for wage and hour regulation. At the same time, care must be taken to distinguish between a predisposition toward communal activism and a desire for federal government activity. For example, many representatives of the moralistic political culture oppose federal aid for urban renewal without in any way opposing community responsibility for urban development. The distinction they make (implicitly, at least) is between what they consider legitimate community responsibility and what they believe to be central government encroachment; or between communitarianism, which they value, and "collectivism," which they abhor. Thus, on some public issues we find certain such representatives taking highly conservative positions despite their positive attitudes toward public activity generally. Such representatives may also prefer government intervention in the social realm—that is, censorship or screening of books and movies—over government intervention in the economy, holding that the former is necessary for the public good and the latter, harmful.

Since the moralistic political culture rests on the fundamental conception that politics exists primarily as a means for coming to grips with the issues and public concerns of civil society, it embraces the notion that politics is ideally a matter of concern for all citizens, not just those who are professionally committed to political careers. Indeed, this political culture considers it the duty of every citizen to participate in the political affairs of his or her commonwealth.

Accordingly, there is a general insistence within this political culture that government service is public service, which places moral obligations upon those who participate in government that are more demanding than the moral obligations of the marketplace. There is an equally general rejection of the notion that the field of politics is a legitimate realm for private economic enrichment. Of course, politicians may benefit economically because of their political careers, but they are not expected to *profit* from political activity; indeed, they are held suspect if they do.

Since the concept of serving the community is the core of the political relationship, politicians are expected to adhere to it even at the expense of individual loyalties and political friendships. Consequently, party regularity is not of prime importance. The political party is considered a useful political device, but it is not valued for its own sake. Regular party ties can be abandoned with relative impunity for third parties, special local parties, or nonpartisan systems if such changes are believed to be helpful in gaining larger political goals. People can even shift from party to party without sanctions if such change is justified by political belief.

In the moralistic political culture, rejection of firm party ties is not to be viewed as a rejection of politics as such. On the contrary, because politics is considered potentially good and healthy within the context of that culture, it is possible to have highly political nonpartisan systems. Certainly nonpartisanship is instituted not to eliminate politics but to improve it, by widening access to public office for those unwilling or unable to gain office through the regular party structure.[5]

In practice, where the moralistic political culture is dominant today, there is considerably more amateur participation in politics. There is also much less of what Americans consider to be corruption in government and less tolerance of those actions considered to be corrupt. Hence politics does not have the taint it so often bears in the individualistic environment.

By virtue of its fundamental outlook, the moralistic political culture creates a greater commitment to active government intervention in the economic and social life of the community. At the same time, the strong commitment to *communitarianism*[6] characteristic of that political culture tends to channel the interest in government intervention into highly localistic paths, such that a willingness to encourage local government intervention to set public standards does not necessarily reflect a concomitant willingness to allow outside governments equal opportunity to intervene. Not infrequently, public officials themselves will seek to initiate new government activities in an effort to come to grips with problems as yet unperceived by a majority of the citizenry. The moralistic political culture is not committed to either change or the status quo *per se* but, rather, will accept either depending upon the morally defined ends to be gained.

The major difficulty of this political culture in adjusting bureaucracy to the political order is tied to the potential conflict between communitarian principles and the necessity for large-scale organization to increase bureaucratic efficiency, a problem that could affect the attitudes of moralistic culture states toward federal activity of certain kinds. Otherwise, the notion of a politically neutral administrative system creates no problem within the moralistic value system and even offers many advantages. Where merit systems are instituted, they are rigidly maintained.

*   *   *

The Traditionalistic Political Culture

The *traditionalistic political culture* is rooted in an ambivalent attitude toward the marketplace coupled with a paternalistic and elitist conception of the commonwealth. It reflects an older, precommercial attitude that accepts a substantially hierarchical society as part of the ordered nature of things, authorizing and expecting those at the top of the social structure to take a special and dominant role in government. Like its moralistic counterpart, the traditionalistic political culture accepts government as an actor with a positive role in the community, but in a very limited sphere—mainly that of securing the continued maintenance of the existing social order. To do so, it functions to confine real political power to a relatively small and self-perpetuating group drawn from an established elite who often inherit their "right" to govern through family ties or social position. Accordingly, social and family ties are paramount in a traditionalistic political culture; in fact, their importance is greater than that of personal ties in the individualistic political culture, where, after all is said and done, a person's first responsibility is to him- or herself. At the same time, those who do not have a definite role to play in politics are not expected to be even minimally active as citizens. In many cases, they are not even expected to vote. In return, they are guaranteed that, outside of the limited sphere of politics, family rights (usually labeled "individual rights") are paramount, not to be taken lightly or ignored. As in the individualistic political culture, those active in politics are expected to benefit personally from their activity, though not necessarily through direct pecuniary gain.

Political parties are of minimal importance in a traditionalistic political culture, inasmuch as they encourage a degree of openness and competition that goes against the fundamental grain of an elite-oriented political order. Their major utility is to recruit people to fill the formal offices of government not desired by the established power-holders. Political competition in a traditionalistic political culture is usually conducted through factional alignments, as an extension of the personalistic politics that is characteristic of the system; hence political systems within the culture tend to have a loose one-party orientation if they have political parties at all.

Practically speaking, a traditionalistic political culture is found only in a society that retains some of the organic characteristics of the preindustrial social order. "Good government" in the political culture involves the maintenance and encouragement of traditional patterns and, if necessary, their adjustment to changing conditions with the least possible upset. Where the traditionalistic political culture is dominant in the United States today, political leaders play conservative and custodial rather than initiatory roles unless pressed strongly from the outside.

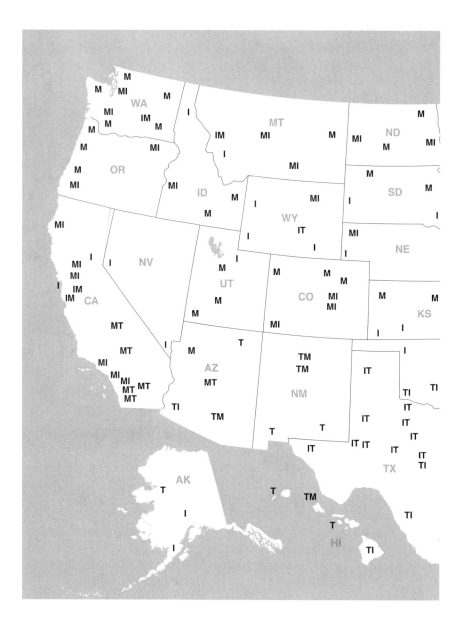

Map 1   The Regional Distribution of Political Cultures Within the States. *Source:* Daniel J. Elazar, *American Federalism: A View from the States*, 3d ed. (New York: Harper and Row Publishers, 1984), pp. 124–25. Reprinted by permission of HarperCollins Publishers.

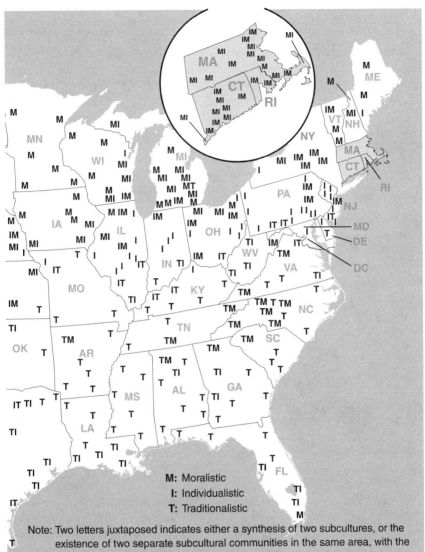

M: Moralistic
I: Individualistic
T: Traditionalistic

Note: Two letters juxtaposed indicates either a synthesis of two subcultures, or the existence of two separate subcultural communities in the same area, with the first dominant and the second secondary.

Whereas the individualistic and moralistic political cultures may encourage the development of bureaucratic systems of organization on the grounds of "rationality" and "efficiency" in government (depending on their particular situations), traditionalistic political cultures tend to be instinctively anti-bureaucratic. The reason is that bureaucracy by its very nature interferes with the fine web of informal interpersonal relationships that lie at the root of the political system and have been developed by following traditional patterns over the years. Where bureaucracy is introduced, it is generally confined to ministerial functions under the aegis of the established power-holders.

* * *

The Distribution and Impact of Political Subcultures

Map 1 on pages 28–29 shows how migrational patterns have led to the concentration of specific political subcultures in particular states and localities. The basic patterns of political culture were set during the period of the rural-land frontier by three great streams of American migration that began on the East Coast and moved westward after the colonial period. Each stream moved from east to west along more or less fixed paths, following lines of least resistance that generally led them due west from the immediately previous area of settlement.

* * *

Political Culture: Some Caveats

By now the reader has no doubt formed his or her own value judgments as to the relative worth of the three political subcultures. For this reason a particular warning against *hasty* judgments must be added here. Each of the three political subcultures contributes something important to the configuration of the American political system, and each possesses certain characteristics that are inherently dangerous to the survival of that system.

The moralistic political culture, for example, is the primary source of the continuing American quest for the good society, yet there is a noticeable tendency toward inflexibility and narrow-mindedness among some of its representatives. The individualistic political culture is the most tolerant of out-and-out political corruption, yet it has also provided the framework for the integration of diverse groups into the mainstream of American life. When representatives of the moralistic political culture, in their striving for a better social order, try to limit individual freedom, they usually come up against representatives of the individualistic political culture, to whom individual freedom is the cornerstone of their pluralistic order, though not for any noble reasons. Conversely, of course, the moralistic political culture acts as a restraint against the tendencies of the individualistic political culture to tolerate anything as long as it is in the marketplace.

The traditionalistic political culture contributes to the search for continuity in a society whose major characteristic is change; yet in the name of continuity, its representatives have denied African-Americans (as well as Native Americans and Latinos) their civil rights. When it is in proper working order, the traditionalistic culture has produced a unique group of first-rate national leaders from among its elites; but without a first-rate elite to draw upon, traditionalistic political-culture systems degenerate into oligarchies of the lowest level. Comparisons like these should induce caution in any evaluation of a subject that, by its very nature, evokes value judgments.

It is equally important to use caution in identifying individuals and groups as belonging to one cultural type or another on the basis of their public political behavior at a given moment in time. Immediate political responses to the issues of the day may reveal the political culture of the respondents, but not necessarily. Often, in fact, people will make what appear to be the same choices for different reasons—especially in public affairs, where the choices available at any give time are usually quite limited. Deeper analysis of what is behind those responses is usually needed. In other words, the names of the political cultures are not substitutes for the terms *conservative* and *liberal*, and should not be taken as such.

* * *

DISCUSSION QUESTIONS

1. How well do you think Elazar's labels describe the political culture in your home state or the state where you attend school?

2. As individuals move around the country, would you expect that regional differences would decline or will new residents tend to adopt the beliefs that are predominant in that part of the country?

3. Considering the definitions Elazar presents in this article, what would you say are the fundamental differences between the three approaches? In what ways might the approaches be more similar than different?

NOTES

1. This section is adapted from Daniel J. Elazar, *American Federalism: A View from the States*, 3d ed. (New York: Harper and Row, 1984).
2. For a fuller description of these political cultures, see Daniel J. Elazar, *Cities of the Prairie* (New York: Basic Books, 1970); Daniel J. Elazar et al., *Cities of the Prairie Revisited* (Lincoln: University of Nebraska Press, 1956); Daniel J. Elazar and Joseph Zikmund II, *The Ecology of American Political Culture: Readings* (New York: Thomas Y. Crowell, 1975); and John Kincaid, ed., *Political Culture, Public Policy and the American States* (Philadelphia: Institute for the Study of Human Issues, 1982).
3. The "good" meaning of *bureaucracy*: Administration of a government chiefly

through bureaus staffed with nonelective officials, selected on the basis of merit. The "bad" meaning: Any administration in which the need to follow complex procedures impedes effective action.

4. Political leaders in such an environment often argue that merit systems are impersonal, rigid, and ultimately inefficient. As Thomas Whelan, former mayor of Jersey City (1963–1971), once remarked: "You have to have the power to hire and fire. Civil Service examinations may measure intelligence but they don't measure courage, drive or curiosity. You wind up with a guy with nine heads who can't even get the men out of the garage." In 1972, Whelan and several other leaders of this highly individualistic city were convicted of various charges of conspiracy and accepting kickbacks on public contracts.

5. In this context, it should be noted that regular party systems are sometimes abandoned in local communities dominated by the indivualistic political culture so that nonpartisan electoral systems can be instituted in an effort to make local governments more "business-like" and to take local administration "out of politics." Such anti-political efforts are generally products of business-dominated reform movements and reflect the view that politics is necessarily "dirty" and illegitimate.

6. On communitarianism, see Robert N. Bellah et al., *Habits of the Heart: Individualism and Commitment in American Life* (New York: Harper and Row, 1985); and Daniel J. Elazar, *The American Constitutional Tradition* (Lincoln: University of Nebraska Press, 1988).

Debating the Issues: What Does It Mean to Be an American?

What does it mean to be an American? This turns out to be a complicated question. Unlike other nations, many of which are defined by a specific religious, ethnic, historical, geographic, or cultural identity, the United States appears to be united by a set of political ideals. As far back as de Tocqueville, scholars have tried to identify the nature of American political culture: is it a commitment to individualism? A belief in equality? A shared set of values about the appropriate role of government? Openness?

Samuel Huntington, a political scientist at Harvard University, argues that American political culture emerged from a combination of Protestantism, English as a common language, and the British traditions of limited government. From these emerged the American Creed, or what Louis Hartz referred to as the liberal tradition. Although we have always been a nation of immigrants, Huntington notes that these immigrants had always assimilated into American political culture: learning English, adopting American political values, self-identifying as American, becoming absorbed into the "melting pot." This process was encouraged by a range of institutional support, including businesses that taught employees English and social organizations that encouraged assimilation and "Americanization."

Huntington sees recent immigration patterns as a threat to American political culture. To him, the recent surge in illegal immigration from Mexico and other Latin American countries, as well as Muslims, will undermine the values that have forged a unique American identity. He believes these recent immigrants, unlike earlier newcomers, tend to retain their old language and national allegiances, resist assimilation, and even oppose key American political institutions and principles. They are aided by multicultural organizations that encourage them to maintain a separate identity apart from the majority culture and see themselves as victims. The result, Huntington fears, will be a balkanized polity, cleaved by language, ethnic, and cultural differences. America could become a "country of two languages, two cultures, and two peoples." That would radically transform the country into something vastly different than the uniqueness that defines Americanism.

Huntington's argument, which he has set out in articles and a book (entitled *Who Are We? The Challenges to America's National Identity*), have generated substantial controversy. His harshest critics have accused him of advocating a racist position that singled out Mexican immigrants for special criticism, and for promoting a form of nativism (a nationalistic and xenophobic ideology). In a review of Huntington's book published in the *New Yorker*, writer Louis Menand critiques

Huntington's view. Menand argues that Huntington has overstated the problem, and that Americans remain, by any standard, the "most patriotic people in the world." Huntington's real problem, according to Menand, is not deterioration of the American Creed, but rather simple change. The American Creed has never been static, and has always embraced change. "Democracy is not a dogma," he writes, "it is an experiment." Further, he argues that fears of multicultural bifurcation are over-blown, and that a broader cultural heterogeneity will strengthen the United States rather than weaken it.

4

"One Nation, Out of Many"

SAMUEL P. HUNTINGTON

America's core culture has primarily been the culture of the seventeenth- and eighteenth-century settlers who founded our nation. The central elements of that culture are the Christian religion; Protestant values, including individualism, the work ethic, and moralism; the English language; British traditions of law, justice, and limits on government power; and a legacy of European art, literature, and philosophy. Out of this culture the early settlers formulated the American Creed, with its principles of liberty, equality, human rights, representative government, and private property. Subsequent generations of immigrants were assimilated into the culture of the founding settlers and modified it, but did not change it fundamentally. It was, after all, Anglo-Protestant culture, values, institutions, and the opportunities they created that attracted more immigrants to America than to all the rest of the world.

America was founded as a Protestant society, and for 200 years almost all Americans practiced Protestantism. With substantial Catholic immigration, first from Germany and Ireland and then Italy and Poland, the proportion of Protestants declined—to about 60 percent of the population by 2000. Protestant beliefs, values, and assumptions, however, have been the core element (along with the English language) of America's settler culture, and they continue to pervade and shape American life, society, and thought. Protestant values have shaped American attitudes toward private and public morality, economic activity, government, and public policy. They have even deeply influenced Catholicism and other religions in America.

Throughout our history, people who were not white, Anglo-Saxon

Protestants have become Americans by adopting America's Anglo-Protestant culture and political values. This benefited them, and it benefited the country. Millions of immigrants and their children achieved wealth, power, and status in American society precisely because they assimilated themselves into the prevailing culture.

One has only to ask: Would America be the America it is today if in the seventeenth and eighteenth centuries it had been settled not by British Protestants but by French, Spanish, or Portuguese Catholics? The answer is no. It would not be America; it would be Quebec, Mexico, or Brazil.

The unfolding of British Protestant culture in America didn't just happen; it was orchestrated by our founders. As immigrants poured in during the late eighteenth century, our forefathers saw the need to "make Americans" of the new arrivals on their shores. "We must," John Jay said in 1797, "see our people more Americanized." At the peak of this effort in 1919, Justice Louis Brandeis declared that Americanization meant the immigrant "adopts the clothes, the manners, and the customs generally prevailing here . . . substitutes for his mother tongue the English language," ensures that "his interests and affections have become deeply rooted here," and comes "into complete harmony with our ideals and aspirations." When he has done all this, the new arrival will have "the national consciousness of an American." The acquisition of American citizenship, the renunciation of foreign allegiances, and the rejection of dual loyalties and nationalities are key components of this process.

During the decades before World War I, the huge wave of immigrants flooding into America generated a major social movement devoted to Americanizing these new arrivals. It involved local, state, and national governments, private organizations, and businesses. Americanization became a key element in the Progressive phase of American politics, and was promoted by Theodore Roosevelt, Woodrow Wilson, and other leaders.

Industrial corporations established schools at their factories to train immigrants in the English language and American values. In almost every city with a significant immigrant population the chamber of commerce had an Americanization program. Henry Ford was a leader in efforts to make immigrants into productive American workers. "These men of many nations must be taught American ways, the English language, and the right way to live," he stated. The Ford Motor Company instituted a six- to eight-month English language course that immigrant employees were compelled to attend, with graduates receiving diplomas qualifying them for citizenship. U.S. Steel and International Harvester sponsored similar programs, and, as one scholar has said, "a good many businessmen inaugurated factory classes, distributed civics lessons in pay envelopes, and even subsidized public evening schools."

A huge number of private nonprofit organizations also became involved in Americanization activities. The YMCA organized classes to teach immigrants English. Ethnic and religious organizations with ties to incoming immigrants actively promoted Americanization. Liberal reformers, conservative businessmen, and concerned citizens founded organizations such as the Committee on Information for Aliens, the North American Civic League for Immigrants, the Chicago League for the Protection of Immigrants, the Educational Alliance of New York City, the Baron de Hirsch Fund (aimed at Jewish immigrants), the Society for Italian Immigrants, and many similar organizations. These groups counseled newcomers, provided evening classes in the English language and American ways, and helped them find jobs and homes.

In due course, more than 30 states passed laws establishing Americanization programs. Connecticut even created a Department of Americanization. The federal government also became active, with the Bureau of Naturalization and the Bureau of Education competing vigorously to further their own assimilation efforts. By 1921 some 3,526 states, cities, towns, and communities were participating in Bureau of Naturalization programs.

The central institution for Americanization was the public school system. Indeed, public schools had been created in the nineteenth century and shaped in considerable part by the perceived need to Americanize and Protestantize immigrants. "People looked to education as the best way to transmit Anglo-American Protestant values and to prevent the collapse of republican institutions," summarizes historian Carl Kaestle. In 1921–22, as many as a thousand communities conducted "special public school programs to Americanize the foreign-born." Between 1915 and 1922, more than 1 million immigrants enrolled in such programs. School systems "saw public education as an instrument to create a unified society out of the multiplying diversity created by immigration," reports Reed Ueda.

Without these Americanizing activities starting in the early 1890s, America's dramatic 1924 reduction in immigration would in all likelihood have been imposed much earlier. Americanization made immigration acceptable to Americans. The success of the movement was manifest when the immigrants and their children rallied to the colors and marched off to fight their country's wars. In World War II in particular, racial, ethnic, and class identities were subordinated to national loyalty, and the identification of Americans with their country reached its highest point in history.

National identity then began to fade. In 1994, 19 scholars of American history and politics were asked to evaluate the level of American unity in 1930, 1950, 1970, and 1990. The year 1950, according to these experts, was the "zenith of American national integration." Since then "cultural and political fragmentation has increased" and "conflict emanating from intensified ethnic and religious consciousness poses the main current challenge to the American nation."

Fanning all of this was the new popularity among liberal elites of the doctrines of "multiculturalism" and "diversity," which elevate subnational, racial, ethnic, cultural, gender, and other identities over national identity, and encourage immigrants to maintain dual identities, loyalties, and citizenships. Multi-culturalism is basically an anti-Western ideology. Multiculturalists argue that white Anglo America has suppressed other cultural alternatives, and that America in the future should not be a society with a single pervasive national culture, but instead should become a "tossed salad" of many starkly different ingredients.

In sharp contrast to their predecessors, American political leaders have recently promoted measures consciously designed to weaken America's cultural identity and strengthen racial, ethnic, and other identities. President Clinton called for a "great revolution" to liberate Americans from their dominant European culture. Vice President Gore interpreted the nation's motto, E pluribus unum (Out of many, one), to mean "out of one, many." By 1992, even some liberals like Arthur Schlesinger, Jr. were warning that the "ethnic upsurge" which had begun "as a gesture of protest against the Anglocentric culture" had become "a cult, and today it threatens to become a counter-revolution against the original theory of America as 'one people,' a common culture, a single nation."

These efforts by members of government to deconstruct the nation they led are, quite possibly, without precedent in human history. Important parts of academia, the media, business, and the professions, joined them in the effort. A study by Paul Vitz of 22 school texts published in the 1970s and 1980s for grades three and six found that only five out of 670 stories and articles in these readers had "any patriotic theme." All five dealt with the American Revolution; none had "anything to do with American history since 1780." In four of the five stories the principal person is a girl, in three the same girl, Sybil Ludington. The 22 books lack any story "featuring Nathan Hale, Patrick Henry, Daniel Boone, or Paul Revere's ride." "Patriotism," Vitz concludes, "is close to nonexistent" in these readers.

The deconstructionist coalition, however, does not include most Americans. In poll after poll, majorities of Americans reject ideas and measures that would lessen national identity and promote subnational identities. Everyday Americans remain deeply patriotic, nationalistic in their outlook, and committed to their national culture, creed, and identity. A major gap has thus developed between portions of our elite and the bulk of our populace over what America is and should be.

Popular opposition to the ideology of multiculturalism developed quickly. During the 1990s, bureaucrats and judges, including some who had earlier backed racial categorization and preferences, began to moderate and even reverse their views. New organizations of scholars and teachers grew up to counter efforts to rewrite American history and school curricula. Energetic "one America" activists and organizations forced votes to end affirmative action and bilingual education.

The American public is overwhelmingly opposed to official multilingualism. In 1986, 81 percent of the American public believed that "anyone who wants to stay in this country should have to learn English." In a 1988 poll, 76 percent of Californians rated speaking English as "very important" in making one an American, and 61 percent believed that the right to vote should be limited to English speakers. In a 1998 poll, 52 percent of Americans strongly supported, and 25 percent somewhat supported, legislation that would require all school instruction to be in English. Despite this clear consensus, legislators have been squeamish on language issues, which has forced proponents of American unity to use ballot initiatives to set the law.

From 1980 to 2000, 12 popular referenda were staged by pro-English or anti-bilingual-education groups. In all these cases political elites and establishment institutions like local newspapers and TV stations, local politicians, universities, labor unions, business federations, and religious groups overwhelmingly opposed the measures, as did heads of minority pressure groups. Yet the average vote in favor of pro-English positions was 65 percent.

In 1988, Presidential candidates George H. W. Bush and Michael Dukakis both opposed the official-English measures on the ballot in Florida, Arizona, and Colorado. In Florida the proposed constitutional amendment was also opposed by the governor, the attorney general, the secretary of state, the *Miami Herald*, the Greater Miami Chamber of Commerce, and many Hispanic organizations, yet it was approved by 86 percent of the voters and carried every county. In the bitter contest in Arizona, an official-English initiative was opposed by the governor, two former governors, both United States senators, the mayor of Phoenix, the Arizona Judges Association, the League of Arizona Cities and Towns, Jewish leaders, and the Arizona Ecumenical Council, yet it passed. In Colorado, the English measure was opposed by the governor, the lieutenant governor, the attorney general, the mayor of Denver, one United States senator, the leading Catholic bishops, the *Denver Post*, the state Democratic Party (the Republicans took no position), and Jesse Jackson. It was approved by 64 percent of Colorado's voters.

As one Stanford University professor commented, "the U.S. English leadership is probably justified in claiming that 'no one is for us but the people.' " A very similar pattern has appeared in referenda on bilingual education. Despite almost universal opposition among elites, 61 percent of California's voters (including majorities in every county except San Francisco) approved an end to bilingual education in 1998.

September 11 gave a major boost to the supporters of America as one people with a common culture. Yet the war to deconstruct our culture has not ended. It remains unresolved today whether America will be a nation of individuals with equal rights sharing a common culture, or an association of racial, ethnic, and cultural groups held together by hopes for material gains.

In this new environment, will today's immigrants assimilate as earlier waves did? Recent immigrants from India, Korea, Japan, and the Philippines—whose educational profiles more closely approximate those of American natives—have generally assimilated rapidly. Indians and Filipinos, of course, have been helped by their knowledge of English.

Latin American immigrants, particularly those from Mexico, have been slower in approximating American norms. In part this is a result of the large numbers and geographical concentration of Mexican arrivals. Also, the educational levels of Mexican immigrants and their descendants have been below that of other immigrants, and below the level of American natives. Moreover, Mexican activists have worked against assimilation.

Muslims, particularly Arab Muslims, also seem slow to assimilate compared with earlier groups. Elsewhere in the world, Muslim minorities have often proved to be "indigestible" by non-Muslim societies. A study of Los Angeles Muslims found ambivalent attitudes toward America: "A significant number of Muslims, particularly immigrant Muslims, do not have close ties or loyalty to the United States." When asked whether they had "closer ties or loyalty to Islamic countries (perhaps your country of birth) or the United States," 45 percent of the immigrants said Islamic countries, 10 percent the United States, and 32 percent "about the same." Among American-born Muslims, 19 percent chose Islamic countries, 38 percent the United States, and 28 percent about the same. Fifty-seven percent of the immigrants and 32 percent of the American-born Muslims said that "if given the choice, [they] would leave the United States to live in an Islamic country." Fifty-two percent of the interviewees said it was very important and 24 percent said it was quite important to replace public schools with Islamic schools.

The current wave of immigration to the U.S. has increased with each decade. During the 1960s, 3 million people entered the country. During the 1980s, 7 million people did. In the 1990s it was over 9 million. The foreign-born percentage of the American population, which was a bit above 5 percent in 1960, more than doubled to close to 12 percent in 2002.

The United States thus appears to face something new in its history: persistent high levels of immigration. The two earlier waves of heavy immigration (1840s and '50s; and 1880s to 1924) subsided as a result of world events. But absent a serious war or economic collapse, over 1 million immigrants are likely to enter the United States each year for the indefinite future. This may cause assimilation to be slower and less complete than it was for past waves of immigration.

That seems to be happening with today's immigration from Latin America, especially from Mexico. Mexican immigration is leading toward a demographic "reconquista" of areas Americans took from Mexico by force in the 1830s and 1840s. Mexican immigration is very different from immigration from other sources, due to its sheer size, its illegality, and its other special qualities. [*Editor's Note:* See Mr. Huntington's earlier feature article on this subject: "The Special Case of Mexican Immigration," *The American Enterprise,* December 2000.]

One reason Mexican immigration is special is simply because there are now so very many arrivals (legal and illegal) from that one country. Thanks to heavy Mexican inflows, for the very first time in history a majority of U.S. immigrants now speak a single non-English language (Spanish). The impact of today's large flow of Mexican immigrants is reinforced by other factors: the proximity of their country of origin; their geographical concentration within the United States; the improbability of their inflow ending or being significantly reduced; the decline of the assimilation movement; and the new enthusiasm of many American elites for multiculturalism, bilingualism, affirmative action, and cultural diversity instead of cultural unity. In addition, the Mexican government now actively promotes the export of its people to the United States while encouraging them to maintain their Mexican culture, identity, and nationality. President Vicente Fox regularly refers to himself as the president of 123 million Mexicans, 100 million in Mexico, 23 million in the United States. The net result is that Mexican immigrants and their progeny have not assimilated into American society as other immigrants did in the past, or as many other immigrants are doing now.

The lags in Mexican assimilation are clearly visible in current American social statistics. Language, education, occupation and income, citizenship, intermarriage, and identity are key criteria that can be used to gauge assimilation, and in these areas Mexicans generally lag behind other immigrants, past and present. In 2003, 89 percent of white and 80 percent of black Americans had graduated from high school, compared to 57 percent of Hispanics. In 2000, 34 percent of Mexican immigrants were high school graduates; subsequent generations of Mexican-Americans continued to lag in educational achievement. The economic position of Mexican immigrants and U.S.-born Mexicans parallels their lagging educational attainment.

The naturalization rate is one important indicator of political assimilation and is lower for Mexicans than for almost any other immigrant group. In 1990, for instance, the naturalization rate for Mexican immigrants in the country at least ten years was 32 percent, in contrast to 86 percent for immigrants from the Soviet Union, 82 percent for arrivals from Ireland, 82 percent for Poles, and 78 percent for Greek immigrants.

As for identity—the ultimate criterion of assimilation—the available evidence is limited and, in some respects, contradictory. Ron Unz states that "a quarter or more of Hispanics have shifted from their traditional Catholic faith to Protestant evangelical churches"—unquestionably a significant manifestation of assimilation. Other evidence, however, suggests a weak identification with America on the part of Mexican immigrants and their descendants. "The biggest problem we have is a cultural clash," the president of the National Council of La Raza said in 1995, "a clash between our values and the values in American society," the former being superior to the latter. One study of 1989–1990 survey data on Mexican-Americans found that "the longer the immigrants were in the United States, the less likely they were to agree that everyone should learn English," and "those more incorporated into mainstream society, the native-born Mexican-Americans, are less supportive of core American values than are the foreign-born." The growing numbers of Hispanics, according to a 1999 report, "help 'Latinize' many Hispanic people who are finding it easier to affirm their heritage . . . they find strength in numbers, as younger generations grow up with more ethnic pride and as a Latin influence starts permeating fields like entertainment, advertising, and politics."

The expansion of the Hispanic media encourages Hispanics to maintain their language and culture. The Mexican-owned Univision is the largest Spanish-language television network in the United States. Its nightly news audiences in New York, Los Angeles, and Chicago rival those of ABC, CBS, NBC, CNN, and Fox. The number of Spanish-language newspapers in the United States more than doubled from 166 in 1990 to 344 in 2003.

Problems in digesting Mexican immigrants would be less urgent if Mexicans were just one group among many. But because legal and illegal Mexicans comprise such a large proportion of our current immigrant flow, any assimilation problems arising within their ranks shape our immigrant experience. The overwhelming influence of Mexicans on America's immigration flow becomes clearly visible if one poses a thought experiment. What if Mexican immigration to the United States somehow abruptly stopped, while other immigration continued as at present? In such a case, illegal entries in particular would diminish dramatically. Agriculture and other businesses in the southwest would be disrupted, but the wages of low-income Americans would rise. Debates over the use of Spanish, and whether English should be made the official language of state and national governments, would fade away. Bilingual education and the controversies it spawns would decline. So also would controversies over welfare and other benefits for immigrants. The debate over whether immigrants are an economic burden on state and federal governments would be decisively resolved in the negative. The average education and skills of the immigrants coming to America would rise to levels unprecedented in American history. Our inflow of immigrants would again become highly diverse, which would increase incentives for all immigrants to learn English and absorb American culture. The possibility of a split between a predominantly Spanish-speaking America and English-speaking America would disappear, and with it a major potential threat to the cultural and possibly political integrity of the United States.

A glimpse of what a splintering of America into English- and Spanish-speaking camps might look like can be found in current-day Miami. Since the 1960s, first Cuban and then other Latin American immigrants have converted Miami from a fairly normal American city into a heavily Hispanic city. By 2000 Spanish was not just the language spoken in most homes in Miami, it was also the principal language of commerce, business, and politics. The local media and communications are increasingly Hispanic. In 1998, a Spanish-language television station became the number one station watched by Miamians—the first time a foreign-language station achieved that rating in a major American city.

The changing linguistic and ethnic makeup of Miami is reflected in the recent history of the *Miami Herald*, one of the most respected papers in the United States. The owners of the Herald first attempted to appeal to Hispanic readers and advertisers with a Spanish supplement, but this attempt to reach Hispanics and Anglos simultaneously, failed. Between 1960 and 1989, the percentage of Miami households reading the Herald fell from 80 percent to 40 percent. Eventually the Herald had to set up a separate Spanish paper, *El Nuevo Herald*.

Is Miami the future for Los Angeles and the southwest generally? In the end, the results could be similar: the creation of a large, distinct, Spanish-speaking community with economic and political resources sufficient to sustain its own Hispanic identity apart from the national identity of other Americans, and also sufficient to significantly influence American politics, government, and society. The process by which this might come about, however, is different. The Hispanization of Miami has been led from the top down by successful Cuban and other Central and South American immigrants. In the southwest, the overwhelming bulk of Spanish-speaking immigrants are Mexican, and have been poor, unskilled, and poorly educated. It appears that many of their offspring are likely to be similar. The pressures toward Hispanization in the southwest thus come from below, whereas those in South Florida came from above.

The persistence of Mexican immigration and the large absolute numbers of Mexicans in the southwest reduce the incentives for cultural assimilation. Mexican-Americans no longer think of themselves as members of a small minority who must accommodate the dominant group and adopt its culture. As their numbers increase, they become more committed to their own ethnic identity and culture. Sustained numerical expansion promotes cultural consolidation, and leads them not to minimize but to glory in the differences between their society and America generally.

The continuation of high levels of Mexican and Hispanic immigration and low rates of assimilation of these immigrants into American society and culture could eventually change America into a country of two languages, two cultures, and two peoples. This will not only transform America. It will also have deep consequences for Hispanics—who will be in America but not of the America that has existed for centuries.

5

"Patriot Games: The New Nativism of Samuel P. Huntington"

Louis Menand

In polls conducted during the past fifteen years, between ninety-six and ninety-eight per cent of all Americans said that they were "very" proud or "quite" proud of their country. When young Americans were asked whether they wanted to do something for their country, eighty-one per cent answered yes. Ninety-two per cent of Americans reported that they believe in God. Eighty-seven per cent said that they took "a great deal" of pride in their work, and although Americans work more hours annually than do people in other industrialized countries, ninety per cent said that they would work harder if it was necessary for the success of their organization. In all these categories, few other nations of comparable size and economic development even come close. By nearly every statistical measure, and by common consent, Americans are the most patriotic people in the world.

Is there a problem here? Samuel P. Huntington . . . believes that there is. The problem is the tiny fraction of Americans in whom national pride, patriotic loyalty, religious faith, and regard for the work ethic might possibly be less than wholehearted. He has identified these people as the heads of transnational corporations, members of the liberal élite, holders of dual citizenship, Mexican-Americans, and what he refers to as "deconstructionists." He thinks that these groups are responsible for an incipient erosion of national identity, a development that he views with an alarm that, while it is virtually unqualified, is somewhat underexplained. Although the erosion of national identity at the hands of multiculturalists and liberal élites is something that people were fretting and fighting about five or ten years ago, a lot of the conviction leaked out of the argument after the attacks of September 11th. This is partly because the public response to the attacks was spontaneously and unequivocally patriotic, suggesting that the divisions animating the so-called "culture wars" ran less deep than the cultural warriors supposed, and partly because the cultural pluralism that had once seemed threatening became, overnight, an all but official attribute of national identity. Inclusiveness turned out to be a flag around which Americans could rally. It was what most distinguished *us* from *them*. The reality, of course, is more complicated than the ideology, but the ideology is what Huntington is worried about, and either his book is a prescient analysis of trends obscure to the rest of us or he has missed the point.

Huntington's name for ideology is "culture." The advantage of the term is that it embraces collective beliefs and assumptions that may not be explicit most of the time; the trouble with it is that it is notoriously expansive. Culture, ultimately, is everything that is not nature. American culture includes American appetites and American dress, American work etiquette and American entertainment, American piety and American promiscuity—all the things that Americans recognize, by their absence, as American when they visit other countries. What Huntington wants to talk about is a specific cluster of American beliefs, habits, assumptions, and institutions. He calls this cluster "America's core culture." It includes, he says, "the Christian religion, Protestant values and moralism, a work ethic, the English language, British traditions of law, justice, and the limits of government power, and a legacy of European art, literature, philosophy, and music," plus "the American Creed with its principles of liberty, equality, individualism, representative government, and private property." . . . This, he maintains, is the culture of the original European settlers; it is the culture to which, until the late twentieth century, every immigrant group assimilated; and it is the culture that is now imperilled.

Huntington's core values are rather abstract. It would probably take many guesses for most of the Americans who score high in the patriotism surveys to come up with these items as the basis for their sentiments. What Americans like about their country, it seems fair to say, is the quality of life, and if the quality of life can be attributed to "a legacy of European art, literature, philosophy, and music" then Americans, even Americans who would be hard-pressed to name a single European philosopher, are in favor of those things, too.

It could be argued that Americans owe the quality of life they enjoy to America's core culture, but Huntington does not argue this. He cares about the core culture principally for its unifying effects, its usefulness as a motive for solidarity. He is, in this book, not interested in values per se; he is interested in national security and national power. He thinks that the erosion or diffusion of *any* cluster of collective ideals, whatever those ideals may be, leads to weakness and vulnerability.

Most readers who are not political scientists know Huntington from his book "The Clash of Civilizations and the Remaking of World Order," which was published in 1996, and which proposed that cultural differences would be the major cause of global tension in the future. The book was translated into thirty-three languages and inspired international conferences; its argument acquired new interest and credibility after the attacks of 2001 and the American response to them. Huntington's thesis could be taken as an answer to Francis Fukuyama's idea of "the end of history." History—that is, conflicts among groups—did not come to an end with the Cold War and the demise of liberalism's main ideological opponent, Huntington argued. The defeat of Communism did not mean that everyone had become a liberal. A civilization's belief that its values have become universal, he warned, has been, historically, the sign that it is on the brink of decline. His book therefore appealed both to people in the West who were anxious about the diversification or erosion of Western culture and to people outside the West who wanted to believe that modernization and Westernization are neither necessary nor inevitable.

The optimal course for the West in a world of potential civilizational conflict, Huntington concluded, was not to reach out to non-Western civilizations with the idea that people in those civilizations are really like us. He thinks that they are not really like us, and that it is both immoral to insist on making other countries conform to Western values (since that must involve trampling on their own values) and naïve to believe that the West speaks a universal language. If differences among civilizations are a perpetual source of rivalry and a potential source of wars, then a group of people whose loyalty to their own culture is attenuated is likely to be worse off relative to other groups. Hence his anxiety about what he thinks is a trend toward cultural diffusion in the United States.

You might think that if cultural difference is what drives people to war, then the world would be a safer place if *every* group's loyalty to its own culture were more attenuated. If you thought that, though, you would be a liberal cosmopolitan idealist, and Huntington would have no use for you. Huntington is a domestic monoculturalist and a global multiculturalist (and an enemy of domestic multiculturalism and global monoculturalism). "Civilizations are the ultimate human tribes," as he put it in "The Clash of Civilizations." The immutable psychic need people have for a shared belief system is precisely the premise of his political theory. You can't fool with immutable psychic needs.

* * *

The bad guys in Huntington's scenario can be divided into two groups. One is composed of intellectuals, people who preach dissent from the values of the "core culture."

* * *

The other group in Huntington's analysis is composed of what could be called the globalists. These are the new immigrants and the transnational businessmen. The new immigrants are people who, as Huntington describes them, "may assimilate into American society without assimilating the core American culture." Many maintain dual citizenship (Huntington calls these people "ampersands"); some do not bother to become American citizens at all, since the difference between the benefits available to citizens and those available to aliens has become smaller and smaller (a trend that originated, Huntington notes, among "unelected judges and administrators"). In a society in which multiculturalism is encouraged, the loyalty of these immigrants to the United States and its core culture is fragile. What distinguishes the new immigration from the old is the exponential increase in global mobility. As Huntington acknowledges, it has always been true that not all immigrants to the United States come to stay. A significant proportion come chiefly to earn money, and eventually they return to the countries they were born in. Transportation today is so cheap and available, though, that people can maintain lives in two nations indefinitely.

Mobility is also what distinguishes the new businessmen, the transnationals. These are, in effect, people without national loyalties at all, not even dual ones, since they identify with their corporations, and their corporations have offices, plants, workers, suppliers, and consumers all over the world. It is no longer in Ford's interest to be thought of as an American company. Ford's market is global, and it conceives of itself as a global entity. These new businessmen "have little need for national loyalty, view national boundaries as obstacles that thankfully are vanishing, and see national governments as residues from the past whose only useful function now is to facilitate the elite's global operations," Huntington says. "The distinction between America and the world is disappearing because of the triumph of America as the only global superpower." This drives him into the same perverse position he got himself into at the end of his attack on the deconstructionists: it is better to have rivals than to be dominant. It is good to compete, but it is bad to win. If we won, we would lose our national identity. The position, though, is consistent with the argument Huntington made in "The Clash of Civilizations"—the argument that nation-states ought to remain inside their own cultural boxes.

The most inflammatory section of "Who Are We?" is the chapter on Mexican immigration. Huntington reports that in 2000 the foreign-born population of the United States included almost eight million people from Mexico. The next country on the list was China, with 1.4 million. Huntington's concern is that Mexican-Americans (and, in Florida, Cuban-Americans) demonstrate less motivation to learn English and assimilate to the Anglo culture than other immigrant groups have historically, and that, thanks to the influence of bilingualism advocates, unelected judges, cosmopolites, and a compliant Congress, it has become less necessary for them to do so. They can remain, for generations, within their own cultural and linguistic enclave, and they are consequently likely to be less loyal to the United States than other hyphenated Americans are. Huntington believes that the United States "could change . . . into a culturally bifurcated Anglo-Hispanic society with two national languages." He can imagine portions of the American Southwest being ceded back to Mexico.

This part of Huntington's book was published first as an article in *Foreign Policy*, and it has already provoked responses, many in the letters column of that journal. Michael Elliott, in his column in *Time*, pointed out that in the Latino National Political Survey, conducted from 1989 to 1990, eighty-four per cent of Mexican-Americans expressed "extremely" or "very" strong love for the United States (against ninety-two per cent of Anglos). Ninety-one per cent said that they were "extremely proud" or "very proud" of the United States. As far as reluctance to learn English is concerned, Richard Alba and Victor Nee, in "Remaking the American Mainstream: Assimilation and Contemporary Immigration," report that in 1990 more than ninety-five per cent of Mexican-Americans between the ages of twenty-five and forty-four who were born in the United States could speak English well. They conclude that although Hispanic-Americans, particularly those who live close to the border, may continue to speak their original language (usually along with English) a generation longer than other groups have tended to do, "by any standard, linguistic assimilation is widespread."

Huntington's account of the nature of Mexican immigration to the United States seems deliberately alarmist. He notes, for example, that since 1975 roughly two-thirds of Mexican immigrants have entered illegally. This is the kind of statistic that is continually cited to suggest a new and dangerous demographic hemorrhaging. But, as Mae Ngai points out, in "Impossible Subjects: Illegal Aliens and the Making of Modern America," a work a hundred times more nuanced than Huntington's, the surge in illegal immigration was the predictable consequence of the reform of the immigration laws in 1965. In the name of liberalizing immigration policy, the new law imposed a uniform quota on all countries, regardless of size. Originally, Western Hemisphere countries were exempted from specific quotas, but the act was amended in 1976, and Mexico was assigned the same annual quota (twenty thousand) as, for example, Belgium. This effectively illegalized a large portion of the Mexican immigrant population. "Legal" and "illegal," as Ngai's book illustrates, are administrative constructions, always subject to change; they do not tell us anything about the desirability of the persons so constructed. (Ngai's analysis also suggests that one reason that Asian-Americans are stereotyped by other Americans as products of a culture that places a high value on education is that the 1965 immigration act gives preference to applicants with professional skills, and, in the nineteen-sixties and seventies, for reasons internal to their own countries, many Asian professionals chose to emigrate. Like professionals from any other culture, they naturally made education a priority for their children.)

Finally, some of Huntington's statistical claims are improperly derived. "Three out of ten Hispanic students drop out of school compared to one in eight blacks and one in fourteen whites," he says, and he cites other studies to argue that Hispanic-Americans are less educationally assimilated than other groups. Educational attainment is not an index of intellectual capacity, though; it is an economic trade-off. The rate of high-school graduation is in part a function of the local economy. For example, according to the Urban Institute and the Manhattan Institute for Policy Research, Florida has one of the worst high-school graduation rates in the United States. This may be because it has a service economy, in which you do not need a diploma to get reasonably steady work. To argue that Hispanic-Americans are disproportionately less likely to finish school, one would have to compare them not with non-Hispanic Americans nationally but with non-Hispanic Americans in the same region. Huntington provides no such comparisons. He is cheered, however, by Hispanic-Americans' high rate of conversion to evangelical Protestantism.

This brings us back to the weird emptiness at the heart of Huntington's analysis, according to which conversion to a fundamentalist faith is counted a good thing just because many other people already share that faith. Huntington never explains, in "Who Are We?," why Protestantism, private enterprise, and the English language are more desirable features of social life or more conducive to self-realization than, say, Judaism, kibbutzim, and Hebrew. He only fears, as an American, their transformation into something different. But how American is that? Huntington's understanding of American culture would be less rigid if he paid more attention to the actual value of his core values. One of the virtues of a liberal democracy is that it is designed to accommodate social and cultural change. Democracy is not a dogma; it is an experiment. That is what Lincoln said in the Gettysburg Address—and there is no more hallowed text in the American Creed than that.

Multiculturalism, in the form associated with people like Clinton and Gore, is part of the democratic experiment. It may have a lot of shortcomings as a political theory, but it is absurd to say that it is anti-Western. Its roots, as Charles Taylor and many other writers have shown, are in the classic texts of Western literature and philosophy. And, unless you are a monoculturalist hysteric, the differences that such multiculturalism celebrates are nearly all completely anodyne. One keeps wondering what Huntington, in his chapter on Mexican-Americans, means by "cultural bifurcation." What is this alien culture that threatens to infect Anglo-Americans? Hispanic-American culture, after all, is a culture derived largely from Spain, which, the last time anyone checked, was in Europe. Here is what we eventually learn (Huntington is quoting from a book called "The Americano Dream," by a Texas businessman named Lionel Sosa): Hispanics are different because "they still put family first, still make room in their lives for activities other than business, are more religious and more community oriented." Pull up the drawbridge!

Insofar as multiculturalism has become, in essence, an official doctrine in public education in the United States, its effects are the opposite of its rhetoric. "Diverse" is what Americans are taught to call themselves as a people, and a whole society cannot think that diversity is good and be all that diverse at the same time. The quickest and most frictionless way to nullify difference is to mainstream it. How culturally unified do Americans need to be, anyway? In an analysis like Huntington's, a nation's strength is a function of the strength of other nations. You don't need microchips if every other country on the planet is still in the Stone Age. Just a little bronze will do. But if the world is becoming more porous, more transnational, more tuned to the same economic, social, and informational frequency—if the globe is more global, which means more Americanized—then the need for national cultural homogeneity is lesser, not greater. The stronger societies will be the more cosmopolitan ones.

Perhaps this sounds like sentimental internationalism. Let's be cynical, then. The people who determine international relations are the political, business, and opinion élites, not the populace. It is overwhelmingly in the interest of those élites today to adapt to an internationalist environment, and they exert a virtually monopolistic control over information, surveillance, and the means of force. People talk about the Internet as a revolutionary populist medium, but the Internet is essentially a marketing tool. They talk about terrorist groups as representatives of a civilization opposed to the West, but most terrorists are dissidents from the civilization they pretend to be fighting for. What this kind of talk mostly reveals is the nonexistence of any genuine alternative to modernization and Westernization. During the past fifty years, the world has undergone two processes. One is de-Stalinization, and the other is decolonization. The second is proving to be much more complicated than the first, and this is because the stamp of the West is all over the rest of the world, and the rest of the world is now putting its stamp on the West. There are no aboriginal civilizations to return to. You can regret the mess, but it's too late to put the colors back in their jars.

And why isn't internationalism, as a number of writers have recently argued, a powerful resource for Americans? The United States doesn't have an exclusive interest in opposing and containing the forces of intolerance, superstition, and fanaticism; the whole world has an interest in opposing and containing those things. On September 12, 2001, the world was with us. Because of our government's mad conviction that it was *our* way of life that was under attack, not the way of life of civilized human beings everywhere, and that only *we* knew what was best to do about it, we squandered our chance to be with the world. The observation is now so obvious as to be banal. That does not make it less painful.

DISCUSSION QUESTIONS

1. Making English a government's official language means that all official documents, ballots, and school instruction would be in English, with no translations provided by the government (although private organizations would be free to provide translations). Should English be the "official" language of the United States? What are the advantages and disadvantages in using only a single language for all government activity? Does having a common language foster assimilation and national unity?

2. Should the United States, as a deliberate strategy, seek to reinforce what it perceives as "shared American values"? If so, how? If not, why not? Should it take the ideology and political values of potential immigrants explicitly into account?

3. A visitor from another country asks you, "What does it mean to be an American?" What do you say?

CHAPTER 2

Constructing the Government:
The Founding and the Constitution

6

"The Nature of American Constitutionalism"
from *The Origins of the American Constitution*

MICHAEL KAMMEN

The Constitution is a remarkably simple document that has provided a frame-work of governance for the United States for nearly 220 years. It establishes a shared sovereignty between the states and the federal government, a separation and checking of powers between three branches of government, qualifications for citizenship and holding office, and a delineation of the rights considered so fun-damental their restriction by the government requires extensive due process and a compelling national or state concern. Yet the Constitution's simple text pro-duces constant controversy over its interpretation and efforts to bend, twist, and nudge its application to changing economic markets, technology, social trends, and family structures. The document's durability and flexibility amidst conflict and social change is a tribute not only to the men who drafted the Constitution in 1787, but to the American people and their willingness to embrace the challenges of self-governance at the time of the Revolution and today.

In the following article Michael Kammen argues that in order to begin to un-derstand the Constitution and the continuous debate surrounding its interpreta-tion, we must look to the history of American constitutionalism. Informed by John Locke's Second Treatise of Government, *the British constitution, and a colonial experience deemed an affront to basic liberties and rights, Americans plunged into the writing of the Constitution as a means to delegate power from the sovereign people to their elected and appointed agents. It is, as Kammen notes, quite remarkable that the American states chose to draft state constitu-tions in the midst of a revolutionary battle of independence, rather than establish provisional governments. It is similarly remarkable that these state constitutions have grown significantly in length over the years and are so readily amended and even rewritten, in contrast to the relatively succinct and difficult-to-amend Constitution of the United States.*

Kammen suggests that the Constitution's simplicity and durability lies in both the historic need for compromise between conflicting interests, as well as the surprising common ground that nevertheless existed over basic principles: the need to protect personal liberty, the commitment to a republican form of government, and the importance of civic virtue for preserving citizen sovereignty. This embrace of basic governing principles could explain the deeper devotion to the U.S. Constitution, in contrast to the state documents, as well might the fear that an amended or completely altered Constitution might prove less malleable and accommodating for the governance of a diverse nation.

The Nature of American Constitutionalism

"Like the Bible, it ought to be read again and again." Franklin Delano Roosevelt made that remark about the U.S. Constitution in March 1937, during one of those cozy "fireside chats" that reached millions of Americans by radio. "It is an easy document to understand," he added. And six months later, speaking to his fellow citizens from the grounds of the Washington Monument on Constitution Day—a widely noted speech because 1937 marked the sesquicentennial of the Constitution, and because the President had provoked the nation with his controversial plan to add as many as six new justices to the Supreme Court—Roosevelt observed that the Constitution was "a layman's document, not a lawyer's contract," a theme that he reiterated several times in the course of this address.

It seems fair to say that Roosevelt's assertions were approximately half true. No one could disagree that the Constitution ought to be read and reread. Few would deny that it was meant to be comprehended by laymen, by ordinary American citizens and aspirants for citizenship. Nevertheless, we must ponder whether it is truly "an easy document to understand." Although the very language of the Constitution is neither technical nor difficult, and although it is notably succinct—one nineteenth-century expert called it "a great code in a small compass"—abundant evidence exists that vast numbers of Americans, ever since 1787, have not understood it as well as they might. Even the so-called experts (judges, lawyers, political leaders, and teachers of constitutional law) have been unable to agree in critical instances about the proper application of key provisions of the Constitution, or about the intentions of those who wrote and approved it. Moreover, we do acknowledge that the Constitution developed from a significant number of compromises, and that the document's ambiguities are, for the most part, not accidental.

Understanding the U.S. Constitution is essential for many reasons. One of the most urgent is that difficult issues are now being and will continue to be settled in accordance with past interpretations and with our jurists' sense of what the founders meant. In order to make such difficult determinations, we begin with the document itself. Quite often, however, we also seek guidance from closely related or contextual documents, such as the notes kept by participants in the Constitutional Convention held at Philadelphia in 1787, from the correspondence of delegates and other prominent leaders during the later 1780s, from *The Federalist* papers, and even from some of the Anti-Federalist tracts written in opposition to the Constitution. In doing so, we essentially scrutinize the origins of American constitutionalism.

If observers want to know what is meant by constitutionalism, they must uncover several layers of historical thought and experience in public affairs. Most obviously we look to the ideas that developed in the United States during the final quarter of the eighteenth century—unquestionably the most brilliant and creative era in the entire history of American political thought. We have in mind particularly, however, a new set of assumptions that developed after 1775 about the very nature of a constitution. Why, for example, when the colonists found themselves nearly in a political state of nature after 1775, did they promptly feel compelled to write state constitutions, many of which contained a bill of rights? The patriots were, after all, preoccupied with fighting a revolution. Why not simply set up provisional governments based upon those they already had and wait until Independence was achieved? If and when the revolution succeeded, there would be time enough to write permanent constitutions.

The revolutionaries did not regard the situation in such casual and pragmatic terms. They shared a strong interest in what they called the science of politics. They knew a reasonable amount about the history of political theory. They believed in the value of ideas applied to problematic developments, and they felt that their circumstances were possibly unique in all of human history. They knew with assurance that their circumstances were changing, and changing rapidly. They wanted self-government, obviously, but they also wanted legitimacy for their newborn governments. Hence a major reason for writing constitutions. They believed in the doctrine of the social contract (about which Jean-Jacques Rousseau had written in 1762) and they believed in government by the consent of the governed: two more reasons for devising written constitutions approved by the people or by their representatives.

The men responsible for composing and revising state constitutions in the decade following 1775 regarded constitutions as social compacts that delineated the fundamental principles upon which the newly formed polities were agreed and to which they pledged themselves. They frequently used the word "experiment" because they believed that they were making institutional innovations that were risky, for they seemed virtually unprecedented. They intended to create republican governments and assumed that to do so successfully required a fair amount of social homogeneity, a high degree of consensus regarding moral values, and a pervasive capacity for virtue, by which they meant unselfish, public-spirited behavior.

Even though they often spoke of liberty, they meant civil liberty rather than natural liberty. The latter implied unrestrained freedom—absolute liberty for the individual to do as he or she pleased. The former, by contrast, meant freedom of action so long as it was not detrimental to others and was beneficial to the common weal. When they spoke of *political* liberty they meant the freedom to be a participant, to vote and hold public office, responsible commitments that ought to be widely shared if republican institutions were to function successfully.

The colonists' experiences throughout the seventeenth and eighteenth centuries had helped to prepare them for this participatory and contractual view of the nature of government. Over and over again, as the circles of settlement expanded, colonists learned to improvise the rules by which they would be governed. They had received charters and had entered into covenants or compacts that may be described as proto-constitutional, i.e., cruder and less complete versions of the constitutional documents that would be formulated in 1776 and subsequently. These colonial charters not only described the structure of government, but frequently explained what officials (often called magistrates) could or could not do.

As a result, by the 1770s American attitudes toward constitutionalism were simultaneously derivative as well as original. On the one hand, they extravagantly admired the British constitution ("unwritten" in the sense that it was not contained in a single document) and declared it to be the ultimate achievement in the entire history of governmental development. On the other hand, as Oscar and Mary Handlin have explained, Americans no longer conceived of constitutions in general as the British had for centuries.

> In the New World the term, constitution, no longer referred to the actual organization of power developed through custom, prescription, and precedent. Instead it had come to mean a written frame of government setting fixed limits on the use of power. The American view was, of course, closely related to the rejection of the old conception that authority descended from the Crown to its officials. In the newer view—that authority was derived from the consent of the governed—the written constitution became the instrument by which the people entrusted power to their agents.[1]

*   *   *

Issues, Aspirations, and Apprehensions in 1787–1788

The major problems that confronted the Constitution-makers, and the issues that separated them from their opponents, can be specified by the key words that recur so frequently in the documents that follow in this collection. The Federalists often refer to the need for much more energy, stability, and efficiency in the national government. They fear anarchy and seek a political system better suited to America's geographical expanse: "an extensive sphere" was Madison's phrase in a letter to Jefferson.

The Anti-Federalists were apprehensive about "unrestrained power" (George Mason's words), about the great risk of national "consolidation" rather than a true confederation, about the failure to include a bill of rights in the new Constitution, about the prospect of too much power in the federal judiciary, about the "tendency to aristocracy" (see the "Federal Farmer"*), about insufficient separation of powers, and a government unresponsive to the needs of diverse and widely scattered people.

Because the two sides disagreed so strongly about the nature of the proposed government—was it genuinely federal or really national?—it is all too easy to lose sight of the common ground that they shared, a common ground that made it possible for many Anti-Federalists to support the Constitution fully even before George Washington's first administration came to a close in 1793. Both sides felt an absolute commitment to republicanism and the protection of personal liberty, as we have already seen. Both sides acknowledged that a science of politics was possible and ought to be pursued, but that "our own experience" (Madison's view, though held by "Brutus"† also) ought to be heeded above all. A majority on both sides accepted the inevitable role that interests would play in public affairs and recognized that public opinion would be a powerful force. The phrase "public opinion" appears eleven times explicitly in *The Federalist* papers, and many other times implicitly or indirectly.

The desire for happiness was invoked constantly. Although admittedly a vague and elusive concept, it clearly meant much more than the safeguarding of property (though the protection of property belonged under the rubric of happiness in the minds of many). For some it simply meant personal contentment; but increasingly there were leaders, such as George Washington, who spoke of "social happiness," which referred to harmony among diverse groups. David Humphreys's "Poem on the Happiness of America" (1786) provides an indication that this notion had national as well as individual and societal connotations.

Although both sides believed that the preservation of liberty was one of the most essential ends of government, the continued existence of chattel slavery in a freedom-loving society created considerable awkwardness for the founders. In 1775–1776, when the revolutionaries had explained the reasons for their rebellion, they frequently referred to a British plot to "enslave" Americans. The constant invocation of that

* [The pen name of Richard Henry Lee of Virginia, a noted Anti-Federalist.]
† [The pen name of Robert Yates, an Anti-Federalist.]

notion has puzzled many students because whatever the wisdom or unwisdom of imperial policy in general, there most certainly was no conspiracy in London to enslave America.

There really should be no mystery about the colonists' usage, however, because as good Lockeans they knew full well the argument in chapter four of John Locke's *Second Treatise of Government*, entitled "Of Slavery" (an argument reiterated in Rousseau's *Social Contract*). "The liberty of man in society," Locke wrote, "is to be under no other legislative power but that established by consent in the commonwealth, nor under the dominion of any will or restraint of any law but what that legislative shall enact according to the trust put in it." The denial of *full* freedom quite simply meant "slavery."

Slavery and the international slave trade were discussed extensively in 1787 at the Constitutional Convention. By then, however, "slavery" was not often used as a theoretical and general synonym for unfreedom. It meant the permanent possession of one person (black) by another (white), usually for life, the slaveowner being entitled to own the children of his or her chattel as well. We must remember that the Convention met in secret session, and that the delegates agreed not to divulge information about their proceedings for fifty years. Consequently not very much was said publicly about slavery in 1787–1788 in connection with the Constitution. Not until 1840, when the U.S. government published James Madison's detailed notes on the Convention debates, did Americans learn just how much had been compromised at Philadelphia in order to placate South Carolina and Georgia. The Constitution essentially protected slavery where it existed, and remained mute about the legality of slavery in territories that might one day become additional states. Accommodation had prevailed in 1787, which meant, as it turned out, postponing for seventy-four years the moral and political crisis of the Union.

Legacies of American Constitutionalism

Although it is difficult for us fully to imagine the complexities of interest group politics, regional rivalries, and ideological differences in 1787, the instrumental achievement of that extraordinary Convention has generally been appreciated over the years. Even such a sardonic mind as H. L. Mencken's conceded as much. "The amazing thing about the Constitution," he wrote, "is that it is as good as it is—that so subtle and complete a document emerged from that long debate. Most of the Framers, obviously, were second-rate men; before and after their session they accomplished nothing in the world. Yet during that session they made an almost perfect job of the work in hand."

Their accomplishment was, indeed, remarkable. The distribution and separation of powers among three branches at the national level, and the development of federalism as a means of apportioning sovereignty between the nation and the states, have received broad recognition and the compliment of imitation by many other nations.

Equally appreciated is the fact that the U.S. Constitution is the oldest written national constitution in the world. (The Massachusetts Constitution of 1780, although amended and revised many times, is even older.) Its endurance is genuinely remarkable. We should therefore note that the framers deserve much of the credit for that endurance, not simply because they transcended their own limitations, * * * but because they contrived to restrict the ease with which the Constitution might be revised or reconsidered. There was considerable talk in 1787–1788 about holding a second convention in order to refine the product of the first. Anti-Federalists and many who were undecided wanted such a course of action. George Washington, however, regarded that idea as impractical. Hamilton, despite his dissatisfaction with many aspects of the Constitution, doubted whether a second convention could possibly be as successful as the first; and Madison feared a serious erosion of what had been accomplished in 1787.

It is easy to forget that the Philadelphia Convention vastly exceeded its authority, and that the men who met there undertook what amounted to a usurpation of legitimate authority. As [President] Franklin Delano Roosevelt pointed out on Constitution Day in 1937, contemporaries who opposed the newly drafted document "insisted that the Constitution itself was unconstitutional under the Articles of Confederation. But the ratifying conventions overruled them." The right of revolution had been explicitly invoked in 1776 and implicitly practiced in 1787. Having done their work, however, most of the delegates did not believe that it ought to be repealed or casually revised.

The complexity of changing or adding to the original document had profound implications for the subsequent history of American constitutionalism. First, it meant that in order to gain acceptance of their handiwork, the Federalists had to commit themselves, unofficially, to the formulation of a bill of rights when the first Congress met in 1789, even though many Federalists felt that such a list of protections was superfluous. They protested that a finite list of specified safeguards would imply that numerous other liberties might not be protected against encroachment by the government. The point, ultimately, is that promulgation of the U.S. Constitution required two sets of compromises rather than one: those that took place among the delegates to the Convention, and the subsequent sense that support for ratification would be rewarded by the explicit enumeration of broad civil liberties.

Next, the existence of various ambiguities in the Constitution meant that explication would subsequently be required by various authorities, such as the Supreme Court. The justices' interpretations would become part of the total "package" that we call American constitutionalism; but the justices did not always agree with one another, and the rest of the nation did not always agree with the justices. Those realities gave rise to an ongoing pattern that might be called conflict-within-consensus.

Some of those disputes and ambiguities involved very basic questions: What are the implications and limits of consent? Once we have participated in the creation of a polity and agreed to abide by its rules, then what? How are we to resolve the conflict that arises when the wishes or needs of a majority diminish the liberties or interests of a minority? This last question was the tough issue faced by the New England states in 1814, when they contemplated secession, and by South Carolina in 1828–1833 when a high tariff designed to protect northern manufacturing threatened economic distress to southern agricultural interests. And that, of course, was the thorny issue that precipitated southern secession and the greatest constitutional crisis of all in 1860–1861.

There is yet another ambiguity, or contradiction, in American constitutional thought—though it is less commonly noticed than the one described in the previous paragraph. As we have observed, the founders were not eager for a second convention, or for easy revisions or additions to their handiwork. They did provide for change; but they made the process complicated and slow. They did not believe that the fundamental law of a nation should be casually altered; and most Americans have accepted that constraint.

Nevertheless, on the *state* level Americans have amended, expanded, revised, and totally rewritten their constitutions with some frequency. A great deal of so-called positive law (i.e., legislative enactments) finds its way into state constitutions, with the result that many modern ones exceed one hundred pages in length. There is no clear explanation for this striking pattern of divergence between constitutionalism on the national and state levels. The curious pattern does suggest, however, that Americans have regarded the U.S. Constitution of 1787 as more nearly permanent than their state constitutions. Perhaps the pattern only tells us that achieving a national consensus for change in a large and diverse society is much more difficult than achieving a statewide consensus for change.

Whatever the explanation for this dualism in American constitutionalism, the paradox does not diminish the historical reality that writers of the federal as well as the first state constitutions all tried to establish charters clearly suited to the cultural assumptions and political realities of the American scene. Even though the founders explored the history of political thought in general and the history of republics in particular, they reached the commonsense conclusion that a constitution must be adapted to the character and customs of a people. Hence the debate in 1787–1788 over the relative merits of "consolidation" versus "confederation." Hence the concern about what sort of governmental system would work most effectively over a large geographical expanse. James

Madison conveyed this sense of American exceptionalism several times in a letter to Thomas Jefferson (then U.S. minister to France) in 1788, when a bill of rights was under consideration.

On August 28, 1788, a month after New York became the eleventh state to ratify the Constitution, George Washington sent Alexander Hamilton a letter from his temporary retirement at Mount Vernon. The future president acknowledged that public affairs were proceeding more smoothly than he had expected. Consequently, he wrote, "I hope the political Machine may be put in motion, without much effort or hazard of miscarrying." As he soon discovered, to put the new constitutional machine in motion would require considerable effort. It did not miscarry because the "machine" had been so soundly designed. A concerted effort would be required, however, to keep the machine successfully in operation. That should not occasion surprise. The founders had assumed an involved citizenry; and the governmental system they created functions best when their assumption is validated. That is the very essence of democratic constitutionalism.

DISCUSSION QUESTIONS

1. In your view, what would Kammen think about recent efforts to amend the Constitution to ban abortion, ban gay marriage, mandate a balanced budget, protect the flag against desecration, and protect victims' rights?

2. Although the flexibility of the Constitution helps explain its longevity, that flexibility comes at a price: ambiguity and gaps in constitutional language. What are some examples of constitutional language that is ambiguous?

3. One reason that Kammen argues it is important to understand the origins of American constitutionalism is that many judges today use their understanding of the Founders' intentions to inform their decisions. To what extent should the Founders' intentions influence modern court decisions? What are the advantages and disadvantages of this "original intent" perspective on jurisprudence?

NOTES

1. Mary Handlin, *The Dimensions of Liberty* (Cambridge, Mass., 1961), p. 55.

7

The Federalist, No. 15

Alexander Hamilton

Despite the deference given the Constitution today, it did not command instant respect in 1787. The fight for ratification was bitter between the Federalists (those who supported the Constitution) and the Anti-Federalists (who feared that the new national government would become too powerful).

The Federalist Papers, *originally written as a series of newspaper editorials intended to persuade New York to ratify the Constitution, remains the most valuable exposition of the political theory underlying the Constitution. In* The Federalist, No. 15, *reprinted below, Alexander Hamilton is at his best arguing for the necessity of a stronger central government than that established under the Articles of Confederation. He points out the practical impossibility of engaging in concerted action when each of the thirteen states retains virtual sovereignty, and the need for a strong central government to hold the new country together politically and economically.*

In the course of the preceding papers I have endeavored, my fellow-citizens, to place before you in a clear and convincing light the importance of Union to your political safety and happiness. * * * [T]he point next in order to be examined is the "insufficiency of the present Confederation to the preservation of the Union." * * * There are material imperfections in our national system and * * * something is necessary to be done to rescue us from impending anarchy. The facts that support this opinion are no longer objects of speculation. They have forced themselves upon the sensibility of the people at large, and have at length extorted . . . a reluctant confession of the reality of those defects in the scheme of our federal government which have been long pointed out and regretted by the intelligent friends of the Union.

We may indeed with propriety be said to have reached almost the last stage of national humiliation. There is scarcely anything that can wound the pride or degrade the character of an independent nation which we do not experience. Are there engagements to the performance of which we are held by every tie respectable among men? These are the subjects of constant and unblushing violation. Do we owe debts to foreigners and to our own citizens contracted in a time of imminent peril for the preservation of our political existence? These remain without any proper or satisfactory provision for their discharge. * * * Are we in a condition to resent or to repel the aggression? We have neither troops, nor treasury, nor government. * * * Is public credit an indispensable resource in time of public danger? We seem to have abandoned its cause as desperate and irretrievable. Is commerce of importance to national wealth? Ours is at the lowest point of declension. Is respectability in the eyes of foreign powers a safeguard against foreign encroachments? The imbecility of our government even forbids them to treat with us. . . . Is private credit the friend and patron of industry? That most useful kind which relates to borrowing and lending is reduced within the narrowest limits, and this still more from an opinion of insecurity than from a scarcity of money. * * *

This is the melancholy situation to which we have been brought by those very maxims and counsels which would now deter us from adopting the proposed Constitution; and which, not content with having conducted us to the brink of a precipice, seem resolved to plunge us into the abyss that awaits us below. Here, my countrymen, impelled by every motive that ought to influence an enlightened people, let us make a firm stand for our safety, our tranquility, our dignity, our reputation. Let us at last break the fatal charm which has too long seduced us from the paths of felicity and prosperity.

* * * While [opponents of the Constitution] admit that the government of the United States is destitute of energy, they contend against conferring upon it those powers which are requisite to supply that energy. * * * This renders a full display of the principal defects of the Confederation necessary in order to show that the evils we experience do not proceed from minute or partial imperfections, but from fundamental errors in the structure of the building, which cannot be amended otherwise than by an alteration in the first principles and main pillars of the fabric.

The great and radical vice in the construction of the existing Confederation is in the principle of LEGISLATION FOR STATES OR GOVERNMENTS, in their CORPORATE OR COLLECTIVE CAPACITIES, and as contradistinguished from the INDIVIDUALS of whom they consist. Though this principle does not run through all the powers delegated to the Union, yet it pervades and governs those on which the efficacy of the rest depends. Except as to the rule of apportionment, the United States have an indefinite discretion to make requisitions for men and money; but they have no authority to raise either by regulations extending to the individual citizens of America. The consequence of this is that though in theory their resolutions concerning those objects are laws constitutionally binding on the members of the Union, yet in practice they are mere recommendations which the States observe or disregard at their option. * * *

There is nothing absurd or impracticable in the idea of a league or alliance between independent nations for certain defined purposes precisely stated in a treaty regulating all the details of time, place, circumstance, and quantity, leaving nothing to future discretion, and depending for its execution on the good faith of the parties. * * *

If the particular States in this country are disposed to stand in a similar relation to each other, and to drop the project of a general DISCRETIONARY SUPERINTENDENCE, the scheme would indeed be pernicious and would entail upon us all the mischiefs which have been enumerated under the first head; but it would have the merit of being, at least, consistent and practicable. Abandoning all views towards a confederate government, this would bring us to a simple alliance offensive and defensive; and would place us in a situation to be alternate friends and enemies of each other, as our mutual jealousies and rivalships, nourished by the intrigues of foreign nations, should prescribe to us.

But if we are unwilling to be placed in this perilous situation; if we still will adhere to the design of a national government, or, which is the same thing, of a superintending power under the direction of a common council, we must resolve to incorporate into our plan those ingredients which may be considered as forming the characteristic difference between a league and a government; we must extend the authority of the Union to the persons of the citizens—the only proper objects of government.

Government implies the power of making laws. It is essential to the idea of a law that it be attended with a sanction; or, in other words, a penalty or punishment for disobedience. If there be no penalty annexed to disobedience, the resolutions or commands which pretend to be laws will, in fact, amount to nothing more than advice or recommendation. This penalty, whatever it may be, can only be inflicted in two ways: by the agency of the courts and ministers of justice, or by military force; by the COERCION of the magistracy, or by the COERCION of arms. The first kind can evidently apply only to men; the last kind must of necessity be employed against bodies politic, or communities, or States. * * * In an association where the general authority is confined to the collective bodies of the communities that compose it, every breach of the laws must involve a state of war; and military execution must become the only instrument of civil obedience. Such a state of things can certainly not deserve the name of government, nor would any prudent man choose to commit his happiness to it.

There was a time when we were told that breaches by the States of the regulations of the federal authority were not to be expected; that a sense of common interest would preside over the conduct of the respective members, and would beget a full compliance with all the constitutional requisitions of the Union. This language, at the present day, would appear as wild as a great part of what we now hear from the same quarter will be thought, when we shall have received further lessons from that best oracle of wisdom, experience. It at all times betrayed an ignorance of the true springs by which human conduct is actuated, and belied the original inducements to the establishment of civil power. Why has government been instituted at all? Because the passions of men will not conform to the dictates of reason and justice without constraint. * * *

In addition to all this * * * it happens that in every political association which is formed upon the principle of uniting in a common interest a number of lesser sovereignties, there will be found a kind of eccentric tendency in the subordinate or inferior orbs by the operation of which there will be a perpetual effort in each to fly off from the common center. This tendency is not difficult to be accounted for. It has its origin in the love of power. Power controlled or abridged is almost always the rival and enemy of that power by which it is controlled or abridged. This simple proposition will teach us how little reason there is to expect that the persons intrusted with the administration of the affairs of the particular members of a confederacy will at all times be ready with perfect good humor and an unbiased regard to the public weal to execute the resolutions or decrees of the general authority. * * *

If, therefore, the measures of the Confederacy cannot be executed without the intervention of the particular administrations, there will be little prospect of their being executed at all. * * * [Each state will evaluate every federal measure in light of its own interests] and in a spirit of interested and suspicious scrutiny, without that knowledge of national circumstances and reasons of state, which is essential to a right judgment, and with that strong predilection in favor of local objects, which can hardly fail to mislead the decision. The same process must be repeated in every member of which the body is constituted; and the execution of the plans, framed by the councils of the whole, will always fluctuate on the discretion of the ill-informed and prejudiced opinion of every part. * * *

In our case the concurrence of thirteen distinct sovereign wills is requisite under the Confederation to the complete execution of every important measure that proceeds from the Union. It has happened as was to have been foreseen. The measures of the Union have not been executed; and the delinquencies of the States have step by step matured themselves to an extreme, which has, at length, arrested all the wheels of the national government and brought them to an awful stand. Congress at this time scarcely possess the means of keeping up the forms of administration, till the States can have time to agree upon a more substantial substitute for the present shadow of a federal government. * * * Each State yielding to the persuasive voice of immediate interest or convenience has successively withdrawn its support, till the frail and tottering edifice seems ready to fall upon our heads and to crush us beneath its ruins.

PUBLIUS

DISCUSSION QUESTIONS

1. Do you think the national government is sufficiently held in check as Hamilton argues, or is the exercise of its authority so vast as to give credence to the Anti-Federalist fears? To put it another way, would the Framers be surprised or pleased with the scope of government powers today?

2. According to Hamilton, what are the weaknesses of a "league" compared to a government?

3. What is the significance of Hamilton's statement that "we must extend the author of the Union to person of the citizens?"

The Federalist, No. 51

James Madison

Such well-known patriots as Patrick Henry—"give me liberty or give me death!"—opposed the new Constitution. The proposed national government was stronger than its predecessor, but this was precisely the problem for the Anti-Federalists. A stronger national government could act in a more concerted manner in matters of foreign affairs and interstate commerce, but it also held the power to oppress the very people who gave it sovereignty. Arguments over this delicate balance of power animated debates over constitutional ratification.

James Madison concurred with Hamilton on the need for a stronger national government, but also recognized the importance of a limited government. In one of the most famous passages of The Federalist Papers, *Madison notes in* The Federalist, No. 5, *"If men were angels, no government would be necessary. If angels were to govern men, neither external nor internal controls on government would be necessary." But because angels do not govern us, Madison argued for the importance of controls on government. Here is where Madison attempts to address the concerns of the Anti-Federalists by arguing for a "double security" against majority tyranny. To achieve this security, the power of government must be divided across (between state and national governments) and within levels of government (among the courts, the president, and Congress). Such a division insured that if any one institution tried to become too powerful, the others would step in to counteract it. This essay remains one of the most eloquent defenses of our system of checks and balances and separation of powers.*

To the People of the State of New York:

To what expedient, then, shall we finally resort for maintaining in practice the necessary partition of power among the several departments as laid down in the Constitution? The only answer that can be given is, that as all these exterior provisions are found to be inadequate, the defect must be supplied by so contriving the interior structure of the government as that its several constituent parts may, by their mutual relations, be the means of keeping each other in their proper places. Without presuming to undertake a full development of this important idea, I will hazard a few general observations, which may perhaps place it in a clearer light, and enable us to form a more correct judgment of the principles and structure of the government planned by the convention.

In order to lay a due foundation for that separate and distinct exercise of the different powers of government, which to a certain extent is admitted on all hands to be essential to the preservation of liberty, it is evident that each department should have a will of its own; and consequently should be so constituted that the members of each should have as little agency as possible in the appointment of the members of the others. Were this principle rigorously adhered to, it would require that all the appointments for the supreme executive, legislative, and judiciary magistracies should be drawn from the same fountain of authority, the people, through channels having no communication whatever with one another. Perhaps such a plan of constructing the several departments would be less difficult in practice than it may in contemplation appear. Some difficulties, however, and some additional expense would attend the execution of it. Some deviations, therefore, from the principle must be admitted. In the constitution of the judiciary department in particular, it might be inexpedient to insist rigorously on the principle: first, because peculiar qualifications being essential in the members, the primary consideration ought to be to select that mode of choice which best secures these qualifications; secondly, because the permanent tenure by which the appointments are held in that department must soon destroy all sense of dependence on the authority conferring them.

It is equally evident, that the members of each department should be as little dependent as possible on those of the others for the emoluments annexed to their offices. Were the executive magistrate or the judges not independent of the legislature in this particular, their independence in every other would be merely nominal.

But the great security against a gradual concentration of the several powers in the same department, consists in giving to those who administer each department the necessary constitutional means and personal motives to resist encroachments of the others. The provision for defence must in this, as in all other cases, be made commensurate to the danger of attack. Ambition must be made to counteract ambition. The interest of the man must be connected with the constitutional rights of the place. It may be a reflection on human nature, that such devices should be necessary to control the abuses of government. But what is government itself, but the greatest of all reflections on human nature? If men were angels, no government would be necessary. If angels were to govern men, neither external nor internal controls on government would be necessary. In framing a government which is to be administered by men over men, the great difficulty lies in this: you must first enable the government to control the governed; and in the next place oblige it to control itself. A dependence on the people is, no doubt, the primary control on the government; but experience has taught mankind the necessity of auxiliary precautions.

This policy of supplying, by opposite and rival interests, the defect of better motives might be traced through the whole system of human affairs, private as well as public. We see it particularly displayed in all the subordinate distributions of power, where the constant aim is to divide and arrange the several offices in such a manner as that each may be a check on the other—that the private interest of every individual may be a sentinel over the public rights. These inventions of prudence cannot be less requisite in the distribution of the supreme powers of the State.

But it is not possible to give to each department an equal power of self-defence. In republican government the legislative authority necessarily predominates. The remedy for this inconveniency is to divide the legislature into different branches; and to render them, by different modes of election and different principles of action, as little connected with each other as the nature of their common functions and their common dependence on the society will admit. It may even be necessary to guard against dangerous encroachments by still further precautions. As the weight of the legislative authority requires that it should be thus divided, the weakness of the executive may require, on the other hand, that it should be fortified. An absolute negative on the legislature appears, at first view, to be the natural defence with which the executive magistrate should be armed. But perhaps it would be neither altogether safe nor alone sufficient. On ordinary occasions it might not be exerted with the requisite firmness, and on extraordinary occasions it might be perfidiously abused. May not this defect of an absolute negative be supplied by some qualified connection between this weaker department and the weaker branch of the stronger department, by which the latter may be led to support the constitutional rights of the former, without being too much detached from the rights of its own department?

If the principles on which these observations are founded be just . . . and they be applied as a criterion to the several State constitutions and to the federal Constitution, it will be found that if the latter does not perfectly correspond with them, the former are infinitely less able to bear such a test.

There are, moreover, two considerations particularly applicable to the federal system of America, which place that system in a very interesting point of view.

First. In a single republic, all the power surrendered by the people is submitted to the administration of a single government; and the usurpations are guarded against by a division of the government into distinct and separate departments. In the compound republic of America, the power surrendered by the people is first divided between two distinct governments, and then the portion allotted to each subdivided among distinct and separate departments. Hence a double security arises to the rights of the people. The different governments will control each other, at the same time that each will be controlled by itself.

Second. It is of great importance in a republic not only to guard the

society against the oppression of its rulers, but to guard one part of the
society against the injustice of the other part. Different interests necessarily exist in different classes of citizens. If a majority be united by a
common interest, the rights of the minority will be insecure. There are
but two methods of providing against this evil: the one by creating a
will in the community independent of the majority—that is, of the society itself; the other by comprehending in the society so many separate
descriptions of citizens as will render an unjust combination of a majority
of the whole very improbable, if not impracticable. The first method
prevails in all governments possessing an hereditary or self-appointed
authority. This, at best, is but a precarious security; because a power
independent of the society may as well espouse the unjust views of the
major, as the rightful interests of the minor party, and may possibly be
turned against both parties. The second method will be exemplified in
the federal republic of the United States. Whilst all authority in it will
be derived from and dependent on the society, the society itself will be
broken into so many parts, interests and classes of citizens, that the rights
of individuals or of the minority will be in little danger from interested
combinations of the majority. In a free government the security for civil
rights must be the same as that for religious rights. It consists in the one
case in the multiplicity of interests and in the other in the multiplicity
of sects. The degree of security in both cases will depend on the number
of interests and sects; and this may be presumed to depend on the extent of country and number of people comprehended under the same
government. This view of the subject must particularly recommend a
proper federal system to all the sincere and considerate friends of republican government, since it shows that in exact proportion as the
territory of the Union may be formed into more circumscribed Confederacies or States, oppressive combinations of a majority will be facilitated; the best security under the republican forms for the rights of
every class of citizens will be diminished; and consequently the stability
and independence of some member of the government, the only other
security, must be proportionally increased. Justice is the end [that is, the
goal] of government. It is the end of civil society. It ever has been and
ever will be pursued until it be obtained, or until liberty be lost in the
pursuit. In a society under the forms of which the stronger faction can
readily unite and oppress the weaker, anarchy may as truly be said to
reign as in a state of nature, where the weaker individual is not secured
against the violence of the stronger; and, as in the latter state even the
stronger individuals are prompted, by the uncertainty of their condition,
to submit to a government which may protect the weak as well as themselves; so, in the former state will the more powerful factions or parties
be gradually induced by a like motive to wish for a government which
will protect all parties, the weaker as well as the more powerful. It can
be little doubted that if the State of Rhode Island was separated from

the Confederacy and left to itself, the insecurity of rights under the popular form of government within such narrow limits would be displayed by such reiterated oppressions of factious majorities that some power altogether independent of the people would soon be called for by the voice of the very factions whose misrule had proved the necessity of it. In the extended republic of the United States and among the great variety of interests, parties, and sects which it embraces, a coalition of a majority of the whole society could seldom take place on any other principles than those of justice and the general good; whilst there being thus less danger to a minor from the will of a major party, there must be less pretext, also, to provide for the security of the former, by introducing into the government a will not dependent on the latter, or, in other words, a will independent of the society itself. It is no less certain than it is important, notwithstanding the contrary opinions which have been entertained, that the larger the society, provided it lie within a practical sphere, the more duly capable it will be of self-government. And happily for the *republican cause*, the practicable sphere may be carried to a very great extent by a judicious modification and mixture of the *federal principle*.

PUBLIUS

DISCUSSION QUESTIONS

1. According to Madison, the principles of "separation of powers" and "checks and balances" operate to limit the authority of the national government. How? Discuss at least one current issue involving these two principles and the constitutional issues at stake.

2. Is the system of "separation of powers" and "checks and balances" too inefficient to handle the challenges posed by the modern and dangerous world? Would the United States be better off with a more efficient form of government that would allow quicker action and more accountability?

Debating the Issues: An Economic Interpretation of the Constitution

> One of the longest-running debates over the Constitution focuses upon the motivation of the Founders in drafting the document. Was the motivation ideological, based upon beliefs of self-governance, the nature of a social contract, and the role of representation? Or was the motivation primarily economic, based upon a need to preserve economic interests that were threatened under the system of governance of the Articles of Confederation? And if the motivation was economic, what economic interests divided the Anti-Federalists from the Federalists in their opposition to or support for the Constitution?
>
> One of the earliest and most controversial efforts to answer the question was written by Charles Beard in 1913. Beard argued that those who favored the Constitution and played the primary role in its drafting were motivated by the need to better protect their substantial "personality" interests—money, public securities, manufacturers, and trade and shipping (or commerce)—in contrast to its opponents who were primarily small farmers (with small real estate holdings) and debtor interests. Not only was its motivation less-than-democratic, Beard argued, but the Constitution was ratified by only one-sixth of the male population because voting was limited to property owners.
>
> Robert Brown takes strong opposition to Beard's thesis. His criticism focuses mainly on Beard's use of historical data and its interpretation, leaving the door open for other interpretations of the motivations behind the Constitution as well as the base of public support for the document.

9

From *An Economic Interpretation of the Constitution of the United States*

Charles A. Beard

The requirements for an economic interpretation of the formation and adoption of the Constitution may be stated in a hypothetical proposition which, although it cannot be verified absolutely from ascertainable data, will at once illustrate the problem and furnish a guide to research and generalization.

It will be admitted without controversy that the Constitution was the creation of a certain number of men, and it was opposed by a certain number of men. Now, if it were possible to have an economic biography of all those connected with its framing and adoption,—perhaps about 160,000 men altogether,—the materials for scientific analysis and classification would be available. Such an economic biography would include a list of the real and personal property owned by all of these men and their families: lands and houses, with incumbrances, money at interest, slaves, capital invested in shipping and manufacturing, and in state and continental securities.

Suppose it could be shown from the classification of the men who supported and opposed the Constitution that there was no line of property division at all; that is, that men owning substantially the same amounts of the same kinds of property were equally divided on the matter of adoption or rejection—it would then become apparent that the Constitution had no ascertainable relation to economic groups or classes, but was the product of some abstract causes remote from the chief business of life—gaining a livelihood.

Suppose, on the other hand, that substantially all of the merchants, money lenders, security holders, manufacturers, shippers, capitalists, and financiers and their professional associates are to be found on one side in support of the Constitution and that substantially all or the major portion of the opposition came from the non-slaveholding farmers and the debtors—would it not be pretty conclusively demonstrated that our fundamental law was not the product of an abstraction known as "the whole people," but of a group of economic interests which must have expected beneficial results from its adoption? Obviously all the facts here desired cannot be discovered, but the data presented in the following chapters bear out the latter hypothesis, and thus a reasonable presumption in favor of the theory is created.

*   *   *

The purpose of such an inquiry is not, of course, to show that the Constitution was made for the personal benefit of the members of the Convention. Far from it. Neither is it of any moment to discover how many hundred thousand dollars accrued to them as a result of the foundation of the new government. The only point here considered is: Did they represent distinct groups whose economic interests they understood and felt in concrete, definite form through their own personal experience with identical property rights, or were they working merely under the guidance of abstract principles of political science?

*   *   *

The Disfranchised

In an examination of the structure of American society in 1787, we first encounter four groups whose economic status had a definite legal expression: the slaves, the indentured servants, the mass of men who could not qualify for voting under the property tests imposed by the state constitutions and laws, and women, disfranchised and subjected to the discriminations of the common law. These groups were, therefore, not represented in the Convention which drafted the Constitution, except under the theory that representation has no relation to voting.

How extensive the disfranchisement really was cannot be determined. In some states, for instance, Pennsylvania and Georgia, propertyless mechanics in the towns could vote; but in other states the freehold qualifications certainly excluded a great number of the adult males.

In no state, apparently, had the working class developed a consciousness of a separate interest or an organization that commanded the attention of the politicians of the time. In turning over the hundreds of pages of writings left by eighteenth-century thinkers one cannot help being impressed with the fact that the existence and special problems of a working class, then already sufficiently numerous to form a considerable portion of society, were outside the realm of politics, except in so far as the future power of the proletariat was foreseen and feared.

When the question of the suffrage was before the Convention, Madison warned his colleagues against the coming industrial masses: "Viewing the subject in its merits alone, the freeholders of the Country would be the safest depositories of Republican liberty. In future times a great majority of the people will not only be without landed [property], but any other sort of property. These will either combine under the influence of their common situation; in which case, the rights of property and the public liberty will not be secure in their hands, or, which is more probable, they will become the tools of opulence and ambition; in which case there will be equal danger on another side."

* * *

It is apparent that a majority of the states placed direct property qualifications on the voters, and the other states eliminated practically all who were not taxpayers. Special safeguards for property were secured in the qualifications imposed on members of the legislatures in New Hampshire, Massachusetts, New York, New Jersey, Maryland, North Carolina, South Carolina, and Georgia. Further safeguards were added by the qualifications imposed in the case of senators in New Hampshire, Massachusetts, New Jersey, New York, Maryland, North Carolina, and South Carolina.

While these qualifications operated to exclude a large portion of the adult males from participating in elections, the wide distribution of real property created an extensive electorate and in most rural regions gave the legislatures a broad popular basis. Far from rendering to personal property that defence which was necessary to the full realization of its rights, these qualifications for electors admitted to the suffrage its most dangerous antagonists: the small farmers and many of the debtors who were the most active in all attempts to depreciate personalty [private property] by legislation. Madison with his usual acumen saw the inadequacy of such defence and pointed out in the Convention that the really serious assaults on property (having in mind of course, personalty) had come from the "freeholders."

Nevertheless, in the election of delegates to the Convention, the representatives of personalty in the legislatures were able by the sheer weight of their combined intelligence and economic power to secure delegates from the urban centres or allied with their interests. Happily for them, all the legislatures which they had to convince had not been elected on the issue of choosing delegates to a national Convention, and did not come from a populace stirred up on that question. The call for the Convention went forth on February 21, 1787, from Congress, and within a few months all the legislatures, except that of Rhode Island, had responded. Thus the heated popular discussion usually incident to such a momentous political undertaking was largely avoided, and an orderly and temperate procedure in the selection of delegates was rendered possible.

* * *

A survey of the economic interests of the members of the Convention presents certain conclusions:

A majority of the members were lawyers by profession.

Most of the members came from towns, on or near the coast, that is, from the regions in which personalty was largely concentrated.

Not one member represented in his immediate personal economic interests the small farming or mechanic classes.

The overwhelming majority of members, at least five-sixths, were immediately, directly, and personally interested in the outcome of their labors at Philadelphia, and were to a greater or less extent economic beneficiaries from the adoption of the Constitution.

1. Public security interests were extensively represented in the Convention. Of the fifty-five members who attended no less than forty appear on the Records of the Treasury Department for sums varying from a few dollars up to more than one hundred thousand dollars. [A list of their names follows.]

It is interesting to note that, with the exception of New York, and possibly Delaware, each state had one or more prominent representatives in the Convention who held more than a negligible amount of securities, and who could therefore speak with feeling and authority on the question of providing in the new Constitution for the full discharge of the public debt: [list of names]

2. Personalty invested in lands for speculation was represented by at least fourteen members: [list of names]

3. Personalty in the form of money loaned at interest was represented by at least twenty-four members: [list of names]

4. Personalty in mercantile, manufacturing, and shipping lines was represented by at least eleven members: [list of names]

5. Personalty in slaves was represented by at least fifteen members: [list of names]

It cannot be said, therefore, that the members of the Convention were "disinterested." On the contrary, we are forced to accept the profoundly significant conclusion that they knew through their personal experiences in economic affairs the precise results which the new government that they were setting up was designed to attain. As a group of doctrinaires, like the Frankfurt assembly of 1848, they would have failed miserably; but as practical men they were able to build the new government upon the only foundations which could be stable: fundamental economic interests.

*   *   *

Conclusions

At the close of this long and arid survey—partaking of the nature of catalogue—it seems worthwhile to bring together the important conclusions for political science which the data presented appear to warrant.

[1.] The movement for the Constitution of the United States was originated and carried through principally by four groups of personalty interests which had been adversely affected under the Articles of Confederation: money, public securities, manufactures, and trade and shipping.

[2.] The first firm steps toward the formation of the Constitution were taken by a small and active group of men immediately interested through their personal possessions in the outcome of their labors.

[3.] No popular vote was taken directly or indirectly on the proposition to call the Convention which drafted the Constitution.

[4.] A large propertyless mass was, under the prevailing suffrage qualifications, excluded at the outset from participation (through representatives) in the work of framing the Constitution.

[5.] The members of the Philadelphia Convention which drafted the Constitution were, with a few exceptions, immediately, directly, and personally interested in, and derived economic advantages from, the establishment of the new system.

[6.] The Constitution was essentially an economic document based upon the concept that the fundamental private rights of property are anterior to government and morally beyond the reach of popular majorities.

[7.] The major portion of the members of the Convention are on record as recognizing the claim of property to a special and defensive position in the Constitution.

[8.] In the ratification of the Constitution, about three-fourths of the adult males failed to vote on the question, having abstained from the elections at which delegates to the state conventions were chosen, either on account of their indifference or their disfranchisement by property qualifications.

[9.] The Constitution was ratified by a vote of probably not more than one-sixth of the adult males.

[10.] It is questionable whether a majority of the voters participating in the elections for the state conventions in New York, Massachusetts, New Hampshire, Virginia, and South Carolina, actually approved the ratification of the Constitution.

[11.] The leaders who supported the Constitution in the ratifying conventions represented the same economic groups as the members of the Philadelphia Convention; and in a large number of instances they were also directly and personally interested in the outcome of their efforts.

[12.] In the ratification, it became manifest that the line of cleavage for and against the Constitution was between substantial personalty interests on the one hand and the small farming and debtor interests on the other.

[13.] The Constitution was not created by "the whole people" as the jurists have said; neither was it created by "the states" as Southern nullifiers long contended; but it was the work of a consolidated group whose interests knew no state boundaries and were truly national in their scope.

10

From *Charles Beard and the Constitution: A Critical Analysis of "An Economic Interpretation of the Constitution"*

Robert E. Brown

Conclusions

At the end of Chapter XI Beard summarized his findings in fourteen paragraphs under the heading of "Conclusions" (pp. 73–74). Actually, these fourteen conclusions merely add up to the two halves of the Beard thesis. One half, that the Constitution originated with and was carried through by personalty interests—money, public securities, manufactures, and commerce—is to be found in paragraphs two, three, six, seven, eight, twelve, thirteen, and fourteen. The other half—that the Constitution was put over undemocratically in an undemocratic society—is expressed in paragraphs four, five, nine, ten, eleven, and fourteen. The lumping of these conclusions under two general headings makes it easier for the reader to see the broad outlines of the Beard thesis.

* * *

If historical method means the gathering of data from primary sources, the critical evaluation of the evidence thus gathered, and the drawing of conclusions consistent with this evidence, then we must conclude that Beard has done great violation to such method in this book. He admitted that the evidence had not been collected which, given the proper use of historical method, should have precluded the writing of the book. Yet he nevertheless proceeded on the assumption that a valid interpretation could be built on secondary writings whose authors had likewise failed to collect the evidence. If we accept Beard's own maxim, "no evidence, no history," and his own admission that the data had never been collected, the answer to whether he used historical method properly is self-evident.

* * *

Finally, the conclusions which he drew were not justified even by the kind of evidence which he used. If we accepted his evidence strictly at face value, it would still not add up to the fact that the Constitution was put over undemocratically in an undemocratic society by personalty. The citing of property qualifications does not prove that a mass of men were disfranchised. And if we accept his figures on property holdings, either we do not know what most of the delegates had in realty and personalty, or we know that realty outnumbered personalty three to one (eighteen to six). Simply showing that a man held public securities is not sufficient to prove that he acted only in terms of his public securities. If we ignore Beard's own generalizations and accept only his evidence, we would have to conclude that most of the property in the country in 1787 was real estate, that real property was widely distributed in rural areas, which included most of the country, and that even the men who were directly concerned with the Constitution, and especially Washington, were large holders of realty.

Perhaps we can never be completely objective in history, but certainly we can be more objective than Beard was in this book. Naturally the historian must always be aware of the biases, the subjectivity, the pitfalls that confront him, but this does not mean that he should not make an effort to overcome these obstacles. Whether Beard had his thesis before he had his evidence, as some have said, is a question that each reader must answer for himself. Certain it is that the evidence does not justify the thesis.

So instead of the Beard interpretation that the Constitution was put over undemocratically in an undemocratic society by personal property, the following fourteen paragraphs are offered as a possible interpretation of the Constitution and as suggestions for future research on that document.

1. The movement for the Constitution was originated and carried through by men who had long been important in both economic and political affairs in their respective states. Some of them owned personalty, more of them owned realty, and if their property was adversely affected by conditions under the Articles of Confederation, so also was the property of the bulk of the people in the country, middle-class farmers as well as town artisans.

2. The movement for the Constitution, like most important movements, was undoubtedly started by a small group of men. They were probably interested personally in the outcome of their labors, but the benefits which they expected were not confined to personal property or, for that matter, strictly to things economic. And if their own interests would be enhanced by a new government, similar interests of other men, whether agricultural or commercial, would also be enhanced.

3. Naturally there was no popular vote on the calling of the convention which drafted the Constitution. Election of delegates by state legislatures was the constitutional method under the Articles of Confederation, and had been the method long established in this country. Del-

egates to the Albany Congress, the Stamp Act Congress, the First Continental Congress, the Second Continental Congress, and subsequent congresses under the Articles were all elected by state legislatures, not by the people. Even the Articles of Confederation had been sanctioned by state legislatures, not by popular vote. This is not to say that the Constitutional Convention should not have been elected directly by the people, but only that such a procedure would have been unusual at the time. Some of the opponents of the Constitution later stressed, without avail, the fact that the Convention had not been directly elected. But at the time the Convention met, the people in general seemed to be about as much concerned over the fact that they had not elected the delegates as the people of this country are now concerned over the fact that they do not elect our delegates to the United Nations.

4. Present evidence seems to indicate that there were no "propertyless masses" who were excluded from the suffrage at the time. Most men were middle-class farmers who owned realty and were qualified voters, and, as the men in the Convention said, mechanics had always voted in the cities. Until credible evidence proves otherwise, we can assume that state legislatures were fairly representative at the time. We cannot condone the fact that a few men were probably disfranchised by prevailing property qualifications, but it makes a great deal of difference to an interpretation of the Constitution whether the disfranchised comprised ninety-five per cent of the adult men or only five per cent. Figures which give percentages of voters in terms of the entire population are misleading, since less than twenty per cent of the people were adult men. And finally, the voting qualifications favored realty, not personalty.

5. If the members of the Convention were directly interested in the outcome of their work and expected to derive benefits from the establishment of the new system, so also did most of the people of the country. We have many statements to the effect that the people in general expected substantial benefits from the labors of the Convention.

6. The Constitution was not just an economic document, although economic factors were undoubtedly important. Since most of the people were middle-class and had private property, practically everybody was interested in the protection of property. A constitution which did not protect property would have been rejected without any question, for the American people had fought the Revolution for the preservation of life, liberty, and property. Many people believed that the Constitution did not go far enough to protect property, and they wrote these views into the amendments to the Constitution. But property was not the only concern of those who wrote and ratified the Constitution, and we would be doing a grave injustice to the political sagacity of the Founding Fathers if we assumed that property or personal gain was their only motive.

7. Naturally the delegates recognized that the protection of property was important under government, but they also recognized that personal

rights were equally important. In fact, persons and property were usually bracketed together as the chief objects of government protection.

8. If three-fourths of the adult males failed to vote on the election of delegates to ratifying conventions, this fact signified indifference, not disfranchisement. We must not confuse those who could *not* vote with those who *could* vote but failed to exercise their right. Many men at the time bewailed the fact that only a small portion of the voters ever exercised their prerogative. But this in itself should stand as evidence that the conflict over the Constitution was not very bitter, for if these people had felt strongly one way or the other, more of them would have voted.

Even if we deny the evidence which I have presented and insist that American society was undemocratic in 1787, we must still accept the fact that the men who wrote the Constitution believed that they were writing it for a democratic society. They did not hide behind an iron curtain of secrecy and devise the kind of conservative government that they wanted without regard to the views and interests of "the people." More than anything else, they were aware that "the people" would have to ratify what they proposed, and that therefore any government which would be acceptable to the people must of necessity incorporate much of what was customary at the time. The men at Philadelphia were practical politicians, not political theorists. They recognized the multitude of different ideas and interests that had to be reconciled and compromised before a constitution would be acceptable. They were far too practical, and represented far too many clashing interests themselves, to fashion a government weighted in favor of personalty or to believe that the people would adopt such a government.

9. If the Constitution was ratified by a vote of only one-sixth of the adult men, that again demonstrates indifference and not disfranchisement. Of the one-fourth of the adult males who voted, nearly two-thirds favored the Constitution. Present evidence does not permit us to say what the popular vote was except as it was measured by the votes of the ratifying conventions.

10. Until we know what the popular vote was, we cannot say that it is questionable whether a majority of the voters in several states favored the Constitution. Too many delegates were sent uninstructed. Neither can we count the towns which did not send delegates on the side of those opposed to the Constitution. Both items would signify indifference rather than sharp conflict over ratification.

11. The ratifying conventions were elected for the specific purpose of adopting or rejecting the Constitution. The people in general had anywhere from several weeks to several months to decide the question. If they did not like the new government, or if they did not know whether they liked it, they could have voted *no* and there would have been no Constitution. Naturally the leaders in the ratifying conventions represented the same interests as the members of the Constitutional Con-

vention—mainly realty and some personalty. But they also represented their constituents in these same interests, especially realty.

12. If the conflict over ratification had been between substantial personality interests on the one hand and small farmers and debtors on the other, there would not have been a constitution. The small farmers comprised such an overwhelming percentage of the voters that they could have rejected the new government without any trouble. Farmers and debtors are not synonymous terms and should not be confused as such. A town-by-town or county-by-county record of the vote would show clearly how the farmers voted.

13. The Constitution was created about as much by the whole people as any government could be which embraced a large area and depended on representation rather than on direct participation. It was also created in part by the states, for as the *Records* show, there was strong state sentiment at the time which had to be appeased by compromise. And it was created by compromising a whole host of interests throughout the country, without which compromises it could never have been adopted.

If the intellectual historians are correct, we cannot explain the Constitution without considering the psychological factors also. Men are motivated by what they believe as well as by what they have. Sometimes their actions can be explained on the basis of what they hope to have or hope that their children will have. Madison understood this fact when he said that the universal hope of acquiring property tended to dispose people to look favorably upon property. It is even possible that some men support a given economic system when they themselves have nothing to gain by it. So we would want to know what the people in 1787 thought of their class status. Did workers and small farmers believe that they were lower-class, or did they, as many workers do now, consider themselves middle-class? Were the common people trying to eliminate the Washingtons, Adamses, Hamiltons, and Pinckneys, or were they trying to join them?

As did Beard's conclusions, these suggestions really add up to two major propositions: the Constitution was adopted in a society which was fundamentally democratic, not undemocratic; and it was adopted by a people who were primarily middle-class property owners, especially farmers who owned realty, not just by the owners of personalty. At present these points seem to be justified by the evidence, but if better evidence in the future disproves or modifies them, we must accept that evidence and change our interpretation accordingly.

After this critical analysis, we should at least not begin future research on this period of American history with the illusion that the Beard thesis of the Constitution is valid. If historians insist on accepting the Beard thesis in spite of this analysis, however, they must do so with the full knowledge that their acceptance is founded on "an act of faith," not an analysis of historical method, and that they are indulging in a "noble dream," not history.

DISCUSSION QUESTIONS

1. Based on these readings, do you think the Framers were governed by self-interest or a commitment to principle, or some combination, when they drafted the Constitution? Explain your answer.

2. What is the contemporary significance of this debate? That is, can you think of any current political debates about whether our political system favors the interests of the economically powerful over poorer people?

3. What does the debate between Beard and Brown say about the use of historical evidence to support one's argument? How can historical evidence be misused and how can historians, or even readers of history, sort out what "really" happened in any specific context?

CHAPTER 3

Federalism

11

The Federalist, No. 46

JAMES MADISON

Some of the most divisive and bitter political battles in our nation's history have occurred over interpretations of the constitutional principle of federalism—the division of powers and functions between the state governments and the national government. The struggle for desegregation and the civil rights of minorities, the legalization of abortion, the selective incorporation of the Bill of Rights into the Fourteenth Amendment, slavery and the Civil War all ultimately turned on the question, "Who has the authority to govern: the states, or the national government?" Our federal system is a delicate balance of power and shared responsibility between nation and states, each with constitutional authority to pass laws, levy taxes, and protect the interests and rights of citizens. It is a dynamic balance of power, easily destabilized by economic crises, political initiatives, and Supreme Court rulings, but often resolved in more recent years by the question, "Who will pay the price for implementing and enforcing government policy?"

The "double security," which James Madison discussed in The Federalist, *No. 51, in the previous chapter, did not satisfy those who feared that the national powers would encroach on state sovereignty. In* The Federalist, *No. 46, Madison went to great lengths to reassure the states that they would continue to wield a high degree of power, arguing that "the first and most natural attachment of the people will be to the governments of their respective states." While recognizing the potential for conflicts between state and federal governments, Madison concluded that the power retained by the states would be sufficient to resist arrogation by the newly established national government.*

I proceed to inquire whether the federal government or the State governments will have the advantage with regard to the predilection and support of the people. Notwithstanding the different modes in which they are appointed, we must consider both of them as substantially dependent on the great body of the citizens of the United States. * * * The federal and State governments are in fact but different agents and trustees of the people, constituted with different powers and designed for different purposes. The adversaries of the Constitution seem to have lost sight of the people altogether in their reasonings on this subject; and to have viewed these different establishments not only as mutual rivals and enemies, but as uncontrolled by any common superior in their efforts to usurp the authorities of each other. These gentlemen must here be reminded of their error. They must be told that the ultimate authority, wherever the derivative may be found, resides in the people alone, and that it will not depend merely on the comparative ambition or address of the different governments whether either, or which of them, will be able to enlarge its sphere of jurisdiction at the expense of the other. Truth, no less than decency, requires that the event in every case should be supposed to depend on the sentiments and sanction of their common constituents.

Many considerations * * * seem to place it beyond doubt that the first and most natural attachment of the people will be to the governments of their respective States. Into the administration of these a greater number of individuals will expect to rise. From the gift of these a greater number of offices and emoluments will flow. By the superintending care of these, all the more domestic and personal interests of the people will be regulated and provided for. With the affairs of these, the people will be more familiarly and minutely conversant. And with the members of these will a greater proportion of the people have the ties of personal acquaintance and friendship, and of family and party attachments; on the side of these, therefore, the popular bias may well be expected most strongly to incline.

The remaining points on which I propose to compare the federal and State governments are the disposition and the faculty they may respectively possess to resist and frustrate the measures of each other.

It has been already proved that the members of the federal will be more dependent on the members of the State governments than the latter will be on the former. It has appeared also that the prepossessions of the people, on whom both will depend, will be more on the side of the State governments than of the federal government. So far as the disposition of each towards the other may be influenced by these causes, the State governments must clearly have the advantage. But in a distinct and very important point of view, the advantage will lie on the same side. The prepossessions, which the members themselves will carry into the federal government, will generally be favorable to the States; whilst it will rarely happen that the members of the State governments will carry into the public councils a bias in favor of the general government. A local spirit will infallibly prevail much more in the members of Congress than a national spirit will prevail in the legislatures of the particular States.

* * * What is the spirit that has in general characterized the proceed-

ings of Congress? A perusal of their journals, as well as the candid acknowledgments of such as have had a seat in that assembly, will inform us that the members have but too frequently displayed the character rather of partisans of their respective States than of impartial guardians of a common interest; that where on one occasion improper sacrifices have been made of local considerations to the aggrandizement of the federal government, the great interests of the nation have suffered on a hundred from an undue attention to the local prejudices, interests, and views of the particular States. I mean not by these reflections to insinuate that the new federal government will not embrace a more enlarged plan of policy than the existing government may have pursued; much less that its views will be as confined as those of the State legislatures; but only that it will partake sufficiently of the spirit of both to be disinclined to invade the rights of the individual States, or the prerogatives of their governments.

Were it admitted, however, that the federal government may feel an equal disposition with the State governments to extend its power beyond the due limits, the latter would still have the advantage in the means of defeating such encroachments. If an act of a particular State, though unfriendly to the national government, be generally popular in that State, and should not too grossly violate the oaths of the State officers, it is executed immediately and, of course, by means on the spot and depending on the State alone. The opposition of the federal government, or the interposition of federal officers, would but inflame the zeal of all parties on the side of the State, and the evil could not be prevented or repaired, if at all, without the employment of means which must always be resorted to with reluctance and difficulty. On the other hand, should an unwarrantable measure of the federal government be unpopular in particular States, which would seldom fail to be the case, or even a warrantable measure be so, which may sometimes be the case, the means of opposition to it are powerful and at hand. The disquietude of the people; their repugnance and, perhaps, refusal to co-operate with the officers of the Union; the frowns of the executive magistracy of the State; the embarrassments created by legislative devices, which would often be added on such occasions, would oppose, in any State, difficulties not to be despised; would form, in a large State, very serious impediments; and where the sentiments of several adjoining States happened to be in unison, would present obstructions which the federal government would hardly be willing to encounter.

But ambitious encroachments of the federal government on the authority of the State governments would not excite the opposition of a single State, or of a few States only. They would be signals of general alarm. Every government would espouse the common cause. A correspondence would be opened. Plans of resistance would be concerted. One spirit would animate and conduct the whole. The same combinations, in short, would result from an apprehension of the federal, as was produced by the dread of a foreign yoke; and unless the projected innovations should be voluntarily renounced, the same appeal to a trial of force would be made in the one case as was made in the other.

The only refuge left for those who prophesy the downfall of the State governments is the visionary supposition that the federal government may previously accumulate a military force for the projects of ambition. The reasonings contained in these papers must have been employed to little purpose indeed, if it could be necessary now to disprove the reality of this danger. That the people and the States should, for a sufficient period of time, elect an uninterrupted succession of men ready to betray both; that the traitors should, throughout this period, uniformly and systematically pursue some fixed plan for the extension of the military establishment; that the governments and the people of the States should silently and patiently behold the gathering storm and continue to supply the materials until it should be prepared to burst on their own heads must appear to everyone more like the incoherent dreams of a delirious jealousy, or the misjudged exaggerations of a counterfeit zeal, than like the sober apprehensions of genuine patriotism. Extravagant as the supposition is, let it, however, be made. Let a regular army, fully equal to the resources of the country, be formed; and let it be entirely at the devotion of the federal government: still it would not be going too far to say that the State governments with the people on their side would be able to repel the danger.

Besides the advantage of being armed, which the Americans possess over the people of almost every other nation, the existence of subordinate governments, to which the people are attached and by which the militia officers are appointed, forms a barrier against the enterprises of ambition, more insurmountable than any which a simple government of any form can admit of.

Let us not insult the free and gallant citizens of America with the suspicion that they would be less able to defend the rights of which they would be in actual possession than the debased subjects of arbitrary power would be to rescue theirs from the hands of their oppressors. Let us rather no longer insult them with the supposition that they can ever reduce themselves to the necessity of making the experiment by a blind and tame submission to the long train of insidious measures which must precede and produce it.

The argument under the present head may be put into a very concise form, which appears altogether conclusive. Either the mode in which the federal government is to be constructed will render it sufficiently dependent on the people, or it will not. On the first supposition, it will be restrained by that dependence from forming schemes obnoxious to their constituents. On the other supposition, it will not possess the confidence of the people, and its schemes of usurpation will be easily defeated by the State governments, who will be supported by the people.

On summing up the considerations stated in this and the last paper, they seem to amount to the most convincing evidence that the powers proposed to be lodged in the federal government are as little formidable to those reserved to the individual States as they are indispensably necessary to accomplish the purposes of the Union; and that all those alarms which have been sounded of a meditated and consequential annihilation of the State governments must, on the most favorable interpretation, be ascribed to the chimerical fears of the authors of them.

PUBLIUS

DISCUSSION QUESTIONS

1. Is Madison right that people are more attached to their state governments than to the national government? Why or why not? If not, would it better facilitate the democratic process if they were more attached to state governments?

2. Would your answer change at all during different political times? For example, are people more attached to the national government in the wake of the terrorist attacks on our country than they were before September 11, 2001?

12

From *The Price of Federalism*

Paul Peterson

In this concise overview of American federalism, Paul Peterson argues that both the early and more modern system of shared sovereignty between the national government and the states have had their disadvantages. From the early period of "dual federalism" to the more modern system of a dominant national govern-ment, the battle over national and state government jurisdiction and power has led to bloodshed and war, the denial of political, social, and economic rights, and regional inequalities among the states.

Nevertheless, Peterson argues, there are advantages to federalism. Federalism has also facilitated capital growth and development, the creation of infrastruc-tures, and social programs that greatly improved the quality of life for millions of Americans. Once the national government took responsibility for guaranteeing civil rights and civil liberties, the states "became the engines of economic devel-opment." Not every state is equally wealthy, but the national government has gradually diminished some of these differences by financing many social and eco-nomic programs. One recent battle over the proper form of federal relations in-volved welfare policy in the 1990s. Republicans in Congress wanted to give back to states the power to devise their own programs, while most Democrats and President Clinton initially wanted to retain a larger degree of federal govern-ment control. However, President Clinton eventually agreed to end welfare as an entitlement and return substantial control over the program to the states. The long-term verdict on this landmark legislation is still an open question and there is considerable debate over the proper balance between federal and state funding for the state-level welfare programs.

These same debates have cropped up in more recent years in homeland secu-rity policy. Ideally, these policies would be run at the national level and resources would be allocated to parts of the country that pose the greatest security risks. However, all states want their share of the federal pie, so resources are not always allocated in the most efficient manner. Federalism also poses challenges for coor-dinating policy for "first responders" in a time of crisis: who is responsible for coming to the aid of people in distress: local, state, or national agencies?

The Price of Early Federalism

As a principle of government, federalism has had a dubious history. It remains on the margins of political respectability even today. I was recently invited to give a presentation on metropolitan government before a United Nations conference. When I offered to discuss how the federal principle could be used to help metropolitan areas govern themselves more effectively, my sponsors politely advised me that this topic would be poorly received. The vast majority of UN members had a unified form of government, I was told, and they saw little of value in federalism. We reached a satisfactory compromise. I replaced "federal" with "two-tier form of government."

Thomas Hobbes, the founder of modern political thought, would have blessed the compromise, for he, too, had little room for federalism in his understanding of the best form of government. Hobbes said that people agreed to have a government over them only because they realized that in a state of nature, that is, when there is no government, life becomes a war of all against all. If no government exists to put malefactors in jail, everyone must become a criminal simply to avoid being a victim. Life becomes "nasty, brutish and short." To avoid the violent state of nature, people need and want rule by a single sovereign. Division of power among multiple sovereigns encourages bickering among them. Conflicts become inevitable, as each sovereign tries to expand its power (if for no other reason than to avoid becoming the prey of competing sovereigns). Government degenerates into anarchy and the world returns to the bitter state of nature from which government originally emerged.

The authors of *The Federalist* papers defended dual sovereignty by turning Hobbes's argument in favor of single sovereignty on its head. While Hobbes said that anything less than a single sovereign would lead to war of all against all, *The Federalist* argued that the best way of preserving liberty was to divide power. If power is concentrated in any one place, it can be used to crush individual liberty. Even in a democracy there can be the tyranny of the majority, the worst kind of tyranny because it is so stifling and complete. A division of power between the national and state governments reduces the possibility that any single majority will be able to control all centers of governmental power. The national government, by defending the country against foreign aggression, prevents external threats to liberty. The state governments, by denying power to any single dictator, reduce threats to liberty from within. As James Madison said in his defense of the Constitution, written on the eve of its ratification,

> The power surrendered by the people is first divided between two distinct governments, and then the portion allotted to each subdivided among distinct and separate departments. Hence a double security arises to the rights of the people. The different governments will control each other, at the same time that each will be controlled by itself. [*The Federalist*, No. 51]

Early federalism was built on the principle of dual sovereignty. The Constitution divided sovereignty between state and nation, each in control of its own sphere. Some even interpreted the Constitution to mean that state legislatures could nullify federal laws. Early federalism also gave both levels of government their own military capacity. Congress was given the power to raise an army and wage war, but states were allowed to maintain their own militia.

The major contribution of early federalism to American liberties took place within a dozen years after the signing of the Constitution. Liberty is never established in a new nation until those in authority have peacefully ceded power to a rival political faction. Those who wrote the Constitution and secured its ratification, known as the Federalists, initially captured control of the main institutions of the national government: Congress, the presidency, and the Supreme Court. Those opposed to the new constitutional order, the antifederalists, had to content themselves with an opposition role in Congress and control over a number of state governments, most notably Virginia's.

The political issues dividing the two parties were serious. The Federalist party favored a strong central government, a powerful central bank that could facilitate economic and industrial development, and a strong, independent executive branch. Federalists had also become increasingly disturbed by the direction the French Revolution had taken. They were alarmed by the execution of thousands, the confiscation of private property, and the movement of French troops across Europe. They called for the creation of a national army and reestablished close ties with Britain.

The antifederalists, who became known as Democratic-Republicans, favored keeping most governmental power in the hands of state governments. They were opposed to a national bank, a strong presidency, and industrial government. They thought the United States would remain a free country only if it remained a land of independent farmers. They bitterly opposed the creation of a national army for fear it would be used to repress political opposition. Impressed by the French Revolution's commitment to the rights of man, they excused its excesses. The greater danger, they thought, was the reassertion of British power, and they denounced the Federalists for seeming to acquiesce in the seizure of U.S. seamen by the British navy.

The conflict between the two sides intensified after George Washington retired to his home in Mount Vernon. In 1800 Thomas Jefferson, founder of the Democratic-Republican party, waged an all-out campaign to defeat Washington's Federalist successor, John Adams. In retrospect, the central issue of the election was democracy itself. Could an opposition party drive a government out of power? Would political leaders accept their defeat?

So bitter was the feud between the two parties that Representative Matthew Lyon, a Democratic-Republican, spit in the face of a Federalist on the floor of Congress. Outside the Congress, pro-French propagandists relentlessly criticized Adams. To silence the opposition, Congress, controlled by the Federalists, passed the Alien and Sedition Acts. One of the Alien Acts gave President Adams the power to deport any foreigners "concerned in any treasonable or secret machinations against the government." The Sedition Act made it illegal to "write, print, utter, or publish . . . any false, scandalous and malicious writing . . . against . . . the Congress of the United States, or the President."

The targets of the Sedition Acts soon became clear. Newspaper editors supporting the Democratic-Republicans were quickly indicted, and ten were brought to trial and convicted by juries under the influence of Federalist judges. Matthew Lyon was sentenced to a four-month jail term for claiming, presumably falsely, that President Adams had an "unbounded thirst for ridiculous pomp, foolish adulation, and selfish avarice." Even George Washington lent his support to this political repression.

Federalism undoubtedly helped the fledgling American democracy survive this first constitutional test. When the Federalists passed the Alien and Sedition Acts, Democratic-Republicans in the Virginia and Kentucky state legislatures passed resolutions nullifying the laws. When it looked as if Jefferson's victory in the election of 1800 might be stripped away by a Federalist-controlled House of Representatives, both sides realized that the Virginia state militia was at least as strong as the remnants of the Continental Army. Lacking the national army they had tried to establish, the Federalists chose not to fight. They acquiesced in their political defeat in part because their opponents had military as well as political power, and because they themselves could retreat to their own regional base of power, the state and local governments of New England and the mid-Atlantic states.

Jefferson claimed his victory was a revolution every bit as comprehensive as the one fought in 1776. The Alien and Sedition Acts were discarded, nullified not by a state legislature but by the results of a national election. President Adams returned to private life without suffering imprisonment or exile. Many years later, he and Jefferson reconciled their differences and developed through correspondence a close friendship. They died on the same day, the fiftieth anniversary of the Declaration of Independence. To both, federalism and liberty seemed closely intertwined.

The price to be paid for early federalism became more evident with the passage of time. To achieve the blessings of liberty, early federalism divided sovereign power. When Virginia and Kentucky nullified the Alien and Sedition Acts, they preserved liberties only by threatening national unity. With the election of Jefferson, the issue was temporarily rendered moot, but the doctrine remained available for use when southerners once again felt threatened by encroaching national power.

The doctrine of nullification was revived in 1830 by John C. Calhoun, sometime senator from South Carolina, who objected to high tariffs that protected northern industry at the expense of southern cotton producers. When Congress raised the tariff, South Carolina's legislature threatened to declare the law null and void. Calhoun, then serving as Andrew Jackson's vice president, argued that liberties could be trampled by national majorities unless states could nullify tyrannical acts. Andrew Jackson, though elected on a state's rights ticket, remained committed to national supremacy. At the annual Democratic banquet honoring the memory of Thomas Jefferson, Calhoun supporters sought to trap Jackson into endorsing the doctrine. But Jackson, aware of the scheme, raised his glass in a dramatic toast to "Our federal union: it must be preserved!" Not to be outdone, Calhoun replied in kind: "The union, next to our liberty, most dear!"

A compromise was found to the overt issue, the tariff, but it was not so easy to resolve the underlying issue of slavery. In the infamous Dred Scott decision, the Supreme Court interpreted federalism to mean that boundaries could not be placed on the movements of masters and slaves. Northern territories could not free slaves that came within their boundaries; to do so deprived masters of their Fifth Amendment right not to be deprived of their property without due process of law. The decision spurred northern states to elect Abraham Lincoln president, which convinced southern whites that their liberties, most dear, were more important than federal union.

To Lincoln, as to Jackson, the union was to be preserved at all costs. Secession meant war. War meant the loss of 1 million lives, the destruction of the southern economy, the emancipation of African Americans from slavery, the demise of the doctrine of nullification, and the end to early federalism. Early federalism, with its doctrine of dual sovereignty, may have initially helped to preserve liberty, but it did so at a terrible price. As Hobbes feared, the price of dual sovereignty was war.

Since the termination of the Civil War, Americans have concluded that they can no longer trust their liberties to federalism. Sovereignty must be concentrated in the hands of the national government. Quite apart from the dangers of civil war, the powers of state and local governments have been used too often by a tyrannical majority to trample the rights of religious, racial, and political minorities. The courts now seem a more reliable institutional shelter for the nation's liberties.

But if federalism is no longer necessary or even conducive to the preservation of liberty, then what is its purpose? Is it merely a relic of an outdated past? Are the majority of the members of the United Nations correct in objecting to the very use of the word?

The Rise of Modern Federalism

The answers to these questions have been gradually articulated in the 130 years following the end of the Civil War. Although the states lost their sovereignty, they remained integral to the workings of American government. Modern federalism no longer meant dual sovereignty and shared military capacity. Modern federalism instead meant only that each level of government had its own independently elected political leaders and its own separate taxing and spending capacity. Equipped with these tools of quasi-sovereignty, each level of government could take all but the most violent of steps to defend its turf.

Although sovereignty and military capacity now rested firmly in the hands of the national government, modern federalism became more complex rather than less so. Power was no longer simply divided between the nation and its states. Cities, counties, towns, school districts, special districts, and a host of additional governmental entities, each with its own elected leaders and taxing authority, assumed new burdens and responsibilities.

Just as the blessings bestowed by early federalism were evident from its inception, so the advantages of modern federalism were clear from the onset. If states and localities were no longer the guarantors of liberty, they became the engines of economic development. By giving state and local governments the autonomy to act independently, the federal system facilitated the rapid growth of an industrial economy that eventually surpassed its European competitors. Canals and railroads were constructed, highways and sewage systems built, schools opened, parks designed, and public safety protected by cities and villages eager to make their locality a boomtown.

The price to be paid for modern federalism did not become evident until government attempted to grapple with the adverse side effects of a burgeoning capitalist economy. Out of a respect for federalism's constitutional status and political durability, social reformers first worked with and through existing components of the federal system, concentrating much of their reform effort on state and local governments. Only gradually did it become clear that state and local governments, for all their ability to work with business leaders to enhance community prosperity, had difficulty meeting the needs of the poor and the needy.

It was ultimately up to the courts to find ways of keeping the price of modern federalism within bounds. Although dual sovereignty no longer meant nullification and secession, much remained to be determined about the respective areas of responsibility of the national and state governments. At first the courts retained remnants of the doctrine of dual sovereignty in order to protect processes of industrialization from governmental intrusion. But with the advent of the New Deal, the constitutional power of the national government expanded so dramatically that the doctrine of dual sovereignty virtually lost all meaning. Court interpretations of the constitutional clauses on commerce and spending have proved to be the most significant.

According to dual sovereignty theory, article 1 of the Constitution gives Congress the power to regulate commerce "among the states," but the regulation of intrastate commerce was to be left to the states. So, for example, in 1895 the Supreme Court said that Congress could not break up a sugar monopoly that had a nationwide impact on the price of sugar, because the monopoly refined its sugar within the state of Pennsylvania. The mere fact that the sugar was to be sold nationwide was only "incidental" to its production. As late as 1935, the Supreme Court, in a 6 to 3 decision, said that Congress could not regulate the sale of poultry because the regulation took effect after the chickens arrived within the state of Illinois, not while they were in transit.

Known as the "sick chicken" case, this decision was one of a series in which the Supreme Court declared unconstitutional legislation passed in the early days of President Franklin Roosevelt's efforts to establish his New Deal programs. Seven of the "nine old men" on the Court had been appointed by Roosevelt's conservative Republican predecessors. By declaring many New Deal programs in violation of the commerce clause, the Supreme Court seemed to be substituting its political views for those of elected officials. In a case denying the federal government the right to protect workers trying to organize a union in the coal industry, the Republican views of the Court seemed to lie just barely below the surface of a technical discussion of the commerce clause. Justice George Sutherland declared, "The relation of employer and employee is a local relation . . . over which the federal government has no legislative control."

The Roosevelt Democrats were furious at decisions that seemed to deny the country's elected officials the right to govern. Not since Dred Scott* had judicial review been in such disrepute. Roosevelt decided to "pack the court" by adding six new judges over and above the nine already on the Court. Although Roosevelt's court-packing scheme did not survive the political uproar on Capitol Hill, its effect on the Supreme Court was noticeable. In the midst of the court-packing debate, Justices Charles Hughes and Owen Roberts, who had agreed with Sutherland's opinion in the coal case, changed their mind and voted to uphold the Wagner Act, a new law designed to facilitate the formation of unions. In his opinion, Hughes did not explicitly overturn the coal miner decision (for which he had voted), but he did say: "When industries organize themselves on a national scale, . . . how can it be maintained that their industrial labor relations constitute a forbidden field into which Congress may not enter?" Relations between employers and their workers, once said to be local, suddenly became part of interstate commerce.

The change of heart by Hughes and Roberts has been called "the switch in time that saved nine." The New Deal majority that emerged on the court was soon augmented by judges appointed by Roosevelt.

---

*[In *Dred Scott v. Sanford* (1857), the Court declared the anti-slavery provision of the Missouri Compromise of 1820 to be unconstitutional.]

Since the New Deal, the definition of interstate commerce has continued to expand. In 1942 a farmer raising twenty-three acres of wheat, all of which might be fed to his own livestock, was said to be in violation of the crop quotas imposed by the Agricultural Adjustment Act of 1938. Since he was feeding his cows himself, he was not buying grain on the open market, thereby depressing the worldwide price of grain. With such a definition of interstate commerce, nothing was local.

The expansion of the meaning of the commerce clause is a well-known part of American political history. The importance to federalism of court interpretations of the "spending clause" is less well known. The constitutional clause in question says that Congress has the power to collect taxes to "provide for the . . . general welfare." But how about Congress's power to collect taxes for the welfare of specific individuals or groups?

The question first arose in a 1923 case, when a childless woman said she could not be asked to pay taxes in order to finance federal grants to states for programs that helped pregnant women. Since she received no benefit from the program, she sued for return of the taxes she had paid to cover its costs. In a decision that has never been reversed, the Supreme Court said that she had suffered no measurable injury and therefore had no right to sue the government. Her taxes were being used for a wide variety of purposes. The amount being spent for this program was too small to be significant. The court's decision to leave spending issues to Congress was restated a decade later when the social security program was also challenged on the grounds that monies were being directed to the elderly, not for the general welfare. Said Justice Benjamin N. Cardozo for a court majority: "The conception of the spending power . . . [must find a point somewhere] between particular and general. . . . There is a middle ground . . . in which discretion is large. The discretion, however, is not confided to the Court. The discretion belongs to Congress, unless the choice is clearly wrong."

The courts have ever since refused to review Congress's power to spend money. They have also conceded to Congress the right to attach any regulations to any aid Congress provides. In 1987 Congress provided a grant to state governments for the maintenance of their highways, but conditioned 5 percent of the funds on state willingness to raise the drinking age from eighteen to twenty-one. The connection between the appropriation and the regulation was based on the assumption that youths under the age of twenty-one are more likely to drive after drinking than those over twenty-one. Presumably, building more roads would only encourage more inebriated young people to drive on them. Despite the fact that the connection between the appropriation and the regulation was problematic, the Supreme Court ruled that Congress could attach any reasonable conditions to its grants to the states. State sovereignty was not violated, because any state could choose not to accept the money.

In short, the courts have virtually given up the doctrine of judicial review when it comes to matters on which Congress can spend money. As a consequence, most national efforts to influence state governments come in the form of federal grants. Federal aid can also be used to influence local governments, such as counties, cities, towns, villages, and school districts. These local governments, from a constitutional point of view, are mere creatures of the state of which they are part. They have no independent sovereignty.

The Contemporary Price of Federalism

If constitutional doctrine has evolved to the point that dual sovereign theory has been put to rest, this does not mean that federalism has come to an end. Although ultimate sovereignty resides with the national government, state and local governments still have certain characteristics and capabilities that make them constituent components of a federal system. * * * Two characteristics of federalism are fundamental. First, citizens elect officials of their choice for each level of government. Unless the authority of each level of government rests in the people, it will become the agent of the other. Second, each level of government raises money through taxation from the citizens residing in the area for which it is responsible. It is hard to see how a system could be regarded as federal unless each level of government can levy taxes on its residents. Unless each level of government can raise its own fiscal resources, it cannot act independently.

Although the constitutional authority of the national government has steadily expanded, state and local governments remain of great practical significance. Almost half of all government spending for domestic (as distinct from foreign and military) purposes is paid for out of taxes raised by state and local governments.

The sharing of control over domestic policy among levels of government has many benefits, but federalism still exacts its price. It can lead to great regional inequalities. Also, the need for establishing cooperative relationships among governments can contribute to great inefficiency in the administration of government programs.

Discussion Questions

1. What is the constitutional basis for federalism?

2. How has the relationship between state governments and the national government changed since the early years of the Republic?

3. Does a federal system serve our needs today? Does the federal government have too much power relative to the states? What would be the advantages and disadvantages of a reduced federal presence in state matters?

13

"Jumping Frogs, Endangered Toads, and California's Medical-Marijuana Law"

George J. Annas

From welfare reform to health care, educational funding to inner-city develop-ment, state governments have sought more control over public policy within their borders. In the 1970s and 1980s, when this devolution of power to the states was called "New Federalism," the debate was pretty simple. Republicans favored devolution because state governments were "closer to the people" and could better determine their needs. Democrats resisted the transfer of power from Washington, fearing that many states would not adequately care for and protect minorities and poor people, or protect the environment without prodding from Washington. To the extent that the courts got involved in the debate, they tended to favor the transfer of power to the states.

The debate over developing power from the national government to the states has grown increasingly complicated in the past several years: the partisan nature of the debate shifted, the Courts have played a larger, but inconsistent role, and issues of "states' rights" increasingly tend to cut across normal ideological and partisan divisions. While Republicans continued to favor greater state control, a Democratic President, Bill Clinton, supported devolution to the states in several areas in the 1990s, especially welfare policy. Since the mid 1990s, the Supreme Court has played a central role in the shift of power to the states, but two recent cases involving medical marijuana (Raich v. Gonzales) and assisted suicide (Gonzales v. Oregon) show how the typical debate between national and state power can shift when a moral dimension is introduced.

In both cases, state voters supported liberal policies (approving medical mari-juana in California and assisted suicide in Oregon). Therefore, the "states' rights" position on federalism in these cases represented the liberal perspective, which in partisan terms means mostly Democratic, rather than the conservative positions on race, labor, market regulation, and welfare that state-centered feder-alism is typically associated with. What's a good liberal or conservative to do? Social liberals supported the medical marijuana law (and thus the minority in Raich) *and the assisted suicide law in Oregon (the majority in* Gonzales). *Moral conservatives were the opposite (pro-*Raich, *anti-*Gonzales). *However, on the central question of federal versus state power, which has been a central ideo-logical divide in this nation since the Federalists and Anti-Federalists battled it out at the Constitutional Convention, liberals and conservatives would have to* *flip their views. So a national-power liberal would have supported the* Raich *decision and opposed the* Gonzales *decision (the opposite of the social liberal), while a state-power conservative would have opposed* Raich *and supported* Gonzales *(which is the reverse of a moral conservative's positions). That means that a national power liberal and the moral conservative would have the same views (national power would be used to regulate medical marijuana and assisted suicide), while states' rights advocates share the views of the social liberals (because voters in California approved medical marijuana and Oregon voters supported assisted suicide).*

Somewhat surprisingly, there was almost no consistency among the eight justices who voted on both cases (William Rehnquist was replaced by John Roberts between the two cases): only Justice O'Connor supported the states' rights position in both cases while Scalia voted as a moral conservative (which runs strongly counter to his previously articulated views on national power and federalism). All of the other six justices mixed their views. The Court as a whole was inconsistent on the question of federalism as well: in the medical marijuana case, the Court upheld Congress's power to regulate the medical use of marijuana under the Controlled Substances Act. But in the assisted suicide case, the Court said that Congress did not give the U.S. Attorney General the power under that same law to limit the drugs that doctors in Oregon could prescribe for use in an assisted suicide.

George Annas looks at the medical marijuana case (and touches on the assisted suicide case) from the perspective of doctors. Writing in the New England Journal of Medicine, *one of the leading medical journals in the nation, Annas points out the "most interesting, and disturbing aspect of the case to physicians" is the Court's reference to "unscrupulous physicians who overprescribe when it is sufficiently profitable to do so." Annas says that such cases are rare and that the California law was narrowly written to make sure that such abuses would not occur. This article is also very useful for its excellent overview of Congress's commerce clause powers and its importance in federalism cases.*

Mark Twain wasn't thinking about federalism or the structure of American government when he wrote "The Celebrated Jumping Frog of Calaveras County."[1] Nonetheless, he would be amused to know that today, almost 150 years later, the Calaveras County Fair and Jumping Frog Jubilee not only has a jumping frog contest but also has its own Frog Welfare Policy. The policy includes a provision for the "Care of Sick or Injured Frogs" and a limitation entitled "Frogs Not Permitted to Participate," which stipulates that "under no circumstances will a frog listed on the endangered species list be permitted to participate in the Frog Jump."[2] This fair, like medical practice, is subject to both state and federal laws. Care of the sick and injured (both frogs and people) is primarily viewed as a matter of state law, whereas protection of endangered species is primarily regulated by Congress under its authority to regulate interstate commerce.

Not to carry the analogy too far, but it is worth recalling that Twain's famous frog, Dan'l Webster, lost his one and only jumping contest because his stomach had been filled with quail shot by a competitor. The loaded-down frog just couldn't jump. Until the California medical-marijuana case, it seemed to many observers that the conservative Rehnquist Court had succeeded in filling the commerce clause with quail shot—and had effectively prevented the federal government from regulating state activities. In the medical-marijuana case, however, a new majority of justices took the lead out of the commerce clause so that the federal government could legitimately claim jurisdiction over just about any activity, including the practice of medicine. The role of the commerce clause in federalism and the implications of the Court's decision in the California medical-marijuana case for physicians are the subjects I explore in this article.

The Commerce Clause

The U.S. Constitution determines the areas over which the federal government has authority. All other areas remain, as they were before the adoption of the Constitution, under the authority of the individual states. Another way to say this is that the states retain all governmental authority they did not delegate to the federal government, including areas such as criminal law and family-law matters. These are part of the state's "police powers," usually defined as the state's sovereign authority to protect the health, safety, and welfare of its residents. Section 8 of Article I of the Constitution contains 18 clauses specifying delegated areas (including the military, currency, postal service, and patenting) over which "Congress shall have power," and these include the commerce clause—"to regulate commerce with foreign nations, and among the several states, and with the Indian tribes."

Until the Great Depression (and the disillusionment with unregulated markets), the Supreme Court took a narrow view of federal authority that could be derived from the commerce clause by ruling consistently that it gave Congress the authority only to regulate activities that directly involved the movement of commercial products (such as pharmaceuticals) from one state to another. Since then, and at least until 1995, the Court's interpretation seemed to be going in the opposite direction: Congress was consistently held to have authority in areas that had almost any relationship at all to commerce.

Guns in Schools and Violence Against Women

Under modern commerce clause doctrine, Congress has authority to regulate in three broad categories of activities: the use of the channels of interstate commerce (e.g., roads, air corridors, and waterways); the instrumentalities of interstate commerce (e.g., trains, trucks, and planes) and persons and things in interstate commerce; and "activities having a substantial relation to interstate commerce."[3] The first two categories are easy ones in that they involve activities that cross state lines. The third category, which does not involve crossing a state line, is the controversial one. The interpretation question involves the meaning and application of the concept of "substantially affecting" interstate commerce.

In a 1937 case that the Court characterized as a "watershed case" it concluded that the real question was one of the degree of effect. Intrastate activities that "have such a close and substantial relation to interstate commerce that their control is essential or appropriate to protect that commerce from burdens and obstructions" are within the power of Congress to regulate.[4] Later, in what has become perhaps its best-known commerce-clause case, the Court held that Congress could enforce a statute that prohibited a farmer from growing wheat on his own farm even if the wheat was never sold but was used only for the farmer's personal consumption. The Court concluded that although one farmer's personal use of home-grown wheat may be trivial (and have no effect on commerce), "taken together with that of many others similarly situated," its effect on interstate commerce (and the market price of wheat) "is far from trivial."[5]

The 1995 case that seemed to presage a states' rights revolution (often referred to as "devolution") involved the federal Gun-Free School Zones Act of 1990, which made it a federal crime "for any individual knowingly to possess a firearm at a place that the individual knows, or has reasonable cause to believe, is a school zone."[3] In a 5-to-4 opinion, written by the late Chief Justice William Rehnquist, the Court held that the statute exceeded Congress's authority under the commerce clause and only the individual states had authority to criminalize the possession of guns in school.[3]

The federal government had argued (and the four justices in the minority agreed) that the costs of violent crime are spread out over the entire population and that the presence of guns in schools threatens "national productivity" by undermining the learning environment, which in turn decreases learning and leads to a less productive citizenry and thus a less productive national economy. The majority of the Court rejected these arguments primarily because they thought that accepting this line of reasoning would make it impossible to define "any limitations on federal power, even in areas such as criminal law enforcement or education, where states historically have been sovereign."[3]

In 2000, in another 5-to-4 opinion written by Rehnquist, using the same rationale, the Court struck down a federal statute, part of the Violence against Women Act of 1994, that provided a federal civil remedy for victims of "gender-motivated violence." In the Court's words:

> Gender-motivated crimes of violence are not, in any sense of the phrase, economic activity. . . . Indeed, if Congress may regulate gender-motivated violence, it would be able to regulate murder or any other type of violence since

gender-motivated violence, as a subset of all violent crime, is certain to have lesser economic impacts than the larger class of which it is a part.[6]

The Court, specifically addressing the question of federalism, concluded that "the Constitution requires a distinction between what is truly national and what is truly local. . . . Indeed, we can think of no better example of the police power, which the Founders denied to the National Government and reposed in the States, than the suppression of violent crime and vindication of its victims."[6]

Medical Marijuana in California

The next commerce-clause case involved physicians, albeit indirectly, and the role assigned to them in California in relation to the protection of patients who used physician-recommended marijuana from criminal prosecution. The question before the Supreme Court in the recent medical-marijuana case (*Gonzalez v. Raich*) was this: Does the commerce clause give Congress the authority to outlaw the local cultivation and use of marijuana for medicine if such cultivation and use complies with the provisions of California law?[7]

The California law, which is similar to laws in at least nine other states, creates an exemption from criminal prosecution for physicians, patients, and primary caregivers who possess or cultivate marijuana for medicinal purposes on the recommendation of a physician. Two patients for whom marijuana had been recommended brought suit to challenge enforcement of the federal Controlled Substances Act after federal Drug Enforcement Administration agents seized and destroyed all six marijuana plants that one of them had been growing for her own medical use in compliance with the California law. The Ninth Circuit Court of Appeals ruled in the plaintiffs' favor, finding that the California law applied to a separate and distinct category of activity, "the intrastate, noncommercial cultivation and possession of *cannabis* for personal medical purposes as recommended by a patient's physician pursuant to valid California state law," as opposed to what it saw as the federal law's purpose, which was to prevent "drug trafficking."[8] In a 6-to-3 opinion, written by Justice John Paul Stevens, with Justice Rehnquist dissenting, the Court reversed the appeals court's opinion and decided that Congress, under the commerce clause, did have authority to enforce its prohibition against marijuana—even state-approved, homegrown, noncommercial marijuana, used only for medicinal purposes on a physician's recommendation.

The majority of the Court decided that the commerce clause gave Congress the same power to regulate homegrown marijuana for personal use that it had to regulate homegrown wheat.[6] The question was whether homegrown marijuana for personal medical consumption substantially affected interstate commerce (albeit illegal commerce) when all affected patients were taken together. The Court concluded that Congress "had a rational basis for concluding that leaving home-consumed marijuana outside federal control" would affect "price and market conditions."[7] The Court also distinguished the guns-in-school and gender-violence cases on the basis that regulation of drugs is "quintessentially economic" when economics is defined as the "production, distribution, and consumption of commodities."[7]

This left only one real question open: Is the fact that marijuana is to be used only for medicinal purposes on the advice of a physician, as the Ninth Circuit Court had decided, sufficient for an exception to be carved out of otherwise legitimate federal authority to control drugs? The Court decided it was not, for several reasons. The first was that Congress itself had determined that marijuana is a Schedule I drug, which it defined as having "no acceptable medical use." The Court acknowledged that Congress might be wrong in this determination, but the issue in this case was not whether marijuana had possible legitimate medical uses but whether Congress had the authority to make the judgment that it had none and to ban all uses of the drug. The dissenting justices argued that personal cultivation and use of marijuana should be beyond the authority of the commerce clause. The Court majority disagreed, stating that if it accepted the dissenting justices' argument, personal cultivation for recreational use would also be beyond congressional authority. This conclusion, the majority argued, could not be sustained:

> One need not have a degree in economics to understand why a nationwide exemption for the vast quantity of marijuana (or other drugs) locally cultivated for personal use (which presumably would include use by friends, neighbors, and family members) may have a substantial impact on the interstate market for this extraordinarily popular substance. The congressional judgment that an exemption for such a significant segment of the total market would undermine the orderly enforcement of the entire [drug] regulatory scheme is entitled to a strong presumption of validity.[7]

The other primary limit to the effect of the California law on interstate commerce is the requirement of a physician's recommendation on the basis of a medical determination that a patient has an "illness for which marijuana provides relief." And the Court's discussion of this limit may be the most interesting, and disturbing, aspect of the case to physicians. Instead of concluding that physicians should be free to use their best medical judgment and that it was up to state medical boards to decide whether specific physicians were failing to live up to reasonable medical standards—as the Court did, for example, in its cases related to restrictive abortion laws[9]—the Court took a totally different approach. In the Court's words, the broad language of the California medical-marijuana law allows "even the most scrupulous doctor to conclude that some recreational uses would be therapeutic. And our cases have taught us that there are some unscrupulous physicians who overprescribe when it is sufficiently profitable to do so."[7]

The California law defines the category of patients who are exempt from criminal prosecution as those suffering from cancer, anorexia, AIDS, chronic pain, spasticity, glaucoma, arthritis, migraine, and "any other chronic or persistent medical symptom that substantially limits the ability of a person to conduct one or more major life activities . . . or if not alleviated may cause serious harm to the patient's safety or physical or mental health." These limits are hardly an invitation for recreational-use recommendations.[7] Regarding "unscrupulous physicians," the Court cited two cases that involve criminal prosecutions of physicians for acting like drug dealers, one from 1919 and the other from 1975, implying that because a few physicians might have been criminally inclined in the past, it was reasonable for Congress (and the Court), on the basis of no actual evidence, to assume that many physicians may be so inclined today. It was not only physicians that the Court found untrustworthy but sick patients and their caregivers as well:

> The exemption for cultivation by patients and caregivers [patients can possess up to 8 oz. of dried marijuana and cultivate up to 6 mature or 12 immature plants] can only increase the supply of marijuana in the California market. The likelihood that all such production will promptly terminate when patients recover or will precisely match the patients' medical needs during their convalescence seems remote; whereas the danger that excesses will satisfy some of the admittedly enormous demand for recreational use seems obvious.[7]

Justice Sandra Day O'Connor's dissent merits comment, because it is especially relevant to the practice of medicine. She argues that the Constitution requires the Court to protect "historic spheres of state sovereignty from excessive federal encroachment" and that one of the virtues of federalism is that it permits the individual states to serve as "laboratories," should they wish, to try "novel social and economic experiments without risk to the rest of the country." Specifically, she argues that the Court's new definition of economic activity is "breathtaking" in its scope, creating exactly what the gun case rejected—a federal police power. She also rejects reliance on the wheat case, noting that under the Agricultural Adjustment Act in question in that case, Congress had exempted the planting of less than 200 bushels (about six tons), and that when Roscoe Filburn, the farmer who challenged the federal statute, himself harvested his wheat, the statute exempted plantings of less than six acres.[5,7]

In O'Connor's words, the wheat case "did not extend Commerce Clause authority to something as modest as the home cook's herb garden."[8] O'Connor is not saying that Congress cannot regulate small quantities of a product produced for personal use, only that the wheat case "did not hold or imply that small-scale production of commodities is always economic, and automatically within Congress' reach." As to potential "exploitation [of the act] by unscrupulous physicians" and patients, O'Connor finds no factual support for this assertion and rejects the conclusion that simply by "piling assertion upon assertion" one can make a case for meeting the "substantiality test" of the guns-in-school and gender-violence cases.[7]

It is important to note that the Court was not taking a position on whether Congress was correct to place marijuana in Schedule I or a position against California's law, any more than it was taking a position in favor of guns in schools or violence against women in the earlier cases. Instead, the Court was ruling only on the question of federal authority under the commerce clause. The Court noted, for example, that California and its supporters may one day prevail by pursuing the democratic process "in the halls of Congress."[7] This seems extremely unlikely. More important is the question not addressed in this case—whether suffering patients have a substantive due-process claim to access to drugs needed to prevent suffering or a valid medical-necessity defense should they be prosecuted for using medical marijuana on a physician's recommendation.[10] Also not addressed was the question that will be decided during the coming year: whether Congress has delegated to the U.S. attorney general its authority to decide what a "legitimate medical use" of an approved drug is in the context of Oregon's law governing physician-assisted suicide.[11,12] What is obvious from this case, however, is that Congress has the authority, under the commerce clause, to regulate both legal and illegal drugs whether or not the drugs in question actually cross state lines. It would also seem reasonable to conclude that Congress has the authority to limit the uses of approved drugs.

Federalism and Endangered Species

Because *Gonzales v. Raich* is a drug case, and because it specifically involves marijuana, the Court's final word on federalism may not yet be in. Whether the "states' rights" movement has any life left after medical marijuana may be determined in the context of the Endangered Species Act. Two U.S. Circuit Courts of Appeals, for example, have recently upheld application of the federal law to protect endangered species that, unlike the descendants of Mark Twain's jumping frog, have no commercial value. Even though the Supreme Court refused to hear appeals from both of the lower courts, the cases help us understand the contemporary reach of congressional power under the commerce clause. One case involves the protection of six tiny creatures that live in caves (the "Cave Species")—three arthropods, a spider, and two beetles—from a commercial developer. The Fifth Circuit Court of Appeals noted that the Cave Species are not themselves an object of economics or commerce, saying: "There is no market for them; any future market is conjecture. If the speculative future medicinal benefits from the Cave Species makes their regulation commercial, then almost anything would be. . . . There is no historic trade in the Cave Species, nor do tourists come to Texas to view them."[13] Nonetheless, the court concluded that Congress had the authority, under the commerce clause, to view life as an "interdependent web" of all species; that destruction of endangered species can be aggregated, like homegrown wheat; and that the destruction of multiple species has a substantial effect on interstate commerce.[13]

The other case, from the District of Columbia Court of Appeals, involves the arroyo south-western toad, whose habitat was threatened by a real-estate developer. In upholding the application of the Endangered Species Act to the case, the appeals court held that the commercial activity being regulated was the housing development itself, as well as the "taking" of the road by the planned commercial development. The court noted that the "company would like us to consider its challenge to the ESA [Endangered Species Act] only as applied to the arroyo toad, which it says has no 'known commercial value'—unlike, for example, Mark Twain's celebrated jumping frogs [sic] of Calaveras County."[14] Instead, the court concluded that application of the Endangered Species Act, far from eroding states' rights, is consistent with "the historic power of the federal government to preserve scarce resources in one locality for the future benefit of all Americans.[14]

On a request for a hearing by the entire appeals court, which was rejected, recently named Chief Justice John Roberts—who at the time was a member of the appeals court—wrote a dissent that was not unlike Justice O'Connor's dissent in the marijuana case. In it he argued that the court's conclusion seemed inconsistent with the guns-in-school and gender-violence cases and that there were real problems with using an analysis of the commerce clause to regulate "the taking of a hapless toad that, for reasons of its own, lives its entire life in California."[15] The case has since been settled. The development is going ahead in a way that protects the toad's habitat.[16]

The Future of the Commerce Clause

Twain's short story has been termed "a living American fairy tale, acted out annually in Calaveras County."[1] In what might be termed a living American government tale, nominees to the Supreme Court are routinely asked to explain their judicial philosophy of constitutional and statutory interpretation to the Senate Judiciary Committee. Asked about his "hapless toad" opinion during the Senate confirmation hearings on his nomination to replace Rehnquist as chief justice, Roberts said: "The whole point of my argument in the dissent was that there was another way to look at this [i.e., the approach taken by the Fifth Circuit Court in the Cave Species case]. . . . I did not say that even in this case that the decision was wrong. . . . I simply said, let's look at those other grounds for decision because that doesn't present this problem." These hearings provide an opportunity for all Americans to review their understanding of our constitutional government and the manner in which it allocates power between the federal government and the 50 states. To the extent that this division of power is determined by the Court's view of the commerce clause, a return to an expansive reading of this clause seems both likely and, given the interdependence of the national and global economies, proper.

Of course, the fact that Congress has authority over a particular subject—such as whether to adopt a system of national licensure for physicians—does not mean that its authority is unlimited or even that Congress will use it. Rather, as Justice Stevens noted, cases such as the California medical-marijuana case lead to other central constitutional questions, as yet unresolved. These questions include whether patients, terminally ill or not, have a constitutional right not to suffer—at least, when their physicians know how to control their pain.[12]

DISCUSSION QUESTIONS

1. *What would you do?* If you were a state legislator or a judge, how would you decide these issues? Specifically, as a matter of policy, do you think that doctors should be able to prescribe marijuana to alleviate pain? Should they be able to prescribe lethal drugs to be used by terminally ill patients? What about as a matter of law? Do you agree with the Supreme Court's decisions on these issues?

2. Do you support a state-centered or nation-centered perspective on federalism? Now go back and look at your answers to the last questions. Did you take positions that were consistent with your views on federalism or as a policy concern?

3. What does Mark Twain's jumping frog represent in Annas's article? Which Supreme Court case breathed life back into the frog and why?

NOTES

1. Charles Neider, ed. The complete short stories of Mark Twain. New York: Hanover House, 1957:1–6.
2. 39th District Agricultural Association. Animal welfare policy (Calaveras County Fair and Jumping Frog Jubilee). April 2003. (Accessed November 3, 2005, at http://www.frogtown.org.)
3. *U.S. v. Lopez*, 514 U.S. 549 (1995).
4. *NLRB v. Jones & Laughlin Steel Corp.*, 301 U.S. 1 (1937).
5. *Wickard v. Filburn*, 317 U.S. 111 (1942).
6. *U.S. v. Morrison*, 529 U.S. 598 (2000).
7. *Gonzales v. Raich*, 125 S.Ct. 2195 (2005).
8. *Raich v. Ashcroft*, 3352 F.3d 1222 (9th Cir. 2003).
9. Annas GJ, Glantz LH, Mariner WK. "The right of privacy protects the doctor-patient relationship." *JAMA* 1900;263:858–61.
10. Annas GJ. "Reefer madness—the federal response to California's medical-marijuana law." *N Engl J Med* 1997;337:435–9.

11. Oregon v. Ashcroft, 368 F.3d 1118 (2004).
12. Annas GJ. "The bell tolls for a constitutional right to physician-assisted suicide." *N Engl J Med* 1997;337:1098–103.
13. *GDF Realty v. Norton*, 326 F.3d 622 (5th Cir. 2003).
14. *Rancho Viejo v. Norton*, 323 F.3d 1062 (D.C. Cir. 2003).
15. *Rancho Viejo v. Norton*, 357 F.3d 1158 (D.C. Cir. 2003).
16. Cummings J. "Environmentalists uncertain on Roberts." *Wall Street Journal*.
August 15, 2005:A3.

DEBATING THE ISSUES: FEDERALISM AND POLICY

For many years, the topic of federalism was viewed as a relatively sleepy, unexciting part of American politics. Sure, it was important to understand federalism's role in the American political system, Madison's "double security," and how intergovernmental relations have evolved. But relations between the national government and the states had settled into a stable system of cooperative federalism in most policy areas, so there were not many new and exciting developments. That all has changed in the past couple of decades. The Supreme Court has generally been shifting power from the national government to the states (but there are exceptions), while new struggles have emerged with "coercive federalism" as the national government tries to shape policy in the states. From education policy and welfare to the environment and taxes, the states are often at odds with Washington, D.C.

Developing this theme, Paul Posner argues that the drive to centralize government at the national level now transcends party lines. He says, "The secular trends toward a more coercive and centralized federalism have survived the passage of both Republican and Democratic Administrations, as well as Democratic and Republican Congresses." Supporters of states rights had hoped for a reduced role for the national government, given the unified Republican control of the presidency and Congress and Republicans' historic support for state power, but the trend under President Bush has been in the opposite direction. This may be especially surprising given the "coercive" tools used by the national government to impose policies on the states. Areas that had been traditionally reserved to the states, such as education, election administration, and welfare, now have an expanded role for the national government.

However, Barry Rabe argues that the states are fighting back, at least in the area of environmental policy. Rather than accepting government pollution standards that are too low and inactivity on issues such as global warming, the states are acting on their own. "The result," Rabe says, "has been a steady increase in intergovernmental conflict from the previous decade." Policies to address climate change, including renewable energy, carbon emissions limits, and carbon "cap and trade" programs, have all been pushed at the state level. States have even started to play a role in international global-warming policy discussions, as the example of the meeting between Arnold Schwarzenegger and Tony Blair illustrates. States have also taken the lead on issues such as electronic waste, mercury emissions, and air pollution more generally.

14

"The Politics of Coercive Federalism in the Bush Era"

PAUL POSNER

Over the past forty years, mandates and preemptions have become among the primary tools relied on by Congress and the president to project national priorities and objectives throughout the intergovernmental system (Kincaid 1990). The trends toward the use of coercive tools have proven to be durable and long lasting, albeit punctuated by episodes of reform. While the enactment of unfunded mandates reform in 1995 most certainly has led to some restraint, the underlying forces prompting national leaders to use these tools have proven to be persistent and compelling. The secular trends toward a more coercive and centralized federalism have survived the passage of both Republican and Democratic Administrations, as well as Democratic and Republican Congresses (Posner 1998).

The beginning of the twenty-first century witnessed the marshalling of new political forces that might be expected to turn away from the instruments of coercive federalism. The ascendancy of George W. Bush to the presidency, in concert with a remarkably unified Republican control of the Congress, presaged a period of unified government presided over by unprecedented conservative political leadership not seen since before the Great Depression. Coupled with the earlier passage of Unfunded Mandate Reform Act as one of the first acts of the 1995 conservative Republican Congress, hopes for the arrest and even reversal of federal policy centralization ran high in many quarters.

This article will explore whether the ascendance of the conservative regime in the White House and the Congress, coming on the heels of the unfunded mandates reform, made a significant difference in reversing the trends toward coercive federalism characterizing previous administrations and congresses. * * *

Coercive Federalism: A Taxonomy

The concept of coercive federalism covers a range of potential federal policy actions with centralizing effects on our system. Intergovernmental regulations can range from direct orders imposed on state and local governments by federal statute to more indirect actions that force state and local policy change as a consequence of other independent federal policies, such as the implications of federal immigration policies for local health clinics. The Advisory Commission on Intergovernmental Relations usefully defined a taxonomy of "federally induced costs" which suggested discrete policy actions the federal government can take to increase state and local costs (ACIR 1994):

- Statutory direct order mandates
- Grant conditions, both program specific and crosscutting
- Total statutory preemption
- Partial statutory preemption
- Federal income tax provisions affecting state and local tax bases
- Regulatory actions taken by federal courts and agencies
- Regulatory delays and nonenforcement
- Federal exposure of state and local governments to liability lawsuits

Given the range of potential actions covered under the rubric of coercive federalism, national actions can be best characterized along a continuum of centralization and fiscal impact that goes well beyond the popular concept of "unfunded mandates." Coercive federal actions in fact span a wide range of tools that also at times include classic elements of cooperative federalism as well, such as the presence of federal grant funding covering some of the costs. The Unfunded Mandates Reform Act (UMRA) of 1995 primarily addressed only one of the instruments of coercive federalism—statutory direct orders—and this relatively narrow definition has served to limit not only our understanding of the implications of national policy decisions for our federal system but also has served to limit the potential effectiveness of this reform in influencing these policy decisions.

The Bush Era: Continuities and Change

At the outset of a new administration, expectations were high for policy change in the intergovernmental system. President Bush himself proved to be more committed to conservative ideological principles than many had expected, given his self-proclaimed profile as a consensus leader with Democratic state legislators in Texas (Portier and Ornstein 2003). The president was able to work with Republican majorities in both House and Senate, albeit with a brief period of Democratic Senate control owing to Vermont Senator Jefford's conversion from a Republican to an Independent. The Republicans controlling the Congress were far more conservative than previous Republican regimes in the Congress. Moreover, the Congress had passed the Unfunded Mandates Act of 1995 which reflected a bipartisan commitment to curb the use of mandates.

Notwithstanding these forces, the period of the Bush presidency in fact witnessed the continuation of the centralization and nationalization of priorities and policies that had characterized previous administrations, both Republican and Democratic. As with those earlier administrations, federalism issues were largely relegated to secondary consideration, often trumped by more compelling national issues and values. It is true that the Bush administration did propose a modicum of decentralization through grant consolidations of community development, state control of the Head Start program, superwaiver proposals,[1] and providing greater state flexibility under Medicaid, albeit accompanied by new funding caps. (Finegold, Wheary, and Schardin 2004). However, the administration put very little "capital" into these initiatives, backing away from these proposals when the going got rough in the Congress. Rather the administration and a Republican Congress defined themselves by major new domestic policy initiatives that constituted major policy departures and federal role expansions. Significant nationalization and centralization of policy occurred in five major areas, many traditionally controlled by state and local governments: education, welfare, homeland security, election administration, and taxation. While many of these actions are covered elsewhere in this volume, it is useful to discuss these decisions along the continuum of coercive federalism.

Education

Perhaps no area has been as sacred to our tradition of federalism and local governance as local control of schools. Given this backdrop, passage of No Child Left Behind (NCLB) with the leadership of President Bush marked a major turning point in the centralization of our federal system. While Democratic support for a stronger federal role was to be expected, the strong leadership of President Bush for federal testing and accountability standards was not only a surprise, but also a reversal of the Republican Congress' position only five years earlier calling for the abolition of the Department of Education. Indeed, Bush lobbied to eliminate the language calling for the department's abolition from the Republican platform in 2002 (Rudalevige 2003). The president's embrace of a strong federal role in education was anything but idiosyncratic, and in fact followed a growing trend in both presidential leadership and public opinion supporting a stronger federal role in education. Following the 1996 presidential election, Republican elites came to realize that defining themselves as the party whose presidential standard bearer carried the tenth amendment in his shirt pocket and whose congressional leaders sought to turn educational leadership back to states and localities was a losing position (Manna 2006).

Skirting the Unfunded Mandates Act, NCLB's requirements were couched as conditions of federal assistance, a category that exempted it from the law's point of order provision.[2] The new mandates were broad reaching indeed, as the testing, teaching, and accountability requirements established a daunting new framework for local education policy and practice. Significant concessions were in fact made to the state and local governments as well. States could define the standards used for tests, parents were consigned to find alternatives for failing schools only among other public schools within the school district, and federal funding rose significantly in the years following passage.[3]

The years of cooperative federalism characterizing the prior period of federal education had succeeded in both promoting greater state and local dependence on ESEA funds as well as gaining state and local buy-in for federal educational policy goals (Peterson, Rabe, and Wong 1986). Indeed, the governors led a coalition of business leaders and others calling for stronger national education standards as early as the 1990 Charlottesville summit with President George H. W. Bush. As the new law was implemented and the costs became more salient during the past five years, however, many state and local officials came to denounce the law as embodying over prescriptive mandates imposed without sufficient funding, and bargaining has ensued in a familiar intergovernmental story line (Ingram 1977).

Welfare Reform

The passage of welfare reform in 1996 marked a signal shift in federal social welfare policy. Converting an open-ended federal grant program into a block grant to the states (called the Temporary Assistance for Needy Families or TANF), the act devolved significant authority to the states to define eligibility and to use funds for a wide range of activities related to supporting lower income persons. While states gained significant authority, the 1996 act did contain major federal mandates, foisting new federal time limits and work participation requirements on states and their welfare recipients. As Jocelyn Johnston notes, the devolutionary rhetoric around the law reduced attention to the stiff requirements imposed (Johnston 2007). At the time of its passage, most states were governed by Republican governors whose policies were congruent with the regulations implicit in the new law.

While popularly celebrated as a triumph of state innovation, in fact the Republicans in the White House and the Congress watched the states as carefully as Democratic committee chairs watched the states during the Reagan block grants of the 1980s. They were concerned that states were undermining the Republican ideological agenda by sidestepping the spirit of the program's work requirements. Under the 1996 act, in fact, states were able to count toward the program's work requirements caseload reductions occurring due to the economy and the program definitions. Twenty states were able to avoid placing additional welfare recipients in work, thanks to this caseload reduction credit. States also shifted the most difficult to place clients to state funding lines, thereby avoiding the work strictures applying to clients served under the federal block grant itself. Finally, reports of states' diversion of block grant funds for other purposes through fiscal substitution inspired concerns by congressional Republicans that states were not faithful partners under the TANF welfare reform process.

The 2006 reauthorization significantly increased the strength of the work mandates associated with the program. The work participation requirements were increased, with the caseload reduction credit no longer available to offset the states' compliance obligations. Moreover, the definition of work activities has narrowed, curtailing the time allowed for education or training to count toward the work requirement. States in compliance under the old rules suddenly find themselves facing the burden of increasing their welfare clients' work participation by more than 100 percent. The challenge is complicated by the fact that those remaining on the rolls following the drop in caseloads across the nation are the most difficult to place in jobs. The new requirement for 90 percent of two-parent families to work a minimum of thirty-five hours a week is acknowledged to be "pretty much unattainable" by Wade Horn, the assistant secretary in the Department of Health and Human Services responsible for the program (Perlman 2006). As with prior recategorizations of block grants, Congress also made significant changes in reporting and oversight over the states, including extending new requirements to cases funded entirely from state dollars.

Election Administration

The Florida election crisis in 2000 clouded the results of the presidential election, precipitating a crisis of legitimacy in our political system. The fallout included congressional action to reform the process of elections administration at the state and local level, culminating in passage of the 2002 Help America Vote Act (HAVA). The act instituted sweeping new federal standards, along with new funding, that regulated significant features of state and local election processes. Congress also provided $3 billion in funding for state and local costs, primarily associated with modernization of election machines, albeit still falling short of actual costs incurred by nearly $800 million (Congressional Research Service 2004).

The HAVA instituted new direct order federal mandates requiring new voting systems, provisional ballots, statewide voter databases, and access to polling places for disabled persons. Federal error rate standards must be met, and voters must be allowed to correct errors. Importantly, the law requires the centralization of the registration and elections process at the state level, specifying new requirements for statewide voter databases and uniform processes for vote definitions across the state (Liebschutz and Palazzolo 2003).

* * *

Tax Policy

Changes in tax policy over the Bush years have had significant, albeit often indirect, consequences on state tax policies and administration. While not mandates in the classic sense and not covered under UMRA, the tax cuts of 2001 and 2003—central to the Bush economic agenda—constituted unilateral federal policy changes to federal-state shared tax bases that threatened to unravel a system of cooperative tax policy and administration that had evolved over many years. While cuts to individual and capital gains tax rates themselves do not threaten the tax bases of states, major changes in depreciation, dividends, and estate taxes presented states with a significant erosion of their income tax bases. Such changes force states to acquiesce and accept their consequences or decouple from the federal tax base. Decoupling complicates the overall system, inhibits sharing of data facilitating tax administration with IRS and adds to the burdens facing taxpayers.

In some respects, unilateral changes to federal income tax bases were a continuation of trends from prior presidential eras. However, tax policy actions broke new ground in some areas. In the estate tax area, an historic agreement was ignored and set aside. The estate tax, originally a state tax, became a shared federal-state regime in 1924, when the federal law was amended to allow a federal tax credit for any estate taxes due under state law (the credit was capped). In this case federal policy makers were intent on providing incentives for states to continue their own estate taxes, rather than displace them by a new federal tax regime. Under the 2001 legislation, the federal estate tax is phased out through 2010 by gradually raising the threshold that triggers the tax (the tax is then reinstated in 2011, but the state credit is not, unless Congress acts). With state revenue losses estimated at as much as $9 billion annually, 20 states have decided to decouple from the federal estate tax laws, complicating tax planning and tax administration.

* * *

Homeland Security

The tragic events of September 11, 2001, forced federal officials to recognize that the intergovernmental system constituted the nation's first line of defense in dealing with the consequences of terrorist attacks. However, the presence of a strong national consensus, many externalities, extensive interdependencies, and high stakes ultimately led the administration and the Congress to adopt intergovernmental grants and mandates that, together, served to centralize emergency preparedness, infrastructure and other state and local services. Many would argue that this is indeed a necessary and appropriate response to a truly national crisis. For instance, the failure of even one state to observe standards for issuance of driver's licenses could compromise the efforts of the other states to provide a more secure identification card. War has been noted to centralize power in our nation before.

*   *   *

The president issued a directive in 2003 requiring the Department of Homeland Security (DHS) to establish national standards for emergency preparedness, governing such areas as equipment, training, exercises and planning assisted with federal funds.[4] The DHS responded by developing a set of guidance documents setting forth standards or "target capabilities" for thirty-six areas of emergency planning and response, keyed to fifteen types of emergencies. The standards were based on a national DHS analysis of nearly four thousand discrete "tasks" involved in responding to these types of disasters. For instance, for pandemic flu, the standards or target capabilities for pandemic flu include how state and local governments are positioned to perform terrorism investigation, mass prophylaxis, and community recovery.

The standards are sweeping in their coverage, fortified by performance measures to specify desired levels of performance by state and local governments. For instance, state and local governments are required to comply with the National Incident Management System to structure their response operations, obligating them to change long standing routines such as eliminating the use of "10" codes for communicating among first responders, choosing "plain English" terms instead (Fiorill 2005).

*   *   *

Other Mandates

The 109th Congress offers a window in to other mandates that have recently been imposed on the state and local sector:[5]

- A requirement for states to collect data on sex offenders including DNA samples and to prepare a statewide sex offender registry database (PL109-299), as a condition attached to receipt of federal law enforcement grants. No appropriations have yet been provided to cover what CBO estimates to be costs of $60 million over a five-year period.
- Prohibition against using federal grant funds for projects where emi-

nent domain is employed to support private use, a response to the Supreme Court's decision in the Kelo case where the use of eminent domain for such purposes was ruled constitutional.[6] The provision was contained in an FY 2006 appropriations act (PL 109-115).[7]

- Federal standards requiring state and local governments using federal foster care funds to visit foster care children monthly (PL 109-299).
- Prohibition of state and local lawsuits against manufacturers or sellers of firearms (PL 109-92).
- Institution of a requirement for states to hold special elections when continuity of government is jeopardized by a national emergency, necessitating some states to amend their constitutions (PL 109-55).
- Preemption of state authority governing citing of certain transmission lines, and citing and operation of onshore liquefied natural gas facilities, energy efficiency, safety of nuclear facilities, and the reliability of electric services (PL 109-58).

*   *   *

Conclusions

Federal actions constituting coercive federalism, including mandates, continue to be a major feature of our system, relied upon by a diverse range of actors to accomplish a wide variety of policy and political goals. The Bush era continues trends observed in prior decades, breaking new ground in the nationalization and centralization of policy in areas that had heretofore largely been untouched by the instruments of coercive federalism. For each of the five major areas covered in this article, cooperative federalism frameworks that had evolved over many years were overturned. Whether it be tax cooperation through tax base sharing and administration, FEMA's highly partnerial model for emergency preparedness, education's accommodation with federal equity goals, state motor vehicle departments' cooperation in commercial drivers licensure, or the largely successful devolution of welfare achieved ten years earlier, the centralizing actions that have unfolded in the past five years mark a major turning point toward a more insistent, demanding federal role with uncertain consequences for program performance and finances.

Ironically, the familiarity and political support spawned by these more cooperative forerunners may very well have paved the way for their more coercive successors. Intergovernmental tensions and consequences have been accentuated by simultaneous federal actions that both increase intergovernmental fiscal burdens through spending mandates and limit revenues available to state and local governments to finance these far-flung federal policy initiatives. The combined effect of these initiatives will work together to encumber a greater share of the fiscal commons for national policy initiatives than we have seen in the past.

One is also impressed with the broad support many of these initiatives attained across both federal and state actors in our system. Policy issues increasingly sweep over federal and state governments alike in waves of enthusiasm that know few political boundaries. In a nationalized media culture, state and national political communities and values have become more integrated, and state and local leaders have become every bit as vulnerable to the same publicly compelling policy stampedes as are national leaders. Jurisdictional boundaries have increasingly become permeable; federal grants have prompted the institutionalization of national values and interests in state governments while state policy innovations increasingly seeded the national agenda with compelling new problem definitions and solutions.

Cross-pressured by overlapping allegiances to national values and interests, state and local officials have become uncertain trumpeters of their own prerogatives in the federal system. Federal and state governments perceive an advantage to "borrowing authority" to engage the resources, authority and legitimacy of other levels of government (Manna 2006). In essence, all levels of government are increasingly engaged in an "opportunistic federalism" where all actors in the system attempt to use one another to achieve particular policy goals, irrespective of traditional boundaries and authority distributions (Conlan 2006). While the Supreme Court has resumed its role in recent times of policing the boundaries, John Kincaid argues that the court has undergone a "federalism fizzle" in ruling against states on recent preemption cases in the past several years (Kincaid 2006).

As the United States faces such vexing challenges as the baby boom retirement and global economic change, marbleized, networked approaches to governance may in fact be necessary to respond to daunting problems. Whether it be health care costs, climate change or education, intergovernmental responses will be necessary. In "borrowing authority," however, it matters whether cooperative or coercive federalism tools are engaged. While perhaps more efficient to respond to insistent national majorities, coercive strategies have the potential to short circuit the feedback loops in our system, curtailing the potential for policy learning through the accretion of experience gained by state and local governments. And most certainly, such strategies also can work to undercut the ability of our system to accommodate the diversity of our nation and the vitality of our federal system.

Notes

1. A superwaiver would give the executive branch authority to override statutory or regulatory regulations in a many low-income programs. It would be initiated at the request of a governor.
2. UMRA provides that any mandate with an uncompensated state and local cost greater than $50 million a year net of savings and direct federal funding can be

stopped by a point of order raised on the House or Senate floor. However, conditions of grants are excluded from UMRA.

3. While not enough to fully cover all incremental costs, federal appropriations for Title 1 increased by 45 percent in the five years since the passage of NCLB, U.S. Office of Management and Budget, *Analytic Perspectives: Budget of the U.S. Government*, Washington, DC: OMB, 2006, 102.

4. Homeland Security Presidential Directive/HSPD-8, December 17, 2003.

5. Sources include the National Conference of State Legislatures, *Mandate Monitor* Washington, DC: NCSL, October 16, 2006, Vol. 4, Issue 4; Congressional Budget Office, A Review of CBO's Activities under the Unfunded Mandate Reform Act, 1996–2005.

6. *Kelo, et al. v. City of New London et al.,* June 23, 2005.

7. Congressional Research Service, *Condemnation of Private Property for Economic Development*, Washington, DC: CRS, December 22, 2005.

References

Advisory Commission on Intergovernmental Relations. 1994. *Federally Induced Costs Affecting State and Local Governments.* Washington, DC: ACIR.

Congressional Research Service. 2004. *Election Reform: The Help America Vote Act and Issues for Congress.* Washington, DC: CRS.

Conlan, Timothy J. 2006. From cooperative to opportunistic federalism: Reflections on the half-century anniversary of the commission on intergovernmental relations. *Public Administration Review* 66: 5 (September/October), 663–676.

Fortier, John C, and Norman J. Ornstein. 2003. President Bush: Legislative strategist. In *The George W. Bush Presidency: An Early Assessment,* ed. Fred I. Greenstein, 139. Baltimore, MD: Johns Hopkins Press.

Finegold, Kenneth, Laura Wherry, and Stephanie Schardin. 2004. *Block Grants: Details of the Bush Proposals*, A-64. Washington, DC: Urban Institute.

Fiorill, Joe. 2005. Local emergency teams resist plain-language radio rules. *Govexec.com*, August 26, 2005.

Ingram, Helen. 1977. Policy implementation through bargaining: The case of grants-in-aid. *Public Policy* 25: 4.

Johnston, Jocelyn. 2007. Welfare reform: A devolutionary success? In *Intergovernmental Management in the 21st Century*, ed. Timothy J. Conlan and Paul L. Posner. Washington, DC: Brookings.

Kincaid, John. 1990. From cooperative to coercive federalism. *Annals of the American Academy of Political and Social Science* 509; 139–152.

———. 2006. State-federal relations: Federal dollars down, federal power up. In *The Book of the States.* Lexington, KY: Council of State Governments.

Liebschutz, Sarah F., and Daniel J. Palazzolo. 2005. The states and the Help America Vote Act. *Publius: The Journal of Federalism* 35 (4).

Manna, Paul. 2006. *School's In.* Washington, DC: Georgetown University Press.

Perlman, Ellen. 2006. Welfare workout. *Governing* 20: 54–57.

Peterson, Paul E., Barry G. Rabe, and Kenneth K. Wong. 1986. *When Federalism Works.* Washington, DC: Brookings.

Posner, Paul L. 1998. *The Politics of Unfunded Mandates: Whither Federalism?* Washington DC: Georgetown University Press.

Rudalevige, Andrew. 2003. No child left behind: Forging a congressional compromise. In *No Child Left Behind? The Politics and Practice of School Accountability*, ed. Paul Peterson and Martin R. West. Washington, DC: Brookings, p. 34.

15

"Environmental Policy and the Bush Era: The Collision Between the Administrative Presidency and State Experimentation"

Barry Rabe

The world has become intimately familiar with the sight of President George W. Bush and British Prime Minister Tony Blair standing side-by-side behind lecterns while remaining shoulder-to-shoulder on pressing international issues such as the Middle East. But a double-take was understandable in July 2006, when Blair flew to Los Angeles for a similarly structured media event but one that replaced Bush with California's Republican Governor, Arnold Schwarzenegger. On this occasion, California and the United Kingdom agreed to collaborate in a number of ways on greenhouse gas reduction to confront global climate change. This included a number of mechanisms to share information and technology but, perhaps more significantly, an agreement to explore the possibility of an emissions trading system that would allow California to work directly with Britain on the design of a cap-and-trade system for carbon releases. This built on years of less-formal contacts between these governments and the fact that the largest American state and second largest member of the European Union have already designed a strikingly similar set of climate policies. In fact, it seemed irrelevant that California is part of a federal system that has scorned the Kyoto Protocol while the United Kingdom has led the EU in ratification and aggressive implementation of Kyoto. Neither the president nor any member of his administration was present at the event and there has been virtually no official comment from Washington, D.C.

One might assume from such a development that the decentralization mantra so pervasive in environmental policy in the late 1980s and throughout the 1990s had reached a new level during the current decade. In some respects, such as climate change policy development and implementation, the American system of environmental federalism is more state-driven than ever before. However, it would be a mistake to assume that this trend holds across various environmental policy areas or that some structured or cooperative set of intergovernmental negotiations have guided these transitions. Despite considerable initial expectation that the Bush administration would build seriously on recent decentral-ization experiments, the third-quarter mark of his Presidency was passed with a very different record, including a number of significant efforts to expand federal—and executive branch—authority. In turn, federal-state conflict over environmental policy may well have reached its highest level in at least two decades.

*   *   *

The State Response

Several bodies of scholarly analysis of federalism might anticipate that states would respond to such evolving federal actions by simply reduc-ing their level of engagement in environmental protection. If environ-mental protection is perceived as a highly redistributive and regulatory activity likely to impose heavy costs on concentrated constituents, states may already have considerable incentive to tread lightly in this area. They might even welcome the recentralization that has occurred in the Bush administration, shifting the venue of policy making in this con-tentious area to the federal government. Indeed, one might expect states to refrain from unilateral policy innovation as well as formally abandon current areas of delegated program implementation and return those du-ties (and costs) to federal agencies. At its extreme, states might take ad-vantage of any opportunity to literally do as little as possible, racing to the bottom as has long been posited by some students of federalism (Crenson 1971; Baumgartner and Jones 1993; Peterson 1995).

The state response to the Bush administration actions in environmen-tal policy does not fit that pattern, however. One does see considerable variation among states and, in such instances as proposals for expanded logging on federal lands or joining lawsuits against the federal govern-ment, disagreements among states about appropriate next steps. But the overall state response entails considerable policy innovation among a wide range of states in a diverse set of areas, an aggressive response by organizations representing state agencies against a number of federal ac-tions, and exploration of litigative strategies to either protect state au-thority or prod the federal government to act in areas of environmental concern. This may reflect a perception in many state capitals that envi-ronmental protection coincides with larger state goals of fostering eco-nomic development and protecting public health. It may also underscore the assessment of political scientist Paul Teske that, contrary to antici-pated races to the bottom that were propelled by dominant interest group pressure, "most areas of state regulations are actually characterized by contested interest group environments within which state institutional actors often make independent policy choices." (Teske 2004, 2005, 369; Rabe and Mundo 2007).

State Definition of American Climate Policy

Long before Arnold Schwarzenegger and Tony Blair joined forces to discuss possible cross-continental collaboration on climate change, states had emerged as the dominant American players in climate policy development. A small number of states began to explore this issue during the 1990s, but the proliferation of state engagement clearly accelerated after the Bush administration decision to abandon the Kyoto Protocol and oppose significant policy proposals at the federal level. As of 2007, more than half of them have active climate programs, many of which involve multiple pieces of legislation.

Collectively, these state efforts involve all of the climate policy tools that have been employed by the European Union and other nations that have ratified the Kyoto Protocol. In the area of renewable energy, twenty-three states representing more than 55 percent of the American population operate renewable portfolio standards that mandate a steady transition from conventional electricity sources to renewables (Rabe and Mundo 2007). In carbon emissions trading, ten Northeastern states are part of an interstate body known as the Regional Greenhouse Gas Initiative (RGGI) that is constructing a carbon cap-and-trade program for that region. California and neighboring western states are exploring the prospects for developing their own version of such a system or even establishing a partnership across the continent. In the area of vehicular emissions, California in 2002 became the first Western government to impose carbon emission standards on new vehicles. This legislation is designed to reduce carbon emissions by approximately 30 percent over the next decade and has been formally embraced by eleven other states. Eleven states have established statewide targets to reduce overall greenhouse gas emissions, including California, New Mexico, and New York. In California, for example, the 2006 Global Warming Solutions Act requires statewide emissions to return to 1990 levels by 2020, with steep reductions in subsequent decades. The legislation authorizes creation of multiple policy tools to seek emission reductions from every major sector, building on the extensive climate policy infrastructure that was already in place (Adams 2006).

Many of these programs remain in early stages of implementation, making it difficult to assess their ability to stabilize emissions in a cost-effective manner. But states have clearly responded to growing concerns about localized impacts of climate change and also frame their policies to achieve multiple benefits, including economic development from cultivation of renewable energy and related environmental improvements such as reduction of conventional air contaminants (Rabe 2004). Although much climate policy activity is concentrated among coastal states, an increasingly diverse set of states have become active, reflected in the passage or expansion in recent years of renewable portfolio standards in such states as Arizona, Colorado, Illinois, Montana, Nevada, Texas, and Wisconsin, among others. In turn, multiple states are increasingly working collaboratively, establishing common policies and seeing potentially significant advantages in advancing regional strategies that operate across state boundaries.

Consistent with the Schwarzenegger-Blair entente, states have also begun to see themselves as players on the international climate policy stage, entering into discussions about possible collaboration with Canadian provinces as well as members of the European Union. It is increasingly recognized that many states generate substantial levels of greenhouse gases; if the fifty states were to secede, 13 would rank among the world's top forty nations in emissions, including Texas in seventh place ahead of the United Kingdom and Canada. In many respects, this climate policy innovation builds on existing state powers and experience but is tailored to the particular greenhouse gas emissions mix and opportunities for blending emissions reduction and economic development in a given jurisdiction.

Aside from some early federal efforts to provide technical support to state policy development that were launched in the George H. W. Bush administration and sustained during the Clinton years, all of this involves unilateral state action in the absence of any significant support or encouragement from the federal government. In fact, states have designed a number of these programs so as to minimize the likelihood of possible federal opposition. State officials involved in RGGI development, for example, readily note that they would benefit handily from federal collaboration and would normally work with the administration and Congress to set up an interstate compact to support this regional effort. But their experience with Washington to date suggests that most federal engagement has been designed to derail their efforts, hence the focus on a loose structure of memoranda-of-understanding among states who then pledge to take identical but unilateral steps rather than a compact that would require federal government approval.

Taking the Lead in Other Areas

Greenhouse gases were not the only environmental threat animating new levels of state engagement during the Bush administration. Virtually every area of environmental protection has been adressed through some form of state action in recent years, whether it entailed policy development where no federal role currently exists or direct challenges to federal policy interpretation. Such engagement is not unprecedented and instead reflects trends that have emerged over past decades. However, states have generally accelerated the pace of policy engagement in recent years, whether attempting to either fill policy vacuums or push back against Bush administration decisions.

As in climate change, states have essentially defined the options for environmental policy in areas such as the management and reuse of electronic waste. On the one hand, states such as Maine and Washington have taken a "producer responsibility" approach to this issue, reflecting a pattern in the European Union whereby computers, televisions, and other electronic goods must be taken back for responsible handling by the manufacturer once their use has ended. On the other hand, states such as California have established a fee structure that collects funds at the point of purchase that are used by the state to oversee reuse and disposal by governmental entities. A growing number of states have become active on this issue, given the absence of engagement from the fedreal government and the growing recognition that the volumes of these wastes are growing at dramatic rates and pose a range of environmental risks if ignored.

At the same time, other state actions constitute a direct response to concern that existing federal strategies are inadequate. Amid the ongoing controversy over Bush administration proposals to manage mercury emissions through the trading system envisioned under the Clean Skies initiative, nearly every state has enacted some form of mercury reduction policies. This represents a direct response to the growing body of scientific evidence that outlines significant public health risks from exposure to mercury contamination, even at levels once deemed to pose little or no risk. Many states have established policies designed to replace or recycle mercury-laden products before they are released into the atmosphere, including automobile switches, medical, and dental products, and thermometers and thermostats.

More recently, states have turned their attention to legislative or administrative strategies designed to impose significant emission reductions on industries that generate high levels of mercury emissions, particularly coal-fired power plants (McCarthy 2006). Such states as Maryland, Michigan, and New York have established policies which call for at least a 90 percent emissions reduction within a decade or less. As of 2007, twenty-one states from all regions had established mercury policies far more stringent than those proposed by the federal government. All of these state policies set far more aggressive reduction targets than Clear Skies and also offer far fewer ways to opt out of the regulation or pursue an emissions trading strategy to achieve the reduction. Many states have opposed emissions trading on this issue largely because mercury emissions tend to settle very quickly and close to their source, leading to concerns about concentrated "mercury sinks" that would be more severe than other pollutants that tend to disperse more widely across jurisdictional boundaries (Pendergrass, 2007). Midwestern states are exploring the possibility of establishing common standards on this issue, much like the RGGI experience in climate change whereby multiple states have worked cooperatively in the absence of any constructive dialogue with the federal government.

Joining Forces in Opposition

States appear to be taking some steps to coordinate their policies, reflected in multi-state collaboration in such areas as greenhouse gas and mercury emission reduction, to either fill federal policy voids or counter federal decisions. They have also made expanded and intensified use of organizations that represent their collective interests. Organizations that represent state environmental agency heads such as ECOS and more specialized units such as the State and Territorial Air Pollution Program Administrators and the Association of Local Air Pollution Control Officials (STAPPA-ALAPCO) have historically seen the promotion of state interests as their primary function. However, they have become increasingly visible during the Bush years, frequently taking the bully pulpit to attack Bush proposals, countering with their own ideas, and joining forces with larger organizations such as the National Conference of State Legislatures on key issues. In effect, they serve much like an opposing body would under a system of executive federalism, even though many of their members belong to the same political party as the president.

ECOS has become particularly outspoken on a wide range of issues, frequently haranguing the federal efforts to expand their workload and control their actions. ECOS regularly enacts resolutions that it uses to confront the administration and Congress and has increasingly turned to establishing specialized work groups that involve multiple states with overlapping interests. On the mercury issue, for example, ECOS has enacted a number of resolutions on its views of state and federal roles and has convened the so-called Quicksilver Caucus of states that want to work collaboratively on this issue. Such groups pursue a range of activities, including the creation of a compendium of state policies on mercury, action plans to establish key goals and target dates for implementation, and creation of ECOS positions that can be used in trying to foster multi-state initiatives and stand in opposition to federal policy.

The tone of resolutions and reports emanating from such bodies underscores the high level of intergovernmental discord in environmental policy. ECOS resolutions on mercury have presented highly critical accounts of the Clear Skies initiatives, just as the executive director of STAPPA-ALAPCO has said that "It is unconscionable EPA is allowing power companies to trade in a powerful neurotoxin—it is unprecedented and illegal" (Vedantam 2006). STAPPA-ALAPCO has gone so far as to publish brochures that suggest a pattern of federal encroachment that threatens state authority to protect air quality in accord with federal and state law as well as drafting model state statutes that can be used to set requirements that are far more rigorous than what has been considered by the federal government. Indeed, it is difficult to understate the stridency of state hostility towards their federal partners, particularly in gatherings involving multiple states. As one state environmental agency official noted in such a setting: "I think EPA may be verging toward irrelevance simply because the basic public trust, of candor, and the fundamental responsibilities of setting appropriate standards to protect public health and address interstate equity issues, are being abandoned" (*Environmental Forum 2003, 59*).

Taking It to the Courts

Although multi-state organizations such as ECOS and STAPPA-ALAPCO are largely confined to advocacy, one other body of state officials has potentially far greater leverage in relations with the federal government. State attorneys generally tend to reach office through partisan elections, oversee substantial staffs, and hold considerable state constitutional powers. They have also increasingly explored new ways to become a presence in many spheres of public policy, including environmental protection (Provost 2003; Derthick 2005). In some instances, they work cooperatively with the state's governor and lead environmental protection agency, but this is not necessarily the case given possible partisan and policy differences. State legal challenges to federal policy interpretations have addressed numerous environmental concerns in recent years, often involving coalitions of 10 or more states that pool resources in bringing a unified suit. These have confronted the federal government in many ways, including challenges to the validity of Bush administration interpretation of federal environmental laws (Dujack 2004).

State litigation has been particularly intensive in systematically responding to Bush administration efforts to interpret clean air policy. This has resulted in protracted court battles on issues such as new source review and mercury policy, producing a patchwork of federal court decisions that thus far has stalled much of what the administration was hoping to accomplish through regulatory reinterpretation. Not all states agree with such a litigative strategy and some may even join forces with their federal counterparts, just as some states like Indiana have embraced the Bush interpretation of new source review with supportive legislation. Nonetheless, this form of collective state litigation has been taken to new levels of intensity over the past half-decade and further reflects intergovernmental discord on environmental policy.

Another type of state litigation strategy involves bringing suit not against federal actions but instead as an attempt to prod the federal government to do something it does not want to do. Perhaps the most prominent example of this strategy involves yet another kind of state engagement in climate change, the *Massachusetts v EPA* case, in which a coalition of twelve states (California, Connecticut, Illinois, Massachusetts, New Jersey, Maine, New Mexico, New York, Oregon, Rhode Island, Vermont, and Washington) attempted to force the federal government to recognize carbon dioxide as an air pollutant under the Clean Air Act Amendments. States successfully carried this issue to the U.S. Supreme

Court, over the objections of the Bush administration. Beyond the immediate question of potential federal acknowledgement of carbon as a pollutant warranting regulatory attention, the April 2007 five-to-four decision upholding the state plaintiffs could have considerable bearing on the constitutionality of a number of state climate provisions, most notably the California-based effort to reduce carbon emissions from vehicles.

It remains to be seen how the 2006 elections will influence this dynamic, given the shift towards Democratic Party control of Congress and increased saliency of climate change as an environmental issue. President Bush acknowledged the threat posed by climate change in his 2007 State of the Union address but gave no indication of any major shift in federal policy. The 110th Congress is awash in proposals to begin to reduce greenhouse gas emissions, but most of these say little or nothing about the potential role of states or the status of existing state programs in the event of new federal legislation. In February 2007, both Senator Dianne Feinstein (D-CA) and National Association of Manufacturers President (and former Michigan Governor) John Engler indicated that federal preemption of established state policies could be a possible component in future federal policy. In turn, there is little evidence that Congress has ever conducted a serious review of the lessons that could be drawn from evolving state climate policy experience. Of the 218 congressional hearings on climate policy and science between 1975 and 2006, only one has given significant attention to state expertise and concerns in contemplating possible federal actions (Rabe 2007). It is unclear whether the 110th Congress will sustain this pattern or initiate a period of intergovernmental deliberation and learning.

Looking Ahead

As in other areas of public policy, courts may be called upon increasingly to address irreconcilable differences between states and the federal government over environmental protection. The 1990s boomlet to forge a new era of collaboration between respective levels of government now seems an artifact, replaced by an intensive set of intergovernmental conflicts. The Bush administration has abandoned its initial commitments to pursue a state-sensitive strategy in favor of an effort to recentralize oversight of environmental policy in a manner entirely consistent with earlier attempts to establish an administrative presidency model. In response, states have demonstrated that they are not prepared to take a back seat to the federal government, probing for areas to pursue innovative opportunities at the same time that they challenge any instances of federal overreach or disengagement that they deem inappropriate. Just as Arnold Schwarzenegger turns increasingly to other governors and heads of state to join common cause, it is not unrealistic to expect states to work increasingly across state and even international boundaries if they continue to find little common ground with the federal government.

DISCUSSION QUESTIONS

1. What are some of the coercive tools used by the national government to impose policies on the states? If you were a member of Congress, which of these tools would you be most likely to use and which would be less attractive?

2. What are the advantages and disadvantages of having the states take the lead on environmental policy? Do you think this development in federalism would change if a Democrat is elected president in 2008?

3. When should the national government step back and let the states have their way and when should it intervene and direct policy, either through coercive federalism or a regulatory approach?

REFERENCES

Adams, Linda. 2006. California Leading the Fight against Global Warming. *ECO States* 23 (Summer): 14–16.

Baumgartner, Frank, and Bryan D. Jones. 1993. *Agendas and Instability in American Politics*. Chicago: University of Chicago Press, 216–234.

Crenson, Matthew A. 1971. *The Un-Politics of Air Pollution*. Baltimore: Johns Hopkins University Press.

Derthick, Martha A. 2005. *Up in Smoke: From Legislation to Litigation in Tobacco Politics*, 2nd edn, Washington, DC: CQ Press.

Dujack, Stephen R. 2004. Prosecutor on a Mission. *Environmental Forum* 21 (May/June): 38–41.

McCarthy, James E. 2006. *Mercury Emissions from Electric Power Plants: States Are Setting Stricter Limits*. Washington, DC: Congressional Research Service.

Pendergrass, John. 2007. States Rolling Out Mercury Cut Plans. *Environmental Forum* 24 (January/February): 10.

Peterson, Paul E. 1995. *The Price of Federalism*. Washington, DC: Brookings Institution.

Provost, Colin. 2003. State Attorneys General, Entrepreneurship, and Consumer Protection in the New Federalism. *Publius* 33 (Spring): 37–53.

Rabe, Barry G. 2004. *Statehouse and Greenhouse*. Washington, DC: Brookings Institution.

———. 2007. *Can Congress Govern the Climate?* Washington, DC: Brookings Institution and John Brademas Center for the Study of Congress.

Rabe, Barry G., and Philip Mundo. 2007. Business Influence in State Environmental Policy. In *Business and Environmental Policy*, eds. Michael E. Kraft, and Sheldon Kamieniecki. Cambridge: MIT Press.

Teske, Paul. 2004. *Regulation in the States*. Washington, DC: Brookings Institution.

———. 2005. Checks, Balances, and Thresholds: State Regulatory Re-enforcement and Federal Preemption. *PS: Political Science and Politics* 38 (July): 367–370.

The Environmental Federalism Debate Heats Up. 2003. *Environmental Forum* 20 (November/December): 50–59.

Vedantam, Shankar. 2006. Clearing the Air? The EPA's Ruling on Mercury Prompts Sharp Criticism. *Washington Post National Weekly Edition*. May 21–27, p. 29.

CHAPTER 4

The Constitutional Framework and the Individual: Civil Liberties and Civil Rights

In the next two selections, Abraham Lincoln and Martin Luther King, Jr., take opposing points of view about how to achieve peaceful change in a civil society. What happens when the fight for justice and equality comes into conflict with the rule of law? Are people ever justified in breaking laws for what they perceive to be the greater good? Is civil disobedience justified in some contexts?

In a speech that he delivered twenty-three years before becoming president, Lincoln argues that the laws must be followed, as without adherence to laws we have no civil society. Change, Lincoln stresses, must come from working within the system. King disagrees, arguing that while people have a moral obligation to follow just laws, they have an equally compelling duty to break unjust laws through nonviolent means. In his "Letter from Birmingham Jail," which he addressed to more-conservative religious leaders in the civil rights movement who were concerned about his tactics, King outlined procedures for distinguishing between just and unjust laws, and for resisting those laws that are unjust. It is ironic that despite Lincoln's admonitions about working within the system, it was under his leadership that the nation fought its bloodiest war precisely because the central issues of states' rights and slavery could not be solved within the system. King, on the other hand, who argued in favor of breaking unjust laws, was actually instrumental in putting pressure on Congress (the "system") to change those laws that he and others in the civil rights movement considered unjust.

Current battles over abortion and the environment show the debate between Lincoln and King to be timeless. Activists in both policy areas have been decried as "radical" or "extremist" because of occasional civil disobedience against legal activities. Some environmentalists have prevented lumber harvesting by putting spikes in trees; some pro-life activists have blocked women's access to abortion clinics. And in the abortion case, as with the Lincoln-King debate, issues of civil rights and civil liberties intersect.

16

"The Perpetuation of Our Political Institutions"

Abraham Lincoln

In the great journal of things happening under the sun, we, the American People, find our account running, under date of the nineteenth century of the Christian era. We find ourselves in the peaceful possession, of the fairest portion of the earth, as regards extent of territory, fertility of soil, and salubrity of climate. We find ourselves under the government of a system of political institutions, conducing more essentially to the ends of civil and religious liberty, than any of which the history of former times tells us. We, when mounting the stage of existence, found ourselves the legal inheritors of these fundamental blessings. We toiled not in the acquirement or establishment of them—they are a legacy bequeathed us, by a *once* hardy, brave, and patriotic, but *now* lamented and departed race of ancestors. Theirs was the task (and nobly they performed it) to possess themselves, and through themselves, us, of this goodly land; and to uprear upon its hills and its valleys, a political edifice of liberty and equal rights; 'tis ours only, to transmit these, the former, unprofaned by the foot of an invader; the latter, undecayed by the lapse of time and untorn by usurpation, to the latest generation that fate shall permit the world to know. This task of gratitude to our fathers, justice to ourselves, duty to posterity, and love for our species in general, all imperatively required us faithfully to perform.

How then shall we perform it? At what point shall we expect the approach of danger? By what means shall we fortify against it? Shall we expect some transatlantic military giant, to step the ocean, and crush us at a blow? Never! All the armies of Europe, Asia and Africa combined, with all the treasure of the earth (our own excepted) in their military chest; with a Buonaparte for a commander, could not by force take a drink from the Ohio, or make a track on the Blue Ridge, in a trial of a thousand years.

At what point then is the approach of danger to be expected? I answer, if it ever reach us, it must spring up amongst us. It cannot come from abroad. If destruction be our lot, we must ourselves be its author and finisher. As a nation of freemen, we must live through all time, or die by suicide.

I hope I am over wary; but if I am not, there is, even now, something of ill-omen amongst us. I mean the increasing disregard for law which pervades the country; the growing disposition to substitute the wild and furious passions, in lieu of the sober judgment of Courts; and the worse than savage mobs, for the executive ministers of justice. This disposition is awfully fearful in any community; and that it now exists in ours, though grating to our feelings to admit, it would be a violation of truth, and an insult to our intelligence, to deny. Accounts of outrages committed by mobs, form the everyday news of the times. They have pervaded the country, from New England to Louisiana; they are neither peculiar to the eternal snows of the former, nor the burning suns of the latter; they are not the creature of climate—neither are they confined to the slaveholding, or the non-slaveholding States. Alike, they spring up among the pleasure hunting masters of Southern slaves, and the order loving citizens of the land of steady habits. Whatever, then, their cause may be, it is common to the whole country.

It would be tedious, as well as useless, to recount the horrors of all of them. Those happening in the State of Mississippi, and at St. Louis, are, perhaps, the most dangerous in example and revolting to humanity. In the Mississippi case, they first commenced by hanging the regular gamblers; a set of men, certainly not following for a livelihood, a very useful, or very honest occupation; but one which, so far from being forbidden by the laws, was actually licensed by an act of the Legislature, passed but a single year before. Next, negroes, suspected of conspiring to raise an insurrection, were caught up and hanged in all parts of the State: then, white men, supposed to be leagued with the negroes; and finally, strangers, from neighboring States, going thither on business, were, in many instances, subjected to the same fate. Thus went on this process of hanging, from gamblers to negroes, from negroes to white citizens, and from these to strangers; till, dead men were seen literally dangling from the boughs of trees upon every road side; and in numbers almost sufficient, to rival the native Spanish moss of the country, as a drapery of the forest.

Turn, then, to that horror-striking scene at St. Louis. A single victim was only sacrificed there. His story is very short; and is, perhaps, the most highly tragic, of anything of its length, that has ever been witnessed in real life. A mulatto man, by the name of McIntosh, was seized in the street, dragged to the suburbs of the city, chained to a tree, and actually burned to death; and all within a single hour from the time he had been a freeman, attending to his own business, and at peace with the world.

Such are the effects of mob law; and such are the scenes, becoming more and more frequent in this land so lately famed for love of law and order; and the stories of which have even now grown too familiar, to attract any thing more than an idle remark.

But you are, perhaps, ready to ask, "What has this to do with the perpetuation of our political institutions?" I answer, it has much to do with it. Its direct consequences are, comparatively speaking, but a small evil; and much of its danger consists, in the proneness of our minds, to regard its direct as its only consequences. Abstractly considered, the hanging of the gamblers at Vicksburg was of but little consequence. They constitute a portion of population that is worse than useless in any community; and their death, if no pernicious example be set by it, is never matter of reasonable regret with anyone. If they were annually swept from the stage of existence by the plague or small pox, honest men would, perhaps, be much profited by the operation. Similar too, is the correct reasoning, in regard to the burning of the negro at St. Louis. He had forfeited his life, by the perpetration of an outrageous murder, upon one of the most worthy and respectable citizens of the city; and had he not died as he did, he must have died by the sentence of the law, in a very short time afterwards. As to him alone, it was as well the way it was, as it could otherwise have been. But the example in either case was fearful. When men take it in their heads today, to hang gamblers, or burn murderers, they should recollect, that, in the confusion usually attending such transactions, they will be as likely to hang or burn someone who is neither a gambler nor a murderer as one who is; and that, acting upon the example they set, the mob of tomorrow, may, and probably will, hang or burn some of them by the very same mistake. And not only so; the innocent, those who have ever set their faces against violations of law in every shape, alike with the guilty, fall victims to the ravages of mob law; and thus it goes on, step by step, till all the walls erected for the defence of the persons and property of individuals, are trodden down, and disregarded. But all this even, is not the full extent of the evil. By such examples, by instances of the perpetrators of such acts going unpunished, the lawless in spirit are encouraged to become lawless in practice; and having been used to no restraint, but dread of punishment, they thus become absolutely unrestrained. Having ever regarded Government as their deadliest bane, they make a jubilee of the suspension of its operations; and pray for nothing so much as its total annihilation. While, on the other hand, good men, men who love tranquility, who desire to abide by the laws, and enjoy their benefits, who would gladly spill their blood in the defence of their country; seeing their property destroyed; their families insulted, and their lives endangered; their persons injured; and seeing nothing in prospect that forebodes a change for the better; become tired of, and disgusted with, a Government that offers them no protection; and are not much averse to a change in which they imagine they have nothing to lose. Thus, then, by the operation of this mobocratic spirit, which all must admit is now abroad in the land, the strongest bulwark of any Government, and particularly of those constituted like ours, may effectually be broken down and destroyed—I mean the *attachment* of the People. Whenever this effect shall be produced among us, whenever the vicious portion of population shall be permitted to gather in bands of hundreds and thousands, and burn churches, ravage and rob provision-stores, throw printing presses into rivers, shoot editors, and hang and burn obnoxious persons at plea- sure, and with impunity, depend on it, this Government cannot last. By such things, the feelings of the best citizens will become more or less alienated from it; and thus it will be left without friends, or with too few, and those few too weak, to make their friendship effectual. At such a time and under such circumstances, men of sufficient talent and am- bition will not be wanting to seize the opportunity, strike the blow, and overturn that fair fabric which for the last half century has been the fondest hope of the lovers of freedom, throughout the world.

I know the American People are *much* attached to their Government; I know they would suffer *much* for its sake; I know they would endure evils long and patiently, before they would ever think of exchanging it for another. Yet, notwithstanding all this, if the laws be continually de- spised and disregarded, if their rights to be secure in their persons and property are held by no better tenure than the caprice of a mob, the alienation of their affections from the Government is the natural conse- quence; and to that, sooner or later, it must come.

Here then, is one point at which danger may be expected.

The question recurs, "how shall we fortify against it?" The answer is simple. Let every American, every lover of liberty, every well-wisher to his posterity, swear by the blood of the Revolution never to violate in the least particular the laws of the country; and never to tolerate their violation by others. As the patriots of seventy-six did to the support of the Declaration of Independence, so to the support of the Constitution and Laws, let every American pledge his life, his property, and his sacred honor; let every man remember that to violate the law is to trample on the blood of his father, and to tear the character of his own, and his children's liberty. Let reverence for the laws be breathed by every Amer- ican mother to the lisping babe that prattles on her lap—let it be taught in schools, in seminaries, and in colleges; let it be written in Primers, spelling books, and in Almanacs; let it be preached from the pulpit, pro- claimed in legislative halls, and enforced in courts of justice. And, in short, let it become the *political religion* of the nation; and let the old and the young, the rich and the poor, the grave and the gay, of all sexes and tongues, and colors and conditions, sacrifice unceasingly upon its altars.

While ever a state of feeling, such as this, shall universally, or even, very generally prevail throughout the nation, vain will be every effort, and fruitless every attempt, to subvert our national freedom.

When I so pressingly urge a strict observance of all the laws, let me not be understood as saying there are no bad laws, nor that grievances may not arise, for the redress of which, no legal provisions have been made. I mean to say no such thing. But I do mean to say that, although bad laws, if they exist, should be repealed as soon as possible, still while they continue in force, for the sake of example they should be religiously observed. So also in unprovided cases. If such arise, let proper legal provisions be made for them with the least possible delay; but, till then, let them, if not too intolerable, be borne with.

There is no grievance that is a fit object of redress by mob law. In any case that arises, as for instance, the promulgation of abolitionism, one of two positions is necessarily true; that is, the thing is right within itself, and therefore deserves the protection of all law and all good citizens; or, it is wrong, and therefore proper to be prohibited by legal enactments; and in neither case, is the interposition of mob law, either necessary, justifiable, or excusable.

* * *

But this state of feeling *must fade, is fading, has faded,* with the circumstances that produced it.

I do not mean to say, that the scenes of the revolution *are now* or *ever will* be entirely forgotten; but that like everything else, they must fade upon the memory of the world, and grow more and more dim by the lapse of time. In history, we hope, they will be read of, and recounted, so long as the bible shall be read; but even granting that they will, their influence *cannot be* what it heretofore has been. Even then, they *cannot be* so universally known, nor so vividly felt, as they were by the generation just gone to rest. At the close of that struggle, nearly every adult male had been a participator in some of its scenes. The consequence was, that of those scenes, in the form of a husband, a father, a son or a brother, *a living history* was to be found in every family—a history bearing the indubitable testimonies of its own authenticity, in the limbs mangled, in the scars of wounds received, in the midst of the very scenes related— a history, too, that could be read and understood alike by all, the wise and the ignorant, the learned and the unlearned. But *those* histories are gone. They *can* be read no more forever. They *were* a fortress of strength; but, what invading foeman could *never do*, the silent artillery of time *has done*; the leveling of its walls. They are gone. They *were* a forest of giant oaks; but the all-resistless hurricane has swept over them, and left only, here and there, a lonely trunk, despoiled of its verdure, shorn of its foliage; unshading and unshaded, to murmur in a few more gentle breezes, and to combat with its mutilated limbs, a few more ruder storms, then to sink, and be no more.

They *were* the pillars of the temple of liberty; and now that they have crumbled away, that temple must fall, unless we, their descendants, supply their places with other pillars, hewn from the solid quarry of sober reason. Passion has helped us; but can do so no more. It will in future be our enemy. Reason, cold, calculating, unimpassioned reason, must furnish all the materials for our future support and defence. Let those materials be molded into *general intelligence, sound morality*, and, in particular, *a reverence for the constitution and laws:* and, that we improved to the last; that we remained free to the last; that we revered his name to the last; that, during his long sleep, we permitted no hostile foot to pass over or desecrate his resting place; shall be that which to learn the last trump shall awaken our WASHINGTON.

Upon these let the proud fabric of freedom rest, as the rock of its basis; and as truly as has been said of the only greater institution, *"the gates of hell shall not prevail against it."*

17

"Letter from Birmingham Jail"

Martin Luther King, Jr.

Source: *Christian Century*, June 12, 1963.

My Dear Fellow Clergymen:

While confined here in the Birmingham City Jail, I came across your recent statement calling my present activities "unwise and untimely." Seldom do I pause to answer criticism of my work and ideas. If I sought to answer all the criticism that cross my desk, my secretaries would have little time for anything other than such correspondence in the course of the day, and I would have no time for constructive work. But since I feel that you are men of genuine goodwill and that your criticisms are sincerely set forth, I want to try to answer your statement in what I hope will be patient and reasonable terms.

I think I should indicate why I am here in Birmingham, since you have been influenced by the view which argues against "outsiders coming in." I have the honor of serving as president of the Southern Christian Leadership Conference, an organization operating in every Southern state, with headquarters in Atlanta, Georgia. We have some eighty-five affiliate organizations across the South, and one of them is the Alabama Christian Movement for Human Rights. Frequently, we share staff, educational, and financial resources with our affiliates. Several months ago the affiliate here in Birmingham asked us to be on call to engage in a nonviolent direct-action program if such were deemed necessary. We readily consented, and when the hour came we lived up to our promise. So I, along with several members of my staff, am here because I was invited here. I am here because I have organizational ties here.

But more basically, I am in Birmingham because injustice exists here. Just as the prophets of the 8th century B.C. left their villages and carried their "thus saith the Lord" far afield, and just as the apostle Paul left his village of Tarsus and carried the gospel of Jesus Christ to the far corners of the Greco-Roman world, so am I compelled to carry the gospel of freedom beyond my own hometown. Like Paul, I must constantly respond to the Macedonian call for aid.*

* [See Acts 16:9.]

Moreover, I am cognizant of the interrelatedness of all communities and states. I cannot sit idly by in Atlanta and not be concerned about what happens in Birmingham. Injustice anywhere is a threat to justice everywhere. We are caught in an inescapable network of mutuality, tied in a single garment of destiny. Whatever affects one directly affects all indirectly. Never again can we afford to live with the narrow, provincial "outside agitator" idea. Anyone who lives inside the United States can never be considered an outsider anywhere within its bounds.

You deplore the demonstrations taking place in Birmingham. But your statement, I am sorry to say, fails to express a similar concern for the conditions that brought about the demonstrations. I am sure that none of you would want to rest content with the superficial kind of social analysis that deals merely with effects and does not grapple with underlying causes. It is unfortunate that demonstrations are taking place in Birmingham, but it is even more unfortunate that the city's white power structure left the Negro community with no alternative.

*   *   *

You may well ask, "Why direct action? Why sit-ins, marches, etc.? Isn't negotiation a better path?" You are quite right in calling for negotiation. Indeed, this is the very purpose of direct action. Nonviolent direct action seeks to foster such a tension that a community which has constantly refused to negotiate is forced to confront the issue. It seeks so to dramatize the issue that it can no longer be ignored. My citing the creation of tension as part of the work of the nonviolent resister may sound rather shocking. But I readily acknowledge that I am not afraid of the word "tension." I have earnestly opposed violent tension, but there is a type of constructive, nonviolent tension which is necessary for growth. Just as Socrates felt that it was necessary to create a tension in the mind so that individuals could shake off the bondage of myths and half-truths and rise to the realm of creative analysis and objective appraisal, so must we see the need for nonviolent gadflies to create the kind of tension in society that will help men rise from the dark depths of prejudice and racism to the majestic heights of understanding and brotherhood.

The purpose of our direct-action program is to create a situation so crisis-packed that it will inevitably open the door to negotiation. I therefore concur with you in your call for negotiation. Too long has our beloved Southland been bogged down in a tragic effort to live in monologue rather than dialogue.

*   *   *

We have waited for more than 340 years for our constitutional and God-given rights. The nations of Asia and Africa are moving with jetlike speed toward gaining political independence, but we still creep at horse-

and-buggy pace toward gaining a cup of coffee at a lunch counter. Perhaps it is easy for those who have never felt the stinging darts of segregation to say "Wait." But when you have seen vicious mobs lynch your mothers and fathers at will and drown your sisters and brothers at whim; when you have seen hate-filled policemen curse, kick, and even kill your black brothers and sisters with impunity; when you see the vast majority of your 20 million Negro brothers smothering in an air-tight cage of poverty in the midst of an affluent society; when you suddenly find your tongue twisted as you seek to explain to your six-year-old daughter why she can't go to the public amusement park that has just been advertised on television, and see tears welling up when she is told that Funtown is closed to colored children, and see ominous clouds of inferiority beginning to form in her little mental sky, and see her beginning to distort her personality by unconsciously developing a bitterness toward white people; when you have to concoct an answer for a five-year-old son asking, "Daddy, why do white people treat colored people so mean?"; when you take a cross-country drive and find it necessary to sleep night after night in the uncomfortable corners of your automobile because no motel will accept you; when you are humiliated day in and day out by nagging signs reading "white" and "colored"; when your first name becomes "nigger," your middle name becomes "boy" (however old you are), and your last name becomes "John," and your wife and mother are never given the respected title "Mrs."; when you are harried by day and haunted by night by the fact that you are a Negro, never quite knowing what to expect next, and are plagued with inner fears and outer resentments; when you are forever fighting a degenerating sense of "nobodiness"—then you will understand why we find it difficult to wait. There comes a time when the cup of endurance runs over, and men are no longer willing to be plunged into an abyss of injustice where they experience the bleakness of corroding despair. I hope, sirs, you can understand our legitimate and unavoidable impatience.

You express a great deal of anxiety over our willingness to break laws. This is certainly a legitimate concern. Since we so diligently urge people to obey the Supreme Court's decision of 1954 outlawing segregation in the public schools, at first glance it may seem rather paradoxical for us consciously to break laws. One may well ask, "How can you advocate breaking some laws and obeying others?" The answer lies in the fact that there are two types of laws: just and unjust. I agree with St. Augustine that "an unjust law is no law at all."

* * *

Let us consider some of the ways in which a law can be unjust. A law is unjust, for example, if the majority group compels a minority group to obey the statute but does not make it binding on itself. By the same token, a law in all probability is just if the majority is itself willing to obey it. Also, a law is unjust if it is inflicted on a minority that, as a result of being denied the right to vote, had no part in enacting or devising the law. Who can say that the legislature of Alabama which set up that state's segregation laws was democratically elected? Throughout Alabama all sorts of devious methods are used to prevent Negroes from becoming registered voters, and there are some counties in which, even though Negroes constitute a majority of the population, not a single Negro is registered. Can any law enacted under such circumstances be considered democratically structured?

Sometimes a law is just on its face and unjust in its application. For instance, I have been arrested on a charge of parading without a permit. Now there is nothing wrong in having an ordinance which requires a permit for a parade. But such an ordinance becomes unjust when it is used to maintain segregation and to deny citizens the First Amendment privilege of peaceful assembly and protest.

I hope you are able to see the distinction I am trying to point out. In no sense do I advocate evading the law, as would the rabid segregationist. That would lead to anarchy. One who breaks an unjust law must do so *openly*, *lovingly*, and with a willingness to accept the penalty. I submit that an individual who breaks a law that conscience tells him is unjust and who willingly accepts the penalty of imprisonment in order to arouse the conscience of the community over its injustice is in reality expressing the highest respect for law.

* * *

I must make two honest confessions to you, my Christian and Jewish brothers. First, I must confess that over the past few years I have been gravely disappointed with the white moderate. I have almost reached the regrettable conclusion that the Negro's great stumbling block in his stride toward freedom is not the White Citizen's Counciler or the Ku Klux Klanner but the white moderate who is more devoted to "order" than to justice; who prefers a negative peace which is the absence of tension to a positive peace which is the presence of justice; who constantly says "I agree with you in the goal you seek, but I cannot agree with your methods"; who paternalistically believes he can set the timetable for another man's freedom; who lives by a mythical concept of time and who constantly advises the Negro to wait for a "more convenient season." Shallow understanding from people of goodwill is more frustrating than absolute misunderstanding from people of ill will. Lukewarm acceptance is much more bewildering than outright rejection.

I had hoped that the white moderate would understand that law and order exist for the purpose of establishing justice and that when they fail in this purpose they block social progress. I had hoped that the white moderate would understand that the present tension in the South is a necessary phase of the transition from an obnoxious negative peace, in which the Negro passively accepted his unjust plight, to a substantive and positive peace, in which all men will respect the dignity and worth of human personality. Actually, we who engage in nonviolent direct action are not the creators of tension. We merely bring to the surface the hidden tension that is already alive. We bring it out in the open where it can be seen and dealt with. Like a boil that can never be cured so long as it is covered up but must be opened with all its pus-flowing ugliness to the natural medicines of air and light, injustice must be exposed, with all the tension its exposure creates, to the light of human conscience and the air of national opinion before it can be cured.

*   *   *

You speak of our activity in Birmingham as extreme. At first I was rather disappointed that fellow clergymen would see my nonviolent efforts as those of an extremist. I began thinking about the fact that I stand in the middle of two opposing forces in the Negro community. One is a force of complacency made up of Negroes who, as a result of long years of oppression, are so completely drained of self-respect and a sense of "somebodiness" that they have adjusted to segregation, and of a few middle-class Negroes who, because of a degree of academic and economic security and because in some ways they profit by segregation, have unconsciously become insensitive to the problems of the masses. The other force is one of bitterness and hatred, and it comes perilously close to advocating violence. It is expressed in the various black nationalist groups that are springing up across the nation, the largest and best-known being Elijah Muhammad's Muslim movement. Nourished by the Negro's frustration over the continued existence of racial discrimination, this movement is made up of people who have lost faith in America, who have absolutely repudiated Christianity, and who have concluded that the white man is an incorrigible "devil."

I have tried to stand between these two forces, saying that we need emulate neither the "do-nothingism" of the complacent nor the hatred of the black nationalist. For there is the more excellent way of love and nonviolent protest. I am grateful to God that, through the influence of the Negro church, the way of nonviolence became an integral part of our struggle.

If this philosophy had not emerged, by now many streets of the South would, I am convinced, be flowing with blood. And I am further convinced that if our white brothers dismiss as "rabble-rousers" and "outside agitators" those of us who employ nonviolent direct action and if they refuse to support our nonviolent efforts, millions of Negroes will, out of frustration and despair, seek solace and security in black nationalist ideologies—a development that would inevitably lead to a frightening racial nightmare.

* * *

Let me take note of my other major disappointment. Though there are some notable exceptions, I have also been disappointed with the white church and its leadership. I do not say this as one of those negative critics who can always find something wrong with the church. I say this as a minister of the gospel, who loves the church; who was nurtured in its bosom; who has been sustained by its spiritual blessings and who will remain true to it as long as the cord of life shall lengthen.

When I was suddenly catapulted into the leadership of the bus protest in Montgomery, Alabama, a few years ago, I felt we would be supported by the white church. I felt that the white ministers, priests, and rabbis of the South would be among our strongest allies. Instead, some have been outright opponents, refusing to understand the freedom movement and misrepresenting its leaders; all too many others have been more cautious than courageous and have remained silent and secure behind stained-glass windows.

In spite of my shattered dreams I came to Birmingham with the hope that the white religious leadership of this community would see the justice of our cause and with deep moral concern would serve as the channel through which our just grievances could reach the power structure. But again I have been disappointed.

I have heard numerous Southern religious leaders admonish their worshipers to comply with a desegregation decision because it is the *law*, but I have longed to hear white ministers declare, "Follow this decree because integration is morally *right* and because the Negro is your brother." In the midst of blatant injustices inflicted upon the Negro I have watched white churchmen stand on the sideline and mouth pious irrelevancies and sanctimonious trivialities. In the midst of a mighty struggle to rid our nation of racial and economic injustice I have heard many ministers say, "Those are social issues with which the gospel has no real concern," and I have watched many churches commit themselves to a completely otherworldly religion which makes a strange, unbiblical distinction between body and soul, between the sacred and the secular.

We are moving toward the close of the twentieth century with a religious community largely adjusted to the status quo—a taillight behind other community agencies rather than a headlight leading men to higher levels of justice.

* * *

But the judgment of God is upon the church as never before. If today's church does not recapture the sacrificial spirit of the early church, it will lose its authenticity, forfeit the loyalty of millions, and be dismissed as an irrelevant social club with no meaning for the twentieth century. Every day I meet young people whose disappointment with the church has turned into outright disgust.

Perhaps I have once again been too optimistic. Is organized religion too inextricably bound to the status quo to save our nation and the world? Perhaps I must turn my faith to the inner spiritual church, the church within the church, as the true *ecclesia* and the hope of the world. But again I am thankful to God that some noble souls from the ranks of organized religion have broken loose from the paralyzing chains of conformity and joined us as active partners in the struggle for freedom. They have left their secure congregations and walked the streets of Albany, Georgia, with us. They have gone down the highways of the South on torturous rides for freedom. Yes, they have gone to jail with us. Some have been kicked out of their churches, have lost the support of their bishops and fellow ministers. But they have acted in the faith that right defeated is stronger than evil triumphant. Their witness has been the spiritual salt that has preserved the true meaning of the gospel in these troubled times. They have carved a tunnel of hope through the dark mountain of disappointment.

I hope the church as a whole will meet the challenge of this decisive hour. But even if the church does not come to the aid of justice, I have no despair about the future. I have no fear about the outcome of our struggle in Birmingham, even if our motives are at present misunderstood. We will reach the goal of freedom in Birmingham and all over the nation, because the goal of America is freedom.

*   *   *

Before closing I feel impelled to mention one other point in your statement that has troubled me profoundly. You warmly commended the Birmingham police force for keeping "order" and "preventing violence." I doubt that you would have so warmly commended the police force if you had seen its angry dogs sinking their teeth into six unarmed, nonviolent Negroes. I doubt that you would so quickly commend the policemen if you were to observe their ugly and inhuman treatment of Negroes here in the City Jail; if you were to watch them push and curse old Negro women and young Negro girls; if you were to see them slap and kick old Negro men and young boys; if you were to observe them, as they did on two occasions, refuse to give us food because we wanted to sing our grace together. I cannot join you in your praise of the Birmingham Police Department.

It is true that the police have exercised discipline in handling the demonstrators. In this sense they have conducted themselves rather "nonviolently" in public. But for what purpose? To preserve the evil system of segregation. Over the past few years I have consistently preached that nonviolence demands that the means we use must be as pure as the ends we seek. I have tried to make clear that it is wrong to use immoral means to attain moral ends. But now I must affirm that it is just as wrong, or perhaps even more so, to use moral means to preserve immoral ends.

Perhaps Mr. Connor and his policemen have been rather nonviolent in public, as was Chief Pritchett in Albany, Georgia, but they have used the moral means of nonviolence to maintain the immoral end of racial injustice. As T. S. Eliot has said, there is no greater treason than to do the right deed for the wrong reason.

I wish you had commended the Negro sit-inners and demonstrators of Birmingham for their sublime courage, their willingness to suffer and their amazing discipline in the midst of great provocation. One day the South will recognize its real heroes. . . . One day the South will know that when these disinherited children of God sat down at lunch counters they were in reality standing up for what is best in the American dream and for the most sacred values in our Judeo-Christian heritage, thereby bringing our nation back to those great wells of democracy which were dug deep by the founding fathers in their formulation of the Constitution and the Declaration of Independence.

DISCUSSION QUESTIONS

1. What are the main points of disagreement between the King and Lincoln views?

2. Many of those involved in social protest movements (from anti-abortion protestors to environmental activists) draw parallels between their efforts and King's legacy of civil disobedience, in an effort to establish their right to disobey laws they find unjust. Are such applications of King's argument legitimate? Why or why not?

18

"In Defense of Prejudice"

Jonathan Rauch

*Some political theorists argue that democracies must not only prevent the intru-
sion of government upon basic liberties, but also must play a positive role in bol-
stering and protecting the rights of all their citizens. The challenge is admirable,
but difficult, as governments in practice are often faced with trade-offs between
the two values. Consider free speech, a right enshrined in the First Amendment.
The right to speak freely is fundamental to democratic governance. Yet it is not
absolute. Is there a line where my right to speak freely impinges upon your wish
not to hear what I have to say, particularly when my words are perceived as offensive, harmful, and prejudicial? What role should the government play in
drawing the line, if any? Should it limit speech in order to protect others from
the insult words can bring? If there is such a line, who decides where it is
drawn?*

*In the following article Jonathan Rauch stands "in defense of prejudice" and
in opposition to those who call for government regulation of speech that is insult-
ing to or stigmatizes individuals based on their sex, race, color, handicap,
religion, sexual orientation; or national and ethnic origin. In the workplace, universities, public school curricula, the media, and criminal law, speech is increasingly regulated by codes aimed at eradicating prejudice. Rauch argues that
regulating speech this way is foolish. In his view, the only way to challenge and
correct prejudice is through the free flow of speech, some of which we might not
want to hear. Government best protects liberty when it works to preserve rather
than prevent the free flow of speech, no matter how distasteful or hurtful that
speech may be.*

The war on prejudice is now, in all likelihood, the most uncontroversial social movement in America. Opposition to "hate speech,"
formerly identified with the liberal left, has become a bipartisan piety.
In the past year, groups and factions that agree on nothing else have
agreed that the public expression of any and all prejudices must be forbidden. On the left, protesters and editorialists have insisted that Francis
L. Lawrence resign as president of Rutgers University for describing
blacks as "a disadvantaged population that doesn't have that genetic,
hereditary background to have a higher average." On the other side of
the ideological divide, Ralph Reed, the executive director of the Christian
Coalition, responded to criticism of the religious right by calling a press

conference to denounce a supposed outbreak of "name-calling, scape-goating, and religious bigotry." Craig Rogers, an evangelical Christian student at California State University, recently filed a $2.5 million sexual-harassment suit against a lesbian professor of psychology, claiming that anti-male bias in one of her lectures violated campus rules and left him feeling "raped and trapped."

In universities and on Capitol Hill, in workplaces and newsrooms, authorities are declaring that there is no place for racism, sexism, homo-phobia, Christian-bashing, and other forms of prejudice in public debate or even in private thought. "Only when racism and other forms of prej-udice are expunged," say the crusaders for sweetness and light, "can minorities be safe and society be fair." So sweet, this dream of a world without prejudice. But the very last thing society should do is seek to utterly eradicate racism and other forms of prejudice.

I suppose I should say, in the customary I-hope-I-don't-sound-too-defensive tone, that I am not a racist and that this is not an article fa-voring racism or any other particular prejudice. It is an article favoring intellectual pluralism, which permits the expression of various forms of bigotry and always will. Although we like to hope that a time will come when no one will believe that people come in types and that each type belongs with its own kind, I doubt such a day will ever arrive. By all indications, *Homo sapiens* is a tribal species for whom "us versus them" comes naturally and must be continually pushed back. Where there is genuine freedom of expression, there will be racist expression. There will also be people who believe that homosexuals are sick or threaten chil-dren or—especially among teenagers—are rightful targets of manly sav-agery. Homosexuality will always be incomprehensible to most people, and what is incomprehensible is feared. As for anti-Semitism, it appears to be a hardier virus than influenza. If you want pluralism, then you get racism and sexism and homophobia, and communism and fascism and xenophobia and tribalism, and that is just for a start. If you want to believe in intellectual freedom and the progress of knowledge and the advancement of science and all those other good things, then you must swallow hard and accept this: for as thickheaded and wayward an ani-mal as us, the realistic question is how to make the best of prejudice, not how to eradicate it.

Indeed, "eradicating prejudice" is so vague a proposition as to be meaningless. Distinguishing prejudice reliably and nonpolitically from non-prejudice, or even defining it crisply, is quite hopeless. We all feel we know prejudice when we see it. But do we? At the University of Michigan, a student said in a classroom discussion that he considered homosexuality a disease treatable with therapy. He was summoned to a formal disciplinary hearing for violating the school's policy against speech that "victimizes" people based on "sexual orientation." Now, the evidence is abundant that this particular hypothesis is wrong, and any

American homosexual can attest to the harm that the student's hypothesis has inflicted on many real people. But was it a statement of prejudice or of misguided belief? Hate speech or hypothesis? Many Americans who do not regard themselves as bigots or haters believe that homosexuality is a treatable disease. They may be wrong, but are they all bigots? I am unwilling to say so, and if you are willing, beware. The line between a prejudiced belief and a merely controversial one is elusive, and the harder you look the more elusive it becomes. "God hates homosexuals" is a statement of fact, not of bias, to those who believe it; "American criminals are disproportionately black" is a statement of bias, not of fact, to those who disbelieve it.

Who is right? You may decide, and so may others, and there is no need to agree. That is the great innovation of intellectual pluralism . . . We cannot know in advance or for sure which belief is prejudice and which is truth, but to advance knowledge we don't need to know. The genius of intellectual pluralism lies not in doing away with prejudices and dogmas but in channeling them—making them socially productive by pitting prejudice against prejudice and dogma against dogma, exposing all to withering public criticism. What survives at the end of the day is our base of knowledge.

* * *

Pluralism is the principle that protects and makes a place in human company for that loneliest and most vulnerable of all minorities, the minority who is hounded and despised among blacks and whites, gays and straights, who is suspect or criminal among every tribe and in every nation of the world, and yet on whom progress depends: the dissident. I am not saying that dissent is always or even usually enlightened. Most of the time it is foolish and self-serving. No dissident has the right to be taken seriously, and the fact that Aryan Nation racists or Nation of Islam anti-Semites are unorthodox does not entitle them to respect. But what goes around comes around. As a supporter of gay marriage, for example, I reject the majority's view of family, and as a Jew I reject its view of God. I try to be civil, but the fact is that most Americans regard my views on marriage as a reckless assault on the most fundamental of all institutions, and many people are more than a little discomfited by the statement "Jesus Christ was no more divine than anybody else" (which is why so few people ever say it). Trap the racists and anti-Semites, and you lay a trap for me too. Hunt for them with eradication in your mind, and you have brought dissent itself within your sights.

The new crusade against prejudice waves aside such warnings. Like earlier crusades against antisocial ideas, the mission is fueled by good (if cocksure) intentions and a genuine sense of urgency. Some kinds of error are held to be intolerable, like pollutants that even in small traces poison the water for a whole town. Some errors are so pernicious as to damage real people's lives, so wrongheaded that no person of right mind or goodwill could support them. Like their forebears of other stripe—the Church in its campaigns against heretics, the McCarthyites in their campaigns against Communists—the modern anti-racist and anti-sexist and anti-homophobic campaigners are totalists, demanding not that misguided ideas and ugly expressions be corrected or criticized but that they be eradicated. They make war not on errors but on error, and like other totalists they act in the name of public safety—the safety, especially, of minorities.

The sweeping implications of this challenge to pluralism are not, I think, well enough understood by the public at large. Indeed, the new brand of totalism has yet even to be properly named. "Multicultural-ism," for instance, is much too broad. "Political correctness" comes closer but is too trendy and snide. For lack of anything else, I will call the new antipluralism "purism," since its major tenet is that society cannot be just until the last traces of invidious prejudice have been scrubbed away. Whatever you call it, the purists' way of seeing things has spread through American intellectual life with remarkable speed, so much so that many people will blink at you uncomprehendingly or even call you a racist (or sexist or homophobe, etc.) if you suggest that expressions of racism should be tolerated or that prejudice has its part to play.

The new purism sets out, to begin with, on a campaign against words, for words are the currency of prejudice, and if prejudice is hurtful then so must be prejudiced words. "We are not safe when these violent words are among us," wrote Mari Matsuda, then a UCLA law professor. Here one imagines gangs of racist words swinging chains and smashing heads in back alleys. To suppress bigoted language seems, at first blush, reasonable, but it quickly leads to a curious result. A peculiar kind of verbal shamanism takes root, as though certain expressions, like curses or magical incantations, carry in themselves the power to hurt or heal—as though words were bigoted rather than people. "Context is everything," people have always said. The use of the word "nigger" in *Huckleberry Finn* does not make the book an "act" of hate speech—or does it? In the new view, this is no longer so clear. The very utterance of the word "nigger" (at least by a non-black) is a racist act. When a *Sacramento Bee* cartoonist put the word "nigger" mockingly in the mouth of a white supremacist, there were howls of protest and 1,400 canceled subscriptions and an editorial apology, even though the word was plainly being invoked against racists, not against blacks.

Faced with escalating demands of verbal absolutism, newspapers issue lists of forbidden words. The expressions "gyp" (derived from "Gypsy") and "Dutch treat" were among the dozens of terms stricken as "offensive" in a much-ridiculed (and later withdrawn) *Los Angeles Times* speech code. The University of Missouri journalism school issued a *Dictionary of Cautionary Words and Phrases*, which included "*Buxom:*

Offensive reference to a woman's chest. Do not use. See 'Woman.' *Codger*: Offensive reference to a senior citizen."

As was bound to happen, purists soon discovered that chasing around after words like "gyp" or "buxom" hardly goes to the roots of the problem. As long as they remain bigoted, bigots will simply find other words. If they can't call you a kike then they will say Jewboy, Judas, or Hebe, and when all those are banned they will press words like "oven" and "lampshade" into their service. The vocabulary of hate is potentially as rich as your dictionary, and all you do by banning language used by cretins is to let them decide what the rest of us may say. The problem, some purists have concluded, must therefore go much deeper than laws: it must go to the deeper level of ideas. Racism, sexism, homophobia, and the rest must be built into the very structure of American society and American patterns of thought, so pervasive yet so insidious that, like water to a fish, they are both omnipresent and unseen. The mere existence of prejudice constructs a society whose very nature is prejudiced.

This line of thinking was pioneered by feminists, who argued that pornography, more than just being expressive, is an act by which men construct an oppressive society. Racial activists quickly picked up the argument. Racist expressions are themselves acts of oppression, they said. "All racist speech constructs the social reality that constrains the liberty of nonwhites because of their race," wrote Charles R. Lawrence III, then a law professor at Stanford. From the purist point of view, a society with even one racist is a racist society, because the idea itself threatens and demeans its targets. They cannot feel wholly safe or wholly welcome as long as racism is present. Pluralism says: There will always be some racists. Marginalize them, ignore them, exploit them, ridicule them, take pains to make their policies illegal, but otherwise leave them alone. Purists say: That's not enough. Society cannot be just until these pervasive and oppressive ideas are searched out and eradicated.

And so what is now under way is a growing drive to eliminate prejudice from every corner of society. I doubt that many people have noticed how far-reaching this anti-pluralist movement is becoming.

In universities: Dozens of universities have adopted codes proscribing speech or other expression that (this is from Stanford's policy, which is more or less representative) "is intended to insult or stigmatize an individual or a small number of individuals on the basis of their sex, race, color, handicap, religion, sexual orientation or national and ethnic origin." Some codes punish only persistent harassment of a targeted individual, but many, following the purist doctrine that even one racist is too many, go much further. At Penn, an administrator declared: "We at the University of Pennsylvania have guaranteed students and the community that they can live in a community free of sexism, racism, and homophobia." Here is the purism that gives "political correctness" its distinctive combination of puffy high-mindedness and authoritarian zeal.

In school curricula: "More fundamental than eliminating racial segregation has to be the removal of racist thinking, assumptions, symbols, and materials in the curriculum," writes theorist Molefi Kete Asante. In practice, the effort to "remove racist thinking" goes well beyond striking egregious references from textbooks. In many cases it becomes a kind of mental engineering in which students are encouraged to see prejudice everywhere; it includes teaching identity politics as an antidote to internalized racism; it rejects mainstream science as "white male" thinking; and it tampers with history, installing such dubious notions as that the ancient Greeks stole their culture from Africa or that an ancient carving of a bird is an example of "African experimental aeronautics."

In criminal law: Consider two crimes. In each, I am beaten brutally; in each, my jaw is smashed and my skull is split in just the same way. However, in the first crime my assailant calls me an "asshole"; in the second he calls me a "queer." In most states, in many localities, and, as of September 1994, in federal cases, these two crimes are treated differently: the crime motivated by bias—or deemed to be so motivated by prosecutors and juries—gets a stiffer punishment. "Longer prison terms for bigots," shrilled Brooklyn Democratic Congressman Charles Schumer, who introduced the federal hate-crimes legislation, and those are what the law now provides. Evidence that the assailant holds prejudiced beliefs, even if he doesn't actually express them while committing an offense, can serve to elevate the crime. Defendants in hate-crimes cases may be grilled on how many black friends they have and whether they have told racist jokes. To increase a prison sentence only because of the defendant's "prejudice" (as gauged by prosecutor and jury) is, of course, to try minds and punish beliefs. Purists say, Well, they are dangerous minds and poisonous beliefs.

In the workplace: Though government cannot constitutionally suppress bigotry directly, it is now busy doing so indirectly by requiring employers to eliminate prejudice. Since the early 1980s, courts and the Equal Employment Opportunity Commission have moved to bar workplace speech deemed to create a hostile or abusive working environment for minorities. The law, held a federal court in 1988, "does require that an employer take prompt action to prevent . . . bigots from expressing their opinions in a way that abuses or offends their co-workers," so as to achieve "the goal of eliminating prejudices and biases from our society." So it was, as UCLA law professor Eugene Volokh notes, that the EEOC charged that a manufacturer's ads using admittedly accurate depictions of samurai, kabuki, and sumo were "racist" and "offensive to people of Japanese origin"; that a Pennsylvania court found that an employer's printing Bible verses on paychecks was religious harassment of Jewish employees; that an employer had to desist using gender-based job titles like "foreman" and "draftsman" after a female employee sued.

On and on the campaign goes, darting from one outbreak of prejudice to another like a cat chasing flies. In the American Bar Association, activists demand that lawyers who express "bias or prejudice" be penalized. In the Education Department, the civil-rights office presses for a ban on computer bulletin board comments that "show hostility toward a person or group based on sex, race or color, including slurs, negative stereotypes, jokes or pranks." In its security checks for government jobs, the FBI takes to asking whether applicants are "free of biases against any class of citizens," whether, for instance, they have told racist jokes or indicated other "prejudices." Joke police! George Orwell, grasping the close relationship of jokes to dissent, said that every joke is a tiny revolution. The purists will have no such rebellions.

The purist campaign reaches, in the end, into the mind itself. In a lecture at the University of New Hampshire, a professor compared writing to sex ("You and the subject become one"); he was suspended and required to apologize, but what was most insidious was the order to undergo university-approved counseling to have his mind straightened out. At the University of Pennsylvania, a law lecturer said, "We have ex-slaves here who should know about the Thirteenth Amendment"; he was banished from campus for a year and required to make a public apology, and he, too, was compelled to attend a "sensitivity and racial awareness" session. Mandatory re-education of alleged bigots is the natural consequence of intellectual purism. Prejudice must be eliminated!

. . . "Nobody escapes," said a Rutgers University report on campus prejudice. Bias and prejudice, it found, cross every conceivable line, from sex to race to politics: "No matter who you are, no matter what the color of your skin, no matter what your gender or sexual orientation, no matter what you believe, no matter how you behave, there is somebody out there who doesn't like people of your kind." Charles Lawrence writes: "Racism is ubiquitous. We are all racists." If he means that most of us think racist thoughts of some sort at one time or another, he is right. If we are going to "eliminate prejudices and biases from our society," then the work of the prejudice police is unending. They are doomed to hunt and hunt and hunt, scour and scour and scour.

What is especially dismaying is that the purists pursue prejudice in the name of protecting minorities. In order to protect people like me (homosexual), they must pursue people like me (dissident). In order to bolster minority self-esteem, they suppress minority opinion. There are, of course, all kinds of practical and legal problems with the purists' campaign: the incursions against the First Amendment; the inevitable abuses by prosecutors and activists who define as "hateful" or "violent" whatever speech they dislike or can score points off of; the lack of any evidence that repressing prejudice eliminates rather than inflames it. But minorities, of all people, ought to remember that by definition we cannot prevail by numbers, and we generally cannot prevail by force. Against the power of ignorant mass opinion and group prejudice and superstition, we have only our voices. If you doubt that minorities' voices are powerful weapons, think of the lengths to which Southern officials went to silence the Reverend Martin Luther King, Jr. (recall that the city commissioner of Montgomery, Alabama, won a $500,000 libel suit, later overturned in *New York Times v. Sullivan* [1964], regarding an advertisement in the *Times* placed by civil-rights leaders who denounced the Montgomery police). Think of how much gay people have improved their lot over twenty-five years simply by refusing to remain silent. Recall the Michigan student who was prosecuted for saying that homosexuality is a treatable disease, and notice that he was black. Under that Michigan speech code, more than twenty blacks were charged with racist speech, while no instance of racist speech by whites was punished. In Florida, the hate-speech law was invoked against a black man who called a policeman a "white cracker"; not so surprisingly, in the first hate-crimes case to reach the Supreme Court, the victim was white and the defendant black.

In the escalating war against "prejudice," the right is already learning to play by the rules that were pioneered by the purist activists of the left. Last year leading Democrats, including the President, criticized the Republican Party for being increasingly in the thrall of the Christian right. Some of the rhetoric was harsh ("fire-breathing Christian radical right"), but it wasn't vicious or even clearly wrong. Never mind: when Democratic Representative Vic Fazio said Republicans were "being forced to the fringes by the aggressive political tactics of the religious right," the chairman of the Republican National Committee, Haley Barbour, said, "Christian-bashing" was "the left's preferred form of religious bigotry." Bigotry! Prejudice! "Christians active in politics are now on the receiving end of an extraordinary campaign of bias and prejudice," said the conservative leader William J. Bennett. One discerns, here, where the new purism leads. Eventually, any criticism of any group will be "prejudice."

DISCUSSION QUESTIONS

1. Do you agree or disagree that some groups need to be protected against offensive or hurtful ideas or speech? How do you define "hurtful" or "offensive"? What is the basis for your position? Where is the First Amendment in this debate?

2. Would a campus newspaper be justified in rejecting a paid advertisement from (a) a group or individual that denied the Holocaust had occurred; (b) a group or individual that argued against any sort of affirmative action; or (c) an environmental group that advocated violence against the property of corporations that polluted the environment? Would you support a "speech code" that prohibited someone from making these arguments on campus? Defend your answer.

150

Debating the Issues: Civil Liberties and the Fight Against Terror

Civil liberties and community safety often have a tense relationship. The difficulty of balancing the two becomes exponentially greater during war or other national crises. The September 11 attacks clearly exposed some key vulnerabilities in the United States: the attackers had blended into the background in several communities, and although law-enforcement authorities came tantalizingly close to connecting the dots in advance, the hijackers were clearly able to exploit the openness of American society. In the wake of the attacks, a number of new laws and actions of the executive branch were defended by supporters as reasonable and necessary measures to safeguard the United States from future threats, while simultaneously being decried by critics as unnecessary, counterproductive, and possibly unconstitutional. Where supporters see a sensible relaxing of walls between the nation's intelligence and law-enforcement agencies, opponents see a shocking erosion of long-cherished civil liberties. Supporters see enhanced secrecy as crucial to the effective investigation of potential terror activity; opponents argue that the new powers claimed by the executive branch are certain to be abused.

The readings in this debate are examples of the scope of the disagreement. David Cole and James Dempsey's analysis is based on three assumptions: the United States should not overreact in times of fear; infringement on basic constitutional values are justifiable only with highly compelling evidence; government policy should not sacrifice the civil liberties of vulnerable minorities to gain security for the majority. In their view, all three of these assumptions were violated by the Bush administration's response after September 11. Rather than viewing terrorism in ethnic or ideological terms, which they believe leads to civil liberties abuses, they propose treating terrorism like any other crime. Standard civil liberties protections in law enforcement should also be present in investigations of terrorism. Terrorism can be thwarted while preserving civil liberties.

To federal judge Richard Posner, writers like Cole and Dempsey are hopelessly naïve and out of touch with the reality of global terrorism. The struggle is in fact ideological, he argues, and it has a strong religious and cultural orientation. Provisions to protect national security may impose a short-term restriction on some aspect of civil liberties, but in the long run national security of the United States increases civil liberties. Posner argues that a balancing method is needed. The stronger the threat, the more leeway should be given to measures that may impinge on civil liberties. In Posner's view, analysts like Cole and Dempsey almost never see a risk as great enough to warrant significant government preventive measures. He believes, instead, that policy makers should seek a balance point. If policy is at the correct balance point, expanding a civil liberty further would result in a greater loss to security than the gain to liberty, while restricting a civil liberty further would result in a greater loss in liberty than the gain to security. Exactly where this balance point lies is situational rather than fixed in stone for all cases.

19

From *Terrorism and the Constitution: Sacrificing Civil Liberties in the Name of National Security*

DAVID COLE AND JAMES X. DEMPSEY

As September 11 dramatically demonstrated, the United States faces a real terrorist threat from abroad. At the same time, however, the United States itself has not been a fertile breeding ground for home-grown terrorism. This may well be because values central to our system of democratic governance make it difficult to nurture within this country the ideological, ethnic, or religious hatred that fuels much terrorism. These values include appreciation of diversity and religious and ethnic tolerance, reflected in our repeated absorption of large influxes of immigrants. They also include constitutional limits on government powers, checks and balances, access to government information, accountability of public officials, and due process accorded in judicial proceedings open to public scrutiny, all of which increase public confidence in government. Perhaps most important is our strong protection for political freedoms of speech and association, with a nearly unlimited right to criticize government and government officials, and a nearly insurmountable presumption against prior censorship, assuring the disaffected that their concerns can be heard without violence.

Unfortunately, much of our official response to the threat of terrorism is incompatible with these core civil liberties values. The 1996 Antiterrorism Act, for example, deems people guilty not only the basis of what they have done, but on the basis of the groups with which they are associated. It denies one of the most fundamental elements of due process—the right to confront one's accusers in open court. And measures taken after September 11 have similarly threatened basic values—criminalizing speech, imposing guilt by association, conducting trials in secret, engaging in ethnic profiling, and intruding on the privacy of innocent persons. The question is whether we can respond effectively to the new threat of terrorism

without jeopardizing the very freedoms that have contributed to our security at home.

The False Trade-Off—Curtailing Liberty Will Not Necessarily Enhance Security

In the ongoing debate over responding to terrorism, many argue that
civil liberties must be sacrificed in order to ensure the safety of our democratic way of life. Something unique about the threat of terrorism, it is
argued, requires us to alter the constitutional balance we have long
struck between government power and personal freedoms. The premise
of this argument—so unquestioningly accepted that it often goes
unstated—is that antiterrorism measures infringing civil liberties will
work. While there are often difficult trade-offs to be made between liberty and security, it does not follow that sacrificing liberties will always,
or even generally, promote security.

Efficacy, of course, does not determine the outcome of the constitutional debate. Even if a police state were efficient, it would not reflect our
fundamental values. But many of the rights we have discussed in this
book actually promote governmental efficacy in defending the common
good. We guarantee the right to confront one's accusers, for example, not
only as an element of human dignity but also because we know that
cross-examination is an effective engine of truth. Relying on untested evidence not only risks convicting the innocent, but it also means that the
search for the truly guilty party may be called off prematurely. We subject
executive decisions to judicial review not only because the judicial system gives a voice to individuals but also because we know that the
adversarial process can produce a fuller factual record, exposing faulty
assumptions, and because deliberative review by life-tenured judges can
protect against the rash decisions resulting from the pressures felt by
elected officials. We reject guilt by association not only to protect political
freedom, but also because a system that holds individuals responsible for
their own actions is more closely tailored to deterring crime. We protect
freedom of speech not only because it allows room for personal self-
expression, but also because the availability of channels for peaceful
change promotes stability. We have more to fear from the pressure cooker
of repressed dissatisfaction than from the cacophony of dissent. For these
reasons, many of the counterterrorism measures that we have criticized
are not only unconstitutional, but are also likely to be counterproductive.

Curtailing civil liberties does not necessarily promote national security. In COINTELPRO, the FBI experimented with the massive monitoring of political dissent. It failed to produce any substantial evidence of
violent conduct, suggesting that politics is a poor guide and extensive
monitoring an ineffective strategy for counterterrorism investigations.
Other more recent examples here and abroad have shown that racial and
ethnic stereotyping is also a poor basis for security policy. The assassin of

Yitzhak Rabin escaped detection because the prime minister's body-guards were on the look-out for Arab assailants. If police had listened only to those who claimed that the Oklahoma City bombing bore the trademarks of Muslim fundamentalists, they might not have captured Timothy McVeigh as he fled from the crime.

Violations of civil liberties often "work" only in a narrow sense: random or door-to-door searches will uncover contraband in some houses, and torture of arrestees will induce some to provide truthful evidence of wrongdoing, including evidence that may allow the prevention of violent attacks. But these "successes" must be balanced against the wasted resources consumed by fruitless random searches and generalized monitoring of groups or movements, the mistakes caused by reliance on faulty coerced confessions, and, most importantly, the tremendous loss of trust in government (and the consequent shutting off of voluntary cooperation) generated by unfocused investigations and the harassment of communities on the basis of stereotypes. On balance, even measured only in terms of effectiveness, there is little evidence that curtailing civil liberties will do more good than harm.[1]

Implications of a New, More Dangerous Terrorism

In every age, dangers can be cited that make limitations on intelligence operations seem imprudent—threats of such an urgent and unique nature that it seems necessary to expand government powers, at least long enough to turn back the new threat. Today's proponents of expanding government power to fight terrorism argue that the terrorism threat now is qualitatively different than in the past. September 11 certainly gave these arguments added weight.

But the heightened risk of terrorism simply means that the consequences of failing to adopt a sound antiterrorism policy are more serious than ever before. It does not tell us what policy to adopt.

Indeed, aspects of the new threat of terrorism point in quite different directions. Before adopting measures that curtail personal freedom, it might be more effective to address the highly destructive products that pose such serious risk to life. The United States and its allies have not done nearly enough to gain control of the nuclear materials of the former Soviet Union, a project that probably would mean far more to national security than curtailing civil liberties. Lethal biological and chemical materials are widely produced and are subject to inadequate controls. A program of stringent federal regulation of anthrax would have no civil liberties implications, but could meaningfully restrict access to such products by both the malevolent and the merely careless.

It is also clear that not nearly enough was done with investigative and protective authorities that existed before the 1996 and 2001 Acts and that had little to do with intrusions on political freedoms. For example, prior to September 11 there were repeated warnings about poor airport security. Documents disclosed by the *New York Times* in January 1999 showed that explosives and guns avoided detection in government tests of airline security, due largely to lax practices on the part of screening personnel.[2] Similarly, it became clear following the embassy bombings in Africa that Washington officials were largely unresponsive to the intense, well-founded, and forcefully expressed concerns of the American ambassador to Kenya, who warned repeatedly that the embassy was insufficiently protected against terrorist attack. Indeed, the CIA repeatedly told the State Department that there was an active terrorist group in Kenya connected to Osama bin Laden, since accused of masterminding the bombings there and in Tanzania.[3]

Despite the wartime rhetoric of stamping out terrorism everywhere, the terrorist threat will never be eliminated. We must develop sound responses. But in doing so, we should be careful not to sacrifice the fundamental principles that characterize our democratic identity. The better course is to adhere to our liberal principles, to use the criminal laws to punish those who plan or carry our violent acts, and to invite critics of our government into the practice of democracy and tolerance.

Reforming FBI Counterterrorism Activities

The principles guiding FBI counterterrorism activities were laid down more than fifty years ago, before World War II, and were codified more than twenty-five years ago, while the Cold War was still under way. At that time, the main national security threat was the Soviet Union, which was understood to be conducting a worldwide campaign against the United States through clandestine means and covert proxies.

At the beginning of the Cold War, the criminal law was thought to be of little relevance to this struggle. The foreign agents conducting or directing hostile actions against the United States were often operating under diplomatic immunity. It was assumed that criminal prosecution would reveal too much classified information, compromising continued counterintelligence efforts. Even with respect to United States citizens suspected of spying in the United States, the presumption was against criminal prosecution. Clandestine disruptive actions and double agent operations were justified as the best means of preventing damage to U.S. interests, on the ground that the criminal law was not available.

Major changes over the last two decades have upset many of the assumptions on which FBI national security activities were founded. The Soviet Union has disintegrated. Human rights protection has emerged as a leading principle of U.S. foreign policy (at least in theory). International law has undergone revolutionary change, to the point where the United States now has at its disposal a range of international sanctions to punish state sponsors of terrorism.

Most importantly, criminal law has assumed a primacy in national security policy. It is now routine to arrest and prosecute suspected spies, through trials in which all of the government's evidence is presented publicly and subject to cross-examination. The Classified Information Procedures Act makes such public prosecutions less risky to ongoing operations, while preserving defendants' rights to confront the evidence against them. U.S. criminal law has been given wide extraterritorial effect, reaching almost any attack anywhere in the world against an American citizen, U.S. government property, or property owned by U.S. corporations. International cooperation in the field of criminal law makes it more likely than ever that terrorism can be dealt with through arrest and prosecution in U.S. courts.

A revised view of intelligence is also demanded by another change: The United States, always a diverse society, has become even more so. Consider just religious diversity. There are 3,000 religious denominations and sects in the United States today. Not only are there more Muslims than Episcopalians in the United States, but there is a diversity within this diversity that defies common assumptions. For example, contrary to popular perception, most Muslims in the United States are not of Arab origin and most persons of Arab descent in the United States are not Muslims.

In the face of such diversity, principles of pluralism, tolerance of dissent, and individual rather than group culpability should guide the development of national security, intelligence, and counterterrorism policy. The alternative is a stereotyping that can ossify or mislead the investigative focus. While the FBI was conducting an intensive investigation of the PLO-affiliated PFLP in the 1980s and 1990s, the U.S. government was promoting the signing of an Israeli-PLO peace accord, and the focus of terrorism concern in the Middle East shifted to anti-PLO Muslim fundamentalists. As soon as the FBI launched a massive campaign against Muslim fundamentalists in the wake of the World Trade Center bombing, the Murrah building in Oklahoma City was blown up by white, native-born ex-GIs. And while the FBI and the INS pursued innocent Arab and Muslim political activists, terrorists careful to avoid any showing of religious or political orientation planned and carried out the September 11 attacks.

Intelligence in a Democratic Society

Improving "intelligence" is obviously a critical factor in preventing future terrorist attacks. Some advocate the clandestine collection, without particular suspicion of wrongdoing, of large quantities of information, the immediate relevance of which may not be clear, in order to piece together a mosaic that might help policy makers anticipate actions of potential adversaries. The tools of this type of intelligence include monitoring of political, ethnic, or religious groups, electronic surveillance without focus on illegal conduct, and the sifting without individualized suspicion of vast databases of information on innocuous transactions. Much of the information generated by these means is inconclusive or unreliable; rarely is it ever subjected to the testing of the adversarial process; and all too often the collection of it intrudes on privacy, due process, or protected political activity.

Inside the United States, we favor another vision of intelligence, one rooted in the concepts of the criminal law. "Intelligence" in this context means the collection and analysis of information about a criminal enterprise that goes beyond what is necessary to solve a particular crime. Intelligence of this type is intended to aid law enforcement agencies in drawing a fuller picture of the enterprise. It allows the government to identify the silent partners, those who provide money for violent attacks or issue the commands. Intelligence allows investigators to link seemingly disparate crimes into a pattern. At its best, intelligence allows the government to anticipate and prevent a group's next dangerous crime, thereby saving lives.

The FBI routinely conducts "intelligence" operations of this second type against organized crime families and drug cartels. It does so subject to the ordinary rules of criminal procedure. The goal of such investigations is to arrest the leaders and to put them on trial for specific crimes. And one of the most important constraints on such criminal intelligence is the public trial—everything done in the name of criminal intelligence must ultimately beat scrutiny in a court of law.

The concept of criminal intelligence can be fully compatible with the Constitution. The First Amendment does not require the FBI to be deaf when someone advocates violence. The Constitution does not require the government to wait until a bomb goes off or even to wait until a bomb factory is brought to its attention—it does, however, require the FBI to focus its investigations on the interdiction of violence and other criminal conduct. Too often, the FBI has not limited itself to uncovering evidence of a crime, but instead has conducted lengthy investigations that consist of routine monitoring and disrupting of lawful political activities.

We live in a world of political, ethnic, and religious violence. There will undoubtedly be more acts of terrorism both here and overseas against U.S. targets. It is incumbent on those who criticize current counterterrorism policies to say how they would go about addressing the threat of terrorism. We believe that an effective counterterrorism policy can be implemented in this country based on traditional criminal procedures directed at crimes of violence, including intelligence gathering aimed at preventing terrorist acts before they occur.[4]

The FBI is at its best when it does criminal investigations. It is at its worst when it acts in a counterintelligence, monitoring mode, secretly pursuing an ethnically, religiously, or ideologically defined target without the constraints and focus of the criminal code and without the expectation that its actions will be subjected to scrutiny in the adversarial context of a public criminal trial.

Counterterrorism investigations should investigate terrorist acts as crimes, regardless of their political motivation. Murder, kidnapping, or bank robbery by terrorists, even murder on a mass scale, is most effectively investigated using the same techniques that are applied to murder, kidnapping, and bank robbery by nonterrorists. By and large, this was the FBI's focus under the Levi domestic security guidelines. The focus on criminal activity was also for some years a central feature of U.S. policy against terrorism abroad. In the 1980s, a major component of the policy was the extension of extraterritorial jurisdiction over crimes of violence committed by terrorists against Americans abroad, so that terrorists could be extradited to the United States to be tried here.

Indeed, the United States has continued to pursue this approach, in tandem with the broader monitoring approach reflected in the 1996 and 2001 antiterrorism laws. Federal prosecutors in New York successfully prosecuted al Qaeda members who carried out the African embassy bombings. If a criminal trial is possible against the hierarchy of entire organized crime families, it is also possible against those members of terrorist organizations who are engaged in carrying out or directly supporting violent activities, at least in situations short of war. In the case of a group having both legitimate and illegitimate activities, the focus should be on identifying and prosecuting all those responsible for the illegal activities, not penalizing innocent support of lawful conduct.

To reform FBI counterterrorism policies and avoid repetitions of CISPES-type cases, it is necessary to redraw the lines between criminal investigations and foreign counterintelligence investigations. Overbroad intelligence monitoring is a diversion from the harder work of identifying real terrorists. The CISPES case after it closed was seen inside and outside the FBI as a waste of resources. Counterintelligence monitoring displaced the search for evidence of crimes. Even though the FBI had an allegation that CISPES was planning terrorist attacks in Dallas, the investigation never actually had as its goal a resolution of that allegation. In the few instances in which the FBI received information concerning other possible violent activity by specific CISPES chapters, agents failed to pursue those allegations. Instead, agents devoted their efforts to identifying all CISPES chapters throughout the United States and monitoring clearly legal activities. If members of CISPES had actually been planning terrorist activity, the investigation conducted by the FBI was not likely to have uncovered it. In the case of those convicted of the first World Trade Center bombing, some of whom were the subject of a counterintelligence investigation prior to the bombing, a similar adherence to the monitoring approach may have contributed to the FBI's failure to pursue the case to an earlier resolution, which could have prevented the 1993 attack.

All antiterrorism investigations in the United States, whether of foreign or domestic groups, should be conducted pursuant to criminal rules, with the goal of arresting people who are planning, supporting, or carrying out violent activities and convicting them in a court of law. Law enforcement must stop framing terrorism investigations in political, religious, or ethnic terms. The FBI still classifies its investigations as "environmental terrorism" ("eco-terrorism") or "Islamic fundamentalist terrorism" or "Puerto Rican terrorism." This only reinforces the notion that the Bureau's role is to monitor politics or to target its efforts based on religion or ethnicity rather than to investigate crime. Instead, once a politically motivated group advocating violence is identified, the goal of the investigation should be to identify those engaged in the criminal enterprise, not to identify those who merely share the ideology.

Such a counterterrorism program would, in many respects, be the exact opposite of what was reflected in the Antiterrorism Act of 1996 and the Patriot Act of 2001. Where those Acts empowered the FBI to investigate a new, broadly defined offense of "support for terrorism," we would propose express legislative limits on the government's discretion to investigate and prosecute First Amendment activities. Where those Acts expanded the concept of support for terrorism to include support for the political and humanitarian activities of groups that also engage in violence, we advocate limiting the crime of support for terrorism, like any crime of aiding and abetting, to support for activities that are themselves crimes. Where those Acts endorsed guilt by association, we would require the FBI to focus its investigations on collecting evidence of individual culpability. Where those Acts allowed the use of secret evidence, we maintain that the government should subject its evidence to the test of cross-examination. And where those Acts adopted a political approach to terrorism, we insist that the FBI must get out of the business of monitoring political activity and associations, foreign and domestic, and instead dedicate itself to the urgent task of identifying those planning violent activities. Only such a transformation can successfully meet the threat of terrorism without sacrificing our political freedoms.

NOTES

1. *Intelligence Activities and the Rights of Americans, Book II, Final Report of the Senate Select Committee to Study Governmental Operations with Respect to Intelligence Activities* 289 (1976).
2. A useful discussion of this and many other issues involving terrorism and civil liberties can be found in Philip B. Heymann, *Terrorism and America* (MIT Press, 1998). This sensitive book serves as a commendable response to the calls of many for substantial curtailment of civil liberties in the name of fighting terrorism. Heymann argues that the current counterintelligence approach of the FBI, properly managed, would produce no intolerable limitations on the First Amendment.
3. Matthew L. Wald, "Tests Show Holes in Airline Security," *The New York Times*, Jan. 11, 1999, at A1.
4. James Risen and Benjamin Weiser, "Before Bombings, Omens and Fears," *The New York Times*, Jan. 9, 1999, at A1.

20

From *Not a Suicide Pact: The Constitution in a Time of National Emergency*

RICHARD A. POSNER

Now, in the early years of the twenty-first century, the nation faces the intertwined menaces of global terrorism and proliferation of weapons of mass destruction. A city can be destroyed by an atomic bomb the size of a melon, which if coated with lead would be undetectable. Large stretches of a city can be rendered uninhabitable, perhaps for decades, merely by the explosion of a conventional bomb that has been coated with radioactive material. Smallpox virus bioengineered to make it even more toxic and vaccines ineffectual, then aerosolized and sprayed in a major airport, might kill millions of people. Our terrorist enemies have the will to do such things and abundant opportunities, because our borders are porous both to enemies and to containers. They will soon have the means as well. The march of technology has increased the variety and lethality of weapons of mass destruction, especially the biological, and also, critically, their accessibility. Aided by the disintegration of the Soviet Union and the acquisition of nuclear weapons by unstable nations (Pakistan and North Korea, soon to be joined, in all likelihood, by Iran), technological progress is making weapons of mass destruction ever more accessible both to terrorist groups (and even individuals) and to hostile nations that are not major powers. The problem of proliferation is more serious today than it was in what now seem the almost halcyon days of the Cold War; it will be even more serious tomorrow.

I am not a Chicken Little, and I agree with those who argue that our vigorous campaign against al-Qaeda and our extensive if chaotic efforts at improving homeland security have bought us a breathing space against terrorist attacks on U.S. territory. But how long will this breathing space last? The terrorists, their leadership decimated and dispersed, may be reeling, but they have not been defeated. In January 2006 Osama bin Laden declared that there would be further terrorist attacks on the United States; it would be reckless to dismiss his declaration as idle boasting. This is not the time to let down our guard.

* * *

The research that I have been conducting for the past several years on catastrophic risks, international terrorism, and national security intelligence has persuaded me that we live in a time of grave and increasing danger, comparable to what the nation faced at the outset of World War II. * * *

* * *

The core meaning of "civil liberties" is freedom from coercive or otherwise intrusive governmental actions designed to secure the nation against real or, sometimes, imagined internal and external enemies. The concern is that such actions may get out of hand, creating a climate of fear, oppressing the innocent, stifling independent thought, and endangering democracy. Civil liberties can even be thought of as weapons of national security, since the government, with its enormous force, is, just like a foreign state, a potential enemy of the people. Civil liberties are also means of bringing the judiciary into the national security conversation, with a perspective that challenges that of the national security experts. The separation of powers has epistemic as well as political significance: competition among branches of government can stimulate thought, correct errors, force experts to explain themselves, expose malfeasance, and combat slack and complacency.

But the more numerous or dangerous the nation's enemies are believed to be, the greater the pressure to curtail civil liberties in favor of executive discretion and unity of command, in order to enable the government to wield its great power more effectively, if less responsibility. The traditional internal enemies are criminals, though in the Civil War they were rebels. The traditional external enemies are foreign states. But at present, with U.S. crime rates well below their historic highs and no major power posing a significant military threat to the nation, the external enemies whom Americans mainly fear are Islamist terrorists. And with good reason: they are numerous, fanatical, implacable, elusive, resourceful, resilient, utterly ruthless, seemingly fearless, apocalyptic in their aims, and eager to get their hands on weapons of mass destruction and use them against us. They did us terrible harm on September 11, 2001, and may do us worse harm in the future. We know little about their current number, leaders, locations, resources, supporters, motivations, and plans; and in part because of our ignorance, we have no strategy for defeating them, only for fighting them. Although our invasion of Afghanistan shortly after the 9/11 attacks and our subsequent vigorous counterterrorist efforts have scattered the leadership of al-Qaeda, as well as depriving the movement of its geographic base (though it has obtained a quasi-sanctuary in Pakistan), we are far from victory. Indeed, it is arguable that we have lost ground since 9/11—that the spectacular success of the 9/11 attacks did more to turn the Muslim world against the West than the vigorous military and police response to Islamist terrorism has done to weaken the terrorist movement. Yet all this is speculation. For all we know, we may be quite safe. But we cannot afford to act on that optimistic assumption.

* * * A military enemy can usually be fought with minimal impairment of civil liberties beyond conscription and the censorship of militarily sensitive information. But terrorists do not field military forces that we can grapple with in the open. And they are not content to operate against us abroad; they penetrate our country by stealth to kill us. Rooting out an invisible enemy in our midst might be fatally inhibited if we felt constrained to strict observance of civil liberties designed in and for eras in which the only serious internal threat (apart from spies) came from common criminals.

* * *

The challenge to constitutional decision making in the era of modern terrorism is to restrike the balance between the interest in liberty from government restraint or interference and the interest in public safety, in recognition of the grave threat that terrorism poses to the nation's security. The scope of a right must be calibrated by reference to the interests that support and oppose it. But how to do this? Ideally, in the case of a right (for example, the right to be free from unreasonable searches and seizures) that could be asserted against government measures for protecting national security, one would like to locate the point at which a slight expansion in the scope of the right would subtract more from public safety than it would add to personal liberty and a slight contraction would subtract more from personal liberty than it would add to public safety. That is the point of balance, and determines the optimal scope of the right. The point shifts continuously as threats to liberty and safety wax and wane. At no time can the exact point be located. Yet to imagine it the object of our quest is useful in underscoring that the balance between liberty and safety must be struck at the margin. One is not to ask whether liberty is more or less important than safety. One is to ask whether a particular security measure harms liberty more or less than it promotes safety.

* * *

In conventional legal terms, the marginal approach equates to decision making guided by a standard and its rejection to decision making guided by a rule. Negligence is a standard, applied in particular cases by balancing the expected accident cost (the cost if the accident occurs discounted by the probability that it will occur) against the cost of preventing the accident; if the former is greater than the latter, the injurer is negligent and therefore liable. A fixed numerical speed limit is a rule, although a rule with exceptions, such as for police cars and other emergency vehicles. Rules, especially ones that allow of no exceptions, are simpler to apply than standards. But by making the outcome of a case depend on one or a few facts (such as the speed at which a car is traveling) rather than on all the relevant circumstances (which might include the design of the highway, the amount of traffic, the time of day, weather conditions, the driver's skills, and the reason he was speeding), rules often make a poor fit with the particular circumstances in which they are applied, and when this is so, exceptions may be allowed in order to improve the fit.

* * *

Although governance by a standard is often unworkable because too many factors are relevant or because the factors are too subjective to be weighed and compared, cases involving a clash between liberty and safety cannot yet be governed by rules. Rules would inevitably favor one over the other, and not enough is known at present to make a categorical judgment on which way to tilt a rule. Better for now, at least, to govern by standard, with the judges feeling their way over the new constitutional terrain created by the 9/11 attacks and the government's responses, deciding cases narrowly, preferably on statutory grounds, hesitating to trundle out the heavy artillery of constitutional invalidation. Eventually, as not only the nature of the terrorist threat but also the consequences for civil liberties of the post-9/11 security measures become clearer, it may become possible to crystallize sensible rules from the standard.

Accurate balancing of competing values requires courts to pay serious attention to risks rather than always insisting on certainty. It would be a mistake to think that a particular measure should be rejected because we do not know whether another terrorist attack on the United States will occur unless that measure is taken and so we cannot be certain that it will actually increase safety. Most safety measures are aimed at reducing risks rather than eliminating certainties, but that doesn't make the measures unwarranted. The fact that one cannot know whether interrogating a particular terrorist will ward off an attack does not make interrogating terrorists valueless. This point is obscured when there is a certain harm on one side of the balance and an uncertain benefit on the other. A terrorist subjected to torture incurs a harm with certainty. But that the torture will yield a benefit for national security is only a probability when the torture begins. The torture may be ineffective either because the person tortured has no useful information to impart or because he is able to withstand the torture; in either case, moreover, he may send his interrogators off on a wild-goose chase by lying.

* * *

A further argument for a light judicial hand in national security matters, at least when the president and the Congress concur on a national security measure, is that while few members of Congress are genuine experts on national security, the total amount of national security expertise in Congress (including congressional staff) is vastly greater than that in the judiciary. Judges aren't *supposed* to know much about national security; at least they don't think they are supposed to know much about it. A related reason for judges to defer to the judgment of the other branches of government in cases of doubt is that the efficacy—the consequences generally—of a security measure adopted to deal with a novel threat cannot be determined if the measure is blocked early on by a constitutional interpretation. The post-9/11 responses to the newly apprehended terrorist threat are entitled to a chance to prove themselves—good or bad.

An important implication of the principle that safety and liberty must be balanced at the margin is that the consequences of particular measures for the protection of national security must be considered in relation to alternative measures that might be taken instead. To argue that the information that could be extracted by torturing terrorists would increase public safety more than it would decrease the "liberty" (in a broad sense) of the tortured person assumes that the information could not be obtained by means that would do less harm to personal liberty. If it could, the incremental benefit of torture would be slight. But the incremental harm might also be rather slight, since forms of coercive interrogation that would not be considered to rise to the level of torture might nevertheless inflict significant emotional distress on the people subjected to them.

*   *   *

The balancing approach that I am advocating to determining the scope of constitutional rights in emergency circumstances highlights the *dynamic* character of constitutional law—the fact that the scope of a constitutional right changes as the relative weights of liberty and safety change. The change may be slow because courts move slowly, in part because of the drag that precedent exerts on judicial innovation. But change there will be. The low crime rate in the 1950s set the stage for the Supreme Court in the 1960s to multiply the rights of criminal defendants; then crime rates rose rapidly (whether or not because of that multiplication) and there was a backlash and the Court curtailed defendants' rights both directly, by redefining constitutional rights, and indirectly, by upholding congressional limitations on those rights. The safer the nation feels, the greater the weight that the courts place on personal liberty relative to public safety. When the nation feels endangered, the balance shifts the other way. The nation felt much safer before the 9/11 attacks than after, just as it felt much safer after the Cold War ended than before, and after the Civil War ended than while it was raging.

Neither in the case of soaring crime rates nor in that of an increased threat of terrorism are judges willing to say that rights are sacrosanct and the nation must either accept greater danger or find some other way to respond. The other ways may be ineffectual or prohibitively costly, and in the crunch most people put safety ahead of liberty. Of course, what the normally self-interested person wants most to do is to put *his* safety ahead of *your* liberty. But when that is not an option, he will usually accept restrictions on his liberty more readily than he will accept enhanced danger to his physical security. Moreover, the people at risk from crime and terrorism are far more numerous than those who face a higher risk of being falsely accused when protections of civil liberties are curtailed, provided they are curtailed only modestly.

*   *   *

Civil libertarians * * * are reluctant to acknowledge that national emergencies in general, or the threat of modern terrorism in particular, justify *any* curtailment of the civil liberties that were accepted on the eve of the emergency. They deny that civil liberties should wax and wane with changes in the danger level. They believe that the Constitution is about protecting individual rights rather than about promoting community interests, a belief that some civil libertarians ground in a quasi-religious veneration of civil liberties coupled with a profound suspicion of the coercive side of government—police, prosecutors, the military, the intelligence community. (The small civil libertarian Right, epitomized by the Cato Institute, extends this suspicion to *all* activities of government.) They base that suspicion on a belief * * * that past curtailments of civil liberties were gratuitous responses to hysterically exaggerated fears. They believe that government always errs on the side of exaggerating threats to national security. And so they believe that the current threat—the terrorist threat—is exaggerated, perhaps deliberately by the Bush administration to promote its political fortunes, and that the laws and institutions in place on September 11, 2001, required no changes in order to be adequate to cope with the current threat. * * * Implicitly they deny that the counterterrorism measures taken since 9/11 may be among the reasons that we haven't been attacked since.

*   *   *

A belief of many civil libertarians that both jostles uneasily with their suspicion of police and prosecutors and, more important, reflects a misunderstanding of modern terrorism is that since acts of terrorism are criminal we should leave it to the criminal law to deal with them. * * * They do not acknowledge that a public trial, or any trial, may come too late. The rather casual attitude of the FBI and other police forces toward ordinary crime—accepting that a great deal of it will occur and being content to limit the crime rate by apprehending and prosecuting a fraction of criminals, thus incapacitating some and deterring some others—is misplaced when it comes to fighting terrorism. Because terrorist attacks are potentially so destructive and also because many terrorists are undeterrable, the emphasis of public policy shifts from punishment after an attack occurs to preventing it from occurring. The line between punishment and prevention blurs when preparatory activity is criminalized, as it is in the criminal-law concepts of attempt and conspiracy. But civil libertarians want to limit the prosecution of preparatory activity, lest it result in punishment of harmless acts, as in the old English crime of "compassing" (imagining) the death of the king. A limitation to completed acts of terrorism, however, would make the criminal law an even less adequate response to terrorism than it is.

* * *

Civil libertarians neglect a genuine lesson of history: that the greatest danger to American civil liberties would be another terrorist attack on the United States, even if it was on a smaller scale than the 9/11 attacks—but it could be on the same or even a much larger scale. The USA PATRIOT Act, which civil libertarians abhor, was passed within weeks of those attacks; it never would have passed, or in all likelihood even have been proposed, had the attacks been thwarted. The other novel measures that the government has adopted to combat the terrorist menace, and that civil libertarians denounce, also would not have been adopted had it not been for 9/11. A minor present curtailment of civil liberties, to the extent that it reduces the probability of a terrorist attack, reduces the likelihood of a major future curtailment of those liberties.* * *

* * *

Constitutional rights are largely created by the Supreme Court, by loose interpretation of the constitutional text. Created as they are in response to the felt needs and conditions of the time, they can be and frequently are modified by the Court in response to changes in those needs and conditions. A constitutional right *should* be modified when changed circumstances indicate that the right no longer strikes a sensible balance between competing constitutional values, such as personal liberty and public safety. A national emergency, such as a war, creates a disequilibrium in the existing system of constitutional rights. Concerns for public safety now weigh more heavily than before. The courts respond by altering the balance, curtailing civil liberties in recognition that the relative weights of the competing interests have changed in favor of safety. That is the pragmatic response, and pragmatism is a dominant feature not only of American culture at large but also of the American judicial culture.

* * *

DISCUSSION QUESTIONS

1. Are Cole and Dempsey correct that counterterrorism can be treated like other crimes rather than be viewed through an ideological or political prism? Or is Posner correct that these are exactly what make terrorism different and ultimately more deadly than other crime?

2. Imagine you are a policy maker trying to implement Posner's balancing framework. What kinds of factors would you take into account in reaching a decision? What kinds of evidence would you want to see?

3. Is the slippery-slope argument that underlies Cole and Dempsey's argument—that we put up with small restrictions on civil liberties only to find further incremental restrictions acceptable, until they add up to significant curtailments—persuasive? How about the inverse of the slippery-slope argument that Posner might find more persuasive—if we do not take steps to protect ourselves, we risk more attacks that could lead to real restrictions on civil liberties?

PART II

Institutions

CHAPTER 5

Congress: The First Branch

21

"Speech to the Electors of Bristol"

Edmund Burke

One often hears a politician say that "I vote my conscience" or "I do the right thing" rather than giving in to political expedience or the temporary whims of the voters. One also suspects that such behavior is relatively uncommon, given the desire of most politicians to stay on the good side of the voters and not be booted from office.

The following selection from Edmund Burke is the classic statement of a representative following his or her conscience, even if it means going against their constituents' wishes. Indeed, the politician who behaves this way is often called a "Burkean trustee." Burke gave this speech after being elected in 1774 to represent Bristol in the House of Commons. Burke argues for independent judgment, saying, "Your Representative owes you, not his industry only, but his judgement (sic); and he betrays, instead of serving you, if he sacrifices it to your opinion."
He also argues for a general, common good rather than local interests as the proper focus of a representative's efforts. He says, "Parliament is a deliberative Assembly of one Nation, with one Interest, that of the whole; where, not local Purposes, not local Prejudices ought to guide, but the general Good, resulting from the general Reason of the whole. You chuse a Member indeed; but when you have chosen him, he is not Member of Bristol, but he is a Member of Parliament."

Burke practiced what he preached and went against his constituents on several issues involving trade (which were quite important in this port city). However, this approach had its political costs—by 1780 it was clear he would not be reelected. So he decided not to run for reelection in Bristol, but instead accepted a safe seat from his parliamentary patron, Lord Rockingham, which he held until his retirement in 1794.

Mr. Edmund Burke's Speech to the Electors of Bristol
[On his being declared by the Sheriffs, duly elected one of the Representatives in Parliament for that City, on Thursday the 3d of November, 1774]

GENTLEMEN,
    I cannot avoid sympathizing strongly with the feelings of the Gentleman who has received the same honour that you have conferred on me. * * *

*   *   *

But how should I appear to the Voters themselves? If I had gone round to the citizens intitled to Freedom, and squeezed them by the hand—"Sir, I humbly beg your Vote—I shall be eternally thankful—may I hope for the honour of your support?—Well!—come—we shall see you at the Council-house."—If I were then to deliver them to my managers, pack them into tallies, vote them off in court, and when I heard from the Bar—"Such a one only! and such a one for ever!—he's my man!"—"Thank you, good Sir—Hah! my worthy friend! thank you kindly—that's an honest fellow—how is your good family?"—Whilst these words were hardly out of my mouth, if I should have wheeled round at once, and told them—"Get you gone, you pack of worthless fellows! you have no votes—you are Usurpers! you are intruders on the rights of real freemen! I will have nothing to do with you! you ought never to have been produced at this Election, and the sheriffs ought not to have admitted you to poll."

Gentlemen, I should make a strange figure, if my conduct had been of this sort. I am not so old an acquaintance of yours as the worthy Gentleman. Indeed I could not have ventured on such kind of freedoms with you. But I am bound, and I will endeavour, to have justice done to the rights of Freemen; even though I should, at the same time, be obliged to vindicate the former part of my antagonist's conduct against his own present inclinations.

I owe myself, in all things, to all the freemen of this city. My particular friends have a demand on me, that I should not deceive their expectations. Never was cause or man supported with more constancy, more activity, more spirit. I have been supported with a zeal indeed and heartiness in my friends, which (if their object had been at all proportioned to their endeavours) could never be sufficiently commended. They supported me upon the most liberal principles. They wished that the members for Bristol should be chosen for the City, and for their Country at large, and not for themselves.

So far they are not disappointed. If I possess nothing else, I am sure I possess the temper that is fit for your service. I know nothing of Bristol, but by the favours I have received, and the virtues I have seen exerted in it.

I shall ever retain, what I now feel, the most perfect and grateful attachment to my friends—and I have no enmities; nor resentment. I never can consider fidelity to engagements, and constancy in friendships, but with the highest approbation; even when those noble qualities are employed against my own pretensions. The Gentleman, who is not fortunate as I have been in this contest, enjoys, in this respect, a consolation full of honour both to himself and to his friends. They have certainly left nothing undone for his service.

As for the trifling petulance, which the rage of party stirs up in little minds, though it should shew itself even in this court, it has not made the slightest impression on me. The highest flight of such clamorous birds is winged in an inferior region of the air. We hear them, and we look upon them, just as you, Gentlemen, when you enjoy the serene air on your lofty rocks, look down upon the Gulls, that skim the mud of your river, when it is exhausted of its tide.

I am sorry I cannot conclude, without saying a word on a topick touched upon by my worthy Colleague. I wish that topick had been passed by; at a time when I have so little leisure to discuss it. But since he has thought proper to throw it out, I owe you a clear explanation of my poor sentiments on that subject.

He tells you, that "the topick of Instructions has occasioned much altercation and uneasiness in this City"; and he expresses himself (if I understand him rightly) in favour of the coercive authority of such instructions.

Certainly, Gentlemen, it ought to be the happiness and glory of a Representative, to live in the strictest union, the closest correspondence, and the most unreserved communication with his constituents. Their wishes ought to have great weight with him; their opinion high respect; their business unremitted attention. It is his duty to sacrifice his repose, his pleasures, his satisfactions, to theirs; and, above all, ever, and in all cases, to prefer their interest to his own. But, his unbiassed opinion, his mature judgement, his enlightened conscience, he ought not to sacrifice to you; to any man, or to any sett of men living. These he does not derive from your pleasure; no, nor from the Law and the Constitution. They are a trust from Providence, for the abuse of which he is deeply answerable. Your Representative owes you, not his industry only, but his judgement; and he betrays, instead of serving you, if he sacrifices it to your opinion.

My worthy Colleague says, his Will ought to be subservient to yours. If that be all, the thing is innocent. If Government were a matter of Will upon any side, yours, without question, ought to be superior. But Government and Legislation are matters of reason and judgement, and not of inclination; and, what sort of reason is that, in which the determination precedes the discussion; in which one sett of men deliberate, and another decide; and where those who form the conclusion are perhaps three hundred miles distant from those who hear the arguments?

To deliver an opinion, is the right of all men; that of Constituents is a weighty and respectable opinion, which a Representative ought always to rejoice to hear; and which he ought always most seriously to consider. But authoritative instructions; Mandates issued, which the Member is bound blindly and implicitly to obey, to vote, and to argue for, though contrary to the clearest conviction of his judgement and conscience; these are things utterly unknown to the laws of this land, and which arise from a fundamental Mistake of the whole order and tenour of our Constitution.

Parliament is not a Congress of Ambassadors from different and hostile interests; which interests each must maintain, as an Agent and Advocate, against other Agents and Advocates; but Parliament is a deliberative Assembly of one Nation, with one Interest, that of the whole; where, not local Purposes, not local Prejudices ought to guide, but the general Good, resulting from the general Reason of the whole. You chuse a Member indeed; but when you have chosen him, he is not Member of Bristol, but he is a Member of Parliament. If the local Constituent should have an Interest, or should form an hasty Opinion, evidently opposite to the real good of the rest of the Community, the Member for that place ought to be as far, as any other, from any endeavour to give it Effect. I beg pardon for saying so much on this subject. I have been unwillingly drawn into it; but I shall ever use a respectful frankness of communication with you. Your faithful friend, your devoted servant, I shall be to the end of my life: A flatterer you do not wish for. On this point of instructions, however, I think it scarcely possible, we ever can have any sort of difference. Perhaps I may give you too much, rather than too little trouble.

From the first hour I was encouraged to court your favour to this happy day of obtaining it, I have never promised you any thing, but humble and persevering endeavours to do my duty. The weight of that duty, I confess, makes me tremble; and whoever well considers what it is, of all things in the world will fly from what has the least likeness to a positive and precipitate engagement. To be a good Member of Parliament, is, let me tell you, no easy task; especially at this time, when there is so strong a disposition to run into the perilous extremes of servile compliance, or wild popularity. To unite circumspection with vigour, is absolutely necessary; but it is extremely difficult. We are now Members for a rich commercial City; this City, however, is but a part of a rich commercial Nation, the Interests of which are various, multiform, and intricate. We are Members for that great Nation, which however is itself but part of a great Empire, extended by our Virtue and our Fortune to the farthest limits of the East and of the West. All these wide-spread Interests must be considered; must be compared; must be reconciled if possible. We are Members for a free Country; and surely we all know, that the machine of a free Constitution is no simple thing; but as intricate and as delicate, as it is valuable. We are Members in a great and ancient Monarchy; and we must preserve religiously, the true legal rights of the Sovereign, which form the Key-stone that binds together the noble and well-constructed Arch of our Empire and our Constitution. A Constitution made up of balanced Powers must ever be a critical thing. As such I mean to touch that part of it which comes within my reach. I know my Inability, and I wish for support from every Quarter. In particular I shall aim at the friendship, and shall cultivate the best Correspondence, of the worthy Colleague you have given me.

I trouble you no farther than once more to thank you all; you, Gentlemen, for your Favours; the Candidates for their temperate and polite behaviour; and the Sheriffs, for a Conduct which may give a Model for all who are in public Stations.

Discussion Questions

1. Is it possible for members of Congress to act as "Burkean trustees" today, or would they not survive politically?

2. Can you think of any examples of Burkean "profiles in courage" in which the politician does the right thing, rather than what is politically popular?

3. What do you think of Burke's claim that "he is not Member of Bristol, but he is a Member of Parliament." How would you feel about your member of Congress if he or she took this view?

4. Are there some issues upon which it may be better to have a representative who behaved like Burke, and others upon which it would be better to listen to the constituents? What would be some examples of each?

22

From *Congress: The Electoral Connection*

David R. Mayhew

Is Edmund Burke right? Are members of Congress motivated by the desire to make good public policy that will best serve the public and national interest, and are they willing to go against their constituents' opinions when they think it is the right thing to do? Political scientist David Mayhew argues the motivation is not so idealistic or complex. Members of Congress simply want to be reelected, and most of their behavior—advertising, credit claiming, and position taking—is designed to make reelection easier. Further, Mayhew argues that the structure of Congress is ideally suited to facilitate the reelection pursuit. Congressional offices and staff advertise member accomplishments, committees allow for the specialization necessary to claim credit for particularistic benefits provided to the district, and the political parties in Congress do not demand loyalty when constituent interests run counter to the party line.

Mayhew's argument is not universally accepted. Many political scientists accept his underlying premise as a given: elected officials are self-interested, and this is manifest in their constant pursuit of reelection. But others disagree with the premise. Motivations, they argue, are far more complex than allowed for by such a simple statement or theory. People often act unselfishly, and members of Congress have been known to vote their consciences even if it means losing an election. Others have pointed out that parties now serve as a stronger constraint on congressional behavior than they did when Mayhew was writing in the early 1970s.

[1.] The organization of Congress meets remarkably well the electoral needs of its members. To put it another way, if a group of planners sat down and tried to design a pair of American national assemblies with the goal of serving members' electoral needs year in and year out, they would be hard pressed to improve on what exists. * * * [2.] Satisfaction of electoral needs requires remarkably little zero-sum conflict among members. That is, one member's gain is not another member's loss; to a remarkable degree members can successfully engage in electorally useful activities without denying other members the opportunity successfully to engage in them. In regard to credit claiming, this second point requires elaboration further on. Its application to advertising is perhaps obvious. The members all have different markets, so that what any one member does is not an inconvenience to any other. There are exceptions here—

House members are sometimes thrown into districts together, senators have to watch the advertising of ambitious House members within their states, and senators from the same state have to keep up with each other—but the case generally holds. With position taking the point is also reasonably clear. As long as congressmen do not attack each other —and they rarely do—any member can champion the most extraordinary causes without inconveniencing any of his colleagues.

* * *

A scrutiny of the basic structural units of Congress will yield evidence to support both these * * * points. First, there are the 535 Capitol Hill *offices*, the small personal empires of the members. * * * The Hill office is a vitally important political unit, part campaign management firm and part political machine. The availability of its staff members for election work in and out of season gives it some of the properties of the former; its casework capabilities, some of the properties of the latter. And there is the franking privilege for use on office emanations. * * * A final comment on congressional offices is perhaps the most important one: office resources are given to all members regardless of party, seniority, or any other qualification. They come with the job.

Second among the structural units are the *committees*. * * * Committee membership can be electorally useful in a number of different ways. Some committees supply good platforms for position taking. The best example over the years is probably the House Un-American Activities Committee (now the Internal Security Committee), whose members have displayed hardly a trace of an interest in legislation. [Theodore] Lowi has a chart showing numbers of days devoted to HUAC public hearings in Congresses from the Eightieth through the Eighty-ninth. It can be read as a supply chart, showing biennial volume of position taking on subversion and related matters; by inference it can also be read as a measure of popular demand (the peak years were 1949–56). Senator Joseph McCarthy used the Senate Government Operations Committee as his investigative base in the Eighty-third Congress; later on in the 1960s Senators Abraham Ribicoff (D., Conn.) and William Proxmire (D., Wis.) used subcommittees of this same unit in catching public attention respectively on auto safety and defense waste. With membership on the Senate Foreign Relations Committee goes a license to make speeches on foreign policy. Some committees perhaps deserve to be designated "cause committees"; membership on them can confer an ostentatious identification with salient public causes. An example is the House Education and Labor Committee, whose members, in Fenno's analysis, have two "strategic premises": "to prosecute policy partisanship" and "to pursue one's individual policy preferences regardless of party." Committee members do a good deal of churning about on education, poverty, and similar matters. In recent years Education and Labor has attracted media-conscious members such as Shirley Chisholm (D., N.Y.), Herman Badillo (D., N.Y.), and Louise Day Hicks (D., Mass.).

Some committees traffic in particularized benefits.

* * *

Specifically, in giving out particularized benefits where the costs are diffuse (falling on taxpayer or consumer) and where in the long run to reward one congressman is not obviously to deprive others, the members follow a policy of universalism. That is, every member, regardless of party or seniority, has a right to his share of benefits. There is evidence of universalism in the distribution of projects on House Public Works, projects on House Interior, projects on Senate Interior, project money on House Appropriations, project money on Senate Appropriations, tax benefits on House Ways and Means, tax benefits on Senate Finance, and (by inference from the reported data) urban renewal projects on House Banking and Currency. The House Interior Committee, in Fenno's account, "takes as its major decision rule a determination to process and pass *all* requests and to do so in such a way as to maximize the chances of passage in the House. Succinctly, then, Interior's major strategic premise is: *to secure House passage of all constituency-supported, Member-sponsored bills.*"

* * *

Particularism also has its position-taking side. On occasion members capture public attention by denouncing the allocation process itself; thus in 1972 a number of liberals held up some Ways and Means "members' bills" on the House floor. But such efforts have little or no effect. Senator Douglas used to offer floor amendments to excise projects from public works appropriations bills, but he had a hard time even getting the Senate to vote on them.

Finally, and very importantly, the committee system aids congressmen simply by allowing a division of labor among members. The parceling out of legislation among small groups of congressmen by subject area has two effects. First, it creates small voting bodies in which membership may be valuable. An attentive interest group will prize more highly the favorable issue positions of members of committees pondering its fortunes than the favorable positions of the general run of congressmen. Second, it creates specialized small-group settings in which individual congressmen can make things happen and be perceived to make things happen. "I put that bill through committee." "That was my amendment." "I talked them around on that." This is the language of credit claiming. It comes easily in the committee setting and also when "expert" committee members handle bills on the floor. To attentive audiences it can be believable. Some political actors follow committee activities closely and mobilize electoral resources to support deserving members.

* * *

The other basic structural units in Congress are the *parties*. The case here will be that the parties, like the offices and committees, are tailored to suit members' electoral needs. They are more useful for what they are not than for what they are.

* * *

What is important to each congressman, and vitally so, is that he be free to take positions that serve his advantage. There is no member of either house who would not be politically injured—or at least who would not think he would be injured—by being made to toe a party line on all policies (unless of course he could determine the line). There is no congressional bloc whose members have identical position needs across all issues. Thus on the school busing issue in the Ninety-second Congress, it was vital to Detroit white liberal Democratic House members that they be free to vote one way and to Detroit black liberal Democrats that they be free to vote the other. In regard to these member needs the best service a party can supply to its congressmen is a negative one; it can leave them alone. And this in general is what the congressional parties do. Party leaders are chosen not to be program salesmen or vote mobilizers, but to be brokers, favor-doers, agenda-setters, and protectors of established institutional routines. Party "pressure" to vote one way or another is minimal. Party "whipping" hardly deserves the name. Leaders in both houses have a habit of counseling members to "vote their constituencies."

DISCUSSION QUESTIONS

1. If members are motivated by the desire to be reelected, is this such a bad thing? After all, shouldn't members of Congress do things that will keep the voters happy? Does the constant quest for reelection have a positive or negative impact on "representation"?

2. How could the institutions of Congress (members' offices, committees, and parties) be changed so that the collective needs of the institution would take precedence over the needs of individual members? Would there be any negative consequences for making these changes?

3. Some have argued that term limits are needed to break the never-ending quest for reelection. Do you think that term limits for members of Congress are a good idea?

23

"Too Much of a Good Thing: More Representative Is Not Necessarily Better"

John R. Hibbing and Elizabeth Theiss-Morse

David Mayhew describes an institution that should be highly responsive to voters. If members of Congress want to get reelected, they need to do what their constituents want them to do. However, John Hibbing and Elizabeth Theiss-Morse argue that having institutions that are too representative may be "too much of a good thing." That is, it may not be in the nation's interest to always do what the public wants, especially when it comes to issues of institutional reform. On questions of reform, the public is usually convinced that the only thing that is preventing ideal policies is that the "people in power" are serving their own interests rather than the public's interests. According to this view, the obvious—but wrong according to Hibbing and Theiss-Morse—solution is to weaken political institutions through "reforms" such as term limits, reducing the salaries of members of Congress, and requiring that Congress balances the federal budget every year. Hibbing and Theiss-Morse argue that these reforms might make people even more disillusioned when they discover that weakening Congress will not solve our nation's problems.

The authors also argue that the public generally do not have a very realistic understanding of the inherent nature of conflict in the political process. The public believes that there is substantial consensus on most issues and only small "fringe" groups disagree on a broad range of issues. If this was true, it is certainly understandable why people are frustrated with Congress. But in reality, as the authors point out, the nation is deeply divided about the proper course of action. This makes conflict and compromise an inherent part of the legislative process and, at the same time, dims the prospects for simple reforms.

Reform sentiments are much in evidence on the American political scene as we approach the end of the [twentieth] century, and improving the way public opinion is represented in political institutions is often the major motivation of reformers. This is clear * * * from the activities of contemporary political elites, and from the mood of ordinary people. Gross dissatisfaction exists with the nature of representation perceived to be offered by the modern political system. People believe the political process has been commandeered by narrow special interests and by political parties whose sole aim is to contradict the other political party. Given the centrality of representation in the U.S. polity, the organizers and contributors to this symposium are to be commended. It is laudable to want to consider ways of improving the system and, thereby, making people happier with their government. Many of the ideas described in the accompanying essays have considerable merit.

We do, however, wish to raise two important cautions: one briefly and the second in greater detail. Perhaps these cautions are not needed; the authors of the accompanying pieces are almost certainly aware of them. Still, general debate often neglects these two points. Therefore, quite apart from whether it is a good idea or a bad idea, say, to reform campaign finance, enact term limits, or move toward proportional representation and away from single-member districts, it is important * * * to keep in mind that 1) "because the people want them" is not a good justification for adopting procedural reforms and 2) actual enactment of the reforms craved by the people will not necessarily leave us with a system that is more liked even by the people who asked for the reforms in the first place. We take each point in turn.

Ignoring the People's Voice on Process Matters Is Not Evil

It would be easy at this point to slip into a discussion of the political acumen possessed by the American public and, relatedly, of the extent to which elected officials and political institutions should listen to the people. But such a discussion has been going on at least since the time of Plato and it is unlikely we would add much to it here. Instead, we merely wish to point out that, whatever the overall talents of the rank and file, political change in the realm of process should *not* be as sensitive to the public's wishes as political change in the realm of policy.

It is one thing to maintain that in a democracy the people should get welfare reform if they want it. It is quite another to maintain that those same people should get term limits if they want them. Process needs to have some relative permanence, some "stickiness." This is the *definiens* of institutional processes. Without this trait, policy legitimacy would be compromised. The U.S. Constitution (like all constitutions) drives home this contention by including much on process (vetoes, impeachments, representational arrangements, terms of officials, minimum qualifications for holding particular offices, etc.) and precious little about policy. What policy proclamations *are* to be found in the Constitution have faced a strong likelihood of being reversed in subsequent actions (slavery and the 13th Amendment; tax policy and the 16th Amendment; prohibition and the 21st Amendment). Constitutions are written not to enshrine policy but to enshrine a system that will then make policy. These systemic structures should not be subjected lightly to popular whimsy.

The Framers took great efforts to insulate processes from the momentary fancies of the people; specifically, they made amending the Constitution difficult. It is not unusual for reformers, therefore, to run up against the Constitution and its main interpreters—the courts. Witness recent decisions undermining the ability of citizens to impose legislative term limits on members of Congress save by constitutional amendment. This uphill battle to enact procedural reform is precisely what the founders intended—and they were wise to do so.

It may be that the people's will should be reflected directly in public policy, perhaps through initiatives or, less drastically, through the actions of citizen-legislators who act as delegates rather than Burkean trustees. But this does not mean that the rules of the system themselves should change with public preferences in the same way health care policy should change with public preferences.

There may be many good reasons to change the processes of government—possibly by making government more representative—but a persuasive defense of process reforms is *not* embedded in the claim that the people are desirous of such reform. Just as the Bill of Rights does not permit a simple majority of the people to make decisions that will restrict basic rights, so the rest of the Constitution does not permit a simple majority of the people to alter willy-nilly the processes of government. There are good reasons for such arrangements.

Be Careful What You Wish For

One important reason we should be glad ordinary people are not in a position to leave their every mark on questions of political process and institutional design is the very good possibility that people will not be happy with the reforms they themselves advocate. The people generally clamor for reforms that would weaken institutions and strengthen the role of the people themselves in policy decisions. They advocate people's courts, an increased number of popular initiatives and referenda, devolution of authority to institutions "closer" to the people, term limits, staff cuts, emaciating the bureaucracy, elimination of committees, cessation of contact between interest groups and elected officials, and a weakening of political parties. These changes would clear the way for people to have greater influence on decisions, and this is what the people want, right?

Actually, our research suggests this is *not* what the people really want. The public does not desire direct democracy; it is not even clear that people desire democracy at all, although they are quite convinced they do. People want no part of a national direct democracy in which they would be asked to register their preferences, probably electronically, on important issues of the day. Proposals for such procedures are received warmly by a very small minority of citizens. Observers who notice the public's enthusiasm for virtually every populist notion sometimes go the next step of assuming the public wants direct democracy. This is simply an inaccurate assumption.

However, the public *does* want institutions to be transformed into something much closer to the people. The public sees a big disconnect between how they want representation to work and how they believe it is working. Strong support of populist government (not direct democracy) has been detected in innumerable polls conducted during the last couple of decades. That the public looks favorably upon this process agenda is beyond dispute. A national survey we conducted in 1992 found strong support for reforms that would limit the impact of the Washington scene on members of Congress.[1] For example, seven out of 10 respondents supported a reduction in congressional salaries, eight out of 10 supported term limitations, and nine out of 10 supported a balanced-budget amendment. What ties these reforms together is the public's desire to make elected officials more like ordinary people. In focus groups we conducted at the same time as the survey, participants stated many times that elected officials in Washington had lost touch with the people. They supported reforms believed to encourage officials to start keeping in touch. Elected officials should balance the budget just like the people back home. Elected officials should live off modest salaries just like the people back home. And elected officials should face the prospect of getting a real job back home rather than staying in Washington for years and years. These reforms would force elected officials to understand the needs of their constituents rather than get swept up in the money and power that run Washington.

If these reforms were put into place, would the public suddenly love Congress? We do not think so. Certain reforms, such as campaign finance reform, may help, since they would diminish the perception that money rules politics in Washington. But the main reason the public is disgruntled with Congress and with politics in Washington is because they are dissatisfied with the processes intrinsic to the operation of a democratic political system—debates, compromises, conflicting information, inefficiency, and slowness. This argument may seem odd on its face, so in the next few paragraphs we provide our interpretation of why the public questions the need for democratic processes.

The public operates under the erroneous assumption that the majority of the American people agrees on policy matters. In focus groups we conducted in 1997, participants adamantly stated that "80 percent of the American people agree on what needs to be done [about serious societal problems], but it's the other 20 percent who have the power." This pervasive and persistent belief in the existence of popular consensus on tough policy issues is, of course, grossly mistaken. Virtually every well-worded survey question dealing with salient policy issues of the day reveals deep divisions in the American public. From welfare reform to health care; from remaining in Bosnia to the taxes-services trade-off; from a constitutional amendment on flag desecration to the situations in which abortion is believed to be properly permitted, the people are at odds with each other.

This level of popular disagreement would be quite unremarkable except for the fact that the people will not admit that the disagreement actually exists. Instead, people project their own particular views, however ill-formed, onto a clear majority of other "real" people. Those (allegedly) few people who allow it to be known that they do not hold these views are dismissed as radical and noisy fringe elements that are accorded far too much influence by polemical parties, self-serving special interests, and spineless, out-of-touch elected officials. Thus, the desire to move the locus of decision making closer to the people is based on a faulty assumption right off the bat. Many believe that if decisions emanated from the people themselves, we would get a welcome break from the fractious politics created by politicians and institutions. Pastoral, common-sensical solutions will instead quietly begin to find their way into the statute books. The artificial conflict to which we have unfortunately become accustomed will be no more and we can then begin to solve problems.

Given people's widespread belief in popular consensus, it is no wonder they despise the existing structure of governmental institutions. All that these institutions—and the people filling them—do is obscure the will of the people by making it look as though there is a great deal of divisiveness afoot. Who then can condone debate and compromise among elected officials if these processes only give disproportionate weight to nefarious fringe elements that are intent upon subverting the desires of healthy, red-blooded Americans? Who then can condone inefficiency and slowness when we all agree on what needs to be done and politicians ought just to do it? Democratic processes merely get in the way. People react positively to the idea that we ought to run government like a business—it would be efficient, frugal, and quick to respond to problems. Of course, what people tend not to realize is that it would also be undemocratic.

Too many people do not understand political conflict: they have not been taught to deal with it; they have not come to realize it is a natural part of a culture such as ours. When they are confronted with it, they conclude it is an indication something is woefully amiss and in need of correction. They jump at any solution perceived to have the potential of reducing conflict; solutions such as giving authority over to potentially autocratic and hierarchical business-like arrangements or to mythically consensual ordinary people.

Our fear is that, if the people were actually given what they want, they might soon be even more disillusioned with the political system than ever. Suppose people *were* made to feel more represented than they are now; suppose authority *were* really pushed toward the common person. The first thing people would learn is that these changes will have done nothing to eliminate political conflict. The deep policy divisions that polls now reveal among the citizenry would be of more consequence since these very views would now be more determinative of public policy. Conflict would still be pervasive. Popular discontent would not have been ameliorated. Quite likely, people would quickly grow ever more cynical about the potential for reform to accomplish what they want it to accomplish.

Instead of allowing the people to strive for the impossible—an open and inclusive democracy that is devoid of conflict—we need to educate the people about the unrealistic nature of their desires. Instead of giving the people every reform for which they agitate, we need to get them to see where their wishes, if granted, are likely to lead them. The people pay lip service to democracy but that is the extent of it. They claim to love democracy more than life itself, but they only love the concept. They do not love the actual practice of democracy because it suggests differences, because it is ponderous, because it revolves around debate (bickering) and compromise (selling out) and divisions (gridlock).

Conclusion

We hasten to point out that we are not opposed to reforms. For what it is worth, we believe the United States polity could certainly benefit from selective modifications to current institutional arrangements. But we *are* opposed to the tendency of many ordinary people to try to enact reforms intended to weaken political institutions even though these same people evince no real plan describing where that power should be transferred. It is often assumed that the people are populists and that they therefore want power in their own hands. As we have indicated, they do not in actuality want power. They only want to know that they could have this power if they wanted it. They only want to know that this power is not being exercised by those who are in a position to use it to their own advantage. They only want decisions to be made nonconflictually. And they are willing to entertain a variety of possible structures (some far from democratic) if those reforms appear to offer hope of bringing about all these somewhat contradictory desires.

Altering representational arrangements should be considered. The current system can and must be improved. The campaign finance system is an embarrassment and the dispute over drawing oddly-shaped districts for the purpose of obtaining majority-minority districts lays bare the very real problems of single member districts. But we should not jump to enact all reforms simply because people think they want them. No one said that in a democracy the people would get to shape processes however they wanted. It is not inconsistent to have democratic governmental structures that are themselves rather impervious to popular sentiments for change in those procedures. What makes the system democratic is the ability of people to influence policy, not the ability of people to influence process.

This is fortunate because the people's ideas about process are fundamentally flawed. People (understandably) think well of the American public writ large, and people (understandably) dislike conflict, so people (nonsensically) assume the two cannot go together in spite of the impressive array of factual evidence indicating that conflict and the American people—indeed any free people, as Madison so eloquently related in *Federalist* 10—go hand in hand. As a result of their misconception, the people will undoubtedly be quite dissatisfied with the actual consequences of most attempts to expand representation via campaign finance reform, term limits, or proportional representation. There may be good reasons to enact such reforms, but, we submit, neither a public likely to be suddenly pleased with the post-reform political system nor a public that is somehow deserving of a direct voice in process reform is one of them.

DISCUSSION QUESTIONS

1. In one of the more provocative claims in their article, Hibbing and Theiss-Morse say, "The public does not desire direct democracy; it is not even clear that people desire democracy at all, although they are quite convinced they do." Do you agree? What evidence do they provide to support this claim?

2. If the public had a more complex understanding of the political process, what types of reforms would they favor?

3. Is it possible to have a political system that is too responsive?

NOTE

1. John R. Hibbing and Elizabeth Theiss-Morse. 1995. *Congress as Public Enemy: Public Attitudes Toward American Political Institutions.* Cambridge: Cambridge University Press.

Debating the Issues: Pork Barrel Politics

Each article in this chapter highlights the importance legislators place on serving their constituents. The strategy might work for reelection, but it may undermine the capacity of Congress to deal effectively with national problems and priorities. The debate over pork barrel politics captures this institutional tension, and illustrates the difficulties of defining "national" interests rather than parochial, or local interests.

Pork may take many forms. The most common legislative vehicle for distributing pork is the "earmark," which identifies specific, targeted spending, usually as part of a larger bill. Transportation bills and water projects are two of the traditional outlets for pork barrel spending, but in recent years even bills funding the war against terrorism, homeland security, and the war in Iraq have been full of pork. One bill that received a lot of negative attention was the airline bailout that sailed through Congress without much debate in the weeks after the terrorist attacks of 9/11. Similar charges of wasteful spending have been made concerning the rebuilding of Iraq as contractors received "no-bid" contracts for securing and restoring oil fields, among other lucrative projects.

The "Citizens Against Government Waste" (CAGW) is an interest group that identifies the pork barrel spending in the federal budget. The first selection is drawn from their *Pig Book* that they publish every year. CAGW defines the criteria that it uses to identify pork and attributes much of the problem of the ballooning federal deficit and debt to Congress's addiction to what it defines as wasteful spending. David Goldston discusses one type of pork that is a little closer to home—academic pork. These are government grants that go directly to the university, rather than being awarded through a competitive, peer-review process. Goldston argues that pork is not likely to go away, despite negative publicity and scandal, for two reasons. First, lobbying is so engrained in the system that it is a "structural change" that perpetuates the production of pork. Second, reforms that focus on disclosing pork is bound to fail because " 'transparency' is an odd way to limit earmarking. The whole point of earmarks is to get public credit for them—at least back home."

Where CAGW sees waste and abuse of the nation's resources, however, Jonathan Cohn views pork as the "glue" of legislating. If it takes a little pork for the home district or state to get important legislation through Congress, so be it. Cohn also questions the motives of budget reform groups that call for greater fiscal discipline in Congress; most of these groups, in his view, are not truly concerned over waste, but are simply against government spending in general. The policies they identify as pork, he argues, can have important national implications: military readiness, road improvements for an Olympic host city, or the development of new agricultural and food products. National interests can be served, in other words, by allowing local interests to take a dip into the pork barrel. Finally, Cohn argues that pork, even according to the critics' own definition, constitutes less than one percent of the overall federal budget.

24

"Party of One: Over a Pork Barrel"

DAVID GOLDSTON

Summer is appropriations season in Washington DC. Congress is beginning to write the spending bills for fiscal year 2008, with the hope of having the House of Representatives and the Senate each vote on their versions before the August recess. The process is likely to be even more politically charged than usual: the new Democratic leadership in Congress will be trying to show that the president stints on domestic priorities, while the president will aim to paint Congress as profligate.

No doubt the age-old battle over congressional "earmarks" will figure prominently in the effort to shape public perceptions of the budget. Indeed, this January the president called on Congress to halve the number of these earmarks, which provide money for a specific project or entity to help a constituent or friend.

Interestingly, Congress itself has been feeling a little queasy about earmarks of late. Although generally it sees earmarks as a fundamental prerogative, an egregious example occasionally makes headlines and cools the ardour for "pork-barrel spending." (The name alone points to the nineteenth-century origins of the practice.) The most recent case was the $200-million "bridge to nowhere"—a project, pushed through by then-chairman of the House Transportation and Infrastructure Committee Don Young (Republican, Alaska), to link a small city and an airport in Alaska that are now connected by ferry. Congress eventually rescinded the money—but not before the span gained mythical status as a symbol of wasteful spending.

Along with other scandals, that incident led the new Congress to change the rules for earmarking as one of its first orders of business. Every earmark must now be publicly listed, along with the name of the legislator who sought it.

But "transparency" is an odd way to limit earmarking. The whole point of earmarks is to get public credit for them—at least back home.

The new rules might act as a brake on the total spending on earmarks, or on particularly embarrassing projects, but they haven't reduced the demand for pork. Members of the House have requested more than 31,000 earmarks for fiscal 2008, probably a record number.

It is safe to assume that the number of earmarks requested in research and development (R&D) programmes has grown apace. The American Association for the Advancement of Science estimates that R&D earmarks grew from about $1.5 billion in fiscal 2002 to about $2.4 billion in fiscal 2006. (Most of the earmarks were for colleges and universities.) That's not a huge number in an R&D budget of more than $140 billion, but it can put a noticeable dent in funding for specific agencies, such as the National Oceanic and Atmospheric Administration, and programmes, such as the Department of Energy's hydrogen effort. Moreover, the rate of growth is a legitimate cause for concern.

Why has "academic pork" grown so rapidly? The most obvious reason is also the most often overlooked: more colleges and universities want it. Earmark requests almost always originate with the beneficiary, not with the representatives. As schools and faculty members have become more entrepreneurial, and as federal funding has come to be seen as a test of prestige, more schools have sought money—often to do the kinds of projects the government isn't otherwise funding or for programmes that aren't strong enough to win awards in traditional grant competitions. And once one school wins some federal cash from Congress, more want to play.

And there are ever more people in Washington DC who want to help them win. Lobbying is a growth industry, generally offering high salaries. It seems that no retiring congressman goes back home anymore; they all stay in Washington and lobby—looking for clients, including research institutions, and encouraging them to seek federal funds. This structural change—a burgeoning "private sector" that needs ever more lobbying clients to thrive—makes it hard to foresee any significant reversal in earmarking trends.

Finally, Congress has bought into the notion that R&D is the key to economic competitiveness. So helping colleges and universities get some federal money is more enticing than it was when institutions of higher education seemed to have little relevance to larger political concerns. And economic development has always been a justification for pork-barrel projects.

With all the factors pushing towards growth in academic pork, the real surprise is that there isn't even more of it. Fortunately, academic pork is still viewed as somewhat suspect, especially among the congressmen who most closely follow science issues. Pork is seen as a way to salve the injustices and inadequacies in the standard grant-making process, not as a sign that the overall system is in need of surgery. Notably, what are arguably the two most prestigious R&D agencies, the National Science Foundation (NSF) and the National Institutes of Health, have never been earmarked—perhaps both an effect and cause of their prestige. (Congress does sometimes push specific large construction projects at the NSF, but those are first proposed by the agency, not Congress, and Congress does not choose where to locate them.)

That doesn't mean that there hasn't been pressure to earmark the two agencies, especially from those who see peer review as a clubby system that benefits only the "haves." In a happy coincidence, some of the "have nots," often schools from the south and Rocky Mountain west, are represented by conservatives who see any form of earmarking as a kind of budgetary incontinence.

Also, Congress has tried to divert some of the earmarking pressure by setting aside competitive funds for institutions in states that do not get a large share of federal R&D funds. The programme began at the NSF decades ago, and Congress has gradually replicated it in other agencies.

So for now, academic earmarks will probably continue to grow, but not without limit. Congress is likely to remain nervous through this political cycle that too much pork will smear it with a reputation for fiscal irresponsibility. And when it comes to academic grant making, Congress still tends to believe, to paraphrase Winston Churchill, that peer review is the worst system except for all the others.

25

"Roll Out the Barrel:
The Case Against the Case Against Pork"

JONATHAN COHN

On most days, the lobby of the U.S. Chamber of Commerce's Washington, D.C., headquarters has a certain rarefied air. But on this Tuesday morning it is thick with the smell of greasy, grilled bacon. The aroma is appropriate, since the breakfast speaker is Republican Representative Bud Shuster of Pennsylvania, chairman of the House Transportation Committee and, his critics say, one of the most shameless promulgators of pork barrel spending in all of Congress. The odor seems even more fitting given that the topic of Shuster's address is the Building Efficient Surface Transportation and Equity Act, the six-year, $217 billion highway-spending package about to pass Congress—and, according to these same critics, the single biggest hunk of pork Washington has seen in a decade.

The critics, of course, are absolutely right. The House version of BESTEA, which hit the floor this week, contains at least $18 billion in so-called "demonstration" and "high-priority" projects. Those are the congressional euphemisms for pork—public works programs of dubious merit, specific to one congressional district, designed to curry favor with its voters. And Shuster's record for bringing home the bacon is indeed legendary. BESTEA's predecessor, which passed in 1991, included $287 million for 13 projects in Shuster's central Pennsylvania district. Today, visitors can see these and other shrines to his legislative clout by driving along the newly built Interstate 99, a shimmering stretch of asphalt the state has officially christened the Bud Shuster Highway.

None of this much bothers the suits at the Chamber of Commerce, who savor every line of Shuster's pitch as if it were just so much more fat-soaked sausage from the buffet table. Money for roads—whether in Shuster's district or anybody else's—means more ways to transport goods and more work for construction companies. But, outside the friendly confines of groups like this, a relentless chorus of high-minded watchdog groups and puritanical public officials complains that pork barrel spending wastes government money. These critics also protest the way pork becomes law in the first place, as last-minute amendments designed to bypass the hearings and debate bills normally require.

To be sure, these arguments are not exactly novel. The very term "pork barrel" is a pre–Civil War term, derived from what was then a readily understandable (but, to modern ears, rather objectionable) analogy between congressmen gobbling up appropriations and slaves grabbing at salt pork distributed from giant barrels. "By the 1870s," William Safire writes in his *Political Dictionary*, "congressmen were regularly referring to 'pork,' and the word became part of the U.S. political lexicon." Criticizing pork, meanwhile, is just as venerable a tradition. Virtually every president from Abraham Lincoln to Ronald Reagan has promised to eliminate pork from the federal budget, and so have most congressmen, much to the satisfaction of muckraking journalists and similarly high-minded voters.

But rarely have the politicians actually meant it, and even more rarely have they succeeded. Until now. Thanks to an endless parade of media exposés on government waste, and a prevailing political consensus in favor of balanced budgets, pork critics have been gaining momentum. In 1994, anti-pork fervor nearly killed President Clinton's crime bill; in 1995, the same sentiment lay behind enactment of the line-item veto, something budget-balancers had sought in vain for more than a decade. A few years ago, a handful of anti-pork legislators took to calling themselves "pork-busters." Thanks to their vigilance, says the nonprofit group Citizens Against Government Waste, the amount of pork in the budget declined by about nine percent in 1998.

The influence of pork-busters reached a new peak in 1997, when they helped defeat a preliminary attempt at BESTEA. They probably won't be able to duplicate the feat this year—Shuster has nearly 400 votes behind his new pork-laden bill, which House Budget Chairman John Kasich has called an "abomination." But pork-busters won a major public relations victory last week when four House Republicans turned on Shuster and accused him of trying to buy them off with pet projects. "I told them my vote was not for sale," said Steve Largent of Oklahoma. "Shuster bought just about everyone," David Hobson of Ohio told *The Washington Post*. Three weeks ago, Republican Senator John McCain of Arizona, Capitol Hill's most determined pork-buster, won passage of an amendment that could cut at least some of the bill's pork. President Clinton has since joined the chorus, saying he too deplores the parochial waste Shuster and his cronies added to the measure.

In the popular telling, episodes like these represent epic struggles of good versus evil—of principled fiscal discipline versus craven political self-interest—with the nation's economic health and public faith in government at stake. But this narrative, related time and again by purveyors of elite wisdom and then repeated mindlessly by everyday citizens, has it exactly backward. The pork-busters are more anti-government than anti-waste. As for pork-barrel spending, it's good for American citizens and American democracy as well. Instead of criticizing it, we should be celebrating it, in all of its gluttonous glory.

Nearly a week has passed since Shuster made his appearance before the Chamber of Commerce, and now it is the pork-busters' turn to be making headlines. In what has become an annual rite of the budget process, Citizens Against Government Waste is staging a press conference near Capitol Hill to release its compilation of pork in the 1997 federal budget—a 40-page, pink-covered booklet it calls the *Pig Book*. (Actually, the pocket-sized, 40-page version is just a summary of the unabridged *Pig Book*, which weighs in at a hefty 170 pages, in single-sided, legal-sized computer printouts.)

CAGW has been fighting this fight for more than a decade, and its steady stream of propaganda, reports, and testimony is in no small part responsible for pork-busting's Beltway resonance. Republican Representative Christopher Cox calls CAGW "the premier waste-fighting organization in America"; the 1995–1996 Congress sought CAGW testimony 20 times. The interest in today's press conference—attended by more than 60 reporters and a dozen television crews—is testimony to the group's high esteem among the Washington press corps, although it doesn't hurt that CAGW has also provided the TV crews with a good photo opportunity.

Like many press conferences in this city, this one features several members of Congress, including McCain and Democratic Senator Russell Feingold. Unlike many press conferences in this city, this one also features a man dressed in a bright pink pig's suit, rubber pig masks free for the media to take, plus a live, charcoal-gray potbellied pig named Porky. For the duration of the event, Porky does little except scarf down some vegetable shreds. But the beast's mere presence gets a few laughs, which is more than can be said for the puns that CAGW's president, Tom Schatz, makes as he rattles off the recipients of this year's "Oinker Awards."

Senator Daniel Inouye of Hawaii secured $127,000 in funding for research on edible seaweed; for this and other appropriations, Schatz says, Inouye (who is of Japanese ancestry) wins "The Sushi Slush Fund Award." Senator Ted Stevens of Alaska sponsored $100,000 for a project called Ship Creek, so he gets "The Up Ship's Creek Award." (Stevens is a double winner: for his other pork, totaling some $477 million since 1991, CAGW also presents him with "The Half Baked Alaska Award.") The Pentagon budget included $3 million for an observatory in South America: "It's supposed to peer back millions of years in time," Schatz says, his deadpan poker face now giving way to a smarmy, half-cocked smile. "Maybe they're looking for a balanced budget." This dubious-sounding project Schatz dubs "The Black Hole Award." And on. And on.

You might think cornball humor like this would earn CAGW the disdain of the famously cynical Washington press corps. But, when Schatz is done, and the question-and-answer period begins, the reporters display barely any skepticism. Instead, that evening, and during the following days, they will heap gobs of attention on the group. They don't flatter or endorse the organization per se, but the coverage shares a common assumption that the group's findings are evidence of political malfeasance. CNN, for example, will use the *Pig Book*'s release as a peg for stories bemoaning the persistence of pork in the federal budget. A story out of Knight Ridder's Washington bureau, which will run in nearly a dozen of the chain's newspapers, basically recapitulates the report. And all this comes on the heels of a front-page *Wall Street Journal* feature—sparked by a similar report from the Tax Foundation—highlighting the profligate pork barreling of the Senate majority leader, Trent Lott of Mississippi. Its headline: "MISSISSIPPI'S SENATORS CONTINUE A TRADITION: GETTING FEDERAL MONEY."

This is typical. Normally jaded Washingtonians, journalists especially, tend to view pork-busters not as ideologues but as politically disinterested watchdogs. Television producers, in particular, regularly summon CAGW experts to validate stories for such waste-focused segments as NBC's "The Fleecing of America" and ABC's "Your Money, Your Choice." While this image has a basis in reality—CAGW truly goes after pork-barreling Republicans with the same fervor it pursues Democrats—it is also a product of the organization's concerted attempt to wrap itself in the flag of nonpartisanship. "No matter how you slice it, pork is always on the menu in the halls of Congress," Schatz said at the press conference. "Some members of Congress simply couldn't resist the lure of easy money and putting partisan political interests over the best interest of taxpayers."

But it's not as if the pork-busters have no partisan or ideological agenda of their own. Some, like the Cato Institute, are explicit about their anti-government predisposition. CAGW is a little more cagey, but it remains true to the spirit of its past chairman, perennial right-wing Republican candidate Alan Keyes, as well as its cofounder, J. Peter Grace, who headed President Reagan's 1984 commission on government waste and whose antipathy to government in general was widely known. "The government is the worst bunch of stupid jerks you've ever run into in your life," he said once at a CAGW fund-raising dinner. "These people just want to spend money, money, money all the time."

That is, of course, a forgivable overstatement of a plausible argument. But it is also an overtly ideological one, and it calls into question the group's reliability when it comes to making delicate distinctions about what is truly wasteful. After all, CAGW is not just against pork, but against much of what the mainstream conservative movement considers bad or overly intrusive public policy—which encompasses an awful lot. In 1995, CAGW was not bashful about embracing the Contract With America, whose expansive definition of waste included many regulatory programs Americans deem quite worthwhile. "Taxpayers . . . demonstrated in two consecutive elections of a Republican Congress that the Washington establishment at its peril ignores the taxpayers' voice," the group's annual report boasts. "CAGW stood shoulder to shoulder with the reformers and enjoyed a sense of accomplishment at this burst of energy from revitalized taxpayers." CAGW's contributor list, not surprisingly, reads like a who's who of conservative interests, from Philip Morris Companies Inc. to the Columbia/HCA Healthcare Foundation Inc.

To be sure, CAGW is not the only Beltway organization whose partisan allegiances belie its nonprofit, nonpartisan status. At least a dozen other groups on both the left and the right do the exact same thing. Anyway, the fact that an argument may be ideologically motivated hardly means it's wrong.

But that doesn't mean it's right, either. Listen closely the next time some smug good-government type starts criticizing pork: it's an awful lot of fuss over what is, in fact, a very small amount of money. In the *Pig Book*, for example, CAGW claims last year's budget included pork worth about $13.2 billion—or, as a pork-buster would say, "$13.2 billion!" Yes, you could feed quite a few hungry people with that much money, or you could give a bigger tax cut. But it's less than one percent of the federal budget.

And it's not even clear that all of the $13.2 billion of waste is really, well, waste. A good chunk of CAGW's $13.2 billion in pork comes from a few dozen big-ticket items, costing tens of millions of dollars each, scattered through various appropriations measures, particularly the Pentagon's. Among the programs: research of a space-based laser ($90 million), transportation improvements in Utah ($14 million), and military construction in Montana ($32 million).

But it's hardly self-evident that these all constitute waste, as the pork-busters suggest. At least some national security experts believe the space-based laser is a necessary defense against rogue nations that might get their hands on nuclear missiles. A lot of that Utah money is to help Salt Lake City prepare for Olympic traffic. And, if you've ever been to Montana, you know that there are a lot of military bases scattered across that vast state—which means a lot of soldiers who need buildings in which to live, eat, and work. In other words, all of these serve some credible purpose.

The wastefulness of the smaller items is similarly open to interpretation. Remember Senator Inouye's "Sushi Slush Fund Award"— the $127,000 for research on edible seaweed in Hawaii? It turns out that aquaculture is an emerging industry in Hawaii and that edible seaweed—known locally as "limu," "ogo," or "sea sprouts"—is "rich in complex carbohydrates and protein and low in calories," according to the *Honolulu Advertiser.* "It's a good source of vitamin A, calcium, and potassium, too."

Yes, the federal government is paying $3 million for a telescope in South America. But it has to, because the telescope is part of a U.S. effort to explore the southern hemisphere sky—which, of course, is only visible from the southern hemisphere. Although the telescope will be located in Chile, it will be operated remotely from the University of North Carolina at Chapel Hill. "When completed, the telescope will hold tremendous promise for scientists and the federal government," the university chancellor said when Republican Senator Lauch Faircloth of North Carolina announced the appropriation. "We at the university also have high hopes for what the project will mean for the North Carolina economy as well as for students of all ages—on this campus, across our state, and beyond."

And Senator Stevens's "Up Ship's Creek Award"? The Ship Creek water project was part of a bill authorizing studies of environmental cleanup across the country. Some $100,000 went to the U.S. Army Corps of Engineers to assess the impact of development on Ship Creek, which is Anchorage's primary source of freshwater. Ironically, according to the Corps of Engineers, the study is exploring not only what kind of environmental precautions are necessary, but whether the federal government really has to pay for them, and whether local private entities might be convinced to foot part of the bill. In other words, one objective of the Ship Creek appropriation was to reduce government waste.

You could argue, as pork-busters do, that, while projects like these may serve some positive function in society—perhaps even deserving of government money—they should not be on the federal dime. Let the Hawaiians pay for their own calcium-rich dinners! Let Alaskans foot the bill for their own water study! But there's a respectable argument that sometimes parochial needs are in fact a legitimate federal interest, particularly when it involves things like pollution and commerce that cross state lines.

Certainly, that's the way a lot of people outside of Washington understand it. Last month, while the national media was busy flogging unthrifty lawmakers, several local newspapers rose to their defense. "We elect people to Congress not only to see to the nation's defense and keep the currency sound but also to bring home some pork," editorialized *The Fort Worth Star-Telegram.* "Pork can mean local jobs, local beautification, local pride, etc." The *Dayton Daily News* defended one project, a museum on the history of flight, that appeared on CAGW's hit list: "It is at the heart of a community effort that has been painstakingly nurtured for years by all manner of Daytonians. It combines the legitimate national purpose of recognizing the history of flight with the top-priority local purpose of getting Dayton recognized as a center of the history of flight." Other papers were more critical: they wanted to know why their congressmen hadn't brought home *more* bacon. "Alaskans aren't going to sit still for being No. 2 for long," *Anchorage Daily News* columnist Mike Doogan wrote in a spirited defense of pork. "We need the money. And we have our pride."

This is not to say that all or even most of what gets called pork is defensible on its own terms. (Did Bedford County, Pennsylvania, which happens to be smack in the middle of Shuster's rural district, really need a new airport when there were two others nearby?) Nor is it to say that the local interest in getting federal money should always trump the national interest in balancing the budget and distributing the federal largesse fairly. (Couldn't the state of Pennsylvania have paid for the Bedford County airport instead?) Nor is it even to say that local interests defending pork aren't being incredibly hypocritical—no one thinks an appropriation is pork when it's his.

No, the point is simply that you can't call something waste just because it makes a clever pun. "From what we can tell," says John Raffetto, communications director for the Senate Transportation Committee, "CAGW does no research to determine what purpose the project serves other than to flip through the pages of the bill and find projects that sound funny. If it sounds funny, that's pork. I have not heard from any member's office that has told me they've received a call from CAGW to ask what purpose that project has served."

Pork-busters concede they lack the time or resources to investigate items thoroughly. "Some may be worthy of consideration," says CAGW media director Jim Campi. "Our concern is that, if the projects went through the process the way they were supposed to, there would be a [better] opportunity to judge them on their merits."

This is the same argument that most animates McCain, Feingold, and other pork-busting lawmakers. But what constitutes a fair appropriations process? CAGW would have everyone believe that a project is pork if it is "not requested by the president" or if it "greatly exceeds the president's budget request or the previous year's funding." Huh? The whole point of the appropriations process is to give Congress a chance to make independent judgments about spending priorities. Particularly when Republicans control one branch of government and Democrats the other—as is the case today—differences will exist. The Republican Congress used to routinely declare the president's budget "dead on arrival." Did this mean the entire congressional budget was pork?

Two other criteria for defining pork are equally shaky. Invoking the familiar pork-busting wisdom, CAGW says a program is pork if it was "not specifically authorized"—meaning it wasn't in the original budget which contains general spending limits, but rather added on as part of the subsequent appropriations process, in which money is specifically allocated to each item. But the rationale for a separate budget and appropriations process is to allow Congress (and, for that matter, the president) an opportunity to change their minds about smaller items, as long as they stay within the broad guidelines of the budget agreement. CAGW also damns any projects "requested by only one chamber of Congress." But, just as Congress can disagree with the president over a project's merit, so the House can disagree with the Senate—that's the reason the architects of the Constitution created two houses in the first place. (Also, keep in mind that one reason the Senate doesn't propose as much pork is that senators—wary of getting stung in the national press for lacking frugality—will often wait to see how much pork the House passes. That way, they end up with the best of both worlds: they can quietly tell supporters that they backed the measure without ever incurring the wrath of pork-busting watchdogs.)

Make no mistake, though: Many pork-barrellers are trying to evade the scrutiny bills get when they move through the normal appropriations process. They stick in small bits of pork after hearings end because they know that nobody is going to vote against a multibillion-dollar bill just because it has a few million dollars of pork tucked in. And they can do so safe in the knowledge that, because there's very little in the way of a paper trail, they will not suffer any public consequences—unless, of course, a watchdog group or enthusiastic reporter manages to find out.

Pork-busters call this strategy sleazy, and it is. But remember, the whole point of our Constitution is to harness mankind's corrupt tendencies and channel them in constructive directions. In an oft-quoted passage of *The Federalist Number 51*, James Madison wrote, "if men were angels, no government would be necessary," and "the private interest of every individual may be a sentinel over the public rights." The Founders believed that sometimes local interests should trump national interests because they recognized it was a way to keep federal power in check. It's true this process lends itself to a skewed distribution of benefits, with disproportionate shares going to powerful lawmakers. But, again, pork is such a small portion of the budget that "equalizing" its distribution would mean only modest funding changes here and there.

Which brings us to the final defense of pork, one Madison would certainly endorse. Even if every single pork-barrel project really were a complete waste of federal money, pork still represents a very cheap way to keep our sputtering legislative process from grinding to a halt. In effect, pork is like putting oil in your car engine: it lubricates the parts and keeps friction to a minimum. This is particularly true when you are talking about controversial measures. "Buying off potential coalition members with spending programs they favor is exactly what the Founders not only expected, but practiced," political scientist James Q. Wilson has argued. He has also written: "If you agree with Madison, you believe in pork."

Think of the NAFTA battle in 1993. Contentious to the bitter end, the fate of the agreement ultimately fell on the shoulders of a handful of congressmen, all of whom privately supported it but feared the political backlash if they voted for it. Clinton gave each of them a little pork— for example, a development bank in border states that ostensibly would provide start-up money for entrepreneurs who had lost jobs because of NAFTA. The bank was just another way to pump some federal money into these districts, but that was the whole point. Thanks to that money, NAFTA became politically viable; these lawmakers could tell their constituents, plausibly and truthfully, that there was something in it for their districts.

To take a more current example, just look at BESTEA. U.S. transportation infrastructure is famously inadequate; the Department of Transportation says unsafe roads cause 30 percent of all traffic fatalities. But, when fiscal conservatives questioned the pork in the original BESTEA last year, the measure failed, forcing Congress to pass an emergency extension. This year, a more permanent, six-year version will likely pass, largely because the appearance of a budget surplus has tipped the scales just enough so that the pork seems tolerable. As John W. Ellwood and Eric M. Patashnik wrote in *The Public Interest* several years ago (in what was the best defense of pork in recent memory): "Favoring legislators with small gifts for their districts in order to achieve great things for the nation is an act not of sin but of statesmanship."

Last week, of course, BESTEA's high pork content had fiscal conservatives downright apoplectic. "Frankly, this bill really is a hog," Kasich said. "It is way over the top." But, without the pork, there might be no highway bill at all. As one highway lobbyist told *National Journal* last year, "The projects are the glue that's going to hold the damn thing together." A former transportation official said: "I've always taken the point of view that every business has some overhead. If that's what it costs to get a significant or a good highway bill, it's worth the price." Kasich would surely be aghast at such logic, but someday he and other fiscal conservatives might find it useful for their own purposes. Remember, they are the ones who say that balancing the budget will likely be impossible without severe and politically risky reforms of entitlements like Medicare. When the time comes to make those tough choices—and they need to pry a few extra votes from the opposition—you can bet they will gladly trade a little pork for *their* greater cause. They might feel guilty about it, but they shouldn't. Pork is good. Pork is virtuous. Pork is the American way.

26

"2007 Pig Book Summary"

CITIZENS AGAINST GOVERNMENT WASTE

Introduction

According to the Chinese calendar, 2007 is the Year of the Pig. Fortunately for American taxpayers, it will be a smaller pig than usual. The 2007 Congressional Pig Book has not been this little since 1999, as only two of the 11 appropriations bills were enacted by Congress and the remaining nine were subject to a moratorium on earmarks. There are no indoor rainforests, National Peanut Festivals, mariachi music grants, or teapot museums to be found.

This year's Pig Book breaks a run of seven consecutive years of record dollar amounts of pork, culminating in $29 billion in the 2006 Congressional Pig Book. This lesser barrel of pork can be attributed to the efforts of Senators Tom Coburn (R-Okla.), Jim DeMint (R-S.C.), and Jeff Sessions (R-Ala.), who prevented the enactment of nine appropriations bills in December, 2006, and the subsequent moratorium on earmarks announced and enforced by the House and Senate Appropriations Committee Chairmen David Obey (D-Wis.) and Robert Byrd (D-W. Va.) in H. J. Res. 20, the bill that funds the government for the remainder of fiscal 2007.

There is still enough pork to cause concern for taxpayers, as 2,658 projects were stuffed into the Defense and Homeland Security Appropriations Acts, at a cost of $13.2 billion. Pork identified in the Pig Book since 1991 totals $252 billion. Defense had 2,618 projects, or 204 less than in 2006, at a cost of $10.8 billion, or 28 percent less than the $14.9 billion in 2006. For homeland security, the totals were $2.4 billion, or 10 percent less than the $2.7 billion in 2006, and 40 projects, or five more than in 2006.

While only two bills were enacted, the states of Alaska and Hawaii, which have been the top two states in pork per capita every year but one since 2000, were served more then their fair share of bacon by Senators Ted Stevens (R-Alaska) and Daniel Inouye (D-Hawaii). In the defense appropriations bill alone, Alaska received $209,900,000, a 127 percent increase over the total of $92,425,000 in 2006.

Based on historical figures, the enactment of H. J. Res. 20 eliminated more than 7,000 earmarks and saved between $12–$15 billion in pork-barrel spending. Unfortunately, in this Year of the Pig, taxpayers are not getting a pork dividend. Instead, Congress took the savings and spent it on other programs.

Despite the moratorium on earmarks, the siren's song of pork is too tempting for some members of Congress, who have called federal agencies to pressure them to divert money to pet projects that were included in committee reports. The Bush Administration told agencies to ignore such oral communications.

While taxpayers should celebrate a reduction in the number and cost of pork-barrel projects, there is still much work that needs to be done to ensure that members of Congress do not return to their piggish ways in the future.

The 24 projects, totaling $2.4 billion, in this year's Congressional Pig Book Summary symbolize the most egregious and blatant examples of pork.

As in previous years, all of the items in the Congressional Pig Book Summary meet at least one of CAGW's seven criteria, but most satisfy at least two:

- Requested by only one chamber of Congress;
- Not specifically authorized;
- Not competitively awarded;
- Not requested by the President;
- Greatly exceeds the President's budget request or the previous year's funding;
- Not the subject of congressional hearings; or
- Serves only a local or special interest.

I. Defense

Efficient and effective operation of the Department of Defense (DOD) is critical to ensuring the security of our nation and the safety of our troops. While American military forces fight for peace and democracy in the Middle East, Pentagon officials struggle to create a lean, mean, war-fighting machine; the good news is that appropriators are winning fewer battles over defense priorities. From fiscal 2006 to fiscal 2007, the number of porkbarrel projects decreased by 7 percent from 2,822 to 2,618, while the total cost went down 28 percent, from $14.9 billion to $10.8 billion.

$1,190,000,000 for full funding of 20 F-22A fighter jets; this barrel of pork is so big that Congress will not even spend it all in one year. The bill funds 20 F-22s per year until 2009. The F-22 was originally designed as an air superiority fighter for use against the Soviet Air Force. Before Congress put the ink on the check, the Government Accountability Office (GAO) sent a 13-page letter on June 20, 2006 to then-House Defense Appropriations Subcommittee Chairman C.W. (Bill) Young urging Congress to stop funding this program due to its high cost and the fact that the aircraft is out of date. The GAO said, "DOD has not demonstrated the need or value for making further investments in the F-22A program." The GAO also noted that the F-22s "are not sufficient to be effective in the current and future national security environment." There are 22 test F-35 aircrafts that are more modern, effective, and cheaper. In 2003, *Popular Science* reported the F-22 had a price tag of $120 million each while the F-35 cost $35 million. In June 2006, the GAO report raised the F-22's numbers, concluding that the multi-year contract would drive per-plane costs up to $183 million from $166 million. The F-35 made its maiden flight in December 2006. Apparently, the F-22 will be stopped only when pigs can fly.

$319,655,000 for projects in the state of then-Senate Defense Appropriations Subcommittee Ranking Member Daniel Inouye (D-Hawaii), including: $20,000,000 for the Army Compatible Use Buffer Program (ACUB); $11,500,000 to fund Pan-STARRS to develop a large aperture telescope with the University of Hawaii to prevent space objects from colliding with Earth; $5,600,000 for the Center of Excellence for Research in Ocean Sciences; $4,500,000 for chitosan bandage component which utilizes natural compounds found in shrimp heads; and $1,000,000 for a wave power electric generating system. The ACUB works on "conservation planning at the ecosystem level to ensure that greater benefits are realized towards species and habitat recovery." The Army's objectives with this program include: "Reduce training restrictions, meet Endangered Species Act recovery responsibilities, prevent development along installation boundaries, and prevent future threatened and endangered species listings." Thanks to programs like ACUB, the ecosystem for oinkers is thriving in Hawaii.

$209,900,000 added for projects in the state of then-Senate Appropriations Committee Chairman Ted Stevens (R-Alaska), an increase of 127 percent over the $92,425,000 for Alaska in the fiscal 2006 defense bill, including: $59,100,000 for upgrades to the Pacific Alaskan Range Complex in Red Flag; $4,000,000 for the Northern Line Extension; and $3,200,000 for HAARP (High Frequency Active Auroral Research Program), which has received $109.1 million in pork since 1995. The Northern Line Extension will provide a direct route from North Pole (pop. 1,778 in 2005) to Delta Junction (pop. 840 in 2000), which is a whopping 82.1 mile drive on one highway between the two villages according to MapQuest. The

Alaska Railroad Corporation said, "The proposed rail line would provide freight and potentially passenger rail services serving commercial interests and communities in or near the project corridor."

$102,000,000 for projects in the state of Senate appropriator Barbara Mikulski (D-Md.) and the district of House appropriator Steny Hoyer (D-Md.), including: $9,500,000 for the Extended ColdWeather Clothing System; $5,000,000 for the Energetics Technology Center; $3,250,000 for the Rotorcraft Survivability Assessment Facility; $2,500,000 for PEM fuel cell tactical generators; $2,000,000 for Life Shield® blast resistant panels, developed by Life Shield Engineered Systems in Maryland; and $1,000,000 for the SureTrak Program.

$72,720,000 added for projects in Nevada by then-Minority Leader Harry Reid (D-Nev.), including: $7,000,000 for the SA-90 airship persistent surveillance program; $3,750,000 for a counter-drug program for the Nevada National Guard; $3,000,000 for large aircraft infrared countermeasures; $1,950,000 for heat dissipation for electronic systems; and $1,300,000 for the study of the structural reliability of smart munitions and lightweight structures at the University of Nevada-Las Vegas. Sen. Reid bragged about securing millions of dollars for money-hungry programs by announcing funding for "Nevada defense projects including operating expenses at Nevada military bases, research projects at state universities, and grants to private companies developing high-tech defense systems in Nevada." This occurred before the time when now-Majority Leader Reid attempted to block expanded earmark reform in the Senate in January 2007, and was embarrassingly defeated when a few Democrats and most Republicans stood up against him.

$59,000,000 for medical research projects ranging from cancer to diabetes to gynecological disease. As important as this research may be, there is no mention as to why these programs should receive money from the Department of Defense. One program which weighs heavily on taxpayers in this category is $1.35 million for the "Obesity in the Military Research Program."

$35,000,000 for Impact Aid, which is described by the website of the Military Impacted Schools Association as "the federal government paying its 'tax bill' to local school districts as a result of the presence of a military installation." The funding included $5,000,000 for Impact Aid for children with disabilities. It is the taxpayers who are impacted by this aid.

$18,300,000 added in the Senate for defense educational programs. Program funding includes $2,000,000 for "Mathematics and Technology Teachers Development" and "Cyber Curriculum for the Education of Children in the Military;" $1,100,000 for the "Reach Out and Read Early Literacy Program;" and $1,000,000 for the "Parents as Teachers Program," which is "a parent education and early childhood development program serving parents throughout pregnancy until their child enters kindergarten."

$8,000,000 added by the Senate for "special assistance to local education agencies." This is a part of the educational arm of the Department of Defense also known as DOD Dependents Education.

$5,500,000 added by the House for the Gallo Center. According to its website, "The Ernest Gallo Clinic and Research Center (EGCRC) at the University of California, San Francisco (USCF) was established in 1980 to study basic neuroscience and the effects of alcohol and drug abuse on the brain." There is no mention of any defense-related research. Apparently, they will serve no pork before its time.

$5,300,000 to study marine mammals, such as whales. The House added $3,500,000 for a program increase and a "marine mammal hearing and echolocation research" program. Scientific Solutions, based in Nashua, N.H., will receive $1,800,000 to fund an "Integrated Marine Mammal Monitoring and Protection system." The Navy claims to be the "world leader in marine mammal research, spending nearly $10 million per year on research to understand how marine mammals hear and how they are affected by sound."

$5,000,000 added in the House for alcohol breath testers. According to the House fiscal 2006 Department of Defense Appropriations Report, "The impact of excessive alcohol use and driving under the influence continues as a leading cause of ground accidents, injury, death, and physical damage across the Services." Out of the $5 million total, $4,500,000 will directly go toward the procurement of Breathscan® alcohol testers. They are already in use at Fort Bliss, Texas as the Army Surgeon General issued individual breathalyzers before the start of the 2006 holiday season.

$3,335,000 added by Sen. John Thune (R-S.D.) for the South Dakota School of Mines and Technology, home of the "Hard Rockers" football team. The school received $2,000,000 for future affordable multi-utility materials for the Army Future Combat System; $500,000 for improvised explosive device simulation in different soils; $300,000 for a control system for laser powder deposition; $285,000 for shielding rocket payloads; and $250,000 for transparent nanocomposite armor. According to a July 12, 2006 press release, the School of Mines has received more than $70 million in congressional appropriations for projects and research since 2001.

$1,650,000 added by Senate appropriator Patty Murray (D-Wash.) to improve the shelf life of vegetables. According to the senator's July 2006 press release, "This project will help our troops in the field get fresh tomatoes . . ." The funding would help "establish and evaluate variant populations of bell pepper, cantaloupe and strawberry." The money is being directed toward Arcadia Biosciences, a company based in Seattle. In all, Sen. Murray claims to have "secured $55 million in federal defense work for Washington state companies in the Fiscal Year 2007 Defense Appropriations bill." On Capitol Hill, Sen. Murray has already extended the shelf life of her own pork products.

$1,000,000 added in the House for the Allen Telescope Array in Mountain View, Calif. This "alien" project is part of SETI (Search for Extraterrestrial Intelligence). SETI describes the telescope as "dedicated to astronomical and simultaneous search for extra-terrestrial intelligence observations." No word on how it will help defend the world against an alien invasion.

$1,000,000 secured by now-Speaker of the House Nancy Pelosi (D-Calif.) to fund the Military Intelligence Service Historic Learning Center. In a September 2006 press release announcing her pork victory, she said the center will serve as an "education center and project to preserve the site of the U.S. Army's first language school established in 1941."

II. Homeland Security

While only two appropriations acts were passed, appropriators squeezed all the pork they could into them. The fiscal 2007 Homeland Security Appropriations Act proved yet again that while the threat of terrorism and natural disasters still exist, so too does Congress's penchant for pork. The number of projects in the bill increased by 14 percent from 35 in fiscal 2006 to 40 in fiscal 2007, while spending decreased 10 percent from $2.7 billion to $2.4 billion, after a 57 percent increase between fiscal 2005 and 2006.

$225,000,000 for port security grants, a 29 percent increase from last year's total. Pork-barrel funding for this program has more than doubled in two years. Established in 2002, the grants are an opportunity for private companies and port authorities to apply for federal financing to improve security at ports. An audit performed by the inspector general of the Department of Homeland Security (DHS) in 2005 revealed that some of the grants "appeared to be for a purpose other than security against an act of terrorism." According to the audit, 95 percent of all international commerce enters the United States through the nation's 360 ports, but nearly 80 percent comes through only 10 ports. While Congress intended the grants to protect ports that have the highest volume of cargo, handle hazardous material, or are located near military facilities, the audit found DHS was distributing the funds in a broad, unfocused manner. As a result, the department "had no assurance that the program is protecting the nation's most critical and vulnerable port infrastructure and assets." Although major ports received funding, so too did smaller ones, including ports in Ludington, Michigan; Martha's Vineyard, Massachusetts; and six located in Arkansas, none of which appeared to meet grant eligibility requirements, according to the audit.

$78,693,000 for a replacement patrol boat to be used until the Fast Response Cutter (FRC) program becomes operational in 2018. The FRC is part of Deepwater, which is run by a joint venture between Northrop

Grumman and Lockheed Martin called Integrated Coast Guard Systems. Deepwater is the Coast Guard's 20-year, $24 billion plan to modernize its fleet, and has come under fire for significant design flaws that will likely increase maintenance costs, limit ships' ability to travel far from port, and ultimately shorten their useful life. Furthermore, DHS Inspector General Richard Skinner stated in a January, 2007 report on Deepwater and its cornerstone ship, the National Security Cutter (NSC), that the Coast Guard had relinquished its oversight authority to contractors. The report's executive summary stated: "The NSC, as designed and constructed, will not meet performance specifications described in the original Deepwater contract. Specifically, due to design deficiencies, the NSC's structure provides insufficient fatigue strength . . . [which will] increase the cutter's maintenance costs and reduce its service life." All in all, Deepwater has proven to be a boondoggle a fact made worse by the critical role it plays in our national security.

$12,000,000 for intercity bus security grants for the improvement of ticket identification, installation of driver shields, enhancement of emergency communications, upgrading facility security, and further implementation of passenger screening. The Intercity Bus Security Grant Program is one of five grant programs that make up the DHS fiscal 2007 Infrastructure Protection Program, designed to offset the cost of protecting the nation's critical infrastructure. For the third year in a row, this program shows up in the Pig Book. Money continues to be directed to profitable, private companies that should be able to fund these measures themselves.

$12,000,000 added by the House for the Rural Domestic Preparedness Consortium in the district of then-House Homeland Security Appropriations Subcommittee Chairman Harold Rogers (R-Ky.). This program is supposed to help protect citizens living in rural areas by training rural emergency responder teams. The funding is to be distributed to an assortment of universities that are not yet known. Meanwhile, funding for the program has increased by 20 percent from last year's level.

$12,000,000 for trucking security grants to continue the Highway-Watch Program, designed to enhance security on the nation's highways. According to the Department of Justice Office of Justice Programs website, the HighwayWatch Program, which is managed by the American Trucking Association, "recruits and trains highway professionals to identify and report security and safety situations on the nation's roads." What happened to the good old-fashioned Highway Patrol? $4,500,000 added in conference for the Secure Border Coordination Office, designed to implement the integration of border security and immigration enforcement. The office is also charged with implementing the Secure Border Initiative (SBInet), a multi-year plan to improve border security with a combination of personnel, infrastructure, and technology, that has come under criticism. In May 2006, then-House Homeland Security Appropriations

Subcommittee Chairman Harold Rogers (R-Ky.) stated, "What we need is a sound, comprehensive strategy that allows us to measure progress. Without a strategic border security plan we are simply planning to fail." Also in May, then-Homeland Security Appropriations Subcommittee Ranking Member Martin Olav Sabo (D-Minn.) wrote to DHS Secretary Michael Chertoff, "I am deeply concerned that the SBInet solicitation is so broad that the government will, in effect, be turning over its responsibility to secure our borders to the private sector."

$3,000,000 added by the House for the Office of the Federal Coordinator (OFC) for Gulf Coast rebuilding. Since Hurricanes Katrina and Rita ravaged much of the Gulf Coast in 2005, the recovery progress has been abysmal. Through the Road Home Program, OFC Director Donald Powell is hoping to "get residents of Louisiana back into their homes as quickly and fairly as possible." However, in a letter to Sudhakar Kesavan, CEO of ICF International, the contractor running the program, Powell expressed concern that the speed of payments to individuals who lost their homes has been sluggish. In December 2006, Powell stated, "As I write this letter, only 92 homeowners have received financial assistance out of over 80,000 applicants, or .1 percent of applicants. This rate must drastically improve." The Road Home Program has considerable problems; appropriating more money will not provide solace to homeowners or taxpayers.

$2,500,000 added in conference for the U.S. Secret Service National Special Security Events Fund. The purpose of the fund is to help plan and coordinate major events, such as national political conventions, international summits, presidential inaugurations, the Super Bowl, and even the Olympics when hosted by the U.S. These events take years to organize; the funding should be treated the same way. If money needs to be allocated, it should be requested in advance, included in the budget, and authorized.

Discussion Questions

1. How would you define pork barrel projects? Are all pork projects contrary to the national interest? How do we distinguish between local projects that are in the national interest and those that are not?

2. Consider the criteria that CAGW uses to define pork. Do these seem reasonable to you? Should anything be added or deleted from the criteria? Is the list objective enough that a liberal Democratic group and conservative Republican group using the criteria would come up with roughly the same list of projects?

3. Again, considering the list of examples, if you were a member of Congress, which of these would you clearly support, which would you clearly oppose, and which would you want to find out more about before deciding?

4. As Mayhew argues, members of Congress face strong incentives to serve constituent needs and claim credit for delivering federal dollars. Pork barrel projects provide the means to do just that. What changes in Congress or the political process might be made to alter legislative behavior, or to change the incentives they face for securing reelection? Do we want members of Congress to be focused primarily on broad national issues rather than local priorities?

CHAPTER 6

The President: From Chief Clerk to Chief Executive

27

"The Power to Persuade"
from *Presidential Power*

RICHARD NEUSTADT

An enduring theme in analyses of the presidency is the gap between what the public expects of the office and the president's actual powers. Neustadt, who wrote the first edition of Presidential Power *in 1960, offered a new way of looking at the office. His main point is that formal powers (the constitutional powers set out in Article II and the statutory powers that Congress grants) are not the president's most important resource. The president cannot, Neustadt concluded, expect to get his way by command—issuing orders to subordinates and other government officials with the expectation of immediate and unquestioning compliance. In a system of "separate institutions sharing power," other political actors have their own independent sources of power and therefore can refuse to comply with presidential orders. Nobody, Neustadt argues, sees things from the president's perspective (or "vantage point"). Legislators, judges, cabinet secretaries, all have their own responsibilities, constituencies, demands of office, and resources, and their interests and the president's will often differ. The key to presidential power is the power to persuade—to convince others that they should comply with the president's wishes because doing so is in their interest. Presidents persuade by bargaining: making deals, reaching compromise positions; in other words, the give and take that is part of politics.*

The limits on command suggest the structure of our government. The constitutional convention of 1787 is supposed to have created a government of "separated powers." It did nothing of the sort. Rather, it created a government of separated institutions *sharing* powers. "I am part of the legislative process," Eisenhower often said in 1959 as a reminder of his veto. Congress, the dispenser of authority and funds, is no less part of the administrative process. Federalism adds another set of separated institutions. The Bill of Rights adds others. Many public purposes can only be achieved by voluntary acts of private institutions; the press, for one, in Douglass Cater's phrase, is a "fourth branch of government." And with the coming of alliances abroad, the separate institutions of a London, or a Bonn, share in the making of American public policy.

What the Constitution separates our political parties do not combine. The parties are themselves composed of separated organizations sharing public authority. The authority consists of nominating powers. Our national parties are confederations of state and local party institutions, with a headquarters that represents the White House, more or less, if the party has a President in office. These confederacies manage presidential nominations. All other public offices depend upon electorates confined within the states. All other nominations are controlled within the states. The President and congressmen who bear one party's label are divided by dependence upon different sets of voters. The differences are sharpest at the stage of nomination. The White House has too small a share in nominating congressmen, and Congress has too little weight in nominating Presidents for party to erase their constitutional separation. Party links are stronger than is frequently supposed, but nominating processes assure the separation.

The separateness of institutions and the sharing of authority prescribe the terms on which a President persuades. When one man shares authority with another, but does not gain or lose his job upon the other's whim, his willingness to act upon the urging of the other turns on whether he conceives the action right for him. The essence of a President's persuasive task is to convince such men that what the White House wants of them is what they ought to do for their sake and on their authority.

Persuasive power, thus defined, amounts to more than charm or reasoned argument. These have their uses for a President, but these are not the whole of his resources. For the men he would induce to do what he wants done on their own responsibility will need or fear some acts by him on his responsibility. If they share his authority, he has some share in theirs. Presidential "powers" may be inconclusive when a President commands, but always remain relevant as he persuades. The status and authority inherent in his office reinforce his logic and his charm.

* * *

A President's authority and status give him great advantages in dealing with the men he would persuade. Each "power" is a vantage point for him in the degree that other men have use for his authority. From the veto to appointments, from publicity to budgeting, and so down a long list, the White House now controls the most encompassing array of vantage points in the American political system. With hardly an exception, the men who share in governing this country are aware that at some time, in some degree, the doing of *their* jobs, the furthering of *their* ambitions, may depend upon the President of the United States. Their need for presidential action, or their fear of it, is bound to be recurrent if not actually continuous. Their need or fear is his advantage.

A President's advantages are greater than mere listing of his "powers" might suggest. The men with whom he deals must deal with him until the last day of his term. Because they have continuing relationships with him, his future, while it lasts, supports his present influence. Even though there is no need or fear of him today, what he could do tomorrow may supply today's advantage. Continuing relationships may convert any "power," any aspect of his status, into vantage points in almost any case. When he induces other men to do what he wants done, a President can trade on their dependence now *and* later.

The President's advantages are checked by the advantages of others. Continuing relationships will pull in both directions. These are relationships of mutual dependence. A President depends upon the men he would persuade; he has to reckon with his need or fear of them. They too will possess status, or authority, or both, else they would be of little use to him. Their vantage points confront his own; their power tempers his.

*   *   *

The power to persuade is the power to bargain. Status and authority yield bargaining advantages. But in a government of "separated institutions sharing powers," they yield them to all sides. With the array of vantage points at his disposal, a President may be far more persuasive than his logic or his charm could make him. But outcomes are not guaranteed by his advantages. There remain the counter pressures those whom he would influence can bring to bear on him from vantage points at their disposal. Command has limited utility; persuasion becomes give-and-take. It is well that the White House holds the vantage points it does. In such a business any President may need them all—and more.

*   *   *

This view of power as akin to bargaining is one we commonly accept in the sphere of congressional relations. Every textbook states and every legislative session demonstrates that save in times like the extraordinary Hundred Days of 1933—times virtually ruled out by definition at mid-century—a President will often be unable to obtain congressional action on his terms or even to halt action he opposes. The reverse is equally accepted: Congress often is frustrated by the President. Their formal powers are so intertwined that neither will accomplish very much, for very long, without the acquiescence of the other. By the same token, though, what one demands the other can resist. The stage is set for that great game, much like collective bargaining, in which each seeks to profit from the other's needs and fears. It is a game played catch-as-catch-can, case by case. And everybody knows the game, observers and participants alike.

* * *

Like our governmental structure as a whole, the executive establishment consists of separated institutions sharing powers. The President heads one of these; Cabinet officers, agency administrators, and military commanders head others. Below the departmental level, virtually independent bureau chiefs head many more. Under mid-century conditions, Federal operations spill across dividing lines on organization charts; almost every policy entangles many agencies; almost every program calls for interagency collaboration. Everything somehow involves the President. But operating agencies owe their existence least of all to one another—and only in some part to him. Each has a separate statutory base; each has its statutes to administer; each deals with a different set of subcommittees at the Capitol. Each has its own peculiar set of clients, friends, and enemies outside the formal government. Each has a different set of specialized careerists inside its own bailiwick. Our Constitution gives the President the "take-care" clause and the appointive power. Our statues give him central budgeting and a degree of personnel control. All agency administrators are responsible to him. But they *also* are responsible to Congress, to their clients, to their staffs, and to themselves. In short, they have five masters. Only after all of those do they owe any loyalty to each other.

"The members of the Cabinet," Charles G. Dawes used to remark, "are a President's natural enemies." Dawes had been Harding's Budget Director, Coolidge's Vice-President, and Hoover's Ambassador to London; he also had been General Pershing's chief assistant for supply in the First World War. The words are highly colored, but Dawes knew whereof he spoke. The men who have to serve so many masters cannot help but be somewhat the "enemy" of any one of them. By the same token, any master wanting service is in some degree the "enemy" of such a servant. A President is likely to want loyal support but not to relish trouble on his doorstep. Yet the more his Cabinet members cleave to him, the more they may need help from him in fending off the wrath of rival masters. Help, though, is synonymous with trouble. Many a Cabinet officer, with loyalty ill-rewarded by his lights and help withheld, has come to view the White House as innately hostile to department heads. Dawes's dictum can be turned around.

* * *

The more an officeholder's status and his "powers" stem from sources independent of the President, the stronger will be his potential pressure *on* the President. Department heads in general have more bargaining power than do most members of the White House staff; but bureau chiefs may have still more, and specialists at upper levels of established career services may have almost unlimited reserves of the enormous power which consists of sitting still. As Franklin Roosevelt once remarked:

> The Treasury is so large and far-flung and ingrained in its practices that I find it almost impossible to get the action and results I want—even with Henry [Morgenthau] there. But the Treasury is not to be compared with the State Department. You should go through the experience of trying to get any changes in the thinking, policy, and action of the career diplomats and then you'd know what a real problem was. But the Treasury and the State Department put together are nothing compared with the Na-a-vy. The admirals are really something to cope with—and I should know. To change anything in the Na-a-vy is like punching a feather bed. You punch it with your right and you punch it with your left until you are finally exhausted, and then you find the damn bed just as it was before you started punching.[1]

* * *

There is a widely held belief in the United States that were it not for folly or for knavery, a reasonable President would need no power other than the logic of his argument. No less a personage than Eisenhower has subscribed to that belief in many a campaign speech and press-conference remark. But faulty reasoning and bad intentions do not cause all quarrels with Presidents. The best of reasoning and of intent cannot compose them all. For in the first place, what the President wants will rarely seem a trifle to the men he wants it from. And in the second place, they will be bound to judge it by the standard of their own responsibilities, not his. However logical his argument according to his lights, their judgment may not bring them to his view.

The men who share in governing this country frequently appear to act as though they were in business for themselves. So, in a real though not entire sense, they are and have to be. When Truman and MacArthur fell to quarreling, for example, the stakes were no less than the substance of American foreign policy, the risks of greater war or military stalemate, the prerogatives of Presidents and field commanders, the pride of a pro-consul and his place in history. Intertwined, inevitably, were other stakes, as well: political stakes for men and factions of both parties; power stakes for interest groups with which they were or wished to be affiliated. And every stake was raised by the apparent discontent in the American public mood. There is no reason to suppose that in such circumstances men of large but differing responsibilities will see all things through the same glasses. On the contrary, it is to be expected that their views of what ought to be done and what they then should do will vary with the differing perspectives their particular responsibilities evoke. Since their duties are not vested in a "team" or a "collegium" but in themselves, as individuals, one must expect that they will see things *for* themselves. Moreover, when they are responsible to many masters and when an event or policy turns loyalty against loyalty—a day by day occurrence in the nature of the case—one must assume that those who have the duties to perform will choose the terms of reconciliation. This is the essence of their personal responsibility. When their own duties pull in opposite directions, who else but they can choose what they will do?

* * *

Outside the Executive Branch the situation is the same, except that loyalty to the President may often matter *less*. . . . And when one comes to congressmen who can do nothing for themselves (or their constituents) save as they are elected, term by term, in districts and through party structures *differing* from those on which a President depends, the case is very clear. An able Eisenhower aide with long congressional experience remarked to me in 1958: "The people on the Hill don't do what they might *like* to do, they do what they think they *have* to do in their own interest as *they* see it. . . ." This states the case precisely.

The essence of a President's persuasive task with congressmen and everybody else, *is to induce them to believe that what he wants of them is what their own appraisal of their own responsibilities requires them to do in their interest, not his.* Because men may differ in their views on public policy, because differences in outlook stem from differences in duty—duty to one's office, one's constituents, oneself—that task is bound to be more like collective bargaining than like a reasoned argument among philosopher kings. Overtly or implicitly, hard bargaining has characterized all illustrations offered up to now. This is the reason why: persuasion deals in the coin of self-interest with men who have some freedom to reject what they find counterfeit.

Let me introduce a case . . . : the European Recovery Program of 1948, the so-called Marshall Plan. This is perhaps the greatest exercise in policy *agreement* since the cold war began. When the then Secretary of State, George Catlett Marshall, spoke at the Harvard commencement in June of 1947, he launched one of the most creative, most imaginative ventures in the history of American foreign relations. What makes this policy most notable for present purposes, however, is that it became effective upon action by the 80th Congress, at the behest of Harry Truman, in the election year of 1948.

Eight months before Marshall spoke at Harvard, the Democrats had lost control of both Houses of Congress for the first time in fourteen years. Truman, whom the Secretary represented, had just finished his second troubled year as President-by-succession. Truman was regarded with so little warmth in his own party that in 1946 he had been urged *not* to participate in the congressional campaign. At the opening of Congress in January 1947, Senator Robert A. Taft, "Mr. Republican," had somewhat the attitude of a President-elect. This was a vision widely shared in Washington, with Truman relegated, thereby, to the role of caretaker-on-term. Moreover, within just two weeks of Marshall's commencement address, Truman was to veto two prized accomplishments of Taft's congressional majority: the Taft-Hartley Act and tax reduction. Yet scarcely ten months later the Marshall Plan was under way on terms to satisfy its sponsors, its authorization completed, its first-year funds in sight, its administering agency in being: all managed by as thorough a display of executive-congressional cooperation as any we have seen since the Second World War. For any President at any time this would have been a great accomplishment. In years before mid-century it would have been enough to make the future reputation of his term. And for a Truman, at this time, enactment of the Marshall Plan appears almost miraculous.

How was the miracle accomplished? How did a President so situated bring it off? In answer, the first thing to note is that he did not do it by himself. Truman had help of a sort no less extraordinary than the outcome. Although each stands for something more complex, the names of Marshall, Vandenberg, . . . Bevin, Stalin, tell the story of that help.

In 1947, two years after V-J Day, General Marshall was something more than Secretary of State. He was a man venerated by the President as "the greatest living American," literally an embodiment of Truman's ideals. He was honored at the Pentagon as an architect of victory. He was thoroughly respected by the Secretary of the Navy, James V. Forrestal, who that year became the first Secretary of Defense. On Capitol Hill Marshall had an enormous fund of respect stemming from his war record as Army Chief of Staff, and in the country generally no officer had come out of the war with a higher reputation for judgment, intellect, and probity. Besides, as Secretary of State, he had behind him the first generation of matured foreign service officers produced by the reforms of the 1920's, and mingled with them, in the departmental service, were some of the ablest of the men drawn by the war from private life to Washington.

*   *   *

Taken together, these are exceptional resources for a Secretary of State. In the circumstances, they were quite as necessary as they obviously are relevant. The Marshall Plan was launched by a "lame duck" Administration "scheduled" to leave office in eighteen months. Marshall's program faced a congressional leadership traditionally isolationist and currently intent upon economy. European aid was viewed with envy by a Pentagon distressed and virtually disarmed through budget cuts, and by domestic agencies intent on enlarged welfare programs. It was not viewed with liking by a Treasury intent on budget surpluses. The plan had need of every asset that could be extracted from the personal position of its nominal author and from the skills of his assistants.

Without the equally remarkable position of the senior Senator from Michigan, Arthur H. Vandenberg, it is hard to see how Marshall's assets could have been enough. Vandenberg was chairman of the Senate Foreign Relations Committee. Actually, he was much more than that. Twenty years a senator, he was the senior member of his party in the Chamber. Assiduously cultivated by F.D.R. and Truman, he was a chief Republican proponent of "bipartisanship" in foreign policy, and consciously conceived himself its living symbol to his party, to the country, and abroad. Moreover, by informal but entirely operative agreement with his colleague Taft, Vandenberg held the acknowledged lead among Senate Republicans in the whole field of international affairs. This acknowledgement meant more in 1947 than it might have meant at any other time. With confidence in the advent of a Republican administration two years hence, most of the gentlemen were in a mood to be responsive and responsible. The war was over, Roosevelt dead, Truman a caretaker, theirs the trust. That the Senator from Michigan saw matters in this light, his diaries make clear. And this was not the outlook from the Senate side alone; the attitudes of House Republicans associated with the Herter Committee and its tours abroad suggest the same mood of responsibility. Vandenberg was not the only source of help on Capitol Hill. But relatively speaking, his position there was as exceptional as Marshall's was downtown.

* * *

At Harvard, Marshall had voiced an idea in general terms. That this was turned into a hard program susceptible of presentation and support is due, in major part, to Ernest Bevin, the British Foreign Secretary. He well deserves the credit he has sometimes been assigned as, in effect, co-author of the Marshall Plan. For Bevin seized on Marshall's Harvard speech and organized a European response with promptness and concreteness beyond the State Department's expectations. What had been virtually a trial balloon to test reactions on both sides of the Atlantic was hailed in London as an invitation to the Europeans to send Washington a bill of particulars. This they promptly organized to do, and the American Administration then organized in turn for its reception without further argument internally about the pros and cons of issuing the "invitation" in the first place. But for Bevin there might have been trouble from the Secretary of the Treasury and others besides.

If Bevin's help was useful at that early stage, Stalin's was vital from first to last. In a mood of self-deprecation Truman once remarked that without Moscow's "crazy" moves "we would never have had our foreign policy . . . we never could have got a thing from Congress." George Kennan, among others, had deplored the anti-Soviet overtone of the case made for the Marshall Plan in Congress and the country, but there is no doubt that this clinched the argument for many segments of American opinion. There also is no doubt that Moscow made the crucial contributions to the case.

*   *   *

The crucial thing to note about this case is that despite compatibility of views on public policy, Truman got no help he did not pay for (except Stalin's). Bevin scarcely could have seized on Marshall's words had Marshall not been plainly backed by Truman. Marshall's interest would not have comported with the exploitation of his prestige by a President who undercut him openly, or subtly, or even inadvertently, at any point. Vandenberg, presumably, could not have backed proposals by a White House which begrudged him deference and access gratifying to his fellow-partisans (and satisfying to himself). Prominent Republicans in private life would not have found it easy to promote a cause identified with Truman's claims on 1948—and neither would the prominent New Dealers then engaged in searching for a substitute.

Truman paid the price required for their services. So far as the record shows, the White House did not falter once in firm support for Marshall and the Marshall Plan. Truman backed his Secretary's gamble on an invitation to all Europe. He made the plan his own in a well-timed address to the Canadians. He lost no opportunity to widen the involvements of his own official family in the cause. Averell Harriman the Secretary of Commerce, Julius Krug the Secretary of the Interior, Edwin Nourse the Economic Council Chairman, James Webb the Director of the Budget—all were made responsible for studies and reports contributing directly to the legislative presentation. Thus these men were committed in advance. Besides, the President continually emphasized to everyone in reach that he did not have doubts, did not desire complications and would foreclose all he could. Reportedly, his emphasis was felt at the Treasury, with good effect. And Truman was at special pains to smooth the way for Vandenberg. The Senator insisted on "no politics" from the Administration side; there was none. He thought a survey of American resources and capacity essential; he got it in the Krug and Harriman reports. Vandenberg expected advance consultation; he received it, step by step, in frequent meetings with the President and weekly conferences with Marshall. He asked for an effective liaison between Congress and agencies concerned; Lovett and others gave him what he wanted. When the Senator decided on the need to change financing and administrative features of the legislation, Truman disregarded Budget Bureau grumbling and acquiesced with grace. When, finally, Vandenberg desired a Republican to head the new administering agency, his candidate, Paul Hoffman, was appointed despite the President's own preference for another. In all of these ways Truman employed the sparse advantages his "powers" and his status then accorded him to gain the sort of help he had to have.

* * *

Had Truman lacked the personal advantages his "powers" and his status gave him, or if he had been maladroit in using them, there probably would not have been a massive European aid program in 1948. . . . The President's own share in this accomplishment was vital. He made his contribution by exploiting his advantages. Truman, in effect, lent Marshall and the rest the perquisites and status of his office. In return they lent him their prestige and their own influence. The transfer multiplied *his* influence despite his limited authority in form and lack of strength politically. Without the wherewithal to make this bargain, Truman could not have contributed to European aid.

* * *

DISCUSSION QUESTIONS

1. Considering recent presidents (Bush and Clinton), identify and discuss some examples of Neustadt's argument that presidents cannot get their way by "command," that they must bargain to get what they want.

2. Can you think of any recent examples where a president has been able to get what he wants by giving a command (that is, to someone not in the military)?

3. How should a president convince a member of Congress to pass a piece of legislation that the president favors?

NOTE

1. Reprinted from Marriner S. Eccles, *Beckoning Frontiers* (New York: Knopf, 1951), p. 336.

2

"Perspectives on the Presidency"
from *The Presidency in a Separated System*

CHARLES O. JONES

Just how powerful is the president? Have the fears of some of the Framers—that the president would degrade into an imperial despot—been realized, or does the separation of powers effectively check the president's ability to misuse the powers of office? Charles Jones argues that we should view the president as only one of the players in American government; the presidency exists only as one part of a set of institutions where responsibility is diffused, where the bulk of political activity takes place independent of the presidency, and where the different players and institutions learn to adjust to the others. Consider, for example, that the Republican 104th Congress (elected in the 1994 midterms) and President Clinton managed to reach compromises on a number of important issues despite early predictions that they would never agree on anything. Or that President George H. W. Bush managed to find a way to work with the Democratic Congress to get some major legislation through during 1991. On the other hand, the more partisan and polarizing presidency of George W. Bush in which more power was centralized in the White House and few bipartisan compromises were reached provides a counter example. Ultimately, Jones argues, the president is only a part of a larger "separated system," in which Congress, the courts, and the bureaucracy can shape policy.

The president is not the presidency. The presidency is not the government. Ours is not a presidential system.

I begin with these starkly negative themes as partial correctives to the more popular interpretations of the United States government as presidency-centered. Presidents themselves learn these refrains on the job, if they do not know them before. President Lyndon B. Johnson, who had impressive political advantages during the early years of his administration, reflected later on what was required to realize the potentialities of the office:

> Every President has to establish with the various sectors of the country what I call "the right to govern." Just being elected to the office does not guarantee him that right. Every President has to inspire the confidence of the people. Every President has to become a leader, and to be a leader he must attract people who are willing to follow him. Every President has to develop a moral underpinning to his power, or he soon discovers that he has no power at all.[1]

To exercise influence, presidents must learn the setting within which it has bearing. [Then] President-elect Bill Clinton recognized the complexities of translating campaign promises into a legislative program during a news conference shortly after his election in 1992:

> It's all very well to say you want an investment tax credit, and quite another thing to make the 15 decisions that have to be made to shape the exact bill you want.
> It's all very well to say . . . that the working poor in this country . . . should be lifted out of poverty by increasing the refundable income tax credit for the working poor, and another thing to answer the five or six questions that define how you get that done.[2]

For presidents, new or experienced, to recognize the limitations of office is commendable. Convincing others to do so is a challenge. Presidents become convenient labels for marking historical time: the Johnson years, the Nixon years, the Reagan years. Media coverage naturally focuses more on the president: there is just one at a time, executive organization is oriented in pyramidal fashion toward the Oval Office, Congress is too diffuse an institution to report on as such, and the Supreme Court leads primarily by indirection. Public interest, too, is directed toward the White House as a symbol of the government. As a result, expectations of a president often far exceed the individual's personal, political, institutional, or constitutional capacities for achievement. Performance seldom matches promise. Presidents who understand how it all works resist the inflated image of power born of high-stakes elections and seek to lower expectations. Politically savvy presidents know instinctively that it is precisely at the moment of great achievement that they must prepare themselves for the setback that will surely follow.

Focusing exclusively on the presidency can lead to a seriously distorted picture of how the national government does its work. The plain fact is that the United States does not have a presidential system. It has a *separated* system. It is odd that it is so commonly thought of as otherwise since schoolchildren learn about the separation of powers and checks and balances. As the author of *Federalist* 51 wrote, "Ambition must be made to counteract ambition." No one, least of all presidents, the Founders reasoned, can be entrusted with excessive authority. Human nature, being what it is, requires "auxiliary precautions" in the form of competing legitimacies.

The acceptance that this is a separated, not a presidential, system, prepares one to appraise how politics works, not to be simply reproachful and reformist. Thus, for example, divided (or split-party) government is accepted as a potential or even likely outcome of a separated system, rooted as it is in the separation of elections. Failure to acknowledge the authenticity of the split-party condition leaves one with little to study and much to reform in the post–World War II period, when the government has been divided more than 60 percent of the time.

Simply put, the role of the president in this separated system of governing varies substantially, depending on his resources, advantages, and strategic position. My strong interest is in how presidents place themselves in an ongoing government and are fitted in by other participants, notably those on Capitol Hill. The central purpose of this book is to explore these "fittings." In pursuing this interest, I have found little value in the presidency-centered, party government perspective, as I will explain below. As a substitute, I propose a separationist, diffused-responsibility perspective that I find more suited to the constitutional, institutional, political, and policy conditions associated with the American system of governing.

*   *   *

The Dominant Perspective

The presidency-centered perspective is consistent with a dominant and well-developed perspective that has been highly influential in evaluating the American political system. The perspective is that of party government, typically one led by a strong or aggressive president. Those advocating this perspective prefer a system in which political parties are stronger than they normally can be in a system of separated elections.

*   *   *

The party government perspective is best summarized in the recommendations made in 1946 by the Committee on Political Parties of the American Political Science Association.

> The party system that is needed must be democratic, responsible and effective. . . .
> An effective party system requires, first, that the parties are able to bring forth programs to which they commit themselves and, second, that the parties possess sufficient internal cohesion to carry out these programs. . . .
> The fundamental requirement of such accountability is a two-party system in which the opposition party acts as the critic of the party in power, developing, defining, and presenting the policy alternatives which are necessary for a true choice in reaching public decisions.[3]

Note the language in this summary: party in power, opposition party, policy alternatives for choice, accountability, internal cohesion, programs to which parties commit themselves. As a whole, it forms a test that a separated system is bound to fail.

I know of very few contemporary advocates of the two-party responsibility model. But I know many analysts who rely on its criteria when judging the political system. One sees this reliance at work when reviewing how elections are interpreted and presidents are evaluated. By this standard, the good campaign and election have the following characteristics:

- Publicly visible issues that are debated by the candidates during the campaign.
- Clear differences between the candidates on the issues, preferably deriving from ideology.
- A substantial victory for the winning candidate, thus demonstrating public support for one set of issue positions.
- A party win accompanying the victory for the president, notably an increase in the presidential party's share of congressional seats and statehouses so that the president's win can be said to have had an impact on other races (the coattail effect).
- A greater than expected win for the victorious party, preferably at both ends of Pennsylvania Avenue.
- A postelection declaration of support and unity from the congressional leaders of the president's party.

The good president, by this perspective, is one who makes government work, one who has a program and uses his resources to get it enacted. The good president is an activist: he sets the agenda, is attentive to the progress being made, and willingly accepts responsibility for what happens. He can behave in this way because he has demonstrable support.

It is not in the least surprising that the real outcomes of separated elections frustrate those who prefer responsible party government. Even a cursory reading of the Constitution suggests that these demanding tests will be met only by coincidence. Even an election that gives one party control of the White House and both houses of Congress in no way guarantees a unified or responsible party outcome. And even when a president and his congressional party leaders appear to agree on policy priorities, the situation may change dramatically following midterm elections. Understandably, advocates of party government are led to propose constitutional reform.

*   *   *

An Alternative Perspective

The alternative perspective for understanding American national politics is bound to be anathema to party responsibility advocates. By the rendition promoted here, responsibility is not focused, it is diffused. Representation is not pure and unidirectional; it is mixed, diluted, and multidirectional. Further, the tracking of policy from inception to implementation discourages the most devoted advocate of responsibility theories. In a system of diffused responsibility, credit will be taken and blame will be avoided by both institutions and both parties. For the mature government (one that has achieved substantial involvement in social and economic life), much of the agenda will be self-generating, that is, resulting from programs already on the books. Thus the desire to propose new programs is often frustrated by demands to sustain existing programs, and substantial debt will constrain both.

Additionally there is the matter of who *should* be held accountable for what and when. This is not a novel issue by any means. It is a part of the common rhetoric of split-party government. Are the Democrats responsible for how medicare has worked because it was a part of Lyndon Johnson's Great Society? Or are the Republicans responsible because their presidents accepted, administered, and revised the program? Is President Carter responsible for creating a Department of Energy or President Reagan responsible for failing to abolish it, or both? The partisan rhetoric on deficits continues to blame the Democrats for supporting spending programs and the Republicans for cutting taxes. It is noteworthy that this level of debate fails to treat more fundamental issues, such as the constitutional roadblocks to defining responsibility. In preventing the tyranny of the majority, the founders also made it difficult to specify accountability.

Diffusion of responsibility, then, is not only a likely result of a separated system but may also be a fair outcome. From what was said above, one has to doubt how reasonable it is to hold one institution or one party accountable for a program that has grown incrementally through decades of single- and split-party control. Yet reforming a government program is bound to be an occasion for holding one or the other of the branches accountable for wrongs being righted. If, however, politics allows crossing the partisan threshold to place both parties on the same side, then agreements may be reached that will permit blame avoidance, credit taking, and, potentially, significant policy change. This is not to say that both sides agree from the start about what to do, in a cabal devoted to irresponsibility (though that process is not unknown). Rather it is to suggest that diffusion of responsibility may permit policy reform that would have been much less likely if one party had to absorb all of the criticism for past performance or blame should the reforms fail when implemented.

Institutional competition is an expected outcome of the constitutional arrangements that facilitate mixed representation and variable electoral horizons. In recent decades this competition has been reinforced by Republicans settling into the White House, the Democrats comfortably occupying the House of Representatives, and, in very recent times, both parties hotly contending for majority status in the Senate. Bargains struck under these conditions have the effect of perpetuating split control by denying opposition candidates (Democratic presidential challengers, Republican congressional challengers) both the issues upon which to campaign and the means for defining accountability.

The participants in this system of mixed representation and diffused responsibility naturally accommodate their political surroundings. Put otherwise, congressional Democrats and presidential Republicans learn how to do their work. Not only does each side adjust to its political circumstances, but both may also be expected to provide themselves with the resources to participate meaningfully in policy politics.

Much of the above suggests that the political and policy strategies of presidents in dealing with Congress will depend on the advantages they have available at any one time. One cannot employ a constant model of the activist president leading a party government. Conditions may encourage the president to work at the margins of president-congressional interaction (for example, where he judges that he has an advantage, as with foreign and defense issues). He may allow members of Congress to take policy initiatives, hanging back to see how the issue develops. He may certify an issue as important, propose a program to satisfy certain group demands, but fail to expend the political capital necessary to get the program enacted. The lame-duck president requires clearer explication. The last months and years of a two-term administration may be one of congressional initiative with presidential response. The point is that having been relieved of testing the system for party responsibility, one can proceed to analyze how presidents perform under variable political and policy conditions.

*   *   *

In a separated system of diffused responsibility, these are the expectations:

- Presidents will enter the White House with variable personal, political, and policy advantages or resources. Presidents are not equally good at comprehending their advantages or identifying how these advantages may work best for purposes of influencing the rest of the government.
- White House and cabinet organization will be quite personal in nature, reflecting the president's assessment of strengths and weaknesses, the challenges the president faces in fitting into the ongoing government, and the political and policy changes that occur during the term of office. There is no formula for organizing the presidency, though certain models can be identified.
- Public support will be an elusive variable in analyzing presidential power. At the very least, its importance for any one president must be considered alongside other advantages. "Going public" does not necessarily carry a special bonus, though presidents with limited advantages otherwise may be forced to rely on this tactic.
- The agenda will be continuous, with many issues derived from programs already being administered. The president surely plays an important role in certifying issues and setting priorities, but Congress and the bureaucracy will also be natural participants. At the very least, therefore, the president will be required to persuade other policy actors that his choices are the right ones. They will do the same with him.
- Lawmaking will vary substantially in terms of initiative, sequence, par-

tisan and institutional interaction, and productivity. The challenge is to comprehend the variable role of the president in a government that is designed for continuity and change.

- Reform will be an especially intricate undertaking since, by constitutional design, the governmental structure is antithetical to efficient goal achievement. Yet many, if not most, reforms seek to achieve efficiency within the basic separated structure. There are not many reforms designed to facilitate the more effective working of split-party government.

DISCUSSION QUESTIONS

1. The conventional wisdom is that presidential power increases (often dramatically) during war and other national crises. How has President George W. Bush's ability to exercise power changed since September 11, 2001? What accounts for this change—is it the rise in his approval ratings, an unwillingness of Congress to oppose him, or something else?

2. How do the last two years—Bush's low popularity, Democratic majorities in Congress, and much partisan conflict between Congress and the president—affect your view of Jones's argument?

3. How can Jones's view of the presidency be squared with the popular view that the president is the most powerful person in the world?

NOTES

1. Lyndon Baines Johnson, *The Vantage Point: Perspectives on the Presidency, 1963–1969* (New York: Holt, Rinehart and Winston, 1971), p. 18.
2. Ruth Marcus, "In Transition Twilight Zone, Clinton's Every Word Scrutinized," *Washington Post*, November 22, 1992, p. A1.
3. American Political Science Association, *Toward a More Responsible Two-Party System* (New York: Rinehart, 1950), pp. 1–2.

DEBATING THE ISSUES: POLITICIZING THE BUREAUCRACY

One of the crucial questions about the executive branch is the degree to which it should be responsive to presidential influence. All presidents complain about bureaucratic obstructionists, who place their agency's mission above presidential policies. On the one hand, democratic legitimacy requires some degree of responsiveness on the part of executive branch agencies; otherwise, even large shifts in public opinion have no effect on what they do. On the other, an overly politicized executive branch can produce poor public policy and unfair implementation, if officials are more concerned about political or partisan consequences than they are about effectiveness or efficiency. Generally, this tension between neutrality and responsiveness is balanced by a competitive civil service, which provides strong job protection for most employees, presidential appointments at the top level, and a Senior Executive Service made up of professional employees who have some protections.

Critics of the Bush administration accuse it of excessive partisanship, and claim that top officials make too many important decisions based on a desire to achieve partisan advantages. Alexis Simendinger, a reporter for the *National Journal*, a Washington, D.C., magazine that covers politics, summarizes these criticisms. Inside the administration, party officials, White House staffers, and executive branch officials worked together closely, pushing beyond what other presidents had done. The White House responds that this is standard practice, and that Democrats have an unusual preoccupation with Karl Rove. Clinton, in fact, brought in political consultant Dick Morris as an advisor, irritating Chief of Staff Leon Panetta, who insisted that Morris be barred from foreign policy deliberations.

James Pfiffner, a political scientist and presidency scholar, offers a different interpretation, calling Bush "the first MBA president." Bush imposed a corporate-like structure on his White House, delegating substantial responsibility to subordinates and emphasizing efficiency and decisiveness (this is consistent with what most practitioners recommend, that a president create administrative structures that are consistent with their own personalities and decision-making processes). This has, in Pfiffner's view, allowed Bush to be decisive and efficient, and was a key factor in many of his legislative and policy successes. At the same time, Pfiffner concludes that Bush has not been a good public administrator, making poor decisions on key appointments (with special scorn heaped on Michael Brown, who ran the Federal Emergency Management Agency during Hurricane Katrina), and failing to deliberate on crucial policy decisions.

29

"The First MBA President: George W. Bush as Public Administrator"

James P. Pfiffner

* * *

President George W. Bush is the nation's first MBA president, and his presidency exhibits both the strengths and weaknesses of his approach to operating as a chief executive officer. He prefers to set a bold direction and delegate administrative matters to his executive team, led by his chief operating officer, Vice President Richard Cheney. The Bush management style is marked by secrecy, speed, and top-down control. Although this approach has brought considerable political success, it also has resulted in administrative failures that have jeopardized the long-term legacy of President Bush's policies.

We usually do not think of the president of the United States primarily as a public administrator. He or she is seen foremost as the political leader of the nation, the symbolic head of state, the director of foreign policy, and the legislative initiator. After a moment's reflection, however, it is apparent that the constitutional provision that "[t]he executive Power shall be vested in a President of the United States of America" makes the president formally the head of the executive branch and thus responsible for its performance in taking care that the laws of the nation are faithfully executed. In addition, the commander-in-chief clause obliges the president to command the armed forces of the United States.

The U.S. Constitution does not specify what level of involvement in administrative matters is appropriate for the president. Hugh Heclo argues that the president must manage the office or else he or she will be trapped by its routines and the expectations of others. According to Heclo, "To manage is something that falls between administering in detail and merely presiding in general" (1999a, 32). Peri Arnold maintains that managerial concerns are essential to the president's "ability to transform ideas and commitments into policies." Management is essential to political leadership, argues Arnold. "Thus the president ought to be concerned with administration, not because he is a manager but because administration is part of the system through which his choices become policy. . . . The president's political and policy concerns come first and lead him to administration. . . . In this view the president is not so much a manager of administration; he is a tactician using it." (1986, 363).

* * *

The Bush administration's impact on public administration is, of course, much broader than the issues addressed in this essay. The administration has undertaken a series of management reforms * * *, it has extended contracting out for governmental services, even in areas of combat and security forces in Iraq; its impact on the economy through its fiscal and budget policies will have far-reaching effects on U.S. economic health; and its changes to the personnel system in the continuing reduction of Title V coverage for U.S. civilian personnel may bring the broadest human resource management changes since the Pendleton Act. Nevertheless, President Bush's administrative decisions in the national security arena have more far-reaching consequences for the United States in history, and President Bush personally has been more intimately involved in national security policy matters than in any of his other public administration responsibilities. Therefore, this essay focuses on President Bush's national security administrative actions rather than the other important areas.

The thrust of the analysis is that President Bush has achieved significant policy victories through secrecy, speed, and tight control of the executive branch by his White House and political appointees. But the ultimate success of his policy victories has been undermined by his neglect of the administrative dimensions of his policies and failure to heed the advice of many career professional public administrators. This essay concludes that George W. Bush has had a profound impact on public administration in the United States, both in the implementation of his policy priorities and in the restructuring of governmental institutions.

The Bush Style of Leadership

President Bush is the first American president to hold a master's degree in business administration (Harvard University, 1975), and according to Donald Kettl, George W. Bush "is the very model of a modern MBA president." (2003, 31). He has also been praised as the "CEO President" (Kessler 2004). Secrecy, speed, and top-down control are all qualities attributed to business management, especially by envious public officials who must cope with the inevitable leaks, dilatory bureaucratic processes, and a system of shared powers. It is not clear, however, that business management experts would embrace Bush's approach to management (Bossidy and Charan 2002; Magretta and Stone 2002; Mintzberg 2004).

President Bush has articulated a bold vision, set priorities, and then delegated the implementation to his vice president (arguably his chief operating officer) and his loyal staff team. In his autobiography, *A Charge to Keep*, he put it this way: "My job is to set the agenda and tone and framework, to lay out the principles by which we operate and make decisions, and then delegate much of the process to them" (quoted in Allen 2004). President Bush prefers short memos, oral briefings, and crisp meetings. His circle of advisers is relatively small. According to American Enterprise Institute president Christopher DeMuth, "It's a too tightly managed decision-making process. When they make decisions, a very small number of people are in the room, and it has a certain effect of constricting the range of alternatives being offered" (Suskind 2004a).

Neither has President Bush sought a broad range of outside advice: "I have no outside advice. Anybody who says they're an outside adviser of this Administration on this particular matter [the war on terror] is not telling the truth" (Lemann 2004, 158). President Bush's first Environmental Protection Agency director, Christine Todd Whitman, felt that the president was even sheltered from his own cabinet. "There is a palace guard, and they want to run interference for him" (Allen and Broder 2004).

Other presidents made flawed decisions because they did not consult broadly enough or conduct systematic deliberations. For example, President Lyndon B. Johnson's escalation of the war in Vietnam and John F. Kennedy's decision to go forward with the Bay of Pigs invasion were both marked by narrow consultation and flawed processes (Burke and Greenstein 1991, Pfiffner 2005b). In contrast, Dwight D. Eisenhower's decision-making process regarding Dien Bien Phu in 1954 and Kennedy's deliberations during the Cuban missile crisis were models of systematic and careful deliberation about going to war. President Bush's deliberations before the war in Afghanistan much more closely approached these positive models than did his series of decisions leading up to the war in Iraq (Pfiffner 2005b).

President Bush's approach to his role as chief executive mirrors that of a chief executive officer of a corporation. He sees himself as tough minded and able to make decisions quickly and leave the details up to his team. His White House staff is legendary for its tight message discipline and absence of unauthorized leaks. President Bush sees himself as one who listens to advice and then makes the tough calls. "I listen to all voices, but mine is the final decision. . . . I'm the decider, and I decide what's best" (White House 2006). In contrast to his father or to Bill Clinton, who would agonize over important decisions, Bush decides and moves on. The detached Bush style resembles the style of President Ronald Reagan, but it contrasts sharply with those of Presidents Franklin Roosevelt and Clinton, who were fascinated with the details of policies and actively sought external advice on the policies of their administrations.

As the nation's first MBA president, President Bush has what he regards as the strengths of a chief executive officer: vision, certainty, and decisiveness. But the defects of this style include a tendency to act without sufficient deliberation, an unwillingness to admit the complexity of many policy issues, and a tendency to consider only a narrow range of alternatives. According to National Security Advisor Condoleezza Rice, "He least likes me to say, 'This is complex' " (Lemann 2002, 177). Bush has described his personal approach to decision making as intuitive: "I just think it's instinctive. I'm not a textbook player. I'm a gut player" (Woodward 2002, 144). He does not believe in elaborate deliberation or explanation of his thinking to his White House staff. As he told Bob Woodward, "I'm the commander—see, I don't need to explain—I do not need to explain why I say things. That's the interesting thing about being the president. Maybe somebody needs to explain to me why they say something, but I don't feel like I owe anybody an explanation" (Woodward 2002, 145–46).

The president has eschewed detailed deliberation, and his White House does not adhere to any regularized policy development process. Former Treasury secretary Paul O'Neill thought that the Bush White House had no serious domestic policy process. "It was a broken process, . . . or rather no process at all; there seemed to be no apparatus to assess policy and deliberate effectively, to create coherent governance" (Suskind 2004b, 97). John DiIulio, who worked in the Bush White House on faith-based initiatives during the first eight months of the administration, said, "There is no precedent in any modern White House for what is going on in this one: a complete lack of a policy apparatus" (Suskind 2003). According to Lawrence Wilkerson, chief of staff to former secretary of state Colin Powell and a career army officer, the national security policy process was even worse: What "I saw for four-plus years was a case that I have never seen in my studies of aberrations, bastardizations, perturbations, changes to the national security decision-making process. What I saw was a cabal between the Vice President of the United States, Richard Cheney, and the Secretary of Defense, Donald Rumsfeld, on critical issues [who] made decisions that the bureaucracy did not know were being made. . . . [T]he bureaucracy often didn't know what it was doing as it moved to carry them out" (2005, 8).

President Bush's strengths as a decisive, CEO-type leader are also a mirror reflection of his weaknesses. Francis Fukuyama comments on the dual nature of President Bush's leadership style:

> Great leadership often involves putting aside self-doubt, bucking conventional wisdom, and listening only to an inner voice that tells you the right thing to do. That is the essence of strong character. The problem is that bad leadership can also flow from these same characteristics: steely determination can become stubbornness; the willingness to flout conventional wisdom can amount to a lack of common sense; the inner voice can become delusional. (2006, 60–61).

President Bush's strengths as leader have led to policy victories, but his weaknesses have led to administrative failures.

Despite President Bush's care in recruiting an experienced and well-credentialed cabinet, he is not about to reverse the trend of the past four decades of power gravitating toward the White House. Early in the Bush administration, all of the major policy priorities were dominated by White House staffers rather than led by the cabinet. As one high-level White House official said during the transition from the first to the second term: "The Bush brand is few priorities, run out of the White House, with no *interference* from the Cabinet. . . . The function of the Bush Cabinet is to provide a chorus of support for White House policies and technical expertise for implementing them" (VandeHei and Kessler 2004; emphasis added).

*   *   *

Reorganization

President Bush undertook the most far-reaching reorganization of the executive branch since the National Security Act of 1947. Although he initially opposed the creation of the Department of Homeland Security and was skeptical of intelligence reorganization, he co-opted the reorganization plans and used them to his political advantage.

Intelligence Reorganization

During the first several years of his administration, President Bush became convinced that the CIA was both incompetent and that elements within the agency were trying to undermine his administration (Brooks 2004; McLaughlin 2005; Novak 2004). High-level officials, particularly Cheney and Rumsfeld, also believed that the CIA was soft, risk averse, and not aggressive enough for the war on terror and that it had made major misjudgments by failing to prevent the 9/11 attacks and being wrong about the presence of weapons of mass destruction in Iraq. President Bush typified his administration's attitude toward dissenting voices when the CIA chief of station in Baghdad wrote a report in 2004 that the war in Iraq was not going well. "What is he, some kind of defeatist?" asked the president (Robinson and Whitelaw 2006).

Because the CIA refused to confirm the administration's claim of a connection between Saddam and al-Qaeda, President Bush concluded that it was not sufficiently responsive. And when leaks to the press seemed to indicate that the CIA disagreed with the administration about some aspects of Iraq policy, he concluded that it was trying to undermine his administration. The consequences included a purge of the top levels of the CIA and the largest reorganization of the intelligence community since the CIA was created in 1947.

President Bush decided to make major changes in the intelligence community. First, he replaced Tenet as director of the CIA with Porter Goss, head of the House Intelligence Committee and an administration loyalist who had been long critical of the CIA. Second, the president signed a bill that directed a major overhaul and reorganization of the intelligence community. The major political impetus for the reorganization came from the 9/11 Commission, which exerted considerable public pressure for the reform. But President Bush used the highly visible reorganization as an opportunity to replace the CIA as the primary intelligence analysis agency for the United States, a stature that it had enjoyed since its creation in 1947.

The new director of national intelligence would report directly to the president and would take over the role (previously played by the director of the CIA) of coordinating the 15 separate intelligence agencies throughout the government. What this meant was that the CIA director would no longer produce the President's Daily Brief or personally brief the president. In addition, the director of national intelligence would control the newly established Counter Terrorism Center and build up his or her own bureaucracy of more than 1,500 personnel, some of them recruited from the CIA. The CIA would play a correspondingly less important role in intelligence analysis, though it would continue to be the home of the newly created Clandestine Service, the new name for the Directorate of Operations. This service would be expanded considerably as the CIA's "humint" (human intelligence, or spying) capacity was built up. The other challenge to the CIA's previous status came from the Pentagon, which allocated more resources to human intelligence and created a parallel clandestine service capacity (Schmitt 2006).

After Goss had spent 18 months at the CIA, the resentment of the remaining career professionals and the disarray at the agency was so great that President Bush replaced Goss with Michael Hayden in 2006. But the CIA was in eclipse. The new director of national intelligence wrote the President's Daily Brief and delivered the daily intelligence briefing to the president. The CIA clandestine services were expanded, but their intelligence analysis function was subordinated to the bureaucracy of the director of national intelligence. And the CIA clandestine service had to share its function with the expanded humint capacity of the Defense Department. As with any large-scale reorganization, its success could not be judged immediately, but it is likely to take years before the overlapping jurisdictions can be sorted out.

The Department of Homeland Security, FEMA, and the Katrina Disaster

President Bush's public image as a competent, MBA-type manager of the executive branch probably suffered most from the disaster wrought by Hurricane Katrina and its devastation of the Gulf Coast, especially New Orleans. The response of the federal government was dilatory and ineffective, and the coordination of federal, state, and local agencies was not successful. The lasting sound bite from the era was Bush's praise for Federal Emergency Management Agency (FEMA) director Michael Brown on September 2, 2005, just as the full range of the government's inadequate response was becoming apparent: "Brownie, you're doing a heck of a job" (Brinkley 2006, 548). Within two weeks, Brown was forced to resign and had become a symbol of incompetent political leadership of a professional agency.

Although President Bush could not have prevented much of the disaster by taking different actions during the crisis, the disaster did have public administration roots, *some of which* can be attributed to the Bush administration. The fundamental problems that Katrina illuminated had grown slowly over the preceding decades. The channeling of the Mississippi River and the loss of wetlands protecting the coast had enabled New Orleans to become a major port and commerce center, but the coastal reengineering had also made the city more vulnerable to major flooding during hurricanes (Brinkley 2006, 9).

Over the preceding decade, many alarms had been sounded about the need for more funding for and reinforcement of the levees that kept the river, lake, and gulf waters at bay. But more importantly, the levees that had been built by the Army Corps of Engineers were poorly designed and based on inadequate soil foundations. Thus, it was not the winds of Katrina that did the most damage, or even flood levees that were overtopped by the rising water, but the structural failure of the dams, which resulted in breaches (especially the 17th Street breach) that caused the inundation of New Orleans. These public administration failures were shared by many elected and appointed officials at all three levels of government over a period of decades.

The public administration failures of the Katrina disaster, in addition to the actions (or inactions) of state and local officials, also stemmed from President Bush's personnel decisions and the creation of the federal Department of Homeland Security. In the aftermath of 9/11, when it became clear that Congress was likely to create a new department, despite the objections of the president, President Bush quickly co-opted the plan by setting up a secret study group to put together a White House plan for a new department. Planning was done literally in the White House basement, in the President's Emergency Operations Center by a group of five White House staffers who designed the administration's proposal for the Department of Homeland Security (Brook et al. 2006, 90). One problem was that the people who were doing the planning did not have an operational understanding of the boxes they were moving around on the organizational chart (Brook et al. 2006, 89–90).

When the new Department of Homeland Security opened its doors in the spring of 2003, it comprised 22 different agencies with 170,000 employees and a $40 billion budget, the largest reorganization of the executive branch since the National Security Act of 1947 created the

Department of Defense, the CIA, and the National Security Council. The reorganization was important as a symbolic statement that the federal government was changing itself substantially to face the new challenge of terrorism. Although the ostensible purpose of the reorganization was to ensure that the disparate agencies would be guided by a secretary with a coherent view of the big picture, the reality of any large reorganization is that the legacy agencies, with their long-established cultures that are not easily changed, are often forced into a marriage that they do not want.

The path of the Department of Homeland Security after its creation was not smooth, and it suffered all of the ills that were predictable in a newly created behemoth of a department. One of these problems was presented by the inclusion of FEMA, which had been established in 1979 when President Jimmy Carter sought to combine a number of different agencies with disaster preparedness and response responsibilities. The agency was designed to be independent rather than subsumed into a larger department, and when President Clinton came into office, he granted it departmental status, with its director reporting directly to the president. He also appointed as its director James Lee Witt, a professional public administrator who had been the director of emergency prepared-ness in Arkansas. Under Witt, FEMA increased its professionalism, fund-ing, and responsibilities.

When Joseph Allbaugh, President Bush's campaign manager, resigned as FEMA's director, Bush filled the position with Allbaugh's deputy, Michael Brown, who had also been Allbaugh's college roommate. Brown had previously been the head of horse-show judging at the International Arabian Horse Association and had padded his résumé in several ways (Brinkley 2006, 246). Thus, part of the problem of FEMA's inade-quate response to Katrina was the lack of professionalism in its po-litical appointees, many of whom had little experience in emergency management.

But part of FEMA's problem was structural and attributable to the cre-ation of the Department of Homeland Security. The leadership of FEMA did not want to be included in the newly created department, fearing that it would be swallowed up in the huge bureaucracy and that its mission of ameliorating natural disasters would be subordinated to fighting terror-ism. Its budget and personnel were cut and shifted to other homeland se-curity priorities. For example, FEMA lost control of its grant making to state and local government when this function was moved to the secre-tary of homeland security's office. This, in turn, severed important con-nections with state and local emergency responders and cut funds for preparedness. In addition, the focus of the grants was shifted to antiter-rorism purposes rather than natural disaster response. The National Re-sponse Plan, mandated by the Homeland Security Act of 2002, was taken from FEMA and given to the Transportation Security Administration. The Office for National Preparedness and the Office for Domestic Preparedness were each brought into the new department but not placed under FEMA.

Each of these losses of bureaucratic resources took a toll on the seasoned career management of FEMA, and the agency suffered a brain drain of its senior career professionals. Thus, the FEMA that faced the catastrophe of Katrina was not the same FEMA that the Bush administration had inherited.

The inadequate federal governmental response to Katrina was the result of a combination of organizational, personnel, and resource decisions of the Bush administration. No level of federal preparedness could have eliminated much of the suffering and damage caused by the natural disaster (and bad engineering), but political appointments at FEMA and the consequences of placing it in the Department of Homeland Security exacerbated the tragedy. The most important things that President Bush could have done in the immediate aftermath of the storm were symbolic in nature and had to do with political leadership rather than public administration. He might have recognized the urgency of the situation more quickly and projected his concern for the victims more effectively. Ironically, political leadership was President Bush's strength, and that is the level at which his actions were not seen as adequate.

Conclusion

President Bush's strengths as a political leader include bold thinking and consistent adherence to his chosen policies. Many perceive him as a strong leader, especially in national security matters. He has infused loyalty in most of his immediate subordinates and delegated sufficient authority for them to carry out his goals. His appointments at the top levels of his administration have been impressive in their racial and gender diversity. His policy successes have been the result his formidable political skills, but his deficiencies as a manager have undermined his policy victories. These deficiencies include his lack of systematic deliberation over policy alternatives and his failure to weigh sufficiently the judgments of military and other public administration professionals.

*   *   *

President Bush's reorganization of the executive branch in the creation of the Department of Homeland Security and the Directorate of National Intelligence skillfully symbolize the administration's response to the post–9/11 security environment. But in the process of making some of the necessary changes, the professionalism of FEMA and the CIA were compromised. Although President Bush's historical legacy cannot yet be judged, his legacy as a public administrator will significantly affect the evaluation of his administration.

Just as he has asserted strong top-down control of the executive branch, President Bush has made extraordinary claims regarding the constitutional power of the president. Although presidents of both parties have sought to enhance and protect executive prerogatives, President Bush's grasp has exceeded that of most of his predecessors in scope and degree, if not in kind.

In his use of signing statements, President Bush has implied that he might not enforce certain parts of laws that he deems to be in conflict with his own constitutional powers. In ordering the National Security Agency to undertake surveillance of Americans in the United States without obtaining warrants, he has refused to follow the mandates of the Foreign Intelligence Surveillance Act. In his assertion of power to imprison "enemy combatants" indefinitely without due process of law, he has attempted to skirt the Fourth Amendment of the Constitution. In his initial establishment of military tribunals, he has ignored the due processes of law traditionally accorded the accused. In his use of "extraordinary rendition" and the establishment of "black sites" in Europe to secretly imprison suspected terrorists, he has flouted international law. In setting aside the Geneva Conventions, he has ignored the treaties signed by the United States and possibly U.S. laws against torture. In addition, his administration has done much to keep the policies and practices of the U.S. government secret from its citizens.

These actions call into question the foundations of a constitutional republic that is accountable to the people. The rule of law is fundamental to a republic because freedom, liberty, and democracy are impossible without it. Secrecy, extraordinary claims to executive power, and an unwillingness to listen to outside advice can be dangerous to a Madisonian system of divided powers. Madison posited that "ambition must be made to counteract ambition," and the executive is fulfilling Madison's expectations of executive assertiveness. Congress, however, has not recently applied the countervailing force that Madison expected. Only the courts, so far, have put up small roadblocks in the path of executive assertions of power.

In its ruling in *Hamdan v. Rumsfeld*, the U.S. Supreme Court refused to allow the executive to create military tribunals without legislative authorization or providing for the due process of law. Most notably, Justice Sandra Day O'Connor declared in *Hamdi v. Rumsfeld* (159 L. Ed. 2d 578 [2004]), "We have long since made clear that a state of war is not a blank check for the President when it comes to the rights of the Nation's citizens."

At the close of the Constitutional Convention in 1787, Benjamin Franklin is reported to have said, in response to a query as to what the framers had created, "A republic, Madam, if you can keep it." Whether the republic will endure depends on whether we can maintain the balance of constitutional powers envisioned by the framers of the Constitution.

* * *

REFERENCES

Allen, Mike. 2004. Management Style Shows Weaknesses. *Washington Post*, June 2.

Allen, Mike, and David S. Broder. 2004. Bush's Leadership Style: Decisive or Simplistic? *Washington Post*, August 30.

Arnold, Peti E. 1986. *Making the Managerial Presidency: Comprehensive Reorganization Planning, 1905–1980*. Princeton, NJ: Princeton University Press.

Bossidy, Larry, and Ram Charan. 2002. *Execution: The Discipline of Getting Things Done*. New York: Random House.

Brinkley, Douglas. 2006. *The Great Deluge: Hurricane Katrina, New Orleans, and the Mississippi Gulf Coast*. New York: Morrow.

Brook, Douglas A., Cynthia L. King, David Anderson, and Joshua Bahr. 2006. *Legislating Civil Service Reform: The Homeland Security Act of 2002*. Monterey, CA: Naval Postgraduate School, Center for Defense Management Reform. www.nps.navy.mil/gsbpp/CDMR/publications.htm [accessed September 25, 2006].

Brooks, David. 2004. The C.I.A. versus Bush. *New York Times*, November 13.

Burke, John P., and Fred I. Grenstein. 1991. *How Presidents Test Reality: Decisions on Vietnam, 1954 and 1965*. New York: Russell Sage Foundation.

Fukuyama, Francis. 2006. *America at the Crossroads: Democracy, Power, and the Neoconservative Legacy*. New Haven, CT: Yale University Press.

Heclo, Hugh. 1999. The Changing Presidential Office. In *The Managerial Presidency*, 2nd ed., edited by James P. Pfiffner, 23–36. College Station: Texas A&M University Press.

Kessler, Ronald. 2004. *A Matter of Character: Inside the White House of George W. Bush*. New York: Sentinel.

Kettl, Donald F. 2003. *Team Bush: Leadership Lessons from the Bush White House*. New York: McGraw-Hill.

Lemann, Nicholas. 2002. Without a Doubt. *New Yorker*, October 14–26. www.newyorker.com/fact/content/articles/021014fa_fact3 [accessed September 27, 2006].

———. 2004. Remember the Alamo. *New Yorker*, October 18. www.newyorker.com/fact/content/?041018fa_fact [accessed September 27, 2006].

Magretta, Joan, and Nat Stone. 2002. *What Management Is: How It Works and Why It's Everyone's Business*. New York: Free Press.

McLaughlin, John. 2005. The CIA Is No "Rogue" Agency. *Washington Post*, November 24.

Mintzberg, Henry. 2004. *Managers, Not MBAs: A Hard Look at the Soft Practice of Managing and Management Development*. San Francisco: Berrett-Koehler.

Novak, Robert D. 2004. "Rogue" CIA. *Washington Post*, November 18.

———. 2005b. Presidential Leadership and Advice about Going to War. Paper prepared for the Conference on Presidential Leadership, Richmond, VA, September 9–10.

Pfiffner, James P. 2005. Presidential Leadership and Advice about Going to War. Paper prepared for the Conference on Presidential Leadership, Richmond, VA, September 9–10.

Robinson, Linda, and Kevin Whitelaw. 2006. Seeking Spies: Why the CIA Is Having Such a Hard Time Keeping Its Best. *U.S. News and World Report*, February 13. www.usnews.com/usnews/news/articles/060213/13cia.htm [accessed September 28, 2006].

Schmitt, Eric. 2006. Clash Foreseen between CIA and Pentagon. *New York Times*, May 10.

Suskind, Ron. 2003. Why Are These Men Laughing? www.ronsuskind.com/articles/000032.html [accessed September 27, 2006].

————. 2004a. Faith, Certainty, and the Presidency of George W. Bush. *New York Times Magazine*, October 17.

————. 2004b. *The Price of Loyalty: George W. Bush, the White House, and the Education of Paul O'Neill.* New York: Simon & Schuster.

VandeHei, Jim, and Glenn Kessler. 2004. President to Consider Changes for New Term. *Washington Post*, November 5.

White House. 2006. President Nominated Rob Portman as OMB Director and Susan Schwab for USTR. News release, April 18. http://www.whitehouse.gov/news/releases/2006/04/20060418-1. html. [accessed September 25, 2006].

Wilkerson, Lawrence. 2005. Weighing the Uniqueness of the Bush Administration's National Security Decision-Making Process: Boon or Danger to American Democracy? Remarks at the New America Foundation Policy Forum, October 19.

Woodward, Bob. 2002. *Bush at War.* New York: Simon & Schuster.

30

"Presidency: Politics Squared"

ALEXIS SIMENDINGER

Monica Goodling learned everything she needed to know about screening candidates for Justice Department jobs during her year as an opposition researcher at the Republican National Committee. If President Bush's critics were looking for a simple testimonial to illustrate how the White House managed to push GOP-centered political considerations deep into the executive branch, Goodling's House testimony last week provided it.

Or maybe just one more example. Democratic committee chairmen are digging into the small type of government contracts that benefited Bush administration friends. They want to know more about White House briefings that encouraged workers in federal agencies to help the GOP. And they want to know much more about White House e-mails written on Republican National Committee accounts—especially the ones that seem to have gone missing.

Goodling explained to lawmakers that her RNC training, including poring over old news clippings and checking voter registrations to identify like-minded Republicans, proved helpful in her subsequent job as an adviser to the attorney general, since she was one of three or four people who screened new hires in the Justice Department. But more important, Goodling told Congress, was her ability after seven years with the Bush team to ferret out—with detailed guidance from those above her—the attributes her bosses at Justice and the White House valued in prospective prosecutors.

"I do acknowledge that I may have gone too far in asking political questions of applicants for career positions," Goodling told the House Judiciary Committee after securing immunity from federal prosecution, "and I may have taken inappropriate political considerations into account on some occasions."

To the administration's critics, stuffing the lower ranks of the Justice Department with conservative Republicans fits right in with their theory that top-level U.S. attorneys were fired because they weren't furthering the electoral prospects of the GOP—an unsavory sort of executive engineering that damaged morale, undercut the administration's credibility, and possibly interfered with delivery of justice.

The ultimate focus of the various investigations is the White House Office of Political Affairs, under the supervision of Karl Rove, Bush's deputy chief of staff and senior political adviser. Goodling didn't recall talking directly to Rove, but she described having regular conversations with his aides about finding attorneys who would be "ideologically compatible" with the president.

It isn't just Democrats who say that the linkage between White House staffers, government functions, and the interests of the Republican Party has become too tight.

"I'm appalled," Republican political consultant Ed Rollins says of the heavy-handed partisan politics that have been revealed in this year's congressional oversight hearings. Rollins was political affairs director in the Reagan administration—the first one to have such a government-funded office. In Rollins's day, firewalls kept the political operatives from having direct contact with executive departments—particularly Justice. "What's happened with this administration is that too many people came in, like the Karl Roves, who had no experience in government," Rollins says. "Campaigns are very separate things, where you're always trying to think politically."

Political scientists who have studied how presidents organize their administrations say that the imposition of campaign-inspired political controls inside the executive branch evolved throughout the twentieth century.

"Institutionalized politics in the White House has been around at least since FDR expanded the Executive Office of the President and brought his close advisers into the White House," said Kathryn Dunn Tenpas, a University of Pennsylvania political scientist who has written extensively on the subject.

President Reagan was the first to put a name to a specialized office that became known as "political affairs." The office was the contact point for all the constituencies that supported Reagan's reelection as well as his role as head of his party. President Clinton elevated the head of his political affairs office to Cabinet-level status, with a seat among senior staff and policy advisers. Bush's creation of a division for Rove, called the Office of

Strategic Initiatives, went the next step, establishing a centralized GOP watchtower over just about all facets of government with one eye on promoting the Republican Party and the other on ways to clobber Democrats.

"Bush has prioritized politics more than any other president because he's expanded the White House Office and all the wings in it," Tenpas said.

Bush's defenders argue that politics are afoot in Washington, all right—the kind practiced by the opposition party during an emotional and unpopular war, as it prepares for a wide-open presidential election in 2008. The same Democrats, they point out, never worked up such a lather over the 103 fundraising coffees hosted inside the Clinton White House, or the hundreds of Lincoln Bedroom sleepovers for generous Democratic donors as Clinton geared up for reelection.

For Democrats now in the congressional majority, "everything is just media-driven" and the organizing principle is, " 'What story can we create today to make the Republicans look bad?' " said longtime Republican strategist Charlie Black, who is close to both Presidents Bush. Rove is "the guy to blame who stole the [2000] election," he added.

Rewards, and Punishments

On George W. Bush's first full day on the job, and again on his 99th day in the Oval Office in 2001, the White House sent Rove, who had transitioned from campaign manager to West Wing senior adviser, to sit in NBC's *Meet the Press* hot seat. During the interviews, Rove wove together Bush's new agenda and his conservative political disposition to respond to questions from moderator Tim Russert.

Asked about Bush's regulatory intentions to weaken his predecessor's limits on arsenic in drinking water, Rove knew that the question was aimed at the president's perceived anti-environmentalism. And because Rove grew up in Utah and the West, he thought he had a firsthand understanding of how arsenic could be a naturally occurring substance in some water supplies and how tougher regulation would not be appreciated by industry or the energy sector.

"This limit of 10 [parts per billion] was arrived at by using a test group of malnourished Taiwanese farmers who drank water that had naturally occurring arsenic concentrations of between 100 and 500 parts per billion," Rove said.

"So we're going to . . . make a determination on the basis of sound science. And it's not going to take us eight years to get it done. We're going to get it done this year."

These were pithy sound bites—"malnourished Taiwanese farmers" was the sort of zinger a political adviser would dream up—but as it turned out, the public disagreed with Bush on the substantive question of allowable poisons in drinking water, and he wound up adopting the

Clinton arsenic rule. By August of his first year, Bush was saying he wished he could get a do-over on arsenic.

Those Rove interviews, which wandered over an expanse of policy questions, were memorable, said Doug Sosnik, who was Clinton's political affairs director in the White House and later his senior adviser, because Rove "was transparent and open about the politics driving the policy." Based on his own experience, Sosnik remembers thinking that such openness was "a big mistake."

"For anyone to say there isn't politics in the White House is ridiculous," Sosnik continued, conceding that the Clinton White House justly earned a reputation for being overtly political while governing. Clinton's campaign finance activities, which sparked federal and congressional investigations, were an example of "pushing all the way to the line without crossing it," he said.

The evolution from the Clinton political operation to the Bush shop holds distinctions with real differences, Clinton's former aides argue. "The problem with this White House is that they conflated the policy and political roles that Rove had so that they are indistinguishable," Sosnik said. "They took the letter of the law and pushed it to at least the line, if not over it, and in the process certainly violated the spirit of it. They got used to it; that was the culture. And they had a supplicant Congress that was their witness protection program. It was a culture where everyone understood the reward system."

That culture—and Bush's ambition to consolidate executive power—has helped erode Bush's credibility and his powers to persuade, suggested Leon Panetta, who was Clinton's second chief of staff, his former budget director, and for 17 years before that a Democratic member of Congress from California. "Every president has that political instinct, but you cannot make everything you do the result of political motivation because you lose the ability to persuade the American people that substantively it is in their interest," he said.

Clinton learned, after his first two nominees were shot down, that the Justice Department was particularly volatile. As numerous aides confided to reporters at the time, Clinton would have loved to replace Attorney General Janet Reno but did not dare. She ended up sticking around for eight years.

"When it comes to the Justice Department, it has to operate in a separate sphere," Panetta added. "You cannot have an attorney general and a Justice Department act as if they're part of the Republican National Committee."

That lesson comes courtesy of John Mitchell. As a reward for Mitchell's prowess as manager of Nixon's 1968 presidential campaign, the president named him attorney general in 1969. By 1977, Mitchell was in prison for his Watergate crimes.

"The Guy They Love to Hate"

The White House response to the chorus of critics, most of them Democrats, is threefold. Politics, it says, is part of governing. Second, the president expects Rove to practice politics because that's his role in the White House, and Bush believes that administration critics take a peculiar pleasure in making Rove a target. And third, the administration may have entertained political considerations before removing the U.S. attorneys, but there was no political interference with their work.

"People use the word 'politics' in strange ways these days," deputy White House press secretary Dana Perino said. "I don't think that's a bad word. To suggest that we should not think about the politics of an issue in terms of the outcome would be foolish."

To the White House, attacks on Rove are at once understandable and still puzzling. "There's this obsession with Karl that is bordering on the weird, and almost the disturbing," Perino said. "He's the guy they love to hate. He's the president's political adviser, so I don't know how they can say what's on the spectrum of 'too political.'"

Aiming Democratic oversight at Rove's behavior is another way of going after the president's remaining hard-core base of conservative support, because Rove is the liaison to that part of Bush's world, said presidential historian Al Felzenberg, who is a former Heritage Foundation fellow, an author, and the former spokesman for the 9/11 commission.

"I have never seen this kind of vitriol over a staff member," he said. "I think the Democrats have decided to focus on Rove because they feel that if they knock the Rove leg out from under the administration, the entire administration will collapse. I think what's driving it is that he's successful. But the legend of Karl Rove comes more from his opponents than it does from him. I don't hear Republicans saying he's indispensable."

"They've Hurt This President"

Presidents have long kept their closest political advisers within arm's reach—Franklin D. Roosevelt relied on Harry Hopkins, for example, and President Truman turned to Clark Clifford—but the institutional White House changes evolved in tandem with the decline of the national political parties as power bases and the rise of candidate-centered campaigns, largely inspired by the shift from caucuses to presidential primaries. Presidents adapted to the shifting reelection terrain by expanding the White House staff and creating teams of political experts to strengthen White House control of executive agencies and to curry votes.

Nixon made substantial organizational changes to the White House aimed at consolidating his reach over Cabinet departments and agencies, as well as his influence over Congress. In elaborate secrecy, Nixon hatched a reorganization plan in 1970 that resulted in the creation of a Domestic Council, as well as the Office of Management and Budget.

Nixon had already asserted his command of foreign policy through Henry Kissinger, and with his reorganization he ensured that every document on domestic affairs and every decision about domestic policy would take place in the West Wing under the supervision of counselor John Ehrlichman.

After Nixon went down in Watergate, the next several presidents formalized the structures that support their role as head of a political party. This brought civil servants under the protection of the Hatch Act, which forbids manipulation by political bosses, and led to safeguards, such as financial disclosure forms.

Reagan established the Office of Political Affairs in the White House and brought in campaign aides Lyn Nofziger and Rollins to run it. As Nofziger recalled before his death, James Baker came to him after Reagan's victory and said, "I want somebody to handle politics, on the political end, as an assistant to the president for political affairs."

Nofziger did not remain in government for long before turning the office over to Rollins, but his initial job description was to maintain contact with the RNC, the state committees, and politically important allies of the president around the country. Once inside the White House, Nofziger told the University of Virginia during a lengthy oral history interview, he realized he wanted to expand his reach into the selection of personnel because Reagan's team "had no concept of the political part of government. They were looking for competent people. I tried to explain to them that the first thing you do is get loyal people, and competence is a bonus."

The power of the advisers depends on the relationships they share with the president, according to interviews with some who have held the positions and according to published studies. For example, President George H. W. Bush was closer to his longtime independent political adviser, Robert Teeter, than he was to his White House political staff. And Bush found in James Baker a hybrid adviser who was accomplished in governing as a Cabinet secretary yet also powerful as a political adviser who ran campaigns and managed the White House staff.

Clinton sought the political advice of James Carville and Paul Begala long after they helped him get elected in 1992, but Carville said from the outset that he had no interest in hiring on with the White House staff. Begala eventually accepted a White House post, and was a senior Clinton adviser when the Monica Lewinsky story became public.

Bush pushed things further by building his White House structure around Rove, who commands a kingdom of 42 people. In addition to Rove's long-range strategic planning and supervision of the Office of Political Affairs, which has a staff of 10 people and direct ties to the RNC, his reach includes the White House offices of Public Liaison and Intergovernmental Affairs. Rove also signs off on personnel picks and presidential appointments, and he has plenty to say about communications and legislation.

In 2005, Bush gave his political architect the add-on title of deputy chief of staff, handling policy. But a year ago, Bush's new chief of staff, Joshua Bolten, nominally trimmed Rove's hold over policy and said that Rove would focus his talents on the midterm elections.

Still, Rove maintains his mythological power by virtue of his ties to the president. Few in government have the standing to "hold him in check," Rollins said. The decisions made by Rove and his colleagues— co-workers who have no desire or ability to reduce his influence—have "hurt this president. And especially in dealing with a place like Justice, which should always have been a place of integrity," Rollins said.

On Guard

To save presidents from themselves and their clever advisers, White House history suggests that checks and balances are essential. Sticklers for policing the commingling of politics and governing are not always the most popular White House staff members. To make an impact they usually need forceful backing from the president, a tough chief of staff, or a vigilant White House counsel.

Rollins remembers that in the Reagan White House, the staff directory spelled out in black and white that no aide was permitted to speak to Justice Department headquarters or to independent agencies. "Only White House Counsel Fred Fielding talked to Justice," Rollins said. "We were very sensitive to the politics and the governing aspects of the game. I think it's all gotten blurred at this point in time."

In Bush's case with the fired U.S. attorneys, Rove aide Scott Jennings, a White House political deputy, thought nothing of using e-mail to contact the attorney general's counselors at Justice. Those communications were sent to the department from his political account at the RNC.

C. Boyden Gray, who was White House counsel under Bush's father, once infuriated James Baker, then secretary of State, by ginning up media pressure to force Baker to sell some stock that Gray believed posed a potential conflict that could embarrass the president. And eight months before the 1992 election, Gray tried to wall off George H. W. Bush's reelection campaign officials—including Charlie Black and Fred Malek, men who maintained lucrative outside business relationships—from high-level White House policy makers and from policy meetings. Prompted by attack ads paid for by Pat Buchanan, a Bush opponent, Gray set up a communications system that funneled all contacts with the campaign team through then–Chief of Staff Samuel Skinner. Gray told reporters he wanted to make sure "they do not have the power to execute anything. . . . They are not making policy."

Panetta remembers, as chief of staff, threatening Clinton with his resignation if the president would not agree to a new firewall. At the time, Clinton thought he needed outside help from Dick Morris, a freewheeling Republican political consultant who was viewed with suspicion by most Democrats and especially by the White House staff. Panetta had discovered that Morris was secretly contacting Clinton's aides about policy issues, outside of the White House chain of command.

The chief of staff set Morris straight, barring him without exception, for example, from involvement in foreign policy. But he also had to lay down some law with his boss. "I told the president, 'I cannot act as your chief of staff in a situation where a political adviser is going to be interfering with my authority,'" Panetta recalled. "He told Clinton that without such backing, he would lose a chief of staff. And the president agreed. Clinton knew what Morris was like."

In or Out?

The Morris example is one reason presidents historically have found it more advantageous to put their closest political advisers on staff, giving them the authority and White House structure to influence events. Although Rove had been an outside political consultant to Bush when he served as Texas governor, he coveted a White House staff role when Bush was inaugurated. "This is what he dreamed of all his life," a former colleague said of Rove's ambitions to advise a president from the West Wing.

The good-government rationale for putting political advisers on the White House payroll is the checks on possible misbehavior: independent scrutiny of conflicts of interest, or any national security risks; application of ethics rules and requirements for annual financial disclosure; and a ban on post-employment lobbying, plus mandates to preserve presidential communications about official business.

In his 2000 book, *The White House Staff: Inside the West Wing and Beyond*, political scientist Bradley Patterson wrote that political advisers who are volunteers or paid by others tend to spend their time trying to push information inside, to the Oval Office, while presidents' on-staff political advisers work to reach outside the White House to bring feedback to the president from various constituencies.

Because Reagan's aides thought of the president as a man who did not spend a lot of time talking politics, his Office of Political Affairs maintained a somewhat separatist air about its business around the White House. Rollins recalled that during Reagan's reelection campaign, the office effectively shut down and moved to the campaign. Fielding issued a memo that the White House staff could have no contact with the campaign other than through Rollins or Baker aide Margaret Tutwiler. "We kept very much at arm's length," he said.

The notion now seems quaint. "I always worried about doing damage to the president, which is the critical thing," Rollins said. Republicans controlled the Senate at the time, but Democrats controlled the House, and Rollins said he feared the harsh scrutiny of the opposing party, working with a vigorous Fourth Estate.

Congressional investigations are a powerful form of oversight. But if the president is in a strong position with the public, he can withstand the scrutiny.

More than three decades ago, Nixon's organizational changes and his expansion of the White House staff to a bloated 560 people raised alarms among Democrats in Congress. Lawmakers held hearings, examined the White House appropriations and a $1.5 million "Special Projects fund," and ordered up federal audits. They made close studies of where Nixon spent taxpayer dollars for political purposes, and Ralph Nader and Public Citizen filed suit to recover more than $10,000 paid to White House aides who they claimed were working for Nixon's reelection.

But at the time, Nixon's critics in Congress confessed to utter frustration that their complaints had little impact on the president. On the Senate floor in September 1970, Sen. Ralph Yarborough, D-Texas, assailed Nixon's jumbo-sized staff and observed that "apparently, there is a long-standing understanding that they do not question our appropriations request as it pertains to the Congress, and we do not stop their appropriations."

Critics of the Bush White House and its politicization of governance argue that self-policing has to be the first check on overreach, followed by external oversight—from Congress, the courts, and an aggressive media. After that, remedies are up to the voters.

Political scientist Tenpas predicts that Bush's successor will balk at replicating the current model. "I think the Office of Strategic Initiatives will go," she said. "It was created for Rove, and I don't know who the next president is going to be, but he or she is not going to hire someone like Karl Rove."

The next president is more likely to search out "a hybrid," she said, meaning an adviser "with suitable skills to governing and campaigning."

The lesson after eight years with the Bush administration may be that hiding the political Wizard of Oz behind a sturdy curtain has advantages. "It is dangerous to reveal the degree to which you really care about politics if you're president," Tenpas added, "because the American people don't want to know the degree to which presidents care about polls, focus groups, strategists, and the political calculus for presidential actions."

And despite the White House condemnations of Democratic critics as consumed in their political theatrics, the president still feels the heat when the head of the opposing national party finds an opening to turn a White House aide into a juicy political target. "The Bush White House continued to put partisan politics ahead of the interests of the American people when it fired U.S. attorneys and inserted politics into ongoing criminal prosecutions," Democratic National Committee Chairman Howard Dean said in March while calling for Attorney General Alberto Gonzales's resignation. "Karl Rove should pack his bags and go, too. His type of leadership doesn't belong in the White House."

DISCUSSION QUESTIONS

1. Is there a "best way" to balance bureaucratic responsiveness with competent administration?

2. Defenders of the Bush administration note that *every* president makes decisions with an eye toward political consequences (citing Clinton, especially), and that Bush has been especially steadfast in his refusal to bend to changes in political winds. Is this a virtue or a liability? How much of your answer depends on what you think about Bush's specific policy decisions?

CHAPTER 7

Bureaucracy in a Democratic System

31

"The Study of Administration"

Woodrow Wilson

Until the late nineteenth century, almost no one paid attention to how the gov-
ernment actually worked. Administrative positions were generally filled by polit-
ical appointees who were supporters of elected officials, and there was little that
resembled "management" in the contemporary sense. There was, however, a
great deal of money distributed at the national level, and as scandals mounted
over the manner in which the money was distributed, the demand for govern-
ment accountability grew.

Reformers argued that government employees should be hired on the basis of
their merit, rather than because of their political allegiance to one candidate or
another. Others called for reforms in the administration of public programs.
Nearly thirty years before he was president, Woodrow Wilson, then a professor at
Bryn Mawr College, wrote an article for the Political Science Quarterly *argu-*
ing that political scientists had neglected the study of public administration (or
the problems involved in managing public programs). He argued that public ad-
ministration should be carried out in accordance with scientific principles of
management and efficiency, an argument that can be heard in contemporary de-
bates over the need to "reinvent" government.

It is the object of administrative study to discover, first, what government can properly and successfully do, and, secondly, how it can do
these proper things with the utmost possible efficiency and at the least
possible cost either of money or of energy. On both these points there is
obviously much need of light among us; and only careful study can
supply that light.

* * *

The science of administration is the latest fruit of that study of the science of politics which was begun some twenty-two hundred years ago. It is a birth of our own century, almost of our own generation.

Why was it so late in coming? Why did it wait till this too busy century of ours to demand attention for itself? Administration is the most obvious part of government; it is government in action; it is the executive, the operative, the most visible side of government, and is of course as old as government itself. It is government in action, and one might very naturally expect to find that government in action had arrested the attention and provoked the scrutiny of writers of politics very early in the history of systematic thought.

But such was not the case. No one wrote systematically of administration as a branch of the science of government until the present century had passed its first youth and had begun to put forth its characteristic flower of systematic knowledge. Up to our own day all the political writers whom we now read had thought, argued, dogmatized only about the *constitution* of government; about the nature of the state, the essence and seat of sovereignty, popular power and kingly prerogative; about the greatest meanings lying at the heart of government, and the high ends set before the purpose of government by man's nature and man's aims. * * * The question was always: Who shall make law, and what shall that law be? The other question, how law should be administered with enlightenment, with equity, with speed, and without fiction, was put aside as "practical detail" which clerks could arrange after doctors had agreed upon principles.

*   *   *

[However,] if difficulties of government action are to be seen gathering in other centuries, they are to be seen culminating in our own.

This is the reason why administrative tasks have nowadays to be so studiously and systematically adjusted to carefully tested standards of policy, the reason why we are having now what we never had before, a science of administration. The weightier debates of constitutional principle are even yet by no means concluded; but they are no longer of more immediate practical moment than questions of administration. It is getting to be harder to *run* a constitution than to frame one.

*   *   *

There is scarcely a single duty of government which was once simple which is not now complex; government once had but a few masters; it now has scores of masters. Majorities formerly only underwent government; they now conduct government. Where government once might follow the whims of a court, it must now follow the views of a nation.

And those views are steadily widening to new conceptions of state duty; so that at the same time that the functions of government are every day becoming more complex and difficult, they are also vastly multiplying in number. Administration is everywhere putting its hands to new undertakings. * * * Seeing every day new things which the state ought to do, the next thing is to see clearly how it ought to do them.

This is why there should be a science of administration which shall seek to straighten the paths of government, to make its business less businesslike, to strengthen and purify its organization, and to crown its dutifulness. This is one reason why there is such a science.

But where has this science grown up? Surely not on this side [of] the sea. Not much impartial scientific method is to be discerned in our administrative practices. The poisonous atmosphere of city government, the crooked secrets of state administration, the confusion, sinecurism, and corruption ever and again discovered in the bureaus at Washington forbid us to believe that any clear conceptions of what constitutes good administration are as yet very widely current in the United States.

* * *

American political history has been a history, not of administrative development, but of legislative oversight—not of progress in governmental organization, but of advance in law-making and political criticism. Consequently, we have reached a time when administrative study and creation are imperatively necessary to the well-being of our governments saddled with the habits of a long period of constitution-making. * * * We have reached * * * the period * * * when the people have to develop administration in accordance with the constitutions they won for themselves in a previous period of struggle with absolute power.

* * *

It is harder for democracy to organize administration than for monarchy. The very completeness of our most cherished political successes in the past embarrasses us. We have enthroned public opinion; and it is forbidden us to hope during its reign for any quick schooling of the sovereign in executive expertness or in the conditions of perfect functional balance in government. The very fact that we have realized popular rule in its fullness has made the task of *organizing* that rule just so much the more difficult. * * * An individual sovereign will adopt a simple plan and carry it out directly: he will have but one opinion, and he will embody that one opinion in one command. But this other sovereign, the people, will have a score of differing opinions. They can agree upon nothing simple: advance must be made through compromise, by a compounding of differences, by a trimming of plans and a suppression of too straightforward principles. There will be a succession of resolves running through a course of years, a dropping fire of commands running through a whole gamut of modifications.

* * *

Wherever regard for public opinion is a first principle of government, practical reform must be slow and all reform must be full of compromises. For wherever public opinion exists it must rule.

* * *

The field of administration is a field of business. It is removed from the hurry and strife of politics; it at most points stands apart even from the debatable ground of constitutional study. It is a part of political life only as the methods of the counting-house are a part of the life of society; only as machinery is part of the manufactured product. But it is, at the same time, raised very far above the dull level of mere technical detail by the fact that through its greater principles it is directly connected with the lasting maxims of political wisdom, the permanent truths of political progress.

The object of administrative study is to rescue executive methods from the confusion and costliness of empirical experiment and set them upon foundations laid deep in stable principle.

* * *

[A]dministration lies outside the proper sphere of *politics*. Administrative questions are not political questions. Although politics sets the tasks for administration, it should not be suffered to manipulate its offices.

* * *

There is another distinction which must be worked into all our conclusions, which, though but another side of that between administration and politics, is not quite so easy to keep sight of: I mean the distinction between *constitutional* and administrative questions, between those governmental adjustments which are essential to constitutional principle and those which are merely instrumental to the possibly changing purposes of a wisely adapting convenience.

* * *

A clear view of the difference between the province of constitutional law and the province of administrative function ought to leave no room for misconception; and it is possible to name some roughly definite criteria upon which such a view can be built. Public administration is detailed and systematic execution of public law. Every particular application of general law is an act of administration. The assessment and raising of taxes, for instance, the hanging of a criminal, the transportation and delivery of the mails, the equipment and recruiting of the army, and navy, etc., are all obviously acts of administration; but the general laws which direct these things to be done are as obviously outside of and above administration. The broad plans of governmental action are not administrative; the detailed execution of such plans is administrative. Constitutions, therefore, properly concern themselves only with those instrumentalities of government which are to control general law. Our federal constitution observes this principle in saying nothing of even the greatest of the purely executive offices, and speaking only of that President of the Union who was to share the legislative and policy-making functions of government, only of those judges of highest jurisdiction who were to interpret and guard its principles, and not of those who were merely to give utterance to them.

*   *   *

There is, [however,] one point at which administrative studies trench on constitutional ground—or at least upon what seems constitutional ground. The study of administration, philosophically viewed, is closely connected with the study of the proper distribution of constitutional authority. To be efficient it must discover the simplest arrangements by which responsibility can be unmistakably fixed upon officials; the best way of dividing authority without hampering it, and responsibility without obscuring it. And this question of the distribution of authority, when taken into the sphere of the higher, the originating functions of government, is obviously a central constitutional question.

*   *   *

To discover the best principle for the distribution of authority is of greater importance, possibly, under a democratic system, where officials serve many masters, than under others where they serve but a few. All sovereigns are suspicious of their servants, and the sovereign people is no exception to the rule; but how is its suspicion to be allayed by *knowledge*? If that suspicion could be clarified into wise vigilance, it would be altogether salutary; if that vigilance could be aided by the unmistakable placing of responsibility, it would be altogether beneficent. Suspicion in itself is never healthful either in the private or in the public mind. *Trust is strength* in all relations of life; and, as it is the office of the constitutional reformer to create conditions of trustfulness, so it is the office of the administrative organizer to fit administration with conditions of clear-cut responsibility which shall insure trustworthiness.

And let me say that large powers and unhampered discretion seem to me the indispensable conditions of responsibility. Public attention must be easily directed, in each case of good or bad administration, to just the man deserving of praise or blame. There is no danger in power, if only it be not irresponsible. If it be divided, dealt out in shares to many, it is obscured; and if it be obscured, it is made irresponsible. But if it be centered in heads of the service and in heads of branches of the service, it is easily watched and brought to book. If to keep his office a man must achieve open and honest success, and if at the same time he feels himself intrusted with large freedom of discretion, the greater his power the less likely is he to abuse it, the more is he nerved and sobered and elevated by it. The less his power, the more safely obscure and unnoticed does he feel his position to be, and the more readily does he relapse into remissness.

Just here we manifestly emerge upon the field of that still larger question—the proper relations between public opinion and administration.

To whom is official trustworthiness to be disclosed, and by whom is it to be rewarded? Is the official to look to the public for his meed of praise and his push of promotion, or only to his superior in office? Are the people to be called in to settle administrative discipline as they are called in to settle constitutional principles? These questions evidently find their root in what is undoubtedly the fundamental problem of this whole study. That problem is: What part shall public opinion take in the conduct of administration?

The right answer seems to be, that public opinion shall play the part of authoritative critic.

But the *method* by which its authority shall be made to tell? Our peculiar American difficulty in organizing administration is not the danger of losing liberty, but the danger of not being able or willing to separate its essentials from its accidents. Our success is made doubtful by that besetting error of ours, the error of trying to do too much by vote. Self-government does not consist in having a hand in everything, any more than housekeeping consists necessarily in cooking dinner with one's own hands. The cook must be trusted with a large discretion as to the management of the fires and the ovens.

*   *   *

The problem is to make public opinion efficient without suffering it to be meddlesome. Directly exercised, in the oversight of the daily details and in the choice of the daily means of government, public criticism is of course a clumsy nuisance, a rustic handling delicate machinery. But as superintending the greater forces of formative policy alike in politics and administration, public criticism is altogether safe and beneficent, altogether indispensable. Let administrative study find the best means for giving public criticism this control and for shutting it out from all other interference.

But is the whole duty of administrative study done when it has taught the people what sort of administration to desire and demand, and how to get what they demand? Ought it not to go on to drill candidates for the public service?

*   *   *

If we are to improve public opinion, which is the motive power of government, we must prepare better officials as the *apparatus* of government. * * * It will be necessary to organize democracy by sending up to the competitive examinations for the civil service men definitely prepared for standing liberal tests as to technical knowledge. A technically schooled civil service will presently have become indispensable.

I know that a corps of civil servants prepared by a special schooling and drilled, after appointment, into a perfected organization, with appropriate hierarchy and characteristic discipline, seems to a great many very thoughtful persons to contain elements which might combine to make an offensive official class—a distinct, semi-corporate body with sympathies divorced from those of a progressive, free-spirited people, and with hearts narrowed to the meanness of a bigoted officialism.

* * *

But to fear the creation of a domineering, illiberal officialism as a result of the studies I am here proposing is to miss altogether the principle upon which I wish most to insist. That principle is, that administration in the United States must be at all points sensitive to public opinion. A body of thoroughly trained officials serving during good behavior we must have in any case: that is a plain business necessity. But the apprehension that such a body will be anything un-American clears away the moment it is asked, What is to constitute good behavior? For that question obviously carries its own answer on its face. Steady, hearty allegiance to the policy of the government they serve will constitute good behavior. That *policy* will have no taint of officialism about it. It will not be the creation of permanent officials, but of statesmen whose responsibility to public opinion will be direct and inevitable. Bureaucracy can exist only where the whole service of the state is removed from the common political life of the people, its chiefs as well as its rank and file. Its motives, its objects, its policy, its standards, must be bureaucratic.

* * *

The ideal for us is a civil service cultured and self-sufficient enough to act with sense and vigor, and yet so intimately connected with the popular thought, by means of elections and constant public counsel, as to find arbitrariness or class spirit quite out of the question.

Having thus viewed in some sort the subject-matter and the objects of this study of administration, what are we to conclude as to the methods best suited to it—the points of view most advantageous for it?

Government is so near us, so much a thing of our daily familiar handling, that we can with difficulty see the need of any philosophical study of it, or the exact point of such study, should it be undertaken. We have been on our feet too long to study now the art of walking. We are a practical people, made so apt, so adept in self-government by centuries of experimental drill that we are scarcely any longer capable of perceiving the awkwardness of the particular system we may be using, just because it is so easy for us to use any system. We do not study the art of governing: we govern. But mere unschooled genius for affairs will not save us from sad blunders in administration. Though democrats by long inheritance and repeated choice, we are still rather crude democrats. Old as democracy is, its organization on a basis of modern ideas and conditions is still an unaccomplished work. The democratic state has yet to be equipped for carrying those enormous burdens of administration which the needs of this industrial and trading age are so fast accumulating.

* * *

We can borrow the science of administration [developed elsewhere] with safety and profit if only we read all fundamental differences of condition into its essential tenets. We have only to filter it through our constitutions, only to put it over a slow fire of criticism and distil away its foreign gases.

* * *

Our own politics must be the touchstone for all theories. The principles on which to base a science of administration for America must be principles which have democratic policy very much at heart. And, to suit American habit, all general theories must, as theories, keep modestly in the background, not in open argument only, but even in our own minds—lest opinions satisfactory only to the standards of the library should be dogmatically used, as if they must be quite as satisfactory to the standards of practical politics as well. Doctrinaire devices must be postponed to tested practices. Arrangements not only sanctioned by conclusive experience elsewhere but also congenial to American habit must be preferred without hesitation to theoretical perfection. In a word, steady, practical statesmanship must come first, closet doctrine second. The cosmopolitan what-to-do must always be commanded by the American how-to-do-it.

Our duty is to supply the best possible life to a *federal* organization, to systems within systems; to make town, city, county, state, and federal governments live with a like strength and an equally assured healthfulness, keeping each unquestionably its own master and yet making all interdependent and co-operative, combining independence with mutual helpfulness. The task is great and important enough to attract the best minds.

This interlacing of local self-government with federal self-government is quite a modern conception. * * * The question for us is, how shall our series of governments within governments be so administered that it shall always be to the interest of the public officer to serve, not his superior alone but the community also, with the best efforts of his talents and the soberest service of his conscience? How shall such service be made to his commonest interest by contributing abundantly to his sustenance, to his dearest interest by furthering his ambition, and to his highest interest by advancing his honor and establishing his character? And how shall this be done alike for the local part and for the national whole?

If we solve this problem we shall again pilot the world.

DISCUSSION QUESTIONS

1. Do you agree with Wilson's central proposition that politics and administration are separate things? Can you think of any examples where the two overlap?

2. George W. Bush's second term has been filled with allegations of "politicized administration," from the firing of several U.S. attorneys for not being sufficiently aggressive in pushing his policy agenda, to the Surgeon General testifying that he had to change policy views when they were not consistent with the president's, to NASA scientists who were not able to express their views on global warming. Do these experiences show that the neutrality and efficiency suggested by Wilson is impossible? Is it possible, or even desirable, to separate politics and administration?

3. Expanding on that last question, should presidents be able to push their policy agenda in implementing policies, or should there be an expectation of neutral efficiency that separates politics from administration?

32

From *Bureaucracy: What Government Agencies Do and Why They Do It*

James Q. Wilson

Woodrow Wilson was merely the first in a long line of reformers to suggest that government might be more efficient if it ran more like a business. The sentiment remains today. Perhaps a more "businesslike" government would issue our income tax refunds more promptly, protect the environment at lower cost, and impose fewer burdens on citizens. The catch is, we want all this at low cost and minimal intrusiveness in our lives, yet we want government bureaucracies to be held strictly accountable for the authority they exercise.

James Q. Wilson argues that government will never operate like a business, nor should it be expected to. His comparison of the Watertown, Massachusetts, Registry of Motor Vehicles (representing any government bureaucracy) with a nearby McDonald's (representing any private profit-seeking organization) shows that the former will most likely never service its clientele as well as the latter. The problem is not bureaucratic laziness, or any of the conventional criticisms of government agencies, but is instead due to the very different characteristics of public versus private enterprises. In order to understand "what government agencies do and why they do it," Wilson argues we must first understand that government bureaucracies operate in a political marketplace, rather than an economic one. The annual revenues and personnel resources of a government agency are determined by elected officials, not by the agency's ability to meet the demands of its customers in a cost-efficient manner. The government agency's internal structure and decision-making procedures are defined by legislation, regulation, and executive orders, while similar decisions in a private business are made by executive officers and management within the organization. And, perhaps most critically, a government agency's goals are often vague, difficult if not impossible to measure, and even contradictory. In business, by contrast, the task is simpler. The basic goal of a private business has always been to maximize the bottom line: profit. While we should not approach the reform of government agencies the way we might a private bureaucracy, Wilson notes we should nevertheless try to make government bureaucracies operate more effectively and efficiently.

By the time the office opens at 8:45 A.M., the line of people waiting to do business at the Registry of Motor Vehicles in Watertown, Massachusetts, often will be twenty-five deep. By midday, especially if it is near the end of the month, the line may extend clear around the building. Inside, motorists wait in slow-moving rows before poorly marked windows to get a driver's license or to register an automobile. When someone gets to the head of the line, he or she is often told by the clerk that it is the wrong line: "Get an application over there and then come back," or "This is only for people getting a new license; if you want to replace one you lost, you have to go to the next window." The customers grumble impatiently. The clerks act harried and sometimes speak brusquely, even rudely. What seems to be a simple transaction may take 45 minutes or even longer. By the time people are photographed for their driver's licenses, they are often scowling. The photographer valiantly tries to get people to smile, but only occasionally succeeds.

Not far away, people also wait in line at a McDonald's fast-food restaurant. There are several lines; each is short, each moves quickly. The menu is clearly displayed on attractive signs. The workers behind the counter are invariably polite. If someone's order cannot be filled immediately, he or she is asked to step aside for a moment while the food is prepared and then is brought back to the head of the line to receive the order. The atmosphere is friendly and good-natured. The room is immaculately clean.

Many people have noticed the difference between getting a driver's license and ordering a Big Mac. Most will explain it by saying that bureaucracies are different from businesses. "Bureaucracies" behave as they do because they are run by unqualified "bureaucrats" and are enmeshed in "rules" and "red tape."

But business firms are also bureaucracies, and McDonald's is a bureaucracy that regulates virtually every detail of its employees' behavior by a complex and all-encompassing set of rules. Its operations manual is six hundred pages long and weighs four pounds. In it one learns that french fries are to be nine-thirty-seconds of an inch thick and that grill workers are to place hamburger patties on the grill from left to right, six to a row for six rows. They are then to flip the third row first, followed by the fourth, fifth, and sixth rows, and finally the first and second. The amount of sauce placed on each bun is precisely specified. Every window must be washed every day. Workers must get down on their hands and knees and pick up litter as soon as it appears. These and countless other rules designed to reduce the workers to interchangeable automata were inculcated in franchise managers at Hamburger University located in a $40 million facility. There are plenty of rules governing the Registry, but they are only a small fraction of the rules that govern every detail of every operation at McDonald's. Indeed, if the DMV manager tried to impose on his employees as demanding a set of rules as those that govern the McDonald's staff, they would probably rebel and he would lose his job.

It is just as hard to explain the differences between the two organizations by reference to the quality or compensation of their employees. The Registry workers are all adults, most with at least a high-school education; the McDonald's employees are mostly teenagers, many still in school. The Registry staff is well-paid compared to the McDonald's workers, most of whom receive only the minimum wage. When labor shortages developed in Massachusetts during the mid-1980s, many McDonald's stores began hiring older people (typically housewives) of the same sort who had long worked for the Registry. They behaved just like the teenagers they replaced.

Not only are the differences between the two organizations not to be explained by reference to "rules" or "red tape" or "incompetent workers," the differences call into question many of the most frequently mentioned complaints about how government agencies are supposed to behave. For example: "Government agencies are big spenders." The Watertown office of the Registry is in a modest building that can barely handle its clientele. The teletype machine used to check information submitted by people requesting a replacement license was antiquated and prone to errors. Three or four clerks often had to wait in line to use equipment described by the office manager as "personally signed by Thomas Edison." No computers or word processors were available to handle the preparation of licenses and registrations; any error made by a clerk while manually typing a form meant starting over again on another form.

Or: "Government agencies hire people regardless of whether they are really needed." Despite the fact that the citizens of Massachusetts probably have more contact with the Registry than with any other state agency, and despite the fact that these citizens complain more about Registry service than about that of any other bureau, the Watertown branch, like all Registry offices, was seriously understaffed. In 1981, the agency lost 400 workers—about 25 percent of its work force—despite the fact that its workload was rising.

Or: "Government agencies are imperialistic, always grasping for new functions." But there is no record of the Registry doing much grasping, even though one could imagine a case being made that the state government could usefully create at Registry offices "one-stop" multi-service centers where people could not only get drivers' licenses but also pay taxes and parking fines, obtain information, and transact other official business. The Registry seemed content to provide one service.

In short, many of the popular stereotypes about government agencies and their members are either questionable or incomplete. To explain why government agencies behave as they do, it is not enough to know that they are "bureaucracies"—that is, it is not enough to know that they are big, or complex, or have rules. What is crucial is that they are *government* bureaucracies. As the preceding chapters should make clear, not all government bureaucracies behave the same way or suffer from the same problems. There may even be registries of motor vehicles in other states that do a better job than the one in Massachusetts. But all government agencies have in common certain characteristics that tend to make their management far more difficult than managing a McDonald's. These common characteristics are the constraints of public agencies.

The key constraints are three in number. To a much greater extent than is true of private bureaucracies, government agencies (1) cannot lawfully retain and devote to the private benefit of their members the earnings of the organization, (2) cannot allocate the factors of production in accordance with the preferences of the organization's administrators, and (3) must serve goals not of the organization's own choosing. Control over revenues, productive factors, and agency goals is all vested to an important degree in entities external to the organization—legislatures, courts, politicians, and interest groups. Given this, agency managers must attend to the demands of these external entities. As a result, government management tends to be driven by the *constraints* on the organization, not the *tasks* of the organization. To say the same thing in other words, whereas business management focuses on the "bottom line" (that is, profits), government management focuses on the "top line" (that is, constraints). Because government managers are not as strongly motivated as private ones to define the tasks of their subordinates, these tasks are often shaped by [other] factors.

* * *

Revenues and Incentives

In the days leading up to September 30, the federal government is Cinderella, courted by legions of individuals and organizations eager to get grants and contracts from the unexpended funds still at the disposal of each agency. At midnight on September 30, the government's coach turns into a pumpkin. That is the moment—the end of the fiscal year—at which every agency, with a few exceptions, must return all unexpended funds to the Treasury Department.

Except for certain quasi-independent government corporations, such as the Tennessee Valley Authority, no agency may keep any surplus revenues (that is, the difference between the funds it received from a congressional appropriation and those it needed to operate during the year). By the same token, any agency that runs out of money before the end of the fiscal year may ask Congress for more (a "supplemental appropriation") instead of being forced to deduct the deficit from any accumulated cash reserves. Because of these fiscal rules agencies do not have a material incentive to economize: Why scrimp and save if you cannot keep the results of your frugality?

Nor can individual bureaucrats lawfully capture for their personal use any revenue surpluses. When a private firm has a good year, many of its officers and workers may receive bonuses. Even if no bonus is paid, these employees may buy stock in the firm so that they can profit from any growth in earnings (and, if they sell the stock in a timely manner, profit from a drop in earnings). Should a public bureaucrat be discovered trying to do what private bureaucrats routinely do, he or she would be charged with corruption.

We take it for granted that bureaucrats should not profit from their offices and nod approvingly when a bureaucrat who has so benefited is indicted and put on trial. But why should we take this view? Once a very different view prevailed. In the seventeenth century, a French colonel would buy his commission from the king, take the king's money to run his regiment, and pocket the profit. At one time a European tax collector was paid by keeping a percentage of the taxes he collected. In this country, some prisons were once managed by giving the warden a sum of money based on how many prisoners were under his control and letting him keep the difference between what he received and what it cost him to feed the prisoners. Such behavior today would be grounds for criminal prosecution. Why? What has changed?

Mostly we the citizenry have changed. We are creatures of the Enlightenment: We believe that the nation ought not to be the property of the sovereign; that laws are intended to rationalize society and (if possible) perfect mankind; and that public service ought to be neutral and disinterested. We worry that a prison warden paid in the old way would have a strong incentive to starve his prisoners in order to maximize his income; that a regiment supported by a greedy colonel would not be properly equipped; and that a tax collector paid on a commission basis would extort excessive taxes from us. These changes reflect our desire to eliminate moral hazards—namely, creating incentives for people to act wrongly. But why should this desire rule out more carefully designed compensation plans that would pay government managers for achieving officially approved goals and would allow efficient agencies to keep any unspent part of their budget for use next year?

Part of the answer is obvious. Often we do not know whether a manager or an agency has achieved the goals we want because either the goals are vague or inconsistent, or their attainment cannot be observed, or both. Bureau chiefs in the Department of State would have to go on welfare if their pay depended on their ability to demonstrate convincingly that they had attained their bureaus' objectives.

But many government agencies have reasonably clear goals toward which progress can be measured. The Social Security Administration, the Postal Service, and the General Services Administration all come to mind. Why not let earnings depend importantly on performance? Why not let agencies keep excess revenues?

* * *

But in part it is because we know that even government agencies with clear goals and readily observable behavior only can be evaluated by making political (and thus conflict-ridden) judgments. If the Welfare Department delivers every benefit check within 24 hours after the application is received, Senator Smith may be pleased but Senator Jones will be irritated because this speedy delivery almost surely would require that the standards of eligibility be relaxed so that many ineligible clients would get money. There is no objective standard by which the trade-off between speed and accuracy in the Welfare Department can be evaluated. Thus we have been unwilling to allow welfare employees to earn large bonuses for achieving either speed or accuracy.

The inability of public managers to capture surplus revenues for their own use alters the pattern of incentives at work in government agencies. Beyond a certain point additional effort does not produce additional earnings. (In this country, Congress from time to time has authorized higher salaries for senior bureaucrats but then put a cap on actual payments to them so that the pay increases were never received. This was done to insure that no bureaucrat would earn more than members of Congress at a time when those members were unwilling to accept the political costs of raising their own salaries. As a result, the pay differential between the top bureaucratic rank and those just below it nearly vanished.) If political constraints reduce the marginal effect of money incentives, then the relative importance of other, nonmonetary incentives will increase. . . .

That bureaucratic performance in most government agencies cannot be linked to monetary benefits is not the whole explanation for the difference between public and private management. There are many examples of private organizations whose members cannot appropriate money surpluses for their own benefit. Private schools ordinarily are run on a nonprofit basis. Neither the headmaster nor the teachers share in the profit of these schools; indeed, most such schools earn no profit at all and instead struggle to keep afloat by soliciting contributions from friends and alumni. Nevertheless, the evidence is quite clear that on the average, private schools, both secular and denominational, do a better job than public ones in educating children. Moreover, as political scientists John Chubb and Terry Moe have pointed out, they do a better job while employing fewer managers. Some other factors are at work. One is the freedom an organization has to acquire and use labor and capital.

Acquiring and Using the Factors of Production

A business firm acquires capital by retaining earnings, borrowing money, or selling shares of ownership; a government agency (with some exceptions) acquires capital by persuading a legislature to appropriate it. A business firm hires, promotes, demotes, and fires personnel with considerable though not perfect freedom; a federal government agency is told by Congress how many persons it can hire and at what rate of pay, by the Office of Personnel Management (OPM) what rules it must follow in selecting and assigning personnel, by the Office of Management and Budget (OMB) how many persons of each rank it may employ, by the Merit Systems Protection Board (MSPB) what procedures it must follow in demoting or discharging personnel, and by the courts whether it has faithfully followed the rules of Congress, OPM, OMB, and MSPB. A business firm purchases goods and services by internally defined procedures (including those that allow it to buy from someone other than the lowest bidder if a more expensive vendor seems more reliable), or to skip the bidding procedure altogether in favor of direct negotiations; a government agency must purchase much of what it uses by formally advertising for bids, accepting the lowest, and keeping the vendor at arm's length. When a business firm develops a good working relationship with a contractor, it often uses that vendor repeatedly without looking for a new one; when a government agency has a satisfactory relationship with a contractor, ordinarily it cannot use the vendor again without putting a new project out for a fresh set of bids. When a business firm finds that certain offices or factories are no longer economical it will close or combine them; when a government agency wishes to shut down a local office or military base often it must get the permission of the legislature (even when formal permission is not necessary, informal consultation is). When a business firm draws up its annual budget each expenditure item can be reviewed as a discretionary amount (except for legally mandated payments of taxes to government and interest to banks and bondholders); when a government agency makes up its budget many of the detailed expenditure items are mandated by the legislature.

All these complexities of doing business in or with the government are well-known to citizens and firms. These complexities in hiring, purchasing, contracting, and budgeting often are said to be the result of the "bureaucracy's love of red tape." But few, if any, of the rules producing this complexity would have been generated by the bureaucracy if left to its own devices, and many are as cordially disliked by the bureaucrats as by their clients. These rules have been imposed on the agencies by external actors, chiefly the legislature. They are not bureaucratic rules but *political* ones. In principle the legislature could allow the Social Security Administration, the Defense Department, or the New York City public school system to follow the same rules as IBM, General Electric, or Harvard University. In practice they could not. The reason is politics, or more precisely, democratic politics.

* * *

Public versus Private Management

What distinguishes public from private organizations is neither their size nor their desire to "plan" (that is, control) their environments but rather the rules under which they acquire and use capital and labor. General Motors acquires capital by selling shares, issuing bonds, or retaining earnings; the Department of Defense acquires it from an annual appropriation by Congress. GM opens and closes plants, subject to certain government regulations, at its own discretion; DOD opens and closes military bases under the watchful guidance of Congress. GM pays its managers with salaries it sets and bonuses tied to its earnings; DOD pays its managers with salaries set by Congress and bonuses (if any) that have no connection with organizational performance. The number of workers in GM is determined by its level of production; the number in DOD by legislation and civil-service rules.

What all this means can be seen by returning to the Registry of Motor Vehicles and McDonald's. Suppose you were just appointed head of the Watertown office of the Registry and you wanted to improve service there so that it more nearly approximated the service at McDonald's. Better service might well require spending more money (on clerks, equipment, and buildings). Why should your political superiors give you that money? It is a cost to them if it requires either higher taxes or taking funds from another agency; offsetting these real and immediate costs are dubious and postponed benefits. If lines become shorter and clients become happier, no legislator will benefit. There may be fewer complaints, but complaints are episodic and have little effect on the career of any given legislator. By contrast, shorter lines and faster service at McDonald's means more customers can be served per hour and thus more money can be earned per hour. A McDonald's manager can estimate the marginal product of the last dollar he or she spends on improving service; the Registry manager can generate no tangible return on any expenditure he or she makes and thus cannot easily justify the expenditure.

Improving service at the Registry may require replacing slow or surly workers with quick and pleasant ones. But you, the manager, can neither hire nor fire them at will. You look enviously at the McDonald's manager who regularly and with little notice replaces poor workers with better ones. Alternatively, you may wish to mount an extensive training program (perhaps creating a Registration University to match McDonald's Hamburger University) that would imbue a culture of service in your employees. But unless the Registry were so large an agency that the legislature would neither notice nor care about funds spent for this purpose—and it is not that large—you would have a tough time convincing anybody that this was not a wasteful expenditure on a frill project.

If somehow your efforts succeed in making Registry clients happier, you can take vicarious pleasure in it; in the unlikely event a client seeks you out to thank you for those efforts, you can bask in a moment's worth of glory. Your colleague at McDonald's who manages to make customers happier may also derive some vicarious satisfaction from the improvement but in addition he or she will earn more money owing to an increase in sales.

In time it will dawn on you that if you improve service too much, clients will start coming to the Watertown office instead of going to the Boston office. As a result, the lines you succeeded in shortening will become longer again. If you wish to keep complaints down, you will have to spend even more on the Watertown office. But if it was hard to persuade the legislature to do that in the past, it is impossible now. Why should the taxpayer be asked to spend more on Watertown when the Boston office, fully staffed (naturally, no one was laid off when the clients disappeared), has no lines at all? From the legislature's point of view the correct level of expenditure is not that which makes one office better than another but that which produces an equal amount of discontent in all offices.

Finally, you remember that your clients have no choice: The Registry offers a monopoly service. It and only it supplies drivers' licenses. In the long run all that matters is that there are not "too many" complaints to the legislature about service. Unlike McDonald's, the Registry need not fear that its clients will take their business to Burger King or to Wendy's. Perhaps you should just relax.

If this were all there is to public management it would be an activity that quickly and inevitably produces cynicism among its practitioners. But this is not the whole story. For one thing, public agencies differ in the kinds of problems they face. For another, many public managers try hard to do a good job even though they face these difficult constraints.

DISCUSSION QUESTIONS

1. Wilson argues that McDonald's and the Department of Motor Vehicles operate differently because of the inherent differences between public and private organizations. Apply his reasoning to other cases, for instance the U.S. Postal Service and Fed Ex, or any other area where the government and the private sector compete for business. Think about the goals of the organizations, who controls them, how you distinguish success from failure, and the consequences of failure.

2. What are the advantages and disadvantages of trying to run the government more like a business? How would you define the basic parameters of a "business-like" government (such as, who are the "customers")?

3. Some critics of government inefficiency argue that nearly every domestic government function—from schools to road building—could
   be run more efficiently if it were "privatized" (or turned over to private contractors). Do you agree? Are there any government functions that do not lend themselves to privatization?

Debating the Issues: Reforming the National Security Bureaucracy

One of the key recommendations to emerge from the various studies and commissions on the 9/11 attacks is a substantial reform of the intelligence community—the various agencies that collect and analyze information from foreign governments and adversaries. The fact that nineteen hijackers could live in the U.S. while planning and then carrying out multiple hijackings was seen as a titanic intelligence failure, with investigators unable to connect dots that were right in front of them. Different threads of warnings were never connected—such as reports from FBI agents about Middle Eastern men receiving suspicious flight training, intelligence alerts that were not passed on to law enforcement agencies, and requests for information that were denied—even though during the summer of 2001 the system was "blinking red," according to then CIA Director George Tenet.

One of the fundamental goals of reform was to increase the efficiency with which information is collected, analyzed, and shared. "Integration" is the key concept. Before 9/11, the intelligence community consisted of over a dozen separate organizations in multiple agencies and each of these units had its own organizational culture, methods, and standards. The Intelligence Reform and Terrorism Prevention Act (IRTPA) of 2004 gave the National Counterterrorism Center (NCTC) the responsibility to promote the sharing and integration of information, improve the "situational awareness" regarding the terrorist threat, more clearly define the roles and responsibilities within the counterterrorism community, and create a library of terrorism information and databases on international terrorist identities. The "progress report" from the NCTC outlines the weaknesses in the counterterrorism community before 9/11, how the NCTC has addressed those problems, and the challenges that remain.

Richard Posner, a federal judge who writes extensively about civil liberties and national security, is much less sanguine about the process of reorganization. He has two concerns. First, we are much too optimistic that *any* reorganization will actually be able to prevent intelligence failures and terrorist attacks. He says, "We are fooled not because our intelligence system is poor, but because surprise attacks are extremely difficult to predict." Second, while it is impossible to prevent intelligence failures, the system can be improved and the reforms we have undertaken are not enough. As long as we have "three distinct, stubborn, and largely incompatible organizational cultures"—military intelligence, the CIA, and the FBI—the clash of cultures and inefficiencies will continue to make integration and coordination far too difficult. He argues that we should spin off military intelligence from the Pentagon and create a new National Security Branch of the FBI that would handle terrorism issues and be free of the "police culture" of the FBI. These new agencies would report to a new Director of Central Intelligence who would operate as the "coordinator or board chairman of the intelligence community," separate from the director of the Central Intelligence Agency. Posner concludes with the warning, "I hope it will not take another terrorist attack to put us back on the right path."

Paul Light emphasizes a different aspect of the preparations for the next terrorist attack. In addition to reforming counterterrorist agencies in the federal government, we need to make sure that people know what to do during and after the next attack. Light cites a survey showing that most Americans think that the U.S. will be attacked again within the next five years, but that it will not happen in their own community. This confidence could lead to complacency and a repeat of the Hurricane Katrina disaster in which citizens did not know what to do or where to go. Light argues that a "citizen-preparedness initiative" with a relatively modest budget in the millions, not billions, of dollars would ensure that people know what to do in various situations. This would enhance the effectiveness of government "first responders" because people would be able to respond more quickly and efficiently if they knew what to expect.

33

From "NCTC and Information Sharing Five Years Since 9/11: A Progress Report"

The performance of the United States Government in the years leading up to the terrorist attacks on September 11, 2001 was hindered by inadequate information sharing between key agencies of the Federal government.

> "Managers should have ensured that information was shared and duties were clearly assigned across agencies, and across the foreign domestic divide."
> —9/11 Commission Report

> "Prior to September 11th, there was a failure to share terrorism-related information rapidly and efficiently within agencies; among entities within the Intelligence Community tasked with producing intelligence to support counterterrorism efforts; and with state, local, and tribal law enforcement."
> —WMD Commission Report

The Intelligence Reform and Terrorism Prevention Act (IRTPA) of 2004 assigned to the National Counterterrorism Center (NCTC) the responsibility "to ensure the agencies, as appropriate, have access to and receive all-source intelligence products needed to execute their counterterrorism plans or perform independent, alternative analysis," and "to ensure that such agencies have access to and receive intelligence needed to accomplish their assigned activities." NCTC statutory authorities are limited to sharing with Federal organizations.

This report focuses on the progress that NCTC, working with its Federal partners, has made in the years since 9/11. It does not address the many efforts by other departments and agencies to improve information sharing at the Federal level and with non-Federal partners.

Complexity

Information sharing in support of the nation's counterterrorism objectives isn't about "flipping a switch"; it involves a diverse landscape of players and technologies, and myriad cultural, security, and policy barriers. Specific challenges include:

- Recognizing and designating "terrorism" information.
- Protecting operationally sensitive information.
- Ensuring that constitutional rights of individuals are not violated through information sharing practices.
- Clarifying roles, responsibilities, and information needs of the members of the counterterrorism community.
- Developing a considered approach to information sharing across Federal, state, and local levels amidst ever-increasing numbers of networks and databases.

* * *

Information Integration

Prior to 9/11

No organization in the US Government had access to the full range of terrorism information available to the various Federal agencies and departments.

Today

Analysts at NCTC have access to dozens of networks and information systems from across the intelligence, law enforcement, military, and homeland security communities, containing many hundreds of data repositories. These systems contain foreign and domestic information pertaining to international terrorism and sensitive operational and law enforcement activities. NCTC is exploring capabilities to help analysts integrate and assimilate this enormous volume of terrorism-related information.

A role-based access philosophy has been adopted to accommodate legal and collector concerns that not all individuals should have access to particularly sensitive information.

*   *   *

Situational Awareness

Prior to 9/11

There was no systematic means of maintaining routine situational awareness regarding the terrorist threat either across the US Government or with foreign partners.

Today

NCTC hosts counterterrorism community-wide secure video teleconferences (SVTCs) three times daily to ensure broad awareness of ongoing operations and newly detected threats. During these SVTCs, participants compare notes, highlight new threats, and debunk erroneous reports.

The NCTC Operations Center, collocated with its CIA and FBI counterparts, works with eleven other counterterrorism community operations centers on a daily basis and up to thirty-four more as events demand.

NCTC provides input to the *President's Daily Brief,* and produces daily the *National Terrorism Bulletin, Senior Executive Threat Report, Threat Matrix,* terrorism situations reports (twice daily), numerous special analysis reports, spot commentaries, threat alerts, advisories, and assessments summarizing the latest intelligence reporting related to terrorism threats.

NCTC provides coordinated counterterrorism community support to national security events, such as the 2004 Olympics, both national Presidential Conventions, and the Presidential Inauguration.

NCTC maintains the US Government database on worldwide terrorist incidents. This unclassified database is available at www.nctc.gov for the benefit of all interested in terrorism.

Enabling All Elements of State Power

Prior to 9/11

The US Government could not bring all elements of state power to bear against the terrorism threat, in part because departments and agencies lacked a common frame of reference. There was no widely available classified electronic library of terrorism information, and classified intelligence dissemination practices did not adequately support the range of US Government organizations involved in counterterrorism activities.

Today

NCTC hosts a classified repository, NCTC Online (NOL), that serves as the counterterrorism community's library of terrorism information. This repository reaches the full range of intelligence, law enforcement, military, homeland security, and other Federal organizations involved in the global war on terrorism. The creation of NOL, coupled with policy changes, has allowed nonintelligence community agencies easier access to counterterrorism information, and has resulted in broad and robust sharing of intelligence information.

Today NOL hosts:

- Over 6,000 users.
- 6 million documents.
- Over 60 contributing departments and agencies.

Business Process and Partnerships

Prior to 9/11

Roles and responsibilities within the counterterrorism community were poorly defined and redundant; information sharing was limited, analysis and production were not coordinated, and dissemination was departmentally focused.

Today

Federal counterterrorism roles and responsibilities are being coordinated across the US Government.

The counterterrorism community Production Planning Board, consisting of representatives from CIA, FBI, DHS, DIA, NSA, NGA, and others, meets daily to plan and coordinate analytic efforts and ensure that all issues receive appropriate resources.

The Interagency Intelligence Committee on Terrorism (IICT) now comprises more than 100 members, meets monthly at NCTC, and actively coordinates critical counterterrorism issues such as emerging threats and threat countermeasures.

Information flow and dissemination have been improved through standardization of the format and use of tearlines, and the elimination of cold-war era rules that restricted the flow of intelligence among departments and agencies of the US Government.

Congress established a Program Manager for the Information Sharing Environment (PM ISE) tasked to improve terrorism information sharing among Federal and non-Federal entities. Federal agencies, in cooperation with the PM ISE are working to integrate business processes to ensure reliable information flow among Federal, state, local, tribal, and private sector entities. NCTC works closely with the PM ISE as an active member of the Information Sharing Council.

NCTC has an active foreign liaison role engaging counterparts, providing sanitized versions of counterterrorism products, hosting conferences, and forward-deploying NCTC officers as warranted.

Terrorist Identities

Prior to 9/11

There were numerous classified databases and approximately a dozen unclassified watchlists containing information about known and suspected international terrorists. These databases and watchlists were neither interoperable nor broadly accessible.

Today

The Terrorist Identities Datamart Environment (TIDE) serves as the central knowledge base for all-source information on international terrorist identities for use by the US counterterrorism community. TIDE distributes a "sensitive but unclassified" extract to the Terrorist Screening Center (TSC). The TSC, in turn, validates this information and provides it to Federal departments and agencies and select foreign governments that use this information to screen for terrorists.

- TIDE contains over 400,000 names/aliases, representing over 300,000 unique individuals.
- To further increase information sharing and decrease the potential for "false positives," additional identifiers are passed to the TSC to aide in screening opportunities.
- TIDE is made available to the majority of the terrorism analytic community via NCTC Online.

Many Difficult Issues Remain

The advancements noted in this report notwithstanding, NCTC and its community partners continue to address many difficult issues:

Privacy—some information vital to the war on terror is intermixed with information about US persons. Ways to use such data while protecting privacy and civil liberties must be identified.

Access—decisions regarding access to information are largely controlled by collectors, thereby creating an inherent tension with analytic elements that need to review information.

Sources and Methods—collectors' ability to obtain vital data must be protected as ways are sought to ensure that intelligence is available to those who need it.

Operational Impact—dissemination of operationally sensitive information must be balanced against the potential adverse impact on intelligence/law enforcement operations.

Liaison Information—US law and policy often are not the only factors governing the ability to share information. Key allies may dictate the extent to which their information may be shared. Violating such guidance could result in the loss of future access to information.

Source Credibility—the act of dissemination lends credibility to information and can force operators to respond to very low credibility information. When information meets dissemination criteria, it should include a clear, standardized credibility assessment.

Information Technology—broad information sharing is a double-edged sword. Consumers of information find themselves quickly overwhelmed by the vast quantity of information. Obtaining tools to search, analyze, and process results is critical.

Access to State, Local, and Tribal Governments and the Private Sector—methods for ensuring that homeland security and terrorism information is shared among non-Federal government entities and the Federal government remain inadequate. The Program Manager for the Information Sharing Environment is working to facilitate two-way information flow.

Data Acquisition—acquiring data that contains terrorism information is often a legally and bureaucratically cumbersome process. Often Secretary-level government officials must approve the data transfer; generally only after many layers of review.

Resolving these issues will require managing an extremely complicated balance between technical, legal, policy, and security issues.

34

"The Reorganized U.S. Intelligence System after One Year"

Richard A. Posner

Congress decreed reorganization of the U.S. intelligence system in the Intelligence Reform and Terrorism Prevention Act of 2004, which the president signed into law in December of that year. The intelligence community has been engaged in implementing the law for a year, since the president appointed Ambassador John Negroponte to be the first director of national intelligence (DNI). A recent article by Scott Shane in the *New York Times* states that "a year after the sweeping government reorganization [of intelligence] began, the [intelligence] agencies . . . remain troubled by high-level turnover, overlapping responsibilities and bureaucratic rivalry," and that the reorganization has "bloated the bureaucracy, adding boxes to the government organization chart without producing clearly defined roles."[1] The question on which I focus in this article is whether these are merely teething troubles—the inevitable transition costs involved in an ambitious government reorganization—or whether they point to fundamental design flaws in the intelligence reorganization.

It is tempting to suppose that all must be well because the DNI has hired able people. Indeed he has. But it is possible that these people could be working equally or even more productively for the individual agencies from which they (largely) came. The reorganization reshuffled rather than augmented the nation's federal intelligence personnel. In evaluating a reorganization, one must always consider the incremental benefits created by it, and compare them with the incremental costs.

The fundamental cause of the ambitious reorganization of the intelligence community that we are living through is not, I believe, some deep flaws in the system as it existed on the eve of the 9/11 attacks. Rather, it is a deep misunderstanding of the limitations of national-security intelligence. It is the kind of misunderstanding that the commissioner of baseball might harbor if he thought it a scandal that 70 percent of the time even the best hitters fail to get a hit, and if he proposed to boost batting averages to 1.000 by reorganizing the leagues. His thinking would be deeply flawed, and his reorganization would fail to raise batting averages, though it might lower them.

Ephraim Kahana, in a recent article, lists Israeli intelligence failures since the founding of the State of Israel in 1948.[2] It is a remarkably long list. Many of the failures, it is true, occurred before Israel's warning-intelligence system was reorganized after the nation's biggest intelligence failure—the Egyptian-Syrian surprise attack of October 1973. But as many occurred afterwards. Israel is reputed to have an excellent intelligence system and one that is on high alert because of the acute threat to its existence posed by the Arab states. Nevertheless, it is fooled repeatedly. And its rate of being fooled seems insensitive to organizational structure.

U.S. intelligence has been fooled repeatedly too. Think only of Pearl Harbor (after which we reorganized our intelligence system); the Tet Offensive of 1968, which put us on the road to eventual defeat in Vietnam; and, of course, the 9/11 attacks. We are fooled not because our intelligence system is poor, but because surprise attacks are extremely difficult to predict. And there are no organizational panaceas. Intelligence misses are a constant; they are not a function of the details of the table of organization. Improvement is possible,[3] but improvement and reorganization are not synonyms.

But failure in a democratic society demands a scapegoat. And because the CIA is a much less popular agency than the military services or the FBI, it is the designated scapegoat for the failure to prevent 9/11 and for the subsequent failure to detect Saddam Hussein's abandonment of his program of weapons of mass destruction (though we may not have heard the last of that). And failure in a democratic society also demands a response that promises, however improbably, to prevent future failures. The preferred response is a reorganization because it is at once dramatic and relatively cheap. And so the 2004 legislation and its subsequent implementation.

Three Organizational Problems

There were flaws in the organization of our intelligence system on the eve of 9/11, and this gave some plausibility to the idea that we needed to reorganize the system. There were in fact three organizational problems in need of solution. The first was the stacking of too many responsibilities on the director of central intelligence (DCI), with insufficient statutory powers. The second was the Defense Department's ownership of the national intelligence agencies (the National Security Agency [NSA], the National Reconnaissance Office [NRO], and the National Geospatial-Intelligence Agency [NGA]). And the third was the FBI's control of domestic intelligence, or in other words, the absence of a U.S. counterpart to Britain's MI5 or Canada's Security Intelligence Service.

The DCI was the head of the CIA, a full-time job because of the size of the agency and because of the sensitivity of many of the missions of the

Directorate of Operations. He was also the president's senior intelligence advisor—itself a full-time job, at least for presidents such as George W. Bush who want to meet frequently with their senior intelligence advisor. And he was the coordinator of the fifteen (actually more) U.S. intelligence agencies, which should also be a full-time job, especially since the DCI had limited statutory powers—particularly over the Defense Department's intelligence agencies—and thus had to operate by cajoling and politicking rather than by command. All this was too much for one person, given the enormous challenge—greater than the challenges that the Cold War had posed for the intelligence community—presented by Islamist terrorism in the era of proliferation of weapons of mass destruction. The DCI and director of the Central Intelligence Agency (DCIA) jobs should have been split and the DCI's powers strengthened, but not to the point of making him the actual administrator, or "czar," of the intelligence community. The DCI's job should have been reconceptualized as that of the coordinator or board chairman of the intelligence community, much as in the British intelligence system. The DCIA would have remained the president's chief intelligence adviser and thus responsible for preparing the President's Daily Brief; those two jobs would be plenty for one person.

The Intelligence Reform Act separated the DCI and DCIA jobs, renaming the DCI the DNI—a cosmetic change, but perhaps justified by a sensible desire to give him domestic intelligence authority without suggesting continuity with the CIA—but went much further, as I am about to explain (and complain about). At the same time, Congress did nothing about the Defense Department's control of the national intelligence agencies and nothing about the FBI's domination of domestic intelligence either. I will return to these omissions, which seem to me unfortunate.

The "much further" was to make the DCI—now DNI—not merely a coordinator or board chairman of the intelligence community, but the president's chief intelligence advisor and the presiding deity of a new bureaucracy, the Directorate of National Intelligence, which may, though I hope will not, engulf many of the responsibilities of the CIA and demote the agency to little more than a spy service, like MI6. The military is making inroads into the CIA as well, and the FBI is trying to. The CIA is embattled—and decentered.

The names of government agencies often don't mean a lot. But there is special significance to the word "central" in the CIA's name. The agency was meant to be the center of the U.S. intelligence system. It was to have most of the spies and most of the analysts, along with significant technical capabilities (NRO and NGA began life as components of the CIA, not of the Defense Department); it would integrate intelligence data obtained by other agencies and present its assessments to the president and other high officials. This still seems to me the right system. It implies, for example, that the National Counterterrorism Center (NCTC) should be inside the CIA (where it began, as the Terrorist Threat Integration Center [TTIC] rather than inside the Directorate of National Intelligence, both to minimize friction with the CIA's Counter-terrorist Center and to keep the analysts close to the operations officers. Returning NCTC to the CIA would give the CIA a significant domestic role, but one of analysis, not operations; and I do not recall that people were much disturbed that the formation of the TTIC put the CIA in the domestic intelligence business. And likewise the new National Counter Proliferation Center seems to me to belong in the CIA, if it belongs anywhere—if it should exist at all—for the proliferation of centers may be another example of the bureaucratic hypertrophy that may eventually strangle the intelligence community. There is also a danger that intelligence tasks that do not fall within the scope of some center will be slighted, and the further danger that centers will survive after the need that gave rise to them has waned.

My analysis further suggests that the head of the CIA should be the president's senior intelligence adviser, not the DNI, and therefore that the Directorate of National Intelligence does not require an analytical capability.

The DNI's staff is climbing toward 1,000; it may have reached or exceeded that number, for all I know, and be en route to 2,000. It has become a new bureaucracy layered on top of the intelligence community, a new agency on top of the fifteen or more previously existing agencies. The DNI finds himself tasked with coordinating the intelligence system, serving as the president's senior intelligence advisor, and managing his own intelligence service. The reorganization may have replicated the main organizational flaw (an overburdened DCI) that it sought to rectify, while doing nothing to rectify the other two organizational flaws that existed before the reorganization (the Defense Department's ownership of the national intelligence agencies and the FBI's domination of domestic intelligence). Ambassador Negroponte appears to have ceded the main coordination role to General Michael Hayden, his principal deputy, producing (to exaggerate slightly) a strange inversion: the number 2 man is the CEO; the number 1 is the presidential advisor.

I am not clear what successes the reorganization has had in its first year. The intelligence community has been poor at getting out its message, an example being Ambassador Negroponte's virtual silence during the debate over the NSA's non-FISA surveillance program, which has stirred up such a storm. But that is a story for another day. (Note the failure of the intelligence community to obtain any credit from either the general public or influential opinion makers for its considerable contribution to our victory in the Cold War—an extraordinary failure of public relations.) I am sure that there have been successes because of the high quality of the persons hired by and detailed to the Directorate of National Intelligence. But I remind the reader of my earlier point that the critical question is not what successes have been achieved, but what successes would not have been achieved without the reorganization.

Clearly there have been setbacks. The departure of Captain John Russack from his post as Program Manager for the Information Sharing Environment, after several months of not being able to assemble a staff, suggests that little progress has been made in solving the stubborn problem of the reluctance, at once technical and cultural, of intelligence agencies to share information with each other. Maybe there has been progress on other fronts, though this is unclear to an outsider such as myself; and it is, to repeat a point that cannot be repeated too often, particularly unclear what, if anything, such improvements as have been made in the intelligence system owe to the reorganization. I have the sense (no stronger assertion is possible) that little progress has been made in exerting control over the intelligence activities of either the military or the FBI and the Department of Homeland Security (DHS).

Before Captain Russack left, he testified before the Senate Judiciary Committee that he intended his staff to be composed mainly of detailees from other agencies rather than permanent employees of the DNI. I was surprised, thinking that detailees were a temporary expedient. I suspect that it would be a mistake for the DNI to make detailees a major component of its staff after it reaches its equilibrium size. This is an area (there are others) in which the seductive analogy of the Goldwater-Nichols reorganization of the armed forces should be resisted. When officers are detailed to the staff of the Joint Chiefs of Staff or otherwise assigned temporarily to joint positions, they are moving within the Defense Department, and if they do not do their joint work well it will reflect adversely on their career prospects. But when the CIA details an officer to the Directorate of National Intelligence, his performance there will not directly affect his career prospects at the CIA, because the DNI is not the ultimate employer of CIA officers; the CIA is. So the DNI may find it difficult to obtain the complete loyalty of its detailees. That will undermine the DNI's effectiveness.

It is tempting to think that, despite all the criticisms that I and others have made of the reorganization of the intelligence system, the government must be doing something right because we haven't been attacked since 9/11. But haven't we? What exactly is going on in Iraq and Afghanistan? And the main thing we did right was to invade Afghanistan and scatter the leadership of al Qaeda, not to reorganize the intelligence community. Moreover, the 9/11 attacks made us hypervigilant about Islamic terrorism; that is a "benefit" that owes nothing to reorganization. A sure sign of the continuing though perhaps inevitable weakness of our counterterrorist intelligence is that we really have no good idea of the capabilities or plans of our terrorist enemies. And a steady drain of experienced intelligence officers to the private sector, whose demand for security personnel soared in the wake of the 9/11 attacks, has weakened the intelligence community, at least temporarily.

My guess, and it is only that, is that in the end the reorganization of the intelligence community will amount to rather little. The continuing debacle that is the Department of Homeland Security, still floundering desperately despite the efforts of its able secretary and his corps of excellent deputies, should make us all suspicious of ambitious reorganizations. That Congress has yet not tried to consolidate the intelligence agencies into a single department, on the model of the Department of Homeland Security, is only a small comfort. The main result of the creation of DHS has been to layer a new bureaucracy over twenty-two separate agencies with a total of 184,000 employees, and the main result of the intelligence reorganization may turn out to be the layering of a new bureaucracy over fifteen or more separate agencies with a total of some 100,000 employees—though this is to exaggerate, since the DNI has no real control over the Defense Department, whose agencies comprise in the aggregate the largest segment of the intelligence community.

When a bureaucratic layer is added on top of a group of agencies, the result is delay, loss or distortion of information from the bottom up, delay and misunderstanding of commands from the top down, turf fights for the attention of the top layer (rival agencies now have a single boss for whose favor they can fight), demoralization of agencies that have been demoted by the insertion of a new layer of command between them and the president, and underspecialization, since the new top echelon can't be expected to be an expert in all the diverse missions of the agencies below. That is one of the lessons of the Hurricane Katrina fiasco. Placing the Federal Emergency Management Agency in DHS inserted between the head of FEMA and the White House an official (the secretary of DHS) who, naturally, because of the breadth of his responsibilities, was not an expert in emergency management. The result was and continues to be needless delay and confusion.

Incompatible Cultures

There is an additional factor, which has been neglected because the people who design government reorganizations are not mindful of the lessons of organization theory. Business mergers often founder on incompatible firm cultures possessed by the merged and merging firms. Mergers of government agencies can founder for the same reason. DHS is the prime current example, but DNI may go the same way. Coordinating, let alone directing, the intelligence system is greatly complicated by the existence of three distinct, stubborn, and largely incompatible organizational cultures that are poorly balanced: military intelligence, civilian national-security intelligence (mainly CIA), and criminal-investigation intelligence (mainly FBI). I discuss their distinctness first, their stubbornness second, and their imbalance third.

No one will deny that the military has a distinctive culture (due to many factors, prominently including its up-and-out promotion system, its discipline, and its strong mission orientation) and views a competing civilian agency such as the CIA with a degree of hostility and disdain, which the agency reciprocates. An aggravating factor is that the military and the CIA are competitors in strategic intelligence and that the military, being at once the customer and the owner of the national intelligence agencies, has no wish to share their spy satellites and other facilities with the agency.

No one will deny that the FBI has a distinctive culture too—and it happens to be one inimical to intelligence gathering. The bureau's conception of intelligence is of information that can be used to obtain a criminal conviction. A crime is committed, having a definite time and place and usually witnesses, and these circumstances enable the investigation to be tightly focused and create a high probability that the information gathered in the investigation will enable a successful prosecution. National security intelligence, especially counterterrorist intelligence, works differently. The aim is to prevent the crime, not punish the criminals. The key to prevention is detection in advance, which requires casting a very wide net, following up on clues, assembling bits of information, and often failing because there is as yet no crime, no definite time and place from which to begin, no witnesses. To speak a bit fancifully, the FBI agents are like dogs, and the CIA officers like cats. The pointer, the retriever, the hound has a definite target, and goes for it. The cat is furtive, slinks about in the dark, pounces unexpectedly at the time and place of its choosing.

There was a noteworthy incident, shortly after the NSA's non-FISA surveillance program came to light last December, that received less attention than it should have. I am referring to leaks by FBI officials, reported in the media, expressing skepticism about the value of the program. These officials complained that the NSA had given the FBI clues to follow up, most of which led nowhere. The bureau's dissatisfaction with this assignment reflected the dominance of the criminal-investigation culture in the bureau, despite Robert Mueller's and Philip Mudd's efforts to change that culture. When a crime has been committed, as I have said, a focused investigation with a high probability of success is possible. That focus and that expectation of success are impossible in national security intelligence concerned with preventing a new round of surprise attacks on the nation. Intelligence is a search for the needle in a haystack. FBI agents don't like being asked to chase down clues gleaned from the NSA's interceptions because 99 out of 100 (probably even a higher percentage) turn out to lead nowhere. That is not what they are accustomed to when they conduct criminal investigations. The agents think that they have better things to do with their time. Maybe they do—maybe the root problem is that we simply don't have enough intelligence officers working on domestic threats.

Organizational cultures are difficult to change, even in business (as I noted), in which competitive pressures are acute, and more so in non-business sectors, such as government. No one wants to be jarred out of his accustomed groove. Changing the FBI's culture from one of criminal investigation to one of criminal investigation plus national security intelligence is particularly unlikely to succeed, for a reason illuminated by the government's inability to alter the organizational culture of our armed forces during the Vietnam War, even though it was plain to many people in government that the culture was poorly suited to the conditions of that war.[4] A particular obstacle was that the culture was optimized for a continuing threat, namely that of a conventional war in Europe. The FBI faces the same problem. Its primary focus is and will remain on criminal investigation, a vital national need. It resists blurring that focus by transforming itself even part way into a national security intelligence agency.

If like the United Kingdom we had a domestic intelligence agency, like MI5, no one would seriously suggest merging it with the FBI, just as no one suggests merging MI5 into Scotland Yard.

What makes coordination of the three competing cultures in the intelligence community—the military, civilian intelligence, and the FBI—so difficult, and maybe impossible, is a profound political imbalance. The military is immensely popular, immensely powerful politically (in part because of its popularity, in part because of the support it receives from defense contractors), accounts for the lion's share of the intelligence budget, is ambitious to expand its intelligence activities under the forceful leadership of Secretary Donald Rumsfeld and Under Secretary Stephen Cambone, and for all these reasons is out of the practical control of the DNI. The FBI is also immensely popular (despite its very poor performance as a domestic intelligence agency—the worst-performing in the run-up to the 9/11 attacks) and politically powerful, and especially resistant to change for the reason mentioned earlier. That leaves the CIA in a situation of considerable vulnerability, as an unpopular agency and therefore a natural scapegoat; and it limits the power of the DNI, who finds cabinet officers (the secretary of defense and the attorney general) between him and the military and bureau intelligence services.

A notable example of the limitations of the DNI's powers, and a dramatic example of the FBI's political strength, is that the improper, as well as obtuse, leaks of which I have just been speaking received no public rebuke from the DNI. Or for that matter from Director Mueller or Attorney General Alberto Gonzales, even though the FBI is part of the Department of Justice and at the very moment that the bureau leakers were deriding the NSA program, the Attorney General was defending it before Congress as essential to the national security (which I believe it is).

My book *Uncertain Shield*[5] documents the FBI's future as an intelligence agency, and the evidence continues to mount up. Recently the *New York Times* published an article on the continuing saga of the FBI's computer struggles.[6] One already knew that the bureau had blown more than $100 million on Virtual Case File, a computer system designed to enable the bureau's agents to share information across field offices and with headquarters. Virtual Case File was abandoned last year in favor of Sentinel, which, we learn from the article, "is still not fully staffed," and "it is not clear that the bureau has a management system in place to prevent the huge cost overruns that plagued previous incarnations of the project"—that is, Virtual Case File. Although it is estimated that Sentinel will cost $500 million or more (surely more), the article reports that the Justice Department's "inspector general's office said it was not yet satisfied that the overhaul [i.e., Sentinel], even if successful, would allow the bureau to share information adequately with other intelligence and law enforcement agencies." So four and a half years after 9/11, the FBI is years away from having computer capabilities adequate to its national security intelligence mission. That is a result not primarily of technical incompetence, but rather of cultural resistance rooted in the autonomy of the bureau's field offices and the reluctance of criminal investigators to leave a documentary trail that might be discoverable in a criminal proceeding.

The nation needs a true domestic intelligence agency, outside the bureau, modeled on MI5 or on the Canadian Security Intelligence Service (CSIS). (I emphasize CSIS because MI5 has a rather scary reputation, having until recently operated with far less sensitivity to civil liberties than would be tolerated in this country.) Here is one organizational change that makes compelling sense, yet was not recommended by the 9/11 Commission or the WMD Commission and was omitted from the Intelligence Reform and Terrorism Prevention Act of 2004. The FBI would retain an intelligence capability, but it would be a capability for intelligence as an adjunct to criminal investigation, which is anyway the bureau's concept of national security intelligence. The National Security Branch would remain in the bureau, corresponding to Scotland Yard's Special Branch. The new agency, corresponding to MI5, would be free from the police culture that dominates the FBI.

The other overdue organizational recommendation, made by a commission headed by Brent Scowcroft and rejected by the Bush administration, is to spin off the national intelligence agencies from the Defense Department, make them their own agency or agencies and by doing so place them under more effective control by the DNI. That would improve the balance among the intelligence cultures by reducing the "twin stars" problem (the secretary of defense and the director of national intelligence circling warily around each other) that is created by the Defense Department's disproportionate weight in the overall intelligence budget. In the case of the NRO and NGA, divesting them from the Defense Department would restore them to approximately their original status, except that they would not be part of the CIA, as they once were.

The culture clash is a factor, though not the only one, in the government's failure to get a good handle on domestic intelligence, a failure reflected in the eruption of a series of unnecessary controversies in recent months. Think of the recent controversies concerning intelligence: the NSA's surveillance program outside of FISA; Dubai Ports World; and the increasing involvement of the Defense Department in domestic intelligence, an involvement not limited to the NSA's program of electronic surveillance of U.S. citizens within the United States. Other Pentagon agencies, notably the Counterintelligence Field Activity (CIFA) have, as described in articles by Walter Pincus in the *Washington Post*, been conducting domestic intelligence on a large scale. Although CIFA's formal mission is to prevent attacks on military installations in the United States, the scale of its activities suggests a broader involvement in domestic security.

Another Pentagon agency that has gotten into the domestic intelligence act is the Information Dominance Center (IDC), which developed the Able Danger data-mining program, a very promising program derailed by the involvement of Admiral John Poindexter and the failure of the administration to explain and defend the program. Another recent article in the *Times* reported

> that the military's counterterrorism effort is hampered by bureaucratic duplication, officials said, citing in particular an overlap between new government centers, including the National Counterterrorism Center . . . The review found that the government-wide national security bureaucracy still does not respond rapidly and effectively to the new requirements of the counterterrorism campaign. The report said more streamlining was necessary across a broad swath of the civilian bureaucracy and military.[7]

All these controversies, even the one over Dubai's now-thwarted acquisition of U.S. port operations, are about protecting the United States from attacks from within—the domain of domestic intelligence. The controversies demonstrate the extraordinary importance and sensitivity of domestic security, which stirs acute fears both of attacks (hence the Dubai controversy) and of civil-liberties abuses (hence the NSA, CIFA, Terrorism Information Awareness, and Able Danger controversies). These fears, however groundless, require focused attention by the leadership of the intelligence community on domestic intelligence and for the further reason that domestic intelligence is a cockpit of conflict among the three separate intelligence cultures that I have described.

I do not sense such focus, or that the DNI is taking a leadership role, though of course he may be operating effectively behind the scenes, concealed from an outsider like myself. (The DNI is invisible to the world outside the national security community, and this I take to be another failure of the community's public relations.) I sense that the cultural imbalance—the Pentagon's huge budget, its control of the national intelligence agencies, the able and aggressive secretary of defense and his able and aggressive under secretary for intelligence, and the FBI's apparent freedom from control by its nominal superiors—is stifling reform on the domestic intelligence front. We not only have no real domestic intelligence agency; we have no official with sole and comprehensive responsibility for domestic intelligence. It is no surprise that gaps in domestic intelligence are being filled by controversial ad hoc initiatives.

* * *

To return to my major theme, that of organization, I am well aware of the political obstacles to taking what I believe to be the sound path to organizational reform. But there is value in speculation. American politics are in continuous flux; what is politically unthinkable one year can in a few years become a political imperative. I hope it will not take another terrorist attack to put us back on the right path: the path that leads to an independent DCI (or DNI), independent national intelligence agencies, a domestic intelligence agency separate from the FBI, and, once more at the center of the spider's web that is national security intelligence, the Central Intelligence Agency.

Notes

1. Scott Shane, "Year into Revamped Spying, Troubles and Some Progress," *New York Times*, February 28, 2006.
2. Ephraim Kahana, "Analyzing Israel's Intelligence Failures," *International Journal of Intelligence and Counterintelligence* 18 (2005): 262.
3. See, for example, John A. Kringen, "How We've Improved Intelligence: Minimizing the Risk of 'Groupthink,' " *Washington Post*, April 3, 2006.
4. R. W. Komer, *Bureaucracy Does Its Thing: Institutional Constraints on U.S.-GVN Performance in Vietnam* (Arlington, VA: RAND, 1972); and John A. Nagl, *Learning to Eat Soup with a Knife: Counterinsurgency Lessons from Malaya and Vietnam* (Chicago: University of Chicago Press, 2005).
5. Richard A. Posner, *Uncertain Shield: The U.S. Intelligence System in the Throes of Reform* (Lanham, MD: Rowman & Littlefield Publishers Inc., 2006).
6. Eric Lichtblau, "Cost Concerns for F.B.I. Overhaul," *New York Times*, March 14, 2006.
7. Thom Hanker, "Study Is Said to Find Overlap in U.S. Counterterror Effort," *New York Times*, March 18, 2006.

35

"Preparing Americans for Disaster"

Paul C. Light

New York—As they ponder the final 9/11 commission report detailing the continued lack of preparedness among federal agencies, Congress and President Bush should also consider the parallel lack of preparedness among the citizenry as a whole.

They might start by addressing the most important lesson that emerged from hurricane Katrina: Despite unrelenting coverage of the chaos that followed the storm, Katrina had virtually no effect on the public's preparedness for disaster.

Americans clearly believe something is coming, however. According to a New York University survey conducted last July, a majority of Americans believe terrorists will hit again within five years.

Yet, Americans also believe disaster will strike just about anywhere but home. Asked last summer why their communities were unlikely targets, most Americans either said their part of the country was too unimportant to attack, terrorists were on the run, or the government would protect them.

Many also said they needed more time and money to prepare, almost half said they did not know exactly what to do and where to turn for help, and two-thirds did not have a plan with family and friends about whom they would contact after a disaster.

Such complacency can only breed the kind of chaos seen on the streets of New Orleans after Katrina. Asked what they would do if a suicide bombing or biological attack occurred in their own communities, Americans said they would go every which way but loose. Some said they would flee, others would volunteer, and still others would contact their friends and family, try to learn more about the event, gather supplies, pray, or lock and load. Americans have never been more dependent on local governments, businesses, and charitable institutions to guide them after disaster strikes.

Unfortunately, according to a second New York University survey conducted in mid-October, Katrina eroded public confidence in the very institutions that they depend upon. Barely a third said their fire departments and charitable organizations were very well prepared to help people in need, less than a fifth said the same about their local police, and barely a tenth said the same about local businesses and governments.

Katrina also created serious doubts about how well the federal government would respond to specific disasters such as terrorist bombings and a flu epidemic. Although the number of Americans who said they know what to expect from a potential disaster almost doubled in the weeks before and after Katrina, many appear to expect government failure. Only 11 percent of Americans said that the federal government was very well prepared for a flu epidemic, for example.

Although some cities such as New York, San Francisco, and Los Angeles are working hard to be prepared for a range of hazards, others simply do not have the time, money, or the motivation to act, and still others suffer from "not in my backyard" syndrome.

Congress should be cautious about giving the Department of Homeland Security yet another responsibility, but it is the logical place to launch an effort to both raise public consciousness and close the preparedness divide between rich and poor.

With a budget in the millions, not billions, such a citizen-preparedness initiative could make an instant impact by merely reconciling the hundreds of federal programs already promoting everything from smoke detectors to evacuation kits. It could also start a long-needed conversation among the thousands of state and local governments, private business, charitable organizations, and first responders who play key roles in citizen education.

However, the most important job right now is to engage Americans in an honest conversation about how to prepare for different kinds of disasters. Too many emergency planners believe that citizens should prepare for every hazard at once. Too many also believe that citizens will panic if they get too much information about the specific threats they face. If nothing else, the New York University surveys show that Americans not only understand the difference between terrorist bombings and flu epidemics, but want more information on what to do in each case.

Such a preparedness initiative need not last forever. It can easily finish its work within a year or two. But it can only succeed if it has the power to speak to the public and is led by a single, nonpartisan executive, not a political crony looking for a plum job.

The cost of increased preparedness is nothing compared to the $35 billion minimum estimates for building new levees in New Orleans or the millions for housing the thousands of citizens who lost their homes in Katrina, but it is every bit as important. Most Americans cannot last on their own after a natural or terrorist disaster for three days. It is just the kind of breach that government should address.

Discussion Questions

1. Why is it so hard to change an organization's culture? Why can't a leader simply say, "This is how it's going to be," and force change?

2. Are there any disadvantages to sharing information (which in these areas will be extremely sensitive and considered top secret)? Are there any good reasons why the FBI, or CIA, or other agency would refuse to provide information to another government organization?

3. Is the only way to overcome the clash of organizational cultures to create independent intelligence-gathering agencies? What are the advantages and disadvantages of this approach?

4. Do you think Light is correct in the "not in my backyard" approach that most Americans currently take toward being prepared for a terrorist attack? Do you think terrorists might strike in your community? What have you done to prepare for that possibility?

CHAPTER 8

The Federal Judiciary

36

The Federalist, No. 78

ALEXANDER HAMILTON

The judiciary, Hamilton wrote in The Federalist, No. 78, *"will always be the least dangerous to the political rights of the Constitution; because it will be least in a capacity to annoy or injure them." The lack of danger Hamilton spoke of stems from the Court's lack of enforcement or policy power, or as Hamilton more eloquently put it, the Court has "no influence over either the sword or the purse": it must rely on the executive branch and state governments to enforce its rulings, and depends on the legislature for its appropriations and rules governing its structure. Critics of "judicial activism" would likely disagree about the weakness of the Court relative to the other branches of government. But Hamilton saw an independent judiciary as an important check on the other branches' ability to assume too much power (the "bulwarks of a limited Constitution against legislative encroachments"). He also argued that the Court, as interpreter of the Constitution, would gain its power from the force of its judgments, which were rooted in the will of the people.*

To the People of the State of New York:

We proceed now to an examination of the judiciary department of the proposed government.

In unfolding the defects of the existing Confederation, the utility and necessity of a federal judicature have been clearly pointed out. It is the less necessary to recapitulate the considerations there urged, as the propriety of the institution in the abstract is not disputed; the only questions which have been raised being relative to the manner of constituting it, and to its extent. To these points, therefore, our observations shall be confined.

The manner of constituting it seems to embrace these several objects:

1ST. The mode of appointing the judges. 2D. The tenure by which they are to hold their places. 3D. The partition of the judiciary authority between different courts, and their relations to each other.

First. As to the mode of appointing the judges; this is the same with that of appointing the officers of the Union in general, and has been so fully discussed in the two last numbers, that nothing can be said here which would not be useless repetition.

Second. As to the tenure by which the judges are to hold their places: this chiefly concerns their duration in office; the provisions for their support; the precautions for their responsibility.

According to the plan of the convention, all judges who may be appointed by the United States are to hold their offices *during good behavior;* which is conformable to the most approved of the State constitutions, and among the rest, to that of this State. Its propriety having been drawn into question by the adversaries of that plan, is no light symptom of the rage for objection, which disorders their imaginations and judgments. The standard of good behavior for the continuance in office of the judicial magistracy is certainly one of the most valuable of the modern improvements in the practice of government. In a monarchy it is an excellent barrier to the despotism of the prince; in a republic it is a no less excellent barrier to the encroachments and oppressions of the representative body. And it is the best expedient which can be devised in any government to secure a steady, upright, and impartial administration of the laws.

Whoever attentively considers the different departments of power must perceive, that, in a government in which they are separated from each other, the judiciary, from the nature of its functions, will always be the least dangerous to the political rights of the Constitution; because it will be least in a capacity to annoy or injure them. The Executive not only dispenses the honors, but holds the sword of the community. The legislature not only commands the purse, but prescribes the rules by which the duties and rights of every citizen are to be regulated. The judiciary, on the contrary, has no influence over either the sword or the purse; no direction either of the strength or of the wealth of the society; and can take no active resolution whatever. It may truly be said to have neither FORCE nor WILL, but merely judgment; and must ultimately depend upon the aid of the executive arm even for the efficacy of its judgments.

This simple view of the matter suggests several important consequences. It proves incontestably that the judiciary is beyond comparison the weakest of the three departments of power that it can never attack with success either of the other two; and that all possible care is requisite to enable it to defend itself against their attacks. It equally proves that though individual oppression may now and then proceed from the courts of justice, the general liberty of the people can never be endangered from that quarter; I mean so long as the judiciary remains truly distinct from both the legislature and the Executive. For I agree, that "there is no liberty, if the power of judging be not separated from the legislative and executive powers." And it proves, in the last place, that as liberty can have nothing to fear from the judiciary alone, but would have every thing to fear from its union with either of the other departments; that as all the effects of such a union must ensue from a dependence of the former on the latter, notwithstanding a nominal and apparent separation; that as, from the natural feebleness of the judiciary it is in continual jeopardy of being overpowered, awed, or influenced by its coordinate branches; and that as nothing can contribute so much to its firmness and independence as permanency in office, this quality may therefore be justly regarded as an indispensable ingredient in its constitution, and, in a great measure, as the citadel of the public justice and the public security.

The complete independence of the courts of justice is peculiarly essential in a limited Constitution. By a limited Constitution, I understand one which contains certain specified exceptions to the legislative authority; such, for instance, as that it shall pass no bills of attainder, no *ex-post-facto* laws, and the like. Limitations of this kind can be preserved in practice no other way than through the medium of courts of justice, whose duty it must be to declare all acts contrary to the manifest tenor of the Constitution void. Without this, all the reservations of particular rights or privileges would amount to nothing.

Some perplexity respecting the rights of the courts to pronounce legislative acts void, because contrary to the constitution, has arisen from an imagination that the doctrine would imply a superiority of the judiciary to the legislative power. It is urged that the authority which can declare the acts of another void must necessarily be superior to the one whose acts may be declared void. As this doctrine is of great importance in all the American constitutions, a brief discussion of the ground on which it rests cannot be unacceptable.

There is no position which depends on clearer principles than that every act of a delegated authority, contrary to the tenor of the commission under which it is exercised, is void. No legislative act, therefore, contrary to the Constitution, can be valid. To deny this would be to affirm that the deputy is greater than his principal; that the servant is above his master; that the representatives of the people are superior to the people themselves; that men acting by virtue of powers may do not only what their powers do not authorize, but what they forbid.

If it be said that the legislative body are themselves the constitutional judges of their own powers, and that the construction they put upon them is conclusive upon the other departments, it may be answered that this cannot be the natural presumption where it is not to be collected from any particular provisions in the Constitution. It is not otherwise to be supposed that the Constitution could intend to enable the representatives of the people to substitute their *will* to that of their constituents. It is far more rational to suppose that the courts were designed to be an intermediate body between the people and the legislature, in order, among other things, to keep the latter within the limits assigned to their authority. The interpretation of the laws is the proper and peculiar province of the courts. A constitution is, in fact, and must be regarded by the judges, as a fundamental law. It therefore belongs to them to ascertain its meaning, as well as the meaning of any particular act proceeding from the legislative body. If there should happen to be an irreconcilable variance between the two, that which has the superior obligation and validity ought, of course, to be preferred; or, in other words, the Constitution ought to be preferred to the statute, the intention of the people to the intention of their agents.

Nor does this conclusion by any means suppose a superiority of the judicial to the legislative power. It only supposes that the power of the people is superior to both; and that where the will of the legislature, declared in its statutes, stands in opposition to that of the people, declared in the Constitution, the judges ought to be governed by the latter rather than the former. They ought to regulate their decisions by the fundamental laws, rather than by those which are not fundamental.

This exercise of judicial discretion, in determining between two contradictory laws, is exemplified in a familiar instance. It not uncommonly happens that there are two statutes existing at one time, clashing in whole or in part with each other, and neither of them containing any repealing clause or expression. In such a case, it is the province of the courts to liquidate and fix their meaning and operation. So far as they can, by any fair construction, be reconciled to each other, reason and law conspire to dictate that this should be done; where this is impracticable, it becomes a matter of necessity to give effect to one in exclusion of the other. The rule which has obtained in the courts for determining their relative validity is, that the last in order of time shall be preferred to the first. But this is a mere rule of construction, not derived from any positive law but from the nature and reason of the thing. It is a rule not enjoined upon the courts by legislative provision but adopted by themselves, as consonant to truth and propriety for the direction of their conduct as interpreters of the law. They thought it reasonable, that between the interfering acts of an *equal* authority, that which was the last indication of its will should have the preference.

But in regard to the interfering acts of a superior and subordinate authority, of an original and derivative power, the nature and reason of the thing indicate the converse of that rule as proper to be followed. They teach us that the prior act of a superior ought to be preferred to the subsequent act of an inferior and subordinate authority; and that accordingly, whenever a particular statute contravenes the Constitution, it will be the duty of the judicial tribunals to adhere to the latter and disregard the former.

It can be of no weight to say that the courts, on the pretence of a repugnancy, may substitute their own pleasure to the constitutional intentions of the legislature. This might as well happen in the case of two contradictory statutes; or it might as well happen in every adjudication upon any single statute. The courts must declare the sense of the law; and if they should be disposed to exercise WILL instead of JUDGMENT, the consequence would equally be the substitution of their pleasure to that of the legislative body. The observation, if it prove any thing, would prove that there ought to be no judges distinct from that body.

If, then, the courts of justice are to be considered as the bulwarks of a limited Constitution against legislative encroachments, this consideration will afford a strong argument for the permanent tenure of judicial offices, since nothing will contribute so much as this to that independent spirit in the judges which must be essential to the faithful performance of so arduous a duty.

This independence of the judges is equally requisite to guard the Constitution and the rights of individuals from the effects of those ill humors, which the arts of designing men or the influence of particular conjunctures sometimes disseminate among the people themselves; and which, though they speedily give place to better information and more deliberate reflection, have a tendency, in the meantime, to occasion dangerous innovations in the government, and serious oppressions of the minor party in the community. Though I trust the friends of the proposed Constitution will never concur with its enemies in questioning that fundamental principle of republican government, which admits the right of the people to alter or abolish the established Constitution whenever they find it inconsistent with their happiness; yet it is not to be inferred from this principle that the representatives of the people, whenever a momentary inclination happens to lay hold of a majority of their constituents, incompatible with the provisions in the existing Constitution, would, on that account, be justifiable in a violation of those provisions; or that the courts would be under a greater obligation to connive at infractions in this shape, than when they had proceeded wholly from the cabals of the representative body. Until the people have by some solemn and authoritative act annulled or changed the established form, it is binding upon themselves collectively, as well as individually; and no presumption, or even knowledge, of their sentiments, can warrant their representatives in a departure from it, prior to such an act. But it is easy to see that it would require an uncommon portion of fortitude in the judges to do their duty as faithful guardians of the Constitution, where legislative invasions of it had been instigated by the major voice of the community.

But it is not with a view to infractions of the Constitution only that the independence of the judges may be an essential safeguard against the effects of occasional ill humors in the society. These sometimes extend no farther than to the injury of the private rights of particular classes of citizens by unjust and partial laws. Here also the firmness of the judicial magistracy is of vast importance in mitigating the severity and confining the operation of such laws. It not only serves to moderate the immediate mischiefs of those which may have been passed, but it operates as a check upon the legislative body in passing them; who, perceiving that obstacles to the success of iniquitous intention are to be expected from the scruples of the courts, are in a manner compelled by the very motives of the injustice they meditate to qualify their attempts. This is a circumstance calculated to have more influence upon the character of our governments, than but few may be aware of. The benefits of the integrity and moderation of the judiciary have already been felt in more States than one; and though they may have displeased those whose sinister expectations they may have disappointed, they must have commanded the esteem and applause of all the virtuous and disinterested. Considerate men of every description ought to prize whatever will tend to beget or fortify that temper in the courts; as no man can be sure that he may not be tomorrow the victim of a spirit of injustice by which he may be a gainer today. And every man must now feel that the inevitable tendency of such a spirit is to sap the foundations of public and private confidence, and to introduce in its stead universal distrust and distress.

That inflexible and uniform adherence to the rights of the Constitution and of individuals, which we perceive to be indispensable in the courts of justice, can certainly not be expected from judges who hold their offices by a temporary commission. Periodical appointments, however regulated or by whomsoever made, would, in some way or other, be fatal to their necessary independence. If the power of making them was committed either to the Executive or legislature, there would be danger of an improper complaisance to the branch which possessed it; if to both, there would be an unwillingness to hazard the displeasure of either; if to the people or to persons chosen by them for the special purpose, there would be too great a disposition to consult popularity, to justify a reliance that nothing would be consulted but the Constitution and the laws.

There is yet a further and a weightier reason for the permanency of the judicial offices, which is deducible from the nature of the qualifications they require. It has been frequently remarked, with great propriety, that a voluminous code of laws is one of the inconveniences necessarily connected with the advantages of a free government. To avoid an arbitrary discretion in the courts, it is indispensable that they should be bound down by strict rules and precedents, which serve to define and point out their duty in every particular case that comes before them; and it will readily be conceived from the variety of controversies which grow out of the folly and wickedness of mankind, that the records of those precedents must unavoidably swell to a very considerable bulk, and must demand long and laborious study to acquire a competent knowledge of them. Hence it is, that there can be but few men in the society who will have sufficient skill in the laws to qualify them for the stations of judges. And making the proper deductions for the ordinary depravity of human nature, the number must be still smaller of those who unite the requisite integrity with the requisite knowledge. These considerations apprise us that the government can have no great option between fit character; and that a temporary duration in office, which would naturally discourage such characters from quitting a lucrative line of practice to accept a seat on the bench, would have a tendency to throw the administration of justice into hands less able, and less well qualified, to conduct it with utility and dignity. In the present circumstances of this country and in those in which it is likely to be for a long time to come, the disadvantages on this score would be greater than they may at first sight appear; but it must be confessed that they are far inferior to those which present themselves under the other aspects of the subject.

Upon the whole, there can be no room to doubt that the convention acted wisely in copying from the models of those constitutions which have established *good behavior* as the tenure of their judicial offices, in point of duration; and that so far from being blamable on this account, their plan would have been inexcusably defective if it had wanted this important feature of good government. The experience of Great Britain affords an illustrious comment on the excellence of the institution.

Publius

Discussion Questions

1. Was Hamilton correct in arguing that the judiciary is the least dangerous branch of government?

2. Critics of the Court often charge that it takes control of issues that should be properly decided in the legislature, while supporters claim that the Court is often the last check against the tyranny of the majority. Who has the stronger case? Can both sides be correct?

3. Hamilton argues that the "power of the people is superior to both" the legislature and the Court, and that the Court upholds the power of the people when it supports the Constitution over a statute that runs counter to the Constitution. Can you think of instances in which Congress may have been a stronger supporter of the "people" than the Court? Is it legitimate to argue that the Court is supporting the will of the people, given that it is an unelected body?

37

"The Court and American Life" from
Storm Center: The Supreme Court in American Politics

David O'Brien

The "textbook" view of the federal judiciary is one in which judges sit in dispassionate review of complex legal questions, render decisions based on a careful reading of constitutional or statutory language, and expect their rulings to be adhered to strictly; the law is the law. This selection shows how unrealistic that picture is: O'Brien notes that the Supreme Court is very much a political institution, whose members pay more attention to the political cycle and public opinion than one might expect. O'Brien reviews the decision-making process in the famous Brown v. Board of Education of Topeka, Kansas, *in which the Court invalidated segregated public schools, as an example of how the Court fits itself into the political process. Throughout the case, Justices delayed their decision, consolidated cases from around the country, and refused to set a firm timetable for implementation, relying instead on the ambiguous standard "with all deliberate speed." Far from being a purely objective arbiter of legal questions, the Court must pay close attention to its own legitimacy, and by extension the likelihood of compliance: it does no good to issue decisions that will be ignored.*

"Why does the Supreme Court pass the school desegregation case?" asked one of Chief Justice Vinson's law clerks in 1952. *Brown v. Board of Education of Topeka, Kansas* had arrived on the Court's docket in 1951, but it was carried over for oral argument the next term and then consolidated with four other cases and reargued in December 1953. The landmark ruling did not come down until May 17, 1954. "Well," Justice Frankfurter explained, "we're holding it for the election"—1952 was a presidential election year. "You're holding it for the election?" The clerk persisted in disbelief. "I thought the Supreme Court was supposed to decide cases without regard to elections." "When you have a major social political issue of this magnitude," timing and public reactions are important considerations, and, Frankfurter continued, "we do not think this is the time to decide it." Similarly, Tom Clark recalled that the Court awaited, over Douglas's dissent, additional cases from the

District of Columbia and other regions, so as "to get a national coverage, rather than a sectional one." Such political considerations are by no means unique. "We often delay adjudication. It's not a question of evading at all," Clark concluded. "It's just the practicalities of life—common sense."

Denied the power of the sword or the purse, the Court must cultivate its institutional prestige. The power of the Court lies in the persuasiveness of its rulings and ultimately rests with other political institutions and public opinion. As an independent force, the Court has no chance to resolve great issues of public policy. *Dred Scott v. Sandford* (1857) and *Brown v. Board of Education* (1954) illustrate the limitations of Supreme Court policy-making. The "great folly," as Senator Henry Cabot Lodge characterized *Dred Scott*, was not the Court's interpretation of the Constitution or the unpersuasive moral position that blacks were not persons under the Constitution. Rather, "the attempt of the Court to settle the slavery question by judicial decision was simple madness." As Lodge explained:

> Slavery involved not only the great moral issue of the right of one man to hold another in bondage and to buy and sell him but it involved also the foundations of a social fabric covering half the country and caused men to feel so deeply that it finally brought them beyond the question of nullification to a point where the life of the Union was at stake and a decision could only be reached by war.[1]

A hundred years later, political struggles within the country and, notably, presidential and congressional leadership in enforcing the Court's school desegregation ruling saved the moral appeal of *Brown* from becoming another "great folly."

Because the Court's decisions are not self-executing, public reactions inevitably weigh on the minds of the justices. Justice Stone, for one, was furious at Chief Justice Hughes's rush to hand down *Powell v. Alabama* (1932). Picketers protested the Scottsboro boys' conviction and death sentence. Stone attributed the Court's rush to judgment to Hughes's "wish to put a stop to the [public] demonstrations around the Court." Opposition to the school desegregation ruling in *Brown* led to bitter, sometimes violent confrontations. In Little Rock, Arkansas, Governor Orval Faubus encouraged disobedience by southern segregationists. The federal National Guard had to be called out to maintain order. The school board in Little Rock unsuccessfully pleaded, in *Cooper v. Aaron* (1958), for the Court's postponement of the implementation of *Brown's* mandate. In the midst of the controversy, Frankfurter worried that Chief Justice Warren's attitude had become "more like that of a fighting politician than that of a judicial statesman." In such confrontations between the Court and the country, "the transcending issue," Frankfurter reminded the brethren, remains that of preserving "the Supreme Court as the authoritative organ of what the Constitution requires." When the justices move too far or too fast in their interpretation of the Constitution, they threaten public acceptance of the Court's legitimacy.

*   *   *

When deciding major issues of public law and policy, justices must consider strategies for getting public acceptance of their rulings. When striking down the doctrine of "separate but equal" facilities in 1954 in *Brown v. Board of Education (Brown I)*, for instance, the Warren Court waited a year before issuing, in *Brown II*, its mandate for "all deliberate speed" in ending racial segregation in public education.

Resistance to the social policy announced in *Brown I* was expected. A rigid timetable for desegregation would only intensify opposition. During oral arguments on *Brown II*, devoted to the question of what kind of decree the Court should issue to enforce *Brown*, Warren confronted the hard fact of southern resistance. The attorney for South Carolina, S. Emory Rogers, pressed for an open-ended decree—one that would not specify when and how desegregation should take place. He boldly proclaimed:

> Mr. Chief Justice, to say we will conform depends on the decree handed down. I am frank to tell you, right now [in] our district I do not think that we will send—[that] the white people of the district will send their children to the Negro schools. It would be unfair to tell the Court that we are going to do that. I do not think it is. But I do think that something can be worked out. We hope so.

"It is not a question of attitude," Warren shot back, "it is a question of conforming to the decree." Their heated exchange continued as follows:

> CHIEF JUSTICE WARREN: But you are not willing to say here that there would be an honest attempt to conform to this decree, if we did leave it to the district court [to implement]?
> MR. ROGERS: No, I am not. Let us get the word "honest" out of there.
> CHIEF JUSTICE WARREN: No, leave it in.
> MR. ROGERS: No, because I would have to tell you that right now we would not conform—we would not send our white children to the Negro schools.[2]

The exchange reinforced Warren's view "that reasonable attempts to start the integration process is [sic] all the court can expect in view of the scope of the problem, and that an order to immediately admit all negroes in white schools would be an absurdity because impossible to obey in many areas. Thus, while total immediate integration might be a reasonable order for Kansas, it would be unreasonable for Virginia, and the district judge might decide that a grade a year or three grades a year is [sic] reasonable compliance in Virginia." Six law clerks were assigned to prepare a segregation research report. They summarized available studies, discussed how school districts in different regions could be desegregated, and projected the effects and reactions to various desegregation plans.

The Court's problem, as one of Reed's law clerks put it, was to frame a decree "so as to allow such divergent results without making it so broad that evasion is encouraged." The clerks agreed that there should be a simple decree but disagreed on whether there should be guidelines for its implementation. One clerk opposed any guidelines. The others thought that their absence "smacks of indecisiveness, and gives the extremists more time to operate." The problem was how precise a guideline should be established. What would constitute "good-faith" compliance? "Although we think a 12-year gradual desegregation plan permissible," they confessed, "we are not certain that the opinion should explicitly sanction it."

At conference, Warren repeated these concerns. Black and Minton thought that a simple decree, without an opinion, was enough. As Black explained, "the less we say the better off we are." The others disagreed. A short, simple opinion seemed advisable for reaffirming *Brown I* and providing guidance for dealing with the inevitable problems of compliance. Harlan wanted *Brown II* expressly to recognize that school desegregation was a local problem to be solved by local authorities. The others also insisted on making clear that school boards and lower courts had flexibility in ending segregation. In Burton's view, "neither this Court nor district courts should act as a school board or formulate the program" for desegregation.

Agreement emerged that the Court should issue a short opinion-decree. In a memorandum, Warren summarized the main points of agreement. The opinion should simply state that *Brown I* held racially segregated public schools to be unconstitutional. *Brown II* should acknowledge that the ruling created various administrative problems, but emphasize that "local school authorities have the primary responsibility for assessing and solving these problems; [and] the courts will have to consider these problems in determining whether the efforts of local school authorities" are in good-faith compliance. The cases, he concluded, should be remanded to the lower courts "for such proceedings and decree necessary and proper to carry out this Court's decision." The justices agreed, and along these lines Warren drafted the Court's short opinion-decree.

The phrase "all deliberate speed" was borrowed from Holmes's opinion in *Virginia v. West Virginia* (1911), a case dealing with how much of the state's public debt, and when, Virginia ought to receive at the time West Virginia broke off and became a state. It was inserted in the final opinion at the suggestion of Frankfurter. Forced integration might lead to a lowering of educational standards. Immediate, court-ordered desegregation, Frankfurter warned, "would make a mockery of the Constitutional adjudication designed to vindicate a claim to equal treatment to achieve 'integrated' but lower educational standards." The Court, he insisted, "does its duty if it gets effectively under way the righting of a wrong. When the wrong is deeply rooted state policy the court does its duty if it decrees measures that reverse the direction of the unconstitutional policy so as to uproot it `with all deliberate speed.'" As much an apology for not setting precise guidelines as a recognition of the limitations of judicial power, the phrase symbolized the Court's bold moral appeal to the country.

Ten years later, after school closings, massive resistance, and continuing litigation, Black complained. "There has been entirely too much deliberation and not enough speed" in complying with *Brown*. "The time for mere 'deliberate speed' has run out." *Brown*'s moral appeal amounted to little more than an invitation for delay.

*   *   *

Twenty years after *Brown*, some schools remained segregated. David Mathews, secretary of the Department of Health, Education, and Welfare, reported to President Ford the results of a survey of half of the nation's primary and secondary public schools, enrolling 91 percent of all students: of these, 42 percent had an "appreciable percentage" of minority students, 16 percent had undertaken desegregation plans, while 26 percent had not, and 7 percent of the school districts remained racially segregated.

For over three decades, problems of implementing and achieving compliance with *Brown* persisted. Litigation by civil rights groups forced change, but it was piecemeal, costly, and modest. The judiciary alone could not achieve desegregation. Evasion and resistance were encouraged by the reluctance of Presidents and Congress to enforce the mandate. Refusing publicly to endorse *Brown*, Eisenhower would not take steps to enforce the decision until violence erupted in Little Rock, Arkansas. He then did so *"not* to enforce integration but to prevent opposition by violence to orders of a court." Later the Kennedy and Johnson administrations lacked congressional authorization and resources to take major initiatives in enforcing school desegregation. Not until 1964, when Congress passed the Civil Rights Act, did the executive branch have such authorization.

Enforcement and implementation required the cooperation and coordination of all three branches. Little progress could be made, as Assistant Attorney General Stephen Pollock has explained, "where historically there had been slavery and a long tradition of discrimination [until] all three branches of the federal government [could] be lined up in support of a movement forward or a requirement for change." The election of Nixon in 1968 then brought changes both in the policies of the executive branch and in the composition of the Court. The simplicity and flexibility of *Brown*, moreover, invited evasion. It produced a continuing struggle over measures, such as gerrymandering school district lines and busing in the 1970s and 1980s, because the mandate itself had evolved from one of ending segregation to one of securing integration in public schools. Republican and Democratic administrations in turn differed on the means and ends of their enforcement policies in promoting integration.

Almost forty years after *Brown*, over 500 school desegregation cases remained in the lower federal courts. At issue in most was whether schools had achieved integration and become free of the vestiges of past segregation. Although lower courts split over how much proof school boards had to show to demonstrate that present *de facto* racial isolation was unrelated to past *de jure* segregation, the Court declined to review major desegregation cases from the mid-1970s to the end of the 1980s. During that time the dynamics of segregation in the country changed, as did the composition and direction of the Court.

* * *

"By itself," the political scientist Robert Dahl observed, "the Court is almost powerless to affect the course of national policy." Another political scientist, Gerald Rosenberg, goes much farther in claiming that "courts can *almost never* be effective producers of significant social reform." *Brown*'s failure to achieve immediate and widespread desegregation is instructive, Rosenberg contends, in developing a model of judicial policy-making on the basis of two opposing theories of judicial power. On the theory of a "Constrainted Court" three institutional factors limit judicial policy-making: "[t]he limited nature of constitutional rights"; "[t]he lack of judicial independence"; and "[t]he judiciary's lack of powers of implementation." On the other hand, a "Dynamic Court" theory emphasizes the judiciary's freedom "from electoral constraints and [other] institutional arrangements that stymie change," and thus enable the courts to take on issues that other political institutions might not or cannot. But neither theory is completely satisfactory, according to Rosenberg, because occasionally courts do bring about social change. The Court may do so when the three institutional restraints identified with the "Constrained Court" theory are absent and at least one of the following conditions exist to support judicial policy-making: when other political institutions and actors offer either (a) incentives or (b) costs to induce compliance; (c) "when judicial decisions can be implemented by the market"; or (d) when the Court's ruling serves as "a shield, cover, or excuse, for persons crucial to implementation who are *willing to act*." On the historical basis of resistance and forced compliance with *Brown*'s mandate, Rosenberg concludes that "*Brown* and its progeny stand for the proposition that courts are impotent to produce significant social reform."

Brown, nonetheless, dramatically and undeniably altered the course of American life in ways and for reasons that Rosenberg underestimates. Neither Congress nor President Eisenhower would have moved to end segregated schools in the 1950s, as their reluctance for a decade to enforce *Brown* underscores. The Court lent moral force and legitimacy to the civil rights movement and to the eventual move by Congress and President Johnson to enforce compliance with *Brown*. More importantly, to argue that the Court is impotent to bring about social change overstates the case. Neither Congress nor the President, any more than the Court, could have singlehandedly dismantled racially segregated public schools. As political scientist Richard Neustadt has argued, presidential power ultimately turns on a President's power of persuasion, the Court's power depends on the persuasiveness of its rulings and the magnitude of change in social behavior mandated. The Court raises the ante in its bid for compliance when it appeals for massive social change through a prescribed course of action, in contrast to when it simply says "no" when striking down a law. The unanimous but ambiguous ruling in *Brown* reflects the justices' awareness that their decisions are not self-enforcing, especially when they deal with highly controversial issues and their rulings depend heavily on other institutions for implementation. Moreover, the ambiguity of *Brown*'s remedial decree was the price of achieving unanimity. Unanimity appeared necessary if the Court was to preserve its institutional prestige while pursuing revolutionary change in social policy. The justices sacrificed their own policy preferences for more precise guidelines, while the Court tolerated lengthy delays in recognition of the costs of open defiance, building consensus, and gaining public acceptance. But in the ensuing decades *Brown*'s mandate was also transformed from that of a simple decree for putting an end to state-imposed segregation into the more vexing one of achieving integrated public schools. With that transformation of *Brown*'s mandate the political dynamics of the desegregation controversy evolved, along with a changing Court and country.

DISCUSSION QUESTIONS

1. In what ways does the Supreme Court take "politics" into account in making decisions? Is this appropriate? What would the alternative be?

2. How does the process of appointment to the Supreme Court shape Court decisions? Should presidents make nominations based on the political views of potential justices?

3. Does O'Brien's argument reflect Hamilton's observations about the power of the Court?

4. In two rulings, in November 2003 and February 2004, the Massachusetts Supreme Court ruled that bans on gay marriage were unconstitutional. This set off a national firestorm of protest, and arguably a backlash against gay marriage. Did the Massachusetts court's ruling damage the court's own public standing by ignoring

the political context of its decision (a nation in which two-thirds of the people are opposed to gay marriage), or did the court do the correct and courageous thing by supporting the basic rights of a minority group? Is there some way the court could have finessed the issue, the way the Supreme Court did in *Brown*?

NOTES

1. Letter to Charles Warren, July 19, 1923, Charles Warren Papers, Box 2, Library of Congress, Manuscripts Division, Washington, D.C.
2. Transcript of Oral Argument, Stanley Reed Papers, Box 43, University of Kentucky, Special Collections Library, Lexington, Kentucky.

38

"Overruling the Court"

Leon Friedman

This article develops another theme that was addressed in Alexander Hamilton's Federalist, No. 78. Hamilton argued that the Supreme Court should be the final interpreter of the Constitution. If Congress passed a law that was clearly unconstitutional, the Court must strike it down. However, as Friedman points out, Congress often disagrees with Supreme Court decisions and will pass legislation that overrules specific decisions (even if the Court claims that it has the final say). These tussles between Congress and the Supreme Court may often go back and forth for several rounds before one of the branches backs down. In general, Congress should have the upper hand if the question concerns statutory interpretation (that is, what a law passed by Congress really means), while the Supreme Court gets the final word concerning Constitutional interpretation. Friedman explores these issues in the context of civil rights legislation in the past twenty years. The Supreme Court has been trying to impose its more narrow conception of civil rights in a series of decisions going back to 1982. On several occasions Congress has passed new legislation to restore the original intention of the 1964 Civil Rights Act and other laws. Friedman argues that the time has come for additional corrective legislation. He outlines five Supreme Court decisions on age discrimination, disability discrimination, language discrimination, lawyers' fees for civil rights cases, and remedies for violence against women that all restrict the scope of civil rights in the United States. Friedman also discusses the types of actions that Congress could take to overturn these decisions. Some changes would be relatively direct, in the case of statutory interpretation; others would be more indirect, when dealing with constitutional issues such as federalism.

One of the myths of our political system is that the Supreme Court has the last word on the scope and meaning of federal law. But time and time again, Congress has shown its dissatisfaction with Supreme Court interpretations of laws it passes—by amending or re-enacting the legislation to clarify its original intent and overrule a contrary Court construction.

The Supreme Court often insists that Congress cannot really "overrule" its decisions on what a law means: The justices' interpretation has to be correct since the Constitution gives final say to the highest court in the land. But Congress certainly has the power to pass a new or revised law that "changes" or "reverses" the meaning or scope of the law as interpreted by the Court, and the legislative history of the new law usually states that it was intended to "overrule" a specific Court decision.

Often the reversal is in highly technical areas, such as the statute of limitations in securities-fraud cases, the jurisdiction of tribal courts on Indian reservations, or the power of state courts to order denaturalization of citizens. But in the last 20 years, a main target of congressional "overruling" has been the Supreme Court's decisions in the area of civil rights. In 1982, for example, Congress amended the Voting Rights Act of 1965 to overrule a narrow Supreme Court holding in *Mobile v. Bolden*, a 1980 decision that addressed whether intentional discrimination must be shown before the act could be invoked. In 1988, Congress overruled another Supreme Court decision (in the 1984 case *Grove City College v. Bell*) by passing the Civil Rights Restoration Act, which broadened the coverage of Title VI of the Civil Rights Act of 1964. The legislative history of that law specifically recited that "certain aspects of recent decisions and opinions of the Supreme Court have unduly narrowed or cast doubt upon" a number of federal civil rights statutes and that "legislative action is necessary to restore the prior consistent and long-standing executive branch interpretations" of those laws.

And in 1991, Congress passed a broad, new Civil Rights Act that specifically reversed no fewer than five Supreme Court cases decided in 1989—decisions that severely restricted and limited workers' rights under federal antidiscrimination laws. Led by Massachusetts Democrat Edward Kennedy in the Senate and New York Republican Hamilton Fish, Jr., in the House, Congress acted to undo those rulings, as well as make other changes to federal law that strengthened the weapons available to workers against discrimination. Despite partisan contention over the language of certain provisions (which led to last-minute-compromise language), President George Bush the elder supported the changes. The new law recited in its preamble that its purpose was "to respond to recent decisions of the Supreme Court by expanding the scope of relevant civil rights statutes in order to provide adequate protection to victims of discrimination."

Given the current Supreme Court's track record in civil rights cases, there can be no doubt that congressional remediation is again necessary. In a series of cases over the past two years, the Court has been giving narrow readings to various federal civil rights laws. And once again, an attentive Congress can and should overrule the Court's decisions if the legislators care about fairness in the operation of government and in the workplace.

The recent cases were decided by identical 5–4 votes: Three conservative justices (William Rehnquist, Antonin Scalia, and Clarence Thomas) were joined by two centrists (Sandra Day O'Connor and Anthony Kennedy) to narrow the reach of the laws at issue. Four liberal justices

(John Paul Stevens, David Souter, Ruth Bader Ginsburg, and Stephen Breyer) dissented in all of the cases, four of which are described below.

- Last year [2000], on the grounds of federalism, the Supreme Court held in *Kimel v. Florida Board of Regents* that persons working for state governments cannot sue in federal court under the Age Discrimination in Employment Act, which Congress adopted in 1967. Such suits, the high court said, were constitutionally barred by the 11th Amendment's prohibition of suits against states in federal court. This ruling removed 3.4 percent of the nation's total workforce from the federal law's protections against age bias—some 5 million state employees across the country.
- On the same basis as the age-discrimination case, the Court held in February of this year that state employees cannot sue in federal court under the Americans with Disabilities Act. In this ruling, *Board of Trustees of the University of Alabama v. Garrett*, state workers who alleged disabilities discrimination were relegated to seeking recourse through state courts, where the available remedies are often much weaker than those provided under federal law.
- In April of this year [2001], the Supreme Court narrowed the reach of Title VI, the 1964 provision that prohibits recipients of federal financial assistance from discriminating on the basis of race, color, or national origin. In *Alexander v. Sandoval*, the Court held that Title VI is violated only if a plaintiff proves that the funded party *intentionally* discriminated on the basis of race—an interpretation that runs contrary to the rule for other civil rights laws (such as Title VII), which require only a showing of a discriminatory impact to trigger enforcement. At the same time, the justices held that neither public nor private recipients of federal financial aid who violate the nation's antidiscrimination regulations can be sued in federal court. Thus the state of Alabama was not vulnerable to suit when it established an "English only" requirement for taking a driver's license exam, even though federal regulations prohibit such restrictions. The only remedy, the Court held, was termination of federal funding to the state entity that violated the regulations (a sanction that entails a complicated administrative process).
- On May 29, the Court decided that civil rights litigants who bring suit against the government or an employer cannot collect attorney fees if the defendant voluntarily ceases the practice complained of or settles the claim before going to trial (the case was *Buckhannon Board and Care Home, Inc., v. West Virginia Department of Health and Human Services*). In 1976, Congress passed the Civil Rights Attorneys Fees Award Act to encourage lawyers to take civil rights cases as "private attorney generals." Such cases "vindicate public policies of the highest order," Congress explained when it passed the law. The act specified that

the legal fees of "prevailing parties" would be paid by the losing party—generally a government that violated the plaintiff's constitutional rights. As Justice Ginsburg pointed out in her dissent in the *Buckhannon* case, Congress enacted the law to "ensure that nonaffluent plaintiffs would have effective access to the Nation's courts to enforce . . . civil rights laws." The effect of the Buckhannon decision is that a government body can tenaciously litigate a case until the last minute, then throw in the towel and evade the requirement of paying attorney fees. Since lawyers can no longer be sure that they'll be paid if they file civil rights suits, this ruling will certainly discourage them from taking on such cases, even those that clearly have merit.

Two of these cases are quite easy to correct. Congress can reverse the Supreme Court's decision about attorney fees by simply amending the civil rights law to provide that a litigant is considered a prevailing party entitled to fees if the lawsuit "was a substantial factor" in remedial action taken by the government and the suit brought by the plaintiff had a "substantial basis in fact and law." That was the rule generally applied by the lower courts before the Supreme Court decision.

The *Sandoval* rule can also be corrected by legislation. Congress could amend Title VI to provide that "any person aggrieved by the violation of any regulation issued pursuant to this act may bring a civil action in an appropriate federal court. Such actions may include suits challenging any discriminatory practice or policy that would be deemed unlawful if it has a disparate impact upon persons protected by this title."

The *Kimel* and *Garrett* decisions are more difficult to attack. The Supreme Court held that the 11th Amendment to the Constitution protects states against suits in federal court for age or disabilities discrimination by their employees. Although Congress cannot overrule a constitutional determination made by the Court, it can condition federal financial assistance on state adherence to federal requirements. In 1987 the Supreme Court held in *South Dakota v. Dole* (a 7–2 decision written by Chief Justice Rehnquist, in which Justice Scalia joined) that Congress could insist that South Dakota increase the minimum drinking age to 21 as a condition of obtaining federal highway funds. In other words, while Congress cannot force states to do its bidding, it in effect may bribe them to follow federal requirements.

Thus Congress could condition federal grants under Medicaid, Medicare, or the Social Security Act on the states' surrendering their 11th Amendment immunity under the federal acts banning discrimination based on age and disability. If a state wished to obtain federal funds under various social-welfare provisions, it would have to accede to the U.S. antidiscrimination laws and waive its immunity from being sued by its employees in federal court. Indeed, the 1986 Civil Rights Remedies Equalization Amendment specifically declared that Congress intended for states to waive their 11th Amendment immunity in order to receive federal financial assistance.

Congress could use the same device to overrule another recent Supreme Court decision: last year's 5–4 holding in *United States v. Morrison* that the civil-remedy provisions of the Violence Against Women Act of 1994 are unconstitutional. The majority held that the law exceeded congressional power under the Constitution's commerce clause—the first time a federal law had been invalidated on that basis since 1936. But Congress can counter the Court's action by ensuring that such civil remedies are available to victims of gender-motivated acts of violence through state courts. How? By making the federal funds that are available through Medicare or Social Security programs contingent on a state's provision of such remedies.

In 1991, Congress and the first President Bush acted courageously to overrule manifestly narrow decisions of the Supreme Court that violated a national consensus against discrimination by government or by employers. Now that the Democrats have control of the Senate, they should make similar corrective legislation one of their first objectives. And who knows? This President Bush might even follow the lead of his father and endorse the changes.

DISCUSSION QUESTIONS

1. The issues discussed here return to some of the themes raised in the chapter on federalism (in terms of the Court playing a role in the institutional balance of power). To what extent should the Supreme Court shape policy in an area such as civil rights, and to what extent should policy be made by Congress or the states?

2. If you think that the Court should play a central role in policy- and lawmaking, how would you answer critics who say that laws should be made by popularly elected institutions and not by unelected judges? If you think that Congress should play a central role, how would you answer those who point to the mid twentieth century and show that Congress was dominated by southern segregationists who killed civil rights legislation for decades? Do the answers to these questions depend, at least in part, on how you view the policy in question and which branch of government would be more sympathetic to your views?

Debating the Issues: Interpreting the Constitution — Originalism or a Living Constitution?

Debates over the federal judiciary's role in the political process often focus on the question of how judges should interpret the Constitution. Should judges apply the document's original meaning as stated by the Framers, or should they use a broader interpretive framework that incorporates a more flexible view? This debate intensified during Earl Warren's tenure as Chief Justice (1953–1969), because of Court decisions that expanded the scope of civil liberties and criminal rights far beyond what strict constructionists thought the Constitution's language authorized. The debate continues in the current Court as an activist, conservative majority has implemented its interpretation of the Constitution over a broad range of cases, in some instances overturning six decades of precedents. The two readings in this section offer contrasting viewpoints from two sitting Supreme Court Justices.

Antonin Scalia, the intellectual force behind the conservative wing of the Court, argues that Justices must be bound by the original meaning of the document, as this is the only neutral principle that allows the judiciary to function as a legal body instead of a political one. The alternative is to embrace an evolving or "Living Constitution," which Scalia criticizes as allowing judges to decide cases on the basis of what seems right at the moment. He says that this "evolutionary" approach does not have any overall guiding principle and therefore "is simply not a practicable constitutional philosophy." He provides several examples of how the Living Constitution approach had produced decisions that stray from the clear meaning of the Constitution in the areas of property rights, the right to bear arms, and the right to confront one's accuser. This last example is especially provocative, given that it concerned the right of an accused child molester to confront the child who accused him of the crime. Scalia also challenges the notion that the Living Constitution approach produces more individual freedoms. Instead, he says, this approach has led to a variety of new restrictions on practices that had previously been allowed in the political process.

Stephen Breyer argues for the Living Constitution approach, but Breyer places it within a broader constitutional and theoretical framework. He argues for a "consequentialist" approach that is rooted in basic constitutional purposes, the most important of which is "active liberty," which he defines as "an active and constant participation in collective power." Breyer applies this framework to a range of difficult constitutional issues, including freedom of speech in the context of campaign finance and privacy rights in the context of rapidly evolving technology. He shows that the plain language of the Constitution does not provide enough guidance to answer these difficult questions. He turns the tables on Scalia, arguing that it is the "literalist" or "originalist" position that will, ironically, lead Justices to rely too heavily on their own personal views while his consequentialist position is actually the view that is more likely to produce judicial restraint. Breyer goes on to criticize the originalist position as fraught with inconsistencies. It is inherently subjective, despite its attempt to emphasize the "objective" words of the Constitution. By relying on the consequentialist perspective, which emphasizes democratic participation and active liberty, Justices are more likely to reach limited conclusions that apply to the facts at hand, while maximizing the positive implications for democracy. Breyer is keenly aware of the Court's place within the political process and wants to use it as a positive tool to improve that process, within the limits of the Constitution.

One observer of the Supreme Court summarized the debate between Scalia and Breyer in these terms: "It is a debate over text versus context. For Justice Scalia, who focuses on text, language is supreme, and the court's job is to derive and apply rules from the words chosen by the Constitution's framers or a statute's drafters. For Justice Breyer, who looks to context, language is only a starting point to an inquiry in which a law's purpose and a decision's likely consequences are the more important elements."[1]

39

"Common-Law Courts in a Civil-Law System: The Role of United States Federal Courts in Interpreting the Constitution and Laws"

ANTONIN SCALIA

I want to say a few words about the distinctive problem of interpreting our Constitution. The problem is distinctive, not because special principles of interpretation apply, but because the usual principles are being applied to an unusual text. Chief Justice Marshall put the point as well as it can be put in *McCulloch* v. *Maryland*:

> A constitution, to contain an accurate detail of all the subdivisions of which its great powers will admit, and of all the means by which they may be carried into execution, would partake of the prolixity of a legal code, and could scarcely be embraced by the human mind. It would probably never be un-

derstood by the public. Its nature, therefore, requires, that only its great outlines should be marked, its important objects designated, and the minor
ingredients which compose the objects be deduced from the nature of the
objects themselves.

In textual interpretation, context is everything, and the context of the
Constitution tells us not to expect nit-picking detail, and to give words
and phrases an expansive rather than narrow interpretation—though
not, of course, an interpretation that the language will not bear.

Take, for example, the provision of the First Amendment that forbids
abridgment of "the freedom of speech, or of the press." That phrase does
not list the full range of communicative expression. Handwritten letters,
for example, are neither speech nor press. Yet surely there is no doubt
they cannot be censored. In this constitutional context, speech and press,
the two most common forms of communication, stand as a sort of syn-
ecdoche for the whole. That is not strict construction, but it is reasonable
construction.

It is curious that most of those who insist that the drafter's intent gives
meaning to a statute reject the drafter's intent as the criterion for interpretation of the Constitution. I reject it for both. I will consult the writings of some men who happened to be Framers—Hamilton's and
Madison's writings in the *Federalist*, for example. I do so, however, not
because they were Framers and therefore their intent is authoritative and
must be the law; but rather because their writings, like those of other
intelligent and informed people of the time, display how the text of the
Constitution was originally understood. Thus, I give equal weight to
Jay's pieces in the *Federalist*, and to Jefferson's writings, even though
neither of them was a Framer. What I look for in the Constitution is
precisely what I look for in a statute: the original meaning of the text,
not what the original draftsmen intended.

But the Great Divide with regard to constitutional interpretation is
not that between Framers' intent and objective meaning; but rather that
between *original* meaning (whether derived from Framers' intent or not)
and *current* meaning. The ascendant school of constitutional interpretation affirms the existence of what is called the "Living Constitution," a
body of law that (unlike normal statutes) grows and changes from age
to age, in order to meet the needs of a changing society. And it is the
judges who determine those needs and "find" that changing law. Seems
familiar, doesn't it? Yes, it is the common law returned, but infinitely
more powerful than what the old common law ever pretended to be, for
now it trumps even the statutes of democratic legislatures. Recall the
words I quoted earlier from the Fourth-of-July speech of the avid codifier
Robert Rantoul: "The judge makes law, by extorting from precedents
something which they do not contain. He extends his precedents, which
were themselves the extension of others, till, by this accommodating
principle, a whole system of law is built up without the authority or

interference of the legislator." Substitute the word "people" for "legislator," and it is a perfect description of what modern American courts have done with the Constitution.

If you go into a constitutional law class, or study a constitutional-law casebook, or read a brief filed in a constitutional-law case, you will rarely find the discussion addressed to the text of the constitutional provision that is at issue, or to the question of what was the originally understood or even the originally intended meaning of that text. Judges simply ask themselves (as a good common-law judge would) what *ought* the result to be, and then proceed to the task of distinguishing (or, if necessary, overruling) any prior Supreme Court cases that stand in the way. Should there be (to take one of the less controversial examples) a constitutional right to die? If so, there is. Should there be a constitutional right to reclaim a biological child put out for adoption by the other parent? Again, if so, there is. If it is good, it is so. Never mind the text that we are supposedly construing; we will smuggle these in, if all else fails, under the Due Process Clause (which, as I have described, is textually incapable of containing them). Moreover, what the Constitution meant yesterday it does not necessarily mean today. As our opinions say in the context of our Eighth Amendment jurisprudence (the Cruel and Unusual Punishments Clause), its meaning changes to reflect "the evolving standards of decency that mark the progress of a maturing society."[2]

This is preeminently a common-law way of making law, and not the way of construing a democratically adopted text. I mentioned earlier a famous English treatise on statutory construction called *Dwarris on Statutes*. The fourth of Dwarris's Maxims was as follows: "An act of Parliament cannot alter by reason of time; but the common law may, since *cessante ratione cessat lex*."[3] This remains (however much it may sometimes be evaded) the formally enunciated rule for statutory construction: statutes do not change. Proposals for "dynamic statutory construction," such as those of Judge Calabresi and Professor Eskridge that I discussed yesterday, are concededly avant-garde. The Constitution, however, even though a democratically adopted text, we formally treat like the common law. What, it is fair to ask, is our justification for doing so?

One would suppose that the rule that a text does not change would apply *a fortiori* to a constitution. If courts felt too much bound by the democratic process to tinker with statutes, when their tinkering could be adjusted by the legislature, how much more should they feel bound not to tinker with a constitution, when their tinkering is virtually irreparable. It surely cannot be said that a constitution naturally suggests changeability; to the contrary, its whole purpose is to prevent change—to embed certain rights in such a manner that future generations cannot take them away. A society that adopts a bill of rights is skeptical that "evolving standards of decency" always "mark progress," and that societies always "mature," as opposed to rot. Neither the text of such a document nor the intent of its framers (whichever you choose) can possibly lead to the conclusion that its only effect is to take the power of changing rights away from the legislature and give it to the courts.

The argument most frequently made in favor of the Living Constitution is a pragmatic one: Such an evolutionary approach is necessary in order to provide the "flexibility" that a changing society requires; the Constitution would have snapped, if it had not been permitted to bend and grow. This might be a persuasive argument if most of the "growing" that the proponents of this approach have brought upon us in the past, and are determined to bring upon us in the future, were the *elimination* of restrictions upon democratic government. But just the opposite is true. Historically, and particularly in the past thirty-five years, the "evolving" Constitution has imposed a vast array of new constraints—new inflexibilities—upon administrative, judicial, and legislative action. To mention only a few things that formerly could be done or not done, as the society desired, but now cannot be done:

> admitting in a state criminal trial evidence of guilt that was obtained by an unlawful search;
> permitting invocation of God at public-school graduations;
> electing one of the two houses of a state legislature the way the United States Senate is elected (i.e., on a basis that does not give all voters numerically equal representation);
> terminating welfare payments as soon as evidence of fraud is received, subject to restoration after hearing if the evidence is satisfactorily refuted;
> imposing property requirements as a condition of voting;
> prohibiting anonymous campaign literature;
> prohibiting pornography.

And the future agenda of constitutional evolutionists is mostly more of the same—the creation of *new* restrictions upon democratic government, rather than the elimination of old ones. *Less* flexibility in government, not *more*. As things now stand, the state and federal governments may either apply capital punishment or abolish it, permit suicide or forbid it—all as the changing times and the changing sentiments of society may demand. But when capital punishment is held to violate the Eighth Amendment, and suicide is held to be protected by the Fourteenth Amendment, all flexibility with regard to those matters will be gone. No, the reality of the matter is that, generally speaking, devotees of the Living Constitution do not seek to faciliate social change but to *prevent* it.

There are, I must admit, a few exceptions to that—a few instances in which, historically, greater flexibility *has been* the result of the process. But those exceptions only serve to refute another argument of the proponents of an evolving Constitution, that evolution will always be in the direction of greater personal liberty. (They consider that a great advantage, for reasons that I do not entirely understand. All government represents a balance between individual freedom and social order, and it is not true that every alteration of that balance in the direction of greater individual freedom is necessarily good.) But in any case, the record of history refutes the proposition that the evolving Constitution will invariably enlarge individual rights. The most obvious refutation is the modern Court's limitation of the constitutional protections afforded to property. The provision prohibiting impairment of the obligation of contracts, for example, has been gutted. I am sure that We the People agree with that development; we value property rights less than the Founders did. So also, we value the right to bear arms less than the Founders (who thought the right of self-defense to be absolutely fundamental), and there will be few tears shed if and when the Second Amendment is held to guarantee nothing more than the State National Guard. But this just shows that the Founders were right when they feared that some (in their view misguided) future generation might wish to abandon liberties that they considered essential, and so sought to protect those liberties in a Bill of Rights. We may *like* the abridgment of property rights, and *like* the elimination of the right to bear arms; but let us not pretend that these are not a *reduction* of *rights*.

Or if property rights are too cold to get your juices flowing, and the right to bear arms too dangerous, let me give another example: Several terms ago a case came before the Supreme Court involving a prosecution for sexual abuse of a young child. The trial court found that the child would be too frightened to testify in the presence of the (presumed) abuser, and so, pursuant to state law, she was permitted to testify with only the prosecutor and defense counsel present, the defendant, the judge, and the jury watching over closed-circuit television. A reasonable enough procedure, and it was held to be constitutional by my Court.[4] I dissented, because the Sixth Amendment provides that "[i]n *all* criminal prosecutions" (let me emphasize the word "all") "the accused shall enjoy the right . . . to be confronted with the witnesses against him." There is no doubt what confrontation meant—or indeed means today. It means face-to-face, not watching from another room. And there is no doubt what one of the major purposes of that provision was: to induce *precisely* that pressure upon the witness which the little girl found it difficult to endure. It is difficult to accuse someone to his face, particularly when you are lying. Now no extrinsic factors have changed since that provision was adopted in 1791. Sexual abuse existed then, as it does now; little children were more easily upset than adults, then as now; a means of placing the defendant out of sight of the witness existed then as now (a screen could easily have been erected that would enable the defendant to see the witness, but not the witness the defendant). But the Sixth Amendment nonetheless gave *all* criminal defendants the right to *confront* the witnesses against them, because that was thought to be an important protection. The only significant thing that *has* changed, I think, is the society's sensitivity to so-called psychic trauma (which is what we are told the child witness in such a situation suffers) and the society's assessment of where the proper balance ought to be struck between the two extremes of a procedure that assures convicting 100 percent of all child abusers, and a procedure that assures acquitting 100 percent of those who have been falsely accused of child abuse. I have no doubt that the society is, as a whole, happy and pleased with what my Court decided. But we should not pretend that the decision did not *eliminate* a liberty that previously existed.

My last remarks may have created the false impression that proponents of the Living Constitution follow the desires of the American people in determining how the Constitution should evolve. They follow nothing so precise; indeed, as a group they follow nothing at all. Perhaps the most glaring defect of Living Constitutionalism, next to its incompatibility with the whole anti-evolutionary purpose of a constitution, is that there is no agreement, and no chance of agreement, upon what is to be the guiding principle of the evolution. *Panta rhei* [all things are in constant flux] is not a sufficiently informative principle of constitutional interpretation. What is it that the judge must consult to determine when, and in what direction, evolution has occurred? Is it the will of the majority, discerned from newspapers, radio talk shows, public opinion polls, and chats at the country club? Is it the philosophy of Hume, or of John Rawls, or of John Stuart Mill, or of Aristotle? As soon as the discussion goes beyond the issue of whether the Constitution is static, the evolutionists divide into as many camps as there are individual views of the good, the true, and the beautiful. I think that is inevitably so, which means that evolutionism is simply not a practicable constitutional philosophy.

I do not suggest, mind you, that originalists always agree upon their answer. There is plenty of room for disagreement as to what original meaning was, and even more as to how that original meaning applies to the situation before the court. But the originalist at least knows what he is looking for: the original meaning of the text. Often, indeed I dare say usually, that is easy to discern and simple to apply. Sometimes (thought not very often) there will be disagreement regarding the original meaning; and sometimes there will be disagreement as to how that original meaning applies to new and unforeseen phenomena. How, for example, does the First Amendment guarantee of "the freedom of speech" apply to new technologies that did not exist when the guarantee was created—to sound trucks, or to government-licensed over-the-air television? In such new fields the Court must follow the trajectory of the First Amendment, so to speak, to determine what it requires—and assuredly that enterprise is not entirely cut-and-dried, but requires the exercise of judgment.

But the difficulties and uncertainties of determining original meaning and applying it to modern circumstances are negligible compared with the difficulties and uncertainties of the philosophy which says that the Constitution *changes*; that the very act which it once prohibited it now permits, and which it once permitted it now forbids; and that the key to that change is unknown and unknowable. The originalist, if he does not have all the answers, has many of them. The Confrontation Clause, for example, requires confrontation. For the evolutionist, however, every question is an open question, every day a new day. No fewer than three of the Justices with whom I have served have maintained that the death penalty is unconstitutional, *even though its use is explicitly contemplated in the Constitution.* The Due Process Clause of the Fifth and Fourteenth Amendments say that no person shall be deprived of life without due process of law; and the Grand Jury Clause of the Fifth Amendment says that no person shall be held to answer for a capital crime without grand jury indictment. No matter. Under the Living Constitution the death penalty may have *become* unconstitutional. And it is up to each Justice to decide for himself (under no standard I can discern) when that occurs.

In the last analysis, however, it probably does not matter what principle, among the innumerable possibilities, the evolutionist proposes to determine in what direction the Living Constitution will grow. For unless the evolutionary dogma is kept a closely held secret among us judges and law professors, it will lead to the result that the Constitution evolves the way the majority wishes. The people will be willing to leave interpretation of the Constitution to a committee of nine lawyers so long as the people believe that it is (like the interpretation of a statute) lawyers' work—requiring a close examination of text, history of the text, traditional understanding of the text, judicial precedent, etc. But if the people come to believe that the Constitution is *not* a text like other texts; if it means, not what it says or what it was understood to mean, but what it *should* mean, in light of the "evolving standards of decency that mark the progress of a maturing society," well then, they will look for qualifications other than impartiality, judgment, and lawyerly acumen in those whom they select to interpret it. More specifically, they will look for people who agree with *them* as to what those evolving standards have evolved to; who agree with *them* as to what the Constitution *ought* to be.

It seems to me that that is where we are heading, or perhaps even where we have arrived. Seventy-five years ago, we believed firmly enough in a rock-solid, unchanging Constitution that we felt it necessary to adopt the Nineteenth Amendment to give women the vote. The battle was not fought in the courts, and few thought that it could be, despite the constitutional guarantee of Equal Protection of the Laws; that provision* did not, when it was adopted, and hence did not in 1920, guarantee equal access to the ballot, but permitted distinctions on the

*[Scalia is referring to the "equal protection clause" of the Fourteenth Amendment, which states, "No state shall . . . deny to any person within its jurisdiction the equal protection of the laws."]

basis not only of age, but of property and of sex. Who can doubt that, if the issue had been deferred until today, the Constitution would be (formally) unamended, and the courts would be the chosen instrumentality of change? The American people have been converted to belief in the Living Constitution, a "morphing" document that means, from age to age, what it ought to mean. And with that conversion has inevitably come the new phenomenon of selecting and confirming federal judges, at all levels, on the basis of their views regarding a whole series of proposals for constitutional evolution. If the courts are free to write the Constitution anew, they will, by God, write it the way the majority wants; the appointment and confirmation process will see to that. This, of course, is the end of the Bill of Rights, whose meaning will be committed to the very body it was meant to protect against: the majority. By trying to make the Constitution do everything that needs doing from age to age, we shall have caused it to do nothing at all.

NOTES

1. Linda Greenhouse, "The Nation: Judicial Intent; the Competing Visions of the Role of the Court." *New York Times,* July 7, 2002, sec. 4, p. 3.
2. *Trop v. Dulles,* 356 U.S. 86, 101 (1958) (plurality opinion).
3. *Rhodes v. Chapman,* 452 U.S. 337, 346 (1981), quoting from Fortunatus Dwarris, *A General Treatise on Statutes, with American Notes and Additions by Platt Potter* (1871), 122.
4. See *Maryland v. Craig,* 497 U.S. 836 (1990).

40

"Our Democratic Constitution"

STEPHEN BREYER

* * * *[Breyer begins with a brief discussion of "ancient" and "modern" liberty.]* * * *

I shall focus upon several contemporary problems that call for governmental action and potential judicial reaction. In each instance I shall argue that, when judges interpret the Constitution, they should place greater emphasis upon the "ancient liberty," i.e., the people's right to "an active and constant participation in collective power." I believe that increased emphasis upon this active liberty will lead to better constitutional law, a law that will promote governmental solutions consistent with individual dignity and community need.

At the same time, my discussion will illustrate an approach to constitutional interpretation that places considerable weight upon consequences—consequences valued in terms of basic constitutional purposes. It disavows a contrary constitutional approach, a more "legalistic" approach that places too much weight upon language, history, tradition, and precedent alone while understating the importance of consequences. If the discussion helps to convince you that the more "consequential" approach has virtue, so much the better.

Three basic views underlie my discussion. First, the Constitution, considered as a whole, creates a framework for a certain kind of government. Its general objectives can be described abstractly as including (1) democratic self-government, (2) dispersion of power (avoiding concentration of too much power in too few hands), (3) individual dignity (through protection of individual liberties), (4) equality before the law (through equal protection of the law), and (5) the rule of law itself.[1]

The Constitution embodies these general objectives in particular provisions. In respect to self-government, for example, Article IV guarantees a "republican Form of Government;" Article I insists that Congress meet at least once a year, that elections take place every two (or six) years, that a census take place every decade; the Fifteenth, Nineteenth, Twenty-fourth, and Twenty-sixth Amendments secure a virtually universal adult suffrage. But a general constitutional objective such as self-government plays a constitutional role beyond the interpretation of an individual provision that refers to it directly. That is because constitutional courts must consider the relation of one phrase to another. They must consider the document as a whole.[2] And consequently the document's handful of general purposes will inform judicial interpretation of many individual provisions that do not refer directly to the general objective in question. My examples seek to show how that is so. And, as I have said, they will suggest a need for judges to pay greater attention to one of those general objectives, namely participatory democratic self-government.

Second, the Court, while always respecting language, tradition, and precedent, nonetheless has emphasized different general constitutional objectives at different periods in its history. Thus one can characterize the early nineteenth century as a period during which the Court helped to establish the authority of the federal government, including the federal judiciary.[3] During the late nineteenth and early twentieth centuries, the Court underemphasized the Constitution's efforts to secure participation by black citizens in representative government—efforts related to the participatory "active" liberty of the ancients.[4] At the same time, it overemphasized protection of property rights, such as an individual's freedom to contract without government interference,[5] to the point where President Franklin Roosevelt commented that the Court's Lochner-era decisions had created a legal "no-man's land" that neither state nor federal regulatory authority had the power to enter.[6]

The New Deal Court and the Warren Court in part reemphasized "active liberty." The former did so by dismantling various Lochner-era distinctions, thereby expanding the scope of democratic self-government.[7] The latter did so by interpreting the Civil War Amendments in light of their purposes and to mean what they say, thereby helping African-Americans become members of the nation's community of self-governing citizens—a community that the Court expanded further in its "one person, one vote" decisions.[8]

More recently, in my view, the Court has again underemphasized the importance of the citizen's active liberty. I will argue for a contemporary reemphasis that better combines "the liberty of the ancients" with that "freedom of governmental restraint" that Constant called "modern."

Third, the real-world consequences of a particular interpretive decision, valued in terms of basic constitutional purposes, play an important role in constitutional decision-making. To that extent, my approach differs from that of judges who would place nearly exclusive interpretive weight upon language, history, tradition and precedent. In truth, the difference is one of degree. Virtually all judges, when interpreting a constitution or a statute, refer at one time or another to language, to history, to tradition, to precedent, to purpose, and to consequences. Even those who take a more literal approach to constitutional interpretation sometimes find consequences and general purposes relevant. But the more "literalist" judge tends to ask those who cannot find an interpretive answer in language, history, tradition, and precedent alone to rethink the problem several times, before making consequences determinative. The more literal judges may hope to find in language, history, tradition, and precedent objective interpretive standards; they may seek to avoid an interpretive subjectivity that could confuse a judge's personal idea of what is good for that which the Constitution demands; and they may believe that these more "original" sources will more readily yield rules that can guide other institutions, including lower courts. These objectives are desirable, but I do not think the literal approach will achieve them, and, in any event, the constitutional price is too high. I hope that my examples will help to show you why that is so, as well as to persuade some of you why it is important to place greater weight upon constitutionally-valued consequences, my consequential focus in this lecture being the affect of a court's decisions upon active liberty.

To recall the fate of Socrates is to understand that the "liberty of the ancients" is not a sufficient condition for human liberty. Nor can (or should) we replicate today the ideal represented by the Athenian agora or the New England town meeting. Nonetheless, today's citizen does participate in democratic self-governing processes. And the "active" liberty to which I refer consists of the Constitution's efforts to secure the citizen's right to do so.

To focus upon that active liberty, to understand it as one of the Constitution's handful of general objectives, will lead judges to consider the constitutionality of statutes with a certain modesty. That modesty embodies an understanding of the judges' own expertise compared, for example, with that of a legislature. It reflects the concern that a judiciary too ready to "correct" legislative error may deprive "the people" of "the political experience and the moral education that come from . . . correcting their own errors."[9] It encompasses that doubt, caution, prudence, and concern—that state of not being "too sure" of oneself—that Learned Hand described as the "spirit of liberty."[10] In a word, it argues for traditional "judicial restraint."

But active liberty argues for more than that. I shall suggest that increased recognition of the Constitution's general democratic participatory objectives can help courts deal more effectively with a range of specific constitutional issues. To show this I shall use examples drawn from the areas of free speech, federalism, privacy, equal protection and statutory interpretation. In each instance, I shall refer to an important modern problem of government that calls for a democratic response. I shall then describe related constitutional implications. I want to draw a picture of some of the different ways that increased judicial focus upon the Constitution's participatory objectives can have a positive effect.

*   *   *

I begin with free speech and campaign finance reform. The campaign finance problem arises out of the recent explosion in campaign costs along with a vast disparity among potential givers. * * * *[Breyer reviews the data on increasing campaign costs]* * * * The upshot is a concern by some that the matter is out of hand—that too few individuals contribute too much money and that, even though money is not the only way to obtain influence, those who give large amounts of money do obtain, or appear to obtain, too much influence. The end result is a marked inequality of participation. That is one important reason why legislatures have sought to regulate the size of campaign contributions.

The basic constitutional question, as you all know, is not the desirability of reform legislation but whether, how, or the extent to which, the First Amendment permits the legislature to impose limitations or ceilings on the amounts individuals or organizations or parties can contribute to a campaign or the kinds of contributions they can make. * * *

One cannot (or, at least, I cannot) find an easy answer to the constitutional questions in language, history, or tradition. The First Amendment's language says that Congress shall not abridge "the freedom of speech." But it does not define "the freedom of speech" in any detail. The nation's founders did not speak directly about campaign contributions. Madison, who decried faction, thought that members of Congress would fairly represent all their constituents, in part because the "electors" would not be the "rich" any "more than the poor."[11] But this kind of statement, while modestly helpful to the campaign reform cause, is hardly determinative.

Neither can I find answers in purely conceptual arguments. Some argue, for example, that "money is speech"; others say "money is not speech." But neither contention helps much. Money is not speech, it is money. But the expenditure of money enables speech; and that expenditure is often necessary to communicate a message, particularly in a political context. A law that forbid the expenditure of money to convey a message could effectively suppress that communication.

Nor does it resolve the matter simply to point out that campaign contribution limits inhibit the political "speech opportunities" of those who wish to contribute more. Indeed, that is so. But the question is whether, in context, such a limitation abridges "the freedom of speech." And to announce that this kind of harm could never prove justified in a political context is simply to state an ultimate constitutional conclusion; it is not to explain the underlying reasons.

To refer to the Constitution's general participatory self-government objective, its protection of "active liberty" is far more helpful. That is because that constitutional goal indicates that the First Amendment's constitutional role is not simply one of protecting the individual's "negative" freedom from governmental restraint. The Amendment in context also forms a necessary part of a constitutional system designed to sustain that democratic self-government. The Amendment helps to sustain the democratic process both by encouraging the exchange of ideas needed to make sound electoral decisions and by encouraging an exchange of views among ordinary citizens necessary to encourage their informed participation in the electoral process. It thereby helps to maintain a form of government open to participation (in Constant's words "by all citizens without exception").

The relevance of this conceptual view lies in the fact that the campaign finance laws also seek to further the latter objective. They hope to democratize the influence that money can bring to bear upon the electoral process, thereby building public confidence in that process, broadening the base of a candidate's meaningful financial support, and encouraging greater public participation. They consequently seek to maintain the integrity of the political process—a process that itself translates political speech into governmental action. Seen in this way, campaign finance laws, despite the limits they impose, help to further the kind of open public political discussion that the First Amendment also seeks to encourage, not simply as an end, but also as a means to achieve a workable democracy.

For this reason, I have argued that a court should approach most campaign finance questions with the understanding that important First Amendment-related interests lie on both sides of the constitutional equation and that a First Amendment presumption hostile to government regulation, such as "strict scrutiny" is consequently out of place.[12] Rather, the Court considering the matter without benefit of presumptions, must look realistically at the legislation's impact, both its negative impact on the ability of some to engage in as much communication as they wish and the positive impact upon the public's confidence, and consequent ability to communicate through (and participate in) the electoral process.

The basic question the Court should ask is one of proportionality. Do the statutes strike a reasonable balance between their electoral speech-restricting and speech-enhancing consequences? Or do you instead impose restrictions on that speech that are disproportionate when measured against their corresponding electoral and speech-related benefits, taking into account the kind, the importance, and the extent of those benefits, as well as the need for the restrictions in order to secure them?

The judicial modesty discussed earlier suggests that, in answering these questions, courts should defer to the legislatures' own answers insofar as those answers reflect empirical matters about which the legislature is comparatively expert, for example, the extent of the campaign finance problem, a matter that directly concerns the realities of political life. But courts cannot defer when evaluating the risk that reform legislation will defeat the very objective of participatory self-government itself, for example, where laws would set limits so low that, by elevating the reputation-related or media-related advantages of incumbency to the point where they would insulate incumbents from effective challenge.

I am not saying that focus upon active liberty will automatically answer the constitutional question in particular campaign finance cases. I argue only that such focus will help courts find a proper route for arriving at an answer. The positive constitutional goal implies a systemic role for the First Amendment; and that role, in turn, suggests a legal framework, i.e., a more particular set of questions for the Court to ask. Modesty suggests where, and how, courts should defer to legislatures in doing so. The suggested inquiry is complex. But courts both here and abroad have engaged in similarly complex inquiries where the constitutionality of electoral laws is at issue. That complexity is demanded by a Constitution that provides for judicial review of the constitutionality of electoral rules while granting Congress the effective power to secure a fair electoral system.

* * * [*The omitted sections apply these same arguments to commercial speech and then discuss recent Supreme Court cases on federalism. The next two sections apply Breyer's argument to privacy and majority-minority districts.*] * * *

I next turn to a different kind of example. It focuses upon current threats to the protection of privacy, defined as "the power to control what others can come to know about you." It seeks to illustrate what active liberty is like in modern America, when we seek to arrive democratically at solutions to important technologically-based problems. And it suggests a need for judicial caution and humility when certain privacy matters, such as the balance between free speech and privacy, are at issue.

First, I must describe the "privacy" problem. That problem is unusually complex. It has clearly become even more so since the terrorist attacks. For one thing, those who agree that privacy is important disagree about why. Some emphasize the need to be left alone, not bothered by others, or that privacy is important because it prevents people from being judged out of context. Some emphasize the way in which relationships of love and friendship depend upon trust, which implies a sharing of information not available to all. Others find connections between privacy and individualism, in that privacy encourages non-conformity. Still others find connections between privacy and equality, in that limitations upon the availability of individualized information lead private businesses to treat all customers alike. For some, or all, of these reasons, legal rules protecting privacy help to assure an individual's dignity.

For another thing, the law protects privacy only because of the way in which technology interacts with different laws. Some laws, such as trespass, wiretapping, eavesdropping, and search-and-seizure laws, protect particular places or sites, such as homes or telephones, from searches and monitoring. Other laws protect not places, but kinds of information, for example laws that forbid the publication of certain personal information even by a person who obtained that information legally. Taken together these laws protect privacy to different degrees depending upon place, individual status, kind of intrusion, and type of information.

Further, technological advances have changed the extent to which present laws can protect privacy. Video cameras now can monitor shopping malls, schools, parks, office buildings, city streets, and other places that present law left unprotected. Scanners and interceptors can overhear virtually any electronic conversation. Thermal imaging devices can detect activities taking place within the home. Computers can record and collate information obtained in any of these ways, or others. This technology means an ability to observe, collate and permanently record a vast amount of information about individuals that the law previously may have made available for collection but which, in practice, could not easily have been recorded and collected. The nature of the current or future privacy threat depends upon how this technological/legal fact will affect differently situated individuals.

These circumstances mean that efforts to revise privacy law to take account of the new technology will involve, in different areas of human activity, the balancing of values in light of prediction about the technological future. If, for example, businesses obtain detailed consumer purchasing information, they may create individualized customer profiles.

Those profiles may invade the customer's privacy. But they may also help firms provide publicly desired products at lower cost. If, for example, medical records are placed online, patient privacy may be compromised. But the ready availability of those records may lower insurance costs or help a patient carried unconscious into an operating room. If, for example, all information about an individual's genetic make-up is completely confidential, that individual's privacy is protected, but suppose a close relative, a nephew or cousin, needs the information to assess his own cancer risk?

Nor does a "consent" requirement automatically answer the dilemmas suggested, for consent forms may be signed without understanding and, in any event, a decision by one individual to release or to deny information can affect others as well.

Legal solutions to these problems will be shaped by what is technologically possible. Should video cameras be programmed to turn off? Recorded images to self-destruct? Computers instructed to delete certain kinds of information? Should cell phones be encrypted? Should web technology, making use of an individual's privacy preferences, automatically negotiate privacy rules with distant web sites as a condition of access?

The complex nature of these problems calls for resolution through a form of participatory democracy. Ideally, that participatory process does not involve legislators, administrators, or judges imposing law from above. Rather, it involves law revision that bubbles up from below. Serious complex changes in law are often made in the context of a national conversation involving, among others, scientists, engineers, businessmen and -women, the media, along with legislators, judges, and many ordinary citizens whose lives the new technology will affect. That conversation takes place through many meetings, symposia, and discussions, through journal articles and media reports, through legislative hearings and court cases. Lawyers participate fully in this discussion, translating specialized knowledge into ordinary English, defining issues, creating consensus. Typically, administrators and legislators then make decisions, with courts later resolving any constitutional issues that those decisions raise. This "conversation" is the participatory democratic process itself.

The presence of this kind of problem and this kind of democratic process helps to explain, because it suggests a need for, judicial caution or modesty. That is why, for example, the Court's decisions so far have hesitated to preempt that process. In one recent case the Court considered a cell phone conversation that an unknown private individual had intercepted with a scanner and delivered to a radio station. A statute forbid the broadcast of that conversation, even though the radio station itself had not planned or participated in the intercept. The Court had to determine the scope of the station's First Amendment right to broadcast given the privacy interests that the statute sought to protect. The Court held that the First Amendment trumped the statute, permitting the radio station to broadcast the information. But the holding was narrow. It focused upon the particular circumstances present, explicitly leaving open broadcaster liability in other, less innocent, circumstances.

The narrowness of the holding itself serves a constitutional purpose. The privacy "conversation" is ongoing. Congress could well rewrite the statute, tailoring it more finely to current technological facts, such as the widespread availability of scanners and the possibility of protecting conversations through encryption. A broader constitutional rule might itself limit legislative options in ways now unforeseeable. And doing so is particularly dangerous where statutory protection of an important personal liberty is at issue.

By way of contrast, the Court held unconstitutional police efforts to use, without a warrant, a thermal imaging device placed on a public sidewalk.[13] The device permitted police to identify activities taking place within a private house. The case required the Court simply to ask whether the residents had a reasonable expectation that their activities within the house would not be disclosed to the public in this way—a well established Fourth Amendment principle. Hence the case asked the Court to pour new technological wine into old bottles; it did not suggest that doing so would significantly interfere with an ongoing democratic policy conversation.

The privacy example suggests more by way of caution. It warns against adopting an overly rigid method of interpreting the constitution—placing weight upon eighteenth-century details to the point where it becomes difficult for a twenty-first-century court to apply the document's underlying values. At a minimum it suggests that courts, in determining the breadth of a constitutional holding, should look to the effect of a holding on the ongoing policy process, distinguishing, as I have suggested, between the "eavesdropping" and the "thermal heat" types of cases. And it makes clear that judicial caution in such matters does not reflect the fact that judges are mitigating their legal concerns with practical considerations. Rather, the Constitution itself is a practical document—a document that authorizes the Court to proceed practically when it examines new laws in light of the Constitution's enduring, underlying values.

My fourth example concerns equal protection and voting rights, an area that has led to considerable constitutional controversy. Some believe that the Constitution prohibits virtually any legislative effort to use race as a basis for drawing electoral district boundaries—unless, for example, the effort seeks to undo earlier invidious race-based discrimination.[14] Others believe that the Constitution does not so severely limit the instances in which a legislature can use race to create majority-minority districts.[15] Without describing in detail the basic argument between the two positions, I wish to point out the relevance to that argument of the Constitution's democratic objective.

That objective suggests a simple, but potentially important, constitutional difference in the electoral area between invidious discrimination, penalizing members of a racial minority, and positive discrimination, assisting members of racial minorities. The Constitution's Fifteenth Amendment prohibits the former, not simply because it violates a basic Fourteenth Amendment principle, namely that the government must treat all citizens with equal respect, but also because it denies minority citizens the opportunity to participate in the self-governing democracy that the Constitution creates. By way of contrast, affirmative discrimination ordinarily seeks to enlarge minority participation in that self-governing democracy. To that extent it is consistent with, indeed furthers, the Constitution's basic democratic objective.[16] That consistency, along with its more benign purposes, helps to mitigate whatever lack of equal respect any such discrimination might show to any disadvantaged member of a majority group.

I am not saying that the mitigation will automatically render any particular discriminatory scheme constitutional. But the presence of this mitigating difference supports the view that courts should not apply the strong presumptions of unconstitutionality that are appropriate where invidious discrimination is at issue. My basic purpose, again, is to suggest that reference to the Constitution's "democratic" objective can help us apply a different basic objective, here that of equal protection. And in the electoral context, the reference suggests increased legislative authority to deal with multiracial issues.

* * * [*This omitted section discusses statutory interpretation. The remainder of the essay draws out the broader implications of a jurisprudence based on broader democratic objectives rather than a more narrow, literalist approach.*] * * *

The instances I have discussed encompass different areas of law—speech, federalism, privacy, equal protection, and statutory interpretation. In each instance, the discussion has focused upon a contemporary social problem—campaign finance, workplace regulation, environmental regulation, information-based technological change, race-based electoral districting, and legislative politics. In each instance, the discussion illustrates how increased focus upon the Constitution's basic democratic objective might make a difference—in refining doctrinal rules, in evaluating consequences, in applying practical cautionary principles, in interacting with other constitutional objectives, and in explicating statutory silences. In each instance, the discussion suggests how that increased focus might mean better law. And "better" in this context means both (a) better able to satisfy the Constitution's purposes and (b) better able to cope with contemporary problems. The discussion, while not proving its point purely through logic or empirical demonstration, uses example to create a pattern. The pattern suggests a need for increased judicial emphasis upon the Constitution's democratic objective.

My discussion emphasizes values underlying specific constitutional phrases, sees the Constitution itself as a single document with certain basic related objectives, and assumes that the latter can inform a judge's understanding of the former. Might that discussion persuade those who prefer to believe that the keys to constitutional interpretation instead lie in specific language, history, tradition, and precedent and who fear that a contrary approach would permit judges too often to act too subjectively?

Perhaps so, for several reasons. First, the area of interpretive disagreement is more limited than many believe. Judges can, and should, decide most cases, including constitutional cases, through the use of language, history, tradition, and precedent. Judges will often agree as to how these factors determine a provision's basic purpose and the result in a particular case. And where they differ, their differences are often differences of modest degree. Only a handful of constitutional issues—though an important handful—are as open in respect to language, history, and basic purpose as those that I have described. And even in respect to those issues, judges must find answers within the limits set by the Constitution's language. Moreover, history, tradition, and precedent remain helpful, even if not determinative.

Second, those more literalist judges who emphasize language, history, tradition, and precedent cannot justify their practices by claiming that is what the Framers wanted, for the Framers did not say specifically what factors judges should emphasize when seeking to interpret the Constitution's open language.[17] Nor is it plausible to believe that those who argued about the Bill of Rights, and made clear that it did not contain an exclusive detailed list, had agreed about what school of interpretive thought should prove dominant in the centuries to come. Indeed, the Constitution itself says that the "enumeration" in the Constitution of some rights "shall not be construed to deny or disparage others retained by the people." Professor Bailyn concludes that the Framers added this language to make clear that "rights, like law itself, should never be fixed, frozen, that new dangers and needs will emerge, and that to respond to these dangers and needs, rights must be newly specified to protect the individual's integrity and inherent dignity."[18] Instead, justification for the literalist's practice itself tends to rest upon consequences. Literalist arguments often seek to show that such an approach will have favorable results, for example, controlling judicial subjectivity.

Third, judges who reject a literalist approach deny that their decisions are subjective and point to important safeguards of objectivity. A decision that emphasizes values, no less than any other, is open to criticism based upon (1) the decision's relation to the other legal principles (precedents, rules, standards, practices, institutional understandings) that it modifies and (2) the decision's consequences, i.e., the way in which the entire bloc of decision-affected legal principles subsequently affects the world. The relevant values, by limiting interpretive possibilities and guiding interpretation, themselves constrain subjectivity, indeed the democratic values that I have emphasized themselves suggest the importance of judicial restraint. An individual constitutional judge's need for consistency over time also constrains subjectivity. That is why Justice O'Connor has explained that need in terms of a constitutional judge's initial decisions creating "footprints" that later decisions almost inevitably will follow.

Fourth, the literalist does not escape subjectivity, for his tools, language, history, and tradition, can provide little objective guidance in the comparatively small set of cases about which I have spoken. In such cases, the Constitution's language is almost always nonspecific. History and tradition are open to competing claims and rival interpretations.[19] Nor does an emphasis upon rules embodied in precedent necessarily produce clarity, particularly in borderline areas or where rules are stated abstractly. Indeed, an emphasis upon language, history, tradition, or prior rules in such cases may simply channel subjectivity into a choice about: Which history? Which tradition? Which rules? It will then produce a decision that is no less subjective but which is far less transparent than a decision that directly addresses consequences in constitutional terms.

Finally, my examples point to offsetting consequences—at least if "literalism" tends to produce the legal doctrines (related to the First Amendment, to federalism, to statutory interpretation, to equal protection) that I have criticized. Those doctrines lead to consequences at least as harmful, from a constitutional perspective, as any increased risk of subjectivity. In the ways that I have set out, they undermine the Constitution's efforts to create a framework for democratic government—a government that, while protecting basic individual liberties, permits individual citizens to govern themselves.

To reemphasize the constitutional importance of democratic self-government may carry with it a practical bonus. We are all aware of figures that show that the public knows ever less about, and is ever less interested in, the processes of government. Foundation reports criticize the lack of high school civics education.[20] Comedians claim that more students know the names of the Three Stooges than the three branches of government. Even law school graduates are ever less inclined to work for government—with the percentage of those entering government (or nongovernment public interest) work declining at one major law school from 12% to 3% over a generation. Indeed, polls show that, over that same period of time, the percentage of the public trusting the government declined at a similar rate.[21]

This trend, however, is not irreversible. Indeed, trust in government has shown a remarkable rebound in response to last month's terrible tragedy [September 11].[22] Courts cannot maintain this upward momentum by themselves. But courts, as highly trusted government institutions, can help some,[23] in part by explaining in terms the public can understand just what the Constitution is about. It is important that the public, trying to cope with the problems of nation, state, and local community, understand that the Constitution does not resolve, and was not intended to resolve, society's problems. Rather, the Constitution provides a framework for the creation of democratically determined solutions, which protect each individual's basic liberties and assures that individual equal respect by government, while securing a democratic form of government. We judges cannot insist that Americans participate in that government, but we can make clear that our Constitution depends upon it. Indeed, participation reinforces that "positive passion for the public good," that John Adams, like so many others, felt a necessary condition for "Republican Government" and any "real Liberty."[24]

That is the democratic ideal. It is as relevant today as it was 200 or 2000 years ago. Today it is embodied in our Constitution. Two thousand years ago, Thucydides, quoting Pericles, set forth a related ideal—relevant in his own time and, with some modifications, still appropriate to recall today. "We Athenians," said Pericles, "do not say that the man who fails to participate in politics is a man who minds his own business. We say that he is a man who has no business here."

DISCUSSION QUESTIONS

1. Critics of the strict-construction, originalist perspective often point to ambiguities in the language of the Constitution. Justice Breyer outlines several of these in his speech. What are some other examples of ambiguous language in the Constitution (look at the Bill of Rights as a start), and what alternative interpretations can you develop?

2. Critics of the Living Constitution, such as Justice Scalia, often argue that judges substitute their own reading of what they think the law should be for what the law is. Justice Breyer replies that subjectivity is even more inherent in the originalist perspective. First, do you think it is possible for Justices to avoid having their own views shape their decisions? If it is impossible, which perspective, Scalia's or Breyer's, is more likely to produce such subjectivity?

3. Should judges take public opinion or changing societal standards into account when ruling on the constitutionality of a statute or practice? Apply your answer to the "confrontation doctrine" that Scalia talks about (the right to confront your accuser, even in the context of a child having to confront the person who sexually molested her or him).

4. Does Breyer's focus on political participation provide Justices with the type of guidance they need to make decisions? Do you think this focus would help restore the public's confidence in political institutions, as Breyer hopes?

5. Consider Scalia's list of activities that are no longer allowed by the Court (the list begins with using illegally obtained evidence in a criminal trial). How would Breyer's approach of active liberty decide these cases? Which do you think is the better outcome? Should this consequentialist approach be the basis for deciding cases before the Court?

6. After considering the arguments, do you find Breyer's or Scalia's more compelling? Which do you think you would be more likely to employ if you were a Justice and why?

NOTES

1. For an in-depth and nuanced discussion of the principles underlying the third and fourth objectives, see generally Ronald Dworkin, *Freedom's Law: The Moral Reading of the American Constitution* 15–35 (1996), and Ronald Dworkin, *Law's Empire* 176–265 (1986).
2. See Jack Rakove, *Original Meanings* 11–13 (1996).
3. See, e.g., *McCulloch v. Maryland*, 4 Wheat 316 (1819); *Marbury v. Madison*, 1 Cranch 137 (1803).
4. See, e.g., *Giles v. Harris*, 189 U.S. 475 (1903); *Civil Rights Cases*, 109 U.S. 3 (1883).
5. See, e.g., *Lochner v. New York*, 198 U.S. 45 (1905).
6. Leuchtenburg, *The Supreme Court Reborn* 103 (1995).
7. See, e.g., *Wickard v. Filburn*, 317 U.S. 111 (1942); *NLRB v. Jones & Laughlin Steel Corp.*, 301 U.S. 1 (1937); *West Coast Hotel Co. v. Parrish*, 300 U.S. 379 (1937).
8. See, e.g., *Baker v. Carr*, 369 U.S. 186 (1962); *Reynolds v. Sims*, 377 U.S. 533 (1964); *Gomillion v. Lightfoot*, 383 U.S. 663 (1966).
9. James Bradley Thayer, *John Marshall* 107 (1901).
10. Learned Hand, *The Spirit of Liberty* 190 (3d ed. 1960); cf. also id., at 109.
11. *The Federalist*, No. 57 (James Madison).
12. See, Nixon, supra n. 22 at 22.
13. *Kyllo v. United States*, 533 U.S. 27 (2001).
14. See, e.g., *Hunt v. Cromartie*, 526 U.S. 541 (1999).
15. See, e.g., *Shaw v. Reno*, 509 U.S. 630 (1993) (White, J., dissenting).
16. Cf. John Hart Ely, *Democracy and Distrust* (1980).
17. Rakove, supra n. 2 at 339-65.
18. Bernard Bailyn, *The Ideological Origins of the American Revolution* (1967).
19. See, e.g., *Alden v. Maine*, 527 U.S. 706 (1999).
20. See, e.g., U.S. Dept. of Educ., Office of Educ. Research and Improvement, Nat'l Ctr. for Educ. Stats., *The NAEP 1998 Civics Report Card* (1999).
21. Lydia Saad, "Americans' Faith in Government Shaken But Not Shattered by Watergate," available at http://www.gallup.com.
22. Tom Shoop, "Trust in Government Up Dramatically, Polls Show," *Government Executive Magazine*, Oct. 1, 2001.
23. See Saad, supra n. 21.
24. John Adams, Letter to Mercy Warren (1776), in *I The Founder's Constitution* 670.

PART III

Political Behavior: Participation

CHAPTER 9

Public Opinion and the Mass Media

41

"Polling the Public" from *Public Opinion in a Democracy*

George Gallup

Assessing public opinion in a democracy of 300 million people is no easy task. George Gallup, who is largely responsible for the development of modern opinion polling, argued that public opinion polls enhance the democratic process by providing elected officials with a picture of what Americans think about current events. Despite Gallup's vigorous defense of his polling techniques and the contribution of polling to democracy, the public opinion poll remains controversial. Some critics charge that public officials pay too much attention to polls, making decisions based on fluctuations in public opinion rather than on informed, independent judgment. Others say that by urging respondents to give an opinion, even if they initially respond that they have no opinion on a question, polls may exaggerate the amount of division in American society. And some critics worry that election-related polls may affect public behavior: if a potential voter hears that her candidate is trailing in the polls, perhaps she becomes demoralized, does not vote, and the poll becomes a self-fulfilling prophecy. In effect, rather than reporting on election news, the poll itself makes news.

We have a national election every two years only. In a world which moves as rapidly as the modern world does, it is often desirable to know the people's will on basic policies at more frequent intervals. We cannot put issues off and say "let them be decided at the next election." World events do not wait on elections. We need to know the will of the people at all times.

If we know the collective will of the people at all times the efficiency of democracy can be increased, because we can substitute specific knowledge of public opinion for blind groping and guesswork. Statesmen who know the true state of public opinion can then formulate plans with a sure knowledge of what the voting public is thinking. They can know what degree of opposition to any proposed plan exists, and what efforts are necessary to gain public acceptance for it. The responsibility for initiating action should, as always, rest with the political leaders of the country. But the collective will or attitude of the people needs to be learned without delay.

The Will of the People

How is the will of the people to be known at all times?

Before I offer an answer to this question, I would like to examine some of the principal channels by which, at the present time, public opinion is expressed.

The most important is of course a national election. An election is the only official and binding expression of the people's judgment. But, as viewed from a strictly objective point of view, elections are a confusing and imperfect way of registering national opinion. In the first place, they come only at infrequent intervals. In the second place, as [James] Bryce pointed out in *The American Commonwealth*, it is virtually impossible to separate issues from candidates. How can we tell whether the public is voting for the man or for his platform? How can we tell whether all the candidate's views are endorsed, or whether some are favored and others opposed by the voters? Because society grows more and more complex, the tendency is to have more and more issues in an election. Some may be discussed; others not. Suppose a candidate for office takes a position on a great many public issues during the campaign. If elected, he inevitably assumes that the public has endorsed all his planks, whereas this may actually not be the case.

*   *   *

The Role of the Elected Representative

A second method by which public opinion now expresses itself is through elected representatives. The legislator is, technically speaking, supposed to represent the interests of all voters in his constituency. But under the two-party system there is a strong temptation for him to represent, and be influenced by, only the voters of his own party. He is subject to the pressure of party discipline and of wishes of party leaders back home. His very continuance in office may depend on giving way to such pressure. Under these circumstances his behavior in Congress is likely to be governed not by what he thinks the voters of his State want, but by what he thinks the leaders of his own party in that State want.

*   *   *

Even in the event that an elected representative does try to perform his duty of representing the whole people, he is confronted with the problem: What is the will of the people? Shall he judge their views by the letters they write him or the telegrams they send him? Too often such expressions of opinion come only from an articulate minority. Shall the congressman judge their views by the visitors or delegations that come to him from his home district?

Pressure Groups and the Whole Nation

Legislators are constantly subject to the influence of organized lobbies and pressure groups. Senator Tydings * * * pointed out recently that the United States is the most fertile soil on earth for the activity of pressure groups. The American people represent a conglomeration of races, all with different cultural backgrounds. Sections and groups struggle with one another to fix national and international policy. And frequently in such struggles, as Senator Tydings pointed out, "self-interest and sectionalism, rather than the promotion of national welfare, dominate the contest." Senator Tydings mentions some twenty important group interests. These include labor, agriculture, veterans, pension plan advocates, chambers of commerce, racial organizations, isolationists and internationalists, high-tariff and low-tariff groups, preparedness and disarmament groups, budget balancers and spending advocates, soft-money associations and hard-money associations, transportation groups and states righters and centralizationists.

The legislator obviously owes a duty to his home district to legislate in its best interests. But he also owes a duty to legislate in the best interests of the whole nation. In order, however, to carry out this second duty he must *know* what the nation thinks. Since he doesn't always know what the voters in his own district think, it is just that much more difficult for him to learn the views of the nation. Yet if he could know those views at all times he could legislate more often in the interest of the whole country.

* * *

The Cross-Section Survey

This effort to discover public opinion has been largely responsible for the introduction of a new instrument for determining public opinion— the cross-section or sampling survey. By means of nationwide studies taken at frequent intervals, research workers are today attempting to measure and give voice to the sentiments of the whole people on vital issues of the day.

Where does this new technique fit into the scheme of things under our form of government? Is it a useful instrument of democracy? Will it prove to be vicious and harmful, or will it contribute to the efficiency of the democratic process?

The sampling referendum is simply a procedure for sounding the opinions of a relatively small number of persons, selected in such manner as to reflect with a high degree of accuracy the views of the whole voting population. In effect such surveys canvass the opinions of a miniature electorate.

Cross-section surveys do not place their chief reliance upon numbers. The technique is based on the fact that a few thousand voters correctly selected will faithfully reflect the views of an electorate of millions of voters. The key to success in this work is the cross section—the proper selection of voters included in the sample. Elaborate precautions must be taken to secure the views of members of all political parties—of rich and poor, old and young, of men and women, farmers and city dwellers, persons of all religious faiths—in short, voters of all types living in every State in the land. And all must be included in correct proportion.

*   *   *

Reliability of Opinion Surveys

Whether opinion surveys will prove to be a useful contribution to democracy depends largely on their reliability in measuring opinion. During the last four years [1935–1939] the sampling procedure, as used in measuring public opinion, has been subjected to many tests. In general these tests indicate that present techniques can attain a high degree of accuracy, and it seems reasonable to assume that with the development of this infant science, the accuracy of its measurements will be constantly improved.

The most practical way at present to measure the accuracy of the sampling referendum is to compare forecasts of elections with election results. Such a test is by no means perfect, because a preelection survey must not only measure opinion in respect to candidates but must also predict just what groups of people will actually take the trouble to cast their ballots. Add to this the problem of measuring the effect of weather on turnout, also the activities of corrupt political machines, and it can easily be seen that election results are by no means a perfect test of the accuracy of this new technique.

*   *   *

Many thoughtful students of government have asked: Why shouldn't the Government itself, rather than private organizations, conduct these sampling surveys? A few political scientists have even suggested the establishment of a permanent federal bureau for sounding public opinion, arguing that if this new technique is a contribution to democracy, the government has a duty to take it over.

The danger in this proposal, as I see it, lies in the temptation it would place in the way of the party in power to conduct surveys to prove itself right and to suppress those which proved it to be wrong. A private organization, on the other hand, must stand or fall not so much on what it reports or fails to report as on the accuracy of its results, and the impartiality of its interpretations. An important requirement in a democracy is complete and reliable news reports of the activities of all branches of the government and of the views of all leaders and parties. But few persons would argue that, for this reason, the government should take over the press, and all its news gathering associations.

*   *   *

Cloture on Debate?

It is sometimes argued that public opinion surveys impose a cloture on debate. When the advocates of one side of an issue are shown to be in the majority, so the argument runs, the other side will lose hope and abandon their cause believing that further efforts are futile.

Again let me say that there is little evidence to support this view. Every election necessarily produces a minority. In 1936 the Republicans polled less than 40 percent of the vote. Yet the fact that the Republicans were defeated badly wasn't enough to lead them to quit the battle. They continued to fight against the New Deal with as much vigor as before. An even better example is afforded by the Socialist Party. For years the Socialist candidate for President has received but a small fraction of the total popular vote, and could count on sure defeat. Yet the Socialist Party continues as a party, and continues to poll about the same number of votes.

Sampling surveys will never impose a cloture on debate so long as it is the nature of public opinion to change. The will of the people is dynamic; opinions are constantly changing. A year ago an overwhelming majority of voters were skeptical of the prospects of the Republican Party in 1940. Today, half the voters think the G.O.P. will win. If elections themselves do not impose cloture on debate, is it likely that opinion surveys will?

Possible Effect on Representative Government

The form of government we live under is a representative form of government. What will be the effect on representative government if the will of the people is known at all times? Will legislators become mere rubber stamps, mere puppets, and the function of representation be lost?

Under a system of frequent opinion measurement, the function of representation is not lost, for two reasons. First, it is well understood that the people have not the time or the inclination to pass on all the problems that confront their leaders. They cannot be expected to express judgment on technical questions of administration and government. They can pass judgment only on basic general policies. As society grows more complex there is a greater and greater need for experts. Once the voters have indicated their approval of a general policy or plan of action, experts are required to carry it out.

Second, it is not the province of the people to initiate legislation, but to decide which of the programs offered they like best. National policies do not spring full-blown from the common people. Leaders, knowing the general will of the people, must take the initiative in forming policies that will carry out the general will and must put them into effect.

Before the advent of the sampling referendum, legislators were not isolated from their constituencies. They read the local newspapers; they toured their districts and talked with voters; they received letters from their home State; they entertained delegations who claimed to speak for large and important blocs of voters. The change that is brought about by sampling referenda is merely one which provides these legislators with a truer measure of opinion in their districts and in the nation.

* * *

How Wise Are the Common People?

The sampling surveys of recent years have provided much evidence concerning the wisdom of the common people. Anyone is free to examine this evidence. And I think that the person who does examine it will come away believing as I do that, collectively, the American people have a remarkably high degree of common sense. These people may not be brilliant or intellectual or particularly well read, but they possess a quality of good sense which is manifested time and again in their expressions of opinion on present-day issues.

* * *

It is not difficult to understand why the conception of the stupidity of the masses has so many adherents. Talk to the first hundred persons whom you happen to meet in the street about many important issues of the day, and the chances are great that you will be struck by their lack of accurate or complete knowledge on these issues. Few of them will likely have sufficient information in this particular field to express a well founded judgment.

But fortunately a democracy does not require that every voter be well informed on every issue. In fact a democracy does not depend so much on the enlightenment of each individual, as upon the quality of the collective judgment or intelligence of thousands of individuals.

* * *

It would of course be foolish to argue that the collective views of the common people always represent the most intelligent and most accurate answer to any question. But results of sampling referenda on hundreds of issues do indicate, in my opinion, that we can place great faith in the collective judgment or intelligence of the people.

The New England Town Meeting Restored

One of the earliest and purest forms of democracy in this country was the New England town meeting. The people gathered in one room to discuss and to vote on the questions of the community. There was a free exchange of opinions in the presence of all the members. The town meeting was a simple and effective way of articulating public opinion, and the decisions made by the meeting kept close to the public will. When a democracy thus operates on a small scale it is able to express itself swiftly and with certainty.

But as communities grew, the town meeting became unwieldy. As a result the common people became less articulate, less able to debate the vital issues in the manner of their New England forefathers. Interest in politics lagged. Opinion had to express itself by the slow and cumbersome method of election, no longer facilitated by the town meeting with its frequent give and take of ideas. The indifference and apathy of voters made it possible for vicious and corrupt political machines to take over the administration of government in many states and cities.

The New England town meeting was valuable because it provided a forum for the exchange of views among all citizens of the community and for a vote on these views. Today, the New England town meeting idea has, in a sense, been restored. The wide distribution of daily newspapers reporting the views of statesmen on issues of the day, the almost universal ownership of radios which bring the whole nation within the hearing of any voice, and now the advent of the sampling referendum which provides a means of determining quickly the response of the public to debate on issues of the day, have in effect created a town meeting on a national scale.

How nearly the goal has been achieved is indicated in the following data recently gathered by the American Institute of Public Opinion. Of the 45,000,000 persons who voted in the last presidential election [1936], approximately 40,000,000 read a daily newspaper, 40,000,000 have radios, and only 2,250,000 of the entire group of voters in the nation neither have a radio nor take a daily newspaper.

This means that the nation is literally in one great room. The newspapers and the radio conduct the debate on national issues, presenting both information and argument on both sides, just as the townsfolk did in person in the old town meeting. And finally, through the process of the sampling referendum, the people, having heard the debate on both sides of every issue, can express their will. After one hundred and fifty years we return to the town meeting. This time the whole nation is within the doors.

DISCUSSION QUESTIONS

1. What are the advantages and disadvantages of modern public opinion polling for policy making and elections?

2. How would our political system change if polls were banned?

3. Imagine you are an elected official. How would you determine when to pay attention to public opinion polls and when to ignore them? In a representative democracy, should you as an elected official *ever* ignore public opinion as revealed in polls?

42

"Choice Words: If You Can't Understand Our Poll Questions, Then How Can We Understand Your Answers?"

RICHARD MORIN

Although polls play a prominent role in contemporary politics, Richard Morin cautions that polls can be "risky." Morin, director of polling for the Washington Post, *notes that minor differences in question wording can—and, during the impeachment of President Clinton, did—result in dramatically different polling results. Other problems arise because people will answer questions "even if they don't really have an opinion or understand the question that has been asked." Ultimately, argues Morin, pollsters and the politicians who rely upon them should be somewhat skeptical of the depth or significance of any individual response.*

If his current government job ends abruptly, President Clinton might think about becoming a pollster. Anyone who ponders the meaning of the word *is* has precisely the right turn of mind to track public opinion in these mindless, mindful times.

Never has polling been so risky—or so much in demand. Never have so many of the rules of polling been bent or broken so cleanly, or so often. Pollsters are sampling public reaction just hours—sometimes minutes—after events occur. Interviewing periods, which traditionally last several days to secure a solid sample, have sometimes shrunk to just a few hours on a single night. Pollsters have been asking questions that were taboo until this past year. Is oral sex really sex? (Yes, said 76 percent of those interviewed in a *Newsweek* poll conducted barely a week after the scandal broke back in January.)

"No living pollster has ever had to poll in a situation like this," said Michael Kagay, the editor of news surveys at the *New York Times.* "We're in uncharted territory." After all, Andrew Johnson had to deal with political enemies, but not pollsters. And Richard Nixon's resignation before impeachment meant that pollsters didn't have a chance to ask whether the Senate should give him the boot.

Clinton has it about right: Words do have different meanings for different people, and these differences matter. At the same time, some seemingly common words and phrases have no meaning at all to many Americans; even on the eve of the impeachment vote last month, nearly a third of the country, didn't know or didn't understand what *impeachment* meant.

Every pollster knows that questions with slightly different wording can produce different results. In the past year, survey researchers learned just how big and baffling those differences can be, particularly when words are used to capture public reaction to an arcane process that no living American—not even [ninety-something Senator] Strom Thurmond—has witnessed in its entirety.

Fear of getting it wrong—coupled with astonishment over the persistent support for Clinton revealed in poll after poll—spawned a flood of novel tests by pollsters to determine precisely the right words to use in our questions.

Last month, less than a week before Clinton was impeached by the House, *The Washington Post* and its polling partner ABC News asked half of a random sampling of Americans whether Clinton should resign if he were impeached or should "fight the charges in the Senate." The other half of the sample was asked a slightly different question: Should Clinton resign if impeached or should he "remain in office and face trial in the Senate?"

The questions are essentially the same. The results were not. Nearly six in 10—59 percent—said Clinton should quit rather than fight impeachment charges in the Senate. But well under half—43 percent—said he should resign when the alternative was to "remain in office and stand trial in the Senate." What gives?

The difference appears to be the word *fight*. America is a peaceable kingdom; we hate it when our parents squabble and are willing to accept just about any alternative—including Clinton's resignation—to spare the country a partisan fight. But when the alternative is less overtly combative—stand trial in the Senate—Americans are less likely to scurry to the resignation option.

Such a fuss over a few words. But it is just more proof that people do not share the same understanding of terms, and that a pollster who ignores this occupational hazard may wind up looking for a new job.

Think I'm exaggerating? Then let's do another test. A month ago, [December 1998], how would you have answered this question: "If the full House votes to send impeachment articles to the Senate for a trial, then do you think it would be better for the country if Bill Clinton resigned from office, or not?"

And how would you have answered this question: "If the full House votes to impeach Bill Clinton, then do you think it would be better for the country if Bill Clinton resigned from office, or not?"

The questions (asked in a *New York Times*/CBS News poll in mid-December) seem virtually identical. But the differences in results were stunning: Forty-three percent said the president should quit if the House sends "impeachment articles to the Senate" while 60 percent said he should quit if the House "votes to impeach."

What's going on here? Kagay says he doesn't know. Neither do I, but here's a guess: Perhaps "impeach" alone was taken as "found guilty" and the phrase "send impeachment articles to the Senate for a trial" suggests that the case isn't over. If only we could do another wording test. . . .

Language problems have challenged pollsters from the very start of the Monica Lewinsky scandal. Among the first: How to describe Monica herself? *The Washington Post*'s first survey questions referred to her as a "21-year-old intern at the White House," as did questions asked by other news organizations. But noting her age was potentially biasing. Highlighting her youthfulness conjured up visions of innocence and victimhood that appeared inconsistent with her apparently aggressive and explicitly amorous conduct with Clinton. In subsequent *Post* poll questions, she became a "former White House intern" of indeterminate age.

Then came the hard part: How to describe what she and Bill were accused of doing in a way that didn't offend, overly titillate or otherwise stampede people into one position or the other? In these early days, details about who did what to whom and where were sketchy but salacious. It clearly wasn't a classic adulterous love affair; love had apparently little to do with it, at least on Clinton's part. Nor was it a one-night stand. It seemed more like the overheated fantasy of a 16-year-old boy or the musings of the White House's favorite pornographer, *Penthouse* magazine publisher Larry Flynt. Piled on top of the sex were the more complex and less easily understood issues of perjury and obstruction of justice. After various iterations, we and other organizations settled on simply "the Lewinsky matter"—nice and neutral, leaving exactly what that meant to the imaginations (or memories) of survey respondents.

One thing is clear, at least in hindsight: Results of hypothetical questions—those that ask what if?—did not hold up in the past 12 months, said political scientist Michael Traugott of the University of Michigan. Last January, pollsters posed questions asking whether Clinton should resign or be impeached if he lied under oath about having an affair with Lewinsky. Clear majorities said he should quit or be impeached.

Fast forward to the eve of the impeachment vote. Nearly everybody believed Clinton had lied under oath about his relationship with Lewinsky, but now healthy majorities said he should not be impeached—a tribute, perhaps, to the White House strategy of drawing out (dare we say stonewalling?) the investigation to allow the public to get used to the idea that their president was a sleazy weasel.

Fortunately, pollsters had time to work out the kinks in question wording. Demand for polling produced a flood of questions of all shades and flavors, and good wording drove out the bad. At times, it seemed even to pollsters that there may be too many questions about the scandal, said Kathy Frankovic, director of surveys for CBS News. Through October [1998], more than 1,000 survey questions specifically mentioned Lewinsky's name—double the number of questions that have ever been asked about the Watergate scandal, Frankovic said.

Polling's new popularity has attracted a tonier class of critic. In the past, mostly assistant professors and aggrieved political operatives or their bosses trashed the public polls. Today, one of the fiercest critics of polling is syndicated columnist Arianna Huffington, the onetime Cambridge University debating champ, A-list socialite and New Age acolyte. A few weeks ago, Huffington revealed in her column that lots of people refuse to talk to pollsters, a problem that's not new (except, apparently, to Huffington).

Actually, I think Huffington has it backward. The real problem is that people are too willing to answer poll questions—dutifully responding to poll takers even if they don't really have an opinion or understand the question that has been asked.

A famous polling experiment illustrates the prevalence of pseudo-opinions: More than 20 years ago, a group of researchers at the University of Cincinnati asked a random sample of local residents whether the 1975 Public Affairs Act should be repealed. About half expressed a view one way or another.

Of course there never was a Public Affairs Act of 1975. Researchers made it up to see how willing people were to express opinions on things they knew absolutely nothing about.

I duplicated that experiment a few years ago in a national survey, and obtained about the same result: Forty-three percent expressed an opinion, with 24 percent saying it should be repealed and 19 percent saying it should not.

But enough about the problems. In hindsight, most experts say that the polls have held up remarkably well. Within a month of the first disclosure, the public moved quickly to this consensus, as captured by the polls: Clinton's a good president but a man of ghastly character who can stay in the White House—but stay away from my house, don't touch my daughter and don't pet the dog.

"It is so striking. The public figured this one out early on and stuck with it," said Thomas E. Mann, director of governmental studies at the Brookings Institution. "If anything, the only changes were these upward blips in support for Clinton in the face of some dramatic development that was certain to presage his collapse."

Mann and others argue that public opinion polls may never have played a more important role in American political life. "This last year illustrates the wisdom of George Gallup's optimism about the use of polls in democracy: to discipline the elites, to constrain the activists, to allow ordinary citizens to register sentiments on a matter of the greatest public importance," Mann said.

Well, hooray for us pollsters! Actually, there is evidence suggesting that all the attention in the past year may have improved the public's opinions of opinion polls and pollsters. And why shouldn't they? These polls have had something for everyone: While Democrats revel in Clinton's high job-approval ratings and otherwise bulletproof presidency, Republicans can point to the equally lopsided majority who think Clinton should be censured and formally reprimanded for his behavior.

A few weeks ago, as bombs fell in Baghdad and talk of impeachment roiled Washington, pollster Nancy Belden took a break from business to attend the annual holiday pageant at her 10-year-old son's school. As she left the auditorium, the steadfast Republican mother of one of her son's classmates approached Belden and clapped her on the shoulder. "Thank heavens for you pollsters," she said.

"I was stunned. I was delighted," Belden laughed. "I've spent many years being beat up on by people who complain that public opinion polling is somewhat thwarting the political process, as opposed to helping it. Suddenly, people are coming up to me at parties and saying thanks for doing what you do. What a relief!"

DISCUSSION QUESTIONS

1. Morin presents striking differences in poll results when a word or a few words in a question are changed. Does this diminish the value of public opinion polls in the democratic process?

2. How might Morin respond to the arguments that George Gallup makes in "Polling the Public"?

3. Try to think of an example where subtly different wording might lead to very different polling results. Why do you think it would have that effect? As a consumer of polls, how would you try to determine what the "true" public opinion is on that issue?

43

"Framing, Agenda Setting, and Priming: The Evolution of Three Media Effects Models"

Dietram A. Scheufele and David Tewksbury

Although everyone has contact with the government nearly every day—attending a public school, driving on public roads, using government-regulated electricity, and so on—few citizens have direct contact with the policymaking process. Because of this distance between the public and policymakers, the behavior of intermediaries between the government and the governed is a significant issue in a democratic polity. The media, in particular the news media, are among the most significant of these intermediaries that tell the people what the government is doing and tell the government what the people want. The central place of the media concerns political advocates from across the political spectrum. The news media can significantly shape public opinion and, ultimately, public policy. To these observers, "media bias" is corrosive to American democracy. And, perhaps even of more immediate concern to these advocates, liberals worry that the media help conservative political causes while conservatives worry about the opposite.

But what, in fact, are the effects of the news media on public opinion? This question has been a central one in the scholarly study of the media for decades. In this selection, Dietram Scheufele and David Tewksbury describe the three major lines of inquiry into media effects. "Agenda setting" means that media emphasis of an issue or politician tends to correlate with the importance the public places on that issue or candidate. "Priming" encourages people to use certain standards rather than others when evaluating an issue or politician. "Framing" suggests that the way an issue or politician is presented will affect public opinion on that issue or politician. As an example, heavy coverage of economic news leads us to think that the economy is an important issue: agenda setting. Heavier coverage of modest income growth than of very low unemployment might suggest to us that the former is a better yardstick to measure government performance: priming. And coverage that suggests that the modest income growth is directly attributable to the actions of one political party may influence how we think about politicians from those parties: framing. Scheufele and Tewksbury discuss the history of media research and some of the complications inherent in that research.

In 1997, Republican pollster Frank Luntz sent out a 222-page memo called "Language of the 21st century" to select members of the U.S. Congress. Parts of the memo soon spread among staffers, members of Congress, and also journalists. Luntz's message was simple: "It's not what you say, it's how you say it" (Luntz, in press). Drawing on various techniques for real-time message testing and focus grouping, Frank Luntz had researched Republican campaign messages and distilled terms and phrases that resonated with specific interpretive schemas among audiences and therefore helped shift people's attitudes. In other words, the effect of the messages was not a function of content differences but of differences in the modes of presentation.

The ideas outlined in the memo were hardly new, of course, and drew on decades of existing research in sociology (Goffman, 1974), economics (Kahneman & Tversky, 1979), psychology (Kahneman & Tversky, 1984), cognitive linguistics (Lakoff, 2004), and communication (Entman, 1991: Iyengar, 1991). But Frank Luntz was the first professional pollster to systematically use the concept of framing as a campaign tool. The Democratic Party soon followed and George Lakoff published *Don't Think of an Elephant* (Lakoff, 2004), a short manual for liberals on how to successfully frame their own messages.

With the emergence of framing as a communication tool for modern campaigns has come a resurgence of academic research on other cognitive campaign effects, such as agenda setting and priming, many of which are thought to be related or at least based on similar premises (for overviews, see McCombs, 2004; Price & Tewksbury, 1997; Scheufele, 2000). * * *

Parsimony Versus Precision: Framing, Agenda Setting, and Priming

The three models we focus on in this issue—framing, agenda setting, and priming—have received significant scholarly attention since they were introduced.

Agenda setting refers to the idea that there is a strong correlation between the emphasis that mass media place on certain issues (e.g., based on relative placement or amount of coverage) and the importance attributed to these issues by mass audiences (McCombs & Shaw, 1972). As defined in the political communication literature, *Priming* refers to "changes in the standards that people use to make political evaluations" (Iyengar & Kinder, 1987, p. 63). Priming occurs when news content suggests to news audiences that they ought to use specific issues as benchmarks for evaluating the performance of leaders and governments. It is often understood as an extension of agenda setting. * * * By making some issues more salient in people's mind (agenda setting), mass media can also shape the considerations that people take into account when making judgments about political candidates or issues (priming).

Framing differs significantly from these accessibility-based models. It is based on the assumption that how an issue is characterized in news reports can have an influence on how it is understood by audiences. Framing is often traced back to roots in both psychology and sociology (Pan & Kosicki, 1993). The psychological origins of framing lie in experimental work by Kahneman and Tversky (1979, 1984), for which Kahneman received the 2002 Nobel Prize in economics (Kahneman, 2003). They examined how different presentations of essentially identical decision-making scenarios influence people's choices and their evaluation of the various options presented to them. * * *

Framing therefore is both a macrolevel and a microlevel construct. (Scheufele, 1999). As a macroconstruct, the term "framing" refers to modes of presentation that journalists and other communicators use to present information in a way that resonates with existing underlying schemas among their audience (Shoemaker & Reese, 1996). This does not mean, of course, that most journalists try to spin a story or deceive their audiences. In fact, framing, for them, is a necessary tool to reduce the complexity of an issue, given the constraints of their respective media related to news holes and airtime (Gans, 1979). Frames, in other words, become invaluable tools for presenting relatively complex issues, such as stem cell research, efficiently and in a way that makes them accessible to lay audiences because they play to existing cognitive schemas. As a microconstruct, framing describes how people use information and presentation features regarding issues as they form impressions.

Sorting Out the Differences

An explication of the relationships between agenda setting (and priming) and framing needs to bridge levels of analysis and answer (a) how news messages are created, (b) how they are processed, and (c) how the effects are produced. The development of a conceptual model that adequately explains the three effects should therefore address the relationships among them related to these three questions. * * *

News Production

The first area of comparison is the production of news messages. Research in this area examines the factors related to frame building and agenda building (Scheufele, 1999, 2000). * * * For example, research in the agenda-setting tradition has identified how issue agendas are built in news production (Gobb & Elder, 1971). * * *

Both frame building and agenda building refer to macroscopic mechanisms that deal with message construction rather than media effects. The activities of interest groups, policymakers, journalists, and other groups interested in shaping media agendas and frames can have an impact on both the volume and character of news messages about a particular issue. * * *

News Processing

How news messages that set agendas and frames are processed by recipients is the second area of comparison between different models of media effects. Here, the question is whether news audiences experience the two processes identically. * * * One point of comparison is the amount of attention to news messages required for the two effects to occur. We could assume that a framing effect occurs when audiences pay substantial attention to news messages. That is, the content and implications of an issue frame are likely to be most apparent to an audience member who pays attention to a news story. A parallel logic could be applied to the agenda-setting process. Information processing theories suggest that people attending to a message and engaging in some level of elaboration of it are most likely to recall information about it later (Eveland, 2004). In short, the accessibility of an issue—and therefore its place on the issue agenda—may be higher when people attend to messages about it. Thus, agenda setting and framing may appear to operate by similar * * * processes. Nonetheless, there is at least one important distinction here. Attention to messages may be more necessary for a framing effect to occur than an agenda-setting effect. Mere exposure may be sufficient for agenda setting, but it is less likely to be so for framing effects.

*   *   *

Locus of Effect

The third central question in the comparison between framing and basic agenda setting is the locus of cognitive effect. In both cases, audiences process information provided by the news media and store it in memory. The traditional agenda-setting approach is based on memory-based models of information processing and therefore an accessibility model (Eagly & Chaiken, 1993). Agenda-setting effects assume that the locus of effect lies with the heightened accessibility an issue receives from its treatment in the news (Price & Tewksbury, 1997). Thus, it is not information *about* the issue that has the effect; it is the fact that the issue has received a certain amount of processing time and attention that carries the effect.

In contrast, the basic framing approach assumes that the locus of effect lies within the description of an issue or the label used in news coverage about the issue. It is the underlying interpretive schemas that have been made applicable to the issue that are the central effect of a frame. The primary difference on the psychological level between agenda setting and priming, on the one hand, and framing, on the other hand, is therefore the difference between *whether* we think about an issue and *how* we think about it.

*   *   *

* * * It certainly seems plausible * * * that *how* people think about an issue (and candidates, in an election setting) has implications for *whether* they think about it, as well. The underappreciated element of traditional agenda-setting research is that it focuses on *problems*, things that need to be fixed. Thus, an integral part of the agenda-setting story is how news reports portray, and how people understand, issues. Research in framing may certainly inform how those processes work and how they influence agenda setting.

An emphasis on attributes of candidates and other figures in the news in some research raises the importance of considering how people think about people and objects (issues). Research in social cognition has observed that people organize information about people's behaviors in a unique way, one that focuses on traits (Newman & Uleman, 1989) and social judgments about people (Hastie & Park, 1986) rather than on discreet behaviors. Information about issues, as objects, on the other hand, is likely to be retained in a different fashion, one that relies more squarely in the retention of facts about problems and solutions (Zaller, 1992). Explanatory models that assume a common processing style and, therefore, media effect for information about people and issues in the news must somehow reconcile these and other differences in the ways people think about people and things. Until they do, we probably ought to be cautious about applying them.

*   *   *

DISCUSSION QUESTIONS

1. Assuming that agenda setting, priming, and framing do exist to some extent, what advice would you give to journalists about how to present the news?

2. What if these three media effects are unequally distributed throughout the population, so that some groups are more influenced than others? Does that have any implications for the place of media in a democracy? For the way journalists do their job?

3. How would you define the role of the news media in a democracy?

4. Should journalists challenge the arguments and facts offered by the individuals they cover? Or should journalists simply present as many sides as possible, allowing each side to make a case, and leave it up to news consumers to determine which case is most convincing?

REFERENCES

Cobb, R. W., & Elder, C. (1971). The politics of agenda-building: An alternative perspective for modern democratic theory. *Journal of Politics, 33*, 892–915.

Eagly, A. H., & Chaiken, S. (1993). *The psychology of attitudes.* Forth Worth, TX: Harcourt Brace.

Entman, R. M. (1991). Framing United-States coverage of international news—Contrasts in narratives of the KAL and Iran Air incidents. *Journal of Communication, 41*(4), 6–27.

Eveland, W. P. (2004). The effects of political discussion in producing informed citizens: The roles of information, motivation, and elaboration. *Political Communication, 21*(2), 177–193.

Gans, H. (1979). *Deciding what's news.* New York: Pantheon Books.

Goffman, E. (1974). *Frame analysis: An essay on the organization of experience.* New York: Harper & Row.

Hastie, R., & Park, B. (1986). The relationship between memory and judgment depends on whether the task is memory-based or on-line. *Psychological Review, 93*, 258–268.

Iyengar, S. (1991). *Is anyone responsible? How television frames political issues.* Chicago: University of Chicago Press.

Iyengar, S., & Kinder, D. R. (1987). *News that matters: Television and American opinion.* Chicago: University of Chicago Press.

Kahneman, D. (2003). Maps of bounded rationality: A perspective on intuitive judgment and choice. In T. Frängsmyr (Ed.), *Les Prix Nobel: The Nobel Prizes 2002* (pp. 449–489). Stockholm: Nobel Foundation.

Kahneman, D., & Tversky, A. (1979). Prospect theory—Analysis of decision under risk. *Econometrica, 47*, 263–291.

Kahneman, D., & Tversky, A. (1984). Choices, values, and frames. *American Psychologist, 39*, 341–350.

Lakoff, G. (2004). *Don't think of an elephant! Know your values and frame the debate.* White River Junction, VT: Chelsea Green.

Luntz, F. (in press). *Words that work: It's not what you say, it's what people hear.* New York: Hyperion.

McCombs, M. E. (2004). *Setting the agenda: The mass media and public opinion.* Malden, MA: Blackwell.

McCombs, M. E., & Shaw, D. L. (1972). The agenda-setting function of mass media. *Public Opinion Quarterly, 36*(2), 176–187.

Newman, L. S., & Uleman, J. S. (1989). Spontaneous trait inferences. In J. S. Uleman & J. A. Bargh (Eds.), *Unintended thought* (pp. 155–188). New York: Guilford.

Pan, Z., & Kosicki, G. M. (1993). Framing analysis: An approach to news discourse. *Political Communication, 10*(1), 55–75.

Price, V., & Tewksbury, D. (1997). News values and public opinion: A theoretical account of media priming and framing. In G. A. Barett & F. J. Boster (Eds.), *Progress in communication sciences: Advances in persuasion* (Vol. 13, pp. 173–212). Greenwich, CT: Ablex.

Scheufele, D. A. (1999). Framing as a theory of media effects. *Journal of Communication, 49*(1), 103–122.

Scheufele, D. A. (2000). Agenda-setting, priming, and framing revisited: Another look at cognitive effects of political communication. *Mass Communication & Society, 3*, 297–316.

Shoemaker, P. J., & Reese, S. D. (1996). *Mediating the message: Theories of influences on mass media content* (2nd ed.). White Plains, NY: Longman.

Zaller, J. (1992). *The nature and origin of mass opinion.* New York: Cambridge University Press.

348

DEBATING THE ISSUES: THE IMPACT OF THE NEW MEDIA ON AMERICAN POLITICS

From the 1960s through the 1980s, when people thought of media and news, they thought of newspapers and, increasingly, the broadcast television networks. Cable news soon emerged to provide an alternative, but one that for the most part followed the same operating procedure as the big networks. Late in the 1980s, talk radio, which had been around for some time, boomed in popularity and hosts such as Rush Limbaugh became household names. Talk radio entertained, informed, and perhaps misinformed. Hosts gleefully tweaked the mainstream media and embraced a much more aggressive, hard-hitting style that was blatantly ideological and partisan. There was, in this new forum, no pretense to being objective but, talk-radio fans would argue, the mainstream media were also not objective—they just pretended to be. The rise of the Internet in the 1990s is the most recent dramatic change in communications technology. The Internet provided new communications alternatives in the form of Web sites and chatrooms. Today, blogs receive most of the attention. In the Democratic party in particular, the "blogosphere" appears to be influencing the decisions of public officials and candidates. And sites like YouTube make it possible for every misstep by a politician to be easily viewed by millions of viewers. Adam Nagourney provides an overview of the changes the Internet has brought to contemporary politics.

Have these new media been a positive force in American democracy? David Perlmutter and Misti McDaniel say they have. New media can force items onto the agenda of the old media. By hammering away at stories and insistently pursuing them, new-media outlets create enough of a buzz around a story that journalists in the traditional media feel obliged to pick up these stories themselves. Control over the agenda—over what gets defined as news and by whom—may be slipping out of the hands of the members of the traditional media. Blogs have the potential, they believe, to provide a powerful check on politicians and to allow for a more participatory democracy.

Markus Prior is not so sure we should celebrate just yet. Information is more abundant than ever, he notes, yet participation and knowledge levels have remained stagnant. Rather than enhance participatory democracy, as advocates of the new media suggest is the norm, the onset of cable television and the Internet has worsened information and participation gaps between those individuals who like to follow the news and those who are more interested in entertainment. A spread of more and more news choices, which sounds democratic, has had nondemocratic effects, Prior argues. Newshounds can dig ever deeper into the news, but other members of the public are increasingly able to ignore the news. Other critics have made a similar argument that new media tend to exacerbate public polarization because readers, viewers, and listeners gravitate to outlets presenting opinions they agree with and ignore those sources that would challenge their views.

44

"Internet Injects Sweeping Change into U.S. Politics"

Adam Nagourney

The transformation of American politics by the Internet is accelerating with the approach of the 2006 Congressional and 2008 White House elections, producing far-reaching changes in the way campaigns approach advertising, fund-raising, the mobilizing of supporters and even the spreading of negative information.

Democrats and Republicans are sharply increasing their use of e-mail, interactive Web sites, candidate and party blogs, and text messaging to raise money, organize get-out-the-vote efforts, and assemble crowds for rallies. The Internet, they say, appears to be far more efficient, and less costly, than the traditional tools of politics, notably door knocking and telephone banks.

Analysts say the campaign television advertisement, already diminishing in influence with the proliferation of cable stations, faces new challenges as campaigns experiment with technology that allows direct messaging to more specific audiences and through unconventional means.

Those include podcasts featuring a daily downloaded message from a candidate and so-called viral attack videos, designed to set off peer-to-peer distribution by e-mail chains, without being associated with any candidate or campaign.

Campaigns are now studying popular Internet social networks, like Friendster and Facebook, as ways to reach groups of potential supporters with similar political views or cultural interests.

President Bush's media consultant, Mark McKinnon, said television advertising, while still crucial to campaigns, had become markedly less influential in persuading voters than it was even two years ago.

"I feel like a woolly mammoth," Mr. McKinnon said.

What the parties and the candidates are undergoing now is in many ways similar to what has happened in other sectors of the nation—including the music industry, newspapers, and retailing—as they try to adjust to, and take advantage of, the Internet as its influence spreads across American society. To a considerable extent, they are responding to, and playing catch up with, bloggers who have demonstrated the power of their forums to harness the energy on both sides of the ideological divide.

Certainly, the Internet was a significant factor in 2004, particularly with the early success in fund-raising and organizing by Howard Dean, a Democratic presidential contender. But officials in both parties say the extent to which the parties have now recognized and rely on the Internet has increased at a staggering rate over the past two years.

The percentage of Americans who went online for election news jumped from 13 percent in the 2002 election cycle to 29 percent in 2004, according to a survey by the Pew Research Center after the last presidential election. A Pew survey released earlier this month found that 50 million Americans go to the Internet for news every day, up from 27 million people in March 2002, a reflection of the fact that the Internet is now available to 70 percent of Americans.

This means, aides said, rethinking every assumption about running a campaign: how to reach different segments of voters, how to get voters to the polls, how to raise money, and the best way to have a candidate interact with the public.

In 2004, John Edwards, a former Democratic senator from North Carolina and his party's vice presidential candidate, spent much of his time talking to voters in living rooms in New Hampshire and Iowa; now he is putting aside hours every week to videotape responses to videotaped questions, the entire exchange posted on his blog.

"The effect of the Internet on politics will be every bit as transformational as television was," said Ken Mehlman, the Republican national chairman. "If you want to get your message out, the old way of paying someone to make a TV ad is insufficient: You need your message out through the Internet, through e-mail, through talk radio."

Michael Cornfield, a political science professor at George Washington University who studies politics and the Internet, said campaigns were actually late in coming to the game.

"Politicians are having a hard time reconciling themselves to a medium where they can't control the message," Professor Cornfield said. "Politics is lagging, but politics is not going to be immune to the digital revolution."

If there was any resistance, it is rapidly melting away.

Mark Warner, the former Democratic governor of Virginia, began preparing for a potential 2008 presidential campaign by hiring a blogging pioneer, Jerome Armstrong, a noteworthy addition to the usual first wave of presidential campaign hiring of political consultants and fund-raisers.

Mr. Warner is now one of at least three potential presidential candidates—the others are the party's 2004 presidential and vice presidential candidates, Senator John Kerry of Massachusetts and Mr. Edwards—who are routinely posting what aides say are their own writings on campaign blogs or on public blogs like the Daily Kos, the nation's largest political blog.

Analysts said that the Internet appeared to be a particularly potent way to appeal to new, young voters, a subject of particular interest to both parties in these politically turbulent times. In the 2004 campaign, 80 percent of people ages 18 to 34 who contributed to Mr. Kerry's campaign made their contributions online, said Carol Darr, director of the Institute for Politics, Democracy and the Internet at George Washington University.

Not incidentally, as it becomes more integrated in American politics, the Internet is being pressed into service for the less seemly side of campaigns.

Both parties have set up Web sites to discredit opponents. In Tennessee, Republicans spotlighted what they described as the lavish spending habits of Representative Harold E. Ford Jr. with a site called www.fancyford.com. That site drew 100,000 hits the first weekend, and extensive coverage in the Tennessee press, which is typically the real goal of creating sites like this. And this weekend, the Republicans launched a new attack site, www.bobsbaggage.com, that is aimed at Senator Robert Menendez of New Jersey and focused on ethics accusations against him.

For their part, Democrats have set up decoy Web sites to post documents with damaging information about Republicans. They described this means of distribution as far more efficient than the more traditional slip of a document to a newspaper reporter.

A senior party official, who was granted anonymity in exchange for describing a clandestine effort, said the party created a site, now defunct, called D.C. Inside Scoop to, among other things, distribute a document written by Senator Mel Martinez, Republican of Florida, discussing the political benefits of the Terri Schiavo case. A second such site, capitol buzz.blogspot.com, spread more mischievous information: the purported sighting of Senator Rick Santorum, a Pennsylvania Republican, parking in a spot reserved for the handicapped.

On the left in particular, bloggers have emerged as something of a police force guarding against disloyalty among Democrats, as Steve Elmendorf, a Democratic consultant, learned after he told *The Washington Post* that bloggers and online donors "are not representative of the majority you need to win elections."

A Daily Kos blogger wrote: "Not one dime, ladies and gentlemen, to anything connected with Steve Elmendorf. Anyone stupid enough to actually give a quote like that deserves to have every single one of his funding sources dry up."

Asked about the episode, Mr. Elmendorf insisted that the posting had not hurt his business, but added, "Since I got attacked on them, I read blogs a lot more and I find them very useful."

One of the big challenges to the campaigns is not only adjusting to the changes of the past two years but also anticipating the kind of technological changes that may be on hand by the next presidential campaign. Among those most cited is the ability of campaigns to beam video advertisements to cellphones.

"All these consultants are still trying to make sense of what blogs are, and I think by 2008 they are going to have a pretty good idea: They are going to be like, 'We're hot and we're hip and we're bloggin',' " said Markos Moulitsas, the founder of the Daily Kos. "But by 2008, the blogs are going to be so institutionalized, it's not going to be funny."

Bloggers, for all the benefits they may bring to both parties, have proved to be a complicating political influence for Democrats. They have tugged the party consistently to the left, particularly on issues like the war, and have been openly critical of such moderate Democrats as Senator Joseph I. Lieberman of Connecticut.

Still, Democrats have been enthusiastic about the potential of this technology to get the party back on track, with many Democratic leaders arguing that the Internet is today for Democrats what talk radio was for Republicans 10 years ago.

"This new media becomes much more important to us because conservatives have been more dominant in traditional media," said Simon Rosenberg, the president of the centrist New Democratic Network. "This stuff becomes really critical for us."

For all the attention being paid to Internet technology, there remain limitations to its reach. Internet use declines markedly among Americans over 65, who tend to be the nation's most reliable voters. Until recently, it tended to be more heavily used by middle- and upper-income people.

And while the Internet is efficient at reaching supporters, who tend to visit and linger at political sites, it has proved to be much less effective at swaying voters who are not interested in politics.

"The holy grail that everybody is looking for right now is how can you use the Internet for persuasion," said Mr. Armstrong, the Warner campaign Internet adviser.

In this age of multitasking, voters are not as captive to a Web site as they may be to a 30-second television advertisement or a campaign mailing. That was a critical lesson of the collapse of Mr. Dean's presidential campaign, after he initially enjoyed great Internet success in raising money and drawing crowds.

"It's very easy to look at something and just click delete," said Carl Forti, a spokesman for the National Republican Congressional Committee. "At least if they are taking out a piece of mail, you know they are taking it out and looking at it on the way to the garbage can."

45

"The Ascent of Blogging"

DAVID D. PERLMUTTER AND MISTI MCDANIEL

New media are not new to those who've grown up with or use them everyday. To 18-year-olds at our journalism school at Louisiana State University, iPods, satellite-reception, Wi-Fi, laptops, cell phones, PDAs, digital photography, and the Internet are technologies as familiar as the wheel and fire. But while ancient innovations took millennia to spread, today a new gadget or idea can catch on globally within a few years.

The ascent of the Web log, Weblog (or blog) is one example. Within five years, online journals of political and personal expression and debate rose from obscurity to become ubiquitous. In examining how the mainstream press has reacted to blogs, we discern lessons about the relationship between technology and journalism:

- Events don't drive new media technology. Rather, new media technology succeeds by finding ways to exploit events.
- News coverage tends to focus on the sexy or "hot" aspects of new media technology, which can obscure other trends that will be potentially more influential in the long run.
- Old media portrays new media technologies as darlings, only to cynically then dethrone them.
- Traditional media's vulnerabilities to such upstarts aren't just technological but are economic and psychological. Mainstream media believe new things might destroy, result in unemployment, or make them obsolete; they don't know how to adapt.
- The best response to blogs by television, radio and print is not to ape them but to determine what blogs do and why they do it well or poorly.

Certainly blogs seem to be everywhere—some estimates put the number of blogs in the tens of millions. According to several Pew studies, of the estimated 120 million U.S. adults who use the Internet, some seven percent have created a blog while more than 30 million look at them regularly. Many blogs are basement setups—scribbled by one, read by few. In contrast, some popular blogs, like Instapundit, Power Line and Daily Kos, receive more daily traffic than many major newspapers or TV news programs.

But blogs aren't talked about just because of their numbers, rather for the news they make while critiquing journalism and tracking events, such as blogging about the rise and fall of presidential candidate Howard Dean, Dan Rather's "memogate," Trent Lott's praise of Strom Thurmond's Dixiecrat campaign, and the South Asian tsunami. In each case—and others—bloggers pushed and prodded old media to change the ways they work. In response, some journalists and news organizations have created blogs and use them for newsgathering, self-reflection, opinion-testing, and interaction with readers, listeners, and viewers.

Though blog-like sites existed during the 1990s—most notably the Drudge Report—blogs were officially born in December 1997, when Jorn Barger, editor of Robot Wisdom.com, created the term "Weblog." In the spring of 1999, Peter Merholz broke "Weblog" into the phrase "we blog" and put it on his homepage. As the term spread, in August 1999 software-maker Pyra Labs released the program Blogger, making blogs user-friendly and generally accessible.

Blogs were not an instant big story in the mainstream media. One of the first hits for "blog" in the press was in October 1999 when Great Britain's *New Statesman* described it as "a Web page, something like a public commonplace book, which is added to each day. . . . If there is any log they resemble, it is the captain's log on a voyage of discovery." The first newspaper reference likely occurred in January 2000 when Canada's *Ottawa Citizen* quoted pop star Sarah McLachlan from her Web site. One of the first broadcast stories about blogs was in May 2000 when National Public Radio's "The Connection" interviewed several bloggers.

Overall, in tracking mainstream media's reporting on blogs between January 1998 and April 2005, we found 16,350 items mentioning the words "Web log," "Weblog," and "blog." In gauging "blog-throughs"—events commonly ascribed to have propelled blogs to media attention—we found that journalists were barely acknowledging blogs in the wake of 9/11.

Blog obscurity changed decisively in 2002, when Senate Majority Leader Trent Lott, while attending a reception for South Carolina Senator Strom Thurmond, made a racially insensitive comment. The item was first mentioned by ABC News and posted on its Web site, but bloggers drumbeat the story into widespread salience. Lott ended up resigning his leadership position under party pressure. Still, as blogs gained stature as agenda-setters, they remained relatively lightly cited by the press.

In 2003, as the presidential primary season kicked off, Howard Dean's team—led by technology-savvy Joe Trippi, Dean's campaign manager—pioneered the campaign blog for the public and the press. Users posted messages to other supporters, and this networking ability enabled them to meet for events. Supporters were encouraged to "decentralize" by starting their Dean Web sites and to raise funds through their blogs. By September 2003 Dean's blog was getting 30,000 unique visitors a day.

When General Wesley Clark entered the race, he cited a "Draft Wes" Web site's popularity and supportive blog comments as one reason to get in. The political parties and many candidates also began blogging. For example, the Democratic National Committee started up "Kicking Ass: Daily Dispatches from the DNC," which promised "frank, one-on-one communication. . . . Blogs make that possible."

Blogs were now being portrayed as voices of the people, political players, and as trip-wires for breaking stories.

Blogs Arrive

2004 was the year of the blog. That word became the most searched-for definition on several online dictionaries. Indeed in our tracking, October 2004 was the time at which 50 percent of blog coverage occurred before and after: In other words there has been as much blog news in the last half-year as in the previous five. What follows are some of the more memorable news stories about blogs:

- As Howard Dean started his political slide out of the race, stories about blogs grew by 50 percent. Instead of seeking disgruntled supporters for face-to-face interviews, reporters cited Dean's bloggers as newspapers carried articles about Dean's blog and how its participants reacted to the campaign's changing fortunes.
- In July 2004 the Democratic National Convention credentialed 35 bloggers. While 15,000 journalists were issued press passes, attention focused on the "bloggeratti."
- Blogging exploded into view on September 8, 2004, when on CBS News's "60 Minutes II" Dan Rather reported a story questioning President George W. Bush's 1970s National Guard service. Offered as evidence were papers, allegedly written by Bush's then-supervisor Lieutenant Colonel Jerry Killian, stating that Bush did not fulfill his service requirements.

Pushing the Rather "memogate" story, bloggers simultaneously displayed their main virtue and vice—speedy deployment of unedited thought. One blogger on freerepublic.com posted his doubt about the memos' authenticity: "They are not in the style that we used when I came in to the USAF. They looked like the style and format we started using about 12 years ago (1992). Our signature blocks were left justified, now they are rigth [sic] of center . . . like the ones they just showed." Bloggers such as Power Line's Scott Johnson launched an investigation of the purported memos. Innovatively, the blog little green footballs posted a file that contrasted a modern Microsoft Word recreation over CBS's version of the disputed papers. The text was almost an exact match.

Within days, the story leapt from new media to the mainstream news media. For two weeks CBS News stood by its reporting, but then admitted that its document examiners could not verify the memos' authenticity. The network launched an investigation to determine how the invalidated material ended up on the air. Eventually four people at CBS were blamed for the error. Rather, who anchored the evening news for 24 years, announced his retirement in November and left his position in March 2005. Many bloggers rejoiced at their power to topple venerable institutions. Freerepublic.com blogger "Rrrod" warned, "NOTE [sic] to old media scum. . . . We are just getting warmed up!"

More big blog news was ahead, including the following incidents:

- When some bloggers heard of Sinclair Broadcasting Group's plan to air an anti-[John] Kerry documentary, they organized letter-writing campaigns and boycotts and again pushed the item until it became a major story in the mainstream media.
- On Election Day, early exit polls indicated John Kerry held a lead over George Bush in a number of key states. Some bloggers pushed a "Kerry is winning big" headline. But the flexibility of the blogosphere was shown when bloggers Hugh Hewitt and Mark Blumenthal (Mystery Pollster) pointed out that exit polls were only scientifically valid in a state until after voting had finished.
- The December tsunami in Southeast Asia contributed to a 39 percent growth in newspaper coverage of blogs. Stories of victims surfaced in blogs, and for the first time traditional media were bypassed as a source as relatives searched for information about loved ones online.

In the tsunami coverage, in particular, old media took another step toward co-opting the new. Uncensored and unedited video surfaced in video blogs (vlogs) and people relied on the Internet to watch scenes from the disaster. Free of Federal Communications Commission regulations, vlogs showed grisly and gripping footage, while TV newscasts often censored their reports to avoid upsetting the American public. WaveofDestruction.org, created by an Australian blogger, posted 25 amateur videos of the event and in five days logged nearly 700,000 visitors. Soon American TV networks vied for broadcast rights. Norwegian editor Oliver Orskaug sold his video for $20,000 to CNN and ABC News.

Even as blogs soared in attention and influence, a blowback from the mainstream media was underway.

- Blame fell on bloggers for leaking the raw exit poll results on Election Day and spreading conspiracy theories afterwards.
- Some bloggers were outed for faking data or retroactively changing posts without notation.
- Some bloggers accepted pay from political candidates or parties but did not reveal the arrangement to their readers.
- Questions arose about whether blogs were, indeed, the "voice of the

people" since most domestic and foreign blog creators are white journalists, professors, lawyers or middle-class professionals.

- CNN was ridiculed for creating an "Inside the Blogs" segment that consisted of people reading blogs on air—an exercise in synergy that drew laughs even from bloggers.
- In March 2005, "The Daily Show" skewered one of the intellectual fathers of blogging, New York University's Jay Rosen, as the program's correspondent satirized the entire idea of amateurs hosting a news and commentary Web site.
- Questions are raised about whether the number of blogs is inflated by ones that are inactive or are spam.

Blogs vs. Old Media

Given what's happened with blogs and journalism, can we say that their upward trend is now in decline? Or are blogs being relegated to places where journalists troll for funny stories or human interest filler? Neither seems a likely outcome.

Blogs are likely to thrive due to their adaptability and innovation. Bloggers' personal style, their technology, the use of open-end sourcing, and their ability to get information and speculation out quickly enable this new media to go around the clunky logistical trails and leadership—bypassing what economists call the "structural rigidity" of the old. Moments after the "60 Minutes II" story aired, for example, ABC News's Peter Jennings was not going to break onto the air and proclaim, "There's something screwy about a story on CBS." And when a few bloggers had an idea about how to speed up and collate information about tsunami victims and survivors, they didn't have to wait for an OK from senior editors or management. Blog failures cost much less than do those of mainstream media, so bloggers can experiment on a whim and do so faster than giant operations.

"Old world panic" is also a problem. At some level, blogs seem a threat to almost everything in the news business. OhmyNews, for example, is a South Korean Web site where anybody can post news stories and editorials; if the content proves popular enough, the author gets paid for it. If such a model becomes dominant, it would mean the end of journalism, not to mention journalism schools. But forcing new technology into old holes doesn't work, either. Reading blogs on TV is artificial and unworkable, as is "hipping up" a newspaper column by calling it a blog or trying to feign technical innovation by telling readers that one's musings were done on a Blackberry (though suspiciously without typos).

Regular media are challenged, too, about how to cover novelties in their business. Journalists noticed blogs late, but interest intensified as bloggers showcased their potential. Now a frenzy of attention by journalists is coupled with mocking. Is this an inevitable cycle—building up what is new to unwarranted levels of praise, then despairing at its flaws, which were evident at the start?

Blogs cannot be stuffed into ill-fitting stereotypes. Blogs represent the divergent voices of millions. Though some news-related blogs have more "hits" than others, blogging lacks both defined leadership and a constituency. Post an item on a blog and comments range from complete agreement to irate dissent. It's messy, but that's what blogs are, and we hope they stay that way.

Certainly traditional journalists have a right to feel as sports stars do when they have to endure catcalls and advice shouted at them by obnoxious fans. And compared with most journalists, a lot of the bloggers have not paid their dues in education, training or experience. But the problems that mainstream journalism is experiencing today have little to do with bloggers. After all, it wasn't bloggers who slashed newsroom budgets for basic beat and investigative reporting. Nor did bloggers create a star system of astronomically paid anchors and pundits. And bloggers were not the ones who reduced coverage of political campaigns and elections to sound- and visual- bytes and horserace handicapping.

Finally, let's step back and take the longer view into this blogger/ mainstream media debate. Once upon a time, as historian Gwenyth L. Jackaway documented, a new medium came along—loud, raucous, uncontrolled and full of unprofessional and discordant voices. It was called radio. The print press of the 1920s and 1930s saw radio as a danger, not only to their livelihoods but also to the future of the republic itself. The *New York Times* fumed, "If the American people . . . were to depend upon scraps of information picked up from air reporting, the problems of a workable democracy would be multiplied incalculably." *Editor & Publisher* asserted that radio was "physically incapable of supplying more than headline material," and thus it was "inconceivable that a medium which is incapable of functioning in the public interest will be allowed to interfere with the established system of news reporting in a democracy."

Print news survived and thrives and radio did not destroy democracy. There will always be a mainstream media, though perhaps blogs will blur into it. But the point worth remembering is that the rise of new media should not make the old media panic or be dismissive or fearful. Rather what is new ought to remind us of the need to grasp ever more tightly ahold of the fundamentals of journalism as we journey forward.

46

"News vs. Entertainment: How Increasing Media Choice Widens Gaps in Political Knowledge and Turnout"

Markus Prior

The rise of new media has brought the question of audience fragmentation and selective exposure to the forefront of scholarly and popular debate. In one of the most widely discussed contributions to this
debate, Sunstein (2001) has proposed that people's increasing ability to
customize their political information will have a polarizing impact on
democracy as media users become less likely to encounter information
that challenges their partisan viewpoints. While this debate is far from
settled, the issue which precedes it is equally important and often side-
stepped: as choice between different media content increases, who continues to access *any type* of political information? Cable television and the
Internet have increased media choice so much in recent decades that
many Americans now live in a high-choice media environment. As media
choice increases, the likelihood of "chance encounters" (Sunstein) *with
any political content* declines significantly for many people * * *. Greater
choice allows politically interested people to access more information
and increase their political knowledge. Yet those who prefer nonpolitical
content can more easily escape the news and therefore pick up less political information than they used to. In a high-choice environment, lack of
motivation, not lack of skills or resources, poses the main obstacle to a
widely informed electorate.

As media choice increases, content preferences thus become the key to
understanding political learning and participation. In a high-choice environment, politics constantly competes with entertainment. Until recently,
the impact of content preferences was limited because media users did
not enjoy much choice between different content. Television quickly became the most popular mass medium in history, but for decades the networks' scheduling ruled out situations in which viewers had to choose
between entertainment and news. Largely unexposed to entertainment
competition, news had its place in the early evening and again before the
late-night shows. Today, as both entertainment and news are available
around the clock on numerous cable channels and web sites, people's

content preferences determine more of what those with cable or Internet access watch, read, and hear.

Distinguishing between people who like news and take advantage of additional information and people who prefer other media content explains a puzzling empirical finding: despite the spectacular rise in available political information, mean levels of political knowledge in the population have essentially remained constant (Delli Carpini and Keeter 1996; Gilens, Vavreck, and Cohen 2004). Yet the fact that average knowledge levels did not change hides important trends: political knowledge has risen in some segments of the electorate, but declined in others. Greater media choice thus widens the "knowledge gap" * * *. [N]umerous studies have examined the diffusion of information in the population and the differences that emerge between more and less informed individuals * * *. According to some of these studies, television works as a "knowledge leveler" (Neuman 1976, 122) because it presents information in less cognitively demanding ways (Eveland and Scheufele 2000; Kwak 1999). To reconcile this effect with the hypothesis that more television widens the knowledge gap, it is necessary to distinguish the effect of news exposure from the effect of the medium itself. In the low-choice broadcast environment, access to the medium and exposure to news were practically one and the same, as less politically interested television viewers had no choice but to watch the news from time to time * * *. As media choice increases, exposure to the news may continue to work as a "knowledge leveler," but the distribution of news exposure itself has become more unequal. Access to the medium no longer implies exposure to the news. Television news narrows the knowledge gap *among its viewers*. For the population as a whole, more channels widen the gap.

The consequences of increasing media choice reach beyond a less equal distribution of political knowledge. Since political knowledge is an important predictor of turnout and since exposure to political information motivates turnout, the shift from a low-choice to a high-choice media environment implies changes in electoral participation as well. Those with a preference for news not only become more knowledgeable, but also vote at higher rates. Those with a stronger interest in other media content vote less.

This study casts doubt on the view that the socioeconomic dimension of the digital divide is the greatest obstacle to an informed and participating electorate. Many casual observers emphasize the great promise new technologies hold for democracy. They deplore current socioeconomic inequalities in access to new media, but predict increasing political knowledge and participation among currently disadvantaged people once these inequalities have been overcome (e.g., National Telecommunications and Information Administration 2002; Negroponte 1995). This ignores that greater media choice leads to greater *voluntary* segmentation of the electorate. The present study suggests that gaps based on socioeconomic status will be eclipsed by preference-based gaps once access to new media becomes cheaper and more widely available. Gaps created by unequal distribution of resources and skills often emerged due to circumstances outside of people's control. The preference-based gaps documented in this article are self-imposed as many people abandon the news for entertainment simply because they like it better. Inequality in political knowledge and turnout increases as a result of voluntary, not circumstantial, consumption decisions.

*   *   *

Theory

The basic premise of this analysis is that people's media environment determines the extent to which their media use is governed by content preferences. According to theories of program choice, viewers have preferences over program characteristics (Bowman 1975; Lehmann 1971) or program types (Youn 1994) and select the program that promises to best satisfy these preferences. The simplest models distinguish between preferences for information and entertainment (Baum 2002; Becker and Schönbach 1989; Rubin 1984). In the low-choice broadcast environment, most people watched news and learned about politics because they were reluctant to turn off the set even if the programs offered at the time did not match their preferences. One study conducted in the early 1970s showed that 40% of the respondents reported watching programs because they appeared on the channel they were already watching or because someone else wanted to see them (LoSciuto 1973). Audience research has proposed a two-stage model according to which people first decide to watch television and then pick the available program they like best. Klein aptly called this model the "Theory of Least Objectionable Program" (1972, 77). If television viewers are routinely "glued to the box" (Barwise, Ehrenberg and Goodhardt 1982) and select the best available program, we can explain why so many Americans watched television news in the 1960s and 70s despite modest political interest. Most television viewing in the broadcast era did not stem from a deliberate choice of a program, but rather was determined by convenience, availability of spare time and the decision to spend that time in front of the TV set. And since broadcast channels offered a solid block of news at the dinner hour and again after primetime, many viewers were routinely exposed to news even though they watched television primarily to be entertained * * *.

Once exposed to television news, people learn about politics (e.g., Neuman, Just, and Crigler 1992; Zhao and Chaffee 1995). Although a captive news audience does not exhibit the same political interest as a self-selected one and therefore may not learn as much, research on passive learning (Krugman and Hartley 1970) suggests that even unmotivated exposure can produce learning (Keeter and Wilson 1986; Zukin and Snyder 1984). * * * Hence, even broadcast viewers who prefer entertainment programs absorb at least basic political knowledge when they happen to tune in when only news is on.

I propose that such accidental exposure should become less likely in a high-choice environment because greater horizontal diversity (the number of genres available at any particular point in time) increases the chance that viewers will find content that matches their preferences. The impact of one's preferences increases, and "indiscriminate viewing" becomes less likely (Youn 1994). Cable subscribers' channel repertoire (the number of frequently viewed channels) is not dramatically higher than that of nonsubscribers (Heeter 1985), but their repertoire reflects a set of channels that are more closely related to their genre preferences. Two-stage viewing behavior thus predicts that news audiences should decrease as more alternatives are offered on other channels. Indeed, local news audiences tend to be smaller when competing entertainment programming is scheduled (Webster 1984; Webster and Newton 1988), Baum and Kernell (1999) show that cable subscribers, especially the less informed among them, are less likely to watch the presidential debates than otherwise similar individuals who receive only broadcast television. According to my first hypothesis, the advent of cable TV increased the knowledge gap between people with a preference for news and people with a preference for other media content.

Internet access should contribute to an increasing knowledge gap as well. Although the two media are undoubtedly different in many respects, access to the Internet, like cable, makes media choice more efficient. Yet, while they both increase media users' content choice, cable TV and the Internet are not perfect substitutes for each other. Compared at least to dial-up Internet service, cable offers greater immediacy and more visuals. The web offers more detailed information and can be customized to a greater extent. Both media, in other words, have unique features, and access to both of them offers users the greatest flexibility. For instance, people with access to both media can watch a campaign speech on cable and then compare online how different newspapers cover the event. Depending on their needs or the issue that interests them, they can actively search a wealth of political information online or passively consume cable politics. Hence, the effects of cable TV and Internet access should be additive and the knowledge gap largest among people with access to both new media.

There are several reasons why exposure to political information increases the likelihood that an individual will cast a vote on election day. Exposure increases political knowledge, which in turn increases turnout (e.g., Delli Carpini and Keeter 1996; Verba, Schlozman, and Brady 1995) because people know where, how, and for whom to vote. Furthermore, knowledgeable people are more likely to perceive differences between candidates and thus less likely to abstain due to indifference (Palfrey and

Poole 1987). Independent of learning effects, exposure to political information on cable news and political web sites is likely to increase people's campaign interest (e.g., Bartels and Rahn 2000). Interest, in turn, affects turnout even when one controls for political knowledge (Verba, Schlozman, and Brady 1995). Entertainment fans with a cable box or Internet connection, on the other hand, will miss both the interest- and the information-based effect of broadcast news on turnout. My second hypothesis thus predicts a widening turnout gap in the current environment, as people who prefer news vote at higher rates and those with other preferences increasingly stay home from the polls.

*   *   *

Conclusion

When speculating about the political implications of new media, pundits and scholars tend to either praise the likely benefits for democracy in the digital age or dwell on the dangers. The optimists claim that the greater availability of political information will lead more people to learn more about politics and increase their involvement in the political process. The pessimists fear that new media will make people apolitical and provide mind-numbing entertainment that keeps citizens from fulfilling their democratic responsibilities. These two predictions are often presented as mutually exclusive. Things will either spiral upwards or spiral downwards; the circle is either virtuous or vicious. The analyses presented here show that both are true. New media do indeed increase political knowledge and involvement in the electoral process among some people, just as the optimists predict. Yet, the evidence supports the pessimists' scenario as well. Other people take advantage of greater choice and tune out of politics completely. Those with a preference for entertainment, once they gain access to new media, become less knowledgeable about politics and less likely to vote. People's media content preferences become the key to understanding the political implications of new media.

*   *   *

The decline in the size of news audiences over the last three decades has been identified as cause for concern by many observers who have generally interpreted it as a sign of waning political interest and a disappearing sense of civic duty. Yet changes in available content can affect news consumption and learning *even in the absence of preference changes.* People's media use may change in a modified media environment, even if their preferences (or political interest or sense of civic duty) remain constant. By this logic, the decreasing size of the news audience is not necessarily an indication of reduced political interest. Interest in politics may simply never have been as high as audience shares for evening news suggested. A combined market share for the three network newscasts of almost 90% takes on a different meaning if one considers that people had hardly any viewing alternatives. It was "politics by default" (Neuman 1996, 19), not politics by choice. Even the mediocre levels of political knowledge during the broadcast era (e.g., Delli Carpini and Keeter 1996), in other words, were partly a result of de facto restrictions of people's freedom to choose their preferred media content.

Ironically, we might have to pin our hopes of creating a reasonably evenly informed electorate on that reviled form of communication, political advertising. Large segments of the electorate in a high-choice environment do not voluntarily watch, read, or listen to political information. Their greatest chance for encounters with the political world occurs when commercials are inserted into their regular entertainment diet. And exposure to political ads can increase viewers' political knowledge (Ansolabehere and Iyengar 1995). At least for the time being, before recording services like TiVo, which automatically skip the commercial breaks, or subscriber-financed premium cable channels without advertising become more widespread, political advertising is more likely than news coverage to reach these viewers.

It might seem counterintuitive that political knowledge has decreased for a substantial portion of the electorate even though the amount of political information has multiplied and is more readily available than ever before. The share of politically uninformed people has risen since we entered the so-called "information age." Television as a medium has often been denigrated as "dumb," but, helped by the features of the broadcast environment, it may have been more successful in reaching less interested segments of the population than the "encyclopedic" Internet. In contrast to the view that politics is simply too difficult and complex to understand, this study shows that motivation, not ability, is the main obstacle that stands between an abundance of political information and a well- and evenly informed public.

When differences in political knowledge and turnout arise from inequality in the distribution of resources and skills, recommendations for how to help the information have-nots are generally uncontroversial. To the extent that knowledge and turnout gaps in the new media environment arise from voluntary consumption decisions, recommendations for how to narrow them, or whether to narrow them at all, become more contestable on normative grounds. As Downs remarked a long time ago, "[t]he loss of freedom involved in forcing people to acquire information would probably far outweigh the benefits to be gained from a better-informed electorate" (1957, 247). Even if a consensus emerged to reduce media choice for the public good, it would still be technically impossible, even temporarily, to put the genie back in the bottle. Avoiding politics will never again be as difficult as it was in the "golden age" of television.

* * *

Discussion Questions

1. Journalists in the traditional media complain that the new media operate without any strong standards of evidence, accuracy, or fair play. Do you agree with these journalists? Should all news-oriented media, whether new or old, use the same standards in determining what to broadcast or publish?

2. Which part or parts of the news media—newspapers, television, Internet, blogs, radio—do you rely on most? Which would you say you trust the most? When you use the Internet for news, do you tend to go to the Web sites connected to print and broadcast media companies?

3. Are you concerned by the findings in Prior's study? If not, why not? If so, can you think of any way to overcome the problem he has identified?

References

Ansolabehere, Stephen, and Shanto Iyengar. 1995. *Going Negative: How Attack Ads Shrink and Polarize the Electorate.* New York: Free Press.
Bartels, Larry M., and Wendy M. Rahn. 2000. "Political Attitudes in the Post-Network Era." Presented at the Annual Meeting of the American Political Science Association, Washington.
Barwise, T. P. A., S. C. Ehrenberg, and G. J. Goodhardt. 1982. "Glued to the Box. Patterns of TV Repeat-Viewing." *Journal of Communication* 32(4):22–29.
Baum, Matthew A. 2002. "Sex, Lies, and War: How Soft News Brings Foreign Policy to the Inattentive Public." *American Political Science Review* 96(1):91–110.
Baum, Matthew A., and Samuel Kernell. 1999. "Has Cable Ended the Golden Age of Presidential Television?" *American Political Science Review* 93(1):99–114.
Becker, Lee B., and Klaus Schönbach. 1989. "When Media Content Diversifies: Anticipating Audience Behaviors." In *Audience Responses to Media Diversification: Coping with Plenty*, ed. Lee B. Becker and Klaus Schönbach. Hillsdale: Lawrence Erlbaum Associates Inc., pp. 1–27.
Bowman, Gary. 1975. "Consumer Choice and Television," *Applied Economics* 7(3): 175–84.
Delli Carpini, Michael X., and Scott Keeter. 1996. *What Americans Know About Politics and Why It Matters.* New Haven: Yale University Press.
Downs, Anthony. 1957. *An Economic Theory of Democracy.* New York: Harper.
Eveland, William P., Jr., and Dietram A. Scheufele. 2000. "Connecting News Media Use with Gaps in Knowledge and Participation." *Political Communication* 17(3):215–37.
Gilens, Martin, Lynn Vavreck, and Martin Cohen. 2004. "See Spot Run: The Rise of Advertising, the Decline of News, and the American Public's Perceptions of Presidential Candidates, 1952–2000." Presented at the Annual Meeting of the Midwest Political Science Association.
Heeter, Carrie. 1985. "Program Selection with Abundance of Choice: A Process Model." *Human Communication Research* 12(1):126–52.

Keeter, Scott, and Harry Wilson. 1986. "Natural Treatment and Control Settings for Research on the Effects of Television." *Communication Research* 13(1):37–53.

Klein, Paul. 1972. "The Television Audience and Program Mediocrity." In *Mass Media and Society*, ed. Alan Wells. Palo Alto: National Press Books, pp. 76–79.

Krugman, Herbert E., and Eugene I. Hartley. 1970. "Passive Learning from Television." *Public Opinion Quarterly* 34(2):184–90.

Kwak, Nojin. 1999. "Revisiting the Knowledge Gap Hypothesis: Education, Motivation, and Media Use." *Communication Research* 26(4):385–413.

Lehmann, Donald R. 1971. "Television Show Preference: Application of a Choice Model." *Journal of Marketing Research* 8(1):47–55.

LoSciuto, Leonard A. 1972. "A National Inventory of Television Viewing Behavior." In *Television and Social Behavior, Television in Day-to-Day Life: Patterns of Use*, ed. Eli A. Rubinstein, George A. Comstock and John P. Murray. Washington: U.S. Government Printing Office, pp. 33–86.

National Telecommunications and Information Administration. 2002. *A Nation Online: How Americans Are Expanding Their Use of the Internet*. Washington: U.S. Department of Commerce.

Negroponte, Nicholas. 1995. *Being Digital*. New York: Knopf.

Neuman, W. Russell. 1976. "Patterns of Recall among Television News Viewers." *Public Opinion Quarterly* 40(1):115–23.

Neuman, W. Russell. 1996. "Political Communication Infrastructure." *The Annals of the American Academy of Political and Social Science* 546(July):9–21.

Neuman, W. Russell, Marion R. Just, and Ana N. Crigler. 1992. *Common Knowledge: News and the Construction of Political Meaning*. Chicago: University of Chicago Press.

Palfrey, Thomas R., and Keith T. Poole. 1987. "The Relationship between Information, Ideology, and Voting Behavior." *American Journal of Political Science* 31(3):511–30.

Rubin, Alan M. 1984. "Ritualized and Instrumental Television Viewing." *Journal of Communication* 34(3):67–77.

Sunstein, Cass R. 2001. *Republic. Com.* Princeton: Princeton University Press.

Verba, Sidney, Kay Lehman Schlozman, and Henry E. Brady. 1995. *Voice and Equality: Civic Voluntarism in American Politics*. Cambridge: Harvard University Press.

Webster, James G. 1984. "Cable Television's Impact on Audience for Local News." *Journalism Quarterly* 61(2):419–22.

Webster, James G., and Gregory D. Newton. 1988. "Structural Determinants of the Television News Audience." *Journal of Broadcasting & Electronic Media* 32(4):381–89.

Youn, Sug-Min. 1994. "Program Type Preference and Program Choice in a Multichannel Situation." *Journal of Broadcasting & Electronic Media* 38(4):465–75.

Zhao, Xinshu, and Steven H. Chaffee. 1995. "Campaign Advertisements Versus Television News as Sources of Political Issue Information." *Public Opinion Quarterly* 59(1):41–65.

Zukin, Cliff, and Robin Snyder. 1984. "Passive Learning: When the Media Environment Is the Message." *Public Opinion Quarterly* 48(3):629–38.

CHAPTER 10

Elections and Voting

47

"The Voice of the People: An Echo" from *The Responsible Electorate*

V. O. KEY, JR.

The votes are cast, the tallies are in, the winning candidate claims victory and a mandate to govern—the people have spoken! But just what have the people said when they cast a plurality of the votes for one candidate? Political scientist V.O. Key, Jr., argued that the voice of the people was nothing more than an echo of the cacophony and hubbub of candidates and parties scrambling for popular support. "Even the most discriminating popular judgment," wrote Key, "can reflect only ambiguity, uncertainty, or even foolishness if those are the qualities of the input into the echo chamber."

So what was the logic of the voting decision? Key argued that the effort among social scientists to develop theories for understanding the voting decision was important because of the ways political candidates and political leaders would respond to them. If research demonstrated that voters are influenced by "images and cultivation of style," rather than the "substance of politics," then that is what candidates will offer the voters. If the people receive only images and style as the input to the echo chamber, then eventually that is all they will come to expect. However, Key argues that contrary to the picture of voters held by many politicians and some academic research of his day, the "voters are not fools" that are easily manipulated by campaign tactics or who vote predictably according to the social groups they are in. Individual voters may behave oddly, he concedes, but "in the large, the electorate behaves about as rationally and responsibly as we should expect." His analysis of presidential elections convinced him that the electorate made decisions based upon a concern for public policy, the performance of government, and the personality of the candidates.

In his reflective moments even the most experienced politician senses a nagging curiosity about why people vote as they do. His power and his position depend upon the outcome of the mysterious rites we perform as opposing candidates harangue the multitudes who finally march to the polls to prolong the rule of their champion, to thrust him, ungratefully, back into the void of private life, or to raise to eminence a new tribune of the people. What kinds of appeals enable a candidate to win the favor of the great god, The People? What circumstances move voters to shift their preferences in this direction or that? What clever propaganda tactic or slogan led to this result? What mannerism of oratory or style of rhetoric produced another outcome? What band of electors rallied to this candidate to save the day for him? What policy of state attracted the devotion of another bloc of voters? What action repelled a third sector of the electorate?

The victorious candidate may claim with assurance that he has the answers to all such questions. He may regard his success as vindication of his beliefs about why voters vote as they do. And he may regard the swing of the vote to him as indubitably a response to the campaign positions he took, as an indication of the acuteness of his intuitive estimates of the mood of the people, and as a ringing manifestation of the esteem in which he is held by a discriminating public. This narcissism assumes its most repulsive form among election winners who have championed intolerance, who have stirred the passions and hatreds of people, or who have advocated causes known by decent men to be outrageous or dangerous in their long-run consequences. No functionary is more repugnant or more arrogant than the unjust man who asserts, with a color of truth, that he speaks from a pedestal of popular approbation.

It thus can be a mischievous error to assume, because a candidate wins, that a majority of the electorate shares his views on public questions, approves his past actions, or has specific expectations about his future conduct. Nor does victory establish that the candidate's campaign strategy, his image, his television style, or his fearless stand against cancer and polio turned the trick. The election returns establish only that the winner attracted a majority of the votes—assuming the existence of a modicum of rectitude in election administration. They tell us precious little about why the plurality was his.

For a glaringly obvious reason, electoral victory cannot be regarded as necessarily a popular ratification of a candidate's outlook. The voice of the people is but an echo. The output of an echo chamber bears an inevitable and invariable relation to the input. As candidates and parties clamor for attention and vie for popular support, the people's verdict can be no more than a selective reflection from among the alternatives and outlooks presented to them. Even the most discriminating popular judgment can reflect only ambiguity, uncertainty, or even foolishness if those are the qualities of the input into the echo chamber. A candidate may win despite his tactics and appeals rather than because of them. If the people can choose only from among rascals, they are certain to choose a rascal.

Scholars, though they have less at stake than do politicians, also have an abiding curiosity about why voters act as they do. In the past quarter of a century [since the 1940s] they have vastly enlarged their capacity to check the hunches born of their curiosities. The invention of the sample survey—the most widely known example of which is the Gallup poll—enabled them to make fairly trustworthy estimates of the characteristics and behaviors of large human populations. This method of mass observation revolutionized the study of politics—as well as the management of political campaigns. The new technique permitted large-scale tests to check the validity of old psychological and sociological theories of human behavior. These tests led to new hunches and new theories about voting behavior, which could, in turn, be checked and which thereby contributed to the extraordinary ferment in the social sciences during recent decades.

The studies of electoral behavior by survey methods cumulate into an imposing body of knowledge which conveys a vivid impression of the variety and subtlety of factors that enter into individual voting decisions. In their first stages in the 1930s the new electoral studies chiefly lent precision and verification to the working maxims of practicing politicians and to some of the crude theories of political speculators. Thus, sample surveys established that people did, indeed, appear to vote their pocketbooks. Yet the demonstration created its embarrassments because it also established that exceptions to the rule were numerous. Not all factory workers, for example, voted alike. How was the behavior of the deviants from "group interest" to be explained? Refinement after refinement of theory and analysis added complexity to the original simple explanation. By introducing a bit of psychological theory it could be demonstrated that factory workers with optimistic expectations tended less to be governed by pocketbook considerations than did those whose outlook was gloomy. When a little social psychology was stirred into the analysis, it could be established that identifications formed early in life, such as attachments to political parties, also reinforced or resisted the pull of the interest of the moment. A sociologist, bringing to play the conceptual tools of his trade, then could show that those factory workers who associate intimately with like-minded persons on the average vote with greater solidarity than do social isolates. Inquiries conducted with great ingenuity along many such lines have enormously broadened our knowledge of the factors associated with the responses of people to the stimuli presented to them by political campaigns.

Yet, by and large, the picture of the voter that emerges from a combination of the folklore of practical politics and the findings of the new electoral studies is not a pretty one. It is not a portrait of citizens moving to considered decision as they play their solemn role of making and unmaking governments. The older tradition from practical politics may regard the voter as an erratic and irrational fellow susceptible to manipulation by skilled humbugs. One need not live through many campaigns to observe politicians, even successful politicians, who act as though they regarded the people as manageable fools. Nor does a heroic conception of the voter emerge from the new analyses of electoral behavior. They can be added up to a conception of voting not as a civic decision but as an almost purely deterministic act. Given knowledge of certain characteristics of a voter—his occupation, his residence, his religion, his national origin, and perhaps certain of his attitudes—one can predict with a high probability the direction of his vote. The actions of persons are made to appear to be only predictable and automatic responses to campaign stimuli.

* * *

Conceptions and theories of the way voters behave do not raise solely arcane problems to be disputed among the democratic and antidemocratic theorists or questions to be settled by the elegant techniques of the analysts of electoral behavior. Rather, they touch upon profound issues at the heart of the problem of the nature and workability of systems of popular government. Obviously the perceptions of the behavior of the electorate held by political leaders, agitators, and activists condition, if they do not fix, the types of appeals politicians employ as they seek popular support. These perceptions—or theories—affect the nature of the input to the echo chamber, if we may revert to our earlier figure, and thereby control its output. They may govern, too, the kinds of actions that governments take as they look forward to the next election. If politicians perceive the electorate as responsive to father images, they will give it father images. If they see voters as most certainly responsive to nonsense, they will give them nonsense. If they see voters as susceptible to delusion, they will delude them. If they see an electorate receptive to the cold, hard realities, they will give it the cold, hard realities.

In short, theories of how voters behave acquire importance not because of their effects on voters, who may proceed blithely unaware of them. They gain significance because of their effects, both potentially and in reality, on candidates and other political leaders. If leaders believe the route to victory is by projection of images and cultivation of styles rather than by advocacy of policies to cope with the problems of the country, they will project images and cultivate styles to the neglect of the substance of politics. They will abdicate their prime function in a democratic system, which amounts, in essence, to the assumption of the risk of trying to persuade us to lift ourselves by our bootstraps.

Among the literary experts on politics there are those who contend that, because of the development of tricks for the manipulation of the masses, practices of political leadership in the management of voters have moved far toward the conversion of election campaigns into obscene parodies of the models set up by democratic idealists. They point to the good old days when politicians were deep thinkers, eloquent orators, and farsighted statesmen. Such estimates of the course of change in social institutions must be regarded with reserve. They may be only manifestations of the inverted optimism of aged and melancholy men who, estopped from hope for the future, see in the past a satisfaction of their yearning for greatness in our political life.

Whatever the trends may have been, the perceptions that leadership elements of democracies hold of the modes of response of the electorate must always be a matter of fundamental significance. Those perceptions determine the nature of the voice of the people, for they determine the character of the input into the echo chamber. While the output may be governed by the nature of the input, over the longer run the properties of the echo chamber may themselves be altered. Fed a steady diet of buncombe [bunkum], the people may come to expect and to respond with highest predictability to buncombe. And those leaders most skilled in the propagation of buncombe may gain lasting advantage in the recurring struggles for popular favor.

The perverse and unorthodox argument of this little book is that voters are not fools. To be sure, many individual voters act in odd ways indeed; yet in the large the electorate behaves about as rationally and responsibly as we should expect, given the clarity of the alternatives presented to it and the character of the information available to it. In American presidential campaigns of recent decades the portrait of the American electorate that develops from the data is not one of an electorate straitjacketed by social determinants or moved by subconscious urges triggered by devilishly skillful propagandists. It is rather one of an electorate moved by concern about central and relevant questions of public policy, of governmental performance, and of executive personality. Propositions so uncompromisingly stated inevitably represent overstatements. Yet to the extent that they can be shown to resemble the reality, they are propositions of basic importance for both the theory and the practice of democracy.

To check the validity of this broad interpretation of the behavior of voters, attention will center on the movements of voters across party lines as they reacted to the issues, events, and candidates of presidential campaigns between 1936 and 1960. Some Democratic voters of one election turned Republican at the next; others stood pat. Some Republicans of one presidential season voted Democratic four years later; others remained loyal Republicans. What motivated these shifts, sometimes large and sometimes small, in voter affection? How did the standpatters differ from the switchers? What led them to stand firmly by their party preference of four years earlier? Were these actions governed by images, moods, and other irrelevancies; or were they expressions of judgments about the sorts of questions that, hopefully, voters will weigh as they responsibly cast their ballots? On these matters evidence is available that is impressive in volume, if not always so complete or so precisely relevant as hindsight would wish. If one perseveres through the analysis of this extensive body of information, the proposition that the voter is not so irrational a fellow after all may become credible.

DISCUSSION QUESTIONS

1. When you go into the voting booth, how do you decide whom to vote for? Is your decision process affected by the nature of the political campaign that has just been completed?

2. Does the 2004 presidential election support Key's view of the electoral process?

48

"Power to the Voters"

RICHARD D. PARKER

We live in a republic, not a pure democracy. That is, rather than have citizens make direct choices on questions of public policy, we delegate that responsibility to elected officials. They make decisions on our behalf, and we exercise control over them through periodic elections. To its supporters, one advantage of a republic is that it can thwart popular ideas that might be built on passionate impulses and reactions rather than thoughtful responses to public problems. Critics of this type of system, though they do not challenge its fundamental legitimacy, argue for more direct public participation in the policy process. This might include allowing voters to indicate their preference for specific public policies on election day, as is allowed in many states via the initiative and referendum processes. Or it might mean a system where citizens, perhaps through the Internet, vote for public policies on an ongoing basis.

Richard Parker falls squarely into what we might call the populist camp. In his view, direct public participation has many public benefits: it emphasizes the equality of voters (rather than the distinction between the mass electorate and political elites); it transcends the traditional left-right orientation of most political debate; and has a positive impact on communities. Contemporary politics, in his view, focuses on minimizing direct participation by the public; elites view public participation as a good thing only under limited conditions. He calls for a "revitalization through democracy," *i.e., using existing democratic processes and channels to reinvigorate participation. His solution calls for a dramatic effort to increase voting turnout: this is, in his view, the only way to create political equality. To accomplish this goal, Parker wants to encourage third parties, impose term limits, and support the ballot initiatives process. The latter two would require constitutional amendments and the first might, depending on the remedy proposed.*

A theme that runs through this article is one of skepticism about the idea of political professionalism. The political process, in Parker's view, should be less friendly to incumbents and public officials in general: "[N]ow is the time to start treating [officials] . . . with a somewhat exaggerated disrespect." On the other hand, Parker has great faith in the virtue of mass participation.

I am, or try to be, a populist democrat. For decades, populism was largely invisible, barely a straw man, in the discourse of the law schools. Well-meaning ideologues of the governing class were accustomed to prescribe—for the people—policies and institutional processes based on an assumption that government of and by the people is—obviously and of course—not to be trusted. Now, that is changing. Populism, today, is a recognized position in legal academia. The ideal is now embraced, its possible implications explored, by a growing band.[1]

Its meaning is, to say the the least, contested. At a minimum, though, my premise is that populism should involve taking popular sovereignty more seriously than has been the practice in legal discourse. More particularly, it ought to involve a renewed emphasis on the value of political equality which—in negotiation with values of political freedom and political community—constitutes the democratic idea. From this it follows that populism ought to involve renewed respect for majority rule as generally the fairest practical guarantor of political equality among persons as well as the most practical way of approximating popular sovereignty over time.

If populism is imagined, above all, in terms of popular sovereignty and political equality, it may acquire a bite that cuts across and shakes up stultified left/right lines of "debate." By the same token, if notions of popular sovereignty and political equality are injected with a populist sensibility—an acceptance and, more, an embrace of ordinariness: ranging from our own ordinariness (and so our deep equality) to the ordinariness of "the people"[2]—these ideas may recover from their torpor of several long decades and acquire, at last, new critical vigor.

What such a re-orientation yields is a back-to-basics approach to the revitalization of democracy. Let me sketch, in three steps, a few fundamental features of this approach.

Mass Political Participation: A Good in Itself

The most potent rationalizations for "governance" of the masses by enlightened elites are, nowadays, packaged as paeans to democracy. Against a backdrop of perfectionist premises, they insist that participation by the mass of real people in the real world of politics has value *only* if other conditions are met—only if reality is radically transformed in one way or another. They deplore the inadequacy (even the "corruption") of democracy as we know it. And they conclude, regretfully of course, that the world is not yet safe for democracy. This line of argument must be rejected at the outset as a barrier, rather than a roadmap, to democratic revitalization.

The most transparently naked rationalization focuses on *outcomes* of political processes. The political empowerment of ordinary people is good, so the argument goes, only insofar as its likely outcomes are good. Today, the argument continues, the masses tend to have "bad values" or, at the very least, a mistaken understanding of their own interests. Hence, bad outcomes. There are, sad to say, some who would call themselves populists who take this line. The assumption of these rationalizers of political elitism is that they know better and, so, that they and their ilk should "lead"—be the "spokesmen" or "advocates" for—ordinary people. For them, political equality is but an "idealistic" fantasy—to be used, if at all, as a cynical smoke screen.

A somewhat more subtle version of the argument focuses on the *quality* of political processes. The participation of the masses in politics is good, it asserts, only so long as the political process is otherwise a good one. Today, it continues, our political process is utterly spoiled—poisoned by a few who, with clever thirty second spots, play on the ignorance, shortsightedness and emotions of the many. Thus, it concludes, the political influence of the many may have to be restricted. Again, there are self-styled populists who make this argument. The assumption is that ordinary people are incompetent dupes in need of enlightened cosseting. Again, political equality is imagined as an "ideal" too fine to flourish as a practice—much less motivate and enable a challenge, even if a messy one, to the few by the many—in the real world.

The most sophisticated version of the argument focuses on *preconditions* of democracy. Mass political participation is good, it claims, only after some level of social and economic empowerment, enlightenment and equality has first been achieved for everyone. Again, there are "populists" who take this line. But at bottom, despite the apparent sophistication, it repeats the other versions of the argument. For it assumes that ordinary people who suffer deprivation and inequality need help from their betters before acting politically on their own. It sees them as victims. It presupposes that they cannot or will not—if and as they choose—help themselves.

In place of these pseudo-democratic rationalizations of elite rule, movement toward a revitalization of democracy requires a different, more positive as well as more realistic, attitude toward mass participation, on a basis of political equality, in democratic rule. It requires an appreciation of such participation in politics as a good in itself. But how so?

The answer, I think, is not to invoke the inherent value of self-government, of autonomy. For in politics there are, after all, going to be winners and losers. The losers do not govern themselves in the same way the winners do. They are governed, instead, by the winners, at least for a time, to a degree and in some respects. The argument from self-government is, as we know, too easily turned by losers in the democratic arena into yet another claim for vindication—and, in the end, a claim for the government of everyone—by an elite of paternalistic protectors.

The answer, rather, lies in an old idea of personal and public hygiene. The idea is that active engagement in political life—win or lose—is good for you and for your community.[3] It is good in the same way that an experience of vitality—regularly summoning and expressing and disciplining your energy (successfully or not) toward a chosen end—is good for you. In an old-fashioned sense, it is good for your "constitution." It is an important way in which you constitute yourself. As participants in the mid-century civil rights movement understood (and as some "civil rights leaders" of the *fin de siècle* seem to have forgotten) political self-help is an indispensable (though not, of course, the exclusive) route to an achievement of respect as well as self-respect.

To be sure, politics can be boring, perverse, even depressing. But physical exercise, too, is often painful. And in a regime of competition among political—if not (yet) social and economic—equals, the gain resulting from the pain is likely all the greater.

Should it be surprising that the prescription for a revitalization of democracy is a promise of revitalization *through* democracy?

The Apex of Political Equality: One Person, One Vote

No one can say, nowadays, that cultural and political elites are un-interested in political equality. In fact, one huge sector of the establishment—the one that nods when it reads editorials in *The New York Times*—talks about no topic more passionately than it does about this one. The focus of its concern, however, is skewed.

The focus is, of course, on equality in the realm of political campaign speech. Indeed, campaign finance reform has surpassed even "minority" rights as *the* cause of the establishment sector I have in mind. But while I support many reform proposals—public financing of campaigns, free television time for candidates, an abolition of "soft money"—I believe we all should be skeptical of claims that such reform would go far toward a goal of political equality.

There is, first, the problem of political advertising "independent" of official campaign organizations.[4] If (as I am convinced) the Supreme Court will never allow a closing of this "loophole"—if wealthy people remain free to spend as much as they want "independently" of the candidate they promote—then it is fatuous to suppose that other reforms will produce anything like political equality in campaign speech. If, on the other hand, "independent" expenditures are somehow shut down—so that the political marketplace is left exclusively to limited spending by campaign organizations—the result would be political *in*equality of another kind. For, then, electoral discourse would be controlled by an even *more* concentrated group: the *coterie* of official campaign managers. Establishment advocates of campaign finance reform tend not to see this as a problem. For their goal is orderly equality among officials of campaign organizations—not among citizens.[5] Nevertheless, as a practical matter, the issue is whether campaign advertising will be dominated by a larger, more fluid and chaotic elite—or a smaller, more tightly organized one, as many reform advocates prefer.

Second, there is the matter of the "free press" exception for media corporations.[6] Plainly, the Court would not permit a limitation (much less a suppression) of speech about candidates by the owners and managers of print and electronic media. They are imagined as "independent" by definition. Indeed, many establishment advocates of campaign finance reform seem surprised that rich people who own newspapers might be regarded as rich people. Their horror at a mixing of "money and politics" tends to disappear abruptly when the money belongs to the owners of *The New York Times*. Nonetheless, so long as the wealthy are free to buy—and then, bluntly or subtly, to support candidates through—such media, participation in campaign debate before a mass audience will be anything but equal.

The problem with focusing our concern about political equality on campaign finance reform is not just the barrier posed by the Supreme Court. Nor is it just that reformers find themselves aspiring to little more than a rearrangement of the elite domination of campaign discourse. There are two deeper problems: On one hand, anything like real equality of *effective* participation in political debate is a chimera. Given the protean nature of "speech," the most that can be imagined (if not hoped for) is a very, very rough equality of opportunity. On the other hand, the assumption underlying the focus on the financing of political advertising is typically an assumption of political inequality—that the mass of ordinary people are passive and rather incompetent consumers (rather than actors), easily duped or swayed (rather than appropriately persuaded) by competing waves of thirty-second spots. If we want to vindicate political equality—as we should if we want to revitalize democracy—we ought to focus, instead, on something that does not, from the very outset, tend to compromise or contradict our goal.

We should focus on the vote. Taking the vote, rather than speech, as the key resource for participation in democratic politics—seeking to promote its use and the effect of using it—is the best way to take political equality seriously. For a focus on voting enables us to begin with a standard of equality that is both strong and established in law: one person, one vote. What's more, equal participation in voting is a practical goal. Not everyone can speak at once or as effectively as everyone else. But everyone can vote at once. And every vote counts as much as every other. Most important, the aspiration to enhance the value of the vote is grounded in a respect for ordinary people—as political actors, indeed as rulers—that is unambiguous.

Strangely, the vote seems now to be out of favor. Across the conventional political spectrum, many denigrate the value of voting and the one person, one vote standard. Some claim voting is irrational. Others purvey a narcissistic notion of "deliberative" democracy to eclipse what they imagine as the tawdry marking of a ballot. Still others claim that "communities"—rather than shifting collections or coalitions of individuals—should somehow express themselves in politics. On the surface, what unites them all is a tendency to idealize democracy and, so, to find its reality disappointing. But what accounts for this idealizing tendency? It is, I think, fear—fear of losing and of trying to win, fear of ordinary people and of their own ordinariness. To them, I would say: Get over it. Get into voting. It will be good for you. And for others as well.

Rock the Vote

How, then, might democracy be revitalized by promoting the use and effect of the vote? The central scandal of American democracy, from my populist point of view, is that most people do not cast a ballot in most elections. To promote use of the vote, the obvious strategy is to promote its effect. If something really significant seems to be at stake, people are more likely to take part. Even if no one believes her own vote will make the difference, she will see value—as have so many, from soldiers to protestors—in doing her part. For the moment, all I can do is gesture toward a few ways of enhancing the effect—and so the value, and so the use—of the vote. With respect to each, I want to encourage not only law reform, but also political action.

First of all, in candidate elections the voters must be presented with a real contest. In 2000, only about 35 seats in the U.S. House of Representatives are said to be in play. In a great many districts, the incumbent faces no (or only nominal) opposition. In other districts—and in many other elections up to and including presidential elections—there frequently seems not much more than a dime's (or perhaps a dollar's) worth of difference between the candidates. Hardly a motivation to cast a ballot.

For this condition, the legal remedy need not go so far as instituting systems of proportional representation. (Such systems tend to funnel power to party elites and, so, should be rejected by populists.) But barriers to entry—from ballot qualification requirements to exclusions from debates[7]—facing "minor" party candidates surely must be lowered. Once a number of "minor" parties gain a foothold, run-off elections should be held. In the run-offs, the two highest vote-getters would be moved to address issues of concern to the others while, at the same time, the principle of popular majority rule would be vindicated. At the same time, the system for drawing legislative districts needs to be transformed. Districting should be taken from the hands of incumbent-friendly politicians and transferred to incumbent-unfriendly commissions. The commissions should be given one overriding instruction: draw and re-draw district lines so as to promote hotly contested elections in as many as possible.

In support of such legal remedies, a political one may now be underway. For the bulk of "alienated" non-voters may now be so huge as to have reached a critical mass. Politicians are more and more likely to take the opportunity to offer the "something different" these non-voters seem to want. In the last decade, candidates ranging from Ross Perot to Jesse Ventura to John McCain to Ralph Nader have done just that and, so, have begun to shake up political business-as-usual. The lesson for democratic populists is: When in doubt, support a maverick.

Second, the suffocating smugness of officialdom must be dispelled. In the last few decades, this pathological condition has become acute. Whether they be elected officials pompously touting "Burkean" notions of representation or civil servants claiming indispensable experience and expertise or judges relying on imagined wisdom and independence, these self-important middlemen—ensconced between voters and lawmaking—now are an incubus, cabining and repressing the political energy essential to popular sovereignty at the ballot box.

The primary legal remedy should be term limits. With respect to elected officials, term limits are an important supplement to the promotion of contested elections. But with respect to unelected officials, they are even more vital. If civil servants and judges (judges!) were limited to no more than fifteen years in office, government in all its nooks and crannies would, to a significant degree, be cracked open to the influence of the voters in periodic elections.

The political remedy, in this case, is largely attitudinal. We must stop acting as the enablers of the inflated arrogance of officialdom. For too long, we have treated officials with exaggerated respect. Now, it is time to start treating them—as they were treated in the early decades of our history—with a somewhat exaggerated disrespect. As reformers of bygone days knew well, regularly exposing the misdeeds, the incompetence, the hypocrisy of officials is not cynicism or nihilism; it is realism, the tonic of democratic lawmaking. (And that goes for lazy Justices and lying Presidents.)

The third and most important way of enhancing the effect, and so the use, of the vote is to eliminate the middlemen entirely. I am referring, of course, to direct democracy, lawmaking by initiative and referendum. What is at stake at the ballot box is, there, about as clear and immediate as can be. Popular support for direct democratic lawmaking, in states that allow it, is strong and consistent. So, however, is elite opposition to it.[8] Today, direct democracy is at a turning point.

The pressing legal challenge, right now, is to resist growing efforts to hem in and hobble the initiative and referendum. That will involve challenges to new infringements on the right to petition, new ballot qualification requirements, and new "interpretations" of arcane rules like the "single subject" standard. Eventually, it is likely also to involve defense against federal constitutional arguments, particularly the claim that direct democracy violates the "republican form of government" clause.[9] (In the 1950s and 1960s, it was exclusively conservatives who insisted that "America is a republic, not a democracy." Now, it is mostly progressives.) While turning back these anti-democratic thrusts, the time is ripe to go on the offensive as well—mending (rather than ending) processes by which proposals for popular lawmaking are drafted and summarized, then extending the initiative and referendum to all fifty states and even experimenting (at first) with "advisory" or "instructive" initiatives and referenda at the federal level.

Politically, beyond exposing elitist assumptions behind the wave of assault on direct democracy, I have one main suggestion: If there is an initiative or referendum proposal that you don't like, oppose it actively. And if it is passed, don't throw up your hands and go to the courts or the newspapers to pontificate about "republican" government. Instead, launch your own initiative campaign to repeal the popularly made law you don't like or to enact one you do like.

My bottom line is this: Democracy will be revitalized when more and more and then more of us give it a try.

DISCUSSION QUESTIONS

1. Do you agree with Parker's argument that increased mass participation is, by definition, a good thing? Is it "elitist" to disagree with him?

2. Is Parker correct in arguing that third parties, term limits, referenda, and increased competitiveness in elections would spur more participation? What positive (and negative) consequences might arise under his proposals?

3. What might the Framers be likely to say about Parker's ideas? Does it matter?

NOTES

1. *See, e.g.,* Akhil Reed Amar & Alan Hirsch, *For the People: What the Constitution Really Says About Your Rights* (1998); Richard D. Parker, *"Here, the People Rule": A Constitutional Populist Manifesto* (1994); Mark V. Tushnet, *Taking the Constitution away from the Courts* (1999); J. M. Balkin, "Populism and Progressivism as Constitutional Categories," 104 Yale L.J. 1935 (1995).
2. *See generally* James Agee & Walker Evans, *Let Us Now Praise Famous Men* (1941); Parker, *supra* note 1; *cf.* Lionel Trilling, *The Liberal Imagination: Essays on Literature and Society* 88 (1950) ("We who are liberal and progressive know that the poor are our equals in every sense except that of being equal to us.").
3. *See* Albert Camus, *The Plague* (1948); *cf.* Hannah Arendt, *The Human Condition,* 22–78 (1958).
4. *See* Buckley v. Valeo, 424 U.S. 1, 39–59 (1976).
5. *See* Richard D. Parker, "Taking Politics Personally," 12 Cardozo Stud. L. & Literature 103, 112 (2000).
6. *See* Austin v. Michigan State Chamber of Commerce, 494 U.S. 652, 668 (1990). The Court opined:

The media exception ensures that [a campaign finance law] does not hinder or prevent the institutional press from reporting on, and publishing editorials about, newsworthy events. A valid distinction thus exists between corporations that are part of the media industry and other corporations that are not involved in the regular business of imparting news to the public. Although the press' unique societal role may not entitle the press to greater protection under the Constitution, it does provide a compelling reason for the State to exempt media corporations from the scope of political expenditure limitations.

Id. (citations omitted).

7. *See, e.g.,* Munro v. Socialist Workers Party, 479 U.S. 189 (1986) (upholding state statute requiring a minor party candidate to get at least 1% of the total votes cast in the primary to be placed on the general election ballot); Forbes v. Arkansas Educ. Television Communication Network Found, 22 F.3d 1423, 1426 (1994) (upholding the right of a public television station to exclude an independent candidate for Congress from participation in a debate even though "[h]e had obtained enough signatures to qualify for the ballot under state law").

8. *See, e.g.,* David S. Broder, *Democracy Derailed: Initiative Campaigns and the Power of Money* (2000).

9. *See, e.g.,* Hans A. Linde, "On Reconstituting 'Republican Government,'" 19 Okla. City U. L. Rev. 193, 199–201 (1994); Hans A. Linde, "When Initiative Lawmaking Is Not 'Republican Government': The Campaign Against Homosexuality," 72 Or. L. Rev. 19 (1993).

49

"The Unpolitical Animal: How Political Science Understands Voters"

Louis Menand

How well do Americans measure up to the ideal of highly informed, engaged, at-tentive, involved citizens? V. O. Key argued that Americans, on the whole, do reasonably well in making sound collective judgments. Writing around the same time as Key, another political scientist, Philip Converse, reached a gloomier con-clusion. Most Americans couldn't be "ideal" citizens because most had minimal and inconsistent political belief systems. To a large part, he concluded, Ameri-cans had a lot of top-of-the-head opinions that had no strong connection to a set of principles. Louis Menand revisits the question addressed by V. O. Key: do elections represent the will of the people? Menand reviews Converse's conclu-sions and then discusses three theories that attempt to make some sense of Amer-icans' failure to behave as ideal citizens. One theory declares that elections are more or less random events in which a large bloc of voters responds to "slogans, misinformation, 'fire alarms' (sensational news), 'October surprises' (last-minute sensational news), random personal associations, and 'gotchas.' " An-other theory posits that voter decisions are guided simply by random events and information, but by elite opinion. Elites do understand the issues and work within ideological frameworks and they find ways to pitch ideas to voters so they gain a governing majority. Elections are thus primarily about the interests and beliefs of rival elite factions. The third theory in part rescues the voter from these unflattering portraits. Here, voters use information shortcuts, especially but not only political party labels, to render verdicts that are substantively meaningful. "People use shortcuts—the social-scientific term is 'heuristics'—to reach judg-ments about political candidates, and, on the whole, these shortcuts are as good as the long and winding road of reading party platforms, listening to candidate debates, and all the other elements of civic duty." Menand concludes that voter decisions may be based on shortcuts that make sense to them—like which candi-date is more optimistic—rather than the weighing and balancing of principles and policy positions that ideologues would prefer.

In every Presidential-election year, there are news stories about unde-cided voters, people who say that they are perplexed about which can-didate's positions make the most sense. They tell reporters things like "I'd like to know more about Bush's plan for education," or "I'm worried that Kerry's ideas about Social Security don't add up." They say that they are thinking about issues like "trust," and whether the candidate cares about people like them. To voters who identify strongly with a political party, the undecided voter is almost an alien life form. For them, a vote for Bush is a vote for a whole philosophy of governance and a vote for Kerry is a vote for a distinctly different philosophy. The difference is obvious to them, and they don't understand how others can't see it, or can decide whom to vote for on the basis of a candidate's personal traits or whether his or her position on a particular issue "makes sense." To an undecided voter, on the other hand, the person who always votes for the Democrat or the Republican, no matter what, must seem like a dangerous fanatic. Which voter is behaving more rationally and responsibly?

If you look to the political professionals, the people whose job it is to know what makes the fish bite, it is clear that, in their view, political philosophy is not the fattest worm. *Winning Elections: Political Campaign Management, Strategy & Tactics* (M. Evans; $49.95) is a collection of articles drawn from the pages of *Campaigns & Elections: The Magazine for People in Politics*. The advice to the political professionals is: Don't assume that your candidate's positions are going to make the difference. "In a competitive political climate," as one article explains, "informed citizens may vote for a candidate based on issues. However, uninformed or undecided voters will often choose the candidate whose name and packaging are most memorable. To make sure your candidate has that 'top-of-mind' voter awareness, a powerful logo is the best place to start." You want to present your candidate in language that voters will understand. They understand colors. "Blue is a positive color for men, signaling authority and control," another article advises. "But it's a negative color for women, who perceive it as distant, cold and aloof. Red is a warm, sentimental color for women—and a sign of danger or anger to men. If you use the wrong colors to the wrong audience, you're sending a mixed message."

It can't be the case, though, that electoral outcomes turn on things like the color of the buttons. Can it? When citizens stand in the privacy of the booth and contemplate the list of those who bid to serve, do they really think, That's the guy with the red logo. A lot of anger there. I'll take my chances with the other one? In Civics 101, the model voter is a citizen vested with the ability to understand the consequences of his or her choice; when these individual rational choices are added up, we know the will of the people. How accurate is this picture?

Skepticism about the competence of the masses to govern themselves is as old as mass self-government. Even so, when that competence began to be measured statistically, around the end of the Second World War, the numbers startled almost everyone. The data were interpreted most powerfully by the political scientist Philip Converse, in an article on "The Nature of Belief Systems in Mass Publics," published in 1964. Forty years later, Converse's conclusions are still the bones at which the science of voting behavior picks.

Converse claimed that only around ten per cent of the public has what can be called, even generously, a political belief system. He named these people "ideologues," by which he meant not that they are fanatics but that they have a reasonable grasp of "what goes with what"—of how a set of opinions adds up to a coherent political philosophy. Non-ideologues may use terms like "liberal" and "conservative," but Converse thought that they basically don't know what they're talking about, and that their beliefs are characterized by what he termed a lack of "constraint": they can't see how one opinion (that taxes should be lower, for example) logically ought to rule out other opinions (such as the belief that there should be more government programs). About forty-two per cent of voters, according to Converse's interpretation of surveys of the 1956 electorate, vote on the basis not of ideology but of perceived self-interest. The rest form political preferences either from their sense of whether times are good or bad (about twenty-five per cent) or from factors that have no discernible "issue content" whatever. Converse put twenty-two per cent of the electorate in this last category. In other words, about twice as many people have no political views as have a coherent political belief system.

Just because someone's opinions don't square with what a political scientist recognizes as a political ideology doesn't mean that those opinions aren't coherent by the lights of some more personal system of beliefs. But Converse found reason to doubt this possibility. When pollsters ask people for their opinion about an issue, people generally feel obliged to have one. Their answer is duly recorded, and it becomes a datum in a report on "public opinion." But, after analyzing the results of surveys conducted over time, in which people tended to give different and randomly inconsistent answers to the same questions, Converse concluded that "very substantial portions of the public" hold opinions that are essentially meaningless—off-the-top-of-the-head responses to questions they have never thought about, derived from no underlying set of principles. These people might as well base their political choices on the weather. And, in fact, many of them do.

Findings about the influence of the weather on voter behavior are among the many surveys and studies that confirm Converse's sense of the inattention of the American electorate. In election years from 1952 to 2000, when people were asked whether they cared who won the Presidential election, between twenty-two and forty-four per cent answered "don't care" or "don't know." In 2000, eighteen per cent said that they decided which Presidential candidate to vote for only in the last two weeks of the campaign; five per cent, enough to swing most elections, decided the day they voted.

Seventy per cent of Americans cannot name their senators or their congressman. Forty-nine per cent believe that the President has the power to suspend the Constitution. Only about thirty per cent name an issue when they explain why they voted the way they did, and only a fifth hold consistent opinions on issues over time. Rephrasing poll questions reveals that many people don't understand the issues that they have just offered an opinion on. According to polls conducted in 1987 and 1989, for example, between twenty and twenty-five per cent of the public thinks that too little is being spent on welfare, and between sixty-three and sixty-five per cent feels that too little is being spent on assistance to the poor. And voters apparently do punish politicians for acts of God. In a paper written in 2004, the Princeton political scientists Christopher Achen and Larry Bartels estimate that "2.8 million people voted against Al Gore in 2000 because their states were too dry or too wet" as a consequence of that year's weather patterns. Achen and Bartels think that these voters cost Gore seven states, any one of which would have given him the election.

All political systems make their claim to legitimacy by some theory, whether it's the divine right of kings or the iron law of history. Divine rights and iron laws are not subject to empirical confirmation, which is one reason that democracy's claims have always seemed superior. What polls and surveys suggest, though, is that the belief that elections express the true preferences of the people may be nearly as imaginary. When you move downward through what Converse called the public's "belief strata," candidates are quickly separated from ideology and issues, and they become attached, in voters' minds, to idiosyncratic clusters of ideas and attitudes. The most widely known fact about George H. W. Bush in the 1992 election was that he hated broccoli. Eighty-six per cent of likely voters in that election knew that the Bushes' dog's name was Millie; only fifteen per cent knew that Bush and Clinton both favored the death penalty. It's not that people know nothing. It's just that politics is not what they know.

In the face of this evidence, three theories have arisen. The first is that electoral outcomes, as far as "the will of the people" is concerned, are essentially arbitrary. The fraction of the electorate that responds to substantive political arguments is hugely outweighed by the fraction that responds to slogans, misinformation, "fire alarms" (sensational news), "October surprises" (last-minute sensational news), random personal associations, and "gotchas." Even when people think that they are thinking in political terms, even when they believe that they are analyzing candidates on the basis of their positions on issues, they are usually operating behind a veil of political ignorance. They simply don't understand, as a practical matter, what it means to be "fiscally conservative," or to have "faith in the private sector," or to pursue an "interventionist foreign policy." They can't hook up positions with policies. From the point of view of democratic theory, American political history is just a random walk through a series of electoral options. Some years, things turn up red; some years, they turn up blue.

A second theory is that although people may not be working with a full deck of information and beliefs, their preferences are dictated by something, and that something is elite opinion. Political campaigns, on this theory, are essentially struggles among the elite, the fraction of a fraction of voters who have the knowledge and the ideological chops to understand the substantive differences between the candidates and to argue their policy implications. These voters communicate their preferences to the rest of the electorate by various cues, low-content phrases and images (warm colors, for instance) to which voters can relate, and these cues determine the outcome of the race. Democracies are really oligarchies with a populist face.

The third theory of democratic politics is the theory that the cues to which most voters respond are, in fact, adequate bases on which to form political preferences. People use shortcuts—the social-scientific term is "heuristics"—to reach judgments about political candidates, and, on the whole, these shortcuts are as good as the long and winding road of reading party platforms, listening to candidate debates, and all the other elements of civic duty. Voters use what Samuel Popkin, one of the proponents of this third theory, calls "low-information rationality"—in other words, gut reasoning—to reach political decisions; and this intuitive form of judgment proves a good enough substitute for its high-information counterpart in reflecting what people want.

An analogy (though one that Popkin is careful to dissociate himself from) would be to buying an expensive item like a house or a stereo system. A tiny fraction of consumers has the knowledge to discriminate among the entire range of available stereo components, and to make an informed choice based on assessments of cost and performance. Most of us rely on the advice of two or three friends who have recently made serious stereo-system purchases, possibly some online screen shopping, and the pitch of the salesman at J&R Music World. We eyeball the product, associate idiosyncratically with the brand name, and choose from the gut. When we ask "experts" for their wisdom, mostly we are hoping for an "objective" ratification of our instinctive desire to buy the coolest-looking stuff. Usually, we're O.K. Our tacit calculation is that the marginal utility of more research is smaller than the benefit of immediate ownership.

On the theory of heuristics, it's roughly the same with candidates: voters don't have the time or the inclination to assess them in depth, so they rely on the advice of experts—television commentators, political activists, Uncle Charlie—combined with their own hunches, to reach a decision. Usually (they feel), they're O.K. If they had spent the time needed for a top-to-toe vetting, they would probably not have chosen differently. Some voters might get it wrong in one direction, choosing the liberal candidate when they in fact preferred a conservative one, but their error is cancelled out by the voters who mistakenly choose the conservative. The will of the people may not be terribly articulate, but it comes out in the wash.

This theory is the most attractive of the three, since it does the most to salvage democratic values from the electoral wreckage Converse described. It gives the mass of voters credit for their decisions by suggesting not only that they can interpret the cues given by the campaigns and the elite opinion-makers but that the other heuristics they use—the candidate seems likable, times are not as good as they were—are actually defensible replacements for informed, logical reasoning. Popkin begins his well-regarded book on the subject, *The Reasoning Voter*, with an example from Gerald Ford's primary campaign against Ronald Reagan in 1976. Visiting a Mexican-American community in Texas, Ford (never a gaffe-free politician) made the mistake of trying to eat a tamale with the corn husk, in which it is traditionally served, still on it. This ethnic misprision made the papers, and when he was asked, after losing to Jimmy Carter in the general election, what the lesson of his defeat was, Ford answered, "Always shuck your tamales." Popkin argues that although familiarity with Mexican-American cuisine is not a prerequisite for favoring policies friendly to Mexican-Americans, Mexican-Americans were justified in concluding that a man who did not know how to eat a tamale was not a man predisposed to put their needs high on his list. The reasoning is illogical: Ford was not running for chef, and it was possible to extrapolate, from his positions, the real difference it would make for Mexican-Americans if he were President rather than Reagan or Carter. But Mexican-Americans, and their sympathizers, felt "in their gut" that Ford was not their man, and that was enough.

The principal shortcut that people use in deciding which candidates to vote for is, of course, the political party. The party is the ultimate Uncle Charlie in American politics. Even elite voters use it when they are confronted, in the voting booth, with candidates whose names they have never seen before. There is nothing in the Constitution requiring candidates to be listed on the ballot with their party affiliations, and, if you think about it, the custom of doing so is vaguely undemocratic. It makes elections a monopoly of the major parties, by giving their candidates an enormous advantage—the advantage of an endorsement right there on the ballot—over everyone else who runs. It is easy to imagine a constitutional challenge to the practice of identifying candidates by party, but it is also easy to imagine how wild the effects would be if voters were confronted by a simple list of names with no identifying tags. Every election would be like an election for student-body president: pure name recognition.

Any time information is lacking or uncertain, a shortcut is generally better than nothing. But the shortcut itself is not a faster way of doing the math; it's a way of skipping the math altogether. My hunch that the coolest-looking stereo component is the best value simply does not reflect an intuitive grasp of electronics. My interest in a stereo is best served if I choose the finest sound for the money, as my interest in an election is best served if I choose the candidate whose policies are most likely to benefit me or the people I care about. But almost no one calculates in so abstract a fashion. Even voters who supported Michael Dukakis in 1988 agreed that he looked ridiculous wearing a weird helmet when he went for a ride in a tank, and a lot of those people felt that, taken together with other evidence of his manner and style of self-expression, the image was not irrelevant to the substance of his campaign. George H. W. Bush underwent a similar moment in 1992, when he was caught showing astonishment at the existence of scanners at supermarket checkout counters. Ideologues opposed to Bush were pleased to propose this as what psychologists call a "fast and frugal" means of assessing the likely effects of his economic policies.

When political scientists interpret these seat-of-the-pants responses as signs that voters are choosing rationally, and that representative government therefore really does reflect the will of the people, they are, in effect, making a heuristic of heuristics. They are not doing the math. Doing the math would mean demonstrating that the voters' intuitive judgments are roughly what they would get if they analyzed the likely effects of candidates' policies, and this is a difficult calculation to perform. One shortcut that voters take, and that generally receives approval from the elite, is pocketbook voting. If they are feeling flush, they vote for the incumbent; if they are feeling strapped, they vote for a change. But, as Larry Bartels, the co-author of the paper on Gore and the weather, has pointed out, pocketbook voting would be rational only if it could be shown that replacing the incumbent did lead, on average, to better economic times. Without such a demonstration, a vote based on the condition of one's pocketbook is no more rational than a vote based on the condition of one's lawn. It's a hunch.

Bartels has also found that when people do focus on specific policies they are often unable to distinguish their own interests. His work, which he summed up in a recent article for *The American Prospect*, concerned public opinion about the estate tax. When people are asked whether they favor Bush's policy of repealing the estate tax, two-thirds say yes—even though the estate tax affects only the wealthiest one or two per cent of the population. Ninety-eight per cent of Americans do not leave estates large enough for the tax to kick in. But people have some notion—Bartels refers to it as "unenlightened self-interest"—that they will be better off if the tax is repealed. What is most remarkable about this opinion is that it is unconstrained by other beliefs. Repeal is supported by sixty-six per cent of people who believe that the income gap between the richest and the poorest Americans has increased in recent decades, and that this is a bad thing. And it's supported by sixty-eight per cent of people who say that the rich pay too little in taxes. Most Americans simply do not make a connection between tax policy and the overall economic condition of the country. Whatever heuristic they are using, it is definitely not doing the math for them. This helps make sense of the fact that the world's greatest democracy has an electorate that continually "chooses" to transfer more and more wealth to a smaller and smaller fraction of itself.

But who *ever* does the math? As Popkin points out, everybody uses heuristics, including the elite. Most of the debate among opinion-makers is conducted in shorthand, and even well-informed voters rely on endorsements and party affiliations to make their choices. The very essence of being an ideologue lies in trusting the label—liberal or conservative, Republican or Democrat. Those are "bundling" terms: they pull together a dozen positions on individual issues under a single handy rubric. They do the work of assessment for you.

It is widely assumed that the upcoming Presidential election will be decided by an electorate that is far more ideological than has historically been the case. Polls indicate much less volatility than usual, supporting the view that the public is divided into starkly antagonistic camps—the "red state-blue state" paradigm. If this is so, it suggests that we have at last moved past Converse's picture of an electoral iceberg, in which ninety per cent of the population is politically underwater. But Morris Fiorina, a political scientist at Stanford, thinks that it is not so, and that the polarized electorate is a product of elite opinion. "The simple truth is that there is no culture war in the United States—no battle for the soul of America rages, at least none that most Americans are aware of," he says in his short book *Culture War? The Myth of a Polarized America* (Longman; $14.95). Public-opinion polls, he argues, show that on most hot-button issues voters in so-called red states do not differ significantly from voters in so-called blue states. Most people identify themselves as moderates, and their responses to survey questions seem to substantiate this self-description. What has become polarized, Fiorina argues, is the elite. The chatter—among political activists, commentators, lobbyists, movie stars, and so on—has become highly ideological. It's a non-stop *Crossfire*, and this means that the candidates themselves come wrapped in more extreme ideological coloring. But Fiorina points out that the ideological position of a candidate is not identical to the position of the people who vote for him or her. He suggests that people generally vote for the candidate whose views strike them as closest to their own, and "closest" is a relative term. With any two candidates, no matter how far out, one will always be "closer" than the other.

Of course, if Converse is correct, and most voters really don't have meaningful political beliefs, even ideological "closeness" is an artifact of survey anxiety, of people's felt need, when they are asked for an opinion, to have one. This absence of "real opinions" is not from lack of brains; it's from lack of interest. "The typical citizen drops down to a lower level of mental performance as soon as he enters the political field," the economic theorist Joseph Schumpeter wrote, in 1942. "He argues and analyzes in a way which he would readily recognize as infantile within the sphere of his real interests. He becomes a primitive again. His thinking is associative and affective." And Fiorina quotes a passage from the political scientist Robert Putnam: "Most men are not political animals. The world of public affairs is not their world. It is alien to them—possibly benevolent, more probably threatening, but nearly always alien. Most men are not interested in politics. Most do not participate in politics."

Man may not be a political animal, but he is certainly a social animal. Voters do respond to the cues of commentators and campaigners, but only when they can match those cues up with the buzz of their own social group. Individual voters are not rational calculators of self-interest (nobody truly is), and may not be very consistent users of heuristic shortcuts, either. But they are not just random particles bouncing off the walls of the voting booth. Voters go into the booth carrying the imprint of the hopes and fears, the prejudices and assumptions of their family, their friends, and their neighbors. For most people, voting may be more meaningful and more understandable as a social act than as a political act.

That it is hard to persuade some people with ideological arguments does not mean that those people cannot be persuaded, but the things that help to convince them are likely to make ideologues sick—things like which candidate is more optimistic. For many liberals, it may have been dismaying to listen to John Kerry and John Edwards, in their speeches at the Democratic National Convention, utter impassioned bromides about how "the sun is rising" and "our best days are still to come." But that is what a very large number of voters want to hear. If they believe it, then Kerry and Edwards will get their votes. The ideas won't matter, and neither will the color of the buttons.

DISCUSSION QUESTIONS

1. What information shortcuts do you think it would be reasonable to use when making voting decisions?

2. Menand is concerned that voters' heuristics might not be reliable if voters actually "did the math." What heuristics do you think might be particularly unreliable guides to voting choices?

3. What, if any, risks are posed to the American political system if voters base their decisions on information shortcuts? Which of the three theories discussed by Menand would be the most troubling for democracy, in your view?

DEBATING THE ISSUES: VOTER FRAUD OR VOTER SUPPRESSION?

The last three national elections have raised many concerns about the voting system and the standards for administering elections in the United States. Charges of impropriety in voting procedures and vote counting as well as complaints that certain voting technologies were systematically likely to produce more voter error or not record voter choices were legion. Massive voter mobilization campaigns on both the political left and right registered millions of new voters. Huge sums were poured into campaign advertising, further stoking the interest of these newly registered voters and the public in general. In such a charged political environment, and with the presidential election widely expected to be close, concerns about the integrity of the process took on a particular urgency. The battle lines again are being drawn in the months leading up to the 2008 election: should we encourage as many people to vote as possible, or will that lead to more fraud? Is this the central question concerning election administration, or are there more fundamental issues?

One argument, presented here by Bob Williams, is that voter fraud and manipulation of the ballot-counting process are the main areas in which reform is needed. He points to voters registered in multiple locations, voting more than once, illegally registered, paid an inducement to vote, to felons voting, and to improper use of provisional ballots and unsecured ballots being counted as symptomatic of the lack of control over the voting process. Williams points to the 2004 Washington gubernatorial election as a key example of an electoral process that is out of control. He urges for more controls on the process of voting, including voter-ID laws and more strict control on the use of provisional ballots.

The opposing argument, presented here by Meg Cox, contends that these complaints about fraud are part of a strategy to discourage or scare away potential voters. Proponents of this argument point to examples that they allege are clear attempts to suppress voter turnout by adding obstacles in the way of voting or interpreting statutes and regulations in the way that is least likely to allow someone's vote to be counted. Voter ID laws are most likely to restrict turnout among the poor and elderly; one study showed that more than 25 million American citizens do not have a government-issued ID with their current address. At the same time, the threat of fraud is minimal: between 2002 and 2006 the Justice Department's efforts to prosecute voter fraud produced only 86 convictions (out of nearly 200 million votes cast nationwide in those elections). The dispute centers around turnout: those complaining about vote suppression say we should err on the side of getting as many people voting as possible, while those complaining about voter fraud ask what the good is in increasing turnout if we cannot be sure that those who voted were indeed supposed to vote.

Phil Keisling has a different perspective. He argues that neither widespread voter fraud (feared by Republicans) or the concern that elections may be stolen by rigging electronic voting machines (feared by Democrats) is much of a concern. Rather, he says, "The biggest problem in American elections isn't deliberate fraud. It's garden-variety human error." As the former secretary of state in Oregon, he had plenty of opportunities to witness the consequences of poorly trained poll workers making bad decisions. Thousands of voters are disenfranchised in every election by such things as poorly designed ballots (for instance, the infamous "butterfly ballot" in Florida, which probably cost Al Gore the 2000 presidential election but was designed by a Democratic county official), forgetting to plug in electronic voting machines, or accidentally erasing votes that could not be recovered. However, Keisling clearly sides with advocates of increasing voter turnout, even if it might mean a small increase in fraud; he says, "The biggest threat to the health of our democracy is low and declining voter participation." Keisling criticizes the debate on voter fraud as a "sad mix of fossilized thinking laced with bipartisan paranoia" and makes a pitch for voting by mail, which has been used in every election in Oregon since 2000.

50

"Election Fraud: Remains Commonplace"

Bob Williams

Joseph Stalin once said, "The people who cast the votes don't decide an election; the people who count the votes do." In the former Soviet Union, the dictator's minions counted the votes and the totals added up according to his wishes. One expects such things in a communist country. Here in the U.S., though, where free and fair elections are an indispensable cornerstone of our republic, sloppy or politically oriented vote counting is not acceptable. Our Founders established the principle of "ballots not bullets," based on the belief that political decisions should be made freely by eligible citizens whose votes would be counted properly. It is up to us to preserve that principle today via election reform.

Through constitutional amendment, we rightly have expanded the voting franchise since our nation's founding. All citizens of voting age can cast a ballot, if they have not lost that right by committing a felony and are mentally competent. Yet, in many places around the country, felons, the deceased, and non-U.S. residents vote. Some people vote twice. The laws that protect the integrity of our elections have been eroding for years, but it took a few whisker-thin races to bring national attention to the problem.

How and why has our election system become so compromised? Some claim incompetency or human error is at the root of the situation. Others point to fraud. Actually, it is both. Yet, there is another factor at work. In *Dirty Little Secrets*, the University of Virginia's Larry Sabato maintains that ignorance plays a huge role: "The fact that voter fraud is generally not recognized as a serious problem by the press, public and law enforcement creates the perfect environment for it to flourish." And flourish it has. Following the 2004 elections, serious questions of various sorts were raised in Ohio, New Mexico, Wisconsin, South Dakota, and elsewhere concerning the integrity of vote counts in close races. Perhaps the largest controversy has been in Washington state with respect to its gubernatorial election.

Wall Street Journal columnist John Rind, author of *Stealing Elections*, writes that the U.S. has a "haphazard, fraud-prone election system befitting an emerging Third World country rather than the world's leading democracy." Democrat Christine Gregoire is Washington's current governor, having won by a mere 133 votes out of more than 2,800,000 cast. Or did she? When the election was first over and the ballots were tallied, Gregoire's challenger, Republican Dino Rossi, had won by 261 votes. A mandatory recount under state law reduced Rossi's margin of victory to just 42 votes, prompting a demand by Democrats for a hand recount, which is expensive and must be paid for by the challenging party. Presidential candidate John Kerry joined groups like MoveOn.org to help raise money for Gregoire and, after the second recount, she was declared the winner by 129 votes. A judge later changed the total to 133.

However, it was not that simple, as reports poured in concerning serious problems at polling places. Various organizations began independent investigations to determine if the complaints were justified. What was discovered proved shocking:

- On at least 10 occasions after the election, King County (which accounts for one-third of the state's votes) found unsecured ballots and, in nine of those cases, election officials added them to the ballot count.
- King County election officials admitted in sworn depositions that they deliberately submitted misleading absentee ballot reconciliation reports—the reports that reconcile the number of voters with the number of ballots cast. With no system in place to track how many absentee ballots were sent out and returned, King County ended up with 875 more absentee votes counted than the number of people who

voted by absentee ballot. Moreover, at least 785 provisional ballots—ballots used by voters whose identification or eligibility to vote is in question—were tabulated improperly, sans verification of voter eligibility. Around the state, an additional 1,033 provisional ballots were identified as improperly tabulated.

- Evidence exists of voter registration drives in state mental institutions, among Alzheimer's patients in extended care facilities, and with felons.
- More than 1,400 felons whose voting rights had not been restored were allowed to vote—including one who voted absentee from his jail cell.
- At least 55,175 ballots were "enhanced" in King County—meaning election workers decided for those voters how they meant to vote for governor if the individual did not select a gubernatorial candidate on his or her ballot.
- In five counties, the secretary of State certified election results even though there were 8,500 more votes cast than voters credited with voting.

Despite this evidence and more, not one law enforcement official in King County has investigated the problems inside the elections department. The district attorney says he will not do anything unless the King County elections director, who is the person at the center of this scandal, brings charges. The U.S. Attorney General will not investigate unless someone can bring him proof of fraud. In his opinion, the items listed above are insufficient.

The Republican Party challenged the results in court, arguing that a new election should be held. The judge in the case disagreed, citing Washington's stringent laws regarding the contesting of elections. He concurred that at least 1,678 illegal votes were cast, but said fraud was not proven in those cases since Republicans could not determine on whose behalf the illegal votes were cast. We are left scratching our heads about how it legally could be determined who people illegally voted for, as candidate selections are supposed to be confidential. Besides, if a voter knowingly cast an illegal ballot, and then testified about who he or she voted for, that individual would be admitting to a felony.

The judge did agree that witnesses for both the Democrats and Republicans had testified to significant errors in the election, including sloppy and misleading voting reports and ballots overlooked until months after the election was over. Yet, since fraud was not argued in this case, he decided to throw out the illegal votes instead of ordering a new election.

In his decision, the judge noted that Washington's election system had been compromised, adding: "This court is not in a position to fix the deficiencies in the election process that we heard about in this courtroom over the past nine days. However, the voters of this state are in a position to demand of their executive and legislative bodies that remedial measures be instituted immediately. And, clearly, the evidence here suggests that the problems require more than just constructing new buildings and hiring more staff."

The judge, by inference, made another observation that underscores something that should be of concern for every state in the nation: the problem posed by the increased use of absentee ballots. "Extraordinary efforts are in place to make it easier to vote," he noted. "But unfortunately, I fear it will be much more difficult to account for those votes in the future."

The move to permit unrestricted voting by absentee ballot is sweeping the nation. This is a dangerous trend because it greatly expands the opportunity to commit fraud. The National Commission on Election Reform, chaired by former presidents Gerald R. Ford and Jimmy Carter, warned in 2001 that voter fraud schemes from the past are even more likely now. According to the Commission's report, "Opportunities to commit such frauds are actually growing because of the trend toward more permissive absentee voting."

In its report, the Florida Department of Law Enforcement agreed: "The lack of in-person, at-the-polls accountability makes absentee ballots the tool of choice for those inclined to commit voter fraud." Former Alabama secretary of State Jim Bennett summarized these concerns, contending that "We don't use guns, tanks, or bullets to put political leaders into power. We simply allow absentee ballot manipulators to undermine and possibly corrupt the system."

This problem arises because of a basic disagreement among state and Federal legislators and administrators over the definition of voter disenfranchisement. One view holds that voters are disenfranchised when the system is too demanding. Its proponents argue that voting should be simple and easy for as many people as possible, voters are on an "honor" system, and election officials must have broad discretionary power, including the ability to "discern voter intent." The second view holds that legal voters are disenfranchised when illegal votes are cast and counted. This side argues that: Voters should have to prove they are eligible; they should properly fill out their ballots, thus avoiding the issue of "discerning voter intent"; and their votes should be counted accurately. Unfortunately for American citizens, the first group has been winning the argument of late.

During the Clinton Administration, for instance, Congress passed the Motor Voter Act, requiring employees at state driver's licensing agencies to ask applicants if they wanted to register to vote. These same employees were forbidden, however, from asking applicants if they were citizens. This makes sense only if the goal is to increase the number of potential voters at the cost of ensuring that people who vote are eligible to do so.

Vote One, Vote All

In recent years, traditional safeguards at the polls, like requirements to show identification, have been eliminated and, with more people voting by absentee ballot, previous safeguards increasingly are not applicable. It should not be surprising, then, that corruption is on the rise. "We the people" have allowed it, whether by silence, inattention, or misunderstanding.

The ballot integrity issues faced by Washington state and many other jurisdictions present significant challenges, but solutions exist. First, criminal prosecution of voter fraud is necessary. More than 60 Federal investigations have been launched in 28 states and one territory since 2001. People have gone to jail already, and others will follow.

Legislative reforms are needed as well. Voter rolls must be cleaned up. To do this, individuals should be required to show proof of citizenship and register in their legal names. This would allow for the removal of names of ineligible felons, dead people, and illegal aliens. Voter ID bills have passed legislatures in five states. The legislation was signed by the governors of Georgia and Indiana, but vetoed by governors in New Jersey, Arizona, and Wisconsin (twice).

Photo identification and a signature should be required of voters prior to casting a ballot, whether they are voting by absentee ballot or at the polls. Even Mexico, whose government spent $1,000,000,000 to clean up its voter rolls, requires this. It is a travesty that our great democracy does not.

Laws should be tightened regarding the use of provisional ballots. According to Federal law, individuals cast provisional ballots if their names are not on the register in their own precincts, or if their voting eligibility is challenged by an election official. The ballot must be verified by the elections department before it is counted. Missouri has the best provisional ballot law on the books: A voter seeking to cast a ballot outside his own precinct is required to show identification, and the election judge will call headquarters to verify eligibility. If a voter insists on casting a ballot at the wrong location, he is given a special ballot allowing him to vote only in those races for which everybody in his state is voting. Also, provisional ballots should be designed to prevent illegal counting prior to verification. They can be a different color or size, or have a unique bar code identifier.

Laws should be tightened regarding ballot enhancement. Under what circumstances should anyone be allowed to determine a voter's intent if it is not made clear on a ballot? Most of us fill out our ballots entirely, but sometimes we purposely choose not to vote for something or somebody. That is our right, but under the laws that allow voter enhancement, election officials can look at our voting pattern and decide to fill in that missing vote for us. This is not right and should be outlawed since it certainly does not represent our vote.

Widespread vote-by-mail should be rolled back. We have seen that it does not increase voter participation, which was the sole purpose behind it. Those of us who love its convenience have to face the fact that it has eroded electoral integrity. Voting by absentee ballot should be the chosen method only for those who truly cannot get to the polls on Election Day.

In addition, military ballots must be sent out in a timely manner. In Washington, thousands of ballots were sent to overseas military too late to be counted in the 2004 election. The state's late primary makes it difficult for county auditors to mail the ballots in time. The remedy is a completely secure Internet balloting procedure, but one has yet to be developed.

Finally, election officials must do their jobs in a timely and law-abiding manner. Strong legislative oversight is necessary to implement the Help America Vote Act passed by Congress in 2002. Some provisions of that law are unlikely to work and they will need to be fixed. For the rest, stiff penalties must be in place for officials who disregard the law.

Untold numbers of Americans have given their lives to protect our precious freedom to vote. Permitting rampant and unchecked election irregularities makes a mockery of this sacrifice. As former Pres. Ronald Reagan once reminded us: "Freedom is never more than one generation away from extinction. We didn't pass it to our children in the bloodstream. It must be fought for, protected, and handed on to them to do the same, or one day we will spend our sunset years telling our children and our children's children what it was once like in the United States where men were free."

51

"Election Fraud, American Style: The Most Effective Voter Suppression Tool Is the Polling Booth Itself"

Phil Keisling

In July 2003, Aviel Rubin, an untenured Johns Hopkins computer-science professor, was asked to analyze some software source code purportedly used in the Accuvote TSx voting machine, manufactured by Diebold. The Ohio-based company is one of several major vendors of "Direct Recording Electronic" (DRE) voting machines that almost 30 million voters, in almost 40 states, will use in the 2006 election.

Rubin and several graduate students quickly realized that Diebold's code was rife with mistakes and vulnerabilities, and laughably easy to hack. Worse, since the same code seemed to underlie every Diebold machine, a skilled hacker could conceivably corrupt every Diebold machine in America. These "first-generation" DREs leave no paper trail; voters have to trust their ballots are being properly recorded and counted.

Rubin has written an engaging memoir of his three years in the vortex of electronic voting controversy. In *Brave New Ballot: The Battle to Safeguard Democracy in the Age of Electronic Voting*, there's unmistakably a "Mr. Rubin Goes to Washington" quality to his narrative arc. Smart, idealistic computer scientist gets outraged about a perceived wrong—and wades right into the shark-infested waters. There are billions of dollars at stake for the DRE vendors. Thousands of election officials have their reputations, even their careers, riding on the machines whose security and reliability Rubin is challenging.

Not that Rubin was a media naïf. Before leaking their report to *The New York Times*, his team spent several hours at a whiteboard coming up with pithy quips. Discomfited vendors and election officials initially belittled Rubin's "freshman homework assignment." When Rubin proved adept at rebutting critics' obfuscations at various public forums and legislative hearings, his integrity came under attack. Nothing like an "Aha! Conflict of interest!" angle—especially with a highly technical subject that few reporters truly understand—to distract from the heart of an issue. (Rubin failed to disclose he was an unpaid advisor, with stock options, for another e-voting company—though the firm was more a hopeful vendor to Diebold than a competitor.)

For Rubin and other critics of DREs, the nightmare scenario is this: Some diabolical (read: corporate and/or Republican) hacker figures out how to steal thousands of votes, in key congressional districts. What could we do? Would we even know? Without a paper trail, could we ever know who had really won?

As Oregon's secretary of state from 1991 until 1999, my job included oversight of elections, and I certainly agree with the importance of a paper trail. (During my tenure, we conducted three major election recounts for Congress, the U.S. Senate, and a contentious statewide ballot initiative.) I'm thankful Oregon is one of the few states where DREs are virtually nonexistent (more on that later).

But is there any tangible evidence, after more than 100 million votes cast on DREs, that a deliberate fraud has actually occurred in any election to date? Rubin offers no specific example. In fairness, his critique doesn't require one. But by focusing on the specter of significant electronic voting fraud, Rubin's critique of America's election system suffers from an even bigger mistake than confusing the elephant's tail with its trunk. In an unintended, but nonetheless real way, Rubin—not to mention the deep conspiracy theorists from whom he distances himself—has fed a hyperactive (and bipartisan) obsession with the perfect election system that ultimately endangers our ability to revitalize the very essence of our democratic system, which is voter participation.

The biggest problem in American elections isn't deliberate fraud. It's garden-variety human error. Election officials keenly understand that mistakes and malfunctioning systems (technical and human) wreak far more havoc than actual fraud. (Al Gore literally lost thousands of Florida votes thanks to the infamous "butterfly ballot" designed by a Democratic county clerk.)

Virtually every DRE problem to date—and there are some doozies—falls into this category. Red-faced election officials in Montgomery County, Md. (Rubin's home state) can't blame Diebold for the debacle during last September's primary when election workers forgot to send "Voter access cards" to the polls. Voters were turned away, or simply left, because they couldn't wait any longer. In desperation, some poll workers gave voters blank pieces of paper for ballots.

The exquisite dilemma, of course, is that DREs, with or without VVPTs (Voter-Verified Paper Trails), won't go away overnight. Billions have been invested in them. As Rubin notes, voters actually like DREs' ATM-like convenience. And even as you read this, controversy and threatened litigation likely rage somewhere in America because one or more congressional candidates, short a few hundred or few thousand votes, will be crying foul.

May I See Your Costco Card?

No study reveals a strong Republican bias toward computer criminals who a) want to risk long prison sentences to commit election fraud and b) have the Ocean's 11–like skill to pull it off. However, the legitimate, if overblown, concern about DRE-related fraud seems to be almost exclusively voiced (so far) by Democrats.

While Democrats fear the machinations of Diebold et al., Republicans have their own version of electoral horror: those vast hordes of non-citizens and illegal immigrants (read: Democrats) eager to take advantage of open voter registration laws. This specter is just as ephemeral—and even less frightening.

The notion that widespread voter registration fraud exists is a long-standing obsession among many Republicans, who for the last few decades have fought virtually every innovation to help citizens overcome bureaucratic and logistical obstacles to exercise their fundamental right to vote.

Sure, registration fraud can happen. But how often? In my home state of Oregon, with two million registered voters, we've had all of a dozen complaints of illegal registration in an entire decade. Exactly two miscreants were found, and both were prosecuted. (One was a British con artist; the other a confused Vietnamese woman.)

False registration is a felony in virtually every state. And just how stupid do people like Rush Limbaugh think illegal immigrants are to avoid being detected by immigration services—so they can then commit two deportable offenses by falsely registering and then voting?

A recent study for the U.S. Election Assistance Commission concluded there was little evidence of the type of polling-place fraud that so alarms the GOP. (This report's release has been delayed for months, reportedly by the EAC's Republican members.)

Since "absence of evidence isn't evidence of absence," to quote Donald Rumsfeld, GOP elected officials are undeterred in trying to impose new, restrictive regulations supposedly meant to combat this phantom threat. For example, Georgia and Arizona have passed laws to require photo identification to register and even vote. The U.S. House of Representatives has passed similar legislation—also mostly along party lines.

These bills have a surface appeal, but quickly raise a host of thorny questions. Must it be a driver's license or other state-issued ID? Can you show a Costco card? A utility bill (with a picture?) And since we're now taking extra time at the polls, longer lines, anyone?

And what about the tens of millions of voters casting absentee ballots? Party operatives, including many Republicans are strongly encouraging people to vote absentee as part of their get-out-the-vote strategies. So now we put photo IDs into the ballot envelopes—and, uh, anyone out there thinking about identity theft?

Fortunately, federal courts have moved quickly to end this nonsense— a superior court judge struck down the Georgia law requiring voters to produce a state–issued voter ID at the polls.

Assume, for a moment, the purest of motives, and focus on the Republicans' ostensible logic. It's not enough to have stiff penalties, or adopt refinements such as random spot checks of voter registration rolls against other government databases. We must prevent that last 0.0001 percent of possible fraud. The goal of a pure, fraud-free election system demands that we do whatever it takes—however cumbersome and expensive.

This is not unlike the worldview that Rubin ultimately embraces, too. As a computer scientist, Rubin literally lives in a world of digital certainty, of ones and zeroes precisely arrayed to produce a desired result. Little wonder the idealist in him seeks a totally secure voting machine, a totally fraud-proof electoral process. But elections, by definition, are inherently incapable of being fraudproof and 100-percent secure. And this is key: After a certain point, efforts to make them so do more harm than good.

A good analogy comes from the biological world. Healthy adults have small quantities of dangerous bacteria in our blood. Yet prescribing massive doses of antibiotics to kill them would ultimately compromise our immune system's natural abilities to counter these and other threats. What kills the bad stuff can also kill the good stuff.

So too with voting. The ability to cast a ballot is the essential democratic freedom. Trying to make the voting process 100 percent error proof inevitably diminishes that freedom. The key to dealing with election fraud is not its elimination, but its strict containment.

Mailing It In

So where does Rubin's quest for the "Perfect DRE" lead him? On page 249, he describes the system he finds most promising. It's the brainchild of cryptographer David Chaum.

"Voters receive two ballots with the candidates' names in different order. Voters mark one of the ballots and keep the other one. Since the authorities running the election would not know which ballot each voter marked, the ballot the voter keeps can be used, through some mathematical manipulations invented by Chaum, to keep the election honest. Furthermore, the marked ballot can be stored in such a way that the voter is able to verify that the vote was counted in the final tally, and the tally can be performed by anyone."

Got that? At least Rubin has the grace to concede that "the details of Chaum's scheme are too complex and technical to list here, and therein lies the rub. . . . A fundamental problem would remain: the public would not understand how the mechanism works."

Bingo. If the public doesn't understand its own election system, what's to make citizens suddenly believe again in the integrity of that system? Would we then start issuing ballots in triplicate and concoct new, ever more complex algorithms? Rubin's logic leads us to ever more sophisticated, technology-centric processes, to fix a problem that's created by an inordinate reliance on complex technology.

The biggest threat to the health of our democracy is low—and declining—voter participation. Even the atypically high turnout in the 2004 presidential election amounted to just over 50 percent of eligible citizens casting ballots. Midterm elections are now attracting just 35 to 40 percent participation. Far, far worse are primary elections, those largely overlooked "first-round" contests where the vast majority of candidates who win the dominant party's nomination are virtual shoo-ins for November. This is now 90 percent of Congress's 435 seats, and perhaps an even higher proportion of our 7,382 state legislative seats. For these contests, turnout has been truly abysmal—in many states 5 to 15 percent of the eligible population.

Various voter suppression tactics (legal and otherwise) contribute to this problem. But the most effective voter suppression tactic is something most Americans consider an untouchable icon: the polling place itself.

In 49 states, the basic premise of elections is that the citizen needs to come to the ballot—and not the other way around. So reformers like Rubin focus on building a better (and more expensive) DRE. Others suggest "early voting" options with additional workers and polling stations set up for days or weeks before Election Day itself. Some even advocate a new national holiday—all to get more voters to come to the ballot.

In other words, spend even more money—and create more opportunities for error (and yes, even fraud) as you rely on evermore complex machines, and even more temporary (often, ill-trained) workers needing to be vigilant at more locations for longer hours.

Far better than going even farther down this rathole (with or without DREs) is to look at an eighteenth-century innovation, the Post Office, and implement Vote by Mail (VBM). Reverse the dynamic: bring the ballot to the voter.

Since 2000, Oregon has conducted all elections by mail, sending a ballot to every registered voter about two weeks before election. Voters can return the ballot by mail or deliver it to an official election site. To prevent fraud, voters must sign the outer envelope. All signatures must be matched to actual voter registration cards before the ballots can be processed. In the 2004 election, Oregon's voter turnout as a percentage of registered voters was 85 percent—the highest in the United States. Even more dramatic, the seemingly dismal 39 percent turnout of registered voters in our state primary also appears to be the nation's highest—compared to states such as Illinois at 21 percent; Pennsylvania at 19 percent, Texas at 10 percent, and Virginia at 4 percent. (By the way, the median age of those who actually voted in Oregon's primary was 60.)

Actually, citizens in all 50 states already vote by mail. More than 80 percent of Washington State voters will cast ballots this way in 2006. In California and several other states, well over 50 percent will do the same.

Rubin's take on Vote by Mail? A casually dismissive half-sentence: "Oregon, where citizens vote by postal mail—another terribly insecure system." Here again, Rubin, like so many other election reformers, falls into the trap of making the (unattainable) perfect the enemy of the good.

Could an individual voter theoretically scam Vote by Mail? Sure—as you can any system. Evidence it's happened in Oregon? One person convicted of forging his wife's signature; another, of voting twice. More to the point: In stark contrast to a DRE world, even if individual or small-scale fraud were to occur, by design a VBM system disperses the risk, rather than concentrates it.

Vote by Mail is good for participation. It's simple to understand. Recounts are easy—by definition, there's a direct paper trail for every vote. And face it. If election night brings rain, snow, or sleet—or sick kids and dinner to get on the table—many (maybe most?) voters would be relieved to know their votes had already been cast by mail. (Question for pundits: What's the "message" voters will be sending if Election 2008 is literally decided by unusually bad weather?)

Today's national debate about how we should vote is still such a sad mix of fossilized thinking laced with bipartisan paranoia. Let's brace ourselves for a flurry of post-election accusations and lawsuits, that might make Florida 2000 look tame by comparison. (Perhaps even pray for one side to win so big, it won't matter as much.) And then, the day after, start figuring this out for real.

52

"Access Denied"

MEG E. COX

In Wisconsin, voter fraud is rampant. Or so thought U.S. Attorney Steven Biskupic, who began a hunt for fraudulent voters after John Kerry won Wisconsin by just 11,000 votes over George W. Bush in 2004, in an election that Republicans claimed was tainted by widespread voter fraud. But by the time he completed his work, Biskupic reported that he had uncovered no conspiracy to commit fraud. His prosecutors ended up charging only 14 people with voting illegally and only four of them, all felons ineligible to vote, were convicted.

Lawmakers in many states are saying that there's only one way to stop this epidemic of fraud: have every voter show ID at the polls—ideally a state-issued photo ID. But experts on elections say that voter fraud of the kind that could be countered by ID requirements is rare. What's more, requiring photo IDs would disenfranchise millions of voters. The supposed remedy, these experts say, would turn out to be far worse than the actual problem.

Since 2002, the Justice Department has made an all-out effort to track down and convict fraudulent voters. By 2006, those efforts had yielded just 86 convictions nationwide, and many of those incidents, like the four Wisconsin cases, would not have been prevented by a voter ID requirement.

Meanwhile, a study by the Brennan Center for Justice (see truthabout fraud.org) found that some 21 million citizens—including a disproportionately large number of African Americans and elderly people—do not have government-issued photo ID. As many as 4.5 million people have a photo ID that lacks their current address or current legal name; many of these are young adults and people with lower income who move frequently. The proof-of-citizenship requirements that some ID advocates propose are especially onerous for married women: 32 million voting-age women do not have documents to prove citizenship that reflect their current legal name.

Proponents of strict voter ID press their case by magnifying the size of the fraud problem while minimizing the impact of voter ID laws. Ohio is one state that strengthened its ID laws after the 2004 election. The League of Women Voters teamed up with a housing advocacy group there to find out how many cases of individual voter fraud had been pursued in relation to the 2004 presidential election. They came up with a statewide total of four, or 0.00004 percent of the nearly 10 million votes cast.

But to hear voter ID proponents tell the story, fraudulent voters were everywhere in Ohio. One master of magnification is Mark "Thor" Hearne of the American Center for Voting Rights. If Web presence is any indicator of an organization's legitimacy, the ACVR should raise eyebrows: its Web site didn't appear until March 2005, and it disappeared exactly two years later. But after the 2004 election, the ACVR was everywhere, testifying at hearings and filing lawsuits that claimed voter fraud.

Hearne, who was national election counsel for Bush-Cheney '04, was called to testify on behalf of the ACVR before the House Administration Committee chaired at the time by Bob Ney (R., Ohio), who is now serving prison time for corruption—when that committee was looking into irregularities in the 2004 election. Hearne claimed that fraud was reported "in every corner" of Ohio, and that "the fraudulent voter registrations totaled in the thousands."

Hearne offered the committee this rhetorical flourish: "Ohio citizens deserve the confidence that they the voters—not trial lawyers, activist judges and special-interest groups soliciting fraudulent votes with crack cocaine—determine the result of Ohio elections." He was inspired to include the last example by the case of a hapless addict who did indeed confess to accepting cocaine in lieu of cash as payment for turning in completed registration forms. (The fraudulent forms were spotted because officials wondered why so many people with names like Mary Poppins and Michael Jackson lived on a single block and had the same handwriting. Presumably this is one of the four cases the League of Women Voters discovered. The addict was charged with a felony, and Mary Poppins didn't get to vote.)

Proponents of strict voter ID laws make their recommendations sound like a matter of common sense. "Every day millions of Americans show a picture ID to pay by check, board a plane or buy alcohol or tobacco," argued Vernon J. Ehlers (R., Mich.) when the U.S. House was preparing its own voter ID bill. "Surely the sanctity of the ballot warrants as much protection as these other activities. Our voting rights are too important to rely on an 'honor system.' " Sound bites like these echoed from coast to coast as the bill skated through the House on a near-perfect party-line vote.

But the analogy is not accurate. First of all, it's not true that you have to have an ID to get on a plane. As George Washington University law professor Spencer Overton pointed out in an interview, "If you don't have an ID [at the airport] there's a different process, more of a search, but you don't need ID. Even in the context of terrorism there are exceptions for people flying without photo ID."

Many of the new voter ID laws, on the other hand, offer no exceptions: some states allow you to vote provisionally if you don't bring your ID to the polls, but require you to bring the ID to the board of elections within a couple of days if you want your vote counted; other states don't allow even this fallback option.

Ehlers's Point about the "honor system" is also disingenuous. Most states do require voters to prove their identity in some way, and those who come to the polls without documentation can sign an affidavit attesting to their identity. If suspicions of fraud surface, the affidavit becomes a tool for investigators. Penalties for voter fraud are so high that it's unlikely many individuals would be willing to risk imprisonment just to add a single vote to their favorite candidate's column.

"If there are so many fraudulent votes out there, more than the legitimate votes that would be excluded, then we can consider voter ID," Overton said. "But let's get the facts on the table to make an assessment instead of using anecdote and inappropriate analogies to analyze the problem."

Overton came to the voter ID conversation by way of his membership on the Commission on Federal Election Reform—called the Carter-Baker Commission because it was chaired by Jimmy Carter and former secretary of state James Baker. The Carter-Baker Commission gave an enormous boost to voter ID proponents in 2005 when it recommended that voters be required to present a REAL ID, a proposed government-issued photo ID that indicates citizenship status. Overton believes that the commission got some bad advice.

"The top experts in the field weren't brought in," Overton said. "People who were brought in included John Fund, a journalist and *Wall Street Journal* political commentator with a particular perspective." (Fund is author of *Stealing Elections: How Voter Fraud Threatens Our Democracy*.) "They didn't bring in academics." Another of the panelists was Colleen McAndrews, an attorney who had fought challenges to the Gray Davis recall in California and served as campaign treasurer for Arnold Schwarzenegger.

The commission held only two hearings, allocating under three hours to voter ID and related issues, and allowed no public comment. The Lawyers' Committee for Civil Rights Under Law issued a press release echoing Overton's concerns: the commission "gave little attention to detail," it said. "There were no separate task forces devoted to any particular aspects of our election system. There was little attempt to gather rigorous empirical data to support any conclusions. The result is a report based on anecdote and supposition, rather than rigorous analysis of real-world facts."

The Carter-Baker deliberations were also shaped by the post-9/11 political context: Congress had just passed the REAL ID Act, which requires states to issue a uniform ID card that indicates citizenship status as well as identity. Overton suggests that in the absence of a careful "cost-benefit analysis," Carter and the commission's Democrats operated on a "hunch" that because "everyone will have photo ID for security purposes, it's not a big deal to ask for ID."

Some of the commissioners, said Overton, "would make the argument that the objective is national security, and therefore encouraging an ID for voting will encourage everyone to get the ID." (Lee Hamilton, chair of the 9/11 Commission, was also a Democratic member of the Carter-Baker Commission.)

Now, though, many states are balking at implementing REAL ID. Arkansas, Maine and Idaho have passed resolutions rejecting the law, and legislation is pending in Congress to repeal the REAL ID Act.

Overton and two other commissioners dissented from the voter ID recommendation (you can read Overton's reasons at carterbakerdissent.com). Commissioner Shirley Malcolm did not, but she said in an interview that her support had been "based on the idea that REAL ID was going to happen." Asked if she would have supported the recommendation if REAL ID hadn't been in the picture, she answered firmly: "No, I would not have."

The dissenters had hoped to make their case in formal statements that would be added to the commission's report. But the heads of the commission announced that the dissents would be limited to 250 words. Overton said that he "felt compelled to write an academic article because the whole debate was reduced to sound bites."

That article, which appeared in the *Michigan Law Review* in January 2007, begins the sort of cost-benefit analysis that was missing from the commission's deliberations. "Policymakers," he challenges in the article, "should await better empirical studies before imposing potentially antidemocratic measures."

Voter ID proponents haven't been waiting for better studies. With the Carter-Baker wind at their back, they continue to push for stricter voter ID laws in state after state while keeping up the steady complaint about voter fraud.

Meanwhile, voting-rights activists have been waiting for the release of a pair of studies requested by the U.S. Election Assistance Commission—one on voter fraud, the other on the impact of voter ID laws.

The voter ID report, completed in June 2006 by researchers at the Eagleton Institute of Politics and the Moritz College of Law, was finally released (but not adopted) by the EAC in March 2007. That was too late for its finding—that strict voter ID requirements correlate with lower voter turnout—to affect the debate over voter ID that preceded the 2006 congressional elections.

The report's authors acknowledge an important limitation of their study: if experts are to assess "the effectiveness of voter ID as a way to protect the integrity of the ballot," then their research "should logically include an estimate of the nature and frequency of vote fraud." Their research didn't do that. Nor did it measure how effective various voter ID rules are for countering fraud.

The Eagleton/Moritz researchers weren't looking at voter fraud because the EAC had hired someone else to cover that topic: Tova Wang, a progressive election reform expert with the Century Foundation, and Job Serebrov, a conservative Arkansas attorney. Wang and Serebrov reviewed literature and legal cases related to voter fraud, and they interviewed elections officials and election law experts from across the country and across the political spectrum. But their final report has never seen the light of day because the EAC has refused to release it.

A summary of Wang and Serebrov's findings submitted in May 2006 and a draft of their final report obtained by the *New York Times* this year provide some clues about the content of the unreleased document. Among the experts the researchers talked to, agreement was all but unanimous that polling-place fraud of the sort that would be prevented by strict voter ID rules is very rare.

Paul DeGregorio, chair of the EAC at the time, told *USA Today* last fall that the agency was sitting on the report because "there was a division of opinion" within the agency. "We've seen places where fraud does occur," he said. By December, EAC staff had written their own report on election fraud, titled "Election Crimes: An Initial Review and Recommendations for Future Study." It is ostensibly based on Wang and Serebrov's research but presents a conclusion opposite theirs: EAC staff write that there is no consensus on individual voter fraud. In support of this reversal, they point to the allegations of massive fraud in Wisconsin that were debunked by U.S. Attorney Biskupic in 2005.

Freedom of Information Act requests haven't succeeded in getting the EAC to cough up the real Wang/Serebrov study; nor have requests from Congress or the press. When I spotted an article in April saying (incorrectly, as it turns out) that the EAC was now making the Wang/Serebrov report available to journalists, I called to ask for a copy. The EAC press liaison sent me the "Election Crimes" document. I think I was supposed to believe that this was the real thing. A colleague who made the same request a month later met with the same result: twice she requested the report authored by Wang and Serebrov and twice a press liaison sent her "Election Crimes," giving no indication that these were two different documents.

Because of contractual obligations, neither Wang nor Serebrov can respond to press inquiries about their findings. But in an April press release protesting the continuing censorship, Wang does discuss her communications with the EAC. She writes that from July 2006, when she and Serebrov submitted their final report, to December 2006, when the "Elections Crimes" document was released, "no member of the EAC Commission or staff contacted me or my coauthor to raise any concerns about the substance of our research."

In an e-mail obtained by the *New York Times*, Serebrov gives his own hint about what was happening behind the scenes; he wrote in the e-mail to an EAC staffer: "I could care less that the results are not what the more conservative members of my party wanted. Neither one of us was willing to conform results for political expediency."

While Wang and Serebrov's conclusions remain buried, the voter ID movement presses on. One house of the Texas legislature has just passed a voter ID measure, and Mississippi lawmakers are poised to do the same.

Discussion Questions

1. If you were an election official, would you abide by a "letter of the law" approach when considering voter registration issues or would you be flexible in order to maximize turnout. What are the advantages and disadvantages of each strategy?

2. Would you approve of a proposal that all voters had to show photo identification at polling places? Do you think that would decrease turnout? If so, is that a reasonable cost?

3. Based on the reports in these articles, identify and defend three reforms you would make to the voting process in the United States.

4. Would you have any concerns with having voting conducted over the Internet or by mail? Are there benefits that outweigh these concerns?

CHAPTER 11

Political Parties

53

"The Decline of Collective Responsibility in American Politics"

Morris P. Fiorina

For more than three decades, political scientists have studied the changing status of American political parties. Morris Fiorina, writing in the early 1980s, suggests that political parties provide many benefits for American democracy, in particular by clarifying policy alternatives and letting citizens know whom to hold accountable when they are dissatisfied with government performance. He sees decline in all the key areas of political-party involvement: the electorate, in government, and in party organizations. He argues that the decline eliminates the motivation for elected members of the parties to define broad policy objectives, leading to diminished political participation and a rise of alienation. Policies are aimed at serving the narrow interests of the various single-issue groups that dominate politics rather than the broad constituencies represented by parties. Without strong political parties to provide electoral accountability, American politics has suffered a "decline in collective responsibility" in Fiorina's view. In the effort to reform the often-corrupt political parties of the late 1800s—often referred to as "machines" led by "bosses"—Fiorina asks us to consider whether we have eliminated the best way to hold elected officials accountable at the ballot box.

Though the Founding Fathers believed in the necessity of establishing a genuinely national government, they took great pains to design one that could not lightly do things *to* its citizens; what government might do *for* its citizens was to be limited to the functions of what we know now as the "watchman state."

* * *

Given the historical record faced by the Founders, their emphasis on constraining government is understandable. But we face a later historical record, one that shows two hundred years of increasing demands for government to act positively. Moreover, developments unforeseen by the Founders increasingly raise the likelihood that the uncoordinated actions of individuals and groups will inflict serious damage on the nation as a whole. The by-products of the industrial and technological revolutions impose physical risks not only on us, but on future generations as well. Resource shortages and international cartels raise the spectre of economic ruin. And the simple proliferation of special interests with their intense, particularistic demands threatens to render us politically incapable of taking actions that might either advance the state of society or prevent foreseeable deteriorations in that state. None of this is to suggest that we should forget about what government can do *to* us—the contemporary concern with the proper scope and methods of government intervention in the social and economic orders is long overdue. But the modern age demands as well that we worry about our ability to make government work *for* us. The problem is that we are gradually losing that ability, and a principal reason for this loss is the steady erosion of *responsibility* in American politics.

* * *

Unfortunately, the importance of responsibility in a democracy is matched by the difficulty of attaining it. In an autocracy, individual responsibility suffices; the location of power in a single individual locates responsibility in that individual as well. But individual responsibility is insufficient whenever more than one person shares governmental authority. We can hold a particular congressman individually responsible for a personal transgression such as bribe-taking. We can even hold a president individually responsible for military moves where he presents Congress and the citizenry with a *fait accompli*. But on most national issues individual responsibility is difficult to assess. If one were to go to Washington, randomly accost a Democratic congressman, and berate him about a 20-percent rate of inflation, imagine the response. More than likely it would run, "Don't blame me. If 'they' had done what I've advocated for *x* years, things would be fine today."

* * *

American institutional structure makes this kind of game-playing all too easy. In order to overcome it we must lay the credit or blame for national conditions on all those who had any hand in bringing them about: some form of *collective responsibility* is essential.

The only way collective responsibility has ever existed, and can exist given our institutions, is through the agency of the political party; in American politics, responsibility requires cohesive parties. This is an old claim to be sure, but its age does not detract from its present relevance. In fact, the continuing decline in public esteem for the parties and continuing efforts to "reform" them out of the political process suggest that old arguments for party responsibility have not been made often enough or, at least, convincingly enough, so I will make these arguments once again in this essay.

A strong political party can generate collective responsibility by creating incentive for leaders, followers, and popular supporters to think and act in collective terms. First, by providing party leaders with the capability (e.g., control of institutional patronage, nominations, and so on) to discipline party members, genuine leadership becomes possible. Legislative output is less likely to be a least common denominator—a residue of myriad conflicting proposals—and more likely to consist of a program actually intended to solve a problem or move the nation in a particular direction. Second, the subordination of individual officeholders to the party lessens their ability to separate themselves from party actions. Like it or not, their performance becomes identified with the performance of the collectivity to which they belong. Third, with individual candidate variation greatly reduced, voters have less incentive to support individuals and more incentive to support or oppose the party as a whole. And fourth, the circle closes as party-line voting in the electorate provides party leaders with the incentive to propose policies that will earn the support of a national majority, and party back-benchers* with the personal incentive to cooperate with leaders in the attempt to compile a good record for the party as a whole.

In the American context, strong parties have traditionally clarified politics in two ways. First, they allow citizens to assess responsibility easily, at least when the government is unified, which it more often was in earlier eras when party meant more than it does today. Citizens need only evaluate the social, economic, and international conditions they observe and make a simple decision for or against change. They do not need to decide whether the energy, inflation, urban, and defense policies advocated by their congressman would be superior to those advocated by [the president]—were any of them to be enacted!

The second way in which strong parties clarify American politics follows from the first. When citizens assess responsibility on the party as a whole, party members have personal incentives to see the party evaluated favorably. They have little to gain from gutting their president's program one day and attacking him for lack of leadership the next, since they share in the president's fate when voters do not differentiate within the party. Put simply, party responsibility provides party members with a personal stake in their collective performance.

* Back-benchers are junior members of the Parliament, who sit in the rear benches of the House of Commons. Here, the term refers to junior members of political parties.

Admittedly, party responsibility is a blunt instrument. The objection immediately arises that party responsibility condemns junior Democratic representatives to suffer electorally for an inflation they could do little to affect. An unhappy situation, true, but unless we accept it, Congress as a whole escapes electoral retribution for an inflation they *could* have done something to affect. Responsibility requires acceptance of both conditions. The choice is between a blunt instrument or none at all.

* * *

In earlier times, when citizens voted for the party, not the person, parties had incentives to nominate good candidates, because poor ones could have harmful fallout on the ticket as a whole. In particular, the existence of presidential coattails (positive and negative) provided an inducement to avoid the nomination of narrowly based candidates, no matter how committed their supporters. And, once in office, the existence of party voting in the electorate provided party members with the incentive to compile a good *party* record. In particular, the tendency of national midterm elections to serve as referenda on the performance of the president provided a clear inducement for congressmen to do what they could to see that their president was perceived as a solid performer. By stimulating electoral phenomena such as coattail effects and mid-term referenda, party transformed some degree of personal ambition into concern with collective performance.

* * *

The Continuing Decline of Party in the United States

Party Organizations

In the United States, party organization has traditionally meant state and local party organization. The national party generally has been a loose confederacy of subnational units that swings into action for a brief period every four years. This characterization remains true today, despite the somewhat greater influence and augmented functions of the national organizations. Though such things are difficult to measure precisely, there is general agreement that the formal party organizations have undergone a secular decline since their peak at the end of the nineteenth century. The prototype of the old-style organization was the urban machine, a form approximated today only in Chicago.

* * *

[Fiorina discusses the reforms of the late nineteenth and early twentieth century.]

In the 1970s two series of reforms further weakened the influence of organized parties in American national politics. The first was a series of legal changes deliberately intended to lessen organized party influence in the presidential nominating process. In the Democratic party, "New Politics" activists captured the national party apparatus and imposed a series of rules changes designed to "open up" the politics of presidential nominations. The Republican party—long more amateur and open than the Democratic party—adopted weaker versions of the Democratic rules changes. In addition, modifications of state electoral laws to conform to the Democratic rules changes (enforced by the federal courts) stimulated Republican rules changes as well.

* * *

A second series of 1970s reforms lessened the role of formal party organizations in the conduct of political campaigns. These are financing regulations growing out of the Federal Election Campaign Act of 1971 as amended in 1974 and 1976. In this case the reforms were aimed at cleaning up corruption in the financing of campaigns; their effects on the parties were a by-product, though many individuals accurately predicted its nature. Serious presidential candidates are now publicly financed. Though the law permits the national party to spend two cents per eligible voter on behalf of the nominee, it also obliges the candidate to set up a finance committee separate from the national party. Between this legally mandated separation and fear of violating spending limits or accounting regulations, for example, the law has the effect of encouraging the candidate to keep his party at arm's length.

* * *

The ultimate results of such reforms are easy to predict. A lesser party role in the nominating and financing of candidates encourages candidates to organize and conduct independent campaigns, which further weakens the role of parties. . . . [I]f parties do not grant nominations, fund their choices, and work for them, why should those choices feel any commitment to their party?

Party in the Electorate

In the citizenry at large, party takes the form of a psychological attachment. The typical American traditionally has been likely to identify with one or the other of the two major parties. Such identifications are transmitted across generations to some degree, and within the individual they tend to be fairly stable. But there is mounting evidence that the basis of identification lies in the individual's experiences (direct and vicarious, through family and social groups) with the parties in the past. Our current party system, of course, is based on the dislocations of the Depression period and the New Deal attempts to alleviate them. Though only a small proportion of those who experienced the Depression directly are active voters today, the general outlines of citizen party identifications much resemble those established at that time.

Again, there is reason to believe that the extent of citizen attachments to parties has undergone a long-term decline from a nineteenth-century high. And again, the New Deal appears to have been a period during which the decline was arrested, even temporarily reversed. But again, the decline of party has reasserted itself in the 1970s.

* * *

As the 1960s wore on, the heretofore stable distribution of citizen party identifications began to change in the general direction of weakened attachments to the parties. Between 1960 and 1976, independents, broadly defined, increased from less than a quarter to more than a third of the voting-age population. Strong identifiers declined from slightly more than a third to about a quarter of the population.

* * *

Indisputably, party in the electorate has declined in recent years. Why? To some extent the electoral decline results from the organizational decline. Few party organizations any longer have the tangible incentives to turn out the faithful and assure their loyalty. Candidates run independent campaigns and deemphasize their partisan ties whenever they see any short-term electoral gain in doing so. If party is increasingly less important in the nomination and election of candidates, it is not surprising that such diminished importance is reflected in the attitudes and behavior of the voter.

Certain long-term sociological and technological trends also appear to work against party in the electorate. The population is younger, and younger citizens traditionally are less attached to the parties than their elders. The population is more highly educated; fewer voters need some means of simplifying the choices they face in the political arena, and party, of course, has been the principal means of simplification. And the media revolution has vastly expanded the amount of information easily available to the citizenry. Candidates would have little incentive to operate campaigns independent of the parties if there were no means to apprise the citizenry of their independence. The media provide the means.

Finally, our present party system is an old one. For increasing numbers of citizens, party attachments based on the Great Depression seem lacking in relevance to the problems of the late twentieth century. Beginning with the racial issue in the 1960s, proceeding to the social issue of the 1970s, and to the energy, environment, and inflation issues of today, the parties have been rent by internal dissension. Sometimes they failed to take stands, at other times they took the wrong ones from the standpoint of the rank and file, and at most times they have failed to solve the new problems in any genuine sense. Since 1965 the parties have done little or nothing to earn the loyalties of modern Americans.

Party in Government

If the organizational capabilities of the parties have weakened, and their psychological ties to the voters have loosened, one would expect predictable consequences for the party in government. In particular, one would expect to see an increasing degree of split party control within and across the levels of American government. The evidence on this point is overwhelming.

* * *

The increased fragmentation of the party in government makes it more difficult for government officeholders to work together than in times past (not that it has ever been terribly easy). Voters meanwhile have a more difficult time attributing responsibility for government performance, and this only further fragments party control. The result is lessened collective responsibility in the system.

What has taken up the slack left by the weakening of the traditional [party] determinants of congressional voting? It appears that a variety of personal and local influences now play a major role in citizen evaluations of their representatives. Along with the expansion of the federal presence in American life, the traditional role of the congressman as an all-purpose ombudsman has greatly expanded. Tens of millions of citizens now are directly affected by federal decisions. Myriad programs provide opportunities to profit from government largesse, and myriad regulations impose costs and/or constraints on citizen activities. And, whether seeking to gain profit or avoid costs, citizens seek the aid of their congressmen. When a court imposes a desegregation plan on an urban school board, the congressional offices immediately are contacted for aid in safeguarding existing sources of funding and in determining eligibility for new ones. When a major employer announces plans to quit an area, the congressional offices immediately are contacted to explore possibilities for using federal programs to persuade the employer to reconsider. Contractors appreciate a good congressional word with DOD [Department of Defense] procurement officers. Local artistic groups cannot survive without NEA [National Endowment for the Arts] funding. And, of course, there are the major individual programs such as social security and veterans' benefits that create a steady demand for congressional information and aid services. Such activities are nonpartisan, nonideological, and, most important, noncontroversial. Moreover, the contribution of the congressman in the realm of district service appears considerably greater than the impact of his or her single vote on major national issues. Constituents respond rationally to this modern state of affairs by weighing nonprogrammatic constituency service heavily when casting their congressional votes. And this emphasis on the part of constituents provides the means for incumbents to solidify their hold on the office. Even if elected by a narrow margin, diligent service activities enable a congressman to neutralize or even convert a portion of those who would otherwise oppose him on policy or ideological grounds. Emphasis on local, nonpartisan factors in congressional voting enables the modern congressman to withstand national swings, whereas yesteryear's uninsulated congressmen were more dependent on preventing the occurrence of the swings.

* * *

[The result is the insulation of the modern congressional member from national forces altogether.]

The withering away of the party organizations and the weakening of party in the electorate have begun to show up as disarray in the party in government. As the electoral fates of congressmen and the president have diverged, their incentives to cooperate have diverged as well. Congressmen have little personal incentive to bear any risk in their president's behalf, since they no longer expect to gain much from his successes or suffer much from his failures. Only those who personally agree with the president's program and/or those who find that program well suited for their particular district support the president. And there are not enough of these to construct the coalitions necessary for action on the major issues now facing the country. By holding only the president responsible for national conditions, the electorate enables officialdom as a whole to escape responsibility. This situation lies at the root of many of the problems that now plague American public life.

Some Consequences of the Decline of Collective Responsibility

The weakening of party has contributed directly to the severity of several of the important problems the nation faces. For some of these, such as the government's inability to deal with inflation and energy, the connections are obvious. But for other problems, such as the growing importance of single-issue politics and the growing alienation of the American citizenry, the connections are more subtle.

Immobilism

As the electoral interdependence of the party in government declines, its ability to act also declines. If responsibility can be shifted to another level or to another officeholder, there is less incentive to stick one's neck out in an attempt to solve a given problem. Leadership becomes more difficult, the ever-present bias toward the short-term solution becomes more pronounced, and the possibility of solving any given problem lessens.

. . . [P]olitical inability to take actions that entail short-run costs ordinarily will result in much higher costs in the long run—we cannot continually depend on the technological fix. So the present American immobilism cannot be dismissed lightly. The sad thing is that the American people appear to understand the depth of our present problems and, at least in principle, appear prepared to sacrifice in furtherance of the long-run good. But they will not have an opportunity to choose between two or more such long-term plans. Although both parties promise tough, equitable policies, in the present state of our politics, neither can deliver.

Single-Issue Politics

In recent years both political analysts and politicians have decried the increased importance of single-issue groups in American politics. Some in fact would claim that the present immobilism in our politics owes more to the rise of single-issue groups than to the decline of party. A little thought, however, should reveal that the two trends are connected. Is single-issue politics a recent phenomenon? The contention is doubtful; such groups have always been active participants in American politics. The gun lobby already was a classic example at the time of President Kennedy's assassination. And however impressive the antiabortionists appear today, remember the temperance movement, which succeeded in getting its constitutional amendment. American history contains numerous forerunners of today's groups, from anti-Masons to abolitionists to the Klan—singularity of purpose is by no means a modern phenomenon. Why, then, do we hear all the contemporary hoopla about single-issue groups? Probably because politicians fear them now more than before and thus allow them to play a larger role in our politics. Why should this be so? Simply because the parties are too weak to protect their members and thus to contain single-issue politics.

In earlier times single-issue groups were under greater pressures to reach accommodations with the parties. After all, the parties nominated candidates, financed candidates, worked for candidates, and, perhaps most important, party voting protected candidates. When a contemporary single-issue group threatens to "get" an officeholder, the threat must be taken seriously.

* * *

Not only did the party organization have greater ability to resist single-issue pressures at the electoral level, but the party in government had greater ability to control the agenda, and thereby contain single-issue pressures at the policy-making level. Today we seem condemned to go through an annual agony over federal abortion funding. There is little doubt that politicians on both sides would prefer to reach some reasonable compromise at the committee level and settle the issue. But in today's decentralized Congress there is no way to put the lid on. In contrast, historians tell us that in the late nineteenth century a large portion of the Republican constituency was far less interested in the tariff and other questions of national economic development than in whether German immigrants should be permitted to teach their native language in their local schools, and whether Catholics and "liturgical Protestants" should be permitted to consume alcohol. Interestingly, however, the national agenda of the period is devoid of such issues. And when they do show up on the state level, the exceptions prove the rule; they produce party splits and striking defeats for the party that allowed them to surface.

In sum, a strong party that is held accountable for the government of a nation-state has both the ability and the incentive to contain particularistic pressures. It controls nominations, elections, and the agenda, and it collectively realizes that small minorities are small minorities no matter how intense they are. But as the parties decline they lose control over nominations and campaigns, they lose the loyalty of the voters, and they lose control of the agenda. Party officeholders cease to be held collectively accountable for party performance, but they become individually exposed to the political pressure of myriad interest groups. The decline of party permits interest groups to wield greater influence, their success encourages the formation of still more interest groups, politics becomes increasingly fragmented, and collective responsibility becomes still more elusive.

Popular Alienation from Government

For at least a decade political analysts have pondered the significance of survey data indicative of a steady increase in the alienation of the American public from the political process. . . . The American public is in a nasty mood, a cynical, distrusting, and resentful mood. The question is, Why?

If the same national problems not only persist but worsen while ever-greater amounts of revenue are directed at them, why shouldn't the typical citizen conclude that most of the money must be wasted by incompetent officials? If narrowly based interest groups increasingly affect our politics, why shouldn't citizens increasingly conclude that the interests run the government? For fifteen years the citizenry has listened to a steady stream of promises but has seen very little in the way of follow-through. An increasing proportion of the electorate does not believe that elections make a difference, a fact that largely explains the much-discussed post-1960 decline in voting turnout.

Continued public disillusionment with the political process poses several real dangers. For one thing, disillusionment begets further disillusionment. Leadership becomes more difficult if citizens do not trust their leaders and will not give them the benefit of a doubt. Policy failure becomes more likely if citizens expect the policy to fail. Waste increases and government competence decreases as citizens disrespect for politics encourages a lesser breed of person to make careers in government. And "government by a few big interests" becomes more than a cliché if citizens increasingly decide the cliché is true and cease participating for that reason.

Finally, there is the real danger that continued disappointment with particular government officials ultimately metamorphoses into disillusionment with government per se. Increasing numbers of citizens believe that government is not simply overextended but perhaps incapable of any further bettering of the world. Yes, government is overextended, inefficiency is pervasive, and ineffectiveness is all too common. But government is one of the few instruments of collective action we have, and even those committed to selective pruning of government programs cannot blithely allow the concept of an activist government to fall into disrepute.

Of late, however, some political commentators have begun to wonder whether contemporary thought places sufficient emphasis on government *for* the people. In stressing participation have we lost sight of *accountability*? Surely, we should be as concerned with what government produces as with how many participate. What good is participation if the citizenry is unable to determine who merits their support?

Participation and responsibility are not logically incompatible, but there is a degree of tension between the two, and the quest for either may be carried to extremes. Participation maximizers find themselves involved with quotas and virtual representation schemes, while responsibility maximizers can find themselves with a closed shop under boss rule. Moreover, both qualities can weaken the democracy they supposedly underpin. Unfettered participation produces Hyde Amendments* and immobilism.

DISCUSSION QUESTIONS

1. How do political parties provide "collective responsibility" and improve the quality of democracy? Do you believe the complaints raised by Fiorina more than twenty-five years ago remain persuasive?

2. Are strong parties in the interest of individual politicians? What might be some reasons why members of Congress would agree to strong parties or would distance themselves from their party's leadership?

---

* The Hyde Amendment, passed in 1976 (three years after *Roe v. Wade*), prohibited using Medicaid funds for abortion.

54

"Needed: A Political Theory for the New Era of Coalition Government in the United States"

James L. Sundquist

Writing in the latter half of the 1980s, James L. Sundquist largely agrees with Morris Fiorina's early-1980s assessment that political parties are weaker than in the past. Sundquist highlights how divided government has become the norm in the United States, but that this was not always so. In the first half of the twentieth century, divided government was rare, but since then, government has been under divided party control more often than not. To Sundquist, this development has shattered much of what political scientists and other observers expected from government. But is this such a bad thing? Sundquist asks whether the divided control of government has had the dire effects that many political scientists might have expected. His answer is: yes. In the age of divided government, he charges, government cannot make policy coherently and cannot respond to public needs effectively. The incentive for both parties, according to Sundquist, is to block and obstruct, and to create an issue for the next campaign, rather than enact good public policy.

On 8 November 1988, when the American voters decreed that Republican George Bush would succeed Ronald Reagan in the White House but the opposition Democratic Party would control both houses of the Congress, it was the sixth time in the last nine presidential elections that the electorate chose to split the government between the parties. As in 1988, so in the earlier elections of 1956, 1968, 1972, 1980, and 1984, the people placed their faith in Republican presidential leadership but voted to retain Democratic majorities in the House of Representatives and in the first three of those elections (as well as in 1988), Democratic majorities in the Senate also.

This is something new in American politics. When Dwight D. Eisenhower took his second oath of office in 1957, he was the first chief executive in seventy-two years—since Grover Cleveland in 1885—to confront on Inauguration Day a Congress of which even one house was controlled by the opposition party. Sometimes the opposition would win majorities in the House or the Senate, or both, at the midterm election, but even such occasions were relatively rare. In the fifty-eight years from 1897 through 1954, the country experienced divided government during only eight years—all in the last half of a presidential term—or 14 percent of the time. Yet in the thirty-six years from 1955 through 1990, the government will have been divided between the parties for twenty-four years—exactly two-thirds of that period.

A generation ago, then, the country passed from a long era of party government, when either the Republican or the Democratic Party controlled both the presidency and the Congress almost all of the time, to an era when the government was divided between the parties most of the time. Under these circumstances, the United States has its own unique version of coalition government—not a coalition voluntarily entered into by the parties but one forced upon them by the accidents of the electoral process.

It is the argument of this article that the advent of the new era has rendered obsolete much of the theory developed by political scientists, from the day of Woodrow Wilson to the 1950s, to explain how the United States government can and should work. That theory identified the political party as the indispensable instrument that brought cohesion and unity, and hence effectiveness, to the government as a whole by linking the executive and legislative branches in a bond of common interest. And, as a corollary, the party made it possible for the president to succeed in his indispensable role as leader and energizer of the governmental process; it accomplished that end because the congressional majorities, while they would not accept the president's leadership by virtue of his constitutional position as chief executive—institutional rivalry would bar that—would accept it in his alternate capacity as head of the political party to which the majorities adhered.

The generations of political scientists who expounded this theory paid little attention to how the government would and should function when the president and the Senate and House majorities were not all of the same party. They could in good conscience disregard that question because intervals of divided government in their experience had been infrequent and short-lived. Whenever the midterm election brought a division of the government, anyone concerned about that could take a deep breath and wait confidently for the next presidential election to put the system back into its proper alignment. As late as 1952 it had always done so in the memory of everybody writing on the subject. But since 1956, that has no longer been a certainty. It has not even been the probability. And that represents a momentous change in the American governmental system, for institutional processes and relationships are profoundly altered when the unifying bond of party disappears.

* * *

The Theory of Party Government and Presidential Leadership

Madison did not expound a new theory to supplant the one that he had been so instrumental in embedding in the Constitution. But without benefit of much explicit doctrine, the nation's political leaders developed in practice the system of party government—as distinct from nonpartisan government—that settled into place in the Jacksonian era and prevailed throughout the next century and a quarter. In each presidential election two national parties sought exactly what the Madisonian theory written into the Constitution was supposed to forestall: the capture of all three of the policy-making elements of the government—the presidency, Senate and House—by the same faction or party, so that the party could carry out its program.

No major party has ever said, "We want only the presidency," or only the Senate or the House. They have always said, "give us *total* responsibility." Since early in the nineteenth century, they have presented their programs formally in official party platforms. Asking for total power in the two elected branches, they have been eager to accept the total responsibility and accountability that would accompany it.

That was the theory of party government; and not only the politicians, but the people accepted it. The parties lined up naturally on opposite sides of whatever were the great issues of the day—creating a national bank, opening the West with turnpikes and railroads and canals financed by the national government, prohibiting slavery in the western territories, raising or lowering tariffs, mobilizing the national government to help the victims of the Great Depression, and so on. The people listened to the arguments of the two parties and made their choices. And when they did, the party they elected had a full opportunity to carry out is mandate, because when the voters chose a president each four years they normally entrusted control of the Congress to the president's party, thus making it fully responsible. From Andrew Jackson's time until the second election of Dwight Eisenhower in 1956, only four presidents— Zachary Taylor elected in 1848, Rutherford B. Hayes in 1876, James A. Garfield in 1880, and Grover Cleveland in 1884—had to confront immediately upon inauguration either a House of Representatives or a Senate organized by the opposition. In the nineteenth century these results may have been largely an artifact of the election process itself. The parties printed separate ballots listing their slates, and the voter selected the ballot of the party he preferred, marked it, and dropped it in the box. Yet after the government-printed, secret ballot came into universal use early in this century, straight-ticket voting and the resultant single-party control of the government continued to prevail. The voters gave the Republican Party responsibility for the entire government in the 1900s, again in the 1920s, and finally in 1952; and they chose the Democratic Party in the 1910s, 1930s, and 1940s. No president in the first half of this century ever had to suffer divided government upon taking office, and few had the problem even after the normal setback to the president's party in the midterm election.

As soon as political science emerged as a scholarly discipline, its adherents began to pronounce and elaborate the theoretical foundation of the system of party government that was in being. Parties were not only natural, since people were bound to organize to advance their differing notions as to the goals and programs of government, but the scholars concluded that they were useful and necessary too. Among their uses was the one that is the concern of this paper: their utility in unifying a government of dispersed powers and thereby making it effective.

*   *   *

By the time the Committee on Political parties of the American Political Science Association made its landmark report in 1950, it could simply assert, without feeling obliged to argue the case, that political parties are "indispensable instruments of government," necessary "to furnish a general kind of direction over the government as a whole" and for "integration of all of the far-flung activities of modern government." It then offered a series of reforms that would make the parties better organized, more tightly disciplined, and hence "more responsible."[1]

*   *   *

Like the Committee on Political Parties, the later writers who saw political parties as the unifying instrument in the governmental system generally agreed that they often failed to perform that function satisfactorily. Decentralized and federal in their organization, without authoritative central institutions, and made up of diverse ideological and cultural elements, the parties lacked discipline. Yet even without the reforms recommended by the committee, the political party was seen as nonetheless succeeding to some degree in bridging the gaps between the separated branches of the government.

*   *   *

And how is that degree of party discipline and responsibility achieved? In the national government, political scientists proclaim with virtual unanimity that it is through presidential leadership. When the party serves its unifying function, it is because the members of the president's party in the Congress recognize the president as not merely the head of the executive branch but as the leader of the band of "brothers in the same political lodge." In enacting as well as in administering the laws, the government cannot move dynamically and prudently without a recognized and accepted prime mover, a leader. And that leader is logically and necessarily the man chosen by the whole national party to carry its standard, and who has done so successfully in the most recent presidential election. Besides, the president has the resources of the entire executive branch to help him to develop coordinated programs. "The President proposes and the Congress disposes" long ago became the catch phrase to describe the legislative process.

* * *

By the 1960s, political science had developed a dominating theory as to how the American constitutional system should—and at its best, did —work. The political party was the institution that unified the separated branches of the government and brought coherence to the policymaking process. And because the president was the leader of his party, he was the chief policy maker of the entire government, presiding directly over the executive branch and indirectly working through and with his party's congressional leadership over the legislative branch as well.

The Old Theory in a New Era

This established theory presupposed one essential condition: there would in fact be a majority party in control of both branches of government. Rereading the literature of the midcentury, one is struck with how easily this condition was taken for granted. The writers could well do so, for in the twentieth century until 1955, the government had been divided between the parties only for four periods of two years each, and in each case in the last half of a presidential term—those of Taft, Wilson, Hoover, and Truman. A scholar who happened to be writing during or immediately after one of these intervals (or who was commenting on state governmental systems) might observe in parenthetical style that divided government could sometimes obscure responsibility, impede leadership, and thus thwart the fulfillment of the party government ideal. But the aberration was passed over quickly, without interrupting the flow of the basic argument. In the normal state of affairs, one party would have control of the policy-making branches of government; the other would be in opposition.

* * *

Divided government invalidates the entire theory of party government and presidential leadership, both elements of it. Divided government requires that the United States "construct a successful government out of antagonisms," which Wilson warned could not be done, and renders impossible the "close synthesis of active parts" that he found necessary. How can a party cast its web over the dispersed organs of government to bring a semblance of unity, in Key's phrase, if it controls but one of the branches? How can the majority party fulfill Burns's "vital function of integration," or rally the government's elements behind Penniman's "common purpose," or provide Rossiter's "bridges across the gaps," or Sorauf's "unifying force" if there is no majority party? How can the president lead the Congress if either or both houses are controlled by the party that fought to defeat him in the last election and has vowed to vanquish him, or his successor as his party's candidate, in the next one? But if the president cannot lead, Rossiter has told us, "weak and disorganized government" must follow. Our "toughest problems," Hyneman has admonished, will in that circumstance remain unsolved.[2]

The question at once arises: In our twenty-two years thus far of forced coalition government, have those gloomy forecasts been fulfilled? Eleven Congresses during the administrations of four presidents would appear to have given ample time for putting the established theory to the test. * * *

My own conclusion is that the predictions of the sages of the earlier generation have been borne out in this modern era of divided or coalition government. True, in the administrations of the four Republican presidents who had to make their peace with House Democratic majorities— and usually Democratic Senate majorities as well—there were significant accomplishments. President Dwight D. Eisenhower achieved a successful bipartisan foreign policy, and President Ronald Reagan managed to carry enough Democrats with him to enact for better or worse the essentials of his economic program in 1981. In subsequent Reagan years, the Congress and the administration collaborated across party lines to enact measures to bring illegal immigration under control, rescue social security, and reform the tax code. But Eisenhower and the Democratic Congress were stalemated on domestic measures throughout his six years of coalition government; the Nixon-Ford period was one of almost unbroken conflict and deadlock on both domestic and foreign issues; and the last seven years of Reagan found the government immobilized on some of the central issues of the day, unwilling to follow the leadership of the President or anyone else and deferring those issues in hope that somehow the 1988 election would resolve matters and render the government functional again.

By common consent, the most conspicuous among the urgent but unresolved problems has been, of course, the federal budget deficit, which has been running at between $150 billion and $200 billion a year since the great tax cut of 1981 took effect. The national debt now stands at well over $2 trillion, more than doubled in seven years of divided government. The United States has suffered the shock of falling from the status of a great creditor nation to the world's largest debtor nation, living on borrowing from abroad. The huge trade deficit, the shortfall in investment, and high interest rates are all blamed on the inability of the government to get the budget deficit under control. For all these reasons, virtually all of the country's responsible leaders—the president, the congressional leaders, and members of both parties in both houses—have for nearly over half a dozen years been proclaiming loudly and in unison that the nation simply cannot go on this way. The experts from outside —in the academic world, the Federal Reserve System, on Wall Street, in foreign countries—likewise agree that these deficits are economically perilous, whether or not they can be termed morally outrageous as well.

But during all that time that the country has seen a virtual consensus on the urgency of this problem, its governmental institutions have floundered in trying to cope with it. President Reagan sent the Congress his program, but the Congress flatly rejected it. The legislators in their turn floated suggestions, but the President killed them by promising a veto if they were passed. The congressional leaders and others pleaded for a summit meeting between the executive and legislative branches to hammer out a common policy. Finally, in November 1986, the meeting took place. But it is a measure of the national predicament that it took a half-trillion-dollar collapse in the stock market—a five-hundred-billion-dollar panic—before the two branches of the U.S. government would even sit down together. It was easier for Mikhail Gorbachev to get a summit meeting with the President of the United States than it was for the Speaker of the United States House of Representatives. And even the domestic summit that was finally held essentially papered over the problem rather than solved it.

Or we can draw examples of the failure of coalition government from international affairs. The country lost a war for the first time in history —in Vietnam—after another period of floundering in search of a policy, with the president pulling in one direction and the Congress in another. And the situation in Nicaragua was throughout the Reagan years almost a replica of Vietnam. The government could adopt no clear and effective policy at all; it could neither take measures strong enough to force the Sandinista government out of power, as the President and his administration wished to do, nor accept that government and make peace with it, as many in the Senate and the House would like. Then there is the Iran-Contra debacle. President Reagan in his own summation of that episode spoke of the "failure" of his policy, of "a policy that went astray," of "the damage that's been done," and he blamed it all on mistrust between the executive and legislative branches.[3]

But, some will argue, even if these or other instances can indeed be considered governmental failures attributable to mistrust between the unwilling partners of a forced coalition, the performance of recent unified government has been no better. The Kennedy and Carter years cannot claim overwhelming success, they will maintain, and while Lyndon Johnson proved to be a spectacular presidential leader of the Congress in the enactment of his Great Society measures in 1964 and 1965, he also led the country into the quagmire of Vietnam that in turn launched a devastating spiral of inflation. That is the difficulty of arguing from cases, as I suggested earlier.

* * * For better or worse, the discussion of the relative merits of unified

over divided government has to be pursued in abstract terms, as it was for the most part in the political science literature cited earlier.

The essence of the theoretical argument in favor of the unified government has been and is: For coherent and timely policies to be adopted and carried out—in short, for government to work effectively, as the established theory held—the president, the Senate, and the House must come into agreement. When the same party controls all three of these power centers, the incentive to reach such agreement is powerful despite the inevitable institutional rivalries and jealousies. The party *does* serve as the bridge or the web, in the metaphors of political science. But in divided government, it is not merely the separated institutions of government that must overcome their built-in rivalries but the opposing parties themselves. And that is bound to be a difficult, arduous process, characterized by conflict, delay, and indecision, and leading frequently to deadlock, inadequate and ineffective policies, or no policies at all.

Competition is the very essence of democratic politics. It gives democracy its meaning, and its vitality. The parties are the instruments of that competition. They are and should be organized for combat, not for collaboration and compromise. They live to win elections in order to advance their philosophies and programs. Therefore, each party strives and must strive to defeat the opposing party. But in a divided government, this healthy competition is translated into an unhealthy, debilitating conflict between the institutions of government themselves. Then, the president and Congress are motivated to try to discredit and defeat each other. Yet these are the institutions that, for anything constructive to happen, simply have to get together.

The average citizen reacts by simply condemning all politicians as a class. "Why don't those people in Washington stop playing politics and just get together and do what's right?" But that is not in the nature of things. Political parties, as the textbooks have always told us, are organized because people have genuine, deep disagreements about the goals and the programs of their societies. If a coalition government is to work, the leaders of committed groups have to be willing to submerge or abandon the very philosophies that caused them to organize their parties in the first place. They have to set aside the principles that are their reason for seeking governmental power. And they will do that only under compulsion of clear and grave necessity—usually, in other words, after deadlock has deteriorated into crisis.

In the American form of coalition government, if the president sends a proposal to Capitol Hill or takes a foreign policy stand, the opposition-controlled House or houses of Congress—unless they are overwhelmed by the president's popularity and standing in the country—simply *must* reject it. Otherwise they are saying the president is a wise and prudent leader. That would only strengthen him and his party for the next election, and how can the men and women of the congressional majority do that, when their whole object is to defeat him when that time arrives? By the same token, if the opposition party in control of Congress initiates a measure, the president has to veto it—or he is saying of his opponents that they are sound and statesmanlike, and so is building them up for the next election.

So when President Reagan sent his budgets to the Congress, the Democrats who controlled both houses had to pronounce them "dead on arrival," as they did. And when they came up with their alternatives, the President had to condemn them and hurl them back. Eventually, when the stream of recrimination and vetoes ran dry each year, some kind of budget was necessarily adopted; but it did not reflect the views of either party, and in terms of the consensus objective of deficit reduction it was a pale and ineffective compromise. Neither party would take responsibility, neither could be held accountable, each could point the finger at the other when the things went wrong.

In such circumstances, the people in their one solemn, sovereign act of voting cannot render a clear verdict and thus set the course of government. Elections lose their purpose and their meaning. The President, all through 1988, was saying, "Don't blame me for the budget deficit. It's those Democrats in Congress." And the Democrats were replying, "Don't blame us. Blame that man in the White House for not giving us the proper leadership." In November, the voters were not able to hold anybody clearly responsible, because, in fact nobody had been.

Our struggles with coalition government have demonstrated also the truth of the established wisdom concerning presidential leadership: in the American system there is simply no substitute for it. The Congress has 535 voting members, organized in two houses and in innumerable committees and subcommittees; every member is in principle the equal of every other member, and nobody can give directions to anybody else and make them stick. Such a body is simply not well designed for making coherent, decisive, coordinated policy. As the old theory told us, the system works best when the president proposes and the Congress disposes, when the president sets the agenda and leads, as everyone expects him to.

But how can leaders lead if followers don't follow? In divided government, presidential leadership becomes all but impossible. The president is not the leader of the congressional majority. He is precisely the opposite—the leader of their opposition, the man they are most dedicated to discredit and defeat. With great fanfare and immense hope, the people elect a president each four years. But then, most of the time these days, they give him a Congress a majority of whose members tried their best to beat him in the last election and will do so again in the next. To lead in those circumstances would be beyond the capability of any mortal. No one should blame presidents when they fail in a time of coalition government. It is the system that is at fault.

Nobody planned it this way. The country in no way made a conscious decision thirty years ago to abandon the responsible-party system that had served it well for almost the whole life of the nation. It was simply an accident of the electoral system. Almost unique in the world, the United States has an electoral process that permits people to split their tickets—to vote one way for president and the other way for Congress, if they so choose. And that is what enough of them have done to produce a divided outcome most of the time of late.

* * *

DISCUSSION QUESTIONS

1. Sundquist emphasizes the problems caused by divided government. Can you identify some potential benefits of having control of government split between the parties?

2. If we grant that divided government is as problematic as Sundquist argues, what are we to do about it? What kinds of reforms might make divided government less likely, and would you favor such reforms? Should Americans be discouraged from splitting their tickets when voting?

3. Public opinion polls show that a majority of Americans vote for candidates of the same party for president and Congress. Yet polls also show that a majority of Americans say they like the idea of divided government. How would you explain this seeming contradiction?

NOTES

1. Committee on Political Parties, *Toward a More Responsible Two-Party System*, supplement to the *American Political Science Review* 44 (September 1950), also published by Rinehart & Co., 1950. Quotation from Rinehart ed., 15, 16.

2. Fortunately for believers in party government, the problem of intra-party cohesion and discipline that so preoccupied the writers of the midcentury has to a large extent been solved by the events. The realignment of the party system since they wrote has produced Democratic and Republican parties that are more homogeneous than at any time within the memory of anyone now living; the minority wings that were once strong enough to disrupt the internal unity of both parties have withered. First to fade were the liberal Republicans, who until a couple of decades ago were potent enough to seriously contest for the presidential nomination; they are now ineffectual remnants that did not even put forward a candidate in 1988. Their mirror-image counterparts, the conservative Democrats, have been vanishing as well, although more slowly. Since the New Deal era, their wing of the party has been virtually confined to the South, and for thirty years its base there has been steadily eroding as conservatives find their political home in the burgeoning Republican Party. New Democratic senators from the South are no longer the Byrds, Robertsons, Eastlands, Russells, Thurmonds, and Hollands, who automatically voted with the Republicans on

major issues and made life miserable for Democratic presidents, Senate majority leaders, and House speakers; for the most part they are people who fit quite comfortably into the moderate-to-liberal national party, such as Terry Sanford, Bob Graham, and Wyche Fowler. (Strom Thurmond himself became a Republican long ago, and the son of Democratic Senator A. Willis Robertson made his race for the presidency in the Republican, not the Democratic, caucuses and primaries.) The same transformation has taken place in the House.

So the Republicans have become a solidly right-of-center party, very much in Ronald Reagan's image. If Republicans ever were to capture the Congress, they would have a little trouble attaining the unity necessary for true party government. And the Democrats, if and when they elect a president, will demonstrate a cohesion that will astound those who recall the schismatic party of thirty or even twenty years ago. Moreover, the reforms of congressional organization and procedures, which have strengthened the position of party leaders, party policy committees, and party caucuses, make it far more likely now that the cohesive Democratic majorities in the Congress would be able to overcome any obstruction that the truncated conservative wing might still attempt.

3. Address to the nation, 12 August 1987, as reported in *New York Times,* 13 August 1987.

55

"Parliamentary Government in the United States?" from *The State of the Parties*

Gerald M. Pomper

Writing in the late 1990s, Gerald Pomper revisits the issues raised by Fiorina and reaches a somewhat more positive assessment of the state of American political parties. Like Fiorina, Pomper believes that political parties should have a strong, prominent place in American politics. Unlike him, he believes that parties have that place. Looking at developments since the 1980s, Pomper argues that parties are today doing nearly everything that political scientists seem to want from them—they are constructing meaningful, coherent policy programs at the congressional level and in the party platforms; they are implementing the promises they make in campaigns; they are strikingly unified in Congress; they present clear, competing visions of the role of government; they are aggressively involved in campaigning, especially through providing campaign funds; and successful presidential candidates are largely those backed by the party rather than outsiders or mavericks. Although the president is obviously still a major institution in American government, Pomper wonders whether the U.S. might be evolving toward its own form of parliamentary government, in which the leadership of government clearly rests in the congressional parties. Suggesting that the presidency is a diminished institution, he asserts that "it may well be time to end the fruitless quest for a presidential savior and instead turn our attention, and our support, to the continuing and emerging strengths of our political parties."

In 1996, the important political decision for American political warriors was not the contest between Bill Clinton and Robert Dole. "For virtually all of the powerful groups behind the Republican Party their overriding goal of keeping control of the House stemmed from their view that that was where the real political power—near- and long-term—lay." Moreover, "Sitting in his office on the sixth floor of the AFL-CIO building on 16th Street, political director Steve Rosenthal said that labor, too, saw the House elections as the most important of 1996—more important than the contest for the Presidency."

These informed activists alert us to a major shift in the character of American politics. To baldly summarize my argument, I suggest that the United States is moving toward a system of parliamentary government, a fundamental change in our constitutional regime. This change is not a total revolution in our institutions, and it will remain incomplete, given the drag of historical tradition. Nevertheless, this trend can be seen if we look beyond the formal definition of parliamentary governments, the union of legislature and executive.

The parliamentary model is evident in both empirical and normative political science. Anthony Downs begins his classic work by defining a political party virtually as a parliamentary coalition, "a team of men seeking to control the governing apparatus by gaining office in a duly constituted election." Normatively, for decades, some political scientists have sought to create a "responsible party system," resembling such parliamentary features as binding party programs and legislative cohesion.

Significant developments toward parliamentary government can be seen in contemporary American politics. The evidence of these trends cannot be found in the formal institutions of the written (capital C) Constitution. Institutional stability, however, may disguise basic change. For example, in formal terms, the president is not chosen until the electoral college meets in December, although we know the outcome within hours of the closing of the polls in early November.

Let us go beyond "literary theory"[1] and compare the present reality of U.S. politics with more general characteristics attributed to parliamentary systems. In the ideal parliamentary model, elections are contests between competitive parties presenting alternative programs, under leaders chosen from and by the parties' legislators or activists. Electoral success is interpreted as a popular mandate in support of these platforms. Using their parliamentary powers, the leaders then enforce party discipline to implement the promised programs.

The United States increasingly evidences these characteristics of parliamentary government. This fundamental change is due to the development of stronger political parties. In particular, I will try to demonstrate transformations of American politics evident in the following six characteristics of the parties:

- The parties present meaningful programs;
- They bridge the institutional separations of national government;
- They reasonably fulfill their promises;
- They act cohesively under strong legislative leadership;
- They have assumed a major role in campaigning; and
- They provide the recruitment base for presidential candidates.

Party Programs

A parliamentary system provides the opportunity to enact party programs. By contrast, in the American system, observers often have doubted that there were party programs, and the multiple checks and balances of American government have made it difficult to enact any coherent policies. For evidence, I examine the major party platforms of 1992–1996, the 1994 Republican Contract with America, and the 1996 Democratic Families First Agenda.

In previous research, we argued that party platforms were meaningful statements and that they were good forecasts of government policy. We found, contrary to cynical belief, that platforms were composed of far more than hot air and empty promises. Rather, a majority of the platforms were relevant defenses and criticisms of the parties' past records and reasonably specific promises of future actions. Moreover, the parties delivered: close to 70 percent of their many specific pledges were actually fulfilled to some degree.

Furthermore, parties have differed in their programs. Examining party manifestos in the major industrial democracies over forty years, 1948–1988, Budge concludes, "American Democrats and Republicans . . . consistently differentiate themselves from each other on such matters as support for welfare, government intervention, foreign aid, and defense, individual initiative and freedom. . . . Indeed, they remain as far apart as many European parties on these points, and more so than many."

In recent years, we might expect platforms to be less important. National conventions have become television exercises rather than occasions for party decision making. The expansion of interest groups has made it more difficult to accomplish policy intentions. Candidate-centered campaigning reduces the incentives to achieve collective, party goals and appears to focus more on individual characteristics than on policy issues.

The party platforms of 1992 provide a test. An independent replication confirms our previous research on platform content. Perhaps surprisingly, this new work indicates that the most recent platforms, like those of previous years, provide significant political and policy statements. These manifestos meet one of the tests of a parliamentary system: meaningful party programs.

The 1992 platforms[2] can be divided into three categories: puff pieces of rhetoric and fact, approvals of one's own party policy record and candidates or disapproval of the opposition, and pledges for future action. The pledges, in turn, can be categorized as being simply rhetorical or general promises or more useful statements of future intentions, such as promises to continue existing policies, expressions of party goals, pledges of action, or quite detailed promises.[3]

Much in the platforms induces yawns and cynicism. The Democrats were fond of such rhetorical statements as "It is time to listen to the grassroots of America." (Actually a difficult task, since most plants are speechless.) The Republicans were prone to vague self-congratulation, as when they boasted, "Republicans recognize the importance of having fathers and mothers in the home." (Possibly even more so if these parents are unemployed, not distracted by jobs?)

Nevertheless, these documents—while hardly models of rational discussion—did provide useful guides to party positions. When the Democrats criticized "the Bush administration's efforts to bankrupt the public school system . . . through private school vouchers," and when the Republicans declared that "American families must be given choice in education," there was an implicit policy debate. Comparison was also facilitated by the similar distributions of platform statements across policy areas. Each party tended to devote about as much attention to particular or related policy areas as its opposition. The only important difference is that Democrats gave far more attention to issues involving women and abortion. Overall, about half of the platforms were potentially useful to the voters in locating the parties on a policy continuum.[4]

The 1994 Contract with America was even more specific. It consisted entirely of promises for the future, potentially focusing attention on public policy. Moreover, the large majority of its fifty-five sentences were reasonably specific promises. Pledges of definite action comprised 42 percent of the total document, and detailed pledges another 27 percent, while less than 4 percent consisted of only vague rhetoric. From the promise of a balanced budget amendment to advocacy of term limits, the Republicans foreshadowed major innovations in American institutions and law. This high degree of specificity can facilitate party accountability to the electorate.

Party as Programmatic Bridge

The great obstacle to party responsibility in the United States has always been the separation of national institutions, the constitutional division between the executive and legislative branches. Party has sometimes been praised as a bridge across this separation, and party reformers have often sought to build stronger institutional ties, even seeking radical constitutional revision to further the goal. Despite these hopes and plans, however, the separation has remained. Presidential parties make promises, but Congress has no institutional responsibility to act on these pledges.

In a parliamentary system, the most current research argues—contrary to Downs—"that office is used as a basis for attaining policy goals, rather than that policy is subordinated to office." In the United States as well, party program rather than institutional discipline may provide the bridge between the legislature and its executive. In previous years, however, we lacked a ready means to compare presidential and congressional programs. Now we have authoritative statements from both institutionalized wings of the parties. The Republican Contract with America marks a major first step toward coherent, interinstitutional programs.

The 1994 contract was far more than a campaign gimmick or an aberrational invention of Newt Gingrich. It was actually a terse condensation of continuing Republican Party doctrine. A majority of these promises had already been anticipated in 1992 and the party endorsed five-sixths of its provisions in 1996.

For example, the 1992 national platform criticized the Democratic Congress for its refusal "to give the President a line-item veto to curb their self-serving porkbarrel projects" and promised adoption of the procedure in a Republican Congress. The 1994 contract repeated the pledge of a "line-item veto to restore fiscal responsibility to an out-of-control Congress," while the 1996 platform reiterated, "A Republican president will fight wasteful spending with the line-item veto which was finally enacted by congressional Republicans this year over bitter Democrat opposition."[5] Republicans built on traditional party doctrine, specified the current party program, and then affirmed accountability for their actions. Building on this achievement in party building, and their claims of legislative "success," the Republicans have already promised to present a new contract for the elections at the turn of the century.

The Democrats imitatively developed a congressional program, the Families First Agenda, for the 1996 election. Intended primarily as a campaign document by the minority party, it is less specific than the Republican contract. Still, 90 of its 204 statements were reasonably precise promises. The legislative Democrats also showed significant and increasing agreement with their presidential wing and platform. By 1996, three-fourths of the congressional agenda was also incorporated into the Clinton program, and the official platform specifically praised the congressional program. The agenda's three sections—"security," "opportunity," and "responsibility"—paralleled those of the national platform (which added "freedom," "peace," and "community"—values presumably shared by congressional Democrats), and many provisions are replicated from one document to another.

The Republican contract with America and the Democratic Families First agenda, then, can be seen as emblems of party responsibility and likely precedents for further development toward parliamentary practice in American politics. Party doctrine has become a bridge across the separation of institutions.

Program Fulfillment

Both Democrats and Republicans, as they held power, followed through on their election promises, as expected in a parliamentary model. Despite the clumsiness of the Clinton administration, and despite the Democrats' loss of their long-term control of Congress in their catastrophic election defeat in 1994, they actually fulfilled most of the 167 reasonably specific pledges in their 1992 manifest.

A few examples illustrate the point. The Democrats promised negative action, in opposing major change in the Clean Air Act—and they stood fast. In their 1993 economic program, the Democrats won action similar to their platform pledge to "make the rich pay their fair share in taxes." Through executive action, the Clinton administration redeemed its promise to reduce U.S. military forces in Europe. The Democrats achieved full action on their promise of "A reasonable waiting period to permit background checks for purchases of handguns."

To be sure, the Democrats have not become latter-day George Washingtons, unable to tell an untruth. There clearly has been no action on the pledge to "limit overall campaign spending and . . . the disproportionate and excessive role of PACs." In other cases, the Democrats did try but were defeated, most notably in their promise of "reform of the health-care system to control costs and make health care affordable." (It is obviously too early to judge fulfillment of 1996 Democratic pledges, made in either the presidential platform or the congressional party Families First Agenda.)

Most impressive are not the failures but the achievements. Altogether, Democrats did accomplish something on nearly 70 percent of their 1992 promises, in contrast to inaction on only 19 percent. In a completely independent analysis, another researcher came to remarkably similar conclusions, calculating Clinton's fulfillment of his campaign promises at the same level, 69 percent (Shaw 1996).[6] I do not believe this record is the result of the virtues of the Democratic Party, which I use for this analysis simply because it controlled the government, nor can this record be explained by Bill Clinton's personal qualities of steadfast commitment to principle. The explanation is that we now have a system in which parties, whatever their names or leaders, make and keep promises.

This conclusion is strengthened if we examine the Republicans. While the GOP of course did not hold the presidency, it did win control of Congress in 1994. In keeping with the model of parliamentary government, Republicans interpreted their impressive victory as an endorsement of the Contract with America, and then they attempted to implement the program. We must remember that the 1994 election cannot be seen as a popular mandate for the Republican manifesto: two-thirds of the public had not even heard of it in November, and only 19 percent expressed support. The contract expressed party ideology, not voter demands.

Despite its extravagant tone and ideological character, the Republicans delivered on their contract just as Democrats fulfilled much of their 1992 platform. Of the more specific pledges, 69 percent were accomplished in large measure[7] (coincidentally, perhaps, the same success rate as the Democrats). Even if we include the rhetorical and unspecific sentences in our test, more than one-half of this party program was accomplished.

Despite the heroics of vetoes and government shutdown, despite bicameralism and the vaunted autonomy of the Senate, and despite popular disapproval, the reality is that most of the Contract with America was implemented. The Republicans accomplished virtually all that they promised in regard to congressional reform, unfunded mandates and welfare, as well as substantial elements of their program in regard to crime, child support, defense, and the social security earnings limit. Defeated on major economic issues, they later achieved many of these goals, including a balanced budget agreement in place of a constitutional amendment, a children's tax credit, and a reduction in capital gains taxes. On these questions, as indeed on the general range of American government, they won the greatest victory of all: they set the agenda for the United States, and the Democratic president eventually followed their lead. Such initiative is what we would expect in a parliamentary system.

* * *

Party Cohesion

Program fulfillment results from party unity. The overall trend in Congress, as expected in a parliamentary system, is toward more party differentiation.[8] One indicator is the proportion of legislative votes in which a majority of one party is opposed to a majority of the other (i.e., "party unity" votes). Not too long ago, in 1969, such party conflict was evident on only about one-third of all roll calls. By 1995, nearly three-fourths of House votes and over two-thirds of Senate roll calls showed these clear party differences. There is another trend—the increasing commitment of representatives and senators to their parties. The average legislator showed party loyalty (expressed as a "party unity score") of less than 60 percent in 1970. In 1996, the degree of loyalty had climbed to 80 percent for Democrats and to an astounding 87 percent for Republicans. Cohesion was still greater on the thirty-three House roll calls in 1995 on final passage of items in the Contract with America. Republicans were unanimous on sixteen of these votes, and the *median* number of Republican dissents was but *one*. Neither the British House of Commons nor the erstwhile Supreme Soviet could rival this record of party unity.

The congressional parties now are ideologically cohesive bodies, even with the occasional but significant split among Democrats on such issues as trade and welfare reform. We need to revise our political language to take account of this ideological cohesion. There are no more "Dixiecrats" or southern conservative Democrats, and therefore there is no meaningful "conservative coalition" in Congress. Supportive evidence is found in the same roll call data: the average southern Democrat supported his or her party 71 percent of the time in 1996, and barely over a tenth of the roll calls found Dixie legislators in opposition to their own party and in alliance with a majority of Republicans. It also seems likely that "liberal Republican" will soon be an oxymoron restricted to that patronized minority holding a pro-choice attitude on abortion, confined to the back of the platform or, so to speak, to the back of the party bus.

Republicans have been acting like a parliamentary party beyond their ideological unity on a party program. The "central leaders efforts during the Contract period were attempts to *impose* a form of party government," which succeeded in winning cooperation from committee chairman and changed roll call behavior as "many Republicans modified their previous preferences in order to accommodate their party colleagues." Beyond programmatic goals, the Republicans have created strong party institutions in Congress, building on previous Democratic reforms.

Even after the Contract with America is completely passed or forgotten, these institutions will likely remain. In their first days in power, as they organized the House, the Republicans centralized power in the hands of the Speaker, abolished institutionalized caucuses of constituency interests, distributed chairmanships on the basis of loyalty to the party program and in disregard of seniority, and changed the ratios of party memberships on committees to foster passage of the party program. Instruments of discipline have become more prevalent and more exercised, including caucus resolutions, committee assignments, aid in securing campaign contributions, and disposition of individual members' bills.

The building of parliamentary party institutions continues. Some of the structural changes in the House have now been adopted by both the Senate and the Democrats, perhaps most significantly the rotation of committee chairmanships, curbing the antiparty influence of seniority. The Republicans have insisted that committees report party bills, even when opposed by the chair, as in the cases of term limits and telecommunications. The party record became the major issue in the 1996 congressional elections, with party leaders Newt Gingrich and Richard Armey doing their best to aid loyalists—but only loyalists—through fund-raising and strong-arming of ideological allies among political action committees.

The party differences and cohesion in Congress partially reflect the enhanced power of legislative leaders. The more fundamental reason for congressional party unity—as in parliamentary systems—is not discipline as much as agreement. Party members vote together because they think the same way. Republicans act as conservatives because they *are* conservatives; Democrats act like liberals or as they now prefer, progressives because they believe in these programs.

*   *   *

The most recent nominating conventions provide further support for the ideological cohesion of the national parties. The CBS/*New York Times* Poll found massive differences between Republican and Democratic delegates on questions involving the scope of government, social issues, and international affairs. A majority of these partisans opposed each other on *all* of ten questions; they were remotely similar on only one issue—international trade—and were in essentially different political worlds (fifty or more percentage points apart) on issues of governmental regulation, the environment, abortion, assault weapons, civil rights, affirmative action, and immigration.

Party Organization

Party unity has another source, related to the recruitment of individual candidates with a common ideology. Unity is also fostered by the development of strong national party organizations, precisely measured by the dollars of election finance. Amid all of the proper concern over the problems of campaign contributions and spending, we have neglected the increasing importance of the parties in providing money, "the mother's milk of politics."

There are two large sources of party money: the direct subsidies provided by the federal election law, and the "soft money" contributions provided for the parties' organizational work. Together, even in 1992, these funds totaled $213 million for the major candidates and their parties.[9] Underlining the impact of this party spending, the Republican and Democratic presidential campaigns in 1992 each spent twice as much money as did billionaire Ross Perot, whose candidacy is often seen as demonstrating the decline of the parties.

An enhanced party role was also evident in the other national elections of 1992. Beyond direct contributions and expenditures, the parties developed a variety of ingenious devices, such as bundling, coordinated spending, and agency agreements, to again become significant players in the election finance game. Overall, in 1992, the six national party committees spent $290 million. (For comparison, total spending in all House and Senate races was $678 million.)[10] The party role became even more evident in 1994, with the victory of a Republican majority originally recruited and financed by Newt Gingrich's GOPAC, a party body disguised as a political action committee.

The party role expanded hugely in 1996, bolstered by the Supreme Court, in its 1996 *Colorado* decision.[11] The Court approved unlimited "independent" spending by political parties on behalf of its candidates. Moreover, four justices explicitly indicated that they were prepared to approve even direct unlimited expenditures by parties, and three other justices are ready to rule on that issue in a future case.

The parties quickly took advantage of the Court's opening. Together, Republican and Democratic party groups spent close to a billion dollars, conservatively 35 percent of all election spending, without even counting the $160 million in federal campaign subsidies for the presidential race.[12]

Despite the commonplace emphasis on "candidate-centered" campaigns, the parties' expenditures were greater than that of all individual House and Senate candidates combined. In discussions of election finance, political action committees receive most of the attention, and condemnation, but the reality is that PACs are of decreasing importance. PACs' money has barely increased since 1988, and they were outspent 2 to 1 by the parties in 1996.[13] The parties now have the muscle to conduct campaigns and present their programs, to act as we would expect of parliamentary contestants.

Party Leadership

Parties need leaders as much as money. In parliamentary governments, leaders achieve power through their party activity. That has always been the case even in America when we look at congressional leadership: a long apprenticeship in the House and Senate has usually been required before one achieves the positions of Speaker, majority and minority leader, and whip. A strong indication of the development of parliamentary politics in the United States is the unrecognized trend toward party recruitment for the presidency, the allegedly separated institution.

* * *

Contrary to the fears of many observers, the new presidential nominating system has developed along with new institutions of party cohesion. Front-runners have great advantages in this new system, but that means that prominent party figures—rather than obscure dark horses stabled in smoke-filled rooms—are most likely to win nomination. Contrary to fears of a personalistic presidency, the candidates chosen in the postreform period tackle tough issues, support their party's program, and agree with their congressional party's leaders on policy positions as much, or even more, than in the past.

Contemporary presidential nominations have become comparable—although not identical—to the choice of leadership in a hypothetical U.S. parliamentary system. Is the selection of Reagan in 1980 that different from the British Tories' choice of Margaret Thatcher to lead the party's turn toward ideological free market conservatism? In a parliamentary system, would not Bush and Dole, Reagan's successors, be the ideal analogues to Britain's John Major? Is the selection of Mondale as the liberal standard-bearer of the liberal Democratic Party that different from the lineage of left-wing leaders in the British Labour Party? Is the Democratic turn toward the electoral center with Clinton not analogous to Labour's replacement of Michael Foot by Neil Kinnock, John Smith, and Tony Blair?

To be sure, American political leadership is still quite open, the parties quite permeable. Presidential nominations do depend greatly on personal coalitions, and popular primaries are the decisive points of decision. Yet it is also true that leadership of the parties is still, and perhaps increasingly, related to prominence within the parties.

Toward Parliamentary Government?

Do these changes amount to parliamentary government in the United States? Certainly not in the most basic definitional sense, since we will surely continue to have separated institutions, in which the president is elected differently from the legislature, and the Senate differently from the House. Unlike a formal parliamentary system, the president will hold his office for a fixed term, regardless of the "votes of confidence" he wins or loses in Congress. By using his veto and the bully pulpit of the White House, Bill Clinton has proven that the president is independent and still "relevant." It is also true that we will never have a system in which a single political party can both promise and deliver a complete and coherent ideological program. As Jones correctly maintains, American government remains a "separated system," in which "serious and continuous in-party and cross-party coalition building typifies policy making." These continuing features were strikingly evident in the adoption of welfare reform in the 104th Congress.

But parliaments also evidence coalition building, particularly in multi-party systems. British parliamentarians can be stalemated by factional and party differences on issues such as Northern Ireland just as the Democrats and Republicans were on health care in the 103d Congress. Achieving a consensual policy on the peace process in Israel's multiparty system is as difficult as achieving a consensual policy on abortion among America's two parties.

* * *

The party basis of parliamentary government will continue, because the ideological basis of intraparty coherence and interparty difference will continue and even be increased with the ongoing departure of moderate legislators of both parties. The need for strong party institutions in Congress will also be furthered by new policy problems, more rapid turnover of membership, and the continuation of split-party control of government.

Of course, the presidency will remain relevant, yet it may also come to be seen as almost superfluous. A principal argument on behalf of Bob Dole's candidacy was that he would sign the legislation passed by a Republican Congress—hardly a testament to presidential leadership. President Clinton fostered his reelection by removing himself from partisan leadership, "triangulating" the White House between congressional Democrats and Republicans, and following the model of patriotic chief of state created by George Washington and prescribed in *The Federalist*: "to guard the community against the effects of faction, precipitancy, or of any impulse unfriendly to the public good."

*   *   *

The absence of presidential initiative is more than a problem of the Clinton administration. Throughout American history, the president has persistently provided the energy of American government, the source of new "regimes" and policy initiatives. Perhaps the lassitude of contemporary politics is only the latest example of the recurrent cycle of presidential initiative, consolidation, and decline. Or, more profoundly, perhaps it marks the decline of the executive office itself as a source of creativity in the government of the United States.

America needs help. It may well be time to end the fruitless quest for a presidential savior and instead turn our attention, and our support, to the continuing and emerging strengths of our political parties. We are developing, almost unnoticed, institutions of semiparliamentary, semiresponsible government. To build a better bridge between the past and the future, perhaps this new form of American government is both inevitable and necessary.

DISCUSSION QUESTIONS

1. Does Pomper address the concerns raised by Fiorina, or are there aspects of his argument that have not been resolved by the changes in political parties identified by Pomper?

2. If the U.S. is evolving toward a semi-parliamentary system, is this a good thing? Pomper suggests that the presidency is weakening. Are there advantages to a system like this compared to a system with a stronger presidency?

3. Pomper was writing before the presidency of George W. Bush. Has the evolution toward congressional-party leadership continued under the Bush presidency?

NOTES

I gratefully acknowledge the help of Andrea Lubin, who performed the content analyses of party platforms included in this essay.
1. The phrase is from Walter Baghot's (1928: 1) classic analysis of the realities of British politics.
2. The texts are found in *The Vision Shared* (Washington, D.C.: Republican National Committee, 1992) and for the less loquacious Democrats, *Congressional Quarterly Weekly Report* 50 (July 18, 1992): 2107–13.
3. Each sentence, or distinct clause within these sentences, constituted the unit of analysis. Because of its great length, only alternate sentences in the Republican platform were included. No selection bias is evident or, given the repetitive char-

acter of the platforms, likely. In total, there are 426 units of analysis in the Democratic platform, 758 in the Republican. For further details on the techniques used, see Pomper and Lederman (1980: 235–48). To avoid contamination or wishful thinking on my part, Lubin did the analysis independently. My later revisions tended to classify the platform sentences as less specific and meaningful than hers, contrary to any optimistic predisposition.

4. The "useful" categories are policy approval and policy criticism, candidate approval and candidate criticism, and future policy promises classified as pledges of continuity, expressions of goals, pledges of action, and detailed pledges.

5. *The Vision Shared* (1992 Republican Platform), p. 46; "Contract with America," in Wilcox (1995: 70): *Restoring the American Dream* (1996 Republican Platform), p. 25.

6. Using the same content categories, Carolyn Shaw (1996), of the University of Texas, lists 150 presidential campaign promises of 1992 in the more specific categories. In regard to fulfillment, she employs the methods of Fishel (1985). With this method, she finds that there was "fully comparable" or "partially comparable" action on 69 percent of Clinton's proposals. This record is higher than that found by Fishel for any president from Kennedy through Reagan.

7. Even this figure underestimates the impact of the Contract with America. I have counted the failure to pass term limits as a defeat, although the Republicans actually promised no more than a floor vote, and I have not given the party credit for achievements in the following Congress.

8. These data are drawn from *Congressional Quarterly Weekly Report* 54 (December 21, 1996): 3461–67.

9. *Congressional Quarterly Weekly Report* 51 (May 15, 1993): 1197.

10. *Congressional Quarterly Weekly Report* 51 (March 20, 1993): 691: Federal Election Commission, *Record* 19 (May 1993): 22.

11. *Colorado Republican Federal Campaign Committee et al. v. Federal Election Commission* (No. 95-489. 1996 U.S. LEXIS 4258).

12. The parties spent $628 million directly, plus at least $263 million and up to $400 million in soft money. For detailed figures, see *Congressional Quarterly Weekly Report* 55 (April 5, 1997): 767–73.

13. For an excellent discussion of 1996 election spending, see Corrado (1997).

Debating the Issues: Red versus Blue America: Are We Polarized?

In 1992, Patrick Buchanan famously stated at the Republican national convention that the United States was in the midst of a culture war that posited traditional, conservative social values against liberal, secular values. Bill Clinton's defeat of President George H. W. Bush seemed to defuse that idea: Clinton was a southern Democrat who had pushed his party toward the ideological center and, although garnering only 43 percent of the vote, he won states in all regions of the country. His 1996 victory was broader, adding states he had lost in 1992. In the 2000 presidential election, however, a striking regional pattern emerged in the results. Al Gore, the Democratic candidate, did well on the coasts and in the upper Midwest, while George W. Bush, the Republican candidate, picked up the remaining states. Many analysts were struck by this "red state/blue state" pattern—named after the coloring of the states on post-election maps—and suggested that it told us something more fundamental about American politics. Indeed, these analysts argued, Patrick Buchanan was in large measure right: the American public was deeply divided and polarized and in many respects living in two different worlds culturally. This polarization showed up not only in voting, but in presidential approval ratings, with the partisan gap in evaluations of Bill Clinton and George W. Bush being larger than for any previous presidents. The 2004 presidential election proved to be a near carbon-copy of 2000: with a few exceptions, the red states stayed red and the blue states stayed blue. President Bush picked up the votes of 78 percent of white, born-again evangelical Christians, while John Kerry received the support of 56 percent of all other voters. Bush received 60 percent of the votes of those individuals attending religious services at least once weekly; Kerry picked up 57 percent of the votes of individuals who attended services a few times a year or not at all. Eighty-five percent of conservatives voted for Bush; the same percentage of liberals voted for Kerry; and moderates split 54–45 percent for Kerry. Among those who believe abortion should be illegal in most or all cases, Bush received 75 percent of the vote. Among those who believe abortion should be legal in most or all cases, Kerry received 66 percent.

Is America deeply polarized along partisan lines? Is there a culture war? Is the red state/blue state split real? Is there division on certain highly charged issues but not on most others? Are the divisions just artifacts of the way that survey questions are worded? In this debate, political scientists James Q. Wilson and Morris Fiorina agree that the political elite—elected leaders, the news media, and interest groups—are polarized, but they disagree on the answers to the rest of the questions. Wilson argues that the cultural split is deep and is reflected in party competition and the public opinion of partisans within and across the red and blue states. Fiorina counters that the idea of a cultural war is vastly exaggerated—there might be a skirmish, but there is no war.

56

"What Culture Wars? Debunking the Myth of a Polarized America"

Morris P. Fiorina

> "There is a religious war going on in this country, a cultural war as critical to the kind of nation we shall be as the Cold War itself, for this war is for the soul of America."

With those ringing words insurgent candidate Pat Buchanan fired up his supporters at the 1992 Republican National Convention. To be sure, not all delegates cheered Buchanan's call to arms, which was at odds with the "kinder, gentler" image that George H.W. Bush had attempted to project. Election analysts later included Buchanan's fiery words among the factors contributing to the defeat of President Bush, albeit one of lesser importance than the slow economy and the repudiation of his "Read my lips, no new taxes" pledge.

In the years since Buchanan's declaration of cultural war, the idea of a clash of cultures has become a common theme in discussions of American politics. The culture war metaphor refers to a displacement of the classic economic conflicts that animated twentieth-century politics in the advanced democracies by newly emergent moral and cultural ones. The literature generally attributes Buchanan's inspiration to a 1991 book, *Culture Wars*, by sociologist James Davison Hunter, who divided Americans into the culturally "orthodox" and the culturally "progressive" and argued that increasing conflict was inevitable.

No one has embraced the concept of the culture war more enthusiastically than journalists, ever alert for subjects that have "news value." Conflict is high in news value. Disagreement, division, polarization, battles, and war make good copy. Agreement, consensus, moderation, compromise, and peace do not. Thus, the notion of a culture war fits well with the news sense of journalists who cover politics. Their reports tell us that contemporary voters are sharply divided on moral issues. As David Broder wrote in the *Washington Post* in November 2000, "The divide went deeper than politics. It reached into the nation's psyche. . . . It was the moral dimension that kept Bush in the race."

Additionally, it is said that close elections do not reflect indifferent or ambivalent voters; rather, such elections reflect evenly matched blocs of deeply committed partisans. According to a February 2002 report in *USA Today*, "When George W. Bush took office, half the country cheered and the other half seethed"; some months later the *Economist* wrote that "such political divisions cannot easily be shifted by any president, let alone in two years, because they reflect deep demographic divisions. . . . The 50-50 nation appears to be made up of two big, separate voting blocks, with only a small number of swing voters in the middle."

The 2000 election brought us the familiar pictorial representation of the culture war in the form of the "red" and "blue" map of the United States. Vast areas of the heartland appeared as Republican red, while coastal and Great Lakes states took on a Democratic blue hue. Pundits reified the colors on the map, treating them as prima facie evidence of deep cultural divisions: Thus "Bush knew that the landslide he had wished for in 2000 . . . had vanished into the values chasm separating the blue states from the red ones" (John Kenneth White, in *The Values Divide*). In the same vein, the *Boston Herald* reported Clinton adviser Paul Begala as saying, on November 18, 2000, that "tens of millions of good people in Middle America voted Republican. But if you look closely at that map you see a more complex picture. You see the state where James Byrd was lynched—dragged behind a pickup truck until his body came apart—it's red. You see the state where Matthew Shepard was crucified on a split-rail fence for the crime of being gay—it's red. You see the state where right-wing extremists blew up a federal office building and murdered scores of federal employees—it's red."

Claims of bitter national division were standard fare after the 2000 elections, and few commentators publicly challenged them. On the contrary, the belief in a fractured nation was expressed even by high-level political operatives. Republican pollster Bill McInturff commented to the *Economist* in January 2001 that "we have two massive colliding forces. One is rural, Christian, religiously conservative. [The other] is socially tolerant, pro-choice, secular, living in New England and the Pacific Coast." And Matthew Dowd, a Bush reelection strategist, explained to the *Los Angeles Times* why Bush has not tried to expand his electoral base: "You've got 80 to 90 percent of the country that look at each other like they are on separate planets."

The journalistic drumbeat continues unabated. A November 2003 report from the Pew Research Center led E. J. Dionne Jr. of the *Washington Post* to comment: "The red states get redder, the blue states get bluer, and the political map of the United States takes on the coloration of the Civil War."

And as the 2004 election approaches, commentators see a continuation, if not an intensification, of the culture war. *Newsweek*'s Howard Fineman wrote in October 2003, "The culture war between the Red and Blue Nations has erupted again—big time—and will last until Election Day next year. Front lines are all over, from the Senate to the Pentagon to Florida to the Virginia suburbs where, at the Bush-Cheney 2004 headquarters, they are blunt about the shape of the battle: 'The country's split 50-50 again,' a top aide told me, 'just as it was in 2000.' "

In sum, observers of contemporary American politics have apparently reached a new consensus around the proposition that old disagreements about economics now pale in comparison to new divisions based on sexuality, morality, and religion, divisions so deep and bitter as to justify talk of war in describing them.

Yet research indicates otherwise. Publicly available databases show that the culture war script embraced by journalists and politicos lies somewhere between simple exaggeration and sheer nonsense. There is no culture war in the United States; no battle for the soul of America rages, at least none that most Americans are aware of.

Certainly, one can find a few warriors who engage in noisy skirmishes. Many of the activists in the political parties and the various cause groups do hate each other and regard themselves as combatants in a war. But their hatreds and battles are not shared by the great mass of Americans—certainly nowhere near "80–90 percent of the country"—who are for the most part moderate in their views and tolerant in their manner. A case in point: To their embarrassment, some GOP senators recently learned that ordinary Americans view gay marriage in somewhat less apocalyptic terms than do the activists in the Republican base.

If swing voters have disappeared, how did the six blue states in which George Bush ran most poorly in 2000 all elect Republican governors in 2002 (and how did Arnold Schwarzenegger run away with the 2003 recall in blue California)? If almost all voters have already made up their minds about their 2004 votes, then why did John Kerry surge to a 14-point trial-heat lead when polls offered voters the prospect of a Kerry-McCain ticket? If voter partisanship has hardened into concrete, why do virtually identical majorities in both red and blue states favor divided control of the presidency and Congress, rather than unified control by their party? Finally, and ironically, if voter positions have become so uncompromising, why did a recent CBS story titled "Polarization in America" report that 76 percent of Republicans, 87 percent of Democrats, and 86 percent of Independents would like to see elected officials compromise more rather than stick to their principles?

Still, how does one account for reports that have almost 90 percent of Republicans planning to vote for Bush and similarly high numbers of Democrats planning to vote for Kerry? The answer is that while voter *positions* have not polarized, their *choices* have. There is no contradiction here; positions and choices are not the same thing. Voter choices are functions of their positions and the positions and actions of the candidates they choose between.

Republican and Democratic elites unquestionably have polarized. But it is a mistake to assume that such elite polarization is equally present in the broader public. It is not. However much they may claim that they are responding to the public, political elites do not take extreme positions because *voters* make them. Rather, by presenting them with polarizing alternatives, elites make voters appear polarized, but the reality shows through clearly when voters have a choice of more moderate alternatives—as with the aforementioned Republican governors.

Republican strategists have bet the Bush presidency on a high-risk gamble. Reports and observation indicate that they are attempting to win in 2004 by getting out the votes of a few million Republican-leaning evangelicals who did not vote in 2000, rather than by attracting some modest proportion of 95 million other non-voting Americans, most of them moderates, not to mention moderate Democratic voters who could have been persuaded to back a genuinely compassionate conservative. Such a strategy leaves no cushion against a negative turn of events and renders the administration vulnerable to a credible Democratic move toward the center. Whether the Democrats can capitalize on their opportunity remains to be seen.

57

"How Divided Are We?"

JAMES Q. WILSON

The 2004 election left our country deeply divided over whether our country is deeply divided. For some, America is indeed a polarized nation, perhaps more so today than at any time in living memory. In this view, yesterday's split over Bill Clinton has given way to today's even more acrimonious split between Americans who detest George Bush and Americans who detest John Kerry, and similar divisions will persist as long as angry liberals and angry conservatives continue to confront each other across the political abyss. Others, however, believe that most Americans are moderate centrists, who, although disagreeing over partisan issues in 2004, harbor no deep ideological hostility. I take the former view.

By polarization I do not have in mind partisan disagreements alone. These have always been with us. Since popular voting began in the 19th century, scarcely any winning candidate has received more than 60 percent of the vote, and very few losers have received less than 40 percent. Inevitably, Americans will differ over who should be in the White House. But this does not necessarily mean they are polarized.

By polarization I mean something else: an intense commitment to a candidate, a culture, or an ideology that sets people in one group definitively apart from people in another, rival group. Such a condition is revealed when a candidate for public office is regarded by a competitor and his supporters not simply as wrong but as corrupt or wicked; when one way of thinking about the world is assumed to be morally superior to any other way; when one set of political beliefs is considered to be entirely correct and a rival set wholly wrong. In extreme form, as defined by Richard Hofstadter in *The Paranoid Style in American Politics* (1965), polarization can entail the belief that the other side is in thrall to a secret conspiracy that is using devious means to obtain control over society. Today's versions might go like this: "Liberals employ their dominance of the media, the universities, and Hollywood to enforce a radically secular agenda"; or, "conservatives, working through the religious Right and the big corporations, conspired with their hired neocon advisers to invade Iraq for the sake of oil."

Polarization is not new to this country. It is hard to imagine a society more divided than ours was in 1800, when pro-British, pro-commerce New Englanders supported John Adams for the presidency while pro-French, pro-agriculture Southerners backed Thomas Jefferson. One sign of this hostility was the passage of the Alien and Sedition Acts in 1798; another was that in 1800, just as in 2000, an extremely close election was settled by a struggle in one state (New York in 1800, Florida in 2000).

The fierce contest between Abraham Lincoln and George McClellan in 1864 signaled another national division, this one over the conduct of the Civil War. But thereafter, until recently, the nation ceased to be polarized in that sense. Even in the half-century from 1948 to (roughly) 1996, marked as it was by sometimes strong expressions of feeling over whether the presidency should go to Harry Truman or Thomas Dewey, to Dwight Eisenhower or Adlai Stevenson, to John F. Kennedy or Richard Nixon, to Nixon or Hubert Humphrey, and so forth, opinion surveys do not indicate widespread detestation of one candidate or the other, or of the people who supported him.

Now they do. Today, many Americans and much of the press regularly speak of the President as a dimwit, a charlatan, or a knave. A former Democratic presidential candidate has asserted that Bush "betrayed" America by launching a war designed to benefit his friends and corporate backers. A senior Democratic Senator has characterized administration policy as a series of "lies, lies, and more lies" and has accused Bush of plotting a "mindless, needless, senseless, and reckless" war. From the other direction, similar expressions of popular disdain have been directed at Senator John Kerry (and before him at President Bill Clinton); if you have not heard them, that may be because (unlike many of my relatives) you do not live in Arkansas or Texas or other locales where the *New York Times* is not read. In these places, Kerry is widely spoken of as a scoundrel.

In the 2004 presidential election, over two-thirds of Kerry voters said they were motivated explicitly by the desire to defeat Bush. By early 2005, President Bush's approval rating, which stood at 94 percent among Republicans, was only 18 percent among Democrats—the largest such gap in the history of the Gallup poll. These data, moreover, were said to reflect a mutual revulsion between whole geographical sections of the country, the so-called Red (Republican) states versus the so-called Blue (Democratic) states. As summed up by the distinguished social scientist who writes humor columns under the name of Dave Barry, residents of Red states are "ignorant racist fascist knuckle-dragging NASCAR-obsessed cousin-marrying roadkill-eating tobacco-juice-dribbling gun-fondling religious fanatic rednecks," while Blue-state residents are "godless unpatriotic pierced-nose Volvo-driving France-loving leftwing Communist latte-sucking tofu-chomping holistic-wacko neurotic vegan weenie perverts."

To be sure, other scholars differ with Dr. Barry. To them, polarization, although a real enough phenomenon, is almost entirely confined to a small number of political elites and members of Congress. In *Culture War?* (2004), which bears the subtitle "The Myth of a Polarized America," Morris Fiorina of Stanford argues that policy differences between voters in Red and Blue states are really quite small, and that most are in general agreement even on issues like abortion and homosexuality.

But the extent of polarization cannot properly be measured by the voting results in Red and Blue states. Many of these states are in fact deeply divided internally between liberal and conservative areas, and gave the nod to one candidate or the other by only a narrow margin. Inferring the views of individual citizens from the gross results of presidential balloting is a questionable procedure.

Nor does Fiorina's analysis capture the very real and very deep division over an issue like abortion. Between 1973, when *Roe v. Wade* was decided, and now, he writes, there has been no change in the degree to which people will or will not accept any one of six reasons to justify an abortion: (1) the woman's health is endangered; (2) she became pregnant because of a rape; (3) there is a strong chance of a fetal defect; (4) the family has a low income; (5) the woman is not married; and (6) the woman simply wants no more children. Fiorina may be right about that. Nevertheless, only about 40 percent of all Americans will support abortion for any of the last three reasons in his series, while over 80 percent will support it for one or another of the first three.

In other words, almost all Americans are for abortion in the case of maternal emergency, but fewer than half if it is simply a matter of the mother's preference. That split—a profoundly important one—has remained in place for over three decades, and it affects how people vote. In 2000 and again in 2004, 70 percent of those who thought abortion should always be legal voted for Al Gore or John Kerry, while over 70 percent of those who thought it should always be illegal voted for George Bush.

Division is just as great over other high-profile issues. Polarization over the war in Iraq, for example, is more pronounced than any war-related controversy in at least a half-century. In the fall of 2005, according to Gallup, 81 percent of Democrats but only 20 percent of Republicans thought the war in Iraq was a mistake. During the Vietnam war, by contrast, itself a famously contentious cause, there was more unanimity across party lines, whether for or against: in late 1968 and early 1969, about equal numbers of Democrats and Republicans thought the intervention there was a mistake. Pretty much the same was true of Korea: in early 1951, 44 percent of Democrats and 61 percent of Republicans thought the war was a mistake—a partisan split, but nowhere near as large as the one over our present campaign in Iraq.

Polarization, then, is real. But what explains its growth? And has it spread beyond the political elites to influence the opinions and attitudes of ordinary Americans?

The answer to the first question, I suspect, can be found in the changing politics of Congress, the new competitiveness of the mass media, and the rise of new interest groups.

That Congress is polarized seems beyond question. When, in 1998, the House deliberated whether to impeach President Clinton, all but four Republican members voted for at least one of the impeachment articles, while only five Democrats voted for even one. In the Senate, 91 percent of Republicans voted to convict on at least one article; every single Democrat voted for acquittal.

The impeachment issue was not an isolated case. In 1993, President Clinton's budget passed both the House and the Senate without a single Republican vote in favor. The same deep partisan split occurred over taxes and supplemental appropriations. Nor was this a blip: since 1950, there has been a steady increase in the percentage of votes in Congress pitting most Democrats against most Republicans.

In the midst of the struggle to pacify Iraq, Howard Dean, the chairman of the Democratic National Committee, said the war could not be won and Nancy Pelosi, the leader of the House Democrats, endorsed the view that American forces should be brought home as soon as possible. By contrast, although there was congressional grumbling (mostly by Republicans) about Korea and complaints (mostly by Democrats) about Vietnam, and although Senator George Aiken of Vermont famously proposed that we declare victory and withdraw, I cannot remember party leaders calling for unconditional surrender.

The reasons for the widening fissures in Congress are not far to seek. Each of the political parties was once a coalition of dissimilar forces: liberal Northern Democrats and conservative Southern Democrats, liberal coastal Republicans and conservative Midwestern Republicans. No longer; the realignments of the South (now overwhelmingly Republican) and of New England (now strongly Democratic) have all but eliminated legislators who deviate from the party's leadership. Conservative Democrats and liberal Republicans are endangered species now approaching extinction. At the same time, the ideological gap between the parties is growing: if there was once a large overlap between Democrats and Republicans—remember "Tweedledum and Tweedledee"?—today that congruence has almost disappeared. By the late 1990s, virtually every Democrat was more liberal than virtually every Republican.

The result has been not only intense partisanship but a sharp rise in congressional incivility. In 1995, a Republican-controlled Senate passed a budget that President Clinton proceeded to veto; in the loggerhead that followed, many federal agencies shut down (in a move that backfired on the Republicans). Congressional debates have seen an increase not only in heated exchanges but in the number of times a representative's words are either ruled out of order or "taken down" (that is, written by the clerk and then read aloud, with the offending member being asked if he or she wishes to withdraw them).

It has been suggested that congressional polarization is exacerbated by new districting arrangements that make each House seat safe for either a Democratic or a Republican incumbent. If only these seats were truly competitive, it is said, more centrist legislators would be elected. That seems plausible, but David C. King of Harvard has shown that it is wrong: in the House, the more competitive the district, the more extreme the views of the winner. This odd finding is apparently the consequence of a nomination process dominated by party activists. In primary races, where turnout is low (and seems to be getting lower), the ideologically motivated tend to exercise a preponderance of influence.

All this suggests a situation very unlike the half-century before the 1990s, if perhaps closer to certain periods in the eighteenth and nineteenth centuries. Then, too, incivility was common in Congress, with members not only passing the most scandalous remarks about each other but on occasion striking their rivals with canes or fists. Such partisan feeling ran highest when Congress was deeply divided over slavery before the Civil War and over Reconstruction after it. Today the issues are different, but the emotions are not dissimilar.

Next, the mass media: Not only are they themselves increasingly polarized, but consumers are well aware of it and act on that awareness. Fewer people now subscribe to newspapers or watch the network evening news. Although some of this decline may be explained by a preference for entertainment over news, some undoubtedly reflects the growing conviction that the mainstream press generally does not tell the truth, or at least not the whole truth.

In part, media bias feeds into, and off, an increase in business competition. In the 1950s, television news amounted to a brief 30-minute interlude in the day's programming, and not a very profitable one at that; for the rest of the time, the three networks supplied us with westerns and situation comedies. Today, television news is a vast, growing, and very profitable venture by the many broadcast and cable outlets that supply news twenty-four hours a day, seven days a week.

The news we get is not only more omnipresent, it is also more competitive and hence often more adversarial. When there were only three television networks, and radio stations were forbidden by the fairness doctrine from broadcasting controversial views, the media gravitated toward the middle of the ideological spectrum, where the large markets could be found. But now that technology has created cable news and the Internet, and now that the fairness doctrine has by and large been repealed, many media outlets find their markets at the ideological extremes.

Here is where the sharper antagonism among political leaders and their advisers and associates comes in. As one journalist has remarked about the change in his profession, "We don't deal in facts [any longer], but in attributed opinions." Or, these days, in unattributed opinions. And those opinions are more intensely rivalrous than was once the case.

The result is that, through commercial as well as ideological self-interest, the media contribute heavily to polarization. Broadcasters are eager for stories to fill their round-the-clock schedules, and at the same time reluctant to trust the government as a source for those stories. Many media outlets are clearly liberal in their orientation; with the arrival of Fox News and the growth of talk radio, many are now just as clearly conservative.

The evidence of liberal bias in the mainstream media is very strong. The Center for Media and Public Affairs (CMPA) has been systematically studying television broadcasts for a quarter-century. In the 2004 presidential campaign, John Kerry received more favorable mentions than any presidential candidate in CMPA's history, especially during the month before election day. This is not new: since 1980 (and setting aside the recent advent of Fox News), the Democratic candidate has received more favorable mentions than the Republican candidate in every race except the 1988 contest between Michael Dukakis and George H. W. Bush. A similarly clear orientation characterizes weekly newsmagazines like *Time* and *Newsweek*.

For its part, talk radio is listened to by about one-sixth of the adult public, and that one-sixth is made up mostly of conservatives.[1] National Public Radio has an audience of about the same size; it is disproportionately liberal. The same breakdown affects cable-television news, where the rivalry is between CNN (and MSNBC) and Fox News. Those who watch

CNN are more likely to be Democrats than Republicans; the reverse is emphatically true of Fox. As for news and opinion on the Internet, which has become an important source for college graduates in particular, it, too, is largely polarized along political and ideological lines, emphasized even more by the culture that has grown up around news blogs.

At one time, our culture was only weakly affected by the media because news organizations had only a few points of access to us and were largely moderate and audience-maximizing enterprises. Today the media have many lines of access, and reflect both the maximization of controversy and the cultivation of niche markets. Once the media talked to us; now they shout at us.

And then there are the interest groups. In the past, the major ones—the National Association of Manufacturers, the Chamber of Commerce, and labor organizations like the AFL-CIO—were concerned with their own material interests. They are still active, but the loudest messages today come from very different sources and have a very different cast to them. They are issued by groups concerned with social and cultural matters like civil rights, managing the environment, alternatives to the public schools, the role of women, access to firearms, and so forth, and they directly influence the way people view politics.

Interest groups preoccupied with material concerns can readily find ways to arrive at compromise solutions to their differences; interest groups divided by issues of rights or morality find compromise very difficult. The positions taken by many of these groups and their supporters, often operating within the two political parties, profoundly affect the selection of candidates for office. In brief, it is hard to imagine someone opposed to abortion receiving the Democratic nomination for President, or someone in favor of it receiving the Republican nomination.

Outside the realm of party politics, interest groups also file briefs in important court cases and can benefit from decisions that in turn help shape the political debate. Abortion became a hot controversy in the 1970s not because the American people were already polarized on the matter but because their (mainly centrist) views were not consulted; instead, national policy was determined by the Supreme Court in a decision, *Roe v. Wade*, that itself reflected a definition of "rights" vigorously promoted by certain well-defined interest groups.

Polarization not only is real and has increased, but it has also spread to rank-and-file voters through elite influence.

In *The Nature and Origins of Mass Opinion* (1992), John R. Zaller of UCLA listed a number of contemporary issues—homosexuality, a nuclear freeze, the war in Vietnam, busing for school integration, the 1990–91 war to expel Iraq from Kuwait—and measured the views held about them by politically aware citizens. (By "politically aware," Zaller meant people who did well answering neutral factual questions about politics.) His findings were illuminating.

Take the Persian Gulf war. Iraq had invaded Kuwait in August 1990. From that point through the congressional elections in November 1990, scarcely any elite voices were raised to warn against anything the United States might contemplate doing in response. Two days after the mid-term elections, however, President George H. W. Bush announced that he was sending many more troops to the Persian Gulf. This provoked strong criticism from some members of Congress, especially Democrats.

As it happens, a major public-opinion survey was under way just as these events were unfolding. Before criticism began to be voiced in Congress, both registered Democrats and registered Republicans had supported Bush's vaguely announced intention of coming to the aid of Kuwait; the more politically aware they were, the greater their support. After the onset of elite criticism, the support of Republican voters went up, but Democratic support flattened out. As Bush became more vigorous in indicating his aims, politically aware voters began to differ sharply, with Democratic support declining and Republican support increasing further.

Much the same pattern can be seen in popular attitudes toward the other issues studied by Zaller. As political awareness increases, attitudes split apart, with, for example, highly aware liberals favoring busing and job guarantees and opposing the war in Vietnam, and highly aware conservatives opposing busing and job guarantees and supporting the war in Vietnam.[2]

But why should this be surprising? To imagine that extremist politics has been confined to the chattering classes is to believe that Congress, the media, and American interest groups operate in an ideological vacuum. I find that assumption implausible.

As for the extent to which these extremist views have spread, that is probably best assessed by looking not at specific issues but at enduring political values and party preferences. In 2004, only 12 percent of Democrats approved of George Bush; at earlier periods, by contrast, three to four times as many Democrats approved of Ronald Reagan, Gerald Ford, Richard Nixon, and Dwight D. Eisenhower. Over the course of about two decades, in other words, party affiliation had come to exercise a critical influence over what people thought about a sitting President.

The same change can be seen in the public's view of military power. Since the late 1980s, Republicans have been more willing than Democrats to say that "the best way to ensure peace is through military strength." By the late 1990s and on into 2003, well over two-thirds of all Republicans agreed with this view, but far fewer than half of all Democrats did. In 2005, three-fourths of all Democrats but fewer than a third of all Republicans told pollsters that good diplomacy was the best way to ensure peace. In the same survey, two-thirds of all Republicans but only one fourth of all Democrats said they would fight for this country "whether it is right or wrong."

Unlike in earlier years, the parties are no longer seen as Tweedledum and Tweedledee. To the contrary, as they sharpen their ideological differences, attentive voters have sharpened their ideological differences. They now like either the Democrats or the Republicans more than they once did, and are less apt to feel neutral toward either one.

How deep does this polarization reach? As measured by opinion polls, the gap between Democrats and Republicans was twice as great in 2004 as in 1972. In fact, rank-and-file Americans disagree more strongly today than did politically active Americans in 1972.

To be sure, this mass polarization involves only a minority of all voters, but the minority is sizable, and a significant part of it is made up of the college-educated. As Marc Hetherington of Vanderbilt puts it: "people with the greatest ability to assimilate new information, those with more formal education, are most affected by elite polarization." And that cohort has undeniably grown.

In 1900, only 10 percent of all young Americans went to high school. My father, in common with many men his age in the early twentieth century, dropped out of school after the eighth grade. Even when I graduated from college, the first in my family to do so, fewer than one-tenth of all Americans over the age of twenty-five had gone that far. Today, 84 percent of adult Americans have graduated from high school and nearly 27 percent have graduated from college. This extraordinary growth in schooling has produced an ever larger audience for political agitation.

Ideologically, an even greater dividing line than undergraduate education is postgraduate education. People who have proceeded beyond college seem to be very different from those who stop with a high-school or college diploma. Thus, about a sixth of all voters describe themselves as liberals, but the figure for those with a postgraduate degree is well over a quarter. In mid-2004, about half of all voters trusted George Bush; less than a third of those with a postgraduate education did. In November of the same year, when over half of all college graduates voted for Bush, well over half of the smaller cohort who had done postgraduate work voted for Kerry. According to the Pew Center for Research on the People and the Press, more than half of all Democrats with a postgraduate education supported the antiwar candidacy of Howard Dean.

The effect of postgraduate education is reinforced by being in a profession. Between 1900 and 1960, write John B. Judis and Ruy Teixeira in *The Emerging Democratic Majority* (2002), professionals voted pretty much the same way as business managers; by 1988, the former began supporting Democrats while the latter supported Republicans. On the other hand, the effect of postgraduate education seems to outweigh the effect of affluence. For most voters, including college graduates, having higher incomes means becoming more conservative; not so for those with a postgraduate education, whose liberal predilections are immune to the wealth effect.

The results of this linkage between ideology, on the one hand, and congressional polarization, media influence, interest-group demands, and education on the other are easily read in the commentary surrounding the 2004 election. In their zeal to denigrate the President, liberals, pronounced one conservative pundit, had "gone quite around the twist." According to liberal spokesmen, conservatives with their "religious intolerance" and their determination to rewrite the Constitution had so befuddled their fellow Americans that a "great nation was felled by a poisonous nut."

If such wholesale slurs are not signs of polarization, then the word has no meaning. To a degree that we cannot precisely measure, and over issues that we cannot exactly list, polarization has seeped down into the public, where it has assumed the form of a culture war. The sociologist James Davison Hunter, who has written about this phenomenon in a mainly religious context, defines culture war as "political and social hostility rooted in different systems of moral understanding." Such conflicts, he writes, which can involve "fundamental ideas about who we are as Americans," are waged both across the religious/secular divide and within religions themselves, where those with an "orthodox" view of moral authority square off against those with a "progressive" view.

To some degree, this terminology is appropriate to today's political situation as well. We are indeed in a culture war in Hunter's sense, though I believe this war is itself but another component, or another symptom, of the larger ideological polarization that has us in its grip. Conservative thinking on political issues has religious roots, but it also has roots that are fully as secular as anything on the Left. By the same token, the liberal attack on conservatives derives in part from an explicitly "progressive" religious orientation—liberal Protestantism or Catholicism, or Reform Judaism—but in part from the same secular sources shared by many conservatives.

But what, one might ask, is wrong with having well-defined parties arguing vigorously about the issues that matter? Is it possible that polarized politics is a good thing, encouraging sharp debate and clear positions? Perhaps that is true on those issues where reasonable compromises can be devised. But there are two limits to such an arrangement.

First, many Americans believe that unbridgeable political differences have prevented leaders from addressing the problems they were elected to address. As a result, distrust of government mounts, leading to an alienation from politics altogether. The steep decline in popular approval of our national officials has many causes, but surely one of them is that ordinary voters agree among themselves more than political elites agree with each other—and the elites are far more numerous than they once were.

In the 1950s, a committee of the American Political Science Association (APSA) argued the case for a "responsible" two-party system. The model the APSA had in mind was the more ideological and therefore more "coherent" party system of Great Britain. At the time, scarcely anyone thought our parties could be transformed in such a supposedly salutary direction. Instead, as Governor George Wallace of Alabama put it in his failed third-party bid for the presidency, there was not a "dime's worth of difference" between Democrats and Republicans.

What Wallace forgot was that, however alike the parties were, the public liked them that way. A half-century ago, Tweedledum and Tweedledee enjoyed the support of the American people; the more different they have become, the greater has been the drop in popular confidence in both them and the federal government.

A final drawback of polarization is more profound. Sharpened debate is arguably helpful with respect to domestic issues, but not for the management of important foreign and military matters. The United States, an unrivaled superpower with unparalleled responsibilities for protecting the peace and defeating terrorists, is now forced to discharge those duties with its own political house in disarray.

We fought World War II as a united nation, even against two enemies (Germany and Italy) that had not attacked us. We began the wars in Korea and Vietnam with some degree of unity, too, although it was eventually whittled away. By the early 1990s, when we expelled Iraq from Kuwait, we had to do so over the objections of congressional critics; the first President Bush avoided putting the issue to Congress altogether. In 2003 we toppled Saddam Hussein in the face of catcalls from many domestic leaders and opinion-makers. Now, in stabilizing Iraq and helping that country create a new free government, we have proceeded despite intense and mounting criticism, much of it voiced by politicians who before the war agreed that Saddam Hussein was an evil menace in possession of weapons of mass destruction and that we had to remove him.

Denmark or Luxembourg can afford to exhibit domestic anguish and uncertainty over military policy; the United States cannot. A divided America encourages our enemies, disheartens our allies, and saps our resolve—potentially to fatal effect. What General Giap of North Vietnam once said of us is even truer today. America cannot be defeated on the battlefield, but it can be defeated at home. Polarization is a force that can defeat us.

NOTES

1. The political disposition of most radio talk-show hosts is explained by William G. Mayer in "Why Talk Radio Is Conservative," *Public Interest*, Summer 2004.
2. True, the "elite effect" may not be felt across the board. With most of the issues Zaller investigated, even well-informed citizens would have had little firsthand experience, and so their minds were of necessity open to the influence of their "betters." Results might have been different had he measured their views on matters about which most Americans believe themselves to be personally well-informed: crime, inflation, drug abuse, or their local schools.

Polarized America?

February 21, 2006
To the editor:
James Q. Wilson (February) takes issue with my demonstration in *Culture War? The Myth of a Polarized America* (with Samuel Abrams and Jeremy Pope) that the polarization evident among the members of the American political class has only a faint reflection in the American public. As a long-time admirer of Wilson's work I am naturally concerned when his take on some aspect of American politics differs from mine. But I believe that his criticisms are a result of misunderstanding. I would like to address two of them.

First, Wilson discounts our red state-blue state comparisons with the comment that "Inferring the views of individual citizens from the gross results of presidential balloting is a questionable procedure." Indeed it is, which is why we did not do that. As we wrote in the book, inferring polarization from close elections is precisely what pundits have done and why their conclusions have been wrong. In contrast, we report detailed analyses of the policy views expressed by voters in 2000 and 2004 and contrary to the claims of Garry Wills, Maureen Dowd, and other op-ed columnists, we find surprisingly small differences between the denizens of the blue states and the red states. As we show in the book and emphasize repeatedly, people's *choices* (as expressed, say, in presidential balloting) can be polarized while their *positions* are not, and the evidence strongly indicates that this is the case.

Moreover, we report that not only are red and blue state citizens surprisingly similar in their views, but other studies find little evidence of growing polarization no matter how one slices and dices the population—affluent v. poor, white v. black v. brown, old v. young, well educated v. the less educated, men v. women, and so on. Like many before him, Wilson confuses partisan *sorting* with polarization—the Democrats have largely shed their conservative southern wing while Republicans have largely shed their liberal Rockefeller wing, resulting in more distinct parties, even while the aggregate distribution of ideology and issue stances among the citizenry remains much the same as in the past.

Second, Wilson criticizes our analysis of Americans' views on the specific issue of abortion, contending that the small numerical differences expressed by people on a General Social Survey scale constitute a significantly larger substantive difference. Although we disagree, even if one accepted Wilson's contention, it would not apply to our supporting analysis of a differently-worded Gallup survey item that yields the same conclusions, or to numerous other survey items that clearly show that most Americans are "pro-choice, buts."

For example, Wilson notes that "70 percent of those who thought abor-

460 Morris P. Fiorina

tion should always be legal voted for Al Gore or John Kerry, while over 70 percent of those who thought it should always be illegal voted for George Bush." True enough, but he does not mention that Gallup repeatedly finds that a majority of the American people place themselves between those polar categories—they think abortion should be "legal only under certain circumstances." Even limiting the analysis to avowed partisans, in 2005 only 30 percent of Democrats thought abortion should always be legal, and fewer than 30 percent of Republicans thought it should always be illegal. One can raise questions about every survey item that has ever been asked, but the cumulative weight of the evidence on Americans' abortion views is overwhelming. Contrary to the wishes of the activists on both sides, the American people prefer a middle ground on abortion, period.

Wilson approvingly cites James Davison Hunter, whose book, *Culture War*, inspired Patrick Buchanan's 1992 speech at the Republican National Convention. In a forthcoming Brookings Institution volume, Hunter now limits his thesis to "somewhere between 10 and 15 percent who occupy these opposing moral and ideological universes." That leaves more than 80 percent of the American public not engaged in the moral and ideological battles reveled in by the political class. Note that Wilson's examples of incivil discourse reference "the press," "a former Democratic presidential candidate," "a senior Democratic Senator," "liberal spokesmen," and "one conservative pundit." Absent from this list are well-intentioned, ordinary working Americans not given to the kind of incendiary remarks that get quoted by journalists.

I share Wilson's concern with the potentially harmful consequences of polarization. But the first step in addressing those concerns is to get the facts correct. I remain convinced that we have done that. If Americans are offered competent, pragmatic candidates with a problem-solving orientation, the shallow popular roots of political polarization will be exposed for all to see.

Morris P. Fiorina
Stanford, California

Discussion Questions

1. According to Wilson, what are the chief factors contributing to polarization and cultural division in the United States? Are these factors likely to change anytime soon? What part, if any, of Wilson's argument would Fiorina agree with?

2. Based on the articles and other information you might have, do you think Fiorina is right that the American public is not deeply split on a range of issues and that they tend to favor more moderate solu-

tions to problems rather than taking extreme positions? Can you think of issues, other than abortion, for which this would be true?

3. If you were an adviser for one of the two major parties, how would you advise them to address the issue of polarization or culture war? Should they emphasize issues where broader consensus might be possible? Or is it the job of political parties to emphasize precisely those issues that might be the most divisive in order to appeal to their strongest supporters? Which is better for voters?

4. Party strategies often talk about changing a party's public image. In your view, what would a party have to do to change its public image significantly? What would convince you that a party had changed?

CHAPTER 12

Groups and Interests

58

"Political Association in the United States" from *Democracy in America*

ALEXIS DE TOCQUEVILLE

The right of political association has long been a cornerstone of American democracy. Alexis de Tocqueville, a French citizen who studied early nineteenth-century American society, argued that the right to associate provides an important check on a majority's power to suppress a political minority. Tocqueville pointed out that allowing citizens to associate in a variety of groups with a variety of crosscutting interests provides a political outlet for all types of political interests, and enables compromises to be reached as each interest group attempts to build support among shifting coalitions. "There is a place for individual independence," Tocqueville argued, in the American system of government. "[A]s in society, all the members are advancing at the same time toward the same goal, but they are not obliged to follow exactly the same path."

Better use has been made of association and this powerful instrument of action has been applied to more varied aims in America than anywhere else in the world.

* * *

The inhabitant of the United States learns from birth that he must rely on himself to combat the ills and trials of life; he is restless and defiant in his outlook toward the authority of society and appeals to its power only when he cannot do without it. The beginnings of this attitude first appear at school, where the children, even in their games, submit to rules settled by themselves and punish offenses which they have defined themselves. The same attitude turns up again in all the affairs of social life. If some obstacle blocks the public road halting the circulation of traffic, the neighbors at once form a deliberative body; this improvised assembly produces an executive authority which remedies the trouble before anyone has thought of the possibility of some previously constituted authority beyond that of those concerned. Where enjoyment is concerned, people associate to make festivities grander and more orderly. Finally, associations are formed to combat exclusively moral troubles: intemperance is fought in common. Public security, trade and industry, and morals and religion all provide the aims for associations in the United States. There is no end which the human will despairs of attaining by the free action of the collective power of individuals.

* * *

The right of association being recognized, citizens can use it in different ways. An association simply consists in the public and formal support of specific doctrines by a certain number of individuals who have undertaken to cooperate in a stated way in order to make these doctrines prevail. Thus the right of association can almost be identified with freedom to write, but already associations are more powerful than the press. When some view is represented by an association, it must take clearer and more precise shape. It counts its supporters and involves them in its cause; these supporters get to know one another, and numbers increase zeal. An association unites the energies of divergent minds and vigorously directs them toward a clearly indicated goal.

Freedom of assembly marks the second stage in the use made of the right of association. When a political association is allowed to form centers of action at certain important places in the country, its activity becomes greater and its influence more widespread. There men meet, active measures are planned, and opinions are expressed with that strength and warmth which the written word can never attain.

But the final stage is the use of association in the sphere of politics. The supporters of an agreed view may meet in electoral colleges and appoint mandatories to represent them in a central assembly. That is, properly speaking, the application of the representative system to one party.

* * *

In our own day freedom of association has become a necessary guarantee against the tyranny of the majority. In the United States, once a party has become predominant, all public power passes into its hands; its close supporters occupy all offices and have control of all organized forces. The most distinguished men of the opposite party, unable to cross the barrier keeping them from power, must be able to establish themselves outside it; the minority must use the whole of its moral authority to oppose the physical power oppressing it. Thus the one danger has to be balanced against a more formidable one.

The omnipotence of the majority seems to me such a danger to the American republics that the dangerous expedient used to curb it is actually something good.

Here I would repeat something which I have put in other words when speaking of municipal freedom: no countries need associations more— to prevent either despotism of parties or the arbitrary rule of a prince —than those with a democratic social state. In aristocratic nations secondary bodies form natural associations which hold abuses of power in check. In countries where such associations do not exist, if private people did not artificially and temporarily create something like them, I see no other dike to hold back tyranny of whatever sort, and a great nation might with impunity be oppressed by some tiny faction or by a single man.

* * *

In America the citizens who form the minority associate in the first place to show their numbers and to lessen the moral authority of the majority, and secondly, by stimulating competition, to discover the arguments most likely to make an impression on the majority, for they always hope to draw the majority over to their side and then to exercise power in its name.

Political associations in the United States are therefore peaceful in their objects and legal in the means used; and when they say that they only wish to prevail legally, in general they are telling the truth.

* * *

The Americans * * * have provided a form of government within their associations, but it is, if I may put it so, a civil government. There is a place for individual independence there; as in society, all the members are advancing at the same time toward the same goal, but they are not obliged to follow exactly the same path. There has been no sacrifice of will or of reason, but rather will and reason are applied to bring success to a common enterprise.

DISCUSSION QUESTIONS

1. Tocqueville argues that "freedom of association has become a necessary guarantee against the tyranny of the majority." Although freedom of association is clearly a central part of any free society, are there features of contemporary American politics that would suggest a rethinking of this benign view?

2. Placing restrictions on interest-group activities is difficult because of the constitutional protections afforded to these groups. The Constitution guarantees the people the right to assemble and to petition government regarding their grievances, and it also guarantees free-

dom of speech. All these are the essence of interest-group activity. Nonetheless, many Americans are uneasy with the influence wielded by organized interest groups. What, if any, restrictions on interest groups would you be comfortable with? Can you think of any instances where the influence of groups should be limited—for example, political extremists like the various militia groups, or large political action committees in electoral campaigns?

59

"The Logic of Collective Action" from *Rise and Decline of Nations*

Mancur Olson

Americans organize at a tremendous rate to pursue common interests in the political arena. Yet not all groups are created equal, and some types of political organizations are much more common than others. In particular, it is far easier to organize groups around narrow economic interests than it is to organize around broad "public goods" interests. Why do some groups organize while others do not?

The nature of collective goods, according to economist Mancur Olson, explains this phenomenon. When a collective good is provided to a group, no member of the group can be denied the benefits of the good. For example, if Congress passes a law that offers subsidies for a new telecommunications technology, any company that produces that technology will benefit from the subsidy. The catch is, any company will benefit even if they did not participate in the collective effort to win the subsidy. Olson argues that "the larger the number of individuals or firms that would benefit from a collective good, the smaller the share of the gains . . . that will accrue to the individual or firm." Hence, the less likely any one member of the group will contribute to the collective effort to secure the collective benefit. For smaller groups, any one member's share of the collective good is larger and more meaningful, so the more likely any one member of the group will be willing to make an individual sacrifice to provide a benefit shared by the entire group. An additional distinction is that in a large group, there is often a tendency to assume someone else will take care of the problem—this is known as the "free rider" problem or, as Olson puts it, "let George do it." This is less likely to happen in smaller groups.

The logic helps to explain the greater difficulty "public interest groups" have in organizing and staying organized to provide such collective goods as clean air, consumer product safety, and banking regulations aimed at promoting inner-city investments by banks. These goods benefit very large numbers of people, but the benefit to any one person, Olson would argue, is not sufficient for them to sacrifice time or money for the effort to succeed, especially if the individual believes that he or she will benefit from the collective good, even if they do not contribute. Olson identifies "selective incentives" as one way in which these larger groups are able to overcome the incentive to free ride.

The Logic

The argument of this book begins with a paradox in the behavior of groups. It has often been taken for granted that if everyone in a group of individuals or firms had some interest in common, then there would be a tendency for the group to seek to further this interest. Thus many students of politics in the United States for a long time supposed that citizens with a common political interest would organize and lobby to serve that interest. Each individual in the population would be in one or more groups and the vector of pressures of these competing groups explained the outcomes of the political process. Similarly, it was often supposed that if workers, farmers, or consumers faced monopolies harmful to their interests, they would eventually attain countervailing power through organizations such as labor unions or farm organizations that obtained market power and protective government action. On a larger scale, huge social classes are often expected to act in the interest of their members; the unalloyed form of this belief is, of course, the Marxian contention that in capitalist societies the bourgeois class runs the government to serve its own interests, and that once the exploitation of the proletariat goes far enough and "false consciousness" has disappeared, the working class will in its own interest revolt and establish a dictatorship of the proletariat. In general, if the individuals in some category or class had a sufficient degree of self-interest and if they all agreed on some common interest, then the group would to some extent also act in a self-interested or group-interested manner.

If we ponder the logic of the familiar assumption described in the preceding paragraph, we can see that it is fundamentally and indisputably faulty. Consider those consumers who agree that they pay higher prices for a product because of some objectionable monopoly or tariff, or those workers who agree that their skill deserves a higher wage. Let us now ask what would be the expedient course of action for an individual consumer who would like to see a boycott to combat a monopoly or a lobby to repeal the tariff, or for an individual worker who would like a strike threat or a minimum wage law that could bring higher wages. If the consumer or worker contributes a few days and a few dollars to organize a boycott or a union or to lobby for favorable legislation, he or she will have sacrificed time and money. What will this sacrifice obtain? The individual will at best succeed in advancing the cause to a small (often imperceptible) degree. In any case he will get only a minute share of the gain from his action. The very fact that the objective or interest is common to or shared by the group entails that the gain from any sacrifice an individual makes to serve this common purpose is shared with everyone in the group. The successful boycott or strike or lobbying action will bring the better price or wage for everyone in the relevant category, so the individual in any large group with a common interest will reap only a minute share of the gains from whatever sacrifices the individual makes to achieve this common interest. Since any gain goes to everyone in the group, those who contribute nothing to the effort will get just as much as those who made a contribution. It pays to "let George do it," but George has little or no incentive to do anything in the group interest either, so (in the absence of factors that are completely left out of the conceptions mentioned in the first paragraph) there will be little, if any, group action. The paradox, then, is that (in the absence of special arrangements or circumstances to which we shall turn later) large groups, at least if they are composed of rational individuals, will *not* act in their group interest.

This paradox is elaborated and set out in a way that lets the reader check every step of the logic in a book I wrote entitled *The Logic of Collective Action*.

* * *

Organizations that provide collective goods to their client groups through political or market action * * * are * * * not supported because of the collective goods they provide, but rather because they have been fortunate enough to find what I have called *selective incentives*. A selective incentive is one that applies selectively to the individuals depending on whether they do or do not contribute to the provision of the collective good.

A selective incentive can be either negative or positive; it can, for example, be a loss or punishment imposed only on those who do *not* help provide the collective good. Tax payments are, of course, obtained with the help of negative selective incentives, since those who are found not to have paid their taxes must then suffer both taxes and penalties. The best-known type of organized interest group in modern democratic societies, the labor union, is also usually supported, in part, through negative selective incentives. Most of the dues in strong unions are obtained through union shop, closed shop, or agency shop arrangements which make dues paying more or less compulsory and automatic. There are often also informal arrangements with the same effect; David McDonald, former president of the United Steel Workers of America, describes one of these arrangements used in the early history of that union. It was, he writes, a technique

> which we called . . . visual education, which was a high-sounding label for a practice much more accurately described as dues picketing. It worked very simply. A group of dues-paying members, selected by the district director (usually more for their size than their tact) would stand at the plant gate with pick handles or baseball bats in hand and confront each worker as he arrived for his shift.[1]

As McDonald's "dues picketing" analogy suggests, picketing during strikes is another negative selective incentive that unions sometimes need; although picketing in industries with established and stable unions is usually peaceful, this is because the union's capacity to close down an enterprise against which it has called a strike is clear to all; the early phase of unionization often involves a great deal of violence on the part of both unions and anti-union employers and scabs.

* * *

Positive selective incentives, although easily overlooked, are also commonplace, as diverse examples in *The Logic* demonstrate. American farm organizations offer prototypical examples. Many of the members of the stronger American farm organizations are members because their dues payments are automatically deducted from the "patronage dividends" of farm cooperatives or are included in the insurance premiums paid to mutual insurance companies associated with the farm organizations. Any number of organizations with urban clients also provide similar positive selective incentives in the form of insurance policies, publications, group air fares, and other private goods made available only to members. The grievance procedures of labor unions usually also offer selective incentives, since the grievances of active members often get most of the attention. The symbiosis between the political power of a lobbying organization and the business institutions associated with it often yields tax or other advantages for the business institution, and the publicity and other information flowing out of the political arm of a movement often generates patterns of preference or trust that make the business activities of the movement more remunerative. The surpluses obtained in such ways in turn provide positive selective incentives that recruit participants for the lobbying efforts.

Small groups, or occasionally large "federal" groups that are made up of many small groups of socially interactive members, have an additional source of both negative and positive selective incentives. Clearly most people value the companionship and respect of those with whom they interact. In modern societies solitary confinement is, apart from the rare death penalty, the harshest legal punishment. The censure or even ostracism of those who fail to bear a share of the burdens of collective action can sometimes be an important selective incentive. An extreme example of this occurs when British unionists refuse to speak to uncooperative colleagues, that is, "send them to Coventry." Similarly, those in a socially interactive group seeking a collective good can give special respect or honor to those who distinguish themselves by their sacrifices in the interest of the group and thereby offer them a positive selective incentive. Since most people apparently prefer relatively like-minded or agreeable and respectable company, and often prefer to associate with those whom they especially admire, they may find it costless to shun those who shirk the collective action and to favor those who over-subscribe.

Social selective incentives can be powerful and inexpensive, but they are available only in certain situations. As I have already indicated, they have little applicability to large groups, except in those cases in which the large groups can be federations of small groups that are capable of social interaction. It also is not possible to organize most large groups in need of a collective good into small, socially interactive subgroups, since most individuals do not have the time needed to maintain a huge number of friends and acquaintances.

The availability of social selective incentives is also limited by the social heterogeneity of some of the groups or categories that would benefit from a collective good. Everyday observation reveals that most socially interactive groups are fairly homogeneous and that many people resist extensive social interaction with those they deem to have lower status or greatly different tastes. Even Bohemian or other nonconformist groups often are made up of individuals who are similar to one another, however much they differ from the rest of society. Since some of the categories of individuals who would benefit from a collective good are socially heterogeneous, the social interaction needed for selective incentives sometimes cannot be arranged even when the number of individuals involved is small.

*   *   *

In short, the political entrepreneurs who attempt to organize collective action will accordingly be more likely to succeed if they strive to organize relatively homogeneous groups. The political managers whose task it is to maintain organized or collusive action similarly will be motivated to use indoctrination and selective recruitment to increase the homogeneity of their client groups. This is true in part because social selective incentives are more likely to be available to the more nearly homogeneous groups, and in part because homogeneity will help achieve consensus.

Information and calculation about a collective good is often itself a collective good. Consider a typical member of a large organization who is deciding how much time to devote to studying the policies or leadership of the organization. The more time the member devotes to this matter, the greater the likelihood that his or her voting and advocacy will favor effective policies and leadership for the organization. This typical member will, however, get only a small share of the gain from the more effective policies and leadership: in the aggregate, the other members will get almost all the gains, so that the individual member does not have an incentive to devote nearly as much time to fact-finding and thinking about the organization as would be in the group interest. Each of the members of the group would be better off if they all could be coerced into spending more time finding out how to vote to make the organization best further their interests. This is dramatically evident in the case of the typical voter in a national election in a large country. The gain to such a voter from studying issues and candidates until it is clear what vote is truly in his or her interest is given by the difference in the value to the individual of the "right" election outcome as compared with the "wrong" outcome, *multiplied by the probability a change in the individual's vote will alter the outcome of the election.* Since the probability that a typical voter will change the outcome of the election is vanishingly small, the typical citizen is usually "rationally ignorant" about public affairs. Often, information about public affairs is so interesting or entertaining that it pays to acquire it for these reasons alone—this appears to be the single most important source of exceptions to the generalization that *typical* citizens are rationally ignorant about public affairs.

Individuals in a few special vocations can receive considerable rewards in private goods if they acquire exceptional knowledge of public goods. Politicians, lobbyists, journalists, and social scientists, for example, may earn more money, power, or prestige from knowledge of this or that public business. Occasionally, exceptional knowledge of public policy can generate exceptional profits in stock exchanges or other markets. Withal, the typical citizen will find that his or her income and life chances will not be improved by zealous study of public affairs, or even of any single collective good.

The limited knowledge of public affairs is in turn necessary to explain the effectiveness of lobbying. If all citizens had obtained and digested all pertinent information, they could not then be swayed by advertising or other persuasion. With perfectly informed citizens, elected officials would not be subject to the blandishments of lobbyists, since the constituents would then know if their interests were betrayed and defeat the unfaithful representative at the next election. Just as lobbies provide collective goods to special-interest groups, so their effectiveness is explained by the imperfect knowledge of citizens, and this in turn is due mainly to the fact that information and calculation about collective goods is also a collective good.

* * *

The fact that the typical individual does not have an incentive to spend much time studying many of his choices concerning collective goods also helps to explain some otherwise inexplicable individual contributions toward the provision of collective goods. The logic of collective action that has been described in this chapter is not immediately apparent to those who have never studied it; if it were, there would be nothing paradoxical in the argument with which this chapter opened, and students to whom the argument is explained would not react with initial skepticism. No doubt the practical implications of this logic for the individual's own choices were often discerned before the logic was ever set out in print, but this does not mean that they were always understood even at the intuitive and practical level. In particular, when the costs of individual contributions to collective action are very small, the individual has little incentive to investigate whether or not to make a contribution or even to exercise intuition. If the individual knows the costs of a contribution to collective action in the interest of a group of which he is a part are trivially small, he may rationally not take the trouble to consider whether the gains are smaller still. This is particularly the case since the size of these gains and the policies that would maximize them are matters about which it is usually not rational for him to investigate.

This consideration of the costs and benefits of calculation about public goods leads to the testable prediction that voluntary contributions toward the provision of collective goods for large groups without selective incentives will often occur when the costs of the individual contributions are negligible, but that they will *not* often occur when the costs of the individual contributions are considerable. In other words, when the costs of individual action to help to obtain a desired collective good are small enough, the result is indeterminate and sometimes goes one way and sometimes the other, but when the costs get larger this indeterminacy disappears. We should accordingly find that more than a few people are willing to take the moment of time needed to sign petitions for causes they support, or to express their opinions in the course of discussion, or to vote for the candidate or party they prefer. Similarly, if the argument here is correct, we should not find many instances where individuals voluntarily contribute substantial sums of resources year after year for the purpose of obtaining some collective good for some large group of which they are a part. Before parting with a large amount of money or time, and particularly before doing so repeatedly, the rational individual will reflect on what this considerable sacrifice will accomplish. If the individual is a typical individual in a large group that would benefit from a collective good, his contribution will not make a perceptible difference in the amount that is provided. The theory here predicts that such contributions become less likely the larger the contribution at issue.

Even when contributions are costly enough to elicit rational calculation, there is still one set of circumstances in which collective action can occur without selective incentives. This set of circumstances becomes evident the moment we think of situations in which there are only a few individuals or firms that would benefit from collective action. Suppose there are two firms of equal size in an industry and no other firms can enter the industry. It still will be the case that a higher price for the industry's product will benefit both firms and that legislation favorable to the industry will help both firms. The higher price and the favorable legislation are then collective goods to this "oligopolistic" industry, even though there are only two in the group that benefit from the collective goods.

Obviously, each of the oligopolists is in a situation in which if it restricts output to raise the industry price, or lobbies for favorable legislation for the industry, it will tend to get half of the benefit. And the cost-benefit ratio of action in the common interest easily could be so favorable that, even though a firm bears the whole cost of its action and gets only half the benefit of this action, it could still profit from acting in the common interest. Thus if the group that would benefit from collective action is sufficiently small and the cost-benefit ratio of collective action for the group sufficiently favorable, there may well be calculated action in the collective interest even without selective incentives.

*   *   *

Untypical as my example of equal-sized firms may be, it makes the general point intuitively obvious: other things being equal, *the larger the number of individuals or firms that would benefit from a collective good, the smaller the share of the gains from action in the group interest that will accrue to the individual or firm that undertakes the action. Thus, in the absence of selective incentives, the incentive for group action diminishes as group size increases, so that large groups are less able to act in their common interest than small ones.* If an additional individual or firm that would value the collective good enters the scene, then the share of the gains from group-oriented action that anyone already in the group might take must diminish. This holds true whatever the relative sizes or valuations of the collective good in the group.

*   *   *

The significance of the logic that has just been set out can best be seen by comparing groups that would have the same net gain from collective action, if they could engage in it, but that vary in size. Suppose there are a million individuals who would gain a thousand dollars each, or a billion in the aggregate, if they were to organize effectively and engage in collective action that had a total cost of a hundred million. If the logic set out above is right, they could not organize or engage in effective collective action without selective incentives. Now suppose that, although the total gain of a billion dollars from collective action and the aggregate cost of a hundred million remain the same, the group is composed instead of five big corporations or five organized municipalities, each of which would gain two hundred million. Collective action is not an absolute certainty even in this case, since each of the five could conceivably expect others to put up the hundred million and hope to gain the collective good worth two hundred million at no cost at all. Yet collective action, perhaps after some delays due to bargaining, seems very likely indeed. In this case any one of the five would gain a hundred million from providing the collective good even if it had to pay the whole cost itself; and the costs of bargaining among five would not be great, so they would sooner or later probably work out an agreement providing for the collective action. The numbers in this example are arbitrary, but roughly similar situations occur often in reality, and the contrast between "small" and "large" groups could be illustrated with an infinite number of diverse examples.

The significance of this argument shows up in a second way if one compares the operations of lobbies or cartels within jurisdictions of vastly different scale, such as a modest municipality on the one hand and a big country on the other. Within the town, the mayor or city council may be influenced by, say, a score of petitioners or a lobbying budget of a thousand dollars. A particular line of business may be in the hands of only a few firms, and if the town is distant enough from other markets only these few would need to agree to create a cartel. In a big country, the resources needed to influence the national government are likely to be much more substantial, and unless the firms are (as they sometimes are) gigantic, many of them would have to cooperate to create an effective cartel. Now suppose that the million individuals in our large group in the previous paragraph were spread out over a hundred thousand towns or jurisdictions, so that each jurisdiction had ten of them, along with the same proportion of citizens in other categories as before. Suppose also that the cost-benefit ratios remained the same, so that there was still a billion dollars to gain across all jurisdictions or ten thousand in each, and that it would still cost a hundred million dollars across all jurisdictions or a thousand in each. It no longer seems out of the question that in many jurisdictions the groups of ten, or subsets of them, would put up the thousand-dollar total needed to get the thousand for each individual. Thus we see that, if all else were equal, small jurisdictions would have more collective action per capita than large ones.

Differences in intensities of preference generate a third type of illustration of the logic at issue. A small number of zealots anxious for a particular collective good are more likely to act collectively to obtain that good than a larger number with the same aggregate willingness to pay. Suppose there are twenty-five individuals, each of whom finds a given collective good worth a thousand dollars in one case, whereas in another there are five thousand, each of whom finds the collective good worth five dollars. Obviously, the argument indicates that there would be a greater likelihood of collective action in the former case than in the latter, even though the aggregate demand for the collective good is the same in both. The great historical significance of small groups of fanatics no doubt owes something to this consideration.

The argument in this chapter predicts that those groups that have access to selective incentives will be more likely to act collectively to obtain collective goods than those that do not, and that smaller groups will have a greater likelihood of engaging in collective action than larger ones. The empirical portions of *The Logic* show that this prediction has been correct for the United States.

*   *   *

DISCUSSION QUESTIONS

1. Besides the size of a group, what other considerations do you think would play a role in people's decision to join a collective endeavor? Are you convinced that the size of a group is as important as Olson argues?

2. Think of your own decisions to join or not join a group. Have you ever been a "free rider?" For example, have there been protests against tuition increases at your school that you supported but did not participate in? If so, what would it have taken to get you to join?

3. If Olson is right, would Tocqueville's view about the role of groups in overcoming the potential tyranny of majority need to be modified?

NOTE

1. David J. McDonald, *Union Man* (New York: Dutton, 1969), p. 121.

60

"Associations Without Members"

Theda Skocpol

One of the hot topics in social science research since the mid-1990s has been the idea of "social capital." Put simply, social capital suggests that involvement in group and social activities generates side benefits that promote the health of the political system. Involvement in these groups tends to contribute to trust, efficacy, and a broader interest and involvement in public affairs. The idea emerged as scholars noted that several measures of public participation in politics—voting turnout, for example—had declined markedly since the early 1960s. At the same time, measures of public disaffection, mistrust, and alienation from politics were growing. Analysts such as the political scientist Robert Putnam noted that, in fact, not only were measures like voting turnout on the downswing, but many indicators of social involvement were drooping. As Putnam famously pointed out, it seemed that even bowling league memberships were dropping and that Americans were increasingly "bowling alone." If in fact involvement broadly speaking was on the decline, then the positive effects of involvement ("social capital") would also be on the decline, with significant impacts on social and political life.

These ideas generated a mountain of research, ranging from studies questioning the thesis of participatory decline, to those trying to explain the decline, to those evaluating the effects of the decline. Theda Skocpol steps into this debate by offering an analysis of how Americans have changed not so much the quantity, but the quality, of their participation. Once, Americans were group members who participated in group activities and group decision making. These associations, in many senses, reflected America's democratic political system, both in terms of their decision making and in terms of their often federal structure. Increasingly, however, the civic world is filled with "associations without members" centered not in communities but in Washington, D.C., led not by ordinary members, but by elite professionals. "Membership" in these organizations usually means little more than writing a check which entitles the check-writer to receive a monthly publication. Meetings and local involvement are absent. Of course, not all associations operate this way, but Skocpol suggests that this is increasingly becoming the norm and that it has had deleterious effects for the political system. She identifies a range of reasons for this transformation, including "racial and gender change; shifts in the political opportunity structure; new techniques and models for building organizations; and recent transformations in U.S. class relations."

In just a third of a century, Americans have dramatically changed their style of civic and political association. A civic world once centered in locally rooted and nationally active membership associations is a relic. Today, Americans volunteer for causes and projects, but only rarely as ongoing members. They send checks to service and advocacy groups run by professionals, often funded by foundations or professional fundraisers. Prime-time airways echo with debates among their spokespersons: the National Abortion Rights Action League debates the National Right to Life Committee; the Concord Coalition takes on the American Association of Retired Persons; and the Environmental Defense Fund counters business groups. Entertained or bemused, disengaged viewers watch as polarized advocates debate.

The largest membership groups of the 1950s were old-line and well-established, with founding dates ranging from 1733 for the Masons to 1939 for the Woman's Division of Christian Service (a Methodist women's association formed from "missionary" societies with nineteenth-century roots). Like most large membership associations throughout American history, most 1950s associations recruited members across class lines. They held regular local meetings and convened periodic assemblies of elected leaders and delegates at the state, regional, or national levels. Engaged in multiple rather than narrowly specialized pursuits, many associations combined social or ritual activities with community service, mutual aid, and involvement in national affairs. Patriotism was a leitmotif; during and after World War II, a passionate and victorious national endeavor, these associations sharply expanded their memberships and renewed the vigor of their local and national activities.

To be sure, very large associations were not the only membership federations that mattered in postwar America. Also prominent were somewhat smaller, elite-dominated civic groups—including male service groups like Rotary, Lions, and Kiwanis, and longstanding female groups like the American Association of University Women and the League of Women Voters. Dozens of ethnically based fraternal and cultural associations flourished, as did African-American fraternal groups like the Prince Hall Masons and the Improved Benevolent and Protective Order of Elks of the World.

For many membership federations, this was a golden era of national as well as community impact. Popularly rooted membership federations rivaled professional and business associations for influence in policy debates. The AFL-CIO was in the thick of struggles about economic and social policies; the American Legion and the Veterans of Foreign Wars advanced veterans' programs; the American Farm Bureau Federation (AFBF) joined other farmers' associations to influence national and state agricultural policies; and the National Congress of Parents and Teachers (PTA) and the General Federation of Women's Clubs were influential on educational, health, and family issues. The results could be decisive, as exemplified by the pivotal role of the American Legion in drafting and lobbying for the GI Bill of 1944.

Then, suddenly, old-line membership federations seemed passé. Upheavals shook America during "the long 1960s," stretching from the mid-1950s through the mid-1970s. The southern Civil Rights movement challenged white racial domination and spurred legislation to enforce legal equality and voting rights for African Americans. Inspired by Civil Rights achievements, additional "rights" movements exploded, promoting equality for women, dignity for homosexuals, the unionization of farm workers, and the mobilization of other nonwhite ethnic minorities. Movements arose to oppose U.S. involvement in the war in Vietnam, champion a new environmentalism, and further other public causes. At the forefront of these groundswells were younger Americans, especially from the growing ranks of college students and university graduates.

The great social movements of the long 1960s were propelled by combinations of grassroots protest, activist radicalism, and professionally led efforts to lobby government and educate the public. Some older membership associations ended up participating and expanding their bases of support, yet the groups that sparked movements were more agile and flexibly structured than pre-existing membership federations.

The upheavals of the 1960s could have left behind a reconfigured civic world, in which some old-line membership associations had declined but others had reoriented and reenergized themselves. Within each great social movement, memberships could have consolidated and groups coalesced into new omnibus federations able to link the grass roots to state, regional, and national leaderships, allowing longstanding American civic traditions to continue in new ways.

But this is not what happened. Instead, the 1960s, 1970s, and 1980s brought extraordinary organizational proliferation and professionalization. At the national level alone, the *Encyclopedia of Associations* listed approximately 6,500 associations in 1958. This total grew by 1990 to almost 23,000. Within the expanding group universe, moreover, new kinds of associations came to the fore: relatively centralized and professionally led organizations focused on policy lobbying and public education.

Another wave of the advocacy explosion involved "public interest" or "citizens" groups seeking to shape public opinion and influence legislation. Citizens' advocacy groups espouse "causes" ranging from environmental protection (for example, the Sierra Club and the Environmental Defense Fund), to the well-being of poor children (the Children's Defense Fund), to reforming politics (Common Cause) and cutting public entitlements (the Concord Coalition).

The Fortunes of Membership Associations

As the associational explosions of 1960 to 1990 took off, America's once large and confident membership federations were not only bypassed in national politics; they also dwindled as locally rooted participant groups. To be sure, some membership associations have been founded or expanded in recent decades. By far the largest is the American Association of Retired Persons (AARP), which now boasts more than 33 million adherents, about one-half of all Americans aged 50 or older. But AARP is not a democratically controlled organization. Launched in 1958 with backing from a teachers' retirement group and an insurance company, the AARP grew rapidly in the 1970s and 1980s by offering commercial discounts to members and establishing a Washington headquarters to monitor and lobby about federal legislation affecting seniors. The AARP has a legislative and policy staff of 165 people, 28 registered lobbyists, and more than 1,200 staff members in the field. After recent efforts to expand its regional and local infrastructure, the AARP involves about 5 to 10 percent of its members in (undemocratic) membership chapters. But for the most part, the AARP national office—covering an entire city block with its own zip code—deals with masses of individual adherents through the mail.

Four additional recently expanded membership associations use modern mass recruitment methods, yet are also rooted in local and state units. Interestingly, these groups are heavily involved in partisan electoral politics. Two recently launched groups are the National Right to Life Committee (founded in 1973) and the Christian Coalition (founded in 1989). They bridge from church congregations, through which they recruit members and activists, to the conservative wing of the Republican Party, through which they exercise political influence. Two old-line membership federations—the National Education Association (founded in 1857) and the National Rifle Association (founded in 1871)—experienced explosive growth after reorienting themselves to take part in partisan politics. The NRA expanded in the 1970s, when right-wing activists opposed to gun control changed what had traditionally been a network of marksmen's clubs into a conservative, Republican-leaning advocacy group fiercely opposed to gun control legislation. During the same period, the NEA burgeoned from a relatively elitist association of public educators into a quasi-union for public school teachers and a stalwart in local, state, and national Democratic Party politics.

Although they fall short of enrolling 1 percent of the adult population, some additional chapter-based membership associations were fueled by the social movements of the 1960s and 1970s. From 1960 to 1990, the Sierra Club (originally created in 1892) ballooned from some 15,000 members to 565,000 members meeting in 378 "local groups." And the National Audubon Society (founded in 1905) went from 30,000 members and 330 chapters in 1958 to about 600,000 members and more than 500 chapters in the 1990s. The National Organization for Women (NOW) reached 1,122 members and 14 chapters within a year of its founding in 1966, and spread across all 50 states with some 125,000 members meeting in 700 chapters by 1978. But notice that these "1960s" movement associations do not match the organizational scope of old-line membership federations. At its post—World War II high point in 1955, for example, the General Federation of Women's Clubs boasted more than 826,000 members meeting in 15,168 local clubs, themselves divided into representative networks within each of the 50 states plus the District of Columbia. By contrast, at its high point in 1993, NOW reported some 280,000 members and 800 chapters, with no intermediate tier of representative governance between the national center and local chapters. These membership associations certainly matter, but mainly as counter-examples to dominant associational trends—of organizations without members.

After nearly a century of civic life rooted in nation-spanning membership federations, why was America's associational universe so transformed? A variety of factors have contributed, including racial and gender change; shifts in the political opportunity structure; new techniques and models for building organizations; and recent transformations in U.S. class relations. Taken together, I suggest, these account for civic America's abrupt and momentous transition from membership to advocacy.

Society Decompartmentalized

Until recent times, most American membership associations enrolled business and professional people together with white-collar folks, farmers, and craft or industrial workers. There was a degree of fellowship across class lines—yet at the price of other kinds of exclusions. With only a few exceptions, old-line associations enrolled either men or women, not both together (although male-only fraternal and veterans' groups often had ties to ladies' auxiliaries). Racial separation was also the rule. Although African Americans did manage to create and greatly expand fraternal associations of their own, they unquestionably resented exclusion by the parallel white fraternals.

Given the pervasiveness of gender and racial separation in classic civic America, established voluntary associations were bound to be shaken after the 1950s. Moreover, changing gender roles and identities blended with other changing values to undercut not just membership appeals but long-standing routes to associational leadership. For example, values of patriotism, brotherhood, and sacrifice had been celebrated by all fraternal groups. During and after each war, the Masons, Knights of Pythias, Elks, Knights of Columbus, Moose, Eagles, and scores of other fraternal groups celebrated and memorialized the contributions of their soldier-members. So did women's auxiliaries, not to mention men's service clubs and trade union "brotherhoods." But "manly" ideals of military service faded after the early 1960s as America's bitter experiences during the war in Vietnam disrupted the intergenerational continuity of male identification with martial brotherliness.

In the past third of a century, female civic leadership has changed as much or more than male leadership. Historically, U.S. women's associations—ranging from female auxiliaries of male groups to independent groups like the General Federation of Women's Clubs, the PTA, and church-connected associations—benefited from the activism of educated wives and mothers. Although a tiny fraction of all U.S. females, higher-educated women were a surprisingly substantial and widespread presence—because the United States was a pioneer in the schooling of girls and the higher education of women. By 1880, some 40,000 American women constituted a third of all students in U.S. institutions of higher learning; women's share rose to nearly half at the early twentieth-century peak in 1920, when some 283,000 women were enrolled in institutions of higher learning. Many higher-educated women of the late 1800s and early 1900s married immediately and stayed out of the paid labor force. Others taught for a time in primary and secondary schools, then got married and stopped teaching (either voluntarily or because school systems would not employ married women). Former teachers accumulated in every community. With skills to make connections within and across communities—and some time on their hands as their children grew older—former teachers and other educated women became mainstays of classic U.S. voluntary life.

Of course, more American women than ever before are now college-educated. But contemporary educated women face new opportunities and constraints. Paid work and family responsibilities are no longer separate spheres, and the occupational structure is less sex-segregated at all levels. Today, even married women with children are very likely to be employed, at least part-time. Despite new time pressures, educated and employed women have certainly not dropped out of civic life. Women employed part-time are more likely to be members of groups or volunteers than housewives; and fully employed women are often drawn into associations or civic projects through work. Yet styles of civic involvement have changed—much to the disadvantage of broad-gauged associations trying to hold regular meetings.

The Lure of Washington, D.C.

The centralization of political change in Washington, D.C. also affected the associational universe. Consider the odyssey of civil rights lawyer Marian Wright Edelman. Fresh from grassroots struggles in Mississippi, she arrived in Washington, D.C. in the late 1960s to lobby for Mississippi's Head Start program. She soon realized that arguing on behalf of children might be the best way to influence legislation and sway public sympathy in favor of the poor, including African Americans. So between 1968 and 1973 Edelman obtained funding from major foundations and developed a new advocacy and policy research association, the Children's Defense Fund (CDF). With a skillful staff, a small national network of individual supporters, ties to social service agencies and foundations, and excellent relationships with the national media, the CDF has been a determined proponent of federal antipoverty programs ever since. The CDF has also worked with Democrats and other liberal advocacy groups to expand such efforts; and during periods of conservative Republican ascendancy, the CDF has been a fierce (if not always successful) defender of federal social programs.

Activists, in short, have gone where the action is. In this same period, congressional committees and their staffs subdivided and multiplied. During the later 1970s and 1980s, the process of group formation became self-reinforcing—not only because groups arose to counter other groups, but also because groups begot more groups. Because businesses and citizens use advocacy groups to influence government outside of parties and between elections, it is not surprising that the contemporary group explosion coincides with waning voter loyalty to the two major political parties. As late as the 1950s, U.S. political parties were networks of local and state organizations through which party officials often brokered nominations, cooperated with locally rooted membership associations, and sometimes directly mobilized voters. The party structure and the associational structure were mutually reinforcing.

Then, demographic shifts, reapportionment struggles, and the social upheavals of the 1960s disrupted old party organizations; and changes in party rules led to nomination elections that favored activists and candidate-centered efforts over backroom brokering by party insiders. Such "reforms" were meant to enhance grassroots participation, but in practice have furthered oligarchical ways of running elections. No longer the preserve of party organizations, U.S. campaigns are now managed by coteries of media consultants, pollsters, direct mail specialists, and—above all—fundraisers. In this revamped electoral arena, advocacy groups have much to offer, hoping to get access to elected officials in return for helping candidates. In low-turnout battles to win party nominations, even groups with modest mail memberships may be able to field enough (paid or unpaid) activists to make a difference. At all stages of the electoral process, advocacy groups with or without members can provide endorsements that may be useful in media or direct mail efforts. And PACs pushing business interests or public interests causes can help candidates raise the huge amounts of money they need to compete.

A New Model of Association-Building

Classic American association-builders took it for granted that the best way to gain national influence, moral or political, was to knit together national, state, and local groups that met regularly and engaged in a degree of representative governance. Leaders who desired to speak on behalf of masses of Americans found it natural to proceed by recruiting self-renewing mass memberships and spreading a network of interactive groups. After the start-up phase, associational budgets usually depended heavily on membership dues and on sales of newsletters or supplies to members and local groups. Supporters had to be continuously recruited through social networks and person-to-person contacts. And if leverage over government was desired, an association had to be able influence legislators, citizens, and newspapers across many districts. For all of these reasons, classic civic entrepreneurs with national ambitions moved quickly to recruit activists and members in every state and across as many towns and cities as possible within each state.

Today, nationally ambitious civic entrepreneurs proceed in quite different ways. When Marian Wright Edelman launched a new advocacy and research group to lobby for the needs of children and the poor, she turned to private foundations for funding and then recruited an expert staff of researchers and lobbyists. In the early 1970s, when John Gardner launched Common Cause as a "national citizens lobby" demanding governmental reforms, he arranged for start-up contributions from several wealthy friends, contacted reporters in the national media, and purchased mailing lists to solicit masses of members giving modest monetary contributions. Patron grants, direct mail techniques, and the capacity to convey images and messages through the mass media have changed the realities of organization building and maintenance.

The very model of civic effectiveness has been up-ended since the 1960s. No longer do civic entrepreneurs think of constructing vast federations and recruiting interactive citizen-members. When a new cause (or tactic) arises, activists envisage opening a national office and managing association-building as well as national projects from the center. Even a group aiming to speak for large numbers of Americans does not absolutely need members. And if mass adherents are recruited through the mail, why hold meetings? From a managerial point of view, interactions with groups of members may be downright inefficient. In the old-time membership federations, annual elections of leaders and a modicum of representative governance went hand in hand with membership dues and interactive meetings. But for the professional executives of today's advocacy organizations, direct mail members can be more appealing because, as Kenneth Godwin and Robert Cameron Mitchell explain, "they contribute without 'meddling'" and "do not take part in leadership selection or policy discussions." This does not mean the new advocacy groups are malevolent; they are just responding rationally to the environment in which they find themselves.

Associational Change and Democracy

This brings us, finally, to what may be the most civically consequential change in late-twentieth-century America: the rise of a very large, highly educated upper middle class in which "expert" professionals are prominent along with businesspeople and managers. When U.S. professionals were a tiny, geographically dispersed stratum, they understood themselves as "trustees of community," in the terminology of Stephen Brint. Working closely with and for nonprofessional fellow citizens in thousands of towns and cities, lawyers, doctors, ministers, and teachers once found it quite natural to join—and eventually help to lead—locally rooted, cross-class voluntary associations. But today's professionals are more likely to see themselves as expert individuals who can best contribute to national well-being by working with other specialists to tackle complex technical or social problems.

Cause-oriented advocacy groups offer busy, privileged Americans a rich menu of opportunities to, in effect, hire other professionals and managers to represent their values and interests in public life. Why should highly trained and economically well-off elites spend years working their way up the leadership ladders of traditional membership federations when they can take leading staff roles at the top, or express their preferences by writing a check?

If America has experienced a great civic transformation from membership to advocacy—so what? Most traditional associations were racially exclusive and gender segregated; and their policy efforts were not always broad-minded. More than a few observers suggest that recent civic reorganizations may be for the best. American public life has been rejuvenated, say the optimists, by social movements and advocacy groups fighting for social rights and an enlarged understanding of the public good.

Local community organizations, neighborhood groups, and grassroots protest movements nowadays tap popular energies and involve people otherwise left out of organized politics. And social interchanges live on in small support groups and occasional volunteering. According to the research of Robert Wuthnow, about 75 million men and women, a remarkable 40 percent of the adult population, report taking part in "a small group that meets regularly and provides caring and support for those who participate in it." Wuthnow estimates that there may be some 3 million such groups, including Bible study groups, 12-step self-help groups, book discussion clubs, singles groups, hobby groups, and disease support groups. Individuals find community, spiritual connection, introspection, and personal gratification in small support groups. Meanwhile, people reach out through volunteering. As many as half of all Americans give time to the community this way, their efforts often coordinated by paid social service professionals. Contemporary volunteering can be intermittent and flexibly structured, an intense one-shot effort or spending "an evening a week on an activity for a few months as time permits, rather than having to make a long-term commitment to an organization."

In the optimistic view, the good civic things Americans once did are still being done—in new ways and in new settings. But if we look at U.S. democracy in its entirety and bring issues of power and social leverage to the fore, then optimists are surely overlooking the downsides of our recently reorganized civic life. Too many valuable aspects of the old civic America are not being reproduced or reinvented in the new public world of memberless organizations.

Despite the multiplicity of voices raised within it, America's new civic universe is remarkably oligarchical. Because today's advocacy groups are staff-heavy and focused on lobbying, research, and media projects, they are managed from the top with few opportunities for member leverage from below. Even when they have hundreds of thousands of adherents, contemporary associations are heavily tilted toward upper-middle-class constituencies. Whether we are talking about memberless advocacy groups, advocacy groups with some chapters, mailing-list associations, or nonprofit institutions, it is hard to escape the conclusion that the wealthiest and best-educated Americans are much more privileged in the new civic world than their (less numerous) counterparts were in the pre-1960s civic world of cross-class membership federations.

Mostly, they involve people in "doing for" others—feeding the needy at a church soup kitchen; tutoring children at an after-school clinic; or guiding visitors at a museum exhibit—rather than in "doing with" fellow citizens. Important as such volunteering may be, it cannot substitute for the central citizenship functions that membership federations performed.

A top-heavy civic world not only encourages "doing for" rather than "doing with." It also distorts national politics and public policymaking. Imagine for a moment what might have happened if the GI Bill of 1944 had been debated and legislated in a civic world configured more like the one that prevailed during the 1993–1994 debates over the national health insurance proposal put forward by the first administration of President Bill Clinton. This is not an entirely fanciful comparison, because goals supported by the vast majority of Americans were at issue in both periods: in the 1940s, care and opportunity for millions of military veterans returning from World War II; in the 1990s, access for all Americans to a modicum of health insurance coverage. Back in the 1940s, moreover, there were elite actors—university presidents, liberal intellectuals, and conservative congressmen—who could have condemned the

GI Bill to the same fate as the 1990s health security plan. University presidents and liberal New Dealers initially favored versions of the GI Bill that would have been bureaucratically complicated, niggardly with public expenditures, and extraordinarily limited in veterans' access to subsidized higher education.

But in the actual civic circumstances of the 1940s, elites did not retain control of public debates or legislative initiatives. Instead, a vast voluntary membership federation, the American Legion, stepped in and drafted a bill to guarantee every one of the returning veterans up to four years of post-high school education, along with family and employment benefits, business loans, and home mortgages. Not only did the Legion draft one of the most generous pieces of social legislation in American history, thousands of local Legion posts and dozens of state organizations mounted a massive public education and lobbying campaign to ensure that even conservative congressional representatives would vote for the new legislation.

Half a century later, the 1990s health security episode played out in a transformed civic universe dominated by advocacy groups, pollsters, and big-money media campaigns. Top-heavy advocacy groups did not mobilize mass support for a sensible reform plan. Hundreds of business and professional groups influenced the Clinton administration's complex policy schemes, and then used a combination of congressional lobbying and media campaigns to block new legislation. Both the artificial polarization and the elitism of today's organized civic universe may help to explain why increasing numbers of Americans are turned off by and pulling back from public life. Large majorities say that wealthy "special interests" dominate the federal government, and many Americans express cynicism about the chances for regular people to make a difference. People may be entertained by advocacy clashes on television, but they are also ignoring many public debates and withdrawing into privatism. Voting less and less, American citizens increasingly act—and claim to feel—like mere spectators in a polity where all the significant action seems to go on above their heads, with their views ignored by pundits and clashing partisans.

From the nineteenth through the mid-twentieth century, American democracy flourished within a unique matrix of state and society. Not only was America the world's first manhood democracy and the first nation in the world to establish mass public education. It also had a uniquely balanced civic life, in which markets expanded but could not subsume civil society, in which governments at multiple levels deliberately and indirectly encouraged federated voluntary associations. National elites had to pay attention to the values and interests of millions of ordinary Americans.

Over the past third of a century, the old civic America has been bypassed and shoved to the side by a gaggle of professionally dominated advocacy groups and nonprofit institutions rarely attached to memberships worthy of the name. Ideals of shared citizenship and possibilities for democratic leverage have been compromised in the process. Since the 1960s, many good things have happened in America. New voices are now heard, and there have been invaluable gains in equality and liberty. But vital links in the nation's associational life have frayed, and we may need to find creative ways to repair those links if America is to avoid becoming a country of detached spectators. There is no going back to the civic world we have lost. But we Americans can and should look for ways to recreate the best of our civic past in new forms suited to a renewed democratic future.

DISCUSSION QUESTIONS

1. What does Skocpol mean by "shifts in the political opportunity structure"?

2. Skocpol is obviously alarmed by the shift in organizational style over the latter half of the twentieth century. What are her concerns? Do you share her concerns? Can you see any advantages to the new model over the old?

3. Do you belong to any national associations that have local group meetings? If so, do you agree that this involvement might generate social capital? What about campus groups? Do you think your involvement in these groups has any "spillover" effect that makes you more likely to be involved elsewhere or increases your sense that your involvement makes a difference?

Debating the Issues: Was Madison Right?

In his famous essay in *The Federalist*, No. 10, future president James Madison expressed concern about the "mischief of factions." It was natural, he argued, for people to organize around a principle or interest they held in common, and the most common motivation for organizing such factions was property—those who had it versus those who did not, creditors versus lenders. The danger in such efforts, however, was that a majority faction might usurp the rights of a minority. In a small direct democracy, where a majority of the people could share a "common passion," the threat was very real. Expand the geographic size of the country, however, and replace direct democracy with a system of elected representatives, separation of powers, and checks and balances, and the threat diminished. The likelihood of any one faction appealing to a majority of citizens in a large republic governed by representatives from diverse geographic regions was remote. To Madison, factions were a natural outgrowth of the differences between people, and the only way to eliminate factions would be to eliminate liberty. Eliminating factions might not be possible or desirable, but the mischief of factions could be controlled with a system of representation based upon varied constituencies that embraced multiple, diverse interests. From the competition of diverse interests would arise compromise and balanced public policy.

Madison's concerns about interests and particularly organized interests have resonated throughout American history. At various times in the U.S., the public has seemed to become especially concerned with the power of interests in politics. One political scientist refers to this as the "ideals vs. institutions" gap—there are times when "what is" is so different from what Americans believe "should be" that pressure mounts to reform lobbying laws, campaign regulations, business practices, and so on. Positions on these issues do not always neatly sort out into the typical liberal and conservative categories. For example, a Democratic senator (Russ Feingold) and Republican senator (John McCain) joined forces to lead the effort for campaign finance reform, but liberal and conservative interest groups joined forces in 2003 to challenge (unsuccessfully) the constitutionality of some of the new law's limits on interest-group campaign advertising.

Was Madison right about the benefits that would emerge from the competition of interests? In the following excerpt from *The Governmental Process*, David Truman answers with an emphatic "yes!" Despite the popular criticism of "special" interests that seem to taint the political process with their dominant influence, Truman argues that such groups have been a common and inevitable feature of American government. Groups form to give individuals a means of self-expression and to help individuals find security in an uncertain world. In fact, the uncertainty of the social environment, and the resulting threat to one's interests, is a chief motivation for groups to form and "taming" this environment is a central concern for group members. Rather than leading to a system ruled by a few dominant powers, Truman suggests the reality is much more fluid. What the critics of group influence fail to recognize is that people have "multiple or overlapping membership" in groups so that "no tolerable normal person is totally absorbed in any group in which he participates." There is balance, in other words, to the views any one member brings to the organization and ultimately to the political process. Further, the potential for a group to form is always present, and "[s]ometimes it may be this possibility of organization that alone gives the potential group a minimum of influence in the political process." Just because someone is not a member of an organized group does not obviate the influence they can bring to bear on the political process. The result, as Madison argued, is a balanced approach to the diverse interests who must compromise to form public policy.

Jonathan Rauch disagrees. He views with pessimism the ever-expanding number of interest groups in the political process. Whether groups claim to represent narrow economic interests or a broader public interest, Rauch does not see balance and compromise as the result of their competition in the political arena. Rather, he sees a nation suffering from "hyperpluralism," or the explosion of groups making claims on government power and resources. When elected officials attempt to reduce budget deficits or to establish new priorities and refocus expenditures, they are overwhelmed by the pressures of a wide range of groups. As a result, government programs are never terminated or restructured; tough budget cuts or tax changes are rarely made; and a very rich democratic country and its government becomes immobile. Rather than the dynamic system of change and compromise envisioned by Truman, Rauch sees a system characterized primarily by inertia because of the power of groups to prevent government action.

61

The Federalist, No. 10

James Madison

To the People of the State of New York:

Among the numerous advantages promised by a well-constructed Union, none deserves to be more accurately developed than its tendency to break and control the violence of faction. The friend of popular governments never finds himself so much alarmed for their character and fate, as when he contemplates their propensity to this dangerous vice. He will not fail, therefore, to set a due value on any plan which, without violating the principles to which he is attached, provides a proper cure for it. The instability, injustice, and confusion introduced into the public councils, have, in truth, been the mortal diseases under which popular governments have everywhere perished; as they continue to be the favorite and fruitful topics from which the adversaries to liberty derive their most specious declamations. The valuable improvements made by the American constitutions on the popular models, both ancient and modern, cannot certainly be too much admired; but it would be an unwarrantable partiality, to contend that they have as effectually obviated the danger on this side, as was wished and expected. Complaints are everywhere heard from our most considerate and virtuous citizens, equally the friends of public and private faith, and of public and personal liberty, that our governments are too unstable; that the public good is disregarded in the conflicts of rival parties; and that measures are too often decided, not according to the rules of justice and the rights of the minor party, but by the superior force of an interested and overbearing majority. However anxiously we may wish that these complaints had no foundation, the evidence of known facts will not permit us to deny that they are in some degree true. It will be found, indeed, on a candid review of our situation, that some of the distresses under which we labor have been erroneously charged on the operation of our governments; but it will be found, at the same time, that other causes will not alone account for many of our heaviest misfortunes; and, particularly, for that prevailing and increasing distrust of public engagements, and alarm for private rights, which are echoed from one end of the continent to the other. These must be chiefly, if not wholly, effects of the unsteadiness and injustice with which a factious spirit has tainted our public administrations.

By a faction, I understand a number of citizens, whether amounting to a majority or minority of the whole, who are united and actuated by some common impulse of passion, or of interest, adverse to the rights of other citizens, or to the permanent and aggregate interests of the community.

There are two methods of curing the mischiefs of faction: the one, by removing its causes; the other, by controlling its effects.

There are again two methods of removing the causes of faction: the one, by destroying the liberty which is essential to its existence; the other, by giving to every citizen the same opinions, the same passions, and the same interests.

It could never be more truly said than of the first remedy, that it is worse than the disease. Liberty is to faction what air is to fire, an aliment without which it instantly expires. But it could not be less folly to abolish liberty, which is essential to political life, because it nourishes faction, than it would be to wish the annihilation of air, which is essential to animal life, because it imparts to fire its destructive agency.

The second expedient is as impracticable as the first would be unwise. As long as the reason of man continues fallible, and he is at liberty to exercise it, different opinions will be formed. As long as the connection subsits between his reason and his self-love, his opinions and his passions will have a reciprocal influence on each other; and the former will be objects to which the latter will attach themselves. The diversity in the faculties of men, from which the rights of property originate, is not less an insuperable obstacle to a uniformity of interests. The protection of these faculties is the first object of government. From the protection of different and unequal faculties of acquiring property, the possession of different degrees and kinds of property immediately results; and from the influence of these on the sentiments and views of the respective proprietors, ensues a division of the society into different interests and parties.

The latent causes of faction are thus sown in the nature of man; and we see them everywhere brought into different degrees of activity, according to the different circumstances of civil society. A zeal for different opinions concerning religion, concerning government, and many other points, as well of speculation as of practice; an attachment to different leaders ambitiously contending for pre-eminence and power; or to persons of other descriptions whose fortunes have been interesting to the human passions, have, in turn, divided mankind into parties, inflamed them with mutual animosity, and rendered them much more disposed to vex and oppress each other than to co-operate for their common good. So strong is this propensity of mankind to fall into mutual animosities, that where no substantial occasion presents itself, the most frivolous and fanciful distinctions have been sufficient to kindle their unfriendly passions and excite their most violent conflicts. But the most common and durable source of factions has been the various and unequal distribution of property. Those who hold and those who are without property have ever formed distinct interests in society. Those who are creditors, and those who are debtors, fall under a like discrimination. A landed interest, a manufacturing interest, a mercantile interest, a moneyed interest, with many lesser interests, grow up of necessity in civilized nations, and divide them into different classes, actuated by different sentiments and views. The regulation of these various and interfering interests forms the principal task of modern legislation, and involves the spirit of party and faction in the necessary and ordinary operations of the government.

No man is allowed to be a judge in his own cause, because his interest would certainly bias his judgment, and, not improbably, corrupt his integrity. With equal, nay with greater reason, a body of men are unfit to be both judges and parties at the same time; yet what are many of the most important acts of legislation, but so many judicial determinations, not indeed concerning the rights of single persons, but concerning the rights of large bodies of citizens? and what are the different classes of legislators but advocates and parties to the causes which they determine? Is a law proposed concerning private debts? It is a question to which the creditors are parties on one side and the debtors on the other. Justice ought to hold the balance between them. Yet the parties are, and must be, themselves the judges; and the most numerous party, or, in other words, the most powerful faction must be expected to prevail. Shall domestic manufactures be encouraged, and in what degree, by restrictions on foreign manufactures? are questions which would be differently decided by the landed and the manufacturing classes, and probably by neither with a sole regard to justice and the public good. The apportionment of taxes on the various descriptions of property is an act which seems to require the most exact impartiality; yet there is, perhaps, no legislative act in which greater opportunity and temptation are given to a predominant party to trample on the rules of justice. Every shilling with which they overburden the inferior number is a shilling saved to their own pockets.

It is in vain to say that enlightened statesmen will be able to adjust these clashing interests and render them all subservient to the public good. Enlightened statesmen will not always be at the helm. Nor, in many cases, can such an adjustment be made at all without taking into view indirect and remote considerations, which will rarely prevail over the immediate interest which one party may find in disregarding the rights of another or the good of the whole.

The inference to which we are brought is, that the *causes* of faction cannot be removed, and that relief is only to be sought in the means of controlling its *effects*.

If a faction consists of less than a majority, relief is supplied by the republican principle, which enables the majority to defeat its sinister views by regular vote. It may clog the administration, it may convulse the society; but it will be unable to execute and mask its violence under the forms of the Constitution. When a majority is included in a faction, the form of popular government, on the other hand, enables it to sacrifice to its ruling passion or interest both the public good and the rights of other citizens. To secure the public good and private rights against the danger of such a faction, and at the same time to preserve the spirit and the form of popular government, is then the great object to which our inquiries are directed. Let me add that it is the great desideratum [desire] by which this form of government can be rescued from the opprobrium under which it has so long labored, and be recommended to the esteem and adoption of mankind.

By what means is this object attainable? Evidently by one of two only. Either the existence of the same passion or interest in a majority at the same time must be prevented, or the majority, having such coexistent passion or interest, must be rendered by their number and local situation unable to concert and carry into effect schemes of oppression. If the impulse and the opportunity be suffered to coincide, we well know that neither moral nor religious motives can be relied on as an adequate control. They are not found to be such on the injustice and violence of individuals, and lose their efficacy in proportion to the number combined together, that is, in proportion as their efficacy becomes needful.

From this view of the subject it may be concluded that a pure democracy, by which I mean a society consisting of a small number of citizens, who assemble and administer the government in person, can admit of no cure for the mischiefs of faction. A common passion or interest will, in almost every case, be felt by a majority of the whole; a communication and concert result from the form of government itself; and there is nothing to check the inducements to sacrifice the weaker party or an obnoxious individual. Hence it is that such democracies have ever been spectacles of turbulence and contention; have ever been found incompatible with personal security or the rights of property; and have in general been as short in their lives as they have been violent in their deaths. Theoretic politicians, who have patronized this species of government, have erroneously supposed that by reducing mankind to a perfect equality in their political rights, they would, at the same time, be perfectly equalized and assimilated in their possessions, their opinions, and their passions.

A republic, by which I mean a government in which the scheme of representation takes place, opens a different prospect, and promises the cure for which we are seeking. Let us examine the points in which it varies from pure democracy, and we shall comprehend both the nature of the cure and the efficacy which it must derive from the Union.

The two great points of difference between a democracy and a republic are: first, the delegation of the government in the latter to a small number of citizens elected by the rest; secondly, the greater number of citizens and greater sphere of country over which the latter may be extended.

The effect of the first difference is, on the one hand, to refine and enlarge the public views, by passing them through the medium of a chosen body of citizens, whose wisdom may best discern the true interest of their country, and whose patriotism and love of justice will be least likely to sacrifice it to temporary or partial considerations. Under such a regulation, it may well happen that the public voice, pronounced by the representatives of the people, will be more consonant to the public good than if pronounced by the people themselves, convened for the purpose. On the other hand, the effect may be inverted. Men of factious tempers, of local prejudices, or of sinister designs, may by intrigue, by corruption, or by other means, first obtain the suffrages, and then betray the interests of the people. The question resulting is, whether small or extensive republics are more favorable to the election of proper guardians of the public weal; and it is clearly decided in favor of the latter by two obvious considerations.

In the first place, it is to be remarked that, however small the republic may be, the representatives must be raised to a certain number in order to guard against the cabals of a few; and that, however large it may be, they must be limited to a certain number in order to guard against the confusion of a multitude. Hence, the number of representatives in the two cases not being in proportion to that of the two constituents, and being proportionally greater in the small republic, it follows that, if the proportion of fit characters be not less in the large than in the small republic, the former will present a greater option and consequently a greater probability of a fit choice.

In the next place, as each representative will be chosen by a greater number of citizens in the large than in the small republic, it will be more difficult for unworthy candidates to practise with success the vicious arts by which elections are too often carried; and the suffrages of the people being more free, will be more likely to centre in men who possess the most attractive merit and the most diffusive and established characters.

It must be confessed that in this, as in most other cases, there is a mean, on both sides of which inconveniences will be found to lie. By enlarging too much the number of electors, you render the representative too little acquainted with all their local circumstances and lesser interests: as by reducing it too much, you render him unduly attached to these, and too little fit to comprehend and pursue great and national objects. The federal Constitution forms a happy combination in this respect; the great and aggregate interests being referred to the national, the local and particular to the State legislatures.

The other point of difference is, the greater number of citizens and extent of territory which may be brought within the compass of republican than of democratic government; and it is this circumstance principally which renders factious combinations less to be dreaded in the former than in the latter. The smaller the society, the fewer probably will be the distinct parties and interests composing it; the fewer the distinct parties and interests, the more frequently will a majority be found of the same party; and the smaller the number of individuals composing a majority, and the smaller the compass within which they are placed, the more easily will they concert and execute their plans of oppression. Extend the sphere, and you take in a greater variety of parties and interests; you make it less probable that a majority of the whole will have a common motive to invade the rights of other citizens; or if such a common motive exists, it will be more difficult for all who feel it to discover their own strength and to act in unison with each other. Besides other impediments, it may be remarked that, where there is a consciousness of unjust or dishonorable purposes, communication is always checked by distrust in proportion to the number whose concurrence is necessary.

Hence, it clearly appears that the same advantage which a republic has over a democracy in controlling the effects of faction is enjoyed by a large over a small republic,—is enjoyed by the Union over the States composing it. Does the advantage consist in the substitution of representatives whose enlightened views and virtuous sentiments render them superior to local prejudices and to schemes of injustice? It will not be denied that the representation of the Union will be most likely to possess these requisite endowments. Does it consist in the greater security afforded by a greater variety of parties, against the event of any one party being able to outnumber and oppress the rest? In an equal degree does the increased variety of parties comprised within the Union, increase this security. Does it, in fine, consist in the greater obstacles opposed to the concert and accomplishment of the secret wishes of an unjust and interested majority? Here, again, the extent of the Union gives it the most palpable advantage.

The influence of factious leaders may kindle a flame within their particular States, but will be unable to spread a general conflagration through the other States. A religious sect may degenerate into a political faction in a part of the Confederacy; but the variety of sects dispersed over the entire face of it must secure the national councils against any danger from that source. A rage for paper money, for an abolition of debts, for an equal division of property, or for any other improper or wicked project, will be less apt to pervade the whole body of the Union than a particular member of it; in the same proportion as such a malady is more likely to taint a particular county or district, than an entire State.

In the extent and proper structure of the Union, therefore, we behold a republican remedy for the diseases most incident to republican government. And according to the degree of pleasure and pride we feel in being republicans, ought to be our zeal in cherishing the spirit and supporting the character of Federalists.

PUBLIUS

62

"The Alleged Mischiefs of Faction" from *The Governmental Process*

David B. Truman

Most accounts of American legislative sessions—national, state, or local—are full of references to the maneuverings and iniquities of various organized groups. Newspaper stories report that a legislative proposal is being promoted by groups of business men or school teachers or farmers or consumers or labor unions or other aggregations of citizens. Cartoonists picture the legislature as completely under the control of sinister, portly, cigar-smoking individuals labeled "special interests," while a diminutive John Q. Public is pushed aside to sulk in futile anger and pathetic frustrations. A member of the legislature rises in righteous anger on the floor of the house or in a press conference to declare that the bill under discussion is being forced through by the "interests," by the most unscrupulous high-pressure "lobby" he has seen in all his years of public life. An investigating committee denounces the activities of a group as deceptive, immoral, and destructive of our constitutional methods and ideals. A chief executive attacks a "lobby" or "pressure group" as the agency responsible for obstructing or emasculating a piece of legislation that he has recommended "in the public interest."

* * *

Such events are familiar even to the casual student of day-to-day politics, if only because they make diverting reading and appear to give the citizen the "low-down" on his government. He tends, along with many of his more sophisticated fellow citizens, to take these things more or less for granted, possibly because they merely confirm his conviction that "as everybody knows, politics is a dirty business." Yet at the same time he is likely to regard the activities of organized groups in political life as somehow outside the proper and normal processes of government, as the lapses of his weak contemporaries whose moral fiber is insufficient to prevent their defaulting on the great traditions of the Founding Fathers. These events appear to be a modern pathology.

Group Pressure and the Founding Fathers

Group pressures, whatever we may wish to call them, are not new in America. One of the earliest pieces of testimony to this effect is essay number 10 of *The Federalist*, which contains James Madison's classic statement of the impact of divergent groups upon government and the reasons for their development. He was arguing the virtues of the proposed Union as a means to "break and control the violence of faction," having in mind, no doubt, the groups involved in such actions of the debtor or propertyless segment of the population as Shays's Rebellion. He defined faction in broader terms, however, as "a number of citizens, whether amounting to a majority or minority of the whole, who are united and actuated by some common impulse of passion, or of interest. . . ."

*   *   *

[Madison's] analysis is not just the brilliant generalization of an armchair philosopher or pamphleteer; it represents as well the distillation from Madison's years of acquaintance with contemporary politics as a member of the Virginia Assembly and of [the Continental] Congress. Using the words "party" and "faction" almost interchangeably, since the political party as we know it had not yet developed, he saw the struggles of such groups as the essence of the political process. One need not concur in all his judgments to agree that the process he described had strong similarities to that of our own day.

The entire effort of which *The Federalist* was a part was one of the most skillful and important examples of pressure group activity in American history. The State ratifying conventions were handled by the Federalists with a skill that might well be the envy of a modern lobbyist. It is easy to overlook the fact that "unless the Federalists had been shrewd in manipulation as they were sound in theory, their arguments could not have prevailed."

*   *   *

Alexis de Tocqueville, perhaps the keenest foreign student ever to write on American institutions, noted as one of the most striking characteristics of the nation the penchant for promoting a bewildering array of projects through organized societies, among them those using political means. "In no country in the world," he observed, "has the principle of association been more successfully used or applied to a greater multitude of objects than in America."[1] De Tocqueville was impressed by the organization of such groups and by their tendency to operate sometimes upon and sometimes parallel to the formal institutions of government. Speaking of the similarity between the representatives of such groups and the members of legislatures, he stated: "It is true that they [delegates of these societies] have not the right, like the others, of making the laws;

but they have the power of attacking those which are in force and of drawing up beforehand those which ought to be enacted."[2]

Since the modern political party was, in the Jackson period, just taking the form that we would recognize today, De Tocqueville does not always distinguish sharply between it and other types of political interest groups. In his discussion of "political associations," however, he gives an account of the antitariff convention held in Philadelphia in October of 1831, the form of which might well have come from the proceedings of a group meeting in an American city today:

> Its debates were public, and they at once assumed a legislative character; the extent of the powers of Congress, the theories of free trade, and the different provisions of the tariff were discussed. At the end of ten days the Convention broke up, having drawn up an address to the American people in which it declared: (1) that Congress had not the right of making a tariff, and that the existing tariff was unconstitutional; (2) that the prohibition of free trade was prejudicial to the interests of any nation, and to those of the American people especially.[3]

Additional evidence might be cited from many quarters to illustrate the long history of group politics in this country. Organized pressures supporting or attacking the charter of the Bank of the United States in Jackson's administration, the peculations surrounding Pendleton's "Palace of Fortune" in the pre–Civil War period, the operations of the railroads and other interests in both national and state legislatures in the latter half of the last century, the political activities of farm groups such as the Grange in the same period—these and others indicate that at no time have the activities of organized political interests not been a part of American politics. Whether they indicate pathology or not, they are certainly not new.

*　*　*

The political interest group is neither a fleeting, transitory newcomer to the political arena nor a localized phenomenon peculiar to one member of the family of nations. The persistence and the dispersion of such organizations indicate rather that we are dealing with a characteristic aspect of our society. That such groups are receiving an increasing measure of popular and technical attention suggests the hypothesis that they are appreciably more significant in the complex and interdependent society of our own day than they were in the simpler, less highly developed community for which our constitutional arrangements were originally designed.

Many people are quite willing to acknowledge the accuracy of these propositions about political groups, but they are worried nevertheless. They are still concerned over the meaning of what they see and read of the activities of such organizations. They observe, for example, that certain farm groups apparently can induce the Government to spend hundreds of millions of dollars to maintain the price of food and to take "surplus" agricultural produce off the market while any urban residents are encountering painful difficulty in stretching their food budgets to provide adequately for their families. They observe that various labor organizations seem to be able to prevent the introduction of cheaper methods into building codes, although the cost of new housing is already beyond the reach of many. Real estate and contractors' trade associations apparently have the power to obstruct various governmental projects for slum clearance and low-cost housing. Veterans' organizations seem able to secure and protect increases in pensions and other benefits almost at will. A church apparently can prevent the appropriation of Federal funds to public schools unless such funds are also given to the schools it operates in competition with the public systems. The Government has declared that stable and friendly European governments cannot be maintained unless Americans buy more goods and services abroad. Yet American shipowners and seamen's unions can secure a statutory requirement that a large proportion of the goods purchased by European countries under the Marshall Plan* must be carried in American ships. Other industries and trade associations can prevent the revision of tariff rates and customs regulations that restrict imports from abroad.

In all these situations the fairly observant citizen sees various groups slugging it out with one another in pursuit of advantages from the Government. Or he sees some of them co-operating with one another to their mutual benefit. He reads of "swarms" of lobbyists "putting pressure on" congressmen and administrators. He has the impression that any group can get what it wants in Washington by deluging officials with mail and telegrams. He may then begin to wonder whether a governmental system like this can survive, whether it can carry its responsibilities in the world and meet the challenges presented by a ruthless dictatorship. He wants to see these external threats effectively met. The sentimental nonsense of the commercial advertisements aside, he values free speech, free elections, representative government, and all that these imply. He fears and resents practices and privileges that seem to place these values in jeopardy.

A common reaction to revelations concerning the more lurid activities of political groups is one of righteous indignation. Such indignation is entirely natural. It is likely, however, to be more comforting than constructive. What we seek are correctives, protections, or controls that will strengthen the practices essential in what we call democracy and that will weaken or eliminate those that really threaten that system. Uncritical anger may do little to achieve that objective, largely because it is likely to be based upon a picture of the governmental process that is a composite of myth and fiction as well as of fact. We shall not begin to achieve con-

*[The U.S. European Recovery Plan after World War II]

trol until we have arrived at a conception of politics that adequately accounts for the operations of political groups. We ned to know what regular patterns are shown by group politics before we can predict its consequences and prescribe for its lapses. We ned to re-examine our notions of how representative government operates in the United States before we can be confident of our statements about the effects of group activities upon it. Just as we should not know how to protect a farm house from lightning unless we knew something of the behavior of electricity, so we cannot hope to protect a governmental system from the results of group organization unless we have an adequate understanding of the political process of which these groups are a part.

*   *   *

There are two elements in this conception of the political process in the United States that are of crucial significance and that require special emphasis. These are, first, the notion of multiple or overlapping membership and, second, the function of unorganized interests, or potential interest groups.

The idea of overlapping membership stems from the conception of a group as a standardized pattern of interactions rather than as a collection of human units. Although the former may appear to be a rather misty abstraction, it is actually far closer to complex reality than the latter notion. he view of a group as an aggregation of individuals abstracts from the observable fact that in any society, and especially a complex one, no single group affiliation accounts for all of the attitudes or interests of any individual except a fanatic or a compulsive neurotic. No tolerably normal person is totally absorbed in any group in which he participates. The diversity of an individual's activities and his attendant interests involve him in a variety of actual and potential groups. Moreover, the fact that the genetic experiences of no two individuals are identical and the consequent fact that the spectra of their attitudes are in varying degrees dissimilar means that the members of a single group will perceive the group's claims in terms of a diversity of frames of reference. Such heterogeneity may be of little significance until such time as these multiple memberships conflict. Then the cohesion and influence of the affected group depend upon the incorporation or accommodation of the conflicting loyalties of any significant segment of the group, an accommodation that may result in altering the original claims. Thus the leaders of a Parent-Teacher Association must take some account of the fact that their proposals must be acceptable to members who also belong to the local taxpayers' league, to the local chamber of commerce, and to the Catholic Church.

*   *   *

We cannot account of an established American political system without the second crucial element in our conception of the political process, the concept of the unorganized interest, or potential interest group. Despite the tremendous number of interest groups existing in the United States, not all interests are organized. If we recall the definition of an interest as a shared attitude, it becomes obvious that continuing interaction resulting in claims upon other groups does not take place on the basis of all such attitudes. One of the commonest interest groups forms, the association, emerges out of severe or prolonged disturbances in the expected relationships of individuals in similar institutionalized groups. As association continues to function as long as it succeeds in ordering these disturbed relationships, as a labor union orders the relationships between management and workers. Not all such expected relationships are simultaneously or in a given short period sufficiently disturbed to produce organization. Therefore only a portion of the interests or attitudes involved in such expectations are represented by organized groups. Similarly, many organized groups—families, businesses, or churches, for example—do not operate continuously as interest groups or as political interest groups.

Any mutual interest, however, any shared attitude, is a potential group. A disturbance in established relationships and expectations anywhere in the society may produce new patterns of interaction aimed at restricting or eliminating he disturbance. Sometimes it may be this possibility of organization that alone gives the potential group a minimum of influence in the political process. Thus . . . the Delta planters in Mississippi "must speak for their Negroes in such programs as health and education,"[4] although the latter are virtually unorganized and are denied the means of active political participation.*

* * *

Obstacles to the development of organized groups from potential ones may be presented by inertia or by the activities of opposed groups, but the possibility that severe disturbances will be created if these submerged, potential interests should organize necessitates some recognition of the existence of these interests and gives them at least a minimum of influence.

More important for present purposes than the potential groups representing separate minority elements are those interests or expectations that are so widely held in the society and are so reflected in the behavior of almost all citizens that they are, so to speak, taken for granted. Such "majority" interests are significant not only because they may become the basis for organized interest groups overlaps extensively the memberships of the various organized interest groups. The resolution of conflicts between the claims of such unorganized interests and those of organized interest groups must grant recognition to the former not only because

*[Until the 1960s, most Southern blacks were denied the right to vote.]

affected individuals may feel strongly attached to them but even more certainly because these interests are widely shared and are a part of many established patterns of behavior the disturbance of which would be difficult and painful. They are likely to be highly valued.

*   *   *

It is thus multiple memberships in potential groups based on widely held and accepted interests that serve as a balance wheel in a going political system like that of the United States. To some people this observation may appear to be a truism and to others a somewhat mystical notion. It is neither. In the first place, neglect of this function of multiple memberships in most discussions of organized interest groups indicates that the observation is not altogether commonplace. Secondly, the statement has no mystical quality; the effective operation of these widely held interests is to be inferred directly from verbal and other behavior in the political sphere. Without the notion of multiple memberships in potential groups it is literally impossible to account for the existence of a viable polity such as that in the United States or to develop a coherent conception of the political process. The strength of these widely held but largely unorganized interests explains the vigor with which propagandists for organized groups attempt to change other attitudes by invoking such interests. Their importance is further evidenced in the recognized function of the means of mass communication, notably the press, in reinforcing widely accepted norms of "public morality."

*   *   *

Thus it is only as the effects of overlapping memberships and the functions of unorganized interests and potential groups are included in the equation that it is accurate to speak of governmental activity as the product or resultant of interest group activity. As [political scientist Arthur F.] Bentley has put it:

> There are limits to the technique of the struggle, this involving also limits to the group demands, all of which is solely a matter of empirical observation. . . . Or, in other words, when the struggle proceeds too harshly at any point there will become insistent in the society a group more powerful than either of those involved which tends to suppress the extreme and annoying methods of the groups in the primary struggle. It is within the embrace of these great lines of activity that the smaller struggles proceed, and the very word struggle has meaning only with reference to its limitations.[5]

To assert that the organization and activity of powerful interest groups constitutes a threat to representative government without measuring their relation to and effects upon the widespread potential groups is to generalize from insufficient data and upon an incomplete conception of the political process. Such an analysis would be as faulty as one that ignoring differences in national systems, predicted identical responses to a given technological change in the United States, Japan, and the Soviet Union.

Notes

1. Alexis de Tocqueville, *Democracy in America*, ed. by Phillips Bradley (New York: Knopf, 1945), Volume I, p. 191.
2. Tocqueville, p. 193.
3. Tocqueville, p. 194.
4. V. O. Key, *Southern Politics in State and Nation* (New York: Knopf, 1949), p. 235.
5. Arthur F. Bentley, *The Process of Government* (Chicago: University of Chicago Press, 1908), p. 372.

62

"The Hyperpluralism Trap"

Jonathan Rauch

Anyone who believes Washington needs to get closer to the people ought to spend a little time with Senator Richard Lugar, the Indiana Republican. "Take a look at the people coming into my office on a normal Tuesday and Wednesday," Lugar said in a speech not long ago. "Almost every organization in our society has a national conference. The typical way of handling this is to come in on a Monday, rev up the troops, give them the bill number and send them up to the Hill. If they can't get in on Tuesday, strike again on Wednesday. I regularly have on Tuesday as many as fifteen constituent groups from Indiana, all of whom have been revved up by some skillful person to cite bills that they don't understand, have never heard of prior to that time, but with a score sheet to report back to headquarters whether I am for or against. It is so routine, it is so fierce, that at some point you [can't be] immune to it."

This is the reality of modern government. The rhetoric of modern politics, alas, is a little different. Take today's standard-issue political stem-winder, which goes something like this: "I think perhaps the most important thing that we understand here in the heartland . . . is the need to reform the political system, to reduce the influence of special interests and give more influence back to the kind of people that are in this crowd tonight by the tens of thousands." That stream of boilerplate is from Bill Clinton (from his election-night speech), but it could have come from almost any politician. It's pitched in a dominant key of political rhetoric today: *standard populism*—that is, someone has taken over the government and "we" must take it back, restore government to the people, etc. But who, exactly, are those thousands of citizens who troop weekly through Senator Lugar's suite, clutching briefing packets and waving scorecards? Standard populism says they are the "special interests," those boils on the skin of democracy, forever interposing themselves between the American people and the people's servants in Washington.

Well, fifty years ago that analysis may have been useful, but not anymore. In America today, the special interests and "the people" have become objectively indistinguishable. Groups are us. As a result, the populist impulse to blame special interests, big corporations and political careerists for our problems—once a tonic—has become Americans' leading political narcotic. Worse, it actually abets the lobbying it so righteously denounces.

Begin with one of the best known yet most underappreciated facts of our time: over the past three or four decades we have busily organized ourselves into interest groups—lobbies, loosely speaking—at an astonishing rate. Interest groups were still fairly sparse in America until about the time of World War II. Then they started proliferating, and in the 1960s the pace of organizing picked up dramatically.

Consider, for instance, the numbers of groups listed in Gale Research's *Encyclopedia of Associations*. The listings have grown from fewer than 5,000 in 1956 to well over 20,000 today. They represent, of course, only a small fraction of America's universe of interest groups. Environmental organizations alone number an estimated 7,000, once you count local clean-up groups and the like; the Washington *Blade*'s resource directory lists more than 400 gay groups, up from 300 at the end of 1990. Between 1961 and 1982 the number of corporate offices in Washington increased tenfold. Even more dramatic was the explosion in the number of public-interest organizations and grass-roots groups. These barely existed at all before the 1960s; today they number in the tens of thousands and collect more than $4 billion per year from 40 million individuals, according to political scientist Ronald Shaiko of American University.

Well, so what? Groups do many good things—provide companionship for the like-minded, collect and disseminate information, sponsor contests, keep the catering industry solvent. Indeed, conventional political theory for much of the postwar period was dominated by a strain known as pluralism, which holds that more groups equals more representation equals better democracy. Yet pluralism missed something. It assumed that the group-forming process was self-balancing and stable, as opposed to self-feeding and unstable. Which is to say, it failed to grasp the danger of what American University political scientist James Thurber aptly calls hyperpluralism.

In economics, inflation is a gradual increase in the price level. Up to a point, if the inflation rate is stable, people can plan around it. But if the rate starts to speed up, people start expecting more inflation. They hoard goods and dump cash, driving the inflation still faster. Eventually, an invisible threshold is crossed: the inflation now feeds on its own growth and undermines the stability of the whole economic system.

What the pluralists missed is that something analogous can happen with interest groups. People see that it pays to organize into groups and angle for benefits, so they do it. But as more groups make more demands, and as even more hungry groups form to compete with all the other groups, the process begins to feed on itself and pick up momentum. At some point there might be so many groups that they choke the political system, sow contention and conflict, even erode society's governability. That's hyperpluralism. And if it is less destabilizing than hyperinflation, it may be more insidious.

The pattern is most visible in smaller social units, such as local school districts, where groups colonize the curriculum—sex education for liberals, values instruction for conservatives, recycling lessons for environmentalists, voluntary silent prayer for Christians. But even among the general population the same forces are at work. Fifty years ago the phrase "the elderly" denoted a demographic category; today, thanks largely to federal pension programs and the American Association of Retired Persons (AARP), it denotes a giant and voracious lobby. In the 1930s the government set up farm-subsidy programs, one per commodity; inevitably, lobbies sprang up to defend each program, so that today American agriculture is fundamentally a collection of interest groups. With the help of group organizers and race-based benefits, loose ethnic distinctions coalesce into hard ethnic lobbies. And so on.

Even more depressing, any attempt to fight back against the proliferating mass of subdivision is foiled by the rhetoric of standard populism and its useful stooge: the special interest. The concept of a "special interest" is at the very core of standard populism—the "them" without which there can be no "us." So widely accepted is this notion, and so useful is it in casual political speech, that most of us talk routinely about special interests without a second thought. We all feel we know a special interest when we see one, if only because it is a group of which we are not a member. Yet buried in the special interest idea is an assumption that is no longer true.

The concept of the special interest is not based on nothing. It is, rather, out of date, an increasingly empty relic of the time of machine politics and political bosses, when special interests were, quite literally, special. Simply because of who they were, they enjoyed access that was available to no one else. But the process of everyone's organizing into more and more groups can go only so far before the very idea of a special interest loses any clear meaning. At some point one must throw up one's hands and concede that the hoary dichotomy between special interests and "us" has become merely rhetoric.

According to a 1990 survey conducted for the American Society of Association Executives, seven out of ten Americans belong to at least one association, and one in four Americans belongs to four or more. Practically everyone who reads these words is a member of an interest group, probably several. Moreover, formal membership tallies omit many people whom we ordinarily think of as being represented by lobbies. For example, the powerful veterans' lobbies enroll only perhaps one-seventh of American veterans, yet the groups lobby on behalf of veterans as a class, and all 27 million veterans share in the benefits. Thus the old era of lobbying by special interests—by a well-connected, plutocratic few —is as dead now as slavery and Prohibition. We Americans have achieved the full democratization of lobbying: influence-peddling for the masses.

The appeal of standard populism today comes precisely from the phony reassurance afforded by its real message: "Other people's groups are the special interests. Less for them—more for you!" Spread that sweet manure around and the natural outgrowth is today's tendency, so evident in the Clinton style, to pander to interest groups frantically while denouncing them furiously. It is the public's style, too: sending ever more checks to the AARP and the National Rifle Association and the National Federation of Independent Business and the National Wildlife Federation and a million others, while railing against special interests. Join and join, blame and blame.

So hyperpluralism makes a hash of the usual sort of standard populist prescription, which calls for "the people" to be given more access to the system, at the expense of powerful Beltway figures who are alleged to have grown arrogant or corrupt or out of touch. Activists and reformers who think the answer to democracy's problems is more access for more of the people need to wake up. Uncontrolled access only breeds more lobbies. It is axiomatic that "the people" (whatever that now means) do not organize to seek government benefits; lobbies do. Every new door to the federal treasury is an opportunity for new groups to queue up for more goodies.

Populists resolutely refuse to confront this truth. Last year, for example, Republicans and the editors of *The Wall Street Journal* campaigned fiercely—and successfully—for new congressional rules making it easier for legislators and groups to demand that bottled-up bills be discharged from committee. The idea was to bring Congress closer to "the people" by weakening the supposedly high-handed barons who rule the Hill. But burying the Free Christmas Tree for Every American Act (or whatever) in committee—while letting members of Congress say they *would* have voted for it—was one of the few remaining ways to hold the door against hungry lobbies clamoring for gifts.

A second brand of populism, *left-populism*, is even more clueless than the standard brand, if that's possible. Many liberals believe the problem is that the wrong groups—the rich, the elites, the giant corporations, etc.—have managed to out-organize the good guys and take control of the system. One version of this model was elaborated by William Greider in his book *Who Will Tell the People*. The New Deal legacy, he writes, "rests upon an idea of interest group bargaining that has gradually been transformed into the random deal-making and permissiveness of the present. The alterations in the system are decisive and . . . the ultimate effects are anti-democratic. People with limited resources, with no real representation in the higher levels of politics, are bound to lose in this environment." So elaborate is the Washington machine of lobbyists, consultants, P.R. experts, political action committees and for-hire think tanks, says Greider, that "powerful economic interests," notably corporations and private wealth, inevitably dominate.

What's appealing about this view is the truism from which it springs: the wealthy enjoy a natural advantage in lobbying, as in almost everything else. Thus many lobbies—even liberal lobbies—are dominated by the comfortable and the wealthy. Consider the case of environmental groups. Anyone who doubts they are major players in Washington today need only look at the massive 1990 Clean Air Act, a piece of legislation that business gladly would have done without. Yet these groups are hardly battalions of the disfranchised. "Readers of *Sierra*, the magazine of the Sierra Club, have household incomes twice that of the average American," notes Senior Economist Terry L. Anderson of the Political Economy Research Center. And *The Economist* notes that "in 1993 the Nature Conservancy, with $915 million in assets, drew 73 percent of its income from rich individuals." When such groups push for emissions controls or pesticide rules, they may be reflecting the priorities of people who buy BMWs and brie more than the priorities of people who buy used Chevies and hamburger. So left-populism's claim to speak for "the people" is often suspect, to say the least.

The larger problem with left-populism, however, is its refusal to see that it is feeding the very problem it decries. Left-populism was supposed to fix the wealth-buys-power problem by organizing the politically disadvantaged into groups: unions, consumer groups, rainbow coalitions and so on. But the strategy has failed. As the left (the unions, the environmentalists) has organized ever more groups, the right (the bosses, the polluters) has followed suit. The group-forming has simply spiraled. This makes a joke of the left-populist prescription, which is to form more "citizens' groups" on the Naderite model, supposedly reinvigorating representative democracy and giving voice to the weak and the silenced. Greider proposes giving people subsidies to spend on political activism: "Giving individual citizens the capacity to deploy political money would inevitably shift power from existing structures and disperse it among the ordinary millions who now feel excluded."

Inevitably, it would do no such thing. Subsidies for activism would perforce go straight into the waiting coffers of (what else?) interest groups, new and old. That just makes matters worse, for if one side organizes more groups, the other side simply redoubles its own mobilization ad infinitum. That escalating cycle is the story of the last three decades. The only winner is the lobbying class. Curiously, then, left-populism has come to serve the very lobbying elites—the Washington lawyers and lobby shops and P.R. pros and interest group execs—whom leftists ought, by rights, to loathe.

The realization that the lobbying class is, to a large extent, both entrepreneurial and in business for itself has fed the third brand of populism, *right-populism*. In the right-populist model, self-serving political careerists have hijacked government and learned to manipulate it for profit. In refreshing contrast to the other two brands of populism, however, this one is in touch with reality. Washington *is* in business for itself, though not only for itself. Legislators and lobbies have an interest in using the tax code to please their constituents, but they also have an interest in churning the tax code to generate campaign contributions and lobbying fees. Luckily for them, those two imperatives generally coincide: the more everyone hunts for tax breaks, the more lobbying jobs there are. Right-populism has tumbled to the fact that so-called public interest and citizens' groups are no more immune to this self-serving logic of lobbying—create conflict, reap rewards—than is any other sort of professional lobby.

Yet right-populism fails to see to the bottom of the problem. It looks into the abyss but flinches. This is not to say that term limits and other procedural fine-tunes may not help; such reforms are no doubt worth trying. But even if noodling with procedures succeeded in diluting the culture of political careerism, it would help (or hurt) mainly at the margins. No, tinkering with the process isn't the answer. What we must do is go straight at the beast itself. We must attack and weaken the lobbies— that is, the *people*'s lobbies.

It sounds so simple: weaken the lobbies! Shove them aside, reclaim the government! "It's just that simple," twinkles Ross Perot. But it's not that simple. Lobbies in Washington have clout because the people who scream when "special interests" are attacked are Medicare recipients defending benefits, farmers defending price supports, small businesses defending subsidized loans, racial groups defending set-asides and so on. Inherently, challenging these groups is no one's idea of fun, which is why politicians so rarely propose to do it. The solution is to strip away lobbies' protections and let competition hammer them. In practice, that means:

Balance the federal budget. It is a hackneyed prescription, but it is the very first thing we should do to curtail the lobbies' ability to rob the future. Deficits empower lobbies by allowing them to raid the nation's scarce reserves of investment capital. Deprived of that ability, they will be forced to compete more fiercely for money, and they'll be unable to steal from the future.

Cut the lobbies' lifelines. Eliminate subsidies and programs, including tax loopholes, by the hundreds. Killing a program here or there is a loser's game; it creates a political uproar without actually making a noticeable difference. The model, rather, should be the 1986 tax reform measure, which proved that a wholesale housecleaning really is possible. Back then, tax loopholes were cleared away by the truckload. The trick was—and is—to do the job with a big package of reforms that politicians can tout back home as real change. That means ditching whole Cabinet departments and abolishing virtually all industry-specific subsidies. Then go after subsidies for the non-needy—wholesale, not retail.

*Promote domestic perestroika.** Lobbies live to lock benefits in and competition out, so government restraints on competition should be removed—not indiscriminately, but determinedly. President Carter's deregulation of transportation industries and interest rates, though imperfectly executed, were good examples. Air travel, trucking and rail shipping are cheaper *and* safer. The affected industries have been more turbulent, but that's exactly the point. Domestic competition shakes up interest groups that settle cozily into Washington.

Encourage foreign competition. This is most important of all. The forces that breed interest groups never abate, and so fighting them requires a constant counterforce. Foreign competition is such a counterforce. Protection invariably benefits the industries and groups with the sharpest lobbyists and the fattest political action committees; stripping away protection forces them to focus more on modernizing and less on lobbying.

No good deed, they say, goes unpunished. We sought to solve pressing social problems, so we gave government vast power to reassign resources. We also sought to look out for ourselves and bring voices to all of our many natures and needs, so we built countless new groups to seek government's resources. What we did not create was a way to control the chain reaction we set off. Swarming interest groups excited government to perpetual activism, and government activism drew new groups to Washington by the thousands. Before we knew it, society itself was turning into a collection of ravenous lobbies.

Why was this not always a problem? Because there used to be control rods containing the chain reaction. Smoke-filled rooms, they were called. On Capitol Hill or in Tammany Hall, you needed to see one of about six people to have any hope of getting what you wanted, and those six people dispensed (and conserved) favors with parsimonious finesse. Seen from today's vantage, smoke-filled rooms and political machines

---

* [1980s Soviet Union program of political and economic reform.]

did a creditable job of keeping a lid on the interest group frenzy—they just didn't do it particularly fairly. That's why we opened up access to anyone who wants to organize and lobby, and opened up power to subcommittee chairs and caucus heads and even junior legislators. In doing so, we abolished the venal gatekeepers. But that was only the good news. The bad news was that we also abolished the gate.

No, we shouldn't go back to smoke-filled rooms. But the way forward is harder than it ever was before. The maladies that now afflict government are ones in which the public is wholly, enthusiastically implicated. Still, there are sprigs and shoots of encouragement all around. There was the surprisingly strong presidential bid of former Senator Paul Tsongas, which built something of a constituency for straight talk. There's the rise of a school of Democrats in Congress—among them Senator Bob Kerrey and retiring Representative Tim Penny—who are willing to drag the White House toward sterner fiscal measures. There was the Clinton-led triumph of NAFTA [North American Free Trade Agreement] last year. Those developments show promise of a political movement that is counterpopulist yet also popular. Maybe—is it too much to hope?—they point beyond the desert of populism.

Discussion Questions

1. Why was Madison concerned about factions? What solutions to the "mischiefs of faction" did he suggest?

2. Can you think of any examples of overlapping group memberships providing overall balance to the political system? How about an example of the emergence of new organizations that had a significant impact on a policy debate? Can you think of instances in which, counter to Truman, a new organization did not emerge, leaving a group unrepresented?

3. Rauch complains that interest groups slow down the policy-making process, but isn't this what the Framers of the Constitution intended? Is the interest-group system as portrayed by Rauch a danger to democracy, or is it in fact implementing the principles implicit in the Constitution?

4. Among the many forms of interest-group activity, campaign contributions seem to provoke some of the harshest criticisms. Is this reasonable? Is there any reason to be more concerned about campaign contributions than about lobbying, lawsuits, funding research, or any other activities groups employ to pursue their cause?

PART IV

Public Policy

CHAPTER 13

Politics and Policy

64

"The Science of Muddling Through"

CHARLES E. LINDBLOM

Today's national government plays a role in virtually every aspect of our lives. It provides health insurance for the elderly and the poor, welfare assistance, veterans' benefits, student loans, and a tax break for home owners paying a mortgage. It regulates the activities of the stock markets, polluting industries, worker safety and worker rights, the quality of our food, and air traffic. These programs and regulatory policies are all designed and implemented by the government to achieve particular goals—such as an expanding economy, healthy citizens, college education, and home ownership. It is important that we know just how the government goes about formulating and implementing public policy, and the consequences of those efforts. Who plays a role in the making of public policy besides elected officials, and what motivates their decision making? Who are the beneficiaries of various public policies, and is the "public interest" being served?

In the article below, the economist and political scientist Charles Lindblom argues that the efforts of scholars to study and improve upon the policy process were flawed because they were based on the assumption that public policy could be made in a "rational" manner. The problem, according to Lindblom, is that decision making for public policy normally proceeds incrementally: policy makers are incapable of defining and developing alternatives that encompass all possible means of achieving explicitly defined goals. Rather, decision makers start with what already exists, goals defined in part by what is known to work and by the interests that are the most vocal and powerful, and changes are made at the margin to achieve these various ends. Further, the way we evaluate any given policy is heavily dependent upon our values and beliefs about what government ought to do and how it ought to be achieved. There is rarely, according to Lindblom, a clear objective standard of a "good" policy that all policy makers and analysts can agree upon. Lindblom's article, originally printed in 1959, was groundbreak-

ing in that it challenged conventional wisdom among analysts that rational com-
prehensive analysis was possible for purposes of formulating public policy.

Suppose an administrator is given responsibility for formulating policy with respect to inflation. He might start by trying to list all related values in order of importance, e.g., full employment, reasonable business profit, protection of small savings, prevention of a stock market crash. Then all possible policy outcomes could be rated as more or less efficient in attaining a maximum of these values. This would of course require a prodigious inquiry into values held by members of society and an equally prodigious set of calculations on how much each value is equal to how much of each other value. He could then proceed to outline all possible policy alternatives. In a third step, he could undertake systematic comparison of his multitude of alternatives to determine which attains the greatest amount of values.

In comparing policies, he would take advantage of any theory available that generalized about classes of policies. In considering inflation, for example, he would compare all policies in the light of the theory of prices. Since no alternatives are beyond his investigation, he would consider strict central control and the abolition of all prices and markets on the one hand and elimination of all public controls with reliance completely on the free market on the other, both in the light of whatever theoretical generalizations he could find on such hypothetical economies.

Finally, he would try to make the choice that would in fact maximize his values.

An alternative line of attack would be to set as his principal objective, either explicitly or without conscious thought, the relatively simple goal of keeping prices level. This objective might be compromised or complicated by only a few other goals, such as full employment. He would in fact disregard most other social values as beyond his present interest, and he would for the moment not even attempt to rank the few values that he regarded as immediately relevant. Were he pressed, he would quickly admit that he was ignoring many related values and many possible important consequences of his policies.

As a second step, he would outline those relatively few policy alternatives that occurred to him. He would then compare them. In comparing his limited number of alternatives, most of them familiar from past controversies, he would not ordinarily find a body of theory precise enough to carry him through a comparison of their respective consequences. Instead he would rely heavily on the record of past experience with small policy steps to predict the consequences of similar steps extended into the future.

Moreover, he would find that the policy alternatives combined objectives or values in different ways. For example, one policy might offer price level stability at the cost of some risk of unemployment; another might offer less price stability but also less risk of unemployment. Hence, the next step in his approach—the final selection—would combine into one the choice among values and the choice among instruments for reaching values. It would not, as in the first method of policy-making, approximate a more mechanical process of choosing the means that best satisfied goals that were previously clarified and ranked. Because practitioners of the second approach expect to achieve their goals only partially, they would expect to repeat endlessly the sequence just described, as conditions and aspirations changed and as accuracy of prediction improved.

By Root or by Branch

For complex problems, the first of these two approaches is of course impossible. Although such an approach can be described, it cannot be practiced except for relatively simple problems and even then only in a somewhat modified form. It assumes intellectual capacities and sources of information that men simply do not possess, and it is even more absurd as an approach to policy when the time and money that can be allocated to a policy problem is limited, as is always the case. Of particular importance to public administrators is the fact that public agencies are in effect usually instructed not to practice the first method. That is to say, their prescribed functions and constraints—the politically or legally possible—restrict their attention to relatively few values and relatively few alternative policies among the countless alternatives that might be imagined. It is the second method that is practiced.

Curiously, however, the literatures of decision-making, policy formulation, planning, and public administration formalize the first approach rather than the second, leaving public administrators who handle complex decisions in the position of practicing what few preach. For emphasis I run some risk of overstatement. True enough, the literature is well aware of limits on man's capacities and of the inevitability that policies will be approached in some such style as the second. But attempts to formalize rational policy formulation—to lay out explicitly the necessary steps in the process—usually describe the first approach and not the second.

The common tendency to describe policy formulation even for complex problems as though it followed the first approach has been strengthened by the attention given to, and success enjoyed by, operations research,* statistical decision theory,† and systems analysis.‡ The hallmarks of these procedures, typical of the first approach, are clarity of

---

* [*Operations research:* type of analysis, based on mathematical models, used to determine the most efficient use of resources for a set of goals.]

† [*Statistical decision theory:* theory that allows one to make choices between alternatives by objectifying problems and analyzing them quantitatively. Also called Bayesian decision theory after Thomas Bayes (1702–1761), who developed the mathematical foundation of inference, the method of using information on a sample to infer characteristics about a population.]

‡ [*Systems analysis:* analysis of systemic data by means of advanced quantitative techniques to aid in selecting the most appropriate course of action among a series of alternatives.]

objective, explicitness of evaluation, a high degree of comprehensiveness of overview, and, wherever possible, quantification of values for mathematical analysis. But these advanced procedures remain largely the appropriate techniques of relatively small-scale problem-solving where the total number of variables to be considered is small and value problems restricted. Charles Hitch, head of the Economics Division of RAND Corporation, one of the leading centers for application of these techniques, has written:

> I would make the empirical generalization from my experience at RAND and elsewhere that operations research is the art of sub-optimizing, i.e., of solving some lower-level problems, and that difficulties increase and our special competence diminishes by an order of magnitude with every level of decision making we attempt to ascend. The sort of simple explicit model which operations researchers are so proficient in using can certainly reflect most of the significant factors influencing traffic control on the George Washington Bridge, but the proportion of the relevant reality which we can represent by any such model or models in studying, say, a major foreign-policy decision, appears to be almost trivial.[1]

Accordingly, I propose in this paper to clarify and formalize the second method, much neglected in the literature. This might be described as the method of *successive limited comparisons*. I will contrast it with the first approach, which might be called the rational-comprehensive method. More impressionistically and briefly—and therefore generally used in this article—they could be characterized as the branch method and root method, the former continually building out from the current situation, step-by-step and by small degrees; the latter starting from fundamentals anew each time, building on the past only as experience is embodied in a theory, and always prepared to start completely from the ground up.

Let us put the characteristics of the two methods side by side in simplest terms.

Rational-Comprehensive (Root)

1a. Clarification of values or objectives distinct from and usually prerequisite to empirical analysis of alternative policies.
2a. Policy-formulation is therefore approached through means-end analysis: First the ends are isolated, then the means to achieve them are sought.
3a. The test of a "good" policy is that it can be shown to be the most appropriate means to desired ends.
4a. Analysis is comprehensive; every important relevant factor is taken into account.
5a. Theory is often heavily relied upon.

Assuming that the root method is familiar and understandable, we proceed directly to clarification of its alternative by contrast. In explaining the second, we shall be describing how most administrators do in fact approach complex questions, for the root method, the "best" way as a blueprint or model, is in fact not workable for complex policy questions, and administrators are forced to use the method of successive limited comparisons.

Intertwining Evaluation and Empirical Analysis (1B)

The quickest way to understand how values are handled in the method of successive limited comparisons is to see how the root method often breaks down in *its* handling of values or objectives. The idea that values should be clarified, and in advance of the examination of alternative policies, is appealing. But what happens when we attempt it for complex social problems? The first difficulty is that on many critical values or objectives, citizens disagree, congressmen disagree, and public administrators disagree. Even where a fairly specific objective is prescribed for the administrator, there remains considerable room for disagreement on sub-objectives. Consider, for example, the conflict with respect to locating public housing, described in Meyerson and Banfield's study of the Chicago Housing Authority—disagreement which occurred despite the clear objective of providing a certain number of public housing units in the city. Similarly conflicting are objectives in highway location, traffic control, minimum wage administration, development of tourist facilities in national parks, or insect control.

Successive Limited Comparisons (Branch)

1b. Selection of value goals and empirical analysis of the needed action are not distinct from one another but are closely intertwined.
2b. Since means and ends are not distinct, means-end analysis is often inappropriate or limited.
3b. The test of a "good" policy is typically that various analysts find themselves directly agreeing on a policy (without their agreeing that it is the most appropriate means to an agreed objective).
4b. Analysis is drastically limited: i) Important possible outcomes are neglected. ii) Important alternative potential policies are neglected. iii) Important affected values are neglected.
5b. A succession of comparisons greatly reduces or eliminates reliance on theory.

Administrators cannot escape these conflicts by ascertaining the majority's preference, for preferences have not been registered on most issues; indeed, there often *are* no preferences in the absence of public discussion sufficient to bring an issue to the attention of the electorate. Furthermore, there is a question of whether intensity of feeling should be considered as well as the number of persons preferring each alternative. By the impossibility of doing otherwise, administrators often are reduced to deciding policy without clarifying objectives first.

Even when an administrator resolves to follow his own values as a criterion for decisions, he often will not know how to rank them when they conflict with one another, as they usually do. Suppose, for example, that an administrator must relocate tenants living in tenements scheduled for destruction. One objective is to empty the buildings fairly promptly, another is to find suitable accommodation for persons displaced, another is to avoid friction with residents in other areas in which a large influx would be unwelcome, another is to deal with all concerned through persuasion if possible, and so on.

How does one state even to himself the relative importance of these partially conflicting values? A simple ranking of them is not enough; one needs ideally to know how much of one value is worth sacrificing for some of another value. The answer is that typically the administrator chooses—and must choose—directly among policies in which these values are combined in different ways. He cannot first clarify his values and then choose among policies.

A more subtle third point underlies both the first two. Social objectives do not always have the same relative values. One objective may be highly prized in one circumstance, another in another circumstance. If, for example, an administrator values highly both the dispatch with which his agency can carry through its projects *and* good public relations, it matters little which of the two possibly conflicting values he favors in some abstract or general sense. Policy questions arise in forms which put to administrators such a question as: Given the degree to which we are or are not already achieving the values of dispatch and the values of good public relations, is it worth sacrificing a little speed for a happier clientele, or is it better to risk offending the clientele so that we can get on with our work? The answer to such a question varies with circumstances.

The value problem is, as the example shows, always a problem of adjustments at a margin. But there is no practicable way to state marginal objectives or values except in terms of particular policies. That one value is preferred to another in one decision situation does not mean that it will be preferred in another decision situation in which it can be had only at great sacrifice of another value. Attempts to rank or order values in general and abstract terms so that they do not shift from decision to decision end up by ignoring the relevant marginal preferences. The significance of this third point thus goes very far. Even if all administrators had at hand an agreed set of values, objectives, and constraints, and an agreed ranking of these values, objectives, and constraints, their marginal values in actual choice situations would be impossible to formulate.

Unable consequently to formulate the relevant values first and then choose among policies to achieve them, administrators must choose directly among alternative policies that offer different marginal combinations of values. Somewhat paradoxically, the only practicable way to disclose one's relevant marginal values even to oneself is to describe the policy one chooses to achieve them. Except roughly and vaguely, I know of no way to describe—or even to understand—what my relative evaluations are for, say, freedom and security, speed and accuracy in governmental decisions, or low taxes and better schools than to describe my preferences among specific policy choices that might be made between the alternatives in each of the pairs.

In summary, two aspects of the process by which values are actually handled can be distinguished. The first is clear: evaluation and empirical analysis are intertwined; that is, one chooses among values and among policies at one and the same time. Put a little more elaborately, one simultaneously chooses a policy to attain certain objectives and chooses the objectives themselves. The second aspect is related but distinct: the administrator focuses his attention on marginal or incremental values. Whether he is aware of it or not, he does not find general formulations of objectives very helpful and in fact makes specific marginal or incremental comparisons. Two policies, X and Y, confront him. Both promise the same degree of attainment of objectives a, b, c, d, and e. But X promises him somewhat more of f than does Y, while Y promises him somewhat more of g than does X. In choosing between them, he is in fact offered the alternative of a marginal or incremental amount of f at the expense of a marginal or incremental amount of g. The only values that are relevant to his choice are these increments by which the two policies differ; and, when he finally chooses between the two marginal values, he does so by making a choice between policies.

As to whether the attempt to clarify objectives in advance of policy selection is more or less rational than the close intertwining of marginal evaluation and empirical analysis, the principal difference established is that for complex problems the first is impossible and irrelevant, and the second is both possible and relevant. The second is possible because the administrator need not try to analyze any values except the values by which alternative policies differ and need not be concerned with them except as they differ marginally. His need for information on values or objectives is drastically reduced as compared with the root method; and his capacity for grasping, comprehending, and relating values to one another is not strained beyond the breaking point.

* * *

Successive Comparison as a System

Successive limited comparisons is, then, indeed a method or system; it is not a failure of method for which administrators ought to apologize. None the less, its imperfections, which have not been explored in this paper, are many. For example, the method is without a built-in safeguard for all relevant values, and it also may lead the decision-maker to over-look excellent policies for no other reason than that they are not sug-gested by the chain of successive policy steps leading up to the present. Hence, it ought to be said that under this method, as well as under some of the most sophisticated variants of the root method—operations re-search, for example—policies will continue to be as foolish as they are wise.

Why then bother to describe the method in all the above detail? Be-cause it is in fact a common method of policy formulation, and is, for complex problems, the principal reliance of administrators as well as of other policy analysts. And because it will be superior to any other decision-making method available for complex problems in many cir-cumstances, certainly superior to a futile attempt at superhuman com-prehensiveness. The reaction of the public administrator to the exposition of method doubtless will be less a discovery of a new method than a better acquaintance with an old. But by becoming more conscious of their practice of this method, administrators might practice it with more skill and know when to extend or constrict its use. (That they sometimes practice it effectively and sometimes not may explain the extremes of opinion on "muddling through," which is both praised as a highly so-phisticated form of problem-solving and denounced as no method at all. For I suspect that in so far as there is a system in what is known as "muddling through," this method is it).

One of the noteworthy incidental consequences of clarification of the method is the light it throws on the suspicion an administrator some-times entertains that a consultant or adviser is not speaking relevantly and responsibly when in fact by all ordinary objective evidence he is. The trouble lies in the fact that most of us approach policy problems within a framework given by our view of a chain of successive policy choices made up to the present. One's thinking about appropriate poli-cies with respect, say, to urban traffic control is greatly influenced by one's knowledge of the incremental steps taken up the present. An ad-ministrator enjoys an intimate knowledge of his past sequences that "outsiders" do not share, and his thinking and that of the "outsider" will consequently be different in ways that may puzzle both. Both may appear to be talking intelligently, yet each may find the other unsatis-factory. The relevance of the policy chain of succession is even more clear when an American tries to discuss, say, antitrust policy with a Swiss, for the chains of policy in the two countries are strikingly different and the two individuals consequently have organized their knowledge in quite different ways.

If this phenomenon is a barrier to communication, an understanding of it promises an enrichment of intellectual interaction in policy formu-lation. Once the source of difference is understood, it will sometimes be stimulating for an administrator to seek out a policy analyst whose recent experience is with a policy chain different from his own.

This raises again a question only briefly discussed above on the merits of like-mindedness among government administrators. While much of organization theory argues the virtues of common values and agreed organizational objectives, for complex problems in which the root method is inapplicable, agencies will want among their own personnel two types of diversification: administrators whose thinking is organized by reference to policy chains other than those familiar to most members of the organization and, even more commonly, administrators whose professional or personal values or interests create diversity of view (perhaps coming from different specialties, social classes, geographical areas) so that, even within a single agency, decision-making can be fragmented and parts of the agency can serve as watchdogs for other parts.

DISCUSSION QUESTIONS

1. When you decide what you will have for dinner this evening do you use the "root" or "branch" method of decision making? How about when you decided which college to attend or which career you might choose?

2. Do you see any problems with incremental decision making? What types of decisions does it tend to favor? Is this a good or a bad thing?

3. Is the comprehensive method of decision making possible, or is it too taxing for the human brain, as Lindblom suggests?

NOTE

1. "Operations Research and National Planning—A Dissent," *Operations Research* 5 (October 1957), p. 718.

65

"American Business, Public Policy, Case Studies, and Political Theory"

Theodore J. Lowi

Before Lowi's article appeared in 1964, many social scientists analyzed public policy through case studies that focused on one particular policy and its implementation. Lowi argued that what the social sciences lacked was a means to cumulate, compare, and contrast the diverse findings of these studies. We needed, in other words, a typology of policy making. In the article below, Lowi argues that different types of public policies produce different patterns of participation. Public policies can be classified as distributive, regulatory, or redistributive, each with its own distinctive "arena of power." For example, public policies that provide benefits to a single congressional district, group, or company can be classified as distributive. In the distributive arena of power, policy beneficiaries are active in seeking to expand or extend their benefits, but there is no real opposition. Rather, legislators build coalitions premised upon "mutual noninterference" interests, and their representatives seek particular benefits, such as a research and development contract, a new highway, or a farm subsidy, but they do not oppose the similar requests of others. The regulatory and redistributive policy arenas also display distinctive dynamics and roles that participants in the process play. Lowi's work was important not only for providing a classification scheme by which social scientists could think more systematically about different public policies, but for proposing that we study "politics" as a consequence of different types of public policy. Traditionally, social scientists have studied politics to see what kinds of policies are produced.

. . . What is needed is a basis for cumulating, comparing, and contrasting diverse findings. Such a framework or interpretative scheme would bring the diverse cases and findings into a more consistent relation to each other and would begin to suggest generalizations sufficiently close to the data to be relevant and sufficiently abstract to be subject to more broadly theoretical treatment.

* * *

The scheme is based upon the following argument: (1) The types of relationships to be found among people are determined by their expectations—by what they hope to achieve or get from relating to others.

(2) In politics, expectations are determined by governmental outputs or policies. (3) Therefore, a political relationship is determined by the type of policy at stake, so that for every type of policy there is likely to be a distinctive type of political relationship. If power is defined as a share in the making of policy, or authoritative allocations, then the political relationship in question is a power relationship or, over time, a power structure.

*   *   *

There are three major categories of public policies in the scheme: distribution, regulation, and redistribution. These types are historically as well as functionally distinct, distribution being almost the exclusive type of national domestic policy from 1789 until virtually 1890. Agitation for regulatory and redistributive policies began at about the same time, but regulation had become an established fact before any headway at all was made in redistribution.

These categories are not mere contrivances for purposes of simplification. They are meant to correspond to real phenomena—so much so that the major hypotheses of the scheme follow directly from the categories and their definitions. Thus, *these areas of policy or government activity constitute real arenas of power.* Each arena tends to develop its own characteristic political structure, political process, elites, and group relations. What remains is to identify these arenas, to formulate hypotheses about the attributes of each, and to test the scheme by how many empirical relationships it can anticipate and explain.

Areas of Policy Defined

(1) In the long run, all governmental policies may be considered redistributive, because in the long run some people pay in taxes more than they receive in services. Or, all may be thought regulatory because, in the long run, a governmental decision on the use of resources can only displace a private decision about the same resource or at least reduce private alternatives about the resource. But politics works in the short run, and in the short run certain kinds of government decisions can be made without regard to limited resources. Policies of this kind are called "distributive," a term first coined for nineteenth-century land policies, but easily extended to include most contemporary public land and resource policies; rivers and harbors ("pork barrel") programs; defense procurement and R & D [research and development]; labor, business, and agricultural "clientele" services; and the traditional tariff. Distributive policies are characterized by the ease with which they can be disaggregated and dispensed unit by small unit, each unit more or less in isolation from other units and from any general rule. "Patronage" in the fullest meaning of the word can be taken as a synonym for "distribu-

tive." These are policies that are virtually not policies at all but are highly individualized decisions that only by accumulation can be called a policy. They are policies in which the indulged and the deprived, the loser and the recipient, need never come into direct confrontation. Indeed, in many instances of distributive policy, the deprived cannot as a class be identified, because the most influential among them can be accommodated by further disaggregation of the stakes.

(2) Regulatory policies are also specific and individual in their impact, but they are not capable of the almost infinite amount of disaggregation typical of distributive policies. Although the laws are stated in general terms ("Arrange the transportation system artistically." "Thou shalt not show favoritism in pricing."), the impact of regulatory decisions is clearly one of directly raising costs and/or reducing or expanding the alternatives of private individuals ("Get off the grass!" "Produce kosher if you advertise kosher!"). Regulatory policies are distinguishable from distributive in that in the short run the regulatory decision involves a direct choice as to who will be indulged and who deprived. Not all applicants for a single television channel or an overseas air route can be propitiated. Enforcement of an unfair labor practice on the part of management weakens management in its dealings with labor. So, while implementation is firm-by-firm and case-by-case, policies cannot be disaggregated to the level of the individual or the single firm (as in distribution), because individual decisions must be made by application of a general rule and therefore become interrelated within the broader standards of law. Decisions cumulate among all individuals affected by the law in roughly the same way. Since the most stable lines of perceived common impact are the basic sectors of the economy, regulatory decisions are cumulative largely along sectoral lines; regulatory policies are usually disaggregable only down to the sector level.

(3) Redistributive policies are like regulatory policies in the sense that relations among broad categories of private individuals are involved and, hence, individual decisions must be interrelated. But on all other counts there are great differences in the nature of impact. The categories of impact are much broader, approaching social classes. They are, crudely speaking, haves and have-nots, bigness and smallness, bourgeoisie and proletariat. The aim involved is not use of property but property itself, not equal treatment but equal possession, not behavior but being. The fact that our income tax is in reality only mildly redistributive does not alter the fact of the aims and the stakes involved in income tax policies. The same goes for our various "welfare state" programs, which are redistributive only for those who entered retirement or unemployment rolls without having contributed at all. The nature of a redistributive issue is not determined by the outcome of a battle over how redistributive a policy is going to be. Expectations about what it *can* be, what it threatens to be, are determinative.

Arenas of Power

Once one posits the general tendency of these areas of policy or governmental activity to develop characteristic political structures, a number of
hypotheses become compelling. And when the various hypotheses are
accumulated, the general contours of each of the three arenas begin
quickly to resemble, respectively, the three "general" theories of political
process identified earlier. The arena that develops around distributive
policies is best characterized in the terms of [E. E.] Schattschneider's
findings. The regulatory arena corresponds to the pluralist school, and
the school's general notions are found to be limited pretty much to this
one arena. The redistributive arena most closely approximates, with
some adaptation, an elitist view of the political process.

(1) The distributive arena can be identified in considerable detail from
Schattschneider's case-study alone. What he and his pluralist successors
did not see was that the traditional structure of tariff politics is also in
largest part the structure of politics of all those diverse policies identified
earlier as distributive. The arena is "pluralistic" only in the sense that a
large number of small, intensely organized interests are operating. In
fact, there is even greater multiplicity of participants here than the
pressure-group model can account for, because essentially it is a politics
of every man for himself. The single person and the single firm are the
major activists.

*   *   *

When a billion-dollar issue can be disaggregated into many millions
of nickel-dime items and each item can be dealt with without regard to
the others, multiplication of interests and of access is inevitable, and so
is reduction of conflict. All of this has the greatest of bearing on the
relations among participants and, therefore, the "power structure." Indeed, coalitions must be built to pass legislation and "make policy," but
what of the nature and basis of the coalitions? In the distributive arena,
political relationships approximate what Schattschneider called "mutual
non-interference"—"a mutuality under which it is proper for each to
seek duties [indulgences] for himself but improper and unfair to oppose
duties [indulgences] sought by others."[1] In the area of rivers and harbors,
references are made to "pork barrel" and "log-rolling," but these collo-
quialisms have not been taken sufficiently seriously. A log-rolling coalition is not one forged of conflict, compromise, and tangential interest
but, on the contrary, one composed of members who have absolutely
nothing in common; and this is possible because the "pork barrel" is a
container for unrelated items. This is the typical form of relationship in
the distributive arena.

The structure of these log-rolling relationships leads typically, though
not always, to Congress; and the structure is relatively stable because all

who have access of any sort usually support whoever are the leaders. And there tend to be "elites" of a peculiar sort in the Congressional committees whose jurisdictions include the subject-matter in question. Until recently, for instance, on tariff matters the House Ways and Means Committee was virtually the government. Much the same can be said for Public Works on rivers and harbors. It is a broker leadership, but "policy" is best understood as cooptation rather than conflict and compromise.

* * *

(2) The regulatory arena could hardly be better identified than in the thousands of pages written for the whole polity by the pluralists. But, unfortunately, some translation is necessary to accommodate pluralism to its more limited universe. The regulatory arena appears to be composed of a multiplicity of groups organized around tangential relations. . . . Within this narrower context of regulatory decisions, one can even go so far as to accept the most extreme pluralist statement that policy tends to be a residue of the interplay of group conflict. This statement can be severely criticized only by use of examples drawn from non-regulatory decisions.

As I argued before, there is no way for regulatory policies to be disaggregated into very large numbers of unrelated items. Because individual regulatory decisions involve direct confrontations of indulged and deprived, the typical political coalition is born of conflict and compromise among tangential interests that usually involve a total sector of the economy. Thus, while the typical basis for coalition in distributive politics is uncommon interests (log-rolling), an entirely different basis is typical in regulatory politics. The pluralist went wrong only in assuming the regulatory type of coalition is *the* coalition.

* * *

What this suggests is that the typical power structure in regulatory politics is far less stable than that in the distributive arena. Since coalitions form around shared interests, the coalitions will shift as the interests change or as conflicts of interest emerge. With such group-based and shifting patterns of conflict built into every regulatory issue, it is in most cases impossible for a Congressional committee, an administrative agency, a peak association governing board, or a social elite to contain all the participants long enough to establish a stable power elite. Policy outcomes seem inevitably to be the residue remaining after all the reductions of demands by all participants have been made in order to extend support to majority size. But a majority-sized coalition of shared interests on one issue could not possibly be entirely appropriate for some other issue. In regulatory decision-making, relationships among group leadership elements and between them on any one or more points of governmental access are too unstable to form a single policy-making elite. As a consequence, decision-making tends to pass from administrative agencies and Congressional committees to Congress, the place where uncertainties in the policy process have always been settled. Congress as an institution is the last resort for breakdowns in bargaining over policy, just as in the case of parties the primary is a last resort for breakdowns in bargaining over nominations. No one leadership group can contain the conflict by an almost infinite subdivision and distribution of the stakes. In the regulatory political process, Congress and the "balance of power" seem to play the classic role attributed to them by the pluralists.

* * *

(3) Issues that involve redistribution cut closer than any others along class lines and activate interests in what are roughly class terms. If there is ever any cohesion within the peak associations, it occurs on redistributive issues, and their rhetoric suggests that they occupy themselves most of the time with these. In a ten-year period just before and after, but not including, the war years [World War II], the Manufacturers' Association of Connecticut, for example, expressed itself overwhelmingly more often on redistributive than on any other types of issues.

* * *

Where the peak associations, led by elements of Mr. Mills's power elite,* have reality, their resources and access are bound to affect power relations. Owing to their stability and the impasse (or equilibrium) in relations among broad classes of the entire society, the political structure of the redistributive arena seems to be highly stabilized, virtually institutionalized. Its stability, unlike that of the distributive arena, derives from shared interests. But in contrast to the regulatory arena, these shared interests are sufficiently stable and clear and consistent to provide the foundation for ideologies.

* * *

. . . Finally, just as the nature of redistributive policies influences politics towards the centralization and stabilization of conflict, so does it further influence the removal of decision-making from Congress. A decentralized and bargaining Congress can cumulate but it cannot balance, and redistributive policies require complex balancing on a very large scale. What [William] Riker has said of budget-making applies here: ". . . legislative governments cannot endure a budget. Its finances must be totted up by party leaders in the legislature itself. In a complex fiscal system, however, haphazard legislative judgments cannot bring revenue

* [According to C. Wright Mills, a small network of individuals, which he called the "power elite," controls the economy, the political system, and the military.]

into even rough alignment with supply. So budgeting is introduced—which transfers financial control to the budget maker. . . ."[2] Congress can provide exceptions to principles and it can implement those principles with elaborate standards of implementation as a condition for the concessions that money-providers will make. But the makers of principles of redistribution seem to be the holders of the "command posts."

None of this suggests a power elite such as Mills would have had us believe existed, but it does suggest a type of stable and continual conflict that can only be understood in class terms. The foundation upon which the social-stratification and power-elite school rested, especially when dealing with national power, was so conceptually weak and empirically unsupported that its critics were led to err in the opposite direction by denying the direct relevance of social and institutional positions and the probability of stable decision-making elites. But the relevance of that approach becomes stronger as the scope of its application is reduced and as the standards for identifying the scope are clarified. But this is equally true of the pluralist school and of those approaches based on a "politics of this-or-that policy."

* * *

DISCUSSION QUESTIONS

1. Provide examples of each type of policy that Lowi discusses (distributive, regulatory, and redistributive).

2. If you were a member of Congress, which type of policy would you try to emphasize if your main interest was in getting reelected?

3. Are there any types of policies that do not seem to fit Lowi's framework? Are there some policies that are in more than one category?

NOTES

1. E. E. Schattschneider, *Politics, Pressure and the Tariff* (New York: 1935), pp. 135–6.
2. William Riker, *Democracy in the United States* (New York: 1953), p. 216.

66

"The Human Factor: Should the Government Put a Price on Your Life?"

Jim Holt

At the core of cost-benefit analysis is the ability to put a dollar value—a price—on the different results and burdens of any government action or policy. Obviously, there are limits to what we are willing to spend to save or preserve life or safety: to dispute this means that you support the expenditure of infinite resources to save even a single life. But if we are not willing to make infinite expenditures, we must then decide how much we will *spend. That forces us to put a value on human life, as otherwise we will never know how much is enough, or what risks are worth taking. Even if money is not the issue, we still face trade-offs: drugs that can treat life-threatening diseases can themselves have fatal side effects, for example, and we must balance lives saved against the risk that some might also be lost.*

How much is enough? As Holt notes, this is an "idiotic question," since most of us would give everything we have to save our own life, or the life of someone close to us. And even an infinite amount of money does us no good personally if we're dead. But we return to the problem that we must decide how much a life is worth when we are considering the effectiveness of policy choices. The federal government uses different methods to determine the monetary value of a life in its cost-benefit models, producing estimates in the $3–4 million range.

How much is your life worth to you? On the face of it, that's an idiotic question. No amount of money could compensate you for the loss of your life, for the simple reason that the money would be no good to you if you were dead. And you might feel, for different reasons, that the dollar value of the lives of your spouse or children—or even a stranger living on the other side of the country—is also infinite. No one should be knowingly sacrificed for a sum of money: that's what we mean when we say that human life is priceless.

But the government set a price for it four years ago: $6.1 million. That's the figure the Environmental Protection Agency came up with when it was trying to decide how far to go in removing arsenic from drinking water. Arsenic can cause diseases, like bladder cancer, that will predictably kill a certain number of people. But reducing the arsenic in water gets more and more expensive as the poison levels approach zero.

How many dollars should be spent to save one "statistical life"? The answer, reasoned the people at the E.P.A., depends on how much that life is worth. And they're not the only ones doing such calculations. The Department of Transportation also puts a price tag on a human life when deciding which road improvements are worth making, although it's the rather more modest one of $3 million.

Presumably, losing your life in a highway smashup is less unpleasant than slowly dying of bladder cancer.

The advantage of this kind of cost-benefit analysis, its proponents declare, is that it promises to make our public policies more rational. But critics find the idea of putting a dollar value on human life preposterous. Part of their case is ethical: it is simply wrong, they say, to count death as a "cost"; no public action that involves lost lives should be evaluated in monetary terms. But they also object to the ways in which the price of life is calculated.

How, exactly, did the E.P.A. arrive at its figure of $6.1 million?

Economists looked at the salaries paid to workers in riskier jobs like mining. They figured out that such workers received, on average, an additional $61 a year for facing an extra 1-in-100,000 risk of accidental death. Evidently, these workers valued their own lives at 100,000 times $61, or $6.1 million. (In 2002, the E.P.A. revised the price of a life downward, to $3.7 million—or if you're older than 70, $2.3 million.)

Ingeniously simple, no? But on closer inspection, you begin to have misgivings about this methodology. In the first place, it is not at all obvious that workers really understand the risks they face in the workplace. Women seem to be much less willing to accept such risks than men. Does that mean their lives should be priced higher? Blacks and nonunionized workers demand little or no risk premium for taking dangerous jobs. Does that mean their lives should be priced lower? Poorer people, for whom an extra dollar is highly valuable, will take less compensation for facing danger. Thus, cost-benefit analysis tells us it is more efficient to locate toxic waste dumps near poorer neighborhoods.

Perhaps the strangest thing about the life-pricing business is the way the lives of future generations become discounted—quite literally. Regulators begin with the assumption that it's better to have $200 in your pocket today—when you can earn interest on it—than a promise of $200 in the future. Equating money with human life, they conclude that a life saved today should count twice as much, in dollar terms, as a life saved 10 years from now; a life saved a century from now scarcely counts at all. That is why cost-benefit analysis might sanction, say, nuclear reactors that provide you and me with cheap energy at the expense of lives lost to cancer decades down the road. But as Frank Ackerman and Lisa Heinzerling point out in their recent book, "Priceless: On Knowing the Price of Everything and the Value of Nothing," it is hardly clear why the same logic should apply to the value of our great-grandchildren. (On the other hand, those future generations may well have developed a cure for cancer, so perhaps we are justified in worrying about them less.)

Champions of cost-benefit analysis—from the controversial Bush administration regulatory guru John D. Graham to the more circumspect liberal law professor Cass Sunstein—maintain that the government is always valuing human life implicitly anyway, so we might as well be forthright about it. Only then, they say, will we be able to stop spending excessively large sums to protect against small risks and vice versa. Most of us, after all, are deficient in rationality: we are excessively fearful of unlikely hazards when those hazards are shockingly unfamiliar or disturbingly involuntary (like dying in a terrorist attack or from something in the drinking water). And we are far too cavalier about much more immediate risks like dying on the highway (which we do at a rate of 117 fatalities per day).

But are ordinary people really being irrational when they seem to "price" their lives differently at different times? Some people even put a *negative* price on their lives—when, for instance, they pay money to engage in a risky activity like mountain climbing. The economist E.J. Mishan, an early authority on cost-benefit analysis, has argued that the value of a human life has no meaning apart from the nature of the risk that is being measured. To say that a human life is "priceless" does not necessarily mean that it is worth more than any amount of money. It may just mean that money is the wrong yardstick to use when our decisions involve the loss of life. Even the most ardent cost-benefit analyst would spend more money to rescue a single actual child than to save 10 "statistical lives."

Discussion Questions

1. Not even Holt really answers the question of how much a life is worth. What factors should go into this evaluation? Age? Income? Future-earnings capacity? What are the implications of concluding that some lives might be "worth" more than others?

2. Is it correct to say that we're not willing to spend an infinite amount to save a life? In an actual life-threatening emergency—a child trapped in a well, people on a sinking ship, a collapsed building, coal miners trapped underground—we probably would spend without limit until we either completed the rescue or knew that the victims were dead. Why aren't we willing to do this in the case of saving potential lives?

3. We could come close to eliminating forty thousand automotive fatalities each year by imposing a nationwide twenty-miles-per-hour speed limit, but such a step is inconceivable. Does this mean we are willing to trade lives for time and convenience? What are the implications of this decision?

Debating the Issues: Global Warming

If you were to describe a problem with potentially devastating consequences, you'd be hard pressed to come up with something more dire than global warming. Over the last century, average global temperatures have risen, as have carbon dioxide emissions as a result of energy production (chiefly from burning fossil fuels: coal, oil, natural gas). A growing scientific literature concludes that this warming is *caused* by increased concentrations of carbon dioxide in the atmosphere. Global warming, according to this school of thought, is man-made (or anthropogenic). If it continues, the earth could face catastrophic changes that would ruin huge tracts of arable land, melt the polar ice caps and glaciers, raise sea levels, flood entire countries, and render much of the globe uninhabitable. What is needed to prevent this is a global effort to drastically reduce the use of fossil fuels through huge increases in efficiency, development of alternative energy sources, and reorienting the entire world away from an oil-based economy. To do less is to threaten human survival. Al Gore made this point in his movie, *An Inconvenient Truth*.

But what if the proponents of anthropogenic climate change are wrong? To do what they ask would require enormous costs, and could depress global economic growth over decades (although this is a matter of dispute). Critics claim that the degree of certainty in the scientific community is overstated in any event, and that there is substantial evidence that we may be in the middle of a natural cycle of climate change that has little to do with human activity.

Either way, though, it's crucial that we get it right. If Al Gore is wrong but we act to slash fossil fuel use anyway, we risk significant economic depression for no good reason, since the climate will follow the same path no matter what we do. We wind up warmer but poorer, a result that has its own serious consequences for global well-being. But if Gore is right and we do nothing, then we risk catastrophe. The increase in wealth we preserve will vanish in any event when New York City and Copenhagen disappear under ten feet of water.

The two readings here address the different sides of this debate. Bjørn Lomborg, a professor of statistics at a Denmark university, criticizes the doomsday scenarios, especially a 2001 report by the International Panel on Climate Change, a body organized by the United Nations. He notes that even if we accept the conclusions that global warming is occurring and is caused by human activity, the costs of cutting carbon dioxide emissions are far greater than even worst-case scenarios about the costs of global warming itself. Cost-benefit analysis shows that many recommendations for how to address the problem are worse than the problem itself, and would hurt developing nations the most without really solving the problem. He concludes that the best way to address global warming is to rely on economic growth; as countries get richer, they can devote more resources to energy efficiency.

Peter Teague and Jeff Navin make a related argument, although they are firmly in the anthropogenic camp. They argue that the key is to find a way to move away from carbon fuels without sacrificing economic growth. Investments in new technologies can both reduce greenhouse gas emission and foster economic development. This makes for good policy *and* good politics.

67

"Global Warming—Are We Doing the Right Thing?"

Bjørn Lomborg

L ast month in Bonn, most of the world's nations (minus the US) reached an agreement to cut carbon emissions. Generally, the deal was widely reported as almost saving the world. Yet, not only is this untrue in the scientific sense—the deal will do almost no good—but it is also unclear whether carbon emission cuts are really the best way for the world to ensure progress on its most important areas.

Global warming is important, environmentally, politically and economically. There is no doubt that mankind has influenced and is still increasing atmospheric concentrations of CO_2 and that this will increase temperature. I will not discuss all the scientific uncertainty, but basically accept the models and predictions from the 2001 report of the UN Climate Panel (IPCC). Yet, we will need to separate hyperbole from realities in order to choose our future optimally.

When the IPCC tells us that the world might warm some 5.8°C over the coming century, this is based on an enormous variety of scenarios and models, where the IPCC has explicitly rejected making predictions about the future, and instead gives us "computer-aided storytelling," basing the development of crucial variables on initial choice and depicting normative scenarios "as one would hope they would emerge." Yet the high-end scenarios seem plainly unlikely. Reasonable analysis * * * suggest that renewables—and especially solar power—will be competitive or even outcompete fossil fuels by mid-century, and this means that carbon emissions are much more likely to follow the low emissions scenarios, causing a warming of about 2–2.5°C.

Moreover, global warming will not decrease food production, it will probably not increase storminess or the frequency of hurricanes, ["there is no general agreement yet among models concerning future changes in midlatitude storms (intensity and frequency) and variability," and "there is some evidence that shows only small changes in the frequency of tropical cyclones."] it will not increase the impact of malaria or indeed cause more deaths. [Mathematical models, merely mapping out suitable temperature zones for mosquitoes, show that global warming in the 2080s could increase the number of people *potentially* exposed to malaria by 2–4 percent (260–320 million people of 8 billion at risk.) Yet, the IPCC points out that most of the additionally exposed would come from middle or high income countries, where a well functioning health sector and developed infrastructure makes actual malaria unlikely. Thus, the global study of *actual* malaria transmission shows "remarkably few changes, even under the most extreme scenarios."] It is even unlikely that it will cause more flood victims, because a much richer world will protect itself better. [The total cost of protection is fairly low, estimated at 0.1 percent of GDP for most nations, though it might be as high as several percent for small island states.]

However, global warming will have serious costs—the total cost is estimated at about $5 trillion. Such estimates are unavoidably uncertain but derive from models assessing the cost of global warming to a wide variety of societal areas such as agriculture, forestry, fisheries, energy, water supply, infrastructure, hurricane damage, drought damage, coast protection, land loss caused by a rise in sea level, loss of wetlands, forest loss, loss of species, loss of human life, pollution and migration.

The consequences of global warming will hit hardest on the developing countries, whereas the industrialized countries may actually benefit from a warming lower than 2–3°C. The developing countries are harder hit primarily because they are poor—giving them less adaptive capacity.

Despite our intuition that we naturally need to do something drastic about such a costly global warming, we should not implement a cure that is actually more costly than the original affliction. Here, economic analyses clearly show that it will be far more expensive to cut CO_2 emissions radically, than to pay the costs of adaptation to the increased temperatures.

The Bonn meeting was generally the implementation of the much more studied Kyoto Protocol, which aims to cut carbon emissions to 5.2 percent below 1990-levels in 2010, or a reduction of almost 30 percent, compared to no-intervention.

The effect of Kyoto (and even more so Bonn) on the climate will be minuscule. All models agree that the Kyoto Protocol will have surprisingly little impact. One model by a lead author of the 1996 IPCC report shows us how an expected temperature increase of 2.1°C in 2100 will be diminished by the protocol to an increase of 1.9°C. Or to put it more clearly, the temperature that we would have experienced in 2094 we have now postponed to 2100. In essence, the Kyoto Protocol does not negate global warming but merely buys the world six years.

*   *   *

If Kyoto is implemented with anything but global emissions trading—a scheme which seems utterly unattainable, and was not at all addressed in Bonn—it will not only be almost inconsequential for the climate, but it will also constitute a poor use of resources. The cost of such a Kyoto pact if implemented, just for the US, will be higher than the cost of solving the single most pressing problem for the world—providing the entire world with clean drinking water and sanitation. It is estimated that the latter would avoid 2 million deaths every year and prevent half a billion people becoming seriously ill each year. If no trading mechanism is implemented for Kyoto, the costs could approach $1 trillion, or almost five times the cost of world-wide water and sanitation coverage. For comparison, the total global aid today is about $50 billion annually.

If we were to go even further—as suggested by many—and curb *global* emissions to the 1990 level, the net cost to the world would seriously escalate to about $4 trillion extra—comparable almost to the cost of global warming itself. Likewise, a temperature increase limit would cost anywhere from $3 to $33 trillion extra.

This emphasizes that we need to be very careful in our willingness to act on global warming. Basically, global warming will be expensive ($5 trillion) and there is very little good we can do about it. Even if we were to handle global warming optimally which would mean cutting emissions a little fairly far into the future, we can only cut the cost very little (about $0.3 trillion). However, if we choose to enact Kyoto or even more ambitious programmes, the world will lose. And this conclusion does not just come from the output from a single model. Almost all the major computer models agree that even when chaotic consequences have been taken into consideration "it is striking that the optimal policy involves little emissions reduction below uncontrolled rates until the middle of the [twenty-first] century at the earliest."

So is it not curious, then, that the typical reporting on global warming tells us all the bad things that could happen from CO_2 emissions, but few or none of the bad things that could come from overly zealous regulation of such emissions? Indeed, why is it that global warming is not discussed with an open attitude, carefully attuned to avoid making big and costly mistakes to be paid for by our descendants, but rather with a fervor more fitting for preachers of opposing religions?

This is an indication that the discussion of global warming is not just a question of choosing the optimal economic path for humanity, but has much deeper, political roots as to what kind of future society we would like. This understanding is clearly laid out in the new 2001 IPCC report. Here IPCC tells us that we should build cars and trains with lower top speeds, and extols the qualities of sail ships, biomass (which "has been the renewable resource base for humankind since time immemorial") and bicycles. Likewise, it is suggested that in order to avoid demand for transport, we should obtain a regionalized economy.

Essentially, what the IPCC suggests—and openly admits—is that we need to change the individual lifestyles, and move away from consumption. We must focus on sharing resources (e.g. through co-ownership), choosing free time instead of wealth, quality instead of quantity, and "increase freedom while containing consumption." Because of climate change we have to remodel our world, and find more "appropriate lifestyles."

The problem—as seen by the IPCC—is, that "the conditions of public acceptance of such options are not often present at the requisite large scale." Actually, it is even "difficult to convince local actors of the significance of climate change and the need for corrective action." IPCC goes as far as suggesting that the reason why we are unwilling to accept slower (or no) cars and regionalized economies with bicycles but no international travel, is that we have been indoctrinated by the media, where we see the TV characters as reference points for our own lives, shaping our values and identities. Consequently, IPCC finds that the media could also help form the path towards a more sustainable world: "Raising awareness among media professionals of the need for greenhouse gas mitigation and the role of the media in shaping lifestyles and aspirations could be an effective way to encourage a wider cultural shift."

But of course, while using global warming as a springboard for other wider policy goals is entirely legitimate, such goals should in all honesty be made explicit. Moreover, it is problematic to have an organization which often quite successfully gathers the most relevant scientific information about global warming, also so clearly promoting a political agenda, which seldom reaches the news headlines.

Thus, the important lesson of the global warming debate is fivefold. First, we have to realize what we are arguing about—do we want to handle global warming in the most efficient way or do we want to use global warming as a stepping stone to other political projects? Before we make this clear to ourselves and others, the debate will continue to be muddled. Personally, I believe that in order to think clearly we should try to the utmost to separate issues, not the least because trying to solve all problems at one go may likely result in making bad solutions for all areas. Thus, I try to address just the issue of global warming.

Second, we should not spend vast amounts of money to cut a tiny slice of the global temperature increase when this constitutes a poor use of resources and when we could probably use these funds far more effectively in the developing world. This connection between resource use on global warming and aiding the Third World actually goes much deeper, because the developing world will experience by far the most damage from global warming. Thus, when we spend resources to mitigate global warming we are in fact and to a large extent helping future inhabitants in the developing world. However, if we spend the same money directly in the Third World we would be helping present inhabitants in the developing world, and through them also their descendants. Since the inhabitants of the Third World are likely to be much richer in the future, and since the return on investments in the developing countries is much higher than those on global warming (about 16 percent to 2 percent), the question really boils down to: *Do we want to help more well-off inhabitants in the Third World a hundred years from now a little or do we want to help poorer inhabitants in the present Third World much more?* To give a feel for the size of the problem—the Kyoto Protocol will likely cost at least $150 billion a year, and possibly much more. UNICEF estimates that just $70–80 billion a year could give all Third World inhabitants access to the basics like health, education, water and sanitation. More important still is the fact that if we could muster such a massive investment in the present-day developing countries this would also give them a much better future position in terms of resources and infrastructure from which to manage a future global warming.

Third, we should realize that the cost of global warming will be substantial—about $5 trillion. Since cutting back CO_2 emissions quickly turns very costly and easily counterproductive, we should focus more of our effort at finding ways of easing the emission of greenhouse gases over the long run. Partly, this means that we need to invest much more in research and development of solar power, fusion and other likely power sources of the future. Given a current US investment in renewable energy research and development of just $200 million, a considerable increase would seem a promising investment to achieve a possible conversion to renewable energy towards the latter part of the century. Partly, this also means that we should be much more open towards other techno-fixes (so-called geoengineering). These suggestions range from fertilizing the ocean (making more algae bind carbon when they die and fall to the ocean floor) and putting sulfur particles into the stratosphere (cooling the earth) to capturing CO_2 from fossil fuel use and returning it to storage in geological formations. Again, if one of these approaches could indeed mitigate (part of) CO_2 emissions or global warming, this would be of tremendous value to the world.

Fourth, we ought to have a look at the cost of global warming in relation to the total world economy. Analysis shows that even if we should choose some of the most inefficient programs to cut carbon emissions, the costs will at most defer growth a couple of years in the middle of the century. Global warming is in this respect still a limited and manageable problem.

Finally, this also underscores that *global warming is not anywhere the most important problem in the world*. What matters is making the developing countries rich and allowing the citizens of developed countries even greater opportunities. [The IPCC report outlines four main scenarios on global economic growth.] If we choose a world focused on economic development within a global setting, the total income over the coming century will be some $900 trillion. However, should we go down a path focusing on the environment, even if we stay within a global setting, humanity will lose some $107 trillion or 12 percent the total, potential income. And should we choose a more regional approach to solving the problems of the twenty-first century, we would stand to lose $140–274 trillion or even more than a quarter of the potential income. Moreover, the loss will mainly be to the detriment of the developing countries—switching from A1 to B1 would cost the developing world a quarter of its total income, forgoing a developing per capita income some 75 percent higher. Again, this should be seen in the light of a total cost of global warming at about $5 trillion and that the optimal global warming policy can save us just $0.3 trillion.

What this illustrates is that if we want to leave a planet with the most possibilities for our descendants, both in the developing and developed world, it is imperative that we focus primarily on the economy and solving our problems in a global context rather than focusing on the environment in a regionalized context. Basically, this puts the spotlight on securing economic growth, especially in the third world while ensuring a global economy, both tasks which the world has set itself within the framework of the World Trade Organization (WTO). If we succeed here, we could increase world income with $107–274 trillion, whereas even if we achieve the absolutely most efficient global warming policies, we can increase wealth with just $0.3 trillion. To put is squarely, what matters to our and our children's future is not primarily decided within the IPCC framework but within the WTO framework.

68

"Global Warming in an Age of Energy Anxiety: Why Progressives Should Shift the Emphasis from Regulation to Investment in Their Political and Policy Approach"

PETER TEAGUE AND JEFF NAVIN

The camera pans in on a scene in a simple American bedroom. An elderly woman sits on the bed, getting dressed to venture out into the cold. She puts on an old coat, over the top of another coat, and then a scarf and hat. Just when we think she's going to get up, she turns off the lamp, lies down, and pulls the covers up.

Fade to black.

Imagine this 30-second ad, narrated by a familiar-sounding voice, describing the higher electricity bills and hardship millions of Americans will face if Congress votes to take action on climate change. Remember how quickly the insurance industry overcame widespread public support for health care reform and destroyed the Clinton plan for universal coverage? Meet the Harry and Louise of global warming.

The Other Global Warming Lesson from California

Environmentalists point to California's new regulations on greenhouse gas emissions, signed into law by Republican Governor Arnold Schwarzenegger, as a sign that federal action on global warming is inevitable. But, last November, California voters offered us another lesson about what it will take to craft politically sustainable solutions to global warming. This lesson has largely been ignored, but is arguably more important.

Proposition 87 would have imposed a tax on oil production in California to support $4 billion in expenditures to develop and promote alternative energy technologies. The ballot initiative, which began with strong approval ratings, and whose proponents spent almost $50 million to secure passage, was defeated by a ten-point margin. Why? Oil companies succeeded in convincing voters that it would increase gas prices.

A recent survey of public opinion research conducted by American Environics for the Nathan Cummings Foundation reveals just how sensitive voters are to energy costs. It also clarifies the complexity of Americans' views on the interconnected issues of energy independence, global warming, taxes, public investment, and jobs. What begins to emerge from the data is a path through, an approach and a vision that might attract sustainable majorities of Americans bringing the power to enact and then defend comprehensive policies to solve global warming.

What the Data Reveals

Americans' anxiety over rising energy costs is a serious challenge to anyone seeking a solution to global warming. The anxiety is real, and the vast majority of Americans perceive these costs as causing financial hardship for their families. Proposals that raise energy prices risk triggering populist anger; Americans uniformly reject government efforts to increase the cost of gasoline or electricity as a way of encouraging certain kinds of behaviors.

Nobody disagrees that regulatory strategies alone will raise energy costs. And raising the price of carbon high enough to have a real effect on global warming—by cutting emissions and by providing sufficient motivation for industry to invest in new technologies—will raise energy costs significantly. One example: The price for carbon debated in the 2007 Senate energy bill would set a price of $7.00/ton, rising to $15.00/ton by 2050; experts estimate that it would take a cost of $150.00/ton to produce the technology necessary to make clean coal a viable future energy source.

With a regulatory-only approach, we will end with a debate between environmentalists arguing about the cost of global warming, and industry economists telling Americans how much more they'll pay for everything from electricity to gasoline to consumer products. And they'll argue that these higher prices will result in job losses.

Policy makers are aware of this challenge and have added provisions to their regulatory bills that are aimed at easing voters' fears. There are proposals for tax rebates and offsets and even the creation of a "Climate Change Credit Corporation" to help voters with the anticipated increase in consumer energy costs. The trouble is that the bills either provide tiny amounts to authorize studies of the problem, or they remain silent about how much help voters can expect. It's important to remember that the proponents of Prop. 87 made a well-supported case that the initiative wouldn't raise energy costs at all. Its defeat demonstrates that it's going to take more than good intentions about global warming and vaguely-worded proposals to convince voters.

The Debate to Come

A recent NPR segment noted that the non-partisan Congressional Budget Office released a report on environmentalists' preferred regulatory approach that says "low-income Americans and coal miners might suffer the most if the government adopts a so called cap and trade program to reduce emissions of green house gasses." The NPR report said, "Consumers will bear the cost of this kind of program. They would face higher prices for electricity, gasoline and other products. Since low-income Americans spend a higher portion of their incomes on such costs, they'll be hit the hardest."

Keep in mind that this was NPR—not Fox News.

The "right-wing populist vs. liberal elite" frame is dropping into place with the help of those calling for the deepest cuts in carbon. The deep-cut mantra, repeated without any real understanding of what might be required to get to 60 or 80 percent reductions in emissions, ignores voters' anxieties. It also reflects the questionable view that these changes can be achieved with little more than trivial disruptions in our lives—a view easier to hold if you're in a financial position to buy carbon credits for your beachfront house.

Labor has indicated a willingness to support action on climate change, but it won't support deep cuts if working people are the most affected. This will leave environmentalists up against the well-financed business lobby. Good luck holding onto moderate Democrats, let alone Republicans—even those who are beginning to understand the need for action on global warming.

History teaches us that regulatory proposals that fail politically often lead to legislative paralysis. In 1993, the public was adamant that action be taken to address health care, and it seemed inevitable that some sort of reform would soon be signed into law. In 1994, the Clinton health care reform proposal failed before coming to a vote. In 1997, the Senate voted 95–0 to reject the United Nations Kyoto framework before it was even fully developed. Voters are still waiting for action on health care *and* global warming.

A More Expansive Approach

Ultimately, the global warming crisis will be solved by the emergence of a new clean energy economy that is also capable of meeting the needs and aspirations of America's—and the world's—growing population. Regulation should be only one piece of a larger set of strategies designed to speed the emergence of that economy, with interlocking investment, tax, and fiscal policies also designed to send the right market signals and prompt private-sector investment and innovation. These policies must both solve the problem of climate change and have the political support to be enacted and sustained.

Good policy is therefore inseparable from good politics. Long-term success will require a broad-based coalition of Americans who see their values in alignment with the transition to the green economy and who will form a political base of support powerful enough to see this transition through decades of well-resourced opposition. This formation is beginning to emerge from some unexpected places.

Witness Mayor Michael Bloomberg's PlaNYC, a 30-year policy blueprint to make New York City a world leader in environmental sustainability. The plan shows an understanding that global warming will be solved as part of a comprehensive package of initiatives to improve the quality of life by simultaneously addressing the need for housing, jobs, clean air, clean water, and public parks. It calls for spending to re-build the city's antiquated infrastructure, retrofit buildings for energy efficiency, and expand public transportation, all while returning what Goldman Sachs estimates will be a 14 percent return on investment.

Compare this bold call to make New York "Greener and Greater" to the mantra of "80 percent cuts" in carbon; there's no doubt which is more likely to inspire a political coalition capable of taking on powerful industry opposition over the course of decades.

Much of the inspiration for the Bloomberg plan came from the Apollo Project, an alliance of trade unionists, grassroots community activists, progressive intellectuals, and local environmentalists. (Full disclosure: Apollo is funded in part by the Nathan Cummings Foundation). Apollo operates nationally and in over 20 locations around the country, including New York City. It has provided much of the basic policy work as well as the relationships and organizing that brought environmental justice, civil rights, faith, labor, and business interests to the table in New York, and is doing the same in places as disparate as Los Angeles, Washington State, Oakland, and Pennsylvania.

At Apollo's core is a common demand for a ten-year, $300 billion public investment in the transition to a clean energy economy. And the Apollo Alliance has produced credible studies showing that this investment would more than pay for itself in increased revenues to the treasury, without even tallying the multiple economic benefits of millions of new jobs, a revitalized manufacturing sector, and reduced reliance on foreign oil.

When compared to the Apollo demand or other budgetary line items, the global warming commitment made by the various presidential contenders looks paltry. Senator Clinton leads the pack, with a new call for a $50 billion energy R&D fund to be spent over an unspecified number of years. But the recent transportation bill authorizes $286 billion, the 2002 farm bill authorized nearly $100 billion in spending, and of course, we've spent over $500 billion on Iraq and Afghanistan since 2001. Global warming experts like U.C. Berkeley's Dan Kammen suggest that the current energy R&D budget, which is less than half what it was in 1979 (in real dollars), should be increased ten-fold, to roughly $30 billion *annually*.

The Case for Investment

Mayor Bloomberg's plan calls both for new fees and regulations to cut greenhouse gas emissions *and* for a $5 billion investment in the city's new green economy. This is in keeping with recommendations from the UN's Intergovernmental Panel on Climate Change (IPCC), as well as virtually every public policy expert on global warming, for a two-pronged approach to deal with the crisis: limit the amount of heat-trapping gases released into the atmosphere and invest in new renewable energy technologies. From the IPCC to the British Government's Stern Review on climate change to last September's special issue of Scientific American on energy policy, energy experts acknowledge the need for major public investment, as well as putting a price on carbon.

Strangely, environmentalists are more quiet on the need for investment, preferring to argue that regulation will drive innovation, which will in turn create jobs and economic opportunity. To the extent that public investment in innovation is mentioned (a survey of environmental web sites and public statements found little on the subject), it seems to be regarded as a hoped-for by-product of the regulatory scheme rather than its core intention. But with a narrow focus on regulation, environmentalists and liberals risk alienating poor and working people with a discredited reliance on the magic of markets—albeit regulated markets—to give us the solutions we need.

What's more likely to happen is what is happening. Regulation, or the promise of regulation, is sending billions of dollars in venture capital chasing short-term gains in the alternative energy field. This investment is as unlikely to produce the long-term technological breakthroughs we'll need as it is to result in the broadly-shared benefits that would drive the creation of sustainable political majorities.

The Politics to Get Us from Here to There

The kinds of large-scale, long-term investments that were instrumental in producing the Internet, the interstate highway system, and the biotech revolution came from government, and for a reason: Private capital won't stay in the game long enough, and the benefits of private investment are likely to be largely private.

On the other hand, broadly shared costs have led to broadly shared benefits, and that's a recipe for strategies that can be maintained overtime, politically and financially. Fortunately, the investments that are likely to speed the development of the right mix of new technologies, create a hundred-year's-worth of good jobs retrofitting our infrastructure, and take current technologies to commercial scale are also the key to a successful, long-term political strategy.

Prior to the 2004 presidential election, the Apollo Alliance asked voters in Pennsylvania what they thought of the proposal to spend billions of taxpayer dollars to speed the transition to a clean energy economy. The results were surprising—74 percent approved, and among white, non-college educated males, classic "Reagan Democrats," the approval rating was 81 percent. In fact, the higher the dollar figure, the more these voters liked the idea. These were the very people who were thought to have bought the conservatives' anti-tax, anti-spending, anti-government message lock, stock, and barrel.

These results were confirmed and our understanding deepened by American Environics' recent review of public opinion data. The analysis revealed that, while the public sees global warming as a threat, they see many other issues as a higher priority. Among those high-priority concerns are the nation's dependence on foreign oil, jobs, and energy costs. Fortunately, these concerns—combined with concern about global warming—create an appetite for the kinds of investments experts agree will be necessary. A policy with enough investment to credibly claim to lead to increased energy independence, reduced energy costs, and job creation will generate the widespread public support necessary for sustained, serious action to solve global warming.

The analysis also reveals that shifting public opinion on the size of government makes it easier to build a case for investment. To be sure, there is no evidence that any sizable segment of the electorate is calling for a dramatic expansion of the size of government. But it appears we have reached a point where the public is less sensitive to congressional spending than they are to regulations that will increase the cost of energy. Today energy costs seem to generate the kind of ire taxes did a decade ago. Based on this analysis, we believe that investment as a frame can help build support for comprehensive global warming legislation.

Where are the advocates for large-scale public investment in the transition to a clean energy economy? Who will make the Churchillian call?

> You ask, what is our aim? I can answer in one word: It is victory, victory at all costs, victory in spite of all terror, victory, however long and hard the road may be; for without victory, there is no survival.

Many proponents of global warming legislation have convinced themselves that a solution containing substantial public investment is not politically viable. But this fear of proposing serious investments backs them into a reliance on regulatory policies that will drive up both energy costs and voter anger. The public opinion data and California's experience with Prop. 87 suggest that it will be better for proponents to risk conservative name-calling, stand up for spending commensurate with the threats and opportunities, and adapt Mayor Bloomberg's vision to the national stage: They should become the champions of a Greener, Greater America.

DISCUSSION QUESTIONS

1. How certain do we need to be about the causes of global warming to be able to make a decision about how to respond? Should we be 80 percent certain that global warming is man-made before embark-

ing on an effort to reshape the global economy? 90 percent? 99 percent? How do we decide? Does your answer depend on the consequences of making the wrong decision?

2. Economies have adapted to other seismic shifts in investment and technology, from the industrial revolution to the computer age. Are Teague and Navin suggesting anything all that revolutionary?

3. Clearly, any action on climate change must involve the global community. Whatever the U.S. does will have minimal impact if we go it alone. What is the best way to achieve an international consensus?

CHAPTER 14

Government and the Economy

69

"Call for Federal Responsibility"

Franklin D. Roosevelt

The national government has always played a role in the economy. Since the late 1700s, the government has provided property for private development, enforced contracts and prohibited the theft of private property, provided subsidies to encourage the growth of particular industries, developed the infrastructure of the growing country, and regulated trade. The question that commands the attention of political leaders and citizens alike today is what the limits of government involvement in the economy ought to be. To what extent should the free market make most economic decisions to maximize efficiency and productivity? Should the government regulate markets in the pursuit of other goals, such as equality, and to address market failures such as monopolies and public goods that are underprovided by the market (such as education and environmental protection)?

This debate reached a peak during the Great Depression, as the nation struggled to define the government's role in reviving the economy, and played a critical role in the 1932 presidential election between the Democratic candidate, Franklin D. Roosevelt, and the Republican president, Herbert Hoover. In the Roosevelt campaign speech printed here, FDR argued that the federal government should play a role in unemployment insurance, housing for the poor, and public works programs to compensate for the hardship of the Great Depression. Hoover, on the other hand, was very much opposed to altering the relationship between government and the private sector, which was "builded up by 150 years of toil of our fathers." It was the extension of freedom and the exercise of individual initiative, Hoover claimed, which made the American economic system strong and which would gradually bring about economic recovery. Roosevelt prevailed, and the resulting New Deal changed the face of government. While the federal government adopted a much more active role in regulating the economy and providing social safety, the central issues discussed by Roosevelt and Hoover are still being debated today.

The first principle I would lay down is that the primary duty rests on the community, through local government and private agencies, to take care of the relief of unemployment. But we then come to a situation where there are so many people out of work that local funds are insufficient.

It seems clear to me that the organized society known as the State comes into the picture at this point. In other words, the obligation of government is extended to the next higher unit.

I [practice] what I preach. In 1930 the state of New York greatly increased its employment service and kept in close touch with the ability of localities to take care of their own unemployed. But by the summer of 1931 it became apparent to me that actual state funds and a state-supervised system were imperative.

I called a special session of the legislature, and they appropriated a fund of $20 million for unemployment relief, this fund to be reimbursed to the state through the doubling of our income taxes. Thus the state of New York became the first among all the states to accept the definite obligation of supplementing local funds where these local funds were insufficient.

The administration of this great work has become a model for the rest of the country. Without setting up any complex machinery or any large overhead, the state of New York is working successfully through local agencies, and, in spite of the fact that over a million people are out of work and in need of aid in this one state alone, we have so far met at least the bare necessities of the case.

This past spring the legislature appropriated another $5 million, and on November 8 the voters will pass on a $30 million bond issue to tide us over this winter and at least up to next summer.

*   *   *

I am very certain that the obligation extends beyond the states and to the federal government itself, if and when it becomes apparent that states and communities are unable to take care of the necessary relief work.

It may interest you to have me read a short quotation from my message to the legislature in 1931:

> What is the State? It is the duly constituted representative of an organized society of human beings, created by them for their mutual protection and well-being. One of the duties of the State is that of caring for those of its citizens who find themselves the victims of such adverse circumstances as make them unable to obtain even the necessities of mere existence without the aid of others.
>
> In broad terms, I assert that modern society, acting through its government, owes the definite obligation to prevent the starvation or the dire want of any of its fellowmen and women who try to maintain themselves but cannot. To these unfortunate citizens aid must be extended by the government, not as a matter of charity but as a matter of social duty.

That principle which I laid down in 1931, I reaffirm. I not only reaffirm it, I go a step further and say that where the State itself is unable successfully to fulfill this obligation which lies upon it, it then becomes the positive duty of the federal government to step in to help.

In the words of our Democratic national platform, the federal government has a "continuous responsibility for human welfare, especially for the protection of children." That duty and responsibility the federal government should carry out promptly, fearlessly, and generously.

It took the present Republican administration in Washington almost three years to recognize this principle. I have recounted to you in other speeches, and it is a matter of general information, that for at least two years after the crash, the only efforts made by the national administration to cope with the distress of unemployment were to deny its existence.

When, finally, this year, after attempts at concealment and minimizing had failed, it was at last forced to recognize the fact of suffering among millions of unemployed, appropriations of federal funds for assistance to states were finally made.

I think it is fair to point out that a complete program of unemployment relief was on my recommendation actually under way in the state of New York over a year ago; and that in Washington relief funds in any large volume were not provided until this summer, and at that they were pushed through at the demand of Congress rather than through the leadership of the President of the United States.

At the same time, I have constantly reiterated my conviction that the expenditures of cities, states, and the federal government must be reduced in the interest of the nation as a whole. I believe that there are many ways in which such reduction of expenditures can take place, but I am utterly unwilling that economy should be practised at the expense of starving people.

We must economize in other ways, but it shall never be said that the American people have refused to provide the necessities of life for those who, through no fault of their own, are unable to feed, clothe, and house themselves. The first obligation of government is the protection of the welfare and well-being, indeed the very existence, of its citizens.

* * *

The next question asks my attitude toward appropriations for public works as an aid to unemployment. I am perfectly clear as to the principles involved in this case also.

From the long-range point of view it would be advisable for governments of all kinds to set up in times of prosperity what might be called a nest egg to be used for public works in times of depression. That is a policy which we should initiate when we get back to good times.

But there is the immediate possibility of helping the emergency through appropriations for public works. One question, however, must be answered first because of the simple fact that these public works cost money.

We all know that government treasuries, whether local or state or federal, are hard put to it to keep their budgets balanced; and, in the case of the federal Treasury, thoroughly unsound financial policies have made its situation not exactly desperate but at least threatening to future stability if the policies of the present administration are continued.

All public works, including federal, must be considered from the point of view of the ability of the government Treasury to pay for them. There are two ways of paying for public works. One is by the sale of bonds. In principle, such bonds should be issued only to pay for self-sustaining projects or for structures which will without question have a useful life over a long period of years. The other method of payment is from current revenues, which in these days means in most cases added taxes. We all know that there is a very definite limit to the increase of taxes above the present level.

From this point, therefore, I can go on and say that, if funds can be properly provided by the federal government for increased appropriations for public works, we must examine the character of these public works. I have already spoken of that type which is self-sustaining. These should be greatly encouraged. The other type is that of public works which are honestly essential to the community. Each case must rest on its own merits.

It is impossible, for example, to say that all parks or all playgrounds are essential. One may be and another may not be. If a school, for instance, has no playground, it is obvious that the furnishing of a playground is a necessity to the community. But if the school already has a playground and some people seek merely to enlarge it, there may be a very definite question as to how necessary that enlargement is.

Let me cite another example. I am much interested in providing better housing accommodations for the poor in our great cities. If a slum area can be torn down and new modern buildings put up, I should call that almost a human necessity; but, on the other hand, the mere erection of new buildings in some other part of the city while allowing the slums to remain raises at once a question of necessity. I am confident that the federal government working in cooperation with states and cities can do much to carry on increased public works and along lines which are sound from the economic and financial point of view.

Now I come to another question. I am asked whether I favor a system of unemployment insurance reserves made compulsory by the states, supplemented by a system of federally coordinated state employment offices to facilitate the reemployment of jobless workers.

The first part of the question is directly answered by the Democratic platform which advocates unemployment insurance under state laws.

This is no new policy for me. I have advocated unemployment insurance in my own state for some time, and, indeed, last year six Eastern governors were my guests at a conference which resulted in the drawing up of what might be called an idea plan of unemployment insurance.

This type of insurance is not a cure-all but it provides at least a cushion to mitigate unemployment in times of depression. It is sound if, after starting it, we stick to the principle of sound insurance financing. It is only where governments, as in some European countries, have failed to live up to these sound principles that unemployment insurance has been an economic failure.

As to the coordinated employment offices, I can only tell you that I was for the bills sponsored by Senator Wagner of my own state and passed by the Congress. They created a nationally coordinated system of employment offices operated by the individual states with the advisory cooperation of joint boards of employers and employees.

To my very great regret this measure was vetoed by the President of the United States. I am certain that the federal government can, by furnishing leadership, stimulate the various states to set up and coordinate practical, useful systems.

70

"Against the Proposed New Deal"

Herbert Hoover

This campaign is more than a contest between two men. It is more than a contest between two parties. It is a contest between two philosophies of government.

We are told by the opposition that we must have a change, that we must have a new deal. It is not the change that comes from normal development of national life to which I object but the proposal to alter the whole foundations of our national life which have been built through generations of testing and struggle, and of the principles upon which we have builded the nation. The expressions our opponents use must refer to important changes in our economic and social system and our system of government, otherwise they are nothing but vacuous words. And I realize that in this time of distress many of our people are asking whether our social and economic system is incapable of that great primary function of providing security and comfort of life to all of the firesides of our 25 million homes in America, whether our social system provides for the fundamental development and progress of our people, whether our form of government is capable of originating and sustaining that security and progress.

This question is the basis upon which our opponents are appealing to the people in their fears and distress. They are proposing changes and so-called new deals which would destroy the very foundations of our American system.

Our people should consider the primary facts before they come to the judgment—not merely through political agitation, the glitter of promise, and the discouragement of temporary hardships—whether they will support changes which radically affect the whole system which has been built up by 150 years of the toil of our fathers. They should not approach the question in the despair with which our opponents would clothe it.

Our economic system has received abnormal shocks during the past three years, which temporarily dislocated its normal functioning. These shocks have in a large sense come from without our borders, but I say to you that our system of government has enabled us to take such strong action as to prevent the disaster which would otherwise have come to our nation. It has enabled us further to develop measures and programs which are now demonstrating their ability to bring about restoration and progress.

We must go deeper than platitudes and emotional appeals of the public platform in the campaign if we will penetrate to the full significance of the changes which our opponents are attempting to float upon the wave of distress and discontent from the difficulties we are passing through. We can find what our opponents would do after searching the record of their appeals to discontent, group and sectional interest. We must search for them in the legislative acts which they sponsored and passed in the Democratic-controlled House of Representatives in the last session of Congress. We must look into measures for which they voted and which were defeated. We must inquire whether or not the presidential and vice-presidential candidates have disavowed these acts. If they have not, we must conclude that they form a portion and are a substantial indication of the profound changes proposed.

And we must look still further than this as to what revolutionary changes have been proposed by the candidates themselves.

We must look into the type of leaders who are campaigning for the Democratic ticket, whose philosophies have been well known all their lives, whose demands for a change in the American system are frank and forceful. I can respect the sincerity of these men in their desire to change our form of government and our social and economic system, though I shall do my best tonight to prove they are wrong. I refer particularly to Senator Norris, Senator La Follette, Senator Cutting, Senator Huey Long, Senator Wheeler, William R. Hearst and other exponents of a social philosophy different from the traditional American one. Unless these men feel assurance of support to their ideas, they certainly would not be supporting these candidates and the Democratic Party. The seal of these men indicates that they have sure confidence that they will have voice in the administration of our government.

I may say at once that the changes proposed from all these Democratic principals and allies are of the most profound and penetrating character. If they are brought about, this will not be the America which we have known in the past.

Let us pause for a moment and examine the American system of government, of social and economic life, which it is now proposed that we should alter. Our system is the product of our race and of our experience in building a nation to heights unparalleled in the whole history of the world. It is a system peculiar to the American people. It differs essentially from all others in the world. It is an American system.

It is founded on the conception that only through ordered liberty, through freedom to the individual, and equal opportunity to the individual will his initiative and enterprise be summoned to spur the march of progress.

It is by the maintenance of equality of opportunity and therefore of a society absolutely fluid in freedom of the movement of its human particles that our individualism departs from the individualism of Europe. We resent class distinction because there can be no rise for the individual through the frozen strata of classes, and no stratification of classes can take place in a mass livened by the free rise of its particles. Thus in our ideals the able and ambitious are able to rise constantly from the bottom to leadership in the community.

This freedom of the individual creates of itself the necessity and the cheerful willingness of men to act cooperatively in a thousand ways and for every purpose as occasion arises; and it permits such voluntary cooperations to be dissolved as soon as they have served their purpose, to be replaced by new voluntary associations for new purposes.

There has thus grown within us, to gigantic importance, a new conception. That is, this voluntary cooperation within the community. Cooperation to perfect the social organization; cooperation for the care of those in distress; cooperation for the advancement of knowledge, of scientific research, of education; for cooperative action in the advancement of many phases of economic life. This is self-government by the people outside of government; it is the most powerful development of individual freedom and equal opportunity that has taken place in the century and a half since our fundamental institutions were founded.

It is in the further development of this cooperation and a sense of its responsibility that we should find solution for many of our complex problems, and not by the extension of government into our economic and social life. The greatest function of government is to build up that cooperation, and its most resolute action should be to deny the extension of bureaucracy. We have developed great agencies of cooperation by the assistance of the government which promote and protect the interests of individuals and the smaller units of business. The Federal Reserve System, in its strengthening and support of the smaller banks; the Farm Board, in its strengthening and support of the farm cooperatives; the Home Loan Banks, in the mobilizing of building and loan associations and savings banks; the Federal Land Banks, in giving independence and strength to land mortgage associations; the great mobilization of relief to distress, the mobilization of business and industry in measures of recovery, and a score of other activities are not socialism—they are the essence of protection to the development of free men.

The primary conception of this whole American system is not the regimentation of men but the cooperation of free men. It is founded upon the conception of responsibility of the individual to the community, of the responsibility of local government to the state, of the state to the national government.

It is founded on a peculiar conception of self-government designed to maintain this equal opportunity to the individual, and through decentralization it brings about and maintains these responsibilities. The centralization of government will undermine responsibilities and will destroy the system.

Our government differs from all previous conceptions, not only in this decentralization but also in the separation of functions between the legislative, executive, and judicial arms of government, in which the independence of the judicial arm is the keystone of the whole structure.

It is founded on a conception that in times of emergency, when forces are running beyond control of individuals or other cooperative action, beyond the control of local communities and of states, then the great reserve powers of the federal government shall be brought into action to protect the community. But when these forces have ceased, there must be a return of state, local, and individual responsibility.

The implacable march of scientific discovery with its train of new inventions presents every year new problems to government and new problems to the social order. Questions often arise whether, in the face of the growth of these new and gigantic tools, democracy can remain master in its own house, can preserve the fundamentals of our American system. I contend that it can; and I contend that this American system of ours has demonstrated its validity and superiority over any other system yet invented by human mind.

It has demonstrated it in the face of the greatest test of our history—that is the emergency which we have faced in the past three years.

When the political and economic weakness of many nations of Europe, the result of the World War and its aftermath, finally culminated in collapse of their institutions, the delicate adjustment of our economic and social life received a shock unparalleled in our history. No one knows that better than you of New York. No one knows its causes better than you. That the crisis was so great that many of the leading banks sought directly or indirectly to convert their assets into gold or its equivalent with the result that they practically ceased to function as credit institutions; that many of our citizens sought flight for their capital to other countries; that many of them attempted to hoard gold in large amounts. These were but indications of the flight of confidence and of the belief that our government could not overcome these forces.

Yet these forces were overcome—perhaps by narrow margins—and this action demonstrates what the courage of a nation can accomplish under the resolute leadership in the Republican Party. And I say the Republican Party, because our opponents before and during the crisis, proposed no constructive program; though some of their members patriotically supported ours. Later on the Democratic House of Representatives did develop the real thought and ideas of the Democratic Party, but it was so destructive that it had to be defeated, for it would have destroyed, not healed.

In spite of all these obstructions, we did succeed. Our form of government did prove itself equal to the task. We saved this nation from a quarter of a century of chaos and degeneration, and we preserved the savings, the insurance policies, gave a fighting chance to men to hold their homes. We saved the integrity of our government and the honesty of the American dollar. And we installed measures which today are bringing back recovery. Employment, agriculture, business—all of these show the steady, if slow, healing of our enormous wound.

I therefore contend that the problem of today is to continue these measures and policies to restore this American system to its normal functioning, to repair the wounds it has received, to correct the weaknesses and evils which would defeat that system. To enter upon a series of deep changes, to embark upon this inchoate new deal which has been propounded in this campaign, would be to undermine and destroy our American system.

DISCUSSION QUESTIONS

1. State governments have always played a role in regulating the economy, from consumer protection to using tax breaks as a way to attract business investment within a state's borders. What kind of economic activities are best regulated at the state level? When should the federal government play a role?

2. Which of the activities that the government performs do you consider essential? Why?

71

"The GDP Myth: Why 'Growth' Isn't Always a Good Thing"

Jonathan Rowe and Judith Silverstein

"Gross Domestic Product," or GDP, is a familiar economic term: It is a standard measure of overall economic activity, or, as Jonathan Rowe and Judith Silverstein write, the amount of money that is spent during a particular period of time. Politicians are quick to take credit when the GDP grows, for it is a sign of economic expansion. And when communities are concerned about the environmental or quality-of-life impact of a new development or industrial site, community and business leaders reassure them by pointing to the economic growth that will result. But is all growth good growth? Rowe and Silverstein argue that GDP is an inaccurate measure of overall economic well-being. Higher GDP does not necessarily mean we are better off, since it includes all types of spending—even spending that results from waste (gasoline burned by people sitting in Los Angeles traffic jams), unhealthy activities (consumption of cholesterol-laden foods, and the cardiologists' bills that often result), or pollution (and the efforts to clean up toxic waste). The impact of this "growth" on the public differs from the perceptions of economists and political leaders, who always portray economic growth as a positive. Rowe and Silverstein urge journalists to stop accepting language such as "economic growth" at face value and force politicians, in particular, to be clear about what has grown in the economy, or what will grow.

George Orwell really did see it coming. "As soon as certain topics are raised," he wrote, "the concrete melts into the abstract." Nowhere does it melt more quickly than in economics. Public discussion of the economy is a hothouse of evasive abstraction. Opinionators and politicians rarely name what they are talking about. Instead they waft into generalities they learned in Economics 101.

The President's [1999] State of the Union Address was a case in point. The President boasted of the "longest peacetime expansion of our history." That's how pols always talk. It sounds like truly wonderful news. But what actually has been expanding? A lot of things can grow, and do. Waistlines grow. Medical bills grow. Traffic, debt, and stress all grow. We can't know whether an "expansion" is good or not unless we know what it includes. Yet the President didn't tell, and the media hordes didn't ask, which was typical too.

A human economy is supposed to advance well-being. That is elementary. Yet politicians and pundits rarely talk about it in those terms. Instead they revert to the language of "expansion," "growth," and the like, which mean something very different. Cut through the boosterism and hysterics, and growth means simply "spending more money." It makes no difference where the money goes, and why. As long as the people spend more of it, the economy is said to "grow."

The technical term for this is "Gross Domestic Product" or GDP, which gives the proceedings an atmosphere of authority and expertise. But it doesn't take a genius to smell the fish. Spending more money doesn't always mean life is getting better. Often it means things are getting worse. This is exceedingly hard for most commentators to grasp. It simply does not fit with the story line we learned in the economics texts. A number of writers have argued, for example, that things are much better than Americans realize, and that only a jaundiced and elitist media obscures this fact. Yes, there is a Cassandra* industry of issue groups on both Left and Right that raise money on dire warnings. Yes, the media gets more attention with bad news than with good. But that doesn't mean Americans are wrong when they tell pollsters that they are concerned about the direction of the nation, even though their own economic fortunes are pretty good. When one looks at what is actually growing in America today, that view makes a lot of sense. Consider a few examples.

The Flab Factor

To put this delicately, Americans are becoming quite ample. Over half of us are overweight. The portion of middle-aged Americans who are clinically obese has doubled since the 1960s; it is now one out of three. The number that is grossly overweight—that is, can't fit into an airline seat—has ballooned 350 percent over the past thirty years.

That's a lot of girth, and a prodigious source of growth. Food is roughly a $700 billion industry in the United States, counting agriculture, supermarkets, restaurants and the rest. Unfortunately, a good deal of that industry ends up inside us Americans. The result is flab, and a diet and weight loss industry of some $32 billion nationwide and—yes—growing. Richard Armey, the House majority leader and an economist, has opined that "the market is rational and the government is dumb." Here's a bit of rationality for him. The food industry spends some $21 billion a year on advertising to goad us to eat more. Then we spend that and half again trying to rid ourselves of the inevitable effects.

When diets and treadmills don't work, which is often, there's always the vacuum pump or knife. Cosmetic surgery is another booming sector,

---

* [This refers to the legendary prophetess Cassandra; in this context, it means one who predicts misfortune.]

and much of it aims to detach unwanted pounds. There were roughly 110,000 liposuctions in the nation last year, at a cost of some $2,000 or more apiece. At five pounds per, that's 275 tons of flab up the tube. Pack it in, vac it off; it's pretty rational, especially if you are in the packing or the vacking business—or if, as in Armey's case, you get campaign contributions from those quarters.

Girth is one growth sector with a bright future. With Channel One and billboards filling schools with junk food ads, and with computers joining TV as a sedentary claim on time, kids are becoming broad of beam like their folks. The Surgeon General says childhood obesity is "epidemic," which is bad for kids but good for growth. Clothing lines for the "husky" child are expanding, as are summer camps for overweight youngsters. Type II diabetes, the kind associated with weight, has quadrupled among kids since 1982, which is a boost for the pharmaco-medical establishment.

Meanwhile, eating disorders such as bulimia have become a growth sector unto themselves. Bulimia may be the trademark affliction of the growth era. It is a disease of literal obedience to the schizoid messages that barrage young girls: indulge yourself wantonly but also be taut and svelte. The teen magazines make the economy grow, and then the treatment for bulimia makes it grow more.

Medical Costs

If Clinton's clunky medical insurance proposal did nothing else, it at least put the medical insurance industry on good behavior for a while. Those days appear to be over. The Health Care Financing Administration says that nationwide, outlays for medical treatment are likely to double over the next decade. Many small employers already are getting hit with hikes of 20 percent or more.

That means more than a sixth of the economy as conventionally measured will be devoted to treating disease. Not only is that major GDP; it's also a product of GDP. C. Everett Koop, the Surgeon General in the Reagan Administration, has said that some 70 percent of the nation's medical bill stems from preventable illnesses—that is, ones that are mainly lifestyle induced. We eat too much, drink too much, smoke too much, watch too much TV, absorb too much stress, and dump too many toxic substances into our air and water.

We are literally growing ourselves sick, and the resulting medical bills make the economy grow more. A study by the American Public Health Association a few years ago found that the United States could cut its medical costs by $17 billion a year if we all cut our daily intake of fat by just 8 grams, the amount in half a cup of premium ice cream.

"One way to reduce health costs is to get people to use the health care system less frequently," Dr. Koop said sensibly—but not rationally by

Armey's standard. If people watched less TV, drove less, ate less but more healthfully, there would be less growth. So instead we resort to high-tech—and expensive—drugs and treatments to undo what we have done.

Such Service

When politicians crow about an expanding economy they make a big assumption—that people actually get something for the money they spend. That's life in the economics textbooks but not in the world we inhabit. W. Steven Albrecht, an accounting professor at Brigham Young University, estimates that white-collar fraud costs us some $200 billion a year. (The yearly take of burglars and robbers is more like $4 billion.) That estimate is probably low. Americans lose at least $40 billion a year to telemarketing fraud alone.

In an era of deregulation and belief in benign "market forces," the toll gets steadily worse. Phone bills and the like have become horrendously complex, for example. The Federal Communications Commission re-ceived 10,000 calls a month in the first five months of last year from people who couldn't understand their bills. The complexity has spawned a practice called "cramming" in which third parties slip phony charges for dating services, psychic help lines and the like into a generic category in the bill. Then there are the no-armed bandits that operate on practi-cally every street corner under the alias "ATM machines." When banks began to install these in the late 1970s they promised lower costs and therefore lower fees. Today we literally have to pay for access to our own money, and increasingly we pay twice. The average bank customer in the United States pays over $150 a year in ATM fees, according to a study by the U.S. Public Interest Research Group. In California alone, ATM users pay over $1.5 billion a year, or as much as people making between $30,000 and $50,000 pay in state income taxes.

In their unfailing instinct for euphemism, economists call this a "ser-vice" industry. Banks pay us 1 to 2 percent for our deposits, loan the money to someone else at up to 18 percent, and then they tax us when we take our own money back. Good service. Next time the pols start touting "tax cuts," let's hope our alert media friends think to ask them about the privatized tax systems like this that take those cuts away.

Pluck the Price-Payer

How do they get away with it? Wise investing doesn't hurt. Banking interests put some $17 million into the last federal elections, not counting in-kind payments, loans and "soft money" contributions to political par-ties and the like. It doesn't take a cynic to suspect a connection between such outlays and the ability of the banks to impose their money-access tax upon the rest of us. When politicians hail the nation's "robust growth," they are talking in part about the robust flow of money to themselves. In California, campaign spending reached half a billion dollars this year, a new record. It is growing faster than major league baseball salaries. In national politics the cost of congressional campaigns has grown four times faster than the economy as a whole; and again, that's not counting "soft money." Few Americans would say that politics has gotten four times better over that time.

It is easy to forget that economically, the campaign finance system works much like the ATM machines: It gets us coming and going. First we provide the money that interest groups pass along to politicians. (The American Bankers Association doesn't pick its money from trees, but rather from us.) Next the pols support policies that enable such interest groups to extract still more from us. The pols get a cut of that extraction in the next round of campaign contributions, and the wheel turns again.

Debt

Americans have a new role in the world. No longer are we the arsenal of democracy, the sturdy producers of Depression-era murals. We are now consumers, the insatiable maws whose buying keeps the world economy afloat. "Amid the turmoil [in Asia]" *The Wall Street Journal* reports, "the U.S. consumer is emerging as a savior of sorts." Jim Hoagland of *The Washington Post* called this consumer "a truly heroic figure."

World salvation is serious business, and the United States fulfills this global obligation the way it has fought its wars—with borrowed money. Consumer debt has burgeoned in the United States. It has grown 73 percent since 1993 and is now some $1.5 trillion, which is about the size of the economy of France. (That doesn't even count home mortgages, which add about $3.8 trillion more.) The average American household has 11 credit cards and owes some $7,000 on them at any given time, plus the car loan and the mortgage.

If Americans feel apprehensive about the future, it just might be in part because they have burdened that future with debt. Yet debt is the Viagra of a growth economy in middle age. It provides an appearance of robust function when in reality we are borrowing ourselves into a financial hole. First the buying itself makes the GDP go up. About half of retail sales today—some $1.4 trillion—are done with debt. Then there's the interest on consumer debt, which comes to over $150 billion a year and growing. Buy a car on time and you can end up paying more for the money than you do for the car. The GDP adds the two together and calls it growth. If Americans paid their bills on time, the money they saved on interest would amount to a 100 percent federal income tax cut for everyone making between $20,000 to $50,000 a year.

But less debt would mean less GDP. It also would mean less business for the satellite industries that have grown up around debt. According to the Small Business Administration, the fastest growing small business in the country over the next decade will be debt collection. Employment there will increase at twice the rate of small business as a whole. Curb debt and you reduce the need for people to collect the debt, which is bad for growth. You also reduce the need for debt counselors and bankruptcy lawyers. Bankruptcies have doubled over this decade, with more to come. "We're going to be happy next year, but nobody else is," said the president of the Bankruptcy Institute, a lawyer's organization.

Consumer debt is another growth sector with a big future. Banks send out over 800 million credit card solicitations every three months, which will come as no surprise to most Americans who receive mail. Today some 28 percent of households making under $10,000 a year have cards, and over half of college students. Students get free T-shirts and Frisbees in college registration lines if they sign up for cards. Of course, many of these students are already in debt for tens of thousands of dollars because of student loans.

In the eyes of the opinion class there is nothing wrong with this. To the contrary, in the words of the *Post*'s Hoagland, it means that we "consumers" will continue to shoulder the world's burdens "by continuing to borrow, spend and consume with impressive single-mindedness." The only danger is that we might become less debt prone, but our banks are on the job. They are starting to punish customers who pay their bills on time. These conscientious citizens are now "freeloaders" who must bear extra fees, shortened grace periods, even cancellation of their cards.

Growing Nowhere

Clichés become that for a reason. When people associate growth with traffic, it's because that's how they experience it in their lives. Traffic is a plague; but it's both a result of growth and also a big source of it. In the strange abstracted world of economics, a plague is good so long as it makes us spend more money.

In California, pace-setter in traffic as in other things, drivers are experts on this subject. Los Angeles has been the most car-congested city in the country for 14 years running, and the rest of the state is not far behind. It's a lot of annoyance, but also a lot of gas. Angelenos alone burn over $800 million a year in gas while they sit in traffic and fume, and Americans generally spend over $4 billion more. That's GDP and the economic future toward which much of urban America is headed.

Cars fume too, of course, which means bad air and respiratory diseases. LA leads the nation, if that's the word, in hospital admissions due to asthma, bronchitis, and other breathing problems, which adds to the state's staggering medical bill. More traffic also means more car crashes. There's a collision almost every minute on California's crowded roads, which helps make car wrecks a $130 billion a year industry in the United States.

Call it the multiplier effect of misery. Yet as the roads become more clogged, the auto makers are pushing sports utility vehicles that burn more gas, take up more space, and do more damage when they crash. But they cost a fortune and that adds to growth. Meanwhile, the traffic takes a heavy toll on the roads themselves. Maintaining them costs some $800 million a year in California, and $20 billion in the nation; California drivers spend some $1.2 billion a year on extra car repairs because the roads are in such bad shape.

That's all GDP. So too is at least part of the $35–$40 billion the nation spends defending the foreign oil supplies that fuel all this misery and havoc.

Stress

Prosperity is supposed to bring satisfaction and peace. But today's version has led the other way. As the GDP has risen and the economy expands, Americans have felt more harried and under siege. Stress is a factor in over 70 percent of all doctor visits, according to the National Institute of Mental Health. "Nearly every patient I see leads a life influenced in some way by inordinate levels of stress," writes Dr. Richard Swenson of the University of Wisconsin Medical School in his book *Margin*. Stress is in large measure a product of the economy. It comes from the barrage of stimuli, the prolixity of choices, the pressures to perform and the multiplying claims upon our attention and time, which drive a rising GDP. Stress also is a producer of growth, in the form of an enlarging treatment industry of counselors, relaxation tapes, seminars, and spas. Sedatives and mood-enhancers of various kinds are roughly a $6 billion industry. Over 28 million Americans now use Prozac and kindred drugs. (Technically, Prozac is for depression. But the lines between depression and stress are blurry at best.) Even kids are taking these drugs; at last count, some one-half million and rising. Whether that's good for kids is questionable; that it's good for growth is not. "Antidepressant makers need a new market as growth slows in the adult segment," *The Wall Street Journal* explained. A Bay Area teenager told what happens when a society redefines a whole generation as a drug market "segment." "Close to half of the 15- to 18-year-olds I know are on Prozac," she wrote in *YO! Magazine*. "Their parents will do anything to get their kids to achieve, behave, clean their rooms—whatever—including supplying them with the latest in personality-altering drugs."

A Simple Question

The more closely one looks the more one understands the feelings of ambiguity in the land. We are glad for jobs and a buoyant stock market. But we are uneasy about the world we are creating in the process. Is growth an unalloyed good when the fastest growing industry of the '90s is gambling? Not entirely coincidentally, the prison business is another booming sector. Since 1980 it has grown five times over. Inmate pay-phone calls alone yield over a billion dollars a year.

Even the mundane and once-innocuous elements of growth can give one pause today. Are we really happy about the aggressive marketing that makes kids obsessed with brand names? Clothing sales go up, but parents have to pay, and others too, sometimes dearly. In January, in Prince George's County, a Washington suburb, three teen-agers were shot within a single 20-minute period. In each case the object of the assault was an Eddie Bauer jacket. Police refer to such incidents as "fashion crime."

It's little wonder that politicians and pundits resort instinctively to the abstract when they talk about the economy. The particulars are turning into a somewhat murky soup. They keep telling us they can solve the nation's problems with more "growth." Yet increasingly problems are what the GDP consists of. This syndrome has become an unacknowledged subtext in much of the daily news. The AP reported recently on a part of eastern Oregon that is the fastest growing in the state. The source of this prosperity? A state prison and a nerve gas incinerator, along with a Wal-Mart distribution center and a railroad maintenance yard. Similarly, there is a pesticide plant in Richmond, California that is owned by the Zeneca Group, an $8 billion corporation that also makes the breast cancer drug tamoxifen. Many researchers believe that pesticides, and the toxins created in the production of them, play a role in breast cancer.

"It's a pretty good deal," a local physician told the *East Bay Express*, a local weekly. "First you cause the cancer, then you profit from curing it." She was overstating of course, but the fact remains: both alleged cause and cure make the GDP go up.

Some economists would dismiss this as wrong headed. If people didn't spend their money on such things as cancer treatments and gas to stand still in traffic, they say, they'd spend it on something else. Growth would be the same or even more. In other words, we shouldn't worry about exactly what is growing because hypothetically it could be something else. The argument approaches professional self-parody. It is fine for those who have the luxury of dealing with the economy through computer models. But for the rest of us who have to deal with the economy in concrete terms, the question of what exactly is expanding matters a great deal.

This doesn't mean the end of growth. Rather, it means the end of the assumption that anything called "growth" is automatically good. It means a need to stop using a euphemistic language that has that assumption built in. Republicans argue, for example, that the government should use the budget surplus for tax cuts because individual Americans will use the money more "rationally" than the awful government would.

Maybe so. But to look at where the money actually goes these days gives one pause. Is it really more "rational" to feed traffic jams as opposed to investing more in other forms of transit? Does the high-growth industry of gambling really do more for the country than the lower growth industry (at least in the short term) of building new inner-city schools with bathrooms that work? Would more Eddie Bauer jackets really do more for the country than better teachers?

We won't even get to these questions unless we start talking about the economy as it is, rather than the way economists tend to think about it. The job is going to fall first to journalists, who frame the first draft of reality for the public mind. They've got to start to articulate the economy as Americans experience it; and to do this, reporters have got to cleanse their minds of the vocabulary and assumptions of economic doctrine and explore the economic dimension of our lives with uncluttered eyes. That's a big assignment, but it starts with a very simple question. The next time a Jack Kemp, say, promises to double the rate of growth, as he did in the vice presidential debate in '96, don't call Brookings or Heritage [political analysis institutes] to find out if it is possible in macroeconomic terms. Reporters must insist on details, as they would with any other story. Exactly what is going to double? Traffic? Consumer debt? Jet skis? The use of mood-altering pharmaceuticals? The next time the Commerce Department releases the GDP figures, don't just call a Wall Street "analyst" for comment. Insist on knowing what those flows of money are leaving in their wake—that is, exactly what is growing and the effects. If official Washington doesn't have this data then find out why not.

People don't experience "growth." They experience the things that growth consists of; and that's where good reporting begins. Until reporters start to look at these issues from the standpoint of those who experience the economy rather than those who pontificate about it, they are going to remain where many readers think they are—in another world.

DISCUSSION QUESTIONS

1. If all growth (increases in spending) is not necessarily good growth, how can we distinguish between "good" growth and "bad" growth? What social factors might we consider? Would it be possible to have agreement on which factors to include? In other words, this may be an interesting theoretical discussion, but would it be politically possible to implement?

2. In public policy debates, analysts often distinguish "economic" indicators—inflation, unemployment, consumer spending—from "social" indicators, such as crime, divorce, school dropout rates, and teen pregnancies. In light of Rowe and Silverstein's argument, is this separation appropriate? Why or why not?

Debating the Issues: Regulating Risk—Government Intrusion or Protecting Society?

Government regulation is everywhere. From the time you wake up in the morning to the time you go to sleep again, government regulations are, usually invisibly, influencing what you do and affecting your quality of life. The dorm room, apartment, or house you live in is governed by scores of regulations, particularly safety-oriented regulations. The school you attend abides by a lengthy list of regulations concerning gender equity, access to buildings for disabled people, the confidentiality of student transcripts, and the dispensing of student financial aid, among many others. Your transportation to and from campus is affected by government regulations of the auto, mass transit, and road construction industries. The water you drink, the food you eat, the medicines you take, the air you breathe—all are subject to reams of government regulations. Is it all too much? Have Americans gotten too used to the government coddling them and protecting them from their own actions?

Roger Scruton clearly believes the answer is yes. Scruton argues that "Nanny" has gone too far in controlling individuals' lives and that, by the same token, individuals have too willingly given away their freedoms to government bureaucrats. While many conservative arguments against government regulations focus on their ineffectiveness or their cost, Scruton takes a more philosophical approach, arguing that as spiritual beings, individuals must accept some risk. Scruton also suggests that the regulatory structure is rampant with hypocrisy. That is, the content of regulations favors the political values and agendas of certain elites. These regulations are not designed to produce the best social outcome but to satisfy the ideological viewpoints of particular groups. Scruton suggests that many traditional or conventional behaviors in terms of marriage, heterosexual orientation, and religious belief, among others, have been shown to have significant health, life, and safety benefits, but fear of making moral choices keeps government elites from acting. If government really wanted to maximize health and safety, Scruton asks, why not push for regulations that encourage these behaviors?

Nurith Aizenman offers a very different perspective. Detailing some alarming conduct by the nation's railroad and trucking industries, Aizenman suggests these industries are treating public safety with contempt and that public regulators are doing very little about it. Focusing on the transportation of hazardous materials, he discusses several cases in which public safety was imperiled and identifies some of the causes that contribute to these safety incidents. Increasingly, these industries are being allowed to self-regulate as government seeks a more "cooperative" business-government partnership.

To Aizenman, the central problem is that regulation has been delegitimized; even liberals, he writes, are afraid to stand up and defend regulation.

72

"What Is Acceptable Risk?"

ROGER SCRUTON

The state of Massachusetts has passed a law against sushi—that is to say, you will be allowed to eat sushi only if it has first been either cooked or frozen, so ceasing, in effect, to be sushi. Why? A minuscule risk exists that sushi, in its normal condition, will make you sick. And this is a risk that the citizens of Massachusetts are no longer allowed to take.

Manufacturers of children's playgrounds now predict that swings in public playgrounds will become a thing of the past, since safety regulations require prohibitively expensive padding beneath them. Indeed, the regulations surrounding children's toys, clothes, and activities are now so strict that it is hard to have an adventurous childhood. In England it is even against the law to allow your child to walk down a country lane to school, since there is a one in a billion chance that he will be abducted.

In the past, the law made a distinction between those risks to health and safety that citizens might voluntarily assume and those from which the state should protect them. Since every act of protection by the state involves a loss of freedom, lawmakers assumed that only in very special cases should the state expropriate our risk taking. In matters of public hygiene, where the risks taken by one person also fall upon others, it seemed legitimate for the state to intervene: for example, the state could compel people to maintain standards of cleanliness in public places or to undergo vaccinations against contagious diseases. But it should not forbid a person to consume a certain product, merely because there is a tiny risk to his own physical well-being. For the state to extend its jurisdiction so far involves a serious invasion of privacy. In matters that affect the citizen alone and that have no adverse consequences on others, the citizen should be free to choose. The state can inform him of the risk, but it should not forbid the choice.

Such, at any rate, was the orthodox position, as defended by John Stuart Mill and the "classical" liberals. But it is not the position adopted by our modern legislators, who do their best to remove both the risk and the freedom to run it. My neighbors are farmers who produce dairy products, livestock, and poultry. Within a few yards of my door is an abundance of milk, eggs, chicken, duck, bacon, beef, and cheese. But I must travel six miles if I am to buy any of these things, and what I buy will have traveled a further 1,000 miles, on average, before reaching me. This is because the state has forbidden me to take the risk of eating my neighbors' products, until they have been processed, packaged and purified, released into the endless stream of global produce, and entirely purged of their local identity and taste. Although the risk of eating the food that grows next door is solely mine, I am not allowed to take it.

The social, environmental, and political costs of such regulation far outweigh any narrow benefit in terms of health. This is especially apparent to someone who lives among farmers and who observes the decline of their industry, the ruination of the landscape, and the dereliction of the farms that has ensued as a result of the criminalization of their traditional economy. However, all protests against over-regulation fall on deaf ears. Governments now regard risk management as their preserve and their priority, and they are prepared to destroy the country's ability to feed itself in an emergency, rather than tolerate one "unnecessary" case of salmonella.

As soon as you look more closely at the matter, however, you discover that modern governments are very selective in the risks that they forbid, and that a law forbidding one risk will often coincide with a law permitting another. Several European governments are currently proposing to outlaw smoking in public places at the same time as legalizing marijuana. Our own government is destroying the local slaughterhouses on which our meat farmers depend on the grounds of wholly invented and unproven risks, while lowering the age of consent for homosexual intercourse and censuring as "homophobic" those who would alert us to the known medical consequences.

In fact, you will quickly discover that Nanny is not concerned with health so much as life-style. She is eager to protect young people from smoking and cites the health risk as her argument. But she does not wish to protect them from homosexual adventures and therefore forbids all discussion of the risk, far greater though it is than the risk attached to cigarettes. Health legislation is being used not to improve the state of the nation's health but to undermine its old, family-based values and to replace them with the antinomian morality of the urban elite.

This is why our government is indifferent to the effect of its legislative zeal on the lives of small farmers. The family farm is the quintessence of old English society, embodying all those virtues of continuity, tradition, patriotism, and local attachment that our ancestors embraced and defended in two world wars.

The farmer is probably the most politically incorrect of Englishmen, and the one most at odds with the media culture that surrounds our government. Hence his way of life can be sacrificed without compunction, and his protests go unheard.

The use of health and safety codes to penalize politically incorrect lifestyles was beautifully exemplified here in rural Wiltshire this last year. Nothing makes Nanny more angry than foxhunting—an offense against the manners, dress code, and morality of the urban elite that has the added taint of being a centuries-old tradition. Nanny is trying hard to make foxhunting illegal. In the meantime, self-appointed policemen patrol the hunts with cameras, looking for evidence of some criminal design. Last year, they photographed the kennel man of the Beaufort Hunt as he left the carcasses of chickens by an earth where some fox cubs lived. This outrageous act caused a national scandal: feeding foxes! Nurturing animals in order to hunt them! The fact that the cubs were orphans, abandoned when their mother was run over by a car, was of no account. Nanny had discovered that people who hunt encourage their quarry to live, sadistically preserving it for a gruesome death. The problem was that no rule in the statute book seemed to condemn it.

At last, after several months of delving, a bureaucrat discovered a piece of European legislation saying that you cannot freely dispose of animal waste without following official guidelines and undergoing official inspections. By leaving out uninspected meat in an uninspected place, the kennel man had committed a crime: the very crime that we all commit when putting out suet for birds. Of course, we bird lovers won't be prosecuted—not yet. So far as I can discover, the case of the Beaufort Hunt was the first and indeed the only time that this particular law has been invoked.

The emphasis on life-style also explains the extraordinary war now being waged against tobacco. Smoking belongs with those old and settled habits—like calling women "ladies," getting drunk on Friday nights with your mates, staying married nevertheless, and having babies in wedlock—that reflect the values of a society shaped by the clear division of sexual roles. It is a symbol of the old order, as portrayed by Hollywood and Ealing Studios in the post-war years, and its very innocence, when set beside cocaine or heroin, gives it the aspect of discarded and parental things.

Furthermore, tobacco advertising has specialized in evoking old ideas of male prowess and female seductiveness: even now, cigarette ads dramatize decidedly un-hip fantasies that stand opposed to the elite culture—after all, the target consumer is the ordinary person, whose fantasies these are. Nor should we forget that tobacco is big business, from which giant corporations make vast profits by the hour. In almost every way, tobacco offends against political correctness, and precisely because it seems to put older people at their ease and enable them to deal confidently with others, it raises the hackles of those who have never achieved that precious condition and whose discomfort is only increased by the sight of others so harmlessly and sociably enjoying themselves.

This is not to deny that tobacco is a risk to health: of course it is. Moreover, it is just about the only product on the market that relentlessly says so. But the health risk does not really explain the vehemence of the attacks on it or the extraordinary attempts by the Environmental Protection Agency and other bureaucracies to portray cigarette smoke as the single most important threat to our children's well-being. For the risk tobacco poses, when compared with those associated with marijuana, automobiles, fatty food, alcohol, or sedentary ways of life, is not actually very serious. Robert A. Levy and Rosalind B. Marimot have shown that smoking reduces the life expectancy of an American 20-year-old by 4.3 years. In an age when people manifestly live too long, why should Nanny be so worried? And why doesn't she turn her attention instead to those products that risk not the physical but the mental and moral health of the consumer: television, for example, or pornography?

It is difficult to avoid the conclusion that what offends about tobacco is not its medical guilt but its moral innocence. It is precisely because it is so harmless, from every point of view other than the medical one, that smoking gets on Nanny's nerves. People don't commit crimes under the influence of smoking, as they do under the influence of drink or drugs. People who smoke have a ready way of putting themselves at ease, of standing back from the world of troubles and taking benign stock of it. Their characters are not distorted or corrupted by their habit, nor is their moral sense betrayed. The smoker is a normal, responsible member of the community, and he can be relied upon, when asked, to put out his [cigarette]. He is not led by his habit into transgressing the established order or the old moral code; on the contrary, his habit has been entirely domesticated by the old sexual morality and recruited to the task of glamorizing it.

Contrast the vehement attacks on tobacco with the pussyfooting over AIDS. The fact that the promiscuous habits of many male homosexuals have greatly advanced this disease has done nothing to make Nanny warn against homosexuality or against exposing young people, even children, to its allure. Indeed, the medical facts about homosexuality are now more or less unmentionable in official circles. They are certainly unmentioned by the British government—in this as in most things a touchstone of political correctness—which has stepped up its campaign not merely to lower the age of consent for homosexual intercourse but also to introduce propaganda into junior schools that will legitimize the "gay" alternative. The medical consequences are brushed aside with advice about condoms and lubricants. Doctors who protest are sneered at, and even in writing this paragraph in *City Journal* I am conscious that I am doing my career as a commentator no good and probably ruling out any prospect of a return to a British university.

For all the fuss over the health and safety effects of various substances, it's interesting to see how little the authorities attend to the health and safety of different life-styles. Statistics show that people live longer, happier, and healthier lives if they are in a stable marriage, if they have the support of a religion, and if they adhere to the traditional sexual code. (Maybe you don't have to be a Darwinian to believe that this is no accident.) But where are the health campaigners and the bureaucrats who are drawing the legislative consequences? Who is agitating for the laws that will privilege these old-fashioned, not to say reactionary, ways of life or for the propaganda campaigns in schools and colleges that will communicate their benefits?

If an article were to appear in a newspaper describing a drug that prolonged life by so much as a year, the medicine would be hailed as a miracle cure. The real miracle cure—religious belief—seems to have a seven-year advantage over atheism, yet it goes unrecognized by Nanny. Indeed, the health consequences of the libertine life-style are, when compared with the consequences of smoking, truly disastrous. Add atheism, relativism, promiscuity, homosexuality, easy divorce, and unstable relationships together, and you probably knock ten years off your life expectancy. But Nanny will never tell you this and will go on reproaching you for your naughty habit of smoking in corners, even if it is the only way, with such a demanding life-style, to obtain in a moment's quiet relief.

Once we see that health legislation is less concerned with physical health than with life-style and the underlying values that life-styles express, we can understand the modern approach to drugs. From the medical point of view, marijuana is at least as dangerous as tobacco, with carcinogenic and cardiological effects comparable with those of ordinary cigarettes and an added danger of brain damage. Moreover, marijuana seems seriously to affect the character and moral responsiveness of those who become addicted to it, and it has a proven association with hard drugs like cocaine and heroin. The connection of all three drugs with crime is well documented by experts and well known to ordinary people. Ask parents what most concerns them among the dangers confronting their children, and you will surely find smoking very low down the list; far higher, and probably nearer the top, will be drugs and the culture that glamorizes them. Hard drugs like heroin kill the user, usually at a young age. But before doing so they rob him of his faculties, his peace of mind, his conscience and consideration for others, his ability to love and be loved. Then they send the body to extinction, already deprived of the soul. And they threaten the lives and the happiness of others— whether parents, lovers, or friends. They present as clear a case as a "classical" liberal could wish for substances whose use should be a crime.

But this is not the message Nanny relays. Drugs are associated with the life-style of which Nanny approves: transgressive, pleasure seeking, contemptuous of stable relationships and objective moral codes. Nanny approves of this life-style because it is subversive of those institutions—marriage, family, local societies, and other "little platoons"—that compete with the state for our loyalties. Where transgression rules, so does the state. Hence in the eyes of the state, the addict is at worst an object of compassion, at best a heroic defender of a valid way of life. His habit is an escape from the intolerable conventions of bourgeois society, and if he lives in a dream world of his own, isn't that his right, in a society that provides no better, or more real, alternative?

Such is the message that is gathering strength among the members of the British political establishment and that corresponds to the emerging reality of our schools. Relentless propaganda against smoking tobacco goes hand in hand with an easy toleration of those who smoke pot, even when they smoke it on the playground. Tobacco users are seeking initiation into the old sexual roles and are therefore subjects of obloquy; marijuana users are preparing themselves for the new, vague, omnisexual life-style, in which real relationships dissolve in a cloud of easy and promiscuous affection. Hence their habit has gained acceptance as no one's business but their own. As far as the health campaigners are concerned, there is no problem. They have averted their eyes, just as they have averted their eyes from the damage done by other habits associated with the youth culture: rock music, for example, which causes widespread deafness; or strobe lights, which cause disorientation of the brain and even epileptic fits.

All this would matter less if the habit of legislation did not encourage a false sense of security. By constantly intervening to save the citizen from self-imposed risk, the legislature creates the impression that everything else is harmless. The citizen need take no care over what he does, so long as he respects the surgeon general's warning and buys in the official market. The state is there to guarantee a risk-free life, and if a risk is not acknowledged by the state, then it doesn't exist. If Nanny sees no harm in pornography or 12-hour doses of television each day or promiscuous but protected sex, then there is no harm in them. Gradually the impression grows that the only risks facing the ordinary citizen are those associated with the old-fashioned life-style glamorized in the Marlboro ads.

Hence the state, by taking charge of risk, massively exposes us to it. The real risks are not those that the state forbids but those that it fosters through its ethos of political correctness. These permitted risks are permitted because it is forbidden to forbid them. To condemn them would be to "marginalize" some valid "alternative" and therefore to interfere with some newly invented or discovered "right." Hence the risks of promiscuity, drug taking, and other habits that short-circuit the rite of passage into adult life are not openly discussed. These practices belong to a culture that has grown under state protection and that is at war with traditional values.

In this way, by being over-protective of the individual, the state undermines society. Almost the entire energy of the health campaigners is devoted to forbidding habits that pose no conceivable social threat, while permitting others that promise social fragmentation. School notice boards now forbid virtually nothing that the young would like to do, save smoking. Their messages about sex, precisely because they are framed exclusively in the language of hygiene, are read as permissions, and their warnings about drugs are noticeably more muted than those relating to tobacco. I am reminded of the scene in *Catch-22* when the hero, going aft to the tail gunner and finding him slumped and bleeding, congratulates himself on the perfect dressing that he applies to the visible wound, only to see a moment later the gunner's guts sliding out from elsewhere.

Of course, a responsible parent would try to prevent his children from smoking. But when the parent takes responsibility, he sees health as part of a larger goal: the long-term fulfillment of his child. This is why it is better, not merely for society but for the individual, too, if education in the taking of risks is left to parents and not appropriated by the state. Wise parents know that their children must grow up and take their place in the community. The child will need nothing so much as the love and trust of others, and these benefits can't be won without a long process of character building and moral education. No sensible parents believe that the future well-being of their child depends entirely on the chemicals that he ingests, or that they can guarantee his happiness merely by ensuring that his bodily functions conform to the surgeon general's requirements.

By attending to the moral and spiritual health of their offspring mothers and fathers provide a far better guarantee of longevity than Nanny can offer. As a parent, it seems to me far more important to keep my children away from television than from "environmental tobacco smoke" and far more important to take them to church than to show them the use of a condom. This makes me a misfit, from the point of view of our official culture. But it is part of what makes me fit into the real culture that surrounds me, the culture that Nanny is trying to kill.

Moreover, those risks against which Nanny warns us are also, in a measure, good for us. It is good that children are surrounded by activities that are permitted but disapproved. For they have to learn to make choices and to know that something may be permitted by the law, and even encouraged by the state, despite being morally wrong. Smoking presents us with an easy apprenticeship in interdiction: a way of showing to a child that something that is not a crime nevertheless ought to be avoided. It belongs, with junk food, pop music, and television, to the world of daily temptations, which is the practice-ground for self-control.

Furthermore there are other risks that a child ought to be encouraged to take, despite the fact that Nanny doesn't like them. Children should not be officiously protected from every kind of danger. Just as their immune systems benefit from contact with hostile bacteria, so do their characters benefit from physical risk. In England, it is now almost impossible for a teacher to lead his class on an expedition, to camp out with his pupils on the moors, or to take them to sea in a boat. All such things occur in the gray area between enterprise and crime, where it is foolhardy for a teacher to trespass. In the world that Nanny is now creating, children encounter danger only on the TV screen, where it is the object of unhealthy and sadistic fantasies, rather than the occasion for cool-headed thinking and resourceful courage.

But this brings us to the crux. Underlying Nanny's attempts to police our way of life is an obsession with the body and its destiny and a refusal to acknowledge that human life is lived, when properly lived, on another plane. You must not smoke, because it harms your body, Nanny asserts (though smoking still leaves the soul in charge and the moral sense undamaged); whereas the harm drugs cause is less important, since drug taking liberates the body. The ecstasy of drugs is a kind of displacement of the soul—a rising up of the body, aided by a physical substance, to usurp the soul's dominion. Similarly, the damage done in the name of sex is done at the body's behest, and by way of overcoming the domain of moral scruples; it is damage done on the body's behalf and in the name of liberation. In all these ways, Nanny promotes the demoralization of the human being and his reconstitution as a purely physical, purely animal thing. Hence Nanny is unable by her very nature to notice that health is promoted far more effectively by a sober, righteous, and godly life than by a fat-free, smoke-free regimen.

But what, in a secular age, should we oppose to Nanny's demoralized vision? It is because people are at a loss for an answer to this question that they capitulate so readily before laws that forbid them to eat sushi, to smoke in public, or to bring up their children as their conscience suggests. In an age when the highest authority is the doctor, and when the state borrows the doctor's white coat, people find themselves insensibly drawn into the vision of themselves as farmyard animals, herded together for their own good.

The answer, it seems to me, is not to deny that we are animals but to recognize that we are animals of a special kind—animals that make themselves by their cooperative efforts into free and spiritual beings. We live by telling our own story, and that story can either ennoble us or demean us. We are ennobled when we learn to coexist with the body on terms, when we subordinate the body's needs to our true loves and loyalties, when we expose it to whatever risks are required by life among friends and neighbors, and when we prevent it from darkening or eclipsing our emotions. No other life is worth living, even if Nanny recommends it. And it is part of the good life that we should not "strive officiously to stay alive," but should recognize the grace of timely death—a death that does not come so late that no one regrets it.

73

"The Case for More Regulation"

NURITH C. AIZENMAN

In March of 1996, all 1,700 residents of Weyauwega, Wisconsin skipped town for three weeks—involuntarily. The reason for their impromptu spring break: an 81-car train carrying propane and sodium hydroxide derailed and exploded just outside the city center, creating a toxic fire so dangerous the entire community had to be evacuated while authorities struggled to contain it. But the Weyauwegans should consider themselves lucky. In Chicago this past August [1997], 19 people were treated for chemical exposure at area hospitals after the hose on a truck pumping sulfur trioxide into a holding tank broke and released a 50-foot-high lethal cloud. And in California several years earlier, 700 people fell ill after a tanker-car full of metam sodium plunged into the Sacramento River, killing all water life within 40 miles and contaminating California's largest reservoir.

These events point to a disturbing trend: serious accidents involving the transport of hazardous materials, or "hazmats," on trucks and trains have become an almost daily occurrence. In 1995 alone, there were 12,712 incidents involving hazardous materials released from trucks and 1,330 from rail cars. But what's really remarkable about these cases is that they were not more disastrous. Considering the recent massive increase in the volume of hazardous materials streaming across our nation's highways and railroads, combined with the industry's cavalier attitude towards safety and the government's cross-your-fingers-and-hope-for-the-best approach to regulation, it's a wonder we haven't witnessed a truly devastating catastrophe. Environmentalists warn it's only a matter of time before we're treated to a tragedy on the scale of the 1984 accident in Bhopal, India—where 3,500 people were suffocated in their sleep by a 20-ton cloud of methyl isocyanate seeping from a Union Carbide plant.

That's not to say there haven't been lots of close calls. Last December, the Department of Transportation's Federal Railroad Administration (FRA) discovered that despite the fact that military bombs being carried aboard a Union Pacific train had broken through their containers and were protruding onto the floor of a flat car, the company had allowed the train to travel from Oklahoma to California through several major terminals without taking any corrective action. As one FRA official noted in an internal memo: "[Union Pacific] needs a big time wake up call. . . . The way we see it, if they can't take care of class A explosives, makes you wonder what they are doing with other HM [hazardous materials]."

And there are plenty of other hazardous materials to wonder about. Between 1990 and 1995, hazmat transport by rail increased 27 percent to almost 1.8 million cars a year, each one carrying a payload that makes the lethal cargo aboard ValuJet flight 592 look like a shipment of fire-retardant blankets. Pick your poison: there are toxic-by-inhalation chemicals like chlorine and hydrogen fluoride, which can roll across miles of countryside in ground-hugging clouds that burn your body tissue, fill your lungs with fluid and cause you to literally drown in your own juices. There are explosives like ammonium nitrate—mix that with a little fuel and it's Oklahoma City time. Then, of course, there are your run-of-the-mill flammables, like liquefied petroleum gas, or propane, which comprises the bulk of the roughly four billion tons of hazardous materials hauled across our highways every year, and which, when released, vaporizes into a volatile gas that can ignite into a jet flame if so much as a spark comes near. And finally, there's the mother of all hazmats, nuclear waste, which could become a lot more familiar if the government goes ahead with plans to open a temporary nuclear materials repository in Nevada. By as early as 1999, up to 100,000 shipments of highly radioactive spent fuel from reactors across the country could begin the long journey to the storage site by rail and truck—in containers whose crash worthiness has been tested almost exclusively through computer simulations. With all these goodies making their way from sea to shining sea, perhaps it's not surprising that even some chemical company executives are reaching for their gas masks. "It scares the living daylights out of me," confides one former DuPont official.

Dying for a Job

The ugly reality of our industrial advances and booming economy is that we need—or at least want—more products made from dangerous substances. Unless we drastically change our consumption habits, one way or another these hazardous materials are going to have to be lugged around the country. But surely our government and industries have taken steps to ensure that the vehicles hauling these toxins are piloted by specially trained experts—crack professionals, alert and ready for the worst, right? Try zombified novices, bleary-eyed and poorly prepared.

To start with, hazardous material transporters are dangerously overworked. At the railroads, the rise in hazardous shipments has been accompanied by large scale downsizing According to a study by an environmental group called The Good Neighbor Project, between 1985 and 1995, Union Pacific, by far the nation's largest hazmat rail carrier, doubled the ratio of its car shipments to workers from 85:1 to 170:1. Freight trains once served by teams of 5 or 6 people are now left in the hands of one engineer and a conductor. This duo is expected to work for up to 12 hours, take 8 hours off (for eating, sleeping, bill paying, etc.), then come back for more. The length of their shifts is bad enough: It's hard to imagine staying focused on your favorite TV show for 12 hours straight, let alone an endless stretch of railroad track—especially as viewed from an overheated, deafeningly loud engine cabin. But to make matters worse, rail workers are generally scheduled without regard to the basic requirements of a normal sleep cycle. Thus an engineer who is happily tucked in bed at 3 A.M. on one morning, is just as likely to find himself at the head of a 70-car train at 3 A.M. on the next—having received no more than two hours advance notice. "I've been forced to go out when I was so exhausted I hallucinated," recalls one Norfolk Southern engineer; "I've seen things that weren't there, almost gone past signals I thought were one color when they were another."

Maybe that's what happened to the engineer of a Union Pacific train who was killed in July after he sped past a rail stop sign near Rossville, Kansas, and collided with an oncoming train. Hazardous materials aboard his train were burned in the crash, and Rossville's residents had to be evacuated. The collision was one of three fatal Union Pacific accidents since June that finally prompted the Federal Railroad Administration to launch an 80-man inspection of the rail company—the most extensive investigation in the agency's history. After a week of probing, the FRA declared itself shocked, shocked, to discover that everyone from dispatchers, to engineers, to yard workers, were being "worked to the bone." Yet for years rail workers' unions have complained about such problems; last spring the Brotherhood of Locomotive Engineers even tried to shut Union Pacific down with a strike over safety, but they were halted by a court order. Still, according to the FRA's spokesman Jim Gower, the FRA "wasn't really aware of the vastness of the problem."

But this was only the tip of the iceberg. The FRA also found that Union Pacific routinely violates the already onerous 12-hour work limit —often keeping workers on duty for up to 17 hours at a stretch. Topping it all off, the agency determined that the training many workers receive is grossly inadequate and in some cases nonexistent—with some employees ordered to operate sophisticated equipment they've never been taught to use.

Among the things a good training program might emphasize would be the importance of watching for smaller problems that could be the harbinger of bigger ones. But even if they were taught to do so, rail workers might be disinclined to report any trouble they find. Many rail companies reward managers with a cash bonus tied [to] the safety record of the track under the manager's jurisdiction. CSX Transportation, for instance, has awarded a total of $4.5 million in company stock since 1995 under its "Take Stock in Safety" program. Sounds like a great incentive system, but the result, according to United Transportation Union's legislative director, J.M. Brunkenhoefer, is that many middle managers strongly discourage the rail workers they supervise from reporting accidents—threatening potential whistle blowers with either layoffs or "investigations" into the whistle blower's responsibility.

Of course, the railroads sometimes run into pesky FRA rules requiring that certain types of accidents be reported, for instance those in which a rail worker is injured seriously. No problem—the companies simply send workers to the doctor with a special note, like one from CSX that asks that "whenever possible, use of equally prudent NON-REPORT-ABLE treatment is encouraged in order to minimize reporting of less significant minor injuries to the Federal Railroad Administration" Among the "reportable" treatments doctors are urged to avoid: "issuing a prescription, injections, closing a wound with sutures, butterfly, staple or steristrip, application of immobilizing cast, sling or splint, . . . [and] restriction of employee's work activity" To be sure, the letter assures doctors that "appropriate treatment should be based upon your professional medical judgment;" but the message from CSX management to the doctor and, more importantly, to its employees couldn't be more blunt: Don't Rock the Boat.

That message was apparently heard loud and dear by the team aboard a CSX train that sideswiped an Amtrak passenger car and caused a derailment near Arlington, Va., this past July. Twice during the train's two-hour journey, crews on passing trains radioed the CSX crew with the warning that one of its flatcars was leaning precariously. Nonetheless, the crew ignored the warning and continued forward because a CSX supervisor had already inspected the car and insisted there was no danger.

Highway to Hell

But intimidated, badly trained and dog-tired as they may be, rail workers are still the envy of truckers. That's because while truckers can only be legally required to drive a mere 10 hours a day, trucking companies routinely—and knowingly—put them on schedules that make a mockery of the law. Consider the timetable of 23-year-old Peter Conway, the driver of a semitrailer loaded with 9,200 gallons of propane headed east on I-287 through New York state in July of 1994. Some time earlier, Conway's truck had been side-lined by a breakdown for 10 hours. Like most truckers, he was being paid by the mile as opposed to the hour, so after his rig was fixed, Conway faced a Hobson's choice: make up the lost time or take a financial hit. He opted to press on. On July 27, Conway's truck drifted off the left shoulder of the highway near White Plains and struck the column of an overpass. The propane leaking from his truck's damaged tank ignited—propelling the container 300 feet through the air onto a nearby house, which was quickly engulfed in flames. Conway was killed, and 23 others were injured. Although Conway had falsified the log book in which he was legally required to enter his work time, federal investigators were able to determine that he had been driving almost continuously for over 35 hours. Their unsurprising conclusion: Conway had dozed off at the wheel.

He's certainly not the first, nor the last, to have done so. A recent government study found that up to 40 percent of truck crashes were probably caused by fatigue. Another study determined that at least 58 percent of truckers had violated hours-of-service rules. In fact, log books are so routinely doctored that truckers have taken to calling them "comic books."

But even if he's awake, there's no guarantee the driver of that monster hazmat truck roaring up behind you on the highway is even marginally competent—or that his rig is remotely safe. Take the case of Willis Curry, a Washington D.C. trucker who, since 1988, has managed to amass 31 citations for such traffic violations as speeding, carrying overweight loads, disobeying red lights and ignoring railroad cross warnings. Back in January, the Department of Transportation's Federal Highway Administration (FHWA) informed Curry's employer of his record and he was promptly fired. But the FHWA waited until April to alert D.C. authorities that his license should be revoked. Two months later Curry, still the proud bearer of a D.C. license and now a driver for a local dump truck company, collided with the car of a young mother and her one-year-old son.

Police determined that the brakes on Curry's dump had failed. This should not have come as a surprise. Curry's vehicle gave a whole new meaning to the term "dump" truck. It had been cited for 28 mechanical safety violations in two random inspections last year. And during the first inspection the truck's wiring was so defective that when the brake pedal was pushed the windshield wipers starting going. On both occasions the truck had been ordered off the road for repairs.

But the story doesn't end there. After Curry's accident, no action was taken to investigate the dump's owner, or to revoke Curry's license. It wasn't until ten days later, when Curry made a routine request for a duplicate license, that a city clerk happened to notice his record and confiscated his license. And Curry quickly managed to win it back, with the proviso that he only drive between 4 A.M. and noon on weekdays. At 2 P.M. the very next week, Curry was once again behind the wheel when the brakes on his dump failed a second time, causing the 30-ton truck to veer out of control and roll over onto a car driven by a teenage honor student. The boy was killed instantly. It is small consolation that Curry's truck wasn't carrying anything more dangerous than sand. Next time we may not be so lucky.

It's hard to say which was the greater menace to society, Curry or his truck. And that's not unusual. On the rare occasions when the Department of Transportation does random roadside inspections, nearly one out of every three rigs they pull over is found to be either unsafe, driven by an unsafe trucker, or both.

Danger Zone

Defective equipment is a problem with which rail workers are also all too familiar. A 1995 surprise inspection of a Union Pacific rail yard in Fort Worth, Texas, found that 37 percent of the rail cars there were faulty—over a third of them with brake problems. And according to Union Pacific itself, 12 percent of the 8,000 plus chemical tank cars it inspected last year turned up "exceptions" like poor positioning of the tops on the cars, or mislabeling of their contents. That wasn't news to rail employees; they say it's not uncommon to work on a train with up to eight "sleeper cars" whose contents, hazardous or otherwise, are unknown to them.

* * *

Just as frightening as the trains themselves are the tracks on which they travel. About 85 percent of rail transport occurs over "dark" areas where there is no automated signaling. Instead, engineers must rely on dispatchers to talk them through their journey. Yet, as the FRA recently "discovered," dispatchers are often unfamiliar with the tracks through which they are expected to guide a train—in many cases they haven't even traveled the route once. So perhaps it's not surprising that a June FRA inspection of Union Pacific found that 80 percent of dispatcher orders contained at least one error.

* * *

A Free Ride

But how does the industry get away with it? Where are all those government regulators conservatives are so fond of disparaging? Turns out they're not nearly as meddlesome as the GOP would have you think. A July study by the General Accounting Office (GAO)—which monitors federal agencies for Congress—found that in just one year, the number of safety inspections conducted by the FRA decreased by 23 percent. And between 1992 and 1995 the percentage of railroads inspected for hazardous materials safety by the FRA fell from 34 percent to 21 percent.

* * *

But the FRA maintains there's no cause for alarm; it's all part of a new "cooperative" way of doing business that began under the Clinton administration. The idea is to move away from using violations and civil penalties as the primary means of obtaining compliance with the regulations. Instead, the agency relies on "partnerships" with the railroad companies. If you're wondering what that means, take a look at the way the FRA has responded to the results of its—admittedly laudable—massive investigation of Union Pacific. You might expect that the agency's discovery that rail employees are being dangerously overworked would prompt it to change the rules governing their schedule. How retro! "New regulations are not the answer," the FRA's Gower patiently explains. Instead, the FRA will simply ask Union Pacific to mend its ways: "After all, it's in their own interest." Union Pacific officials agree—pointing out that they're hiring an additional 2,600 employees this year. But just how much relief will those new hires be able to provide for the company's exhausted 54,000-strong work force? Officials like Barry Sweedler at the National Transportation Safety Board (NTSB)—the independent agency responsible for investigating accidents and making recommendations to transportation regulators—think the FRA is being naive. "What you have today is an industry that's willing to accept a certain number of collisions every year," observes Sweedler.

* * *

Many of the FRA-mandated innovations that are actually in use were required by the FRA only after fatal foot-dragging. That was the case with a backup braking system called a "two-way end-of-train device" that allows an engineer to use a radio signal to apply brakes from the back of his train if his locomotive brakes fail. The FRA did not mandate use of the devices on all trains traveling through mountainous terrain until February of 1996—seven years after the NTSB first recommended them, and only after a runaway train had derailed at the bottom of the steep Cajon Pass in California not once, but twice. Similarly, while the FRA has (after over a decade of urging by the NTSB) finally conceded the considerable potential of using satellite-based proximity warning systems to alert engineers, and even apply the brakes, when one train is speeding or about to collide with another, the agency is now merely helping the rail companies run pilot projects—rather than insisting that they install it on a timetable.

* * *

The Department of Transportation's record on hazmat trucking is just as deplorable. As you may have gathered from the case of dump truck driver Willis Curry, enforcement of the law by the Department's Federal Highway Administration is laughable. A March study by the Department's Inspector General—a sort of in-house independent watchdog—found that in 1995, only 2.5 percent of trucking companies were reviewed by the Federal Highway Administration (FHWA) to see if they complied with safety rules. What's more, about two-thirds of the nation's interstate carriers have never been rated for safety. Most alarming, the Inspector General determined that 22 percent of trucking companies with high rates of on-the-road violations and accidents had never been rated for safety, and 42 percent had not been rated in the past two years.

*   *   *

When the FHWA bothers to conduct inspections, it tends to favor the velvet-fist-in-the-velvet-glove approach. According to the Inspector General, FHWA inspectors consistently underreport violations, and low-ball fines. For instance, the penalties for 81 carriers surveyed did not include over half of the major violations found during their inspection. But the FHWA had a ready explanation for this dismal performance: "we're a regulatory agency, not an enforcement agency."

The trucking companies clearly share that impression. To get a sense of how little they fear the FHWA, you need only consider that in the Inspector General's survey, over a third of the companies deemed unsatisfactory by FHWA inspectors had to be inspected and scolded two more times before they cleaned up their act. Moreover—and this is the clincher—most of these delinquent companies were allowed to keep their trucks on the road even while they continued to fail one inspection after another. To cite just one example, a Missouri hazardous materials carrier continued to operate without interruption despite the fact that it had failed two general inspections—and despite the fact that one out of every two of its trucks had to be pulled out of service when stopped for random inspections along the road. It's enough to drive long-time highway safety advocate Gerald Donaldson to distruction. "Words fail me on the extent of the FHWA's ineptness," he sighs.

*   *   *

Among the other possible improvements that could make hazardous materials trucks safer that the Department of Transportation has chosen to ignore: anti-lock brakes, a better internal compartment system to prevent the liquid in tankers from violently sloshing around and causing the truck to roll over, technology to keep the top and bottom ports of tankers from springing a leak when such rollovers do occur; and steel head shields like those used to such great effect on train tank cars. Many of these changes have long been advocated by the National Transportation Safety Board (NTSB) based on its investigation of serious accidents. But, once again, the Department of Transportation simply buries its head in the sand.

Regulation Redeemed

* * *

* * * It's time to re-think the conventional wisdom that regulation is a bad word. In recent years, conservatives have largely succeeded in convincing us that regulators are our number one enemy, strangling businesses with yards of expensive and impractical red tape. And the conservative cause has actually been helped by many liberals—who are quick to defend whatever regulation exists, without bothering to check how well it's working. Meanwhile, the Department of Transportation has all too readily absorbed the mood in Washington, speaking proudly of its new "partnership" with trucking and rail companies, as if having good relations with those industries were the primary goal. It's not. The government's duty is to protect the public—and it is falling seriously short.

Of course, it's not hard to understand why the regulators have lost sight of their mission: Like most of us, they don't enjoy hearing complaints from the people they work with, and no one howls louder than the industries being regulated. But both the government and the public need to start greeting those protests with a hefty grain of salt. From the dangerous overworking of employees, to the appalling condition of their vehicles, to the lack of inspections and penalties for safety violations, to the failure to install new life-saving technologies, the troubles plaguing the transport of hazardous materials by train and truck provide a dramatic illustration of how the real problem can be not too much government regulation, but far too little. If you think this lesson only applies to trucks and trains, just consider what smarter and tougher regulation could have done for the folks aboard ValuJet flight 592 [Improper labeling and packing of oxygen canisters led to the death of all 110 passengers and crew members on this 1996 flight.] And by the way, how do you feel about that hamburger in your freezer?

Discussion Questions

1. Do you agree with Scruton that government tries to insulate individuals too much from risk? Can you think of some examples?

2. Is Scruton right to argue that if government is to have regulation, it should have a broader moral content? He suggests that government chooses to regulate certain things (e.g., tobacco use) because it assuages the moral perspective of those implementing the regulations, but government won't consider regulating other behavior that may have even more serious health consequences. How would you draw the line between what government should and shouldn't be able to regulate?

3. One argument against excessive regulations is that they are a costly way of protecting people against miniscule risk—for example, the remote chance that we might contract cancer from food additives—while ignoring much larger risks, such as reckless driving, suicide, and prescription-drug interactions. What determines the sorts of risk that the public will accept? What determines the risks that we demand protection from?

CHAPTER 15

Government and Society

74

"Growing American Inequality: Sources and Remedies"

GARY BURTLESS

How much, if anything, should the federal government do to promote greater income equality among its citizens? Ignoring the increasing income gap between the richest and poorest Americans, argues Gary Burtless, is a mistake. When more and more Americans see themselves as falling behind, they will show less confidence in political leaders and in government. In addition, income inequalities threaten public health, with larger gaps between rich and poor associated with higher mortality rates and higher incidence of disease. Burtless dismisses the argument that income inequality provides an incentive for the poorest Americans to work harder and earn more, citing evidence that the income of poor Americans has declined in recent years. Public policies that target the working poor—such as the 1986 Tax Reform Act, which eliminated taxes for many low-income Americans and increased the Earned Income Tax Credit—have elevated income levels. But there has been no comparable political support for the "non-working" poor, and critics charge that the EITC program is riddled with fraud. The 1996 welfare reform, moreover, has been particularly harsh, in Burtless's view. To begin the process of bridging the wage gap, he proposes efforts to bring the nonworking poor into the workforce, and publicly subsidized health care to ease the difficulties of poverty and provide the means for individual families to work their way out of poverty.

Over the past two decades the United States has experienced a startling increase in inequality. The incomes of poor Americans shrank and those of the middle class stagnated while the incomes of the richest families continued to grow. The well-being of families up and down the income scale has increased over the past five years, but the average income of the poorest Americans remains well below where it was at the end of the 1970s.

From the end of World War II until the 1970s, the percentage difference in average cash income between well-to-do and middle-class American families generally declined. In the 1980s, the gap began to widen noticeably. Better measurement of rich families' incomes accounts for some of the apparent jump in the early 1990s, but the gap between middle- and high-income families almost certainly increased after 1992. The cash income difference between middle-income and poor families followed a similar trend. After narrowing for several decades after World War II, largely because of increased wages and improved Social Security and welfare benefits for the poor, the gap began widening in the early 1970s. * * * [T]he trend in inequality has not been driven solely by worsening poverty among the poor or by spectacular income gains among the wealthy. It has been produced by growing disparities between Americans at every level of the income ladder.

Soaring inequality has not been confined to the United States. Rich nations around the world have seen inequality grow since the late 1970s. But the jump in income inequality has been particularly rapid in the United States—and it came on top of a higher initial level of inequality.

Should We Care?

Many Americans are not terribly concerned about income inequality or about the need for public policies to temper inequality. Although public opinion polls find that large majorities of residents in five European countries and Japan believe the government should guarantee each citizen a minimum standard of living, only about a quarter of Americans agree. By and large, Americans tend to believe that people bear primary responsibility for supporting themselves. U.S. citizens are also more likely to believe their society offers an equal opportunity for people who work hard to get ahead. Given these views, why should Americans be concerned about mounting inequality?

One reason for concern is that growing income disparities may undermine Americans' sense of social cohesion. Even if they are indifferent about the abstract principle of economic equality, most Americans probably believe in the ideals of political and legal equality. But greater inequality has almost certainly produced wider discrepancies in political influence and legal bargaining power. In 1979 the income of an American at the 95th percentile of the income distribution was three times the median income and thirteen times the income of an American at the 5th percentile. By 1996 an American at the 95th percentile had an income almost four times the median income and twenty-three times the income of the person at the 5th percentile. The growing income gap between rich, middle-class, and poor and its consequences for the distribution of political influence may contribute to Americans' dwindling confidence that their elected officials care very much about the views of ordinary citizens. According to polling experts Karlyn Bowman and Everett Ladd, in 1960 only a quarter of U.S. respondents agreed with the statement, "I don't think public officials care much about what people like me think." By 1996, the share who agreed had climbed to 60 percent.

Inequality may also affect public health. Demographers and public health researchers have found mounting though controversial evidence that greater inequality can boost mortality rates and contribute to poor health. Countries and communities with above-average inequality have higher mortality rates than countries or communities with comparable incomes and poverty rates but lower inequality. According to one public health researcher, low-income Americans have death rates comparable to those in Bangladesh, one of the world's poorest countries, even though absolute incomes, average consumption, and health care spending are much higher among America's poor than they are in Bangladesh. The possible link between public health and inequality may help explain why the United States, one of the world's wealthiest countries, does not have the longest average life span or the lowest infant mortality rate. If the benefits of U.S. income growth after 1979 had been more equally shared, the average health and life spans of Americans, especially poor Americans, might have improved faster than they did.

Defenders of American economic and political institutions correctly point out that inequality plays a crucial role in creating incentives for people to improve their situations through saving, hard work, and additional schooling. They argue that wage and income disparities must sometimes widen to send correct signals to people to save more, work harder, change jobs, or get a better education. In the long run, poor people might enjoy higher absolute incomes in a society where income disparities are permitted to widen than one where law and social convention keep income differentials small. According to this argument, widening inequality is in the best long-term interest of the poor themselves.

For poor people in the United States, however, the theoretical advantages of greater inequality have proved elusive over the past two decades. Their absolute incomes have not improved; they have declined. Their absolute incomes do not exceed those of low-income residents in countries with less inequality; typically they are lower than those of people in a comparable position in other rich countries. The efficiency advantages, if any, of growing U.S. inequality have not been enjoyed by the poor, at least so far. They have flowed to people much further up the income scale.

Why Has Inequality Increased?

Researchers on income inequality agree on two key facts. Greater family income inequality is closely connected to wider disparities in worker pay—disparities that in turn are associated with rising pay premiums for education, job experience, and occupational skills. In addition, shifts in family composition, specifically the continuing growth of single-parent families and the shrinking fraction of married-couple families, have reinforced the effects of widening wage inequality.

How much of the increase in family income inequality is attributable to rising wage disparities? Both male and female workers saw hourly pay disparities increase over the past two decades, though on average men saw their real earnings fall, while women got a raise. The hourly wage of workers at the 10th percentile fell 16 percent between 1979 and 1997. At the upper end of the pay ladder, wages at the 90th percentile rose 2 percent for men and 24 percent for women. Changes in annual earnings mirrored this pattern. Workers at the bottom of the pay scale saw their yearly labor incomes sink while workers at the top saw their annual pay increase. The gains were especially large among highly paid women.

One way to assess the impact of rising wage disparities on overall income inequality is to calculate how much overall inequality would have changed if wage disparities had remained unchanged. My calculation, using a standard statistical measure of income inequality known as the Gini coefficient, suggests that if male annual earnings disparities had remained unchanged between 1979 and 1996, personal income inequality would have increased about 72 percent of the actual jump. This means that the increase in men's earnings inequality explains about 28 percent of the overall increase in inequality. A similar calculation implies that despite the large increase in pay disparities among women, only about 5 percent of the increase in income inequality can be explained by growing earnings disparities among women. We can combine these two calculations to see what would have happened if male and female earnings inequality had both remained constant after 1979. This third set of calculations suggests that two-thirds of the increase in personal income inequality would have occurred, even without a change in pay disparities. An implication of this finding is that just one-third of the increase in personal income inequality was due to the growth of male and female earnings disparities. Most of the growth was due to some other set of factors.

One factor was the changing American household. In 1979, 74 percent of adults and children lived in married-couple households. By 1996, this share had fallen to 65 percent. Inequality and the incidence of poverty are much lower in married-couple households than in single-adult households. If the percentage of Americans living in married-couple families had remained unchanged after 1979, about one-fifth of the 1979–96 jump in inequality would have been avoided.

Another trend has pushed up income disparities. Women who are married to high-income husbands are increasingly likely to hold year-round jobs and earn high incomes themselves. The increased correlation between husbands' and wives' earnings has widened the income gap between affluent dual-earner families and the rest of the population. If the husband-wife earnings correlation had remained unchanged, about one-eighth of the rise in overall inequality since 1979 would have been avoided. In other words, roughly 13 percent of the increase in income inequality can be traced to the growing correlation between husbands' and wives' earned income.

Policy Response

Though critics of U.S. social policy often overlook the fact, policymakers have not stood still in the face of momentous changes in the income distribution. The direction of policy has shifted noticeably since the early 1980s.

The shift began under President Reagan, who attempted to scale back and reorient welfare programs targeted on the working-age poor. His goal was to make the programs less attractive to potential applicants by cutting benefits or making benefits harder to get. One important policy change, later reversed, was to scale back payments to poor families with a working adult. Reagan thought welfare benefits should be focused on the nonworking poor. He expected working adults to support themselves.

The steep decline in hourly wages of low-skill workers made this view increasingly untenable. Measured in inflation-adjusted dollars, the minimum wage fell more than 30 percent over the 1980s, and wages paid to unskilled young men fell almost as fast. Few breadwinners can support families on wages of $5 or $6 an hour.

Congress and the president responded by reforming tax policy toward low-income families and broadening eligibility for publicly financed health benefits. The Tax Reform Act of 1986 removed millions of low-income Americans from the income tax rolls and boosted the tax rebates low-income workers receive under the Earned Income Tax Credit. The EITC was further liberalized in 1990 and 1993, greatly increasing the credits flowing to low-income breadwinners and their children. Spending on the credit increased elevenfold in the decade after 1986, reaching more than $21 billion by 1996. The credit, payable to breadwinners even if they owe no federal income taxes, has raised the incomes of millions of families with extremely low earnings.

The EITC is the most distinctive American policy innovation on behalf of the working poor, and several European countries may eventually adopt a variant of it. While most cash assistance goes to people who do not work, the EITC goes only to low-income people who do work. In 1997 the credit provided as much as $3,656 to a breadwinner with two or more dependents. For a parent working full time in a minimum-wage job, the EITC can increase net earnings nearly 40 percent.

The idea behind the credit is to encourage work by increasing the incomes available to low-wage breadwinners who have dependent children. Instead of shrinking as a recipient's earnings grow, the credit rises, at least up to a limit. At low earnings levels the credit increases by 34¢ or 40¢ for each extra dollar earned. Most labor economists who have examined the credit conclude that it has contributed to the sudden and sizable increase in job holding among unmarried mothers.

Congress has also liberalized the eligibility requirements for Medicaid health insurance to include a broad population of low-income children with working parents. Until the late 1980s, working-age families with children were usually eligible for health protection only if the families were collecting public assistance. Children typically lost their eligibility for free health insurance when the family breadwinner returned to work. The Medicaid liberalizations of the late 1980s and early 1990s meant that many children were enrolled in the program even if their parents had modest earnings and were not collecting public assistance.

Some state governments have established new programs to provide subsidized health insurance to members of working-poor families, including the adult breadwinners. Congress passed legislation in 1997 offering states generous federal subsidies to establish or enlarge health insurance programs for the working poor and near-poor.

As U.S. policy has expanded tax and health benefits for the working poor, state and federal policymakers have slashed cash assistance to the nonworking poor. General assistance, which provides cash aid to childless adults, has been scaled back or eliminated in several states. Aid to Families with Dependent Children was eliminated in 1996 and replaced with Temporary Assistance to Needy Families (TANF). The new federal program pressures all states to curtail cash benefits to poor parents who are capable of working. The head of each family on welfare is required to work within two years after assistance payments begin. Work-hour requirements are stringent, and states face increasingly harsh penalties for failing to meet them. The law stipulates that the great majority of families may receive benefits for no longer than five years and permits states to impose even shorter time limits. Over a dozen states have already done so.

The new welfare law—and the new state welfare policies that preceded it—helped produce an unprecedented drop in the nation's child welfare rolls. Since peaking in 1994, the number of families collecting public assistance for children has dropped more than 2 million, or 40 percent.

In sum, U.S. policy has become much less generous to the nonworking (but working-age) poor, while it has become much more generous to working-poor adults with children. For many low-wage breadwinners with children, the recent policy changes—the increased generosity of the EITC, Medicaid, state-supported health plans, and child care subsidies —have offset the loss of potential earnings due to shrinking hourly wages.

The reforms are having other economic effects. Poor breadwinners with children have been induced to enter the work force—and stay there. Their entry contributes to the downward pressure on the wages of the least skilled. In effect, public subsidies to the working poor and cuts in welfare benefits to the nonworking poor have helped keep employers' costs low and thus helped fuel employers' creation of poorly paid jobs.

Future Directions

U.S. policies toward low-income, working-age families are not so callous that struggling families have been left wholly on their own to cope with declining wages. But they are not so generous that poor, working-age Americans have shared equally in the prosperity of the past two decades.

Different policies, such as those adopted in Western Europe, would have yielded different results. Some differences, including lower poverty rates and higher wages, make Western Europe a more pleasant place to live, especially for the poor. But others, including high unemployment, are unwelcome. It is not obvious that most Americans, even liberals, would prefer the European approach or approve the policies needed to achieve it.

While the current U.S. policy mix broadly reflects the preferences of U.S. voters, it is haphazard and fails to reach some of those who most need help. Two new policies could aid working-age people who have suffered the worst cuts in hourly pay. The first would assure some of the long-term unemployed a job at a modest wage. The second would make work subsidies more uniformly available and would provide them in a form that most voters approve.

Because public assistance to the nonworking but able-bodied poor is being drastically curtailed, it makes sense to assure at least some poor adults that they will be able to find jobs at a modest wage, however bad the local job market. In some cases this may involve creating publicly subsidized jobs that pay a little less than the minimum wage. It seems particularly important to extend this offer to parents who face the loss of cash public assistance. If voters and policymakers want unskilled parents to begin supporting themselves through jobs, they should assure these parents that some jobs will be available, at least eventually, even when unemployment is high.

For poorly paid breadwinners, it is essential to improve the rewards from working. One possibility is to make a basic package of subsidized health insurance available to all children and young adults. Many Americans regard health insurance for children as a fair and acceptable way to help those in need.

Most health insurance for children is either publicly subsidized through Medicaid or privately provided through employer health plans. When insurance is financed by employers, most of the cost to employers shows up as lower money wages paid to workers. By publicly assuming some or all of the cost of paying for a basic health package for children, we could push employers to boost the wages they pay to insured workers who have child dependents. Such a move would have a greater impact on the pay of low-wage workers, for whom health insurance represents a big fraction of compensation, than on the pay of high-wage workers.

About 15 percent of all children (and nearly a quarter of poor children) have no health insurance. For these children and their working parents, publicly subsidized child health insurance would directly improve well-being and reduce out-of-pocket spending on medical care. It would also greatly increase the reward to work. Parents who do not work qualify for free medical insurance for themselves and for their children under Medicaid. Some lose this insurance when they accept a job that pays modest but above-poverty-level wages. A public health insurance package for all children would reduce or eliminate this penalty for accepting a job.

American economic progress over the past two decades has been quite uneven. Families and workers at the top of the economic ladder have enjoyed rising incomes. Families in the middle have made much smaller income gains. Workers at the bottom have suffered a sharp erosion in their relative income position. For some low-income workers, new public policies have helped offset the loss of wages with larger earnings supplements and better health insurance. But many low-wage workers have not benefited from these policies. Humane public policy should try to assure that the most vulnerable Americans share at least modestly in the nation's prosperity.

DISCUSSION QUESTIONS

1. According to the AFL-CIO, the average pay of working Americans grew by 68 percent over a recent twenty-year period. The pay of an average major-company CEO, by contrast, grew by 1,600 percent during the same period, and was more than 420 times higher than the wage of an average worker. These statistics seem to confirm Burtless's assessment that any "efficiency advantages . . . of growing U.S. inequality . . . have flowed to people much further up the

income scale." Similarly, people often bemoan the fact that a top movie or sports star will earn in one movie or one season more than a teacher or nurse might earn in a lifetime. Are these differences in income simply the sign of a highly competitive free-market economy? Should government be concerned with these differentials? If so, what kind of government policy might address the concern?

2. To some, "reducing wage inequalities" is simply another way of saying "income redistribution." How would a policy geared toward reducing wage inequalities affect the economic incentives faced by individuals? Might we reduce the incentive for people to work hard, invest in their education, and take risks?

75

"Objections to These Unions"

Jonathan Rauch

One of the most controversial and politically significant issues in the past few years is same-sex marriage. Jonathan Rauch is less interested in the electoral impact of the same-sex marriage issue than in trying to understand why people are opposed to this form of marriage. He suggests two reasons: the simple anti-homosexual position and the not-so-simple view based on tradition. The latter is rooted in the gut-level feeling that marriage between two men or two women is simply wrong because marriage has always been between a man and a woman: no law can change this basic institution because it has roots that are deeper and older than any government or law. Rauch situates this argument within the political thought of F. A. Hayek, one of the great conservative thinkers of the twentieth century. Hayek warns that changing traditions and customs may lead to social chaos. This is precisely one of the arguments made against same-sex marriage: it will undermine the institution of marriage. Rauch replies that other changes have had a far greater impact on undermining the institution of marriage, such as allowing women to own property, the abolition of arranged marriages, legalized contraception, and "no-fault" divorce law. While recognizing the legitimacy of the concerns about same-sex marriage, Rauch concludes that the fears of its negative impact are overstated and the benefits of same-sex marriage for gays and lesbians outweigh the costs for heterosexuals.

There are only two objections to same-sex marriage that are intellectually honest and internally consistent. One is the simple anti-gay position: "It is the law's job to stigmatize and disadvantage homosexuals, and the marriage ban is a means to that end." The other is the argument from tradition—which turns out, on inspection, not to be so simple.

Many Americans may agree that there are plausible, even compelling, reasons to allow same-sex marriage, and that many of the objections to such unions are overwrought, unfair, or misguided. And yet they draw back. They have reservations that are hard to pin down but that seem not a whit less powerful for that. They may cite religion or culture, but the roots of their misgivings go even deeper. Press them, and they might say something like this:

"I understand how hard it must be to live a marriageless life, or at least I try to understand. I see that some of the objections to same-sex marriage are more about excluding gays than about defending marriage.

Believe me, I am no homophobe; I want gay people to have joy and comfort. I respect their relationships and their love, even if they are not what I would want for myself.

"But look. No matter how I come at this question, I keep bumping into the same wall. For the entire history of civilization, marriage has been between men and women. In every religion, every culture, every society—maybe with some minor and rare exceptions, none of them part of our own heritage—marriage has been reserved for the union of male and female. All the words in the world cannot change that. Same-sex marriage would not be an incremental tweak but a radical reform, a break with all of Western history.

"I'm sorry. I am not prepared to take that step, not when we are talking about civilization's bedrock institution. I don't know that I can even give you good reasons. It is just that what you are asking for is too much."

Perhaps it doesn't matter what marriage is for, or perhaps we can't know exactly what marriage is for. Perhaps it is enough simply to say that marriage is as it is, and you can't just make it something else. I call this the Hayekian argument, for Friedrich August von Hayek, one of the 20th century's great economists and philosophers.

Hayek the Conservative?

Hayek—Austrian by birth, British by adoption, winner of the 1974 Nobel Memorial Prize in Economic Sciences—is generally known as one of the leading theoreticians of free market economics and, more broadly, of libertarian (he always said "liberal") social thought. He was eloquent in his defense of the dynamic change that markets bring, but many people are less aware of a deeply traditionalist, conservative strand in his thinking, a strand that traces its lineage back at least to Edmund Burke, the 18th-century English philosopher and politician. Burke famously poured scorn on the French Revolution and its claims to be inventing a new and enlightened social order. The attempt to reinvent society on abstract principles would result not in Utopia, he contended, but in tyranny. For Burke, the existing order might be flawed, even in some respects evil, but it had an organic sense to it; throwing the whole system out the window would bring greater flaws and larger evils.

Outside Britain and America, few people listened. The French Revolution inspired generations of reformers to propose their own Utopian social experiments. Communism was one such, fascism another; today, radical Islamism (the political philosophy, not the religion) is yet one more. "The attempt to make heaven on earth invariably produces hell," wrote Karl Popper, another great Austrian-British philosopher, in 1945, when the totalitarian night looked darkest. He and Hayek came of age in the same intellectual climate, when not only Marxists and fascists but many mainstream Western intellectuals took for granted that a handful of smart people could make better social decisions than could chaotic markets, blind traditions, or crude majorities.

It was in opposition to this "fatal conceit," as he called it, that Hayek organized much of his career. He vigorously argued the case for the dynamism and "spontaneous order" of free markets, but he asserted just as vigorously that the dynamism and freedom of constant change were possible only within a restraining framework of rules and customs and institutions that, for the most part, do not change, or change at a speed they themselves set. No expert or political leader can possibly have enough knowledge to get up every morning and order the world from scratch; decide whether to wear clothing, which side of the street to drive on, what counts as mine and what as yours. "Every man growing up in a given culture will find in himself rules, or may discover that he acts in accordance with rules and will similarly recognize the actions of others as conforming or not conforming to various rules," Hayek wrote in *Law, Legislation, and Liberty*. The rules, he added, are not necessarily innate or unchangeable, but "they are part of a cultural heritage which is likely to be fairly constant, especially so long as they are not articulated in words and therefore also are not discussed or consciously examined."

Tradition Over Reason

Hayek the economist is famous for the insight that, in a market system, the prices generated by impersonal forces may not make sense from any one person's point of view, but they encode far more economic information than even the cleverest person or the most powerful computer could ever hope to organize. In a similar fashion, Hayek the social philosopher wrote that human societies' complicated web of culture, traditions, and institutions embodies far more cultural knowledge than anyone person could master. Like prices, the customs generated by societies over time may seem irrational or arbitrary. But the very fact that these customs have evolved and survived to come down to us implies that a practical logic may be embedded in them that might not be apparent from even a sophisticated analysis. And the web of custom cannot be torn apart and reordered at will, because once its internal logic is violated it may fall apart.

It was on this point that Hayek was particularly outspoken: Intellectuals and visionaries who seek to deconstruct and rationally rebuild social traditions will produce not a better order but chaos. In his 1952 book *The Counter-Revolution of Science: Studies in the Abuse of Reason*, Hayek made a statement that demands to be quoted in full and read at least twice:

> It may indeed prove to be far the most difficult and not the least important task for human reason rationally to comprehend its own limitations. It is essential for the growth of reason that as individuals we should bow to forces and obey principles which we cannot hope fully to understand, yet on which

the advance and even the preservation of civilization depends. Historically this has been achieved by the influence of the various religious creeds and by traditions and superstitions which made man submit to those forces by an appeal to his emotions rather than to his reason. The most dangerous stage in the growth of civilization may well be that in which man has come to regard all these beliefs as superstitions and refuses to accept or to submit to anything which he does not rationally understand. The rationalist whose reason is not sufficient to teach him those limitations of the powers of conscious reason, and who despises all the institutions and customs which have not been consciously designed, would thus become the destroyer of the civilization built upon them. This may well prove a hurdle which man will repeatedly reach, only to be thrown back into barbarism.

For secular intellectuals who are unhappy with the evolved framework of marriage and who are excluded from it—in other words, for people like me—the Hayekian argument is very challenging. The age-old stigmas attached to illegitimacy and out-of-wedlock pregnancy were crude and unfair to women and children. On the male side, shotgun marriages were coercive and intrusive and often made poor matches. The shame associated with divorce seemed to make no sense at all. But when modern societies abolished the stigmas on illegitimacy, divorce, and all the rest, whole portions of the social structure just caved in.

Not long ago I had dinner with a friend who is a devout Christian. He has a heart of gold, knows and likes gay people, and has warmed to the idea of civil unions. But when I asked him about gay marriage, he replied with a firm no. I asked if he imagined there was anything I could say that might budge him. He thought for a moment and then said no again. Why? Because, he said, male-female marriage is a sacrament from God. It predates the Constitution and every other law of man. We could not, in that sense, change it even if we wanted to. I asked if it might alter his conclusion to reflect that legal marriage is a secular institution, that the separation of church and state requires us to distinguish God's law from civil law, and that we must refrain from using law to impose one group's religious precepts on the rest of society. He shook his head. No, he said. This is bigger than that.

I felt he had not answered my argument. His God is not mine, and in a secular country, law can and should be influenced by religious teachings but must not enforce them. Yet in a deeper way, it was I who had not answered his argument. No doubt the government has the right to set the law of marriage without kowtowing to, say, the Vatican. But that does not make it wise for the government to disregard the centuries of tradition—of accumulated social knowledge—that the teachings of the world's great religions embody. None of those religions sanctions same-sex marriage.

My friend understood the church-state distinction perfectly well. He was saying there are traditions and traditions. Male-female marriage is one of the most hallowed. Whether you call it a sacrament from God or part of Western civilization's cultural DNA, you are saying essentially the same thing: that for many people a same-sex union, whatever else it may be, can never be a marriage, and that no judge or legislature can change this fact.

Here the advocates of same-sex marriage face peril coming from two directions. On the one side, the Hayekian argument warns of unintended and perhaps grave social consequences if, thinking we're smarter than our customs, we decide to rearrange the core elements of marriage. The current rules for marriage may not be the best ones, and they may even be unfair. But they are all we have, and you cannot reengineer the formula without causing unforeseen results, possibly including the implosion of the institution itself. On the other side, political realism warns that we could do serious damage to the legitimacy of marital law if we rewrote it with disregard for what a large share of Americans recognize as marriage.

If some state passed a law allowing you to marry a Volkswagen, the result would be to make a joke of the law. Certainly legal gay marriage would not seem so silly, but people who found it offensive or illegitimate might just ignore it or, in effect, boycott it. Civil and social marriage would fall out of step. That might not be the end of the world—the vast majority of marriages would be just as they were before—but it could not do marriage, or the law any good either. In such an environment, same-sex marriage would offer little beyond legal arrangements that could be provided just as well through civil unions, and it would come at a price in diminished respect for the law.

Call those, then, the problem of unintended consequences and the problem of legitimacy. They are the toughest problems same-sex marriage has to contend with. But they are not intractable.

The Decoy of Traditional Marriage

The Hayekian position really comes in two quite different versions, one much more sweeping than the other. In its strong version, the Hayekian argument implies that no reforms of longstanding institutions or customs should ever be undertaken, because any legal or political meddling would interfere with the natural evolution of social mores. One would thus have had to say, a century and a half ago, that slavery should not be abolished, because it was customary in almost all human societies. More recently, one would have had to say that the federal government was wrong to step in and end racial segregation instead of letting it evolve at its own pace.

Obviously, neither Hayek nor any reputable follower of his would defend every cultural practice simply on the grounds that it must exist for a reason. Hayekians would point out that slavery violated a fundamental tenet of justice and was intolerably cruel. In calling for slavery's abolition, they would do what they must do to be human: They would establish a moral standpoint from which to judge social rules and reforms. They thus would acknowledge that sometimes society must make changes in the name of fairness or decency, even if there are bound to be hidden costs.

If the ban on same-sex marriage were only mildly unfair or if the costs of lifting it were certain to be catastrophic, then the ban could stand on Hayekian grounds. But if there is any social policy today that has a claim to being scaldingly inhumane, it is the ban on gay marriage. Marriage, after all, is the most fundamental institution of society and, for most people, an indispensable element of the pursuit of happiness. For the same reason that tinkering with marriage should not be undertaken lightly (marriage is important to personal and social well-being), barring a whole class of people from marrying imposes an extraordinary deprivation. Not so long ago, it was illegal in certain parts of the United States for blacks to marry whites; no one would call this a trivial disfranchisement. For many years, the champions of women's suffrage were patted on the head and told, "Your rallies and petitions are all very charming, but you don't really need to vote, do you?" It didn't wash. The strong Hayekian argument has traction only against a weak moral claim.

To rule out a moral and emotional claim as powerful as the right to marry for love, saying that bad things might happen is not enough. Bad things always might happen. People predicted that bad things would happen if contraception became legal and widespread, and indeed bad things did happen, but that did not make legalizing contraception the wrong thing to do; and, in any case, good things happened too. Unintended consequences can also be positive, after all.

Besides, by now the traditional understanding of marriage, however you define it, has been tampered with in all kinds of ways, some of them more consequential than gay marriage is likely to be. No-fault divorce dealt a severe blow to, "till death do us part," which was certainly an essential element of the traditional meaning of marriage.

It is hard to think of a bigger affront to tradition than allowing married women to own property independently of their husbands. In *What Is Marriage For?*, her history of marriage, the journalist E. J. Graff quotes a 19th-century New York legislator as saying that allowing wives to own property would affront both God and nature, "degrading the holy bonds of matrimony [and] striking at the root of those divinely ordained principles upon which is built the superstructure of our society." In 1844 a New York legislative committee said that permitting married women to control their own property would lead to "infidelity in the marriage bed, a high rate of divorce, and increased female criminality" and would turn marriage "from its high and holy purpose" into something arranged for "convenience and sensuality." A British parliamentarian denounced the proposal as "contrary not only to the law of England but to the law of God."

Graff assembles other quotations in the same vein, and goes on to add, wryly, "The funny thing, of course, is that those jeremiads were right." Allowing married women to control their economic destinies did indeed open the door to today's high divorce rates; but it also transformed marriage into something less like servitude for women and more in keeping with liberal principles of equality in personhood and citizenship.

An off-the-cuff list of fundamental changes to marriage would include not only divorce and property reform but also the abolition of polygamy, the fading of dowries, the abolition of childhood betrothals, the elimination of parents' right to choose mates for their children or to veto their children's choices, the legalization of interracial marriage, the legalization of contraception, the criminalization of marital rape (an offense that wasn't even recognized until recently), and of course the very concept of civil marriage. Surely it is unfair to say that marriage may be reformed for the sake of anyone and everyone except homosexuals, who must respect the dictates of tradition.

Some people will argue that permitting same-sex marriage would be a more fundamental change than any of the earlier ones. Perhaps so; but equally possible is that we forget today just how unnatural and destabilizing and contrary to the meaning of marriage it once seemed, for example, to put the wife on a par, legally, with the husband. Anyway, even if it is true that gay marriage constitutes a more radical definitional change than earlier innovations, in an important respect it stands out as one of the narrowest of reforms. All the earlier alterations directly affected many or all married couples, whereas same-sex marriage would directly pertain to only a small minority. It isn't certain that allowing same-sex couples to marry would have any noticeable effect on heterosexual marriage at all.

True, you never know what might happen when you tinker with tradition. A catastrophe cannot be ruled out. It is worth bearing in mind, though, that predictions of disaster if open homosexuals are integrated into traditionally straight institutions have a perfect track record: They are always wrong. When openly gay couples began making homes together in suburban neighborhoods, the result was not Sodom on every street corner; when openly gay executives began turning up in corporate jobs, stud collars did not replace neckties. I vividly remember, when I lived in London in 1995, the forecasts of morale and unit cohesion crumbling if open homosexuals were allowed to serve in the British armed forces. But when integration came (under court order), the whole thing turned out to be a nonevent. Again and again, the homosexual threat turns out to be imaginary; straights have far less to fear from gay inclusion than gays do from exclusion.

Jeopardizing Marriage's Universality

So the extreme Hayekian position—never reform anything—is unten-able. And that point was made resoundingly by no less an authority than F. A. Hayek himself. In a 1960 essay called "Why I Am Not a Conserva-tive," he took pains to argue that his position was as far from that of reac-tionary traditionalists as from that of utopian rationalists. "Though there is a need for a 'brake on the vehicle of progress,' " he said, "I personally cannot be content with simply helping to apply the brake." Classical lib-eralism, he writes, "has never been a backward-looking doctrine." To the contrary, it recognizes, as reactionary conservatism often fails to, that change is a constant and the world cannot be stopped in its tracks.

His own liberalism, Hayek wrote, "shares with conservatism a distrust of reason to the extent that the liberal is very much aware that we do not know all the answers," but the liberal, unlike the reactionary con-servative, does not imagine that simply clinging to the past or "claiming the authority of supernatural sources of knowledge" is any kind of an-swer. We must move ahead, but humbly and with respect for our own fallibility.

And there are times, Hayek said (in *Law, Legislation, and Liberty*), when what he called "grown law" requires correction by legislation. "It may be due simply to the recognition that some past development was based on error or that it produced consequences later recognized as unjust," he wrote. "But the most frequent cause is probably that the development of the law has lain in the hands of members of a particular class whose tra-ditional views made them regard as just what could not meet the more general requirements of justice . . . Such occasions when it is recognized that some hereto accepted rules are unjust in the light of more general principles of justice may well require the revision not only of single rules but of whole sections of the established system of case law."

That passage, I think, could have been written with gay marriage in mind. The old view that homosexuals were heterosexuals who needed punishment or prayer or treatment has been exposed as an error. What homosexuals need is the love of another homosexual. The ban on same-sex marriage, hallowed though it is, no longer accords with liberal justice or the meaning of marriage as it is practiced today. Something has to give. Standing still is not an option.

Hayek himself, then, was a partisan of the milder version of Hayekian-ism. This version is not so much a prescription as an attitude. Respect tra-dition. Reject utopianism. Plan for mistakes rather than for perfection. If reform is needed, look for paths that follow the terrain of custom, if pos-sible. If someone promises to remake society on rational or supernatural or theological principles, run in the opposite direction. In sum: Move ahead, but be careful.

Good advice. But not advice, particularly, against gay marriage. Remember Hayek's admonition against dogmatic conservatism. In a shifting current, holding your course can be just as dangerous as oversteering. Conservatives, in their panic to stop same-sex marriage, jeopardize marriage's universality and ultimately its legitimacy. They are taking risks, and big ones, and unnecessary ones. The liberal tradition and the *Declaration of Independence* are not currents you want to set marriage against.

It is worth recalling that Burke, the patron saint of social conservatism and the scourge of the French Revolution, supported the American Revolution. He distinguished between a revolt that aimed to overthrow established rights and principles and a revolt that aimed to restore them. Many of the American founders, incidentally, made exactly the same distinction. Whatever else they may have been, they were not Utopian social engineers. Whether a modern-day Burke or Jefferson would support gay marriage, I cannot begin to say; but I am confident they would, at least, have understood and carefully weighed the possibility that to preserve the liberal foundation of civil marriage, we may find it necessary to adjust its boundaries.

Discussion Questions

1. The idea that same-sex marriage radically redefines the institution of marriage is a key premise of the traditional argument. If you find this premise persuasive, why so? If not, explain why not.

2. Is protecting the institution of marriage an important societal goal? If so, how could that be accomplished? Is this an appropriate area for government involvement? In a society where individualism and equality are said to be important values, should marriage convey any legal benefits or advantages that are not available to single people?

3. Should the strong public opposition to same-sex marriage be a factor in whether states allow this form of marriage? Or is this an issue where public opinion should be less relevant? If so, why?

76

"Providing Social Security Benefits in the Future: A Review of the Social Security System and Plans to Reform It"

David C. John

There is wide agreement that Social Security requires major reforms if it is to continue to provide economic security to retirees. The baby boom generation will be retiring soon and the amount of money paid in benefits will exceed payroll taxes that are used to fund the system by 2017. The program has been running a surplus for the past two decades, but the government has been spending this money and giving the Social Security trust fund special Treasury bonds that will be repaid with general revenue between 2017 and 2042, when the bonds will be gone. By 2030 there will be only 2.2 workers for every retiree, which means that this "pay as you go" program will be facing a series of increasingly difficult choices about how to meet its obligations.

At the heart of the debate are two contrasting perspective of what the Social Security system should accomplish, both deeply rooted in American political culture: Should we view Social Security as a national guarantee of basic income for all individuals in their retirement, no matter what? Or should Social Security be an individualistic program that permits people to succeed—or fail—based on the choices that they make? To put it another way, is Social Security a social welfare program or an investment program? David John weighs into this controversy by outlining some principles for Social Security reform, providing an overview of five plans for reform, and then discussing the central characteristics of the Social Security program that are necessary for understanding the debate over reform. John is a strong supporter of personal retirement accounts (PRA), which would allow workers to invest a portion of their Social Security taxes. However, as John notes, none of these plans addresses the "transition problem." That is, because Social Security is a "pay as you go" program—today's workers pay for the Social Security benefits of today's retirees—if today's workers are allowed to take a portion of their Social Security taxes and put them in a PRA, this means that there will be even less money to pay for the current obligations to retirees than under the current system, at least for the next several decades. John writes, "Neither the current system nor any of the proposed reform plans comes close to closing the gap."

Social Security is the best-loved American government program, but how it works and is financed is almost completely unknown. Most Americans have a vague idea that they pay taxes for their benefits and that their benefits are linked somehow to their earnings. Many also know that the program is in trouble and needs to be "fixed" sometime soon to deal with the retirement of the baby boomers. Beyond this, their knowledge of the facts is severely limited and often colored by rumors and stories.

Most politicians exploit this lack of knowledge and limit their statements on Social Security to platitudes and vague promises. To make matters worse, reformers tend either to be content with similar platitudes or to speak in such detail that few outside the policy world can understand what they are saying. The simple fact is that today's Social Security is extremely complex, and any reform plan that is more than fine words will be similarly complex.

This paper attempts to simplify the reform debate by comparing various plans (including the current system) side by side. Each of the six sections of this paper compares how the current system and the reform plans handle a specific subject. Only reform plans that have been scored by Social Security's Office of the Chief Actuary are included in this comparison, using numbers contained in the 2003 Report of the Social Security Trustees. * * *

While looking at just one or two sections of special interest may be tempting, this approach would probably be misleading. For the best effect, each section should be considered together with the other sections in order to form a complete picture of the plan. Using simply one section by itself to judge an entire plan will not yield an accurate result.

Seven Important Rules for Real Social Security Reform

Information in this side-by-side comparison is based on Social Security's scoring memos for each plan and conclusions that can be drawn from information contained in those memos. While there are many good points in the reform plans examined in this analysis, this is not an endorsement of any proposal by the author or The Heritage Foundation. Instead, this comparison provides details of specific plans. However, it would be wise for reformers to follow a set of general principles to ensure that any Social Security reform both resolves Social Security's problems and provides workers with greater retirement security. Those principles are listed below.

This comparison of plans makes no effort to examine whether the Social Security reform plans included in it meet or violate any or all of the principles.

Principles for Social Security Reform

- **The benefits of current retirees and those close to retirement must not be reduced.** The government has a moral contract with those who currently receive Social Security retirement benefits, as well as with those who are so close to retirement, that they have no other options for building a retirement nest egg. If the benefits of younger workers cannot be maintained given the need to curb the burgeoning cost of the program, then they should have the opportunity to make up the difference by investing a portion of their Social Security taxes in a personal retirement account.
- **The rate of return on a worker's Social Security taxes must be improved.** Today's workers receive very poor returns on their Social Security payroll taxes. As a general rule, the younger a worker is or the lower his or her income, the lower his or her rate of return will be. Reform must provide a better retirement income to future retirees without increasing Social Security taxes. The best way to do this is to allow workers to divert a portion of their existing Social Security taxes into a personal retirement account that can earn significantly more than Social Security can pay.
- **Americans must be able to use Social Security to build a nest egg for the future.** A well-designed retirement system includes three elements: regular monthly retirement income, dependent's insurance, and the ability to save for retirement. Today's Social Security system provides a stable level of retirement income and does provide benefits for dependents. But it does not allow workers to accumulate cash savings to fulfill their own retirement goals or to pass on to their heirs. Workers should be able to use Social Security to build a cash nest egg that can be used to increase their retirement income or to build a better economic future for their families. The best way to do this is to establish, within the framework of Social Security, a system of personal retirement accounts.
- **Personal retirement accounts must guarantee an adequate minimum income.** Seniors must be able to count on a reasonable and predictable minimum level of monthly income, regardless of what happens in the investment markets.
- **Workers should be allowed to fund their Social Security personal retirement accounts by allocating some of their existing payroll tax dollars to them.** Workers should not be required to pay twice for their benefits—once through existing payroll taxes and again through additional income taxes or contributions used to fund a personal retirement account. Moreover, many working Americans can save little after paying existing payroll taxes and so cannot be expected to make additional contributions to a personal account. Thus Congress should allow Americans to divert a portion of the taxes that they currently pay for Social Security retirement benefits into personal retirement accounts.

- **For currently employed workers, participation in the new accounts must be voluntary.** No one should be forced into a system of personal retirement accounts. Instead, currently employed workers must be allowed to choose between today's Social Security and one that offers personal retirement accounts.
- **Any Social Security reform plan must be realistic, cost-effective and reduce the unfunded liabilities of the current system.** True Social Security reform will provide an improved total retirement benefit. But it should also reduce Social Security's huge unfunded liabilities by a greater level than the "transition" cost needed to finance benefits for retirees during the reform. Like paying points to obtain a better mortgage, Social Security reform should lead to a net reduction in liabilities.

The Social Security System and Plans for Reform

The Current System

Social Security currently pays an inflation-indexed monthly retirement and survivors' benefit, based on a worker's highest 35 years of earnings. Past earnings are indexed for average wage growth in the economy before calculating the benefit. The benefit formula is progressive, meaning that lower-income workers receive a benefit equal to a higher proportion of their average income than upper-income workers receive. The program is expected to continue to collect more in payroll taxes than it pays out in benefits until about 2018.

Unused payroll taxes are borrowed by the federal government and replaced by special-issue Treasury bonds. After the system begins to pay out more than it receives, the federal government will cover the resulting cash flow deficits by repaying the special-issue Treasury bonds out of general revenues. When the bonds run out in about 2042, Social Security benefits will automatically be reduced to a level equal to incoming revenue. This is projected to require a 27 percent reduction in 2042, with greater reductions after that.

The DeMint Plan

Representative Jim DeMint (R-SC) has introduced a voluntary personal retirement account (PRA) plan that would establish progressively funded voluntary individual accounts for workers under age 55 on January 1, 2005. The amount that goes into each worker's account would vary according to income, with lower-income workers able to save a higher percentage. For average-income workers, the account would equal about 5.1 percent of income.

The government would pay the difference between the monthly benefit that can be financed from an annuity paid for by using all or some of the PRA and the amount that the current system promises. The sum of the annuity and the government-paid portion of Social Security would be guaranteed at least to equal benefits promised under the current system, and 35 percent of PRA assets would be invested in government bonds to help pay for any Social Security cash flow deficits. This proportion would be reduced gradually in the future. General revenue money would be used to pay for additional cash flow deficits.

The Graham Plan

Senator Lindsay Graham (R-SC) has proposed a plan that would give workers under age 55 (in 2004) three options. (Workers above the age of 55 would be required to remain in the current system and would receive full benefits.)

Under *Option 1*, workers would establish PRAs funded with part of their existing payroll taxes, equal to 4 percent of pay up to a maximum of $1,300 per year. Workers' benefits would be reduced by changing the benefit indexing formula from the current wage growth index to one based on consumer prices. Over time, this change would reduce benefits for workers at all income levels, but the effect on lower-income workers would be eased by a mandated minimum benefit of at least 120 percent of the poverty level for workers with a 35-year work history. The government-paid monthly benefit would be further reduced to reflect the value of the PRA. This reduction would be calculated using the average earnings of government bonds so that, if the PRA earned more than government bonds, the total monthly benefit would be higher. Option 1 also raises survivor benefits to 75 percent of the couple's benefit for many survivors.

Option 2 is essentially the same as Option 1, but without PRAs. The government would pay all benefits for workers who choose this option. Option 2 includes both the basic benefit reduction and the minimum benefit requirement.

Option 3 pays the same level of benefits promised under current law, but workers who select this option would pay higher payroll taxes in return. Initially, the payroll tax rate for retirement and survivors benefits would increase from 12.4 percent of income to 14.4 percent of income (counting both the worker's and the employer's shares of the tax). In subsequent years, the tax rate would continue to climb in 0.25 percent increments.

The Smith Plan

Representative Nick Smith (R–MI) has proposed a voluntary PRA plan that would create personal retirement savings accounts funded with an amount equal to 2.5 percent of income, paid out of existing payroll taxes. This would increase to 2.75 percent of income in 2025 and could become larger after 2038 if Social Security has surplus cash flows. Retirement and survivors' benefits would be reduced by an amount equal to the value of lifetime account contributions plus a specified interest rate.

The Smith plan would also make many changes in Social Security's benefit formula, mainly affecting middle-income and upper-income workers. These changes would eventually result in most workers receiving a flat monthly benefit of about $550 in 2004 dollars. It would also gradually increase the retirement age for full benefits and require that all newly hired local and state workers be covered by Social Security. The Smith plan transfers $866 billion from general revenues to Social Security between 2007 and 2013 to help cover cash flow deficits and allows additional general revenue transfers when needed after that.

The Ferrara Plan

Peter Ferrara, Director of the International Center for Law and Economics, has proposed a plan that would create voluntary PRAs that would be funded according to a progressive formula that allows lower-income workers to save a higher proportion of their payroll taxes than upper-income workers. Average-income workers could save about 6.4 percent of their income. Workers would be guaranteed that the total of their PRA-generated benefits and government-paid monthly benefits would at least equal the benefits promised under the current system.

Any Social Security cash flow deficits that remain would be financed through general revenue transfers equal to a 1 percent reduction in the growth rate of all government spending for eight years, the corporate income taxes deemed to result from the investment of personal account contributions, and issuing about $1.4 trillion in "off-budget" bonds. Under the Ferrara plan, these bonds would be considered a replacement for the existing system's unfunded liability and thus would not increase the federal debt.

The Orszag-Diamond Plan

Peter Orszag, Senior Fellow at the Brookings Institution, and Peter Diamond, Institute Professor of Economics at the Massachusetts Institute of Technology, have developed a plan that does not include any form of PRA or government investment of Social Security trust fund money in private markets. Instead, it gradually changes the benefit formula to reduce benefits for moderate-income and upper-income workers and requires that all state and local government workers come under Social Security. It would also gradually reduce benefits by raising the age at which workers could receive full benefits. Workers could still retire earlier, but at lower benefits. Benefits would increase for lower-income workers, widows, and the disabled.

In addition, the plan would gradually increase the payroll tax for all workers from the current 12.4 percent of income to 15.36 percent of income in 2078. It would also raise the earnings threshold on Social Security taxes—thus requiring higher-income workers to pay additional payroll taxes—and impose a new 3 percent tax on income above the earnings threshold. Workers would not receive any credit toward benefits for income covered by this new tax.

*   *   *

1. Personal Retirement Accounts

What Is This, and Why Is It Important?

Allowing workers to invest a portion of their Social Security taxes is the only alternative to raising Social Security taxes or reducing Social Security benefits. However, personal retirement accounts are not all equal. The money that goes into the PRAs could come from diverting a portion of existing Social Security taxes or from some other source.

Similarly, the size of the accounts (usually expressed as a percentage of the worker's pay) is important. While larger accounts would temporarily increase the amount of additional funds required to pay benefits to retirees, they would also accumulate a pool of money faster than smaller accounts and finance a greater portion of benefits in future years. This can reduce the amount of additional tax dollars needed in future decades.

Finally, how the PRAs are invested is important. Even though they show steady growth over time stocks and commercial bonds are generally more volatile than government bonds. Investing a portion of the PRAs in government bonds makes the accounts slightly less volatile while providing some of the additional dollars needed to pay benefits to current retirees.

2. Retirement and Survivors Benefits

What Is This, and Why Is It Important?

Other than creating personal retirement accounts that allow workers to self-fund all or a portion of their Social Security retirement benefits, most reform plans deal with the program's coming deficits by either changing the level of retirement benefits promised or finding ways to increase program revenues. This section examines how various reform plans treat promised retirement benefits.

Social Security uses a complex formula to calculate an individual worker's retirement benefits. Subtle changes in this formula can cause a large change in benefits over time. For instance, changing how past income is indexed to a constant purchasing power will have only a minor impact for the first several years. However, the effect is cumulative and after several decades will result in major changes in benefits.

Similarly, seemingly minor changes in "bend points"[1] or other aspects of the benefit formula can, over the long term, cause major changes in benefits for upper-income and/or moderate-income workers. It is even possible to use the benefit formula to approximate an increase in the full retirement age without actually raising it. Thus, a plan could still allow workers to quality for "full retirement benefits" at 65, 66, or 67 but award them full retirement benefits (as defined under the current system) only if they wait to retire until a later age.

The first question that any plan must answer is whether it would pay the full level of benefits promised under the current system. If so, it must deal with how to pay the cost, since the current system cannot afford to pay for all of the promised benefits. Other important questions include whether the plan proposes benefit changes (usually reductions) if workers do not choose to have a personal retirement account, protects lower-income workers (who more often have an interrupted work history) by instituting some sort of minimum benefit level, and/or addresses the low benefits for certain lower-income, widowed, and disabled workers under the current system.

3. Payroll Taxes

What Is This, and Why Is It Important?

Increasing Social Security payroll taxes would be one way to pay projected cash flow deficits. This method is closer to the self-funding that has characterized the system so far, but raising payroll taxes has significant drawbacks. Alternatives to payroll tax increases include instituting some form of personal retirement account to increase the return on taxes, reducing benefits, and using significant amounts of general revenue money to cover Social Security's cash flow deficits.

Currently, all workers pay 5.3 percent of their income to pay for Social Security retirement and survivors benefits. In 2004, this tax will be paid on the first $87,700 of an employee's income.[2] Employers match this tax for a total of 10.6 percent of each worker's income. In addition, both employer and employee pay an additional 0.9 percent of the worker's income (1.8 percent total) for Social Security disability benefits. Thus, the employer and employee pay a total Social Security payroll tax of 12.4 percent.[3]

Additional payroll taxes could be collected in three ways:

- The overall tax rate could be increased. However, this imposes higher taxes on all income groups and could reduce employment in the economy by making it more expensive to hire additional workers.

- The tax could be imposed on income levels above the threshold, currently at $87,700. In the short run, this would increase revenues, but since retirement benefits are paid on all income taxed for Social Security, it would also eventually increase the amount of benefits the system would have to pay each year and offset the amount raised through the higher taxes.
- Payroll taxes could be disconnected from the benefit formula. This could take the form of a new tax paid on income above the current $87,700 earnings threshold, collecting taxes on income up to the $87,700 level but counting only income up to $60,000 or some other level toward benefits, or some combination of the two. In either case, this type of tax would break the link between taxes and income that has existed since Social Security began in 1935. To date, neither the right nor the left has been willing to break this link for fear that it would be the first step toward turning Social Security into a welfare system. Both sides have worried that such a move—or even the perception of such a move—would undermine the program's widespread support among the American people.

4. Social Security's Unfunded Liability

What Is This, and Why Is It Important?

Both the current Social Security system and every plan to reform it will require significant amounts of general revenue money in addition to the amount collected through payroll taxes. This additional money is necessary to reduce the difference between what Social Security currently owes and what it will be able to pay.

In the reform plans, the transition cost represents a major reduction from the unfunded liability of the current program. Even though the reform plans are expensive, all of them would require less additional money than the current system. However, both the amount and the timing of this additional money would vary depending on the plan.

The amount of additional money that is needed can be measured according to two different systems. Both measurements give valuable information.

Present value reflects the idea that a dollar today has more value to a person than that same dollar has sometime in the future. It gives an idea of when the additional money is needed by giving greater weight to money needed in the near future than to an equal amount needed further in the future. In addition to showing the amount of money needed, a higher present value number indicates that money is needed sooner rather than later. [The present value of the unfunded liability ranges from $929 billion in the Orszag-Diamond plan to $7.6 trillion in the Ferrara plan.]

The *sum of the deficits* indicates the total amount of additional money that will be needed. This measure gives $100 needed today the same weight as $100 needed in 15 years. This measure adds up only the future cash flow deficits; it does not include cash flow surpluses because the government does not have any way to save or invest that money for future use. Using both of these measurements gives a better picture of the situation than using just one. [The sum of the deficits of the unfunded liability ranges from $7.1 trillion in the Graham plan to $16.4 trillion in the Ferrara plan.]

Paying for the current system or any of the reform plans will require Congress to balance Social Security's needs against those of the rest of the economy. In general, as more additional dollars are needed for the current system or a reform plan, less money will be available for other government programs and the private sector.

As this burden on the general federal budget increases and persists, Congress would find it increasingly more difficult to come up with that money, and it would become increasingly less likely that such a plan would really be paid for on schedule. This is especially true for the current system, which will incur the massive deficits to pay all of the promised benefits.

*   *   *

5. Paying for Social Security's Unfunded Liability

What Is This, and Why Is It Important?

Both the current Social Security program and all of the proposed reform plans will require large amounts of general revenue money to cover the annual cash flow deficits. Exactly when that money is first needed, how many years it will be needed, and the total amount that will be needed varies from plan to plan. Avoiding use of general revenue money would require either reducing Social Security benefits enough to eliminate the annual deficits or imposing new taxes to generate sufficient revenue. Neither the current system nor any of the proposed reform plans comes close to closing the gap.

Some plans do specify sources for the needed general revenues, but these are handicapped by the fact that no Congress can bind the hands of a future Congress. Thus, even if Congress did pass a plan that specified the source of the needed general revenues, a future Congress could change the plan by a majority vote. The only way to avoid this uncertainty would be for Congress to pass and the states to ratify the plan as a constitutional amendment—which would be prohibitively difficult.

In short, both the current system and all known reform plans would have to find the necessary general revenues from some combination of four sources: borrowing additional money collecting more taxes than needed to fund the rest of the government, reducing other government spending, or reducing Social Security benefits more than is called for under either current law or any of the reform plans.

The most important thing to remember is that the existing Social Security system and the reform plans all face this problem. This is not a weakness that is limited to PRA plans or any other reform plan. The only question is when the cash flow deficits begin and how large they will be.

Current Law

Current law makes no provision for funding Social Security's unfunded liability. The program has no credit line with the U.S. Treasury, and when its trust fund promises are exhausted, current law will require it to reduce benefits.

The DeMint Plan

While some press releases connected with Representative DeMint's plan suggest that some of its general revenue needs could be generated by reducing the growth of federal spending, no language specifying where the general revenues would come from is included in his legislation.

The Graham Plan

Senator Graham's plan includes a commission that would recommend reductions in corporate welfare and redirect the savings to reduce his plans unfunded liability. At best, a reduction in corporate welfare would generate only part of the needed general revenue. The commission would produce a legislative proposal that would then be considered by Congress.

Because the commission would be created by the same legislation that implements Graham's Social Security reforms, its recommendations could not even be considered until after the plan is enacted. As a result, passage of the Graham plan does not guarantee that these revenues would be available. Regardless of what the commission recommended, a future Congress could reject the proposed cuts in corporate welfare. In that case, Congress would have to come up with another method to raise the needed revenue.

The Smith Plan

Other than the proposed benefit changes that would partially reduce Social Security's unfunded liability, the Smith plan does not specify how it would pay cash flow deficits.

The Ferrara Plan

The Ferrara plan includes three mechanisms designed to create the needed general revenues.

First, it would mandate a 1 percent reduction in the growth of all federal spending (including entitlements such as Social Security) for at least 8 years and redirect that revenue to Social Security. Since Congress cannot legally force a subsequent Congress to follow a set course of action, the only enforcement mechanism available is a constitutional amendment. As a result, the Ferrara plan simply appropriates to Social Security the amount of revenue that would result if Congress were to reduce spending growth. In practice, a future Congress could choose not to reduce spending growth and, instead, just let the deficit grow larger or generate the necessary revenue in some other way.

Second, the Ferrara plan would transfer to Social Security the amount of corporate income taxes that could potentially result from the investment of personal accounts in corporate stocks and bonds. This is not a new or higher tax. This transfer is intended to reflect the taxes that would be paid at the current 35 percent corporate tax rate. Since SSA does not conduct dynamic scoring, this transfer is based on the static assumption that two-thirds of the stocks and bonds held through personal accounts reflect domestic corporate investment.

Third, the Ferrara plan would borrow about $1.4 trillion in special off-budget bonds. However, there is no practical way to create off-budget bonds that would not count against the federal debt. Even if there were, such a move would reduce the amount of transparency in the federal budget.

The Orszag-Diamond Plan

While the Orszag-Diamond plan includes both some benefit reductions and benefit increases for widows, the disabled, and low-income workers, the two elements of the plan are roughly equal. It reduces Social Security's unfunded liability using tax increases contained in the plan, including an increase in the payroll tax rate, a gradual increase in the amount of income subject to Social Security taxes, and a new 3 percent tax on any salary income not subject to Social Security taxes.

6. Making Social Security a Better Deal for Workers

What Is This, and Why Is It Important?

In the long run, a reform plan should do more than just preserve the current Social Security system with its many flaws. While a key requirement of any reform plan is to provide a stable, guaranteed, and adequate level of benefits at an affordable cost, it should do more.

The current system fails to allow workers to build any form of nest egg for the future. Instead, it is the highest single tax for about 80 percent of workers. In return, each worker receives a life annuity that ends with the death(s) of the worker, the surviving spouse (if there is one), or young children (if any). In today's world, where two-earner families are increasingly the norm, the current system even limits survivor benefits to the higher of either the deceased spouses benefits or the surviving spouses benefits. Whichever account is lower, no matter how long that spouse worked, is marked paid in full and extinguished.

At a minimum, a reform plan should allow workers to pass on some of what they earned and paid in Social Security taxes to improve their spouse's retirement benefits. It should also allow workers the flexibility to use their entire account for retirement benefits or take a smaller retirement benefit and use the balance to pay for a grandchild's college education, start a small business, or pass on money to a later generation.

In judging whether each proposed reform would be better for America's workers, readers may differ sharply. However, while most summaries and studies examine Social Security reform from the viewpoint of federal budget impact, tax rates, and the survivability of the system, few consider the overall impact of reform on the workers it was designed to benefit in the first place. Social Security should not be reformed or "saved" for its own sake, but only if it more effectively provides the benefits workers need at a price they can afford.

DISCUSSION QUESTIONS

1. The only plan that does not include partial privatization is the Orszag-Diamond plan. This could be called the "tough medicine" plan because the solvency of Social Security is accomplished through benefit reductions and tax increases. It is the only one of the plans that is funded through cuts and tax increases. Is the tough medicine worth it, or do you agree with John that PRAs must be part of the overall reform?

2. One alternative to partial privatization that is not mentioned here is to have the federal government invest the Social Security surplus in the stock market or corporate bonds (as every state retirement system in the country does). This would, in theory, provide a high investment return, but critics claim it would also give the government too much leverage (as a large shareholder) over the activities of private corporations. Would this be a legitimate role for the government to play in the economy? Can you think of other ways in which the existing system could be reformed, other than turning portions of the fund over to individuals?

3. Are the broad objectives initially established for Social Security— income security for old age, income redistribution, and risk sharing across the population and across generations—still appropriate today? Are individuals more able to plan for and manage their retirement income today than in the 1930s or even the 1980s? Why or why not? What do you see as the major advantages and disadvantages of the current Social Security system and the plan for partial privatization?

NOTES

1. The benefit formula used by the current Social Security system develops an "average indexed monthly earnings" for each worker by indexing his or her highest 35 years' earnings covered by Social Security taxes according to the growth in wages that has occurred between the date they were earned and the date that the benefit calculation is being made. In the next step, the actual retirement benefit is calculated. In 2003, the formula paid benefits equal to 90 percent of the first $606 of a worker's average indexed monthly earnings, 32 percent of the amount between $606 and $3,653, and 15 percent of any indexed earnings above $3,653. The divisions between the 90 percent, 32 percent, and 15 percent levels are called bend points.
2. This threshold is indexed and changes each year.
3. Although the federal government considers the employer's matching share as a separate item, most employers add their portions of the Social Security tax to a worker's salary when calculating the true cost of an employee.

Debating the Issues: Health Care Reform

The health care system in the United States presents a paradox: it provides the best health care in the world to the people who have insurance, but for the 40 to 45 million Americans who do not have insurance, health care can be a challenge. Millions of people use the emergency room as their family doctor, which is not a very efficient way to provide health care. Millions more postpone receiving needed medical attention because they have no way of paying for it. Consequently, our nation spends twice as much on health care (as a percentage of GDP) as many other industrialized countries, while our overall health outcomes are not notably better and in several instances worse.

Paul Krugman and Robin Wells argue that a single-payer system, in which the federal government would handle all purchasing of medical care, is the best remedy for these problems. They argue that a public system based on universal coverage would result in lower administrative costs, because in the current system private insurers spend substantial amounts of money trying to weed out undesirable—i.e., expensive—customers and trying to be restrictive in the types of services and treatments they will cover under their policies. In addition, a single-payer system would allow the government to be a powerful negotiator, indeed the only negotiator, with medical suppliers, in particular the pharmaceutical companies.

Grace-Marie Turner sees the Krugman-Wells approach as a giant step in the wrong direction. The problem with American health care, she argues, is that consumers have become too distant from their medical decisions. The solution is to give consumers more control over their health care, which will also mean being made aware of the costs of the decisions they are making. She supports a proposal made by President Bush that would provide incentives for individuals to purchase insurance that they would carry with them—the policies would not be owned by their employers or by the government. Consumers would have free reign to shop for exactly the policy they preferred, as they now do with other types of insurance. Some advocates of this plan couple it with a requirement that individuals purchase or be covered by insurance, again, as many states require individuals to do if they wish to drive an automobile.

Jacob Hacker argues that both the Krugman-Wells and Turner approaches are wishful thinking. The reality, he writes, is that obstacles to reform prevent the complete restructuring of the health care system envisioned by those authors. Resistance to change by vested interests, satisfaction with what works in the system now, and government budgetary constraints are all reasons the dramatic overhauls are not likely to succeed. Instead, Hacker argues, the way forward is to build on the current system. He would maintain the current employer-based insurance system, where both Krugman-Wells and Turner would dismantle it. To do that, he would build upon the Medicare system—the health care system for elderly Americans—to cover those who did not receive coverage through an employer. Employers could provide insurance to their workers through this new add-on to Medicare. Any remaining uninsured individuals would be required to purchase insurance, either privately or through the revised Medicare program.

77

"The Health Care Crisis and What to Do About It"

Paul Krugman and Robin Wells

Thirteen years ago Bill Clinton became president partly because he promised to do something about rising health care costs. Although Clinton's chances of reforming the U.S. health care system looked quite good at first, the effort soon ran aground. Since then a combination of factors—the unwillingness of other politicians to confront the insurance and other lobbies that so successfully frustrated the Clinton effort, a temporary remission in the growth of health care spending as HMOs briefly managed to limit cost increases, and the general distraction of a nation focused first on the gloriousness of getting rich, then on terrorism—have kept health care off the top of the agenda.

But medical costs are once again rising rapidly, forcing health care back into political prominence. Indeed, the problem of medical costs is so pervasive that it underlies three quite different policy crises. First is the increasingly rapid unraveling of employer-based health insurance. Second is the plight of Medicaid, an increasingly crucial program that is under both fiscal and political attack. Third is the long-term problem of the federal government's solvency, which is, as we'll explain, largely a problem of health care costs.

The good news is that we know more about the economics of health care than we did when Clinton tried and failed to remake the system. There's now a large body of evidence on what works and what doesn't work in health care, and it's not hard to see how to make dramatic improvements in U.S. practice. As we'll see, the evidence clearly shows that the key problem with the U.S. health care system is its fragmentation. A history of failed attempts to introduce universal health insurance has left us with a system in which the government pays directly or indirectly for more than half of the nation's health care, but the actual delivery both of insurance and of care is undertaken by a crazy quilt of private insurers, for-profit hospitals, and other players who add cost without adding value. A Canadian-style single-payer system, in which the government directly provides insurance, would almost surely be both cheaper and more effective than what we now have. And we could do even better if we learned from "integrated" systems, like the Veterans Administration, that directly provide some health care as well as medical insurance.

The bad news is that Washington currently seems incapable of accepting what the evidence on health care says. In particular, the Bush administration is under the influence of both industry lobbyists, especially those representing the drug companies, and a free-market ideology that is wholly inappropriate to health care issues. As a result, it seems determined to pursue policies that will increase the fragmentation of our system and swell the ranks of the uninsured.

Before we talk about reform, however, let's talk about the current state of the U.S. health care system. Let us begin by asking a seemingly naive question: What's wrong with spending ever more on health care?

Is Health Care Spending a Problem?

In 1960 the United States spent only 5.2 percent of GDP on health care. By 2004 that number had risen to 16 percent. At this point America spends more on health care than it does on food. But what's wrong with that?

The starting point for any discussion of rising health care costs has to be the realization that these rising costs are, in an important sense, a sign of progress. Here's how the Congressional Budget Office puts it, in the latest edition of its annual publication *The Long-Term Budget Outlook:*

> Growth in health care spending has outstripped economic growth regardless of the source of its funding. . . . The major factor associated with that growth has been the development and increasing use of new medical technology. . . . In the health care field, unlike in many sectors of the economy, technology advances have generally raised costs rather than lowered them.

Notice the three points in that quote. First, health care spending is rising rapidly "regardless of the source of its funding." Translation: although much health care is paid for by the government, this isn't a simple case of runaway government spending, because private spending is rising at a comparably fast clip. "Comparing common benefits," says the Kaiser Family Foundation,

> changes in Medicare spending in the last three decades has largely tracked the growth rate in private health insurance premiums. Typically, Medicare increases have been lower than those of private health insurance.

Second, "new medical technology" is the major factor in rising spending: we spend more on medicine because there's more that medicine can do. Third, in medical care, "technological advances have generally raised costs rather than lowered them": although new technology surely produces cost savings in medicine, as elsewhere, the additional spending that takes place as a result of the expansion of medical possibilities outweighs those savings.

So far, this sounds like a happy story. We've found new ways to help people, and are spending more to take advantage of the opportunity. Why not view rising medical spending, like rising spending on, say, home entertainment systems, simply as a rational response to expanded choice? We would suggest two answers.

The first is that the U.S. health care system is extremely inefficient, and this inefficiency becomes more costly as the health care sector becomes a larger fraction of the economy. Suppose, for example, that we believe that 30 percent of U.S. health care spending is wasted, and always has been. In 1960, when health care was only 5.2 percent of GDP, that meant waste equal to only 1.5 percent of GDP. Now that the share of health care in the economy has more than tripled, so has the waste.

This inefficiency is a bad thing in itself. What makes it literally fatal to thousands of Americans each year is that the inefficiency of our health care system exacerbates a second problem: our health care system often makes irrational choices, and rising costs exacerbate those irrationalities. Specifically, American health care tends to divide the population into insiders and outsiders. Insiders, who have good insurance, receive everything modern medicine can provide, no matter how expensive. Outsiders, who have poor insurance or none at all, receive very little. To take just one example, one study found that among Americans diagnosed with colorectal cancer, those without insurance were 70 percent more likely than those with insurance to die over the next three years.

In response to new medical technology, the system spends even more on insiders. But it compensates for higher spending on insiders, in part, by consigning more people to outsider status—robbing Peter of basic care in order to pay for Paul's state-of-the-art treatment. Thus we have the cruel paradox that medical progress is bad for many Americans' health.

* * *

* * * The only way modern medical care can be made available to anyone other than the very rich is through health insurance. Yet it's very difficult for the private sector to provide such insurance, because health insurance suffers from a particularly acute case of a well-known economic problem known as adverse selection. Here's how it works: imagine an insurer who offered policies to anyone, with the annual premium set to cover the average person's health care expenses, plus the administrative costs of running the insurance company. Who would sign up? The answer, unfortunately, is that the insurer's customers wouldn't be a representative sample of the population. Healthy people, with little reason to expect high medical bills, would probably shun policies priced to reflect the average person's health costs. On the other hand, unhealthy people would find the policies very attractive.

You can see where this is going. The insurance company would quickly find that because its clientele was tilted toward those with high medical costs, its actual costs per customer were much higher than those of the average member of the population. So it would have to raise premiums to cover those higher costs. However, this would disproportionately drive off its healthier customers, leaving it with an even less healthy customer base, requiring a further rise in premiums, and so on.

Insurance companies deal with these problems, to some extent, by carefully screening applicants to identify those with a high risk of needing expensive treatment, and either rejecting such applicants or charging them higher premiums. But such screening is itself expensive. Furthermore, it tends to screen out exactly those who most need insurance.

Most advanced countries have dealt with the defects of private health insurance in a straightforward way, by making health insurance a government service. Through Medicare, the United States has in effect done the same thing for its seniors. We also have Medicaid, a means-tested program that provides health insurance to many of the poor and near poor. But nonelderly, nonpoor Americans are on their own. In practice, only a tiny fraction of nonelderly Americans (5.3 percent in 2003) buy private insurance for themselves. The rest of those not covered by Medicare or Medicaid get insurance, if at all, through their employers.

* * *

Health care costs at current levels override the incentives that have historically supported employer-based health insurance. Now that health costs loom so large, companies that provide generous benefits are in effect paying some of their workers much more than the going wage—or, more to the point, more than competitors pay similar workers. Inevitably, this creates pressure to reduce or eliminate health benefits. And companies that can't cut benefits enough to stay competitive—such as GM—find their very existence at risk.

Rising health costs have also ended the ability of employer-based insurance plans to avoid the problem of adverse selection. Anecdotal evidence suggests that workers who know they have health problems actively seek out jobs with companies that still offer generous benefits. On the other side, employers are starting to make hiring decisions based on likely health costs. For example, an internal Wal-Mart memo, reported by *The New York Times* in October, suggested adding tasks requiring physical exertion to jobs that don't really require it as a way to screen out individuals with potential health risks.

So rising health care costs are undermining the institution of employer-based coverage. We'd suggest that the drop in the number of insured so far only hints at the scale of the problem: we may well be seeing the whole institution unraveling.

*   *   *

Single-Payer and Beyond

How do we know that the U.S. health care system is highly inefficient? An important part of the evidence takes the form of international comparisons. * * * We spend far more on health care than other advanced countries—almost twice as much per capita as France, almost two and a half times as much as Britain. Yet we do considerably worse even than the British on basic measures of health performance, such as life expectancy and infant mortality.

*   *   *

So why does U.S. health care cost so much? Part of the answer is that doctors, like other highly skilled workers, are paid much more in the United States than in other advanced countries. But the main source of high U.S. costs is probably the unique degree to which the U.S. system relies on private rather than public health insurance, reflected in the uniquely high U.S. share of private spending in total health care expenditure.

Over the years since the failure of the Clinton health plan, a great deal of evidence has accumulated on the relative merits of private and public health insurance. As far as we have been able to ascertain, all of that evidence indicates that public insurance of the kind available in several European countries and others such as Taiwan achieves equal or better results at much lower cost. This conclusion applies to comparisons within the United States as well as across countries. For example, a study conducted by researchers at the Urban Institute found that

> per capita spending for an adult Medicaid beneficiary in poor health would rise from $9,615 to $14,785 if the person were insured privately and received services consistent with private utilization levels and private provider payment rates.

The cost advantage of public health insurance appears to arise from two main sources. The first is lower administrative costs. Private insurers spend large sums fighting adverse selection, trying to identify and screen out high-cost customers. Systems such as Medicare, which covers every American sixty-five or older, or the Canadian single-payer system, which covers everyone, avoid these costs. In 2003 Medicare spent less than 2 percent of its resources on administration, while private insurance companies spent more than 13 percent.

At the same time, the fragmentation of a system that relies largely on private insurance leads both to administrative complexity because of differences in coverage among individuals and to what is, in effect, a zero-sum struggle between different players in the system, each trying to stick others with the bill. Many estimates suggest that the paperwork imposed on health care providers by the fragmentation of the U.S. system costs several times as much as the direct costs borne by the insurers.

The second source of savings in a system of public health insurance is the ability to bargain with suppliers, especially drug companies, for lower prices. Residents of the United States notoriously pay much higher prices for prescription drugs than residents of other advanced countries, including Canada. What is less known is that both Medicaid and, to an even greater extent, the Veterans' Administration, get discounts similar to or greater than those received by the Canadian health system.

We're talking about large cost savings. Indeed, the available evidence suggests that if the United States were to replace its current complex mix of health insurance systems with standardized, universal coverage, the savings would be so large that we could cover all those currently uninsured, yet end up spending less overall. That's what happened in Taiwan, which adopted a single-payer system in 1995: the percentage of the population with health insurance soared from 57 percent to 97 percent, yet health care costs actually grew more slowly than one would have predicted from trends before the change in system.

If U.S. politicians could be persuaded of the advantages of a public health insurance system, the next step would be to convince them of the virtues, in at least some cases, of honest-to-God socialized medicine, in which government employees provide the care as well as the money. Exhibit A for the advantages of government provision is the Veterans' Administration, which runs its own hospitals and clinics, and provides some of the best-quality health care in America at far lower cost than the private sector. How does the VA do it? It turns out that there are many advantages to having a single health care organization provide individuals with what amounts to lifetime care. For example, the VA has taken the lead in introducing electronic medical records, which it can do far more easily than a private hospital chain because its patients stay with it for decades. The VA also invests heavily and systematically in preventive care, because unlike private health care providers it can expect to realize financial benefits from measures that keep its clients out of the hospital.

In summary, then, the obvious way to make the U.S. health care system more efficient is to make it more like the systems of other advanced countries, and more like the most efficient parts of our own system. That means a shift from private insurance to public insurance, and greater government involvement in the provision of health care—if not publicly run hospitals and clinics, at least a much larger government role in creating integrated record-keeping and quality control. Such a system would probably allow individuals to purchase additional medical care, as they can in Britain (although not in Canada). But the core of the system would be government insurance—"Medicare for all," as Ted Kennedy puts it.

* * *

Can We Fix Health Care?

Health policy experts know a lot more about the economics of health care now than they did when Bill Clinton tried to remake the U.S. health care system. And there's overwhelming evidence that the United States could get better health care at lower cost if we were willing to put that knowledge into practice. But the political obstacles remain daunting. * * *

Even liberal economists and scholars at progressive think tanks tend to shy away from proposing a straightforward system of national health insurance. Instead, they propose fairly complex compromise plans. * * * The main reason for not proposing single-payer is political fear: reformers believe that private insurers are too powerful to be cut out of the loop, and that a single-payer plan would be too easily demonized by business and political propagandists as "big government."

These are the same political calculations that led Bill Clinton to reject a single-payer system in 1993, even though his advisers believed that a single-payer system would be the least expensive way to provide universal coverage. Instead, he proposed a complex plan designed to preserve a role for private health insurers. But the plan backfired. The insurers opposed it anyway, most famously with their "Harry and Louise" ads. And the plan's complexity left the public baffled.

We believe that * * * it would be politically smarter as well as economically superior to go for broke: to propose a straightforward single-payer system, and try to sell voters on the huge advantages such a system would bring. But this would mean taking on the drug and insurance companies rather than trying to co-opt them, and even progressive policy wonks, let alone Democratic politicians, still seem too timid to do that.

* * *

NOTE

1. "Medicaid: A Lower-Cost Approach to Serving a High-Cost Population," policy brief by the Kaiser Commission on Medicaid and the Uninsured, March 2004.

78

"Toward Free-Market Health Care"

Grace-Marie Turner

Our health care sector must change to meet the challenges of a 21st century economy. Consumers, not just in the United States but in all developed countries, are demanding a much greater role in decisions involving their health care.

People can find on the Internet a wealth of information about diseases, diagnoses, and treatment options, but all too often, they must fight bureaucracies and paperwork all along the way. Women especially believe that they, rather than a corporate human resources director, could make better decisions involving health coverage for their families if only they were given the chance.

In addition, many who have health insurance are worried that if they lose their jobs, they will lose their health insurance. And with the cost of health insurance and health care rising every year, they fear they would not be able to afford coverage on their own. The middle class is increasingly afraid that they are one premium payment away from joining the ranks of the uninsured.

Meanwhile, our system of tying health insurance to the workplace is becoming antiquated with a workforce that is increasingly independent and mobile. The Labor Department reports that four in ten Americans change jobs every year. With this kind of job mobility, it is extremely difficult to tie health insurance to the workplace and expect people to have continuity of coverage. People lose their jobs, and they lose their health insurance. We need a system that allows people to have health insurance that is portable; insurance that they can own and control; insurance that they, and not a politician or a human resources department, decide is right for them and their families.

This move toward more individual control over health care decisions and health care spending is part of the global movement toward health care consumerism. Giving people more power and control over their health care and health insurance creates new incentives for people to be more engaged in managing their health.

Many companies realize this and are instituting new programs to give employees incentives to better manage their health spending. And they are creating new programs for those with chronic illnesses, like diabetes and asthma, to be partners in managing their care. A number of studies have shown that if people are given the tools, the information, and the incentive to manage their care, outcomes can be dramatically improved.

Leading the Way

America can lead the way in creating a health care system that fits with our 21st century economy by putting in place new policies that allow innovation to continue and that is better able to respond to consumer demands and preferences. But public policy changes are needed to lead us in a new direction.

Our health sector is like a giant ship: It takes a great deal of effort to change direction, but even a small change can lead to a very different destination over time. For the past six years, the health sector has been moving toward more free-market solutions, introducing patient choice and competition into a system that had been largely dominated by top-down, centralized management. A few very familiar examples:

- Consumers have new incentives to become partners in managing their health costs through financing options like Health Savings Accounts and company-based Health Reimbursement Arrangements. Both individuals and companies are saving money on health costs as a result.
- Choice and competition also have been introduced in public programs like Medicare and Medicaid, showing that people can choose among competing health plans that have new incentives to offer better benefits at lower costs.

Threats to the Free Market in Health Care

Competition is working, but there are threats on the horizon. The new leadership in Congress is setting a clear agenda that involves expanding government health care programs and cutting back the initiatives begun over the past several years to bring more competition and patient choice into private and public programs.

Key committee chairmen want to expand government coverage of children, putting children in families earning up to $83,000 a year and "children" as old as age 25 into government-run plans. In addition, Senator Ted Kennedy (D–MA) has put as his top priority enacting legislation that would put all Americans on government-run health care through Medicare-for-All. Others are working to expand Medicaid to more middle-income Americans, shifting tens of tens of millions of Americans into government health care.

Innovative Solutions

So what can we do?

The health care initiative that President Bush offered during his State of the Union address in 2007 could usher in the changes that would continue to make the U.S. the leader in quality health care while addressing the growing problem of the uninsured and middle-class anxiety about high health costs.

The President would give families the opportunity to own health insurance that is portable from job to job, and he would free up some of their tax money to help them buy the coverage. The White House estimates his plan also would give a tax cut to 100 million working Americans and provide health insurance to up to 9 million more Americans without any new long-term costs to the federal treasury. The dynamic changes in the marketplace for health insurance would transform the system to offer health insurance that is more affordable, flexible, and portable.

The centerpiece of Mr. Bush's plan is a new standard deduction for health insurance. It would be available to any taxpayer who buys qualifying health insurance. Families would get a new $15,000 standard tax deduction, and individuals would get $7,500. You need not itemize and will get the full deduction even if the policy you buy costs less as long as it meets certain minimum requirements for catastrophic coverage. Families earning $50,000 a year could save more than $4,300 in income and payroll taxes and use the tax savings to buy health insurance.

What about the uninsured, especially those with lower incomes? The White House says the proposal would lower the average tax bill of a family without coverage by $3,350. This would mean $3,350 of their pay would be available to buy insurance instead of going to taxes.

But for many of the insured, this still would not be enough, so there is a second part to the President's plan involving the states: Health and Human Services Secretary Mike Leavitt (former governor of Utah) is meeting with every governor to find out what his or her state needs to create "Affordable Choices" in health insurance. Secretary Leavitt wants to help states make basic, affordable private health insurance policies available to their citizens. This could include, for example, grants in the form of vouchers or refundable tax credits to help low-income people purchase private health insurance.

The President's proposal was very innovative and took the policy community by surprise with its boldness. The President described his basic philosophy to enthusiastic applause on both sides of the aisle during his State of the Union Address when he said, "in all we do, we must remember that the best healthcare decisions are made not by government and insurance companies, but by patients and their doctors."

Changing the Conversation

This changes the whole conversation in the health policy debate. No longer are we simply talking about how much or how little to expand government programs. We now can have a new national debate over how to engage the power of consumers in transforming our health sector to become more efficient, more responsive to their needs, and more affordable. In addressing the core problem of our current dysfunctional tax treatment of health insurance, the President has won support from *The Washington Post, The Wall Street Journal,* and experts from think tanks as traditionally divergent as the Urban Institute and The Heritage Foundation.

Does everyone like this? No, of course not. Congressional leaders have said the proposal is dead on arrival. It is such a new and creative idea that it will take time for people to analyze and digest the plan and its implications.

- Many are fearful that it will accelerate the decline of employment-based health insurance by giving a tax break to individuals who buy coverage on their own. But job-based coverage already is declining. This will give employers and employees a new negotiating tool to bargain for insurance that offers the best value.
- Others say it doesn't do enough for the uninsured and that tax credits rather than a tax deduction would be better. Using some of the "Affordable Choices" money, states can put new resources on the table to provide state-based tax credits, vouchers, or other new subsidies to the uninsured to supplement the federal tax break.

There are many more details than we can get into here and which will be addressed over time, but what's the bottom line? The President's plan is a win/win/win/win/win:

- It is a win for the uninsured because it offers millions more Americans the chance to buy health insurance with the tax savings they will receive from the new standard deduction and likely new state subsidies.
- It is a win for states because they will have more flexibility with the new "Affordable Choices" state initiative to direct federal resources to meet the needs of citizens to get affordable health insurance.
- It is a win for employees because they now have the opportunity to buy health insurance that they can own and take with them from job to job, and it gives them more control over decisions involving their health insurance and health care.
- The health sector wins because this eliminates one of the major hidden forces driving up the cost of health insurance and gives the market new incentives to make insurance more affordable.
- Taxpayers win because 80 percent of them will receive a tax cut when they take the new $15,000 family deduction.

Sharpening the Debate

This idea sharpens the debate between those who believe that the answer to the problems in the health sector lies in much more government involvement through expansion of public programs and those who believe that the free market can and does have much more potential to get health insurance costs down and provide people with greater access to coverage and more choices.

Incentives work, and competition works. What we need to do is engage the power of consumers to transform our health sector to become more efficient, more responsive to consumer needs, and more affordable.

79

"Health Care for America"

Jacob S. Hacker

America's $2.2-trillion-a-year medical complex is enormously wasteful, ill-targeted, inefficient, and unfair. The best medical care is extremely good, but the Rube Goldberg system through which that care is financed is extremely bad—and falling apart. One out of three nonelderly Americans spend some time without health insurance every two years, and the majority of those remain uninsured for more than nine months.[1] Meanwhile, runaway health costs have become an increasingly grave threat, not just to the security of family finances, but also to corporate America's bottom line. The United States spends much more as a share of its economy on health care than any other nation, and yet all this spending has failed to buy Americans the one thing that health insurance is supposed to provide: health security.

Health insecurity is not confined to one part of the population. It is experienced by all Americans: those without insurance as well as those who risk losing coverage; those who are impoverished as well as those with higher incomes who experience catastrophic costs; those who are sick or injured as well as those who are just one sickness or injury away from financial calamity. As health care costs have skyrocketed and the proportion of Americans with stable benefits has eroded, health insecurity has become a shared American experience, felt by those who thought they had it made as well as those just struggling to get by.

This growing problem is pushing health care reform back onto the agenda of American politics after more than a decade of neglect. And yet, nothing guarantees that this debate will end differently than previous battles. Again and again in the 20th century—most recently, in the early 1990s—efforts to make health insurance an integral piece of the American social fabric were stymied. The stakes are too high to allow reform to be blocked again. America's economy, the finances of its middle class, the quality of its medical care, and the health of its citizens all hang in the balance.

To avoid the dismal fate of previous reform campaigns, a successful agenda must take seriously the political constraints and organizational realities that have hamstrung reform efforts in the past. Limits on public budgets, resistance to measures that might be seen as taking away what Americans already have, and the embedded realities of the present system all stand squarely in the path of grand policy redesigns—from single-payer national health insurance, to individual mandates requiring that everyone purchase private coverage, to a universe of individualized Health Savings Accounts. Instead, the most promising route forward is to build on the most popular elements of the present structure— Medicare and employment-based health insurance for well-compensated workers—through a series of large-scale changes that are straightforward, politically doable, self-reinforcing, and guaranteed to produce expanded health security.

A True Guarantee of Affordable Health Care

Health Care for America embodies this strategy.[2] It would extend insurance to all non-elderly Americans through a new Medicare-like program and workplace health insurance, while creating an effective framework for controlling medical costs and improving health outcomes to guarantee affordable, quality care to all. It is at once comprehensive, realistic, consistent with American values and beliefs, and grounded in the best elements of the present system. It combines employer and personal responsibility with a strong public commitment to ensuring that American workers and their families and American employers can afford coverage. It promises better care, lower costs, more choice, healthier citizens, and immensely stronger guarantees for workers and their families. And it promises real savings for employers and state governments—without unraveling existing sources of health security, without forcing workers to obtain coverage on their own, and without pressuring patients into Health Savings Accounts or tightly managed health maintenance organizations (HMOs).

What Health Care for America would do is simple: every legal resident of the United States who lacks access to Medicare or good workplace coverage would be able to buy into the "Health Care for America Plan," a new public insurance pool modeled after Medicare. This new program would team up with Medicare to bargain for lower prices and upgrade the quality of care so that every enrollee would have access to either an affordable Medicare-like plan with free choice of providers or to a selection of comprehensive private plans.

At the same time, employers would be asked to either provide coverage as good as this new plan or, failing that, make a relatively modest payroll-based contribution to the Health Care for America Plan to help finance coverage for their workers. At a stroke, then, no one with a direct or family tie to the workforce would remain uninsured. The self-employed could buy into the plan by paying the same payroll-based contribution; those without workplace ties would be able to buy into Health Care for America by paying an income-related premium. The states would be given powerful incentives to enroll any remaining uninsured.

Equally important is what Health Care for America would *not* do. It would not eliminate private employment-based insurance. It would not allow employers to retreat from the financing of a reasonable share of the cost of health insurance. It would not leave Americans coping with ever-higher private insurance premiums with an inadequate voucher, or pressure them to enroll in HMOs that do not cover care from the doctors they know and trust. It would not break up the large insurance groups in the public and private sectors that are best capable of pooling risks today. And it certainly would not encourage individualized Health Savings Accounts that threaten to further fragment the insurance market and leave Americans even less protected against medical costs. Instead, Health Care for America would preserve what works in American health financing and replace what does not—through a simple yet comprehensive strategy that holds out the best promise of controlling costs, improving quality, and guaranteeing health security.

Health Care for America is not single payer—a vision that, for both political and budgetary reasons, is unlikely to be achieved in the near future. Nonetheless, Health Care for America does embody many of the key virtues of a universal Medicare-like program. At heart, it rests on the time-tested idea of social insurance, the notion that major financial risks should be pooled as widely as possible across rich and poor, healthy and sick, young and old. Health Care for America would create a large publicly overseen insurance pool that would bargain for lower prices, capitalize on the vast administrative efficiencies of a single insurer, and use its reach and purchasing power to spearhead improvements in the quality and cost-effectiveness of medical care.

Health Care for America also rests on the conviction that the Medicare model has a proven track record—and a huge amount of untapped potential—when it comes to controlling costs and improving care. Sustaining Medicare's vital promise to the aged and disabled does not require abandoning the Medicare model, as critics of the program frequently claim. It requires extending the model to those without secure workplace coverage, filling some of the glaring gaps that remain in Medicare, and allowing the two programs to work jointly to hold down costs and improve the quality of care.

Health Care for America would be good not just for American families, but also for American corporations. It would make it easier for firms to provide coverage on their own by reducing the burden of uncompensated care and the cost to employers of covering workers' employed dependents (because all employers would be required to contribute to the cost of covering their own workers). It would also offer substantial savings to employers that decided to buy into the Health Care for America Plan—an option that many small and low-wage employers would likely seize. Employers that chose to enroll their workers would be free to supplement Health Care for America benefits, allowing them to provide better coverage at a lower cost. Yet, unlike many other approaches promising business savings, this approach would guarantee that every employer either provided good private coverage or enrolled its workers in a broad insurance pool and contributed to its cost.

If one word captures the essence of Health Care for America, it is "guaranteed." Health Care for America would guarantee coverage; it would guarantee a generous package of benefits; it would guarantee greater choice; and it would guarantee real savings and improved quality. The lack of such guarantees is at the heart of health insecurity in the United States today. To fulfill these guarantees, Health Care for America would create a new public-private partnership with powerful built-in incentives to control costs while improving quality. The stakeholders in our crumbling system would forge a new and stronger social contract for the 21st century.

How Health Care for America Would Provide Affordable Coverage to All

Health Care for America has just three central elements:

- the new Health Care for America Plan, which would be open to any legal U.S. resident without good workplace coverage;[3]
- a requirement that employers (and the self-employed) either purchase coverage comparable to Health Care for America for all their workers or pay a relatively modest payroll contribution (6% of payroll) to fund Health Care for America coverage for all their employees;
- a requirement that Americans who remain without insurance take responsibility for their and their families' health by purchasing private coverage or buying into the Health Care for America Plan.[4]

The benefits of the Health Care for America Plan would be comprehensive. Besides Medicare benefits, the plan would cover mental health and maternal and child health and include strict limits on total out-of-pocket spending. (Medicare currently lacks such limits, and Health Care for America would authorize a study of how best to incorporate cost-sharing limits into Medicare in the future.) Health Care for America would also provide drug coverage directly, rather than solely through private plans. And it would allow Medicare to provide drug coverage directly on behalf of the elderly and disabled as well. In addition, a new independent Benefits Advisory Commission would be created to determine what both the Health Care for America Plan and Medicare should cover going forward, allowing the harmonization of the two programs' benefits over time. To encourage better health, preventive and well-child care and covered screenings would be provided to all beneficiaries at no out-of-pocket charge.

The Health Care for America Plan would provide extensive assistance to enrollees to help them afford coverage. For those enrolled in the plan at their place of work, anyone whose income was below 200% of the poverty level would pay no additional premiums. (The poverty line in 2006 was roughly $10,000 for an individual and $20,000 for a family of four.) The maximum monthly premium—phased in between 200% and 300% of the poverty level—would be $70 for an individual, $140 for a couple, $130 for a single-parent family, and $200 for all other families.

In sum, every American with a direct or family tie to the workforce—a group that includes more than 80% of the currently uninsured and more than 90% of all non-elderly Americans—would be automatically covered by either private insurance or the Health Care for America Plan.[5] Employers, in turn, would contribute a share of earnings on behalf of every individual or family enrolled in Health Care for America. And Americans with family incomes above 200% of the poverty level who enrolled in Health Care for America through their place of work would pay a monthly premium based on family income, as just detailed.

Non-elderly beneficiaries of Medicaid and S-CHIP (the State Children's Health Insurance Program) would be enrolled in the Health Care for America Plan, either through their employers if working or individually if not. Enrollment in the plan would relieve the states of a significant share of the burden of these programs, providing states with strong incentives to streamline enrollment. To ensure that former Medicaid and S-CHIP beneficiaries received coverage at least as generous as that which they had enjoyed previously, the states would be required to provide wraparound benefits. (States could also elect to pay Health Care for America to provide such wraparound coverage.) Moreover, all low-income enrollees in the Health Care for America Plan would receive cost-sharing subsidies to ensure that co-payments or deductibles did not deter them from seeking necessary care.

For the small share of people without direct or family ties to the workforce and ineligible for Medicaid, S-CHIP, or Medicare, the Health Care for America Plan would be available as an attractive new coverage option. Premiums would again be based on income, ranging from no premium in the case of those with incomes below the poverty line to the average actuarial cost of coverage for all enrollees in Health Care for America in the case of those with incomes above 400% of the poverty level. In other words, Health Care for America would allow higher-income individuals without workplace ties to buy into the program for a premium that did not vary with age, region, or health status (a so-called community-rated premium).

Coverage under the Health Care for America Plan would be continuous and guaranteed. Once an individual or family was enrolled, they would remain covered unless they gained qualified private workplace coverage.

Building on the Best Aspects of Workplace Insurance While Filling the Gaps

Health Care for America capitalizes on the untapped potential of workplace insurance to ensure that virtually everyone has coverage. But while employers would play an important role in making Health Care for America work, they would not be asked to make an open-ended commitment. Most, in fact, would save money under the plan, and employers as a whole would reap substantial savings, especially over time.

* * *

For most workers with good coverage, Health Care for America would change little—besides eliminating the very real threat of *losing* coverage. Employers that provide generous insurance are largely big corporations with high wages, precisely the employers most likely to continue to sponsor tax-favored coverage, rather than pay the payroll-based contribution to enroll their workers in the Health Care for America Plan. Thus, enrollees in the Health Care for America Plan would mostly be current beneficiaries of Medicaid and S-CHIP, low-wage employees, and the working uninsured, as well as early retirees, contingent workers, and the self-employed. All these groups have weak access to employment-based insurance and insecure access to *any* insurance, and all would be vastly better off because of Health Care for America.

* * *

For non-workers ineligible for Medicaid, S-CHIP, or Medicare—including early retirees—states would be required to set up effective enrollment and outreach systems that enrolled people when they sought state assistance or obtained hospital care. States would also be encouraged to subsidize the (community-rated) premiums paid by higher-income non-workers, especially those that were temporarily unemployed. In the case of early retirees, employers could contribute to the cost of the Health Care for American Plan on a tax-free basis. Most employers would find this a much less expensive way of providing retiree coverage, which is currently unraveling due to rising costs.

In sum, Health Care for America would level the playing field, ensuring that every firm made at least a modest contribution to the cost of coverage for every worker. Meanwhile, Americans without ties to the workforce would be enrolled in the Health Care for America Plan through an individual buy-in, through state antipoverty and unemployment insurance programs, or through new efforts to reach the uninsured when they sought medical care without insurance.

Using the Medicare Model to Contain Costs and Improve Quality

The other side of Health Care for America's pragmatic approach is its commitment to build on the success and potential of Medicare, America's most popular and familiar health program. For millions of Americans who are now uninsured or lack secure or affordable workplace coverage, the Health Care for America Plan would be an extremely attractive option. Through it, roughly half of non-elderly Americans would have access to a good public insurance plan with free choice of providers. At the same time, the Health Care for America Plan would give enrollees access to a range of high-quality comprehensive health plans that would offer broad, easily comparable benefits.

*   *   *

Because Medicare and the Health Care for America Plan would bargain jointly for lower prices and join forces to improve quality, they would have enormous combined leverage to hold down costs. Cross-national evidence and the historical experience of Medicare show conclusively that concentrated purchasing power is by far the most effective means by which to restrain the price of medical services. Other nations spend much less for the same medical services than we do because their insurance systems bargain for lower prices. And though Medicare covers less than a seventh of the U.S. population, it has still controlled costs substantially better than the private sector, especially since the introduction of payment controls in the mid-1980s.

*   *   *

The Health Care for America proposal promises to restrain costs not just because it creates a large public insurance pool. The structure of the proposal also ensures that the sector best able to control costs is rewarded with additional patients over time. Because employers covering approximately half of workers would continue to provide private insurance, employers and insurers would be free to experiment with their own cost-control strategies, so long as these strategies did not involve cutting benefits or shifting more costs onto workers. And if employers and insurers effectively held down costs, then private insurance would become increasingly attractive in comparison with the Health Care for America

Plan. If, by contrast, private premiums were not kept in line, an increasing share of employers would enroll their workers in the Health Care for America Plan.

Thus, rather than a constant tug of war, Health Care for America would create a constructive public–private dynamic that would reward the sector best able to control costs—and without holding the health security of ordinary Americans in the balance.

Health Care for America's Realistic Financing

Health Care for America would require new federal spending. But because the majority of workers who now have employment-based coverage would retain private workplace insurance when the new Health Care for America Plan was in place, federal spending would be much lower than it would be under a universal Medicare plan. Furthermore, most of the necessary financing would come from those benefiting directly from the new Health Care for America Plan—namely, from employers that make the payroll-based contribution for guaranteed health insurance for their workers and from higher-income individuals who pay income-related premiums when enrolling in the Health Care for America Plan.

A good deal of the additional financing would come from the reduction of federal spending for S-CHIP and Medicaid, and from the redirection of current state spending on these programs. (Despite requiring that the states continue to contribute to the cost of public health insurance, this proposal would still provide substantial savings to the states.) In addition, the movement of workers from tax-favored private coverage into Health Care for America would reduce federal tax subsidies for employment-based insurance. And payroll and income tax receipts would rise due to the substitution of wages for health benefits among firms that pay less for insurance than they would have without reform.

The remaining federal costs could be financed by various combinations of liquor and tobacco taxes and other dedicated levies and general revenues. Past estimates suggest that this approach has a relatively modest net federal cost compared with other comprehensive proposals, many of which would cover fewer Americans.[6] Moreover, Health Care for America requires much less new tax financing (even including the payroll-based contribution) than a single-payer proposal.

* * *

Why Health Care for America Is What Americans Want

Americans are ready for a bold proposal for change like Health Care for America. Most believe the present system is broken, and most are willing to support fundamental change even if it means new taxes or an enhanced government role. Americans do not believe they should be on their own when it comes to health care. They want employers to remain in the game, and they are skeptical of measures, such as Health Savings Accounts, that would shift more costs and risks onto them. Overwhelming majorities of *insured* Americans worry that they won't be able to afford care in the future, and a substantial majority of those who currently have insurance fear losing coverage altogether.[7]

*   *   *

To pass the test of public opinion, a reform proposal should be simple, rest on familiar foundations, and not be threatening to those Americans relatively happy with their coverage today. Health Care for America is such a proposal. It contains no complex purchasing pools or complicated new tax credits, no tough new incentives for HMO enrollment, and no unpopular changes in the tax treatment of health benefits. Instead, it builds on the most popular elements of the present system, changing little for most Americans with secure insurance today, except to promise them true health security at last.

*   *   *

Discussion Questions

1. What do you see as the main strengths and weaknesses of these three competing plans?

2. Economists would tell us that there is no such thing as "free" health care—ultimately, someone has to pay for it. One of the premises of market-oriented approaches like Turner's is that if people do not bear the cost purchasing something, they tend to overuse it. For example, people might go to see a doctor much more quickly when the visit is viewed as "free" than if they had to pay something for the visit. Do you believe this is a problem in health care? How if at all should market and price considerations be part of the equation when deciding on health care?

3. One complaint about the current system is that decisions about what care will and will not be provided is being made by bureaucrats in insurance companies. Ultimately, though, someone has to make these decisions, and they are hard decisions. Critics of single-payer plans warn that "rationing" of health care will be even worse where government has a larger role. There is simply no way to afford every possible procedure for every person from the beginning of their life until their very old age. Some procedures might be considered optional, or cosmetic, too expensive given their likelihood of success or the amount of improvement they will provide. If you were determining health care policy, where would you have these

decisions made? By whom? How can you be sure those individuals have an incentive to approve the right amount of health care, neither being too stingy nor too generous? And how would you determine what the "right amount" is, assuming that the answer cannot be to cover every single expense and procedure?

4. Only in health care is the idea of a single payer seriously considered in the United States. Is health care in some way so fundamentally different that this solution would be offered in that industry but in no other?

NOTES

1. Families USA, *One in Three: Nonelderly Americans Without Health Insurance, 2002–2003* (Washington, D.C.: Families USA, 2005), available online at www.familiesusa.org/assets/pdfs/82million_uninsured_report6fdc.pdf.

2. This proposal builds on a plan developed in 2001 for the "Covering America" project sponsored by the Robert Wood Johnson Foundation. Although key features of the proposal have not changed, a number of provisions have been altered or updated. Readers interested in the earlier proposal ("Medicare Plus") and the cost and coverage estimates for this earlier proposal that were produced by the Lewin Group can find them at www.greatriskshift.com/ideas.html.

3. For simplicity, legal U.S. residents are hereafter referred to as "Americans."

4. All Americans would eventually be required to show proof of coverage by attaching a standard insurance verification form to their federal income tax return. Because all workers and their families would be enrolled automatically in either Health Care for America or employer-sponsored plans, the individual mandate would have true significance only for the small share of Americans who both lack ties to the workforce and are currently ineligible for Medicaid or S-CHIP (the State Children's Health Insurance Program). To reach those in this population who do not file tax returns, states would be given powerful incentives to enroll non-workers in Health Care for America. They would also be encouraged to subsidize Health Care for America coverage for the temporarily unemployed, and to establish mechanisms for enrolling the uninsured in Health Care for America when they sought care.

5. The estimate of the share of the non-elderly population with ties to the workforce is drawn from the 2006 Current Population Survey and represents the proportion of non-elderly individuals living in households with positive earnings. The exact share is 94%.

6. As part of the Agenda for Shared Prosperity project, the Economic Policy Institute plans to commission independent estimates of the cost and coverage impact of the Health Care for America proposal.

7. For a good recent compendium of polls, see Ruy Teixeira, "What the Public Really Wants on Health Care," The Century Foundation, December 4, 2006, available online at http://tcf.org/publications/healthcare/wptw.healthcare.pdf.

CHAPTER 16

Foreign Policy and World Politics

80

"The Age of Open Society"

George Soros

"Globalization" refers, generally speaking, to the diffusion of interests and ide-
ologies across national borders. Proponents of globalization point to the hope that
it will encourage global economic development, and foster universal human
rights that are not dependent on where someone happens to live. Critics fall into
two camps. One consists of those who fear that globalization will undermine na-
tional sovereignty and lead to a "one world" government that leaves everyone at
the mercy of distant bureaucrats and officials. The other camp consists of those
who see globalization as a smokescreen for corporate hegemony, where multina-
tional corporations exploit workers in countries with low wages, few job protec-
tions, and lax environmental regulation, all in the name of higher profits.

George Soros believes that economic globalization and political globalization
are out of sync: although capital and markets move freely across national bound-
aries, political institutions do not. A global "open society" would, in his view,
insure that the political and social needs of all countries are met (not simply the
needs of industrialized nations, whose interests tend to dominate international
markets), and would foster the development of stable political and financial insti-
tutions. This would require a broad international organization, either as part of
the United Nations or as an independent institution. It would have to be based
on the idea that there are interests that transcend questions of national sover-
eignty.

Global politics and global economics are dangerously out of sync.
Although we live in a global economy characterized by free trade
and the free movement of capital, our politics are still based on the sovereignty of the state. International institutions exist, but their powers are
limited by how much authority states are willing to confer on them. At
the same time, the powers of the state are limited by the freedom of

capital to escape taxation and regulation by moving elsewhere. This is particularly true of the countries at the periphery of the global capitalist system, whose economic destiny depends on what happens at the center.

This state of affairs would be sustainable if the market mechanism could be trusted to satisfy social needs. But that is not the case.

We need to find international political arrangements that can meet the requirements of an increasingly interdependent world. These arrangements ought to be built on the principles of open society. A perfect society is beyond our reach. We must content ourselves with the next best thing: a society that holds itself open to improvement. We need institutions that allow people of different views, interests, and backgrounds to live together in peace. These institutions should assure the greatest degree of freedom compatible with the common interest. Many mature democracies come close to qualifying as open societies. But they refuse to accept openness as a universal principle.

How could this principle of openness be translated into practice? By the open societies of the world forming an alliance for this purpose. The alliance would have two distinct but interrelated goals: to foster the development of open society within individual countries; and to establish international laws, rules of conduct, and institutions to implement these norms.

It is contrary to the principles of open society to dictate from the outside how a society should govern itself. Yet the matter cannot be left entirely to the state, either. The state can be an instrument of oppression. To the extent possible, outside help should take the form of incentives; the evolution of open society requires aid for economic and institutional development. Punitive measures, though sometimes unavoidable, tend to be counterproductive.

Unfortunately, positive intervention is out of favor because of an excessive faith in the magic of the marketplace. There is an alliance of democratic countries, NATO, capable of military intervention, but there is no similar alliance to engage in constructive intervention. This open-society alliance ought to have a much broader membership than NATO, and it must include nongovernmental members as well as heads of state. As former U.S. Secretary of State Henry Kissinger points out, states have interests but no principles; we cannot rely on them to implement the principle of openness.

Democratic governments are, however, responsive to the wishes of their electorates. Therefore, the impulse for the alliance has to come from the people, not from their leaders. Citizens living in open societies must recognize a global open society as something worth sacrifice. This responsibility rests in particular with the United States, the sole surviving superpower and the dominant force in the global capitalist system. There can be no global open society without its leadership. But the United States has become carried away by its success and fails to see why it should subordinate its self-interest to some nebulous common principle. The United States jealously guards its sovereignty and behaves as if it ought to be the sole arbiter of right and wrong. Washington will have to undergo a significant change of heart before it is ready to lead an open-society alliance.

The alliance, if it comes to pass, must not lose sight of its own fallibity. Foreign aid, though very valuable, is notoriously inefficient. Rule-based incentives are more promising. The international financial architecture needs to be redesigned to help give underdeveloped countries a leg up. Incentives would be conditional on each country's success in establishing open political and financial institutions.

The alliance could act within the United Nations, or it could go it alone. But a commitment to such an alliance would offer an opportunity to reform the United Nations. The noble intentions annunciated in the preamble of the U.N. Charter can never be attained as long as the United Nations remains a rigid association of sovereign states. But there is ample room for improvement, and an open-society alliance would be a start. Perhaps one day, then, historians will look back at these years to come as the Age of Open Society.

DISCUSSION QUESTIONS

1. Is Soros's suggestion about an open society practical? Do you think there are circumstances under which nations would agree to such a proposal?

2. How, if at all, will globalization change notions about national identity? Do you think that, twenty-five or fifty years from now, being a U.S. citizen—or a citizen of any other country—will have the same meaning as it does now?

81

"Reality Check"

Peter D. Sutherland

Peter Sutherland confronts the arguments against globalization. Over the past few years, protesters have disrupted meetings of international economic organizations (especially the World Trade Organization, an institution created to foster global free trade). Susan George, a critic of the World Trade Organization, gave the flavor of the arguments against globalization in a recent article in the journal The Nation: *" 'Free trade' as managed by the World Trade Organization and reinvigorated at the recent negotiations in Doha is largely the freedom of the fox in the henhouse. Despite the advance on generic drugs for pandemics like AIDS, tuberculosis and malaria, the South's needs are shelved and the transnationals continue to run the show according to their own preferred rules." Sutherland has little patience with such protests, and believes that protesters are motivated by a simplistic and inaccurate view of what globalization is about: "The notion that globalization is an international conspiracy on the part of industrial-country governments and large firms to marginalize the poorest nations, to exploit low wages and social costs wherever they may be found . . . and even to undermine human rights and cut away democratic processes that stand in the way of ever more open markets is, of course, utter nonsense." He disagrees that international trade organizations ignore the needs of poor countries, and argues that increased global trade is (and has been) the most effective mechanism of economic development. At the same time, he offers some suggestions on how to ensure that existing institutions are strengthened.*

The Seattle Ministerial Conference of the World Trade Organization (WTO) demonstrated with disturbing force the huge confusions that haunt the public mind and much of global politics about the nature of trade and the process now known as globalization. The notion that globalization is an international conspiracy on the part of industrial-country governments and large firms to marginalize the poorest nations, to exploit low wages and social costs wherever they may be found, to diminish cultures in the interests of an Anglo-Saxon model of lifestyle and language, and even to undermine human rights and cut away democratic processes that stand in the way of ever more open markets is, of course, utter nonsense. Yet the Seattle demonstrations vividly exhibited the worrying tendency to equate these concerns and others to the existence and potential development of the World Trade Organization, the institutional and legal face of the world trade system.

This outpouring of misconceived, ill-understood propaganda against a system that has brought vast gains to most nations over the past few decades is extraordinarily dangerous. It is a threat to the prospects of a better life for many millions, perhaps billions, of people at the start of the new millennium. If left unquestioned and unchallenged in the interests of political correctness or political advantage, this sentiment could set the cause of economic and social development back 20 years. This threat is made all the more serious by the difficult new challenges facing governments today. Still, Seattle showed more clearly some of the institutional difficulties of managing effective decision-making processes, with over 100 countries truly interested and involved in managing the geopolitical realities of the 21st century.

The Biggest Straw Man

In order to understand the dangers implied by attacks on the WTO, one must first distinguish between "globalization" and the World Trade Organization. Neither as a body of international law nor as a governmental institution can the WTO be regarded as synonymous with globalization. The WTO, like its predecessor the General Agreement on Tariffs and Trade (GATT), is a collection of rules and undertakings voluntarily entered into and implemented by governments on the basis of consensus among those governments to provide a predictable, stable, and secure environment in which all types of firms can trade and invest. A small transfer of national sovereignty (insofar as any purely intergovernmental structure can affect sovereignty) in the interest of internationally enforceable disciplines brings economic gains for all and prevents economic muscle from being the sole arbiter of commercial advantage. It is easy to argue that in a period when business is as likely to be conducted at the global level as at the national, the WTO recovers a degree of sovereignty for governments that otherwise find themselves no longer able to influence significant aspects of their economic future.

Of course, open and secure markets have encouraged global trade and investment. They have provided jobs, consumer choice, and rising personal wealth in large parts of the world, including many developing countries. Governments everywhere want to see their firms able to trade, and they actively seek inward investment by foreign firms. But that is not the whole story of globalization. The WTO has had only a marginal effect on other significant elements, most of which relate to the mobility of people, information, culture, technology and capital. Air transport, telecommunications, the media, and now the internet are four of the most crucial drivers of globalization. While they are not without their dangers or inadequacies, few would seriously argue that they have not brought widespread benefits. These innovations represent the positive face of the global economy.

Are the more troublesome aspects of globalization really a reflection of the trading system, or do they represent quite different policy failures, including poor education and training, misplaced and inefficient government intervention in industry, corruption in both the public and private sectors, poor governance, crime, lack of transparency in regulatory systems, inadequate or inappropriate social security and pensions systems, and so on? Admittedly, the trading system has not always provided the right results; for instance, it ought to be able to deliver more for the least-developed countries, even if it cannot solve all their problems. However, equating the WTO with the difficulties of the global economy risks damaging a system which has given much and still has more to offer. Such thinking also neglects the importance of the WTO's fundamental role in simply facilitating trade and investment. The tendency to turn to the trade rules to resolve every challenge facing mankind—the environment, human rights, and labor standards—is almost as dangerous as the desire to dismantle the system in order to halt a process of globalization that is beyond the realm of any institution.

Fruits of the Uruguay Round

The first thing governments need to do in the current atmosphere of sometimes dubiously motivated protest and fear is to stop apologizing for the WTO and start defending it. The GATT helped create three decades of remarkably healthy economic growth. It succeeded in a low-profile manner because, in the 1950s and 1960s, high customs duties could be brought down steadily without attracting much political controversy. By the time the Uruguay Round was launched in 1986, the world was left with the hard cases of international trade. Negotiators finally had to face up to protectionism in the most sensitive industries of the developed countries, particularly in textiles, clothing, footwear, agriculture, steel, and automobiles. They also came to realize that the next stages of reducing protection and opening markets, and thus re-establishing the kind of trade growth spurred by the GATT, would mean moving some of the focus of negotiation from conditions at the border (such as tariffs and quota restrictions) to the heart of domestic regulation and sectoral support.

Immense political effort was required at the highest levels of government, but the Uruguay Round succeeded and established the WTO in the process. The advances made on all fronts cannot be underestimated. Policies in agriculture underwent a revolution: all market-access restrictions were translated into transparent tariffs, and the process of winding back the most distorting features of domestic support and export subsidies was initiated. A higher level of practical liberalization for farm goods might have been preferred, but the fundamental policy changes are irreversible and provide the basis to go further next time. Similarly, in textiles and clothing all the countries maintaining heavy quantitative controls on imports are committed to phasing them out. It will take nearly ten years, but the agreement at Uruguay marked a fundamental change of heart and direction.

Many other trade rules were amended, clarified, or added to the system. The practice of "negotiating" so-called "voluntary export restraints" affecting automobiles, steel, cutlery, and many other products for which consumers were forced to pay far more than was reasonable was outlawed. Some of the most damaging features of anti-dumping practices were cut back. Modern rules on technical barriers to trade and health and safety regulation were also put in place.

An agreement requiring intellectual property rights to be available and enforceable in all WTO countries was concluded for the first time, despite doubts and difficulties in some industrial and developing countries. There were two final jewels in the crown. First, an agreement on trade in services brought GATT-like disciplines and concessions in sectors as diverse as banking, telecommunications, professional services, travel, tourism, and the audio-visual industry. Financial services and telecommunications were the subject of additional valuable packages of concessions in the past three years, and the new negotiations, beginning this year, will take the process of progressive liberalization in the services sector much further. Second, the entire body of WTO disciplines and concessions was made enforceable through a tough dispute-settlement procedure that has now been used in nearly 200 cases.

It has become almost an article of faith that while all of these developments were good for the industrialized countries and some of the more advanced developing countries, many poorer countries lost out. Some critics suggest that these countries did not benefit from the results of the round, and that they were, in fact, further marginalized and impoverished. According to these critics, such marginalization is not surprising because developing countries had little or no voice in the negotiations that culminated in agreement at the end of 1993.

Such a position is an insult to the abilities of the many developing country trade negotiators who participated fully in the Uruguay Round. Although I took responsibility at a comparatively late stage, I can attest to the effectiveness and strength of purpose of these officials and ministers from poorer nations. They had considerable influence on the original development of the Uruguay Round agenda; worked assiduously through the eight-year process of examination and elucidation of issues, and negotiation of texts; and were in the foreground during the tough final months of bargaining. Certainly the United States, the European Union, and Japan were more influential, and many of the Uruguay Round texts pay particular attention to their interests. But the developing countries succeeded for the first time in any trade round in melding an influence on the final outcome quite disproportionate to their share of world trade. The WTO is very much their institution and the rules of world trade are as much their rules as those of the industrial countries.

Myths and Realities

So, if it is untrue that developing countries were ignored in the establishment of the WTO, is it at least true that they saw few practical benefits in terms of trade and investment? Again, the answer is no. A few measures demonstrating the longterm trends rather than the shortterm aberrations bolster the point. Are developing countries benefiting from more open industrial-country markets? The answer is yes; despite the fall in trade during 1997 because of the drop in commodity prices and the Asian financial crisis, the share of developing countries and the transition economies in the imports of developed countries increased to 25 percent in 1998 from 22.8 percent in 1994. Has the developing countries' share in world trade grown? Again, yes. Despite the setbacks of 1997–1998, the latest WTO figures show that the share of developing countries in world exports of manufactures in 1998 was one percent higher than in 1994, and 6.4 percent higher than in 1990. The same overall growth trend can be observed for merchandise exports generally as well as agricultural products.

What about investment? Have developing countries seen an inward flow of productive investment, as they should if they offer more open markets with stable trade regimes based upon WTO disciplines? As with trade, the picture is mixed, with considerable variations in performance. However, figures from the UN Conference on Trade and Development show that overall inward foreign direct investment (FDI) flows to the developing world rose steadily and consistently from an average of US$35 billion a year in the period 1987–92 to US$166 billion in 1998. Taken as a percentage of gross fixed capital formation, FDI inflows to developing countries rose from an average of 3.9 percent in the period 1987–92 to 10.3 percent in 1998.

There is nothing fundamentally wrong with the system that calls for a wholesale rethinking on behalf of the developing countries. It is accepted that some developing countries have had difficulty in implementing some Uruguay Round commitments. Political and conceptual difficulties have hampered the implementation of certain intellectual property commitments in countries like India. In some of the poorest economies, the absence of solid institutional and technological infrastructure has made the implementation of agreements such as those on customs valuation and health and safety standards difficult. But patience and the right kind of technical assistance can resolve such problems over time. They are not evidence of a systemic failure in the WTO.

Indeed, many developing countries are successfully integrating themselves into the global economy through their commitment to WTO obligations. The failure of the Seattle meeting effectively blocked the continuation of that process or, at the very least, reduced opportunities for further progress. Essentially all that remains is the potential for negotiations on trade in services and agriculture that were mandated in the Uruguay Round agreements. This is not a small agenda, and any successful conclusion in the near future remains in question.

What has been lost or suspended is a larger and, in some respects more urgent, agenda. Developing countries have clearly been denied much that they rightly expected in the implementation of Uruguay Round commitments. They had reasonable demands that industrial countries implement in better faith the agreement to phase out textiles and clothing quotas. The agricultural agreement should have brought them more commercial advantage than has been the case. Antidumping legislation has continued to operate too stringently to the disadvantage of poorer countries. On the other hand, these countries have sometimes had difficulties in meeting their own obligations. That is hardly surprising since they have been required to go much further, much faster than was ever expected of industrial countries. In most cases, additional time needed for implementation of commitments should willingly be provided along with generous technical assistance efforts and the necessary funding for institutional capacity-building.

The least developed countries have been denied the duty-free treatment in market access that has long been promised and discussed in the context of a new round. The entire world has lost the commercial opportunities that would have sprung from global tariff and non-tariff-barrier negotiations covering industrial products. It is estimated that a 50 percent reduction in industrial tariffs would raise some US$270 billion in global income per year, and that developing countries could benefit from as much as 95 percent of the gains from liberalizing trade in manufactures.

Before the Next Round

Perhaps those opportunities will re-emerge, but the immediate priority is not to rush to launch a new round. Governments need to learn the lessons of the Seattle meeting and prepare the ground for the multilateral trading system to move forward on the basis of willing consensus among governments. I would propose four major areas as needing profound reconsideration.

First, coherence in trade policymaking is needed. Until now, this has tended to mean cooperation between the secretariats of the WTO and other major international institutions like the World Bank and the International Monetary Fund. Coherence should now take on a different meaning. It should ensure that the stances of WTO member governments in trade negotiations reflect a domestic consensus. Government departments must coordinate effectively among themselves so that, for instance, environmental, public health, or development concerns are factored into trade-policy decision-making early on. Governments must listen to and work with many different constituencies in an open and transparent manner. Only then can the WTO be clear of the foolish charge that it is some form of government-business conspiracy.

Second, negotiations and decision-making within the WTO itself need to become more coherent and effective. This may require a high level management structure in Geneva, perhaps based upon a restricted constituency-based management or advisory board. Senior policymakers should come to Geneva regularly to set the body's business in the fullest context, including financial development, environmental concerns, and other considerations. Moreover, both the preparatory process and the Seattle ministerial meeting demonstrated that while full transparency is vital—and the institution will have to steel itself to become yet more open—efficient and effective decision-making is necessary if continued paralysis is to be avoided. Of course, negotiating positions may often be so far apart that compromise is simply not possible. Recent history suggests, however, that the techniques of negotiating in a multilateral environment are either inoperable or have been forgotten.

Third, careful consideration must now be given to the speed and intensity with which a new round or any other effort to extend the trading system is pursued. There can be little doubt that the Seattle meeting was both premature and over-burdened with proposals that were poorly thought-out, unnecessary, or premature. Is there really an urgent need to launch a broad-based new trade round in the immediate future? If one believes that neither agriculture nor services negotiations can progress outside such a round, then perhaps the answer is a qualified "yes." But, if the reality is such that an early start would be unlikely to move forward with any conviction, then perhaps governments should take a deep breath and await a more propitious time. Nothing would damage the WTO's image further than another failed attempt to initiate a round.

Fourth, regardless of a new round, governments must now live up to their responsibilities and start energetically defending the principles on which the WTO is based. A "human face" for the trading system is appropriate if it does not serve to undermine the foundations of the system and the huge gains it has provided humanity over the past 50 years. It is perfectly possible to understand and respond to the concerns of those who doubt the value of the system without holding it hostage to local politics. The critics must understand that however justified their causes, the world would not be a better place without the WTO and without continued efforts to make it still more effective for all its members.

This is a turning point for the global trading system. How governments respond to the challenges raised by the Seattle Ministerial Conference could have an overwhelming influence on the contribution that the institution can have on the creation of a better society in the future. Globalization remains a fact and an opportunity. The WTO is one of the most effective instruments at our disposal for translating the opportunity into the reality of improved welfare for billions of citizens. There is no question that it could be a better instrument. But it is the best that we have at our disposal and are likely to have in the future. Governments must learn to use it wisely, change it carefully, and support it convincingly.

DISCUSSION QUESTIONS

1. Many critics of globalization argue that allowing goods and capital to move freely across borders serves only to move jobs to countries with the cheapest (and most exploitable) labor force. Supporters argue that these jobs, even though they might not pay much by Western standards, still provide much better opportunities than would otherwise be available. Who do you think has the better case?

2. Does your campus have organizations active in "anti-sweatshop" organizations? (These groups, among other things, have encouraged universities to insure that clothing and other gear with university symbols are not made by child labor or in dangerous factories). What impact have these organizations had on student opinion?

3. What is the alternative to globalization? What costs are associated with, for example, protecting domestic jobs from being exported? What are the benefits of such protection?

DEBATING THE ISSUES: FOREIGN POLICY—A WAR ON TERROR

How serious is the threat of global terror? Are we engaged in a global struggle with radical Islamists willing to use terror tactics—even weapons of mass destruction—in an effort to undermine Western values? Or are Al Qaeda and related groups especially dangerous criminal organizations, which can be fought and subdued through intelligence and law enforcement? Ian Lustick argues that the threat of terrorism is vastly overestimated. To Lustick, the "war on terror" is mostly a rhetorical device, used by government leaders to justify their own policies. When political leaders point out the obvious—John Kerry saying in 2004 that we would never be able to eliminate terrorism, and that we have to learn how to control it—he was, in Lustick's words, "smothered." The biggest problem with conceiving of a "war on terror," Lustick concludes, is that it produces counterproductive and wasteful policies. Instead of implementing programs that might actually succeed in protecting the country, political leaders pander to sensationalism and stoke needless fear in the public.

Frank Gaffney takes the exact opposite view. Gaffney, a former Reagan Administration defense department official, views radical Islamists (a group he calls "Islamofascists") as a grave threat to the West. In his view, we are engaged in a global struggle with "adherents to a totalitarian ideology bent on world domination and the destruction of all who stand in the way of that goal." The contrast with Lustick's position could not be clearer.

We also provide the unclassified portion of the July 2007 National Intelligence Estimate, which consists of a consensus summary of the views of the intelligence community. It concludes that the U.S. faces "a persistent and evolving terrorist threat over the next three years," from possible domestic cells and increased efforts by Al Qaeda (al-Qa'ida) to place members inside the country. Al Qaeda will continue its efforts to obtain nuclear, biological, and chemical weapons, and will use them if it has the opportunity.

82

"Are We Trapped in the War on Terror?"

Ian Lustick

The war in Iraq has become politically radioactive. It's a burden to any politician associated with it. Not so the War on Terror. It continues to attract the allegiance of every politician in the country, whether as a justification for keeping U.S. troops in Iraq to win in a central front in the War on Terror or as a justification for withdrawing those troops to win the really crucial battles in the War on Terror at home or in Afghanistan.

What accounts for the stupendous success of the War on Terror as a political program, as a frame of reference for policy and as undisputed champion in the battle for increases in discretionary funding over the last five years? Certainly it is not the scale of the threat to the homeland. Since 9/11, there has been no evidence of any serious terrorist threat from Islamic extremists inside America—no sleeper cells, no attacks, no evidence of serious planning or preparation for an attack. This, despite red-teaming analyses (and monthly shootings in schools and shopping malls) that show how easy it is, or would be, for terrorists bent on killing Americans to do so. This absence of evidence of a big domestic terror threat is even more instructive thanks to the unprecedentedly exhaustive, constant, unrestrained and heavily funded scrutiny of anyone and anything that law enforcement agencies have had even the vaguest reason to imagine might be suspect.

For many the absence of attacks is truly puzzling. What has puzzled me more, however, is how to explain a nearly universal allegiance of Americans to the War on Terror—the steady polling numbers showing support for it, the often panicky concern that it is not being prosecuted successfully enough, its dominance of the political landscape and the $650 billion that we have so far spent on it. Answering this question means understanding how the War on Terror was triggered and how it sustains itself.

The official mantra is that we fight in Iraq because it is the central front in the War on Terror. The exact opposite is the case. We are trapped in fighting an unwinnable and essentially nonsensical "War on Terror" *because* its invention was required in order to fight in Iraq. When we were struck on September 11, 2001, the U.S. military budget was the equal of the military budgets of the next 24 most powerful countries. That structural fact of military unipolarity, by sharply reducing the perception of the costs of military adventures, made it likely that the United States would fight some kind of war abroad. However, in the first eight months of the George W. Bush administration the State Department, the uniformed military and the intelligence community blocked efforts inspired by the Project for the New American Century, and led Vice President Dick Cheney and Defense Secretary Donald Rumsfeld to launch a war in Iraq as the first stage of a radical transformation of U.S. foreign policy toward global hegemony and military unilateralism. But when 9/11 produced an immense amount of political capital for a president peculiarly ready to accept the role offered him by that supremacist cabal—of anointed Churchillian savior in a global, epochal "War on Terror"—the cabal had exactly what it needed. As they spun it, the global War on Terror divided the world into those with us and those against us. Coupled with the principle of preemption, this radical division of the world into our camp and the enemy camp rendered automatically any country or group not with us as subject to attack by the United States at will. In this way, although Iraq had absolutely nothing to do with 9/11, the cabal was able to devise and implement the formula linking the September attacks to its long-cherished goal: forcible regime change in Iraq as a model for a series of quick neo-imperialist wars to revolutionize American foreign policy and accomplish conservative political objectives at home. Thus the latent propensity of the United States to go to war, born of immense military preponderance, was exploited by the supremacists, able to portray their long-sought invasion of Iraq as a requirement of a global War on Terror.

After years of slaughter in Iraq, the neocon fantasy of a series of cheap, fast imperial wars is dead. But the War on Terror lives on stronger than ever. How did it take on a life of its own and trap the entire political class and most Americans into public beliefs about the need to fight a global War on Terror as our first priority, even when there is no evidence of an enemy present in the United States?

Consider how the Congress responded to the War on Terror. In the summer of 2003, a list of 160 potential targets for terrorists was drawn up to be protected, triggering intense efforts by representatives and senators in Congress and their constituents to find targets in their districts that could generate funding. The result? Widening definitions of potential targets and mushrooming increases in the number of infrastructure and other assets deemed worthy of protection—up to 1,849 such targets in late 2003, 28,360 in 2004, 77,769 in 2005 and up to an estimated 300,000 in our national assets database today, including the Sears Tower in Chicago but also the Indiana Apple and Pork Festival.

Across the country virtually every lobby and interest group cast its traditional objectives and funding proposals as more important than ever, given the imperatives of the War on Terror. In exuberant press releases of the National Rifle Association, the War on Terror means more Americans should own and carry firearms to defend the country and themselves against terrorists. According to the gun-control lobby, fighting the War on Terror means passing strict gun-control laws to keep assault weapons out of the hands of terrorists. Schools of veterinary medicine called for quadrupling their funding. Who else would train veterinarians to defend the country against terrorists using hoof-and-mouth disease to decimate our cattle herds? Pediatricians declared that more funding was required to train pediatricians as first responders to terrorist attacks, since treating children as victims is not the same as treating adults. Pharmacists advocated the creation of pharmaceutical SWAT teams to respond quickly with appropriate drugs to the victims of terrorist attacks. Aside from the swarms of beltway-bandit consulting firms and huge corporate investments in counterterrorism activities, universities across the country created graduate programs in homeland security and institutes on terrorism and counterterrorism, all raising huge catcher's mitts into the air for the billions of dollars of grants and contracts blowing in the wind.

As these and other groups found counterterrorism slogans effective in raising revenue, they became even more committed to the War on Terror, convincing those who had been slow to define themselves as part of the war to do so quickly or lose out.

The same imperative—translate your agenda into War on Terror requirements or be starved of funds—and its spiraling consequences, surged across the government affecting all agencies. Bureaucrats unable to think of a way to describe their activities in War on Terror terms were virtually disqualified from budget increases and probably doomed to cuts. With billions of dollars a year in state and local funding, the Department of Homeland Security devised a list of 15 national planning scenarios to help guide its allocations. To qualify for Homeland Security funding, state and local governments had to describe how they would use these funds to meet one of those chosen 15 scenarios. What was the process that produced this list? It was in part deeply political, driven by competition among agencies, states and localities that knew funding opportunities would depend on exactly which scenarios were included or excluded—with anthrax, a chemical attack on a sports stadium and hoof-and-mouth disease included but attacks on liquid-natural-gas tankers and the spreading of West Nile virus excluded. Most instructive of all in this process was the unwillingness to define the enemy posing the terrorist threat. Why? Because if a particular enemy were identified certain scenarios profitable for some of the funding competitors would be disqualified. Thus the enemy in these scenarios is officially referred to as the "universal adversary"; in other words, it's Satan. This is how the War on Terror drives the country from responding to threats to preparing for vulnerabilities, producing an irrational and doomed strategic posture that treats any bad thing that could happen as a national-security imperative.

Of course, this entire dynamic is accelerated by the hallowed principle of CYA, Cover Your Ass. Each policy maker knows that if there is another attack no one will be able to predict where and when it will be; but after it occurs, it will be easy to discover who it was who did not approve some project or level of funding that could have prevented it.

Finally, apart from the merciless competition among politicians posing as War on Terror warriors—think of the bizarre public posturing about Abu Dhabi controlling our ports—there is no more important energy source for the War on Terror than the media. I don't mean just the films and television shows thriving on exciting images of maniacal but brilliant Middle East terrorists ready to destroy the country if not for a few heroes operating to protect us in an otherwise incompetent government. I am also talking about the news media.

When a blizzard bears down on a large American city, the local news media has a field day. Ratings rise. Announcers are barely able to contain their excitement. Meteorologists become celebrities. They warn of the storm event of the century. Viewers are glued to their sets. Soon, however, the blizzard dumps its snow and passes, or fizzles and is forgotten. Either way, the blizzard story ends. Ratings for local news shows return to normal, and anchors shift their attention back to murders, fires and auto accidents.

When it comes to the War on Terror, however, the "blizzard of the century" is always about to hit and never goes away. For the national media this is as good as it gets. Officially the terrorist threat level is always and everywhere no less than "elevated." Absent any actual attacks or detectable threats, government agencies manufacture pseudo-victories over alleged or sting-produced plots to justify hundreds of billions of dollars worth of mostly silly expenditures. With every lost soul captured by the FBI and presented as the latest incarnation of Muhammad Atta, the news media and the entertainment industry fairly exult, thriving on fears stoked by evocations of 9/11 and the ready availability of disaster scenarios too varied to be thwarted but too frightening to be ignored. Compounded by media sensationalism, these fears then provide irresistible opportunities for ambitious politicians to attack one another for failing to protect the terrorist target *du jour*: ports, border crossings, the milk supply, cattle herds, liquid-natural-gas tankers, nuclear power plants, drinking water, tunnels, bridges or subways. The result of such sensationalist coverage, accompanied by advice from academic or corporate experts anxious to sell their counterterrorism schemes to a terrified public and a cover-your-ass-obsessed government bureaucracy are more waves of support for increased funding for the War on Terror. But every precaution against the terrorists quickly produces speculation about what grounds the terrorist could use, thereby fueling more cycles of anxiety, blame, expert counterterrorist advice and increased funding.

These are the vicious cycles, the self-powering dynamics that have produced a widespread hysteria over non-existent "sleeper cells" and a vulnerability to bad things happening not seen here since the anti-communist frenzy of the McCarthy era. How humiliating! The country that was able to adjust psychologically, politically and militarily to the real capacity of the Soviet enemy to incinerate our cities on a moment's notice has been reduced to moaning, wasting resources and spinning in circles by ragged bands of Muslim fanatics.

We have been and are still being suckered big time. Before the attacks, al-Qaeda was a shattered remnant of a failed movement dropping into the dustbin of history, the equivalent of the Aryan Nations on the American political scene. But the diabolical strikes against the twin towers and the Pentagon saved them. Well, not really. What saved them from political oblivion, and lifted them to a protagonist declared as equivalent in potency and world-historic importance to Nazi Germany and Imperial Japan, was the American reaction to those attacks. Our invasion of Iraq, cast within a global War on Terror, was for them the "crusade" that makes their world of "jihad" appear not just real but compellingly real to hundreds of millions of Muslims. The Bush administration launched the War on Terror, but it was a war fought according to Osama's script. Now our army is broken and demoralized in an Iraq war that breeds al-Qaeda recruits and turns their propaganda into reality. Meanwhile, the very strength of American democracy and free enterprise—motivating every faction in America to turn the War on Terror to its own interest—is hijacked and turned against us by our adversaries just as effectively as they hit us with our own airplanes in 9/11.

We want to arm wrestle with our enemies. Why not? We have more economic and political and military muscle than any state in history. But that is precisely why they fight us with judo, using our strength against us. They hijack our planes to attack our buildings. They use our passionate patriotism to propel us into a war in the Middle East that precisely serves their interests and was the main reason for their attack. And they hijack Madisonian democracy itself to create a vortex of aggrandizing exploitation of the War on Terror for self-interested agendas that spin our country out of control.

One of the things that the War on Terror does to defend itself is to prevent itself from being known. Consider what happened to John Kerry when he said something true about it in October 2004. He said that the War on Terror was inappropriate, that the terrorism threat, though real, had been exaggerated; that it is a nuisance, akin to prostitution and organized crime, something that we have to control through systematic law enforcement. The War on Terror immediately smothered this argument. Both Republicans and Kerry's Democratic handlers forced an immediate retreat. In his debate with President Bush, Senator Kerry sought to prove he did not have a "pre-9/11 mentality" by intensifying his War on Terror rhetoric. In the televised presidential debate, he declared he wasn't going to just hunt down the terrorists and "bring them to justice," he was going to "kill them."

Indeed, in a whole host of ways the War on Terror suppresses knowledge of itself. For example, it does not allow the American people to see Osama bin Laden, for if we knew and understood him, we would understand that a "War on Terror" is exactly *not* how we can combat him and what he stands for. So almost no one in America is aware of a passage at the end of Bin Laden's famous tape on November 1, 2004, released right before the election. It is easy, he said,

> for us to provoke and bait this administration. All we have to do is to send two mujahidin [jihadists] to the furthest point east to raise a piece of cloth on which is written al-Qaeda, in order to make the generals race there to cause America to suffer human, economic and political losses without their achieving for it anything of note other than some benefits for their private companies. . . .
>
> So we are continuing this policy of bleeding America to the point of bankruptcy . . . . That being said, . . . when one scrutinizes the results, one cannot say that al-Qaeda is the sole factor in achieving these spectacular gains.
>
> Rather the policy of the White House that demands the opening of war fronts to keep busy their various corporations, whether they be working in the field of arms or oil or reconstruction, has helped al-Qaeda to achieve these enormous results.
>
> And so it appears to some analysts and diplomats that the White House and we are playing as one team toward the economic goals of the United States, even if the intentions differ . . . for example, al-Qaeda spent $500,000 on the events [the 9/11 attacks], while America, in the incident and its aftermath lost—according to the lowest estimate—more than $500 billion. Meaning that every dollar of al-Qaeda defeated a million dollars by the permission of Allah, besides the loss of a huge number of jobs.

As Seif al-Adl, al-Qaeda's security chief, put it, "The Americans took the bait and fell into our trap." Until we know our current enemy as we came to know the Soviet Union and then use that knowledge to adopt, as we did then, an appropriate long-term, sustainable, *reality-based* strategy, we will be unable to focus properly on security problems that do exist. Indeed, we will remain "Trapped in the War on Terror."

* * *

83

"Islamofascism and the War for the Free World"

Frank Gaffney

This contribution was originally presented to the House International Relations Committee Subcommittee on international Terrorism and Nonproliferation on 7 September 2006.

Mr. Chairman, it is a privilege to be afforded the opportunity to contribute to this Committee's deliberations about what is, arguably, the most important issues of our time: the nature of the conflict in which we find ourselves and what it will take for us to prevail in it.

Clarity About the Enemy

This war is not just about Iraq, any more than it is simply a "war on terror." To be sure, we are fighting in Iraq and we are contending with the use of terror as an asymmetric weapon. It is, however, a serious misunderstanding of the nature of this war and a grave disservice to the American people to confine our thinking about it just to the theater or front that is Iraq and what we "do" about it in isolation. The same is true of the characterization that our enemy is "terror" or "terrorists."

Rather, we are in the midst of the latest in a series of death-struggles between, on the one hand, a totalitarian ideology bent on world domination and the destruction of all who stand in the way of that goal and, on the other, freedom-loving peoples. I call it the War for the Free World.

As President Bush and his senior subordinates have pointed out in recent days, contemporary totalitarians have much in common with their predecessors, the Fascists, Nazis and Communists. For example, today's enemies amount to an ideological vanguard or cadre that constitute a relatively small percentage of a much larger population. Like their forerunners, today's totalitarians seek to dominate the latter through violence, coercion and indoctrination. As ever, propaganda, repression, financial rewards and the prospect of future glory are used to establish and maintain effective control of the base. Once that has been accomplished, our generation's totalitarians will inevitably attempt to conquer other populations and lands, as well.

There is, of course, an important difference between the current crop of totalitarians and their predecessors: Those that threaten us most immediately cloak their cause, and justify their aggressive behavior, with a patina of religion. For this reason, I believe they are most accurately described as 'Islamofascists' (or Islamist, for short). President Bush has used a variation on the theme, calling them 'Islamic fascists.'

Why the Ideological Aspect Matters

It is imperative to appreciate the ideological character of our enemy for two reasons:

First, recognizing that we are up against a totalitarian political movement permits a strategically vital distinction to be drawn between the vast majority of Muslims around the world who practice their faith in a tolerant, peaceable manner, consistent with the laws and values of civil societies, and the Islamofascists who do not. The latter seek to subjugate such Muslims and non-Muslims alike under a Taliban-style form of repressive religious rule they describe as Shari'a.

Clarity on this point is made more difficult by three factors: 1) the concerted efforts of some to obscure this distinction (about which I will have more to say in a moment); 2) the fact that Islamofascists find in some passages of the Koran and certain traditions in Islam justification for their behavior; and 3) by the success the Islamofascists have had in suppressing public expressions of opposition from Muslims who do not subscribe to their Islamist creed. For the moment, however, such a distinction clearly does exist and it behooves us to help Muslim opponents of the Islamofascists survive and prevail over our common foes.

Secondly, recognizing that we are up against a totalitarian ideology is essential to the adoption of instruments of warfare appropriate to defeating its adherents. The U.S. military and our homeland defenders have important roles to play in carrying the fight to the enemy and protecting us against their predations here. They must be equipped with the wherewithal to do so.

For the former, this requires a substantial and sustained ramp-up in defense spending, sufficient personnel and training and the steady support of the American people for the troops and their mission. The latter must be given intelligence, law enforcement and civil defense tools of sufficient quality, utility and flexibility to meet the dynamic threats of today and tomorrow. I would put in this category measures like those contained in the Patriot Act, the recently disclosed Terrorism Surveillance Program and bank transaction monitoring effort.

These steps, while absolutely necessary, are not likely to be sufficient. In the final analysis, though, this war will be won or lost at the political and ideological level.

*   *   *

The Enemy Within

Finally, Mr. Chairman, we must recognize that America's current totalitarian foe enjoys an advantage of which its forerunners could only have dreamt: Thanks in large measure to an investment by Saudi Arabia going back three decades and costing many tens of billions of dollars, there is in place in this country an apparatus that is at best sympathetic to the Islamists, and at worst an incipient Fifth Column.

This apparatus has a substantial organizational footprint all across the United States. Its elements include: mosques and associated religious schools (madrassas), by some estimates 80% of which have their financing provided by Saudi Arabia; indoctrination efforts on college campuses; recruitment programs run under the guise of prison and military chaplain programs; and front organizations responsible for political influence operations aimed at professional, ecumenical, media and governmental targets. The Bush Administration, the Congress and the press must be alive to the danger posed by such entities and their activities. This is especially true insofar as these organizations have realized that, by cloaking themselves as adherents to a religion rather than an ideological movement, they can exploit civil liberties afforded by tolerant liberal democracies to undermine them.

Yet, to an astonishing degree, nearly five years into the active phase of this War for the Free World, we continue to treat many of these organizations notably, the Council on American-Islamic Relations, the Islamic Society of North America, the Muslim Students Associations and others associated with and/or funded by the Saudi-directed Muslim World League as though they are what they purport to be: legitimate leaders of the Muslim-American and Arab-American communities and both necessary and valued interlocutors with those communities.

In my view, such organizations do not represent the majority of this country's Muslims or Arabs. It is a strategic mistake of the first order to legitimate their bid to do so by: having senior U.S. government officials meet with and seek the counsel of their representatives, allowing such groups to shape let alone dictate policy or entrust to them such tasks as "Muslim sensitivity training" for the FBI, military or other agencies. The Islamist footprint in America places a special premium on having robust intelligence sources and methods and effective cooperation between the intelligence and law enforcement communities. Since U.S. soil is also a theater in the War for the Free World, it behooves us to ensure that the Commander-in-Chief's inherent powers to intercept and monitor battle-field communications remains unencumbered, even when at least one of the parties to such communications is in the United States.

Conclusion

In short, Mr. Chairman, we confront a complex, multifaceted and increasingly dangerous world. Islamofascists are on the march. They benefit from the statesponsorship of oil-rich regimes that subscribe to one strain or another of this totalitarian ideology. Such wealth and the determination to destroy us that is a central purpose of our enemies makes it all other things being equal just a matter of time before their attacks on us and/or our allies are inflicted with weapons of mass destruction.

To make matters worse, governments that are not themselves Islamist (such as that of Vladimir Putin in Russia, the Communist Chinese, Kim Jong Il's regime in North Korea and Hugo Chavez's in Venezuela) are aiding and abetting the Islamofascists.

This combination of factors leaves us no choice but to get far more serious about this war than we have been to date. Serious in terms of the nature of the enemy. Serious in terms of what it will take to defeat it from a vastly larger investment in our military to the mobilization of our people, resources and energies. And serious about adopting the policies and programs, including counter-ideological political warfare-related ones, necessary to ensure that we prevail in this War for the Free World.

I hope that my observations today will help this Committee and the Congress play their respective, indispensable roles in achieving that level of seriousness.

84

National Intelligence Estimate: The Terrorist Threat to the U.S. Homeland, July 2007

National Intelligence Estimates and the NIE Process

National Intelligence Estimates (NIEs) are the Intelligence Community's (IC) most authoritative written judgments on national security issues and designed to help U.S. civilian and military leaders develop policies to protect U.S. national security interests. NIEs usually provide information on the current state of play but are primarily "estimative"—that is, they make judgments about the likely course of future events and identify the implications for U.S. policy.

The NIEs are typically requested by senior civilian and military policy-makers, Congressional leaders and at times are initiated by the National Intelligence Council (NIC). Before a NIE is drafted, the relevant National Intelligence Officer is responsible for producing a concept paper, or terms of reference (TOR), and circulates it throughout the Intelligence Community for comment. The TOR defines the key estimative questions, determines drafting responsibilities, and sets the drafting and publication schedule. One or more IC analysts are usually assigned to produce the initial text. The NIC then meets to critique the draft before it is circulated to the broader IC. Representatives from the relevant IC agencies meet to hone and coordinate line-by-line the full text of the NIE. Working with their Agencies, representatives also assign the level of confidence they have in key judgments. IC representatives discuss the quality of sources with collectors, and the National Clandestine Service vets the sources used to ensure the draft does not include any that have been recalled or otherwise seriously questioned.

All NIEs are reviewed by National Intelligence Board, which is chaired by the DNI and is composed of the heads of relevant IC agencies. Once approved by the NIB, NIEs are briefed to the President and senior policy-makers. The whole process of producing NIEs normally takes at least several months.

The NIC has undertaken a number of steps to improve the NIE process under the DNI. These steps are in accordance with the goals and recommendations set out in the Senate Select Committee on Intelligence and WMD Commission reports and the 2004 Intelligence Reform and Prevention of Terrorism Act. Most notably, over the last two years the IC has:

- *Created new procedures to integrate formal reviews of source reporting and technical judgments.* The Director of CIA, as the National HUMINT Manager, as well as the Directors of NSA, NGA, and DIA and the Assistant Secretary/INR are now required to submit formal assessments that highlight the strengths, weaknesses, and overall credibility of their sources used in developing the critical judgments of the NIE.
- *Applied more rigorous standards.* A textbox is incorporated into all NIEs that explains what we mean by such terms as "we judge" and that clarifies the difference between judgments of likelihood and confidence levels. We have made a concerted effort to not only highlight differences among agencies but to explain the reasons for such differences and to display them prominently in the Key Judgments.

* * *

What We Mean When We Say: An Explanation of
Estimative Language

When we use words such as "we judge" or "we assess"—
terms we use synonymously—as well as "we estimate,"
"likely" or "indicate," we are trying to convey an analytical
assessment or judgment. These assessments, which are
based on incomplete or at times fragmentary information
are not a fact, proof, or knowledge. Some analytical judgments are based directly on collected information; others
rest on previous judgments, which serve as building blocks.
In either type of judgment, we do not have "evidence" that
shows something to be a fact or that definitively links two
items or issues.

Intelligence judgments pertaining to likelihood are intended
to reflect the Community's sense of the probability of a development or event. Assigning precise numerical ratings to
such judgments would imply more rigor than we intend.
The chart below provides a rough idea of the relationship of
terms to each other.

Remote	Unlikely	Even chance	Probably, Likely	Almost certainly

We do not intend the term "unlikely" to imply an event will
not happen. We use "probably" and "likely" to indicate
there is a greater than even chance. We use words such as

"we cannot dismiss," "we cannot rule out," and "we cannot
discount" to reflect an unlikely—or even remote—event
whose consequences are such it warrants mentioning.
Words such as "may be" and "suggest" are used to reflect
situations in which we are unable to assess the likelihood
generally because relevant information is nonexistent,
sketchy, or fragmented.

In addition to using words within a judgment to convey degrees of likelihood, we also ascribe "high," "moderate," or
"low" confidence levels based on the scope and quality of
information supporting our judgments.

- "High confidence" generally indicates our judgments are based on high-quality information and/or the nature of the issue makes it possible to render a solid judgment.
- "Moderate confidence" generally means the information is interpreted in various ways, we have alternative views, or the information is credible and plausible but not corroborated sufficiently to warrant a higher level of confidence.
- "Low confidence" generally means the information is scant, questionable, or very fragmented and it is difficult to make solid analytic inferences, or we have significant concerns or problems with the sources.

Key Judgments

We judge the U.S. Homeland will face a persistent and evolving terrorist threat over the next three years. The main threat comes from Islamic terrorist groups and cells, especially al-Qa'ida, driven by their undiminished intent to attack the Homeland and a continued effort by these terrorist groups to adapt and improve their capabilities.

We assess that greatly increased worldwide counterterrorism efforts over the past five years have constrained the ability of al-Qa'ida to attack the U.S. Homeland again and have led terrorist groups to perceive the Homeland as a harder target to strike than on 9/11. These measures have helped disrupt known plots against the United States since 9/11.

- We are concerned, however, that this level of international cooperation may wane as 9/11 becomes a more distant memory and perceptions of the threat diverge.

Al-Qa'ida is and will remain the most serious terrorist threat to the Homeland, as its central leadership continues to plan high-impact plots, while pushing others in extremist Sunni communities to mimic its efforts and to supplement its capabilities. We assess the group has protected or regenerated key elements of its Homeland attack capability, including: a safehaven in the Pakistan Federally Administered Tribal Areas (FATA), operational lieutenants, and its top leadership. Although we have discovered only a handful of individuals in the United States with ties to al-Qa'ida senior leadership since 9/11, we judge that al-Qa'ida will intensify its efforts to put operatives here.

- As a result, we judge that the United States currently is in a heightened threat environment.

We assess that al-Qa'ida will continue to enhance its capabilities to attack the Homeland through greater cooperation with regional terrorist groups. Of note, we assess that al-Qa'ida will probably seek to leverage the contacts and capabilities of al-Qa'ida in Iraq (AQI), its most visible and capable affiliate and the only one known to have expressed a desire to attack the Homeland. In addition, we assess that its association with AQI helps al-Qa'ida to energize the broader Sunni extremist community, raise resources, and to recruit and indoctrinate operatives, including for Homeland attacks.

We assess that al-Qa'ida's Homeland plotting is likely to continue to focus on prominent political, economic, and infrastructure targets with the goal of producing mass casualties, visually dramatic destruction, significant economic aftershocks, and/or fear among the U.S. population. The group is proficient with conventional small arms and improvised explosive devices, and is innovative in creating new capabilities and overcoming security obstacles.

- We assess that al-Qa'ida will continue to try to acquire and employ chemical, biological, radiological, or nuclear material in attacks and would not hesitate to use them if it develops what it deems is sufficient capability.

We assess Lebanese Hizballah, which has conducted anti-U.S. attacks outside the United States in the past, may be more likely to consider attacking the Homeland over the next three years if it perceives the United States as posing a direct threat to the group or Iran.

We assess that the spread of radical—especially Salafi—Internet sites, increasingly aggressive anti-U.S. rhetoric and actions, and the growing number of radical, self-generating cells in Western countries indicate that the radical and violent segment of the West's Muslim population is expanding, including in the United States. The arrest and prosecution by U.S. law enforcement of a small number of violent Islamic extremists inside the United States—who are becoming more connected ideologically, virtually, and/or in a physical sense to the global extremist movement—points to the possibility that others may become sufficiently radicalized that they will view the use of violence here as legitimate. We assess that this internal Muslim terrorist threat is not likely to be as severe as it is in Europe, however.

We assess that other, non-Muslim terrorist groups—often referred to as "single-issue" groups by the FBI—probably will conduct attacks over the next three years given their violent histories, but we assess this violence is likely to be on a small scale.

We assess that globalization trends and recent technological advances will continue to enable even small numbers of alienated people to find and connect with one another, justify and intensify their anger, and mobilize resources to attack—all without requiring a centralized terrorist organization, training camp, or leader.

- The ability to detect broader and more diverse terrorist plotting in this environment will challenge current U.S. defensive efforts and the tools we use to detect and disrupt plots. It will also require greater understanding of how suspect activities at the local level relate to strategic threat information and how best to identify indicators of terrorist activity in the midst of legitimate interactions.

DISCUSSION QUESTIONS

1. As with the issue of global warming, it is important to have the right response to the terror threat. If we overreact, we impose costs and reduce civil liberties for no real purpose. If we underreact, we are at risk of a catastrophic attack. How do you balance the risks against the costs?

2. The actual "intelligence" portion of the NIE is shorter than the introductory material, which explains how it was derived and what the various terms mean. It is a very cautious document, full of caveats and qualifications. This is intentional. Why do you think the document was phrased this way?

3. If Lustick is right, would you conclude that we could safely and significantly scale back our counterterrorism efforts? Critics of the Bush Administration have accused the president of ignoring evidence that Al Qaeda was actively planning a terror attack, provided in an August 2001 National Intelligence Estimate. What incentives would policy makers have to respond to Lustick's argument?

Appendix

Marbury v. Madison (1803)

The power of judicial review—the authority of the federal courts to determine the constitutionality of state and federal legislative acts—was established early in the nation's history in the case of Marbury v. Madison *(1803). While the doctrine of judicial review is now firmly entrenched in the American judicial process, the outcome of* Marbury *was by no means a sure thing. The doctrine had been outlined in* The Federalist, *No. 78, and had been relied upon implicitly in earlier, lower federal court cases, but there were certainly sentiments among some of the Founders to suggest that only Congress ought to be able to judge the constitutionality of its acts.*

The facts leading up to the decision in Marbury v. Madison *tell an intensely political story. Efforts to reform the federal judiciary had been ongoing with the Federalist administration of President Adams. Following the defeat of the Federalist party in 1800, and the election of Thomas Jefferson as president, the Federalist Congress passed an act reforming the judiciary. The act gave outgoing President Adams authority to appoint several Federalist justices of the peace before Jefferson's term as president began. This would have enabled the Federalist party to retain a large measure of power.*

Marbury was appointed to be a justice of the peace by President Adams, but his commission, signed by the president and sealed by the secretary of state, without which he could not assume office, was not delivered to him before President Jefferson took office March 4, 1803. Jefferson refused to order James Madison, his secretary of state, to deliver the commission. Marbury, in turn, filed an action in the U.S. Supreme Court seeking an order—called a writ of mandamus—directing the secretary of state to compel the delivery of the commission.

The Constitution grants the Supreme Court original jurisdiction in only a limited number of cases—those involving ambassadors, public ministers, and those in which a state is a party; in the remaining cases, the Court has authority only as an appellate court. When it acts according to its original jurisdiction, the Court exercises initial authority over a controversy, just like a trial court, as distinguished from the more limited authority it exercises when a case is presented as an appeal from a lower court's decision.

In 1789, Congress passed legislation setting up the federal courts, called the Judiciary Act of 1789. That legislation gave the Supreme Court the original authority to "issue writs of mandamus in cases warranted by the principles and usage of law. . . ." Thus, the ultimate question in Marbury v. Madison *was whether Congress could, by statute, enlarge the original jurisdiction of the Court.*

The Court first considered whether Marbury's appointment was complete—and therefore irrevocable—before Jefferson took office. Under the law, the appointment was deemed complete when the president signed the commission and the secretary of state sealed it; the appointment was a completed fact at that time, and was not dependent upon delivery. Therefore, the Court found that Marbury was entitled to his commission. The Court then decided that by withholding the commission, Secretary of State Madison was violating Marbury's legal rights. The remaining question was whether the Supreme Court could issue an order compelling the delivery of the commission.

CHIEF JUSTICE MARSHALL delivered the opinion of the Court.

. . . It is, then, the opinion of the Court,

1st. That by signing the commission of Mr. Marbury, the President of the United States appointed him a justice of peace for the county of Washington, in the District of Columbia; and that the seal of the United States, affixed thereto by the Secretary of State, is conclusive testimony of the verity of the signature, and of the completion of the appointment, and that the appointment conferred on him a legal right to the office for the space of five years.

2d. That, having this legal title to the office, he has a consequent right to the commission; a refusal to deliver which is a plain violation of that right, for which the laws of his country afford him a remedy.

It remains to be inquired whether,

3d. He is entitled to the remedy for which he applies. This depends on,

1st. The nature of the writ applied for; and,

2d. The power of this court.

* * *

This . . . is a plain case for a mandamus, either to deliver the commission, or a copy of it from the record; and it only remains to be inquired,

Whether it can issue from this court.

The act to establish the judicial courts of the United States authorizes the Supreme Court "to issue writs of mandamus in cases warranted by the principles and usages of law, to any courts appointed, or persons holding office, under the authority of the United States."

The Secretary of State, being a person holding an office under the authority of the United States, is precisely within the letter of the description, and if this court is not authorized to issue a writ of mandamus to such an officer, it must be because the law is unconstitutional, and therefore absolutely incapable of conferring the authority, and assigning the duties which its words purport to confer and assign.

The constitution vests the whole judicial power of the United States in one Supreme Court, and such inferior courts as congress shall, from time to time, ordain and establish. This power is expressly extended to all cases arising under the laws of the United States; and, consequently, in some form, may be exercised over the present case; because the right claimed is given by a law of the United States.

In the distribution of this power it is declared that "the Supreme Court shall have original jurisdiction in all cases affecting ambassadors, other public ministers and consuls, and those in which a state shall be a party. In all other cases, the Supreme Court shall have appellate jurisdiction."

*   *   *

To enable this court, then, to issue a mandamus, it must be shown to be an exercise of appellate jurisdiction, or to be necessary to enable them to exercise appellate jurisdiction.

*   *   *

It is the essential criterion of appellate jurisdiction, that it revises and corrects the proceedings in a cause already instituted, and does not create that cause. . . . [Y]et to issue such a writ to an officer for the delivery of a paper, is in effect the same as to sustain an original action for that paper, and, therefore, seems not to belong to appellate, but to original jurisdiction.

The authority, therefore, given to the Supreme Court, by the act establishing the judicial courts of the United States, to issue writs of mandamus to public officers, appears not to be warranted by the constitution; and it becomes necessary to inquire whether a jurisdiction so conferred can be exercised.

The question, whether an act, repugnant to the constitution, can become the law of the land, is a question deeply interesting to the United States; but, happily, not of an intricacy proportioned to its interest. It seems only necessary to recognize certain principles, supposed to have been long and well established, to decide it.

That the people have an original right to establish, for their future government, such principles, as, in their opinion, shall most conduce to their own happiness is the basis on which the whole American fabric has been erected. The exercise of this original right is a very great exertion; nor can it, nor ought it, to be frequently repeated. The principles, therefore, so established, are deemed fundamental. And as the authority from which they proceed is supreme, and can seldom act, they are designed to be permanent.

This original and supreme will organizes the government, and assigns to different departments their respective powers. It may either stop here, or establish certain limits not to be transcended by those departments.

The government of the United States is of the latter description. The powers of the legislature are defined and limited; and that those limits may not be mistaken, or forgotten, the constitution is written. To what purpose are powers limited, and to what purpose is that limitation committed to writing, if these limits may, at any time, be passed by those intended to be restrained? The distinction between a government with limited and unlimited powers is abolished, if those limits do not confine the persons on whom they are imposed, and if acts prohibited and acts allowed, are of equal obligation. It is a proposition too plain to be contested, that the constitution controls any legislative act repugnant to it; or, that the legislature may alter the constitution by an ordinary act.

Between these alternatives there is no middle ground. The constitution is either a superior paramount law, unchangeable by ordinary means, or it is on a level with ordinary legislative acts, and, like other acts, is alterable when the legislature shall please to alter it.

If the former part of the alternative be true, then a legislative act contrary to the constitution is not law: if the latter part be true, then written constitutions are absurd attempts, on the part of the people, to limit a power in its own nature illimitable.

Certainly all those who have framed written constitutions contemplate them as forming the fundamental and paramount law of the nation, and, consequently, the theory of every such government must be, that an act of the legislature, repugnant to the constitution, is void.

This theory is essentially attached to a written constitution, and, is consequently, to be considered, by this court, as one of the fundamental principles of our society. It is not therefore to be lost sight of in the further consideration of this subject.

If an act of the legislature, repugnant to the constitution, is void, does it, notwithstanding its invalidity, bind the courts, and oblige them to give it effect? Or, in other words, though it be not law, does it constitute a rule as operative as if it was a law? This would be to overthrow in fact what was established in theory; and would seem, at first view, an absurdity too gross to be insisted on.

* * *

It is emphatically the province and duty of the judicial department to say what the law is. Those who apply the rule to particular cases, must of necessity expound and interpret that rule. If two laws conflict with each other, the courts must decide on the operation of each.

So if a law be in opposition to the constitution; if both the law and the constitution apply to a particular case, so that the court must either decide that case conformably to the law, disregarding the constitution; or conformably to the constitution, disregarding the law; the court must determine which of these conflicting rules governs the case. This is of the very essence of judicial duty.

If, then, the courts are to regard the constitution, and the constitution is superior to any ordinary act of the legislature, the constitution, and not such ordinary act, must govern the case to which they both apply.

Those, then, who controvert the principle that the constitution is to be considered, in court, as a paramount law, are reduced to the necessity of maintaining that courts must close their eyes on the constitution, and see only the law.

This doctrine would subvert the very foundation of all written constitutions. It would declare that an act which, according to the principles and theory of our government, is entirely void, is yet, in practice, completely obligatory. It would declare that if the legislature shall do what is expressly forbidden, such act, notwithstanding the express prohibition, is in reality effectual. It would be giving to the legislature a practical and real omnipotence, with the same breath which professes to restrict their powers within narrow limits. It is prescribing limits, and declaring that those limits may be passed at pleasure.

That it thus reduces to nothing what we have deemed the greatest improvement on political institutions, a written constitution, would of itself be sufficient, in America, where written constitutions have been viewed with so much reverence, for rejecting the construction. But the peculiar expressions of the constitution of the United States furnish additional arguments in favour of its rejection.

The judicial power of the United States is extended to all cases arising under the constitution.

Could it be the intention of those who gave this power, to say that in using it the constitution should not be looked into? That a case arising under the constitution should be decided without examining the instrument under which it arises?

This is too extravagant to be maintained.

In some cases, then, the constitution must be looked into by the judges.

. . . [I]t is apparent, that the framers of the constitution contemplated that instrument as a rule for the government of courts, as well as of the legislature.

Why otherwise does it direct the judges to take an oath to support it? This oath certainly applies in an especial manner, to their conduct in their official character. How immoral to impose it on them, if they were to be used as the instruments, and the knowing instruments, for violating what they swear to support!

The oath of office, too, imposed by the legislature, is completely demonstrative of the legislative opinion on this subject.

* * *

Why does a judge swear to discharge his duties agreeably to the constitution of the United States, if that constitution forms no rule for his government? If it is closed upon him, and cannot be inspected by him?

If such be the real state of things, this is worse than solemn mockery. To prescribe, or to take this oath, becomes equally a crime.

It is also not entirely unworthy of observation, that in declaring what shall be the supreme law of the land, the constitution itself is first mentioned; and not the laws of the United States generally, but those only which shall be made in pursuance of the constitution, have that rank.

Thus, the particular phraseology of the constitution of the United States confirms and strengthens the principle, supposed to be essential to all written constitutions, that a law repugnant to the constitution is void; and that courts, as well as other departments, are bound by that instrument.

McCulloch v. Maryland (1819)

Early in the nation's history, the United States Supreme Court interpreted the powers of the national government expansively. The first Supreme Court case to directly address the scope of federal authority under the Constitution was McCulloch v. Maryland *(1819). The facts were straightforward: Congress created the Bank of the United States—to the dismay of many states who viewed the creation of a national bank as a threat to the operation of banks within their own state borders. As a result, when a branch of the Bank of the United States was opened in Maryland, that state attempted to limit the bank's ability to do business under a law that imposed taxes on all banks not chartered by the state.*

In an opinion authored by Chief Justice Marshall, the Court considered two questions: whether Congress had the authority to create a national bank; and whether Maryland could in turn tax it. Marshall's answer to these two questions defends an expansive theory of implied powers for the national government and propounds the principle of national supremacy with an eloquence rarely found in judicial decisions.

CHIEF JUSTICE JOHN MARSHALL delivered the opinion of the Court.

The first question made in the cause is, has Congress power to incorporate a bank? The power now contested was exercised by the first Congress elected under the present constitution. The bill for incorporating the Bank of the United States did not steal upon an unsuspecting legislature, and pass unobserved. Its principle was completely understood, and was opposed with equal zeal and ability. . . . In discussing this question, the counsel for the state of Maryland have deemed it of some importance, in the construction of the constitution, to consider that instrument not as emanating from the people, but as the act of sovereign and independent states. The powers of the general government, it has been said, are delegated by the states, who alone are truly sovereign; and must be exercised in subordination to the states, who alone possess supreme dominion. . . . No political dreamer was ever wild enough to think of breaking down the lines which separate the states, and of compounding the American people into one common mass. Of consequence, when they act, they act in their states. But the measures they adopt do not, on that account, cease to be the measures of the people themselves, or become the measures of the state governments.

From these conventions the constitution derives its whole authority. The government proceeds directly from the people; is "ordained and established" in the name of the people; and is declared to be ordained, "in order to form a more perfect union, establish justice, insure domestic tranquility, and secure the blessings of liberty to themselves and to their posterity." The assent of the states, in their sovereign capacity, is implied in calling a convention, and thus submitting that instrument to the people. But the people were at perfect liberty to accept or reject it; and their act was final. It required not the affirmance, and could not be negatived, by the state governments. The constitution, when thus adopted, was of complete obligation, and bound the state sovereignties.

The government of the Union, then (whatever may be the influence of this fact on the case), is, emphatically, and truly, a government of the people. In form and in substance it emanates from them. Its powers are granted by them, and are to be exercised directly on them, and for their benefit.

This government is acknowledged by all to be one of enumerated powers. The principle, that it can exercise only the powers granted to it, is now universally admitted. But the question respecting the extent of the powers actually granted, is perpetually arising, and will probably continue to arise, as long as our system shall exist. The government of the United States though limited in its powers, is supreme; and its laws, when made in pursuance of the constitution, form the supreme law of the land, "anything in the constitution or laws of any state to the contrary notwithstanding."

* * *

A constitution, to contain an accurate detail of all the subdivisions of which its great powers will admit, and of all the means by which they may be carried into execution, would partake of the prolixity of a legal code, and could scarcely be embraced by the human mind. It would probably never be understood by the public. Its nature, therefore, requires, that only its great outlines should be marked, its important objects designated, and the minor ingredients which compose those objects be deduced from the nature of the objects themselves. . . . in considering this question, then, we must never forget, that it is a constitution we are expounding.

Although, among the enumerated powers of government, we do not find the word "bank" or "incorporation," we find the great powers to lay and collect taxes; to borrow money; to regulate commerce; to declare and conduct a war; and to raise and support armies and navies. The sword and the purse, all the external relations, and no inconsiderable portion of the industry of the nation, are entrusted to its government. . . . [I]t may with great reason be contended, that a government, entrusted with such ample powers, on the due execution of which the happiness and prosperity of the nation so vitally depends, must also be entrusted with ample means for their execution. The power being given, it is the interest of the nation to facilitate its execution. It can never be their interest, and cannot be presumed to have been their intention, to clog and embarrass its execution by withholding the most appropriate means. . . . It is, then, the subject of fair inquiry, how far such means may be employed.

The government which has a right to do an act, and has imposed on it the duty of performing that act, must, according to the dictates of reason, be allowed to select the means.

* * *

But the constitution of the United States has not left the right of Congress to employ the necessary means, for the execution of the powers conferred on the government, to general reasoning. To its enumeration of powers is added that of making "all laws which shall be necessary and proper, for carrying into execution the foregoing powers, and all other powers vested by this constitution, in the government of the United States, or in any department [or officer] thereof."

The counsel for the state of Maryland have urged various arguments, to prove that this clause . . . is really restrictive of the general right, which might otherwise be implied, of selecting means for executing the enumerated powers.

. . . [Maryland argues that] Congress is not empowered by it to make all laws, which may have relation to the powers conferred on the government, but such only as may be "necessary and proper" for carrying them into execution. The word "necessary" is considered as controlling the whole sentence, and as limiting the right to pass laws for the execution of the granted powers, to such as are indispensable, and without which the power would be nugatory. That it excludes the choice of means, and leaves to Congress, in each case, that only which is most direct and simple.

Is it true, that this is the sense in which the word "necessary" is always used? . . . We think it does not. If reference be had to its use, in the common affairs of the world, or in approved authors, we find that it frequently imports no more than that one thing is convenient, or useful, or essential to another. To employ the means necessary to an end, is generally understood as employing any means calculated to produce the end, and not as being confined to those single means, without which the end would be entirely unattainable.

Let this be done in the case under consideration. The subject is the execution of those great powers on which the welfare of a nation essentially depends. It must have been the intention of those who gave these powers, to insure, as far as human prudence could insure, their beneficial execution. This could not be done by confiding the choice of means to such narrow limits as not to leave it in the power of Congress to adopt any which might be appropriate, and which were conducive to the end. This provision is made in a constitution intended to endure for ages to come, and consequently, to be adapted to the various crises of human affairs. To have prescribed the means by which government should, in all future time, execute its powers, would have been to change, entirely, the character of the instrument, and give it the properties of a legal code. It would have been an unwise attempt to provide, by immutable rules, for exigencies which, if foreseen at all, must have been seen dimly, and which can be best provided for as they occur. To have declared that the best means shall not be used, but those alone without which the power given would be nugatory, would have been to deprive the legislature of the capacity to avail itself of experience, to exercise its reason, and to accommodate its legislation to circumstances. If we apply this principle of construction to any of the powers of the government, we shall find it so pernicious in its operation that we shall be compelled to discard it.

*   *   *

We admit, as all must admit, that the powers of the government are limited, and that its limits are not to be transcended. But we think the sound construction of the constitution must allow to the national legislature that discretion, with respect to the means by which the powers it confers are to be carried into execution, which will enable that body to perform the high duties assigned to it, in the manner most beneficial to the people. Let the end be legitimate, let it be within the scope of the constitution, and all means which are appropriate, which are plainly adapted to that end, which are not prohibited, but consist with the letter and spirit of the constitution, are constitutional.

*   *   *

It being the opinion of the court that the act incorporating the bank is constitutional, and that the power of establishing a branch in the state of Maryland might be properly exercised by the bank itself, we proceed to inquire: Whether the state of Maryland may, without violating the constitution, tax that branch?

That the power of taxation is one of vital importance; that it is retained by the states; that it is not abridged by the grant of a similar power to the government of the Union; that it is to be concurrently exercised by the two governments; are truths which have never been denied. But, such is the paramount character of the constitution that its capacity to withdraw any subject from the action of even this power, is admitted. . . . [T]he paramount character [of the Constitution] would seem to restrain, as it certainly may restrain, a state from such other exercise of this power as is in its nature incompatible with, and repugnant to, the constitutional laws of the Union. A law, absolutely repugnant to another, as entirely repeals that other as if express terms of repeal were used.

* * *

This great principle is, that the constitution and the laws made in pursuance thereof are supreme; that they control the constitution and laws of the respective states, and cannot be controlled by them. From this, which may be almost termed an axiom, other propositions are adduced as corollaries, on the truth or error of which, and on their application to this case, the cause has been supposed to depend. These are, 1st. That a power to create implies a power to preserve. 2d. That a power to destroy, if wielded by a different hand, is hostile to, and incompatible with, these powers to create and to preserve. 3d. That where this repugnance exists, that authority which is supreme must control, not yield to that over which it is supreme.

. . . [T]axation is said to be an absolute power, which acknowledges no other limits than those expressly prescribed in the constitution, and like sovereign powers of every other description, is trusted to the discretion of those who use it. But the very terms of this argument admit that the sovereignty of the state, in the article of taxation itself, is subordinate to, and may be controlled by the constitution of the United States. How far it has been controlled by that instrument must be a question of construction. In making this construction, no principle not declared can be admissible, which would defeat the legitimate operations of a supreme government.

* * *

All subjects over which the sovereign power of a state extends, are objects of taxation; but those over which it does not extend, are, upon the soundest principles, exempt from taxation. . . . The sovereignty of a state extends to everything which exists by its own authority, or is introduced by its permission; but does it extend to those means which are employed by Congress to carry into execution—powers conferred on that body by the people of the United States? We think it demonstrable that it does not. Those powers are not given by the people of a single state. They are given by the people of the United States, to a government whose laws, made in pursuance of the constitution, are declared to be supreme. Consequently, the people of a single state cannot confer a sovereignty which will extend over them.

If we apply the principle for which the state of Maryland contends, to the constitution generally, we shall find it capable of changing totally the character of that instrument. We shall find it capable of arresting all the measures of the government, and of prostrating it at the foot of the states. The American people have declared their constitution, and the laws made in pursuance thereof, to be supreme; but this principle would transfer the supremacy, in fact, to the states. If the controlling power of the states be established; if their supremacy as to taxation be acknowledged; what is to restrain their exercising this control in any shape they may please to give it? Their sovereignty is not confined to taxation. That is not the only mode in which it might be displayed. The question is, in truth, a question of supremacy; and if the right of the states to tax the means employed by the general government be conceded, the declaration that the constitution, and the laws made in pursuance thereof, shall be the supreme law of the land, is empty and unmeaning declamation.

* * *

We are unanimously of opinion, that the law passed by the legislature of Maryland, imposing a tax on the Bank of the United States, is unconstitutional and void. This opinion does not deprive the states of any resources which they originally possessed. It does not extend to a tax paid by the real property of the bank, in common with other real property within the state, nor to a tax imposed on the interest which the citizens of Maryland may hold in this institution, in common with other property of the same description throughout the state. But this is a tax on the operations of the bank, and is, consequently, a tax on the operation of an instrument employed by the government of the Union to carry its powers into execution. Such a tax must be unconstitutional.

Reversed.

Barron v. Baltimore (1833)

The declaration made in Barron v. Baltimore *(1833) that citizenship had a dual aspect—state and national—set the terms of the Supreme Court's interpretation of the Bill of Rights for nearly a century. The reasoning of the case*

proved persuasive even after the adoption of the Fourteenth Amendment, as the
federal courts refused to extend the protections of the federal Constitution to
citizens aggrieved by the actions of state or local governments.

Barron brought suit in a federal court claiming that the city of Baltimore
had appropriated his property for a public purpose without paying him just
compensation. He asserted that the Fifth Amendment to the Constitution op-
erated as a constraint upon both state and federal governments.

CHIEF JUSTICE JOHN MARSHALL delivered the opinion of the Court.

. . . The question presented is, we think, of great importance, but not
of much difficulty. The constitution was ordained and established by the
people of the United States for themselves, for their own government,
and not for the government of the individual states. Each state established a constitution for itself, and in that constitution, provided such
limitations and restrictions on the powers of its particular government,
as its judgment dictated. The people of the United States framed such a
government for the United States as they supposed best adapted to their
situation and best calculated to promote their interests. The powers they
conferred on this government were to be exercised by itself; and the
limitations on power, if expressed in general terms, are naturally, and,
we think, necessarily, applicable to the government created by the instrument. They are limitations of power granted in the instrument itself; not of distinct governments, framed by different persons and for
different purposes.

If these propositions be correct, the fifth amendment must be understood as restraining the power of the general government, not as applicable to the states. In their several constitutions, they have imposed such
restrictions on their respective governments, as their own wisdom suggested; such as they deemed most proper for themselves. It is a subject
on which they judge exclusively, and with which others interfere no
further than they are supposed to have a common interest.

* * *

Had the people of the several states, or any of them, required changes
in their constitutions; had they required additional safe-guards to liberty
from the apprehended encroachments of their particular governments; the
remedy was in their own hands, and could have been applied by themselves. A convention could have been assembled by the discontented
state, and the required improvements could have been made by itself.
. . . Had Congress engaged in the extraordinary occupation of improving the constitutions of the several states, by affording the people
additional protection from the exercise of power by their own governments, in matters which concerned themselves alone, they would have
declared this purpose in plain and intelligible language.

But it is universally understood, it is a part of the history of the day, that the great revolution which established the constitution of the United States, was not effected without immense opposition. Serious fears were extensively entertained, that those powers which the patriot statesmen, who then watched over the interests of our country, deemed essential to union, and to the attainment of those unvaluable objects for which union was sought, might be exercised in a manner dangerous to liberty. In almost every convention by which the constitution was adopted, amendments to guard against the abuse of power were recommended. These amendments demanded security against the apprehended encroachments of the general government—not against those of the local governments. In compliance with a sentiment thus generally expressed, to quiet fears thus extensively entertained, amendments were proposed by the required majority in congress, and adopted by the states. These amendments contain no expression indicating an intention to apply them to the state governments. This court cannot so apply them.

We are of opinion, that the provision in the fifth amendment to the constitution, declaring that private property shall not be taken for public use, without just compensation, is intended solely as a limitation on the exercise of power by the government of the United States, and is not applicable to the legislation of the states. We are, therefore, of opinion, that there is no repugnancy between the several acts of the general assembly of Maryland, given in evidence by the defendants at the trial of this cause, in the court of that state, and the constitution of the United States. This court, therefore, has no jurisdiction of the cause, and it is dismissed.

This cause came on to be heard, on the transcript of the record from the court of appeals for the western shore of the state of Maryland, and was argued by counsel: On consideration whereof, it is the opinion of this court, that there is no repugnancy between the several acts of the general assembly of Maryland, given in evidence by the defendants at the trial of this cause in the court of that state, and the constitution of the United States; whereupon, it is ordered and adjudged by this court, that this writ of error be and the same is hereby dismissed, for the want of jurisdiction.

Roe v. Wade (1973)

One of the most significant changes in constitutional interpretation in the last three decades has been the Court's willingness to look beyond the explicit language of the Bill of Rights to find unenumerated rights, such as the right to privacy. In discovering such rights, the Court has engaged in what is known as substantive due process analysis—defining and articulating fundamental rights—distinct from its efforts to define the scope of procedural due process, when it decides what procedures the state and federal governments must follow to be fair in their treatment of citizens. The Court's move into the substantive due process area has generated much of the political discussion over the proper role of the Court in constitutional interpretation.

The case that has been the focal point for this debate is Roe v. Wade, *the 1973 case that held that a woman's right to privacy protected her decision to have an abortion. The right to privacy in matters relating to contraception and childbearing had been recognized in the 1965 decision of* Griswold v. Connecticut, *and was extended in subsequent decisions culminating in* Roe. *The theoretical issue of concern here relates back to the incorporation issue: Should the Supreme Court be able to prohibit the states not only from violating the express guarantees contained in the Bill of Rights, but its implied guarantees as well?*

Texas law prohibited abortions except for "the purpose of saving the life of the mother." The plaintiff challenged the constitutionality of the statute, claiming that it infringed upon her substantive due process right to privacy.

JUSTICE BLACKMUN delivered the opinion of the Court.

. . . [We] forthwith acknowledge our awareness of the sensitive and emotional nature of the abortion controversy, of the vigorous opposing views, and the deep and seemingly absolute convictions that the subject inspires. One's philosophy, one's experiences, one's exposure to the raw edges of human existence, one's religious training, one's attitudes toward life and family and their values, and the moral standards one establishes and seeks to observe, are all likely to affect one's thinking [about] abortion. In addition, population growth, pollution, poverty, and racial overtones tend to complicate and not to simplify the problem. Our task, of course, is to resolve the issue by constitutional measurement, free of emotion and of predilection. We seek earnestly to do this, and, because we do, we have inquired into, and in this opinion place some emphasis upon, medical and medical-legal history and what that history reveals about man's attitudes toward the abortion procedure over the centuries.

*   *   *

[*The Court here reviewed ancient and contemporary attitudes toward abortion, observing that restrictive laws date primarily from the late nineteenth century. The Court also reviewed the possible state interests in restricting abortions, including discouraging illicit sexual conduct, limiting access to a hazardous medical procedure, and the states' general interests in protecting fetal life. The Court addressed only the third interest as a current legitimate interest of the state.*]

. . . The Constitution does not explicitly mention any right of privacy. In a line of decisions, however, . . . the Court has recognized that a right of personal privacy, or a guarantee of certain areas or zones of privacy, does exist under the Constitution. . . . This right of privacy, whether it be founded in the Fourteenth Amendment's concept of personal liberty and restrictions upon state action, as we feel it is, or, as the District Court determined, in the Ninth Amendment's reservation of rights to the people, is broad enough to encompass a woman's decision whether or not to terminate her pregnancy. The detriment that the State would impose upon the pregnant woman by denying this choice altogether is apparent. Specific and direct harm medically diagnosable even in early pregnancy may be involved. Maternity, or additional offspring, may force upon the woman a distressful life and future. Psychological harm may be imminent. Mental and physical health may be taxed by child care. There is also the distress, for all concerned, associated with the unwanted child, and there is the problem of bringing a child into a family already unable, psychologically and otherwise, to care for it. In other cases, as in this one, the additional difficulties and continuing stigma of unwed motherhood may be involved. All these are factors the woman and her responsible physician necessarily will consider in consultation.

On the basis of elements such as these, appellants and some amici [friends of the Court] argue that the woman's right is absolute and that she is entitled to terminate her pregnancy at whatever time, in whatever way, and for whatever reason she alone chooses. With this we do not agree. Appellants' arguments that Texas either has no valid interest at all in regulating the abortion decision, or no interest strong enough to support any limitation upon the woman's sole determination, is unpersuasive. The Court's decisions recognizing a right of privacy also acknowledge that some state regulation in areas protected by that right is appropriate. As noted above, a State may properly assert important interests in safeguarding health, in maintaining medical standards, and in protecting potential life. At some point in pregnancy, these respective interests become sufficiently compelling to sustain regulation of the factors that govern the abortion decision. The privacy right involved, therefor, cannot be said to be absolute. In fact, it is not clear to us that the claim asserted by some amici that one has an unlimited right to do with one's body as one pleases bears a close relationship to the right of privacy previously articulated in the Court's decisions.

* * *

We therefore conclude that the right of personal privacy includes the abortion decision, but that this right is not unqualified and must be considered against state interests in regulation.

Where certain "fundamental rights" are involved, the Court has held that regulation limiting these rights may be justified only by a "compelling state interest," and that legislative enactments must be narrowly drawn to express only the legitimate state interests at stake.

. . . The District Court held that the appellee failed to meet his burden of demonstrating that the Texas statute's infringement upon Roe's rights was necessary to support a compelling state interest. . . . Appellee argues that the State's determination to recognize and protect prenatal life from and after conception constitutes a compelling state interest. As noted above, we do not agree fully with either formulation.

The appellee and certain amici argue that the fetus is a "person" within the language and meaning of the Fourteenth Amendment. In support of this they outline at length and in detail the well-known facts of fetal development. If this suggestion of personhood is established, the appellant's case, of course, collapses, for the fetus' right to life is then guaranteed specifically by the Amendment. The appellant conceded as much on reargument. On the other hand, the appellee conceded on reargument that no case could be cited that holds that a fetus is a person within the meaning of the Fourteenth Amendment.

The Constitution does not define "person" in so many words. Section 1 of the Fourteenth Amendment contains three references to "person." The first, in defining "citizens," speaks of "persons born or naturalized in the United States." The word also appears both in the Due Process Clause and in the Equal Protection Clause. "Person" is used in other places in the Constitution. . . . But in nearly all these instances, the use of the word is such that it has application only postnatally. None indicates, with any assurance, that it has any possible pre-natal application.

All this, together with our observation, that throughout the major portion of the 19th century prevailing legal abortion practices were far freer than they are today, persuades us that the word "person," as used in the Fourteenth Amendment, does not include the unborn.

. . . The pregnant woman cannot be isolated in her privacy. She carries an embryo and, later, a fetus, if one accepts the medical definitions of the developing young in the human uterus. . . . The situation therefore is inherently different from marital intimacy, or bedroom possession of obscene material, or marriage, or procreation, or education, with which [earlier cases defining the right to privacy] were concerned. As we have intimated above, it is reasonable and appropriate for a State to decide that at some point in time another interest, that of health of the mother or that of potential human life, becomes significantly involved. The woman's privacy is no longer sole and any right of privacy she possesses must be measured accordingly.

Texas urges that, apart from the Fourteenth Amendment, life begins at conception and is present throughout pregnancy, and that, therefore, the State has a compelling interest in protecting that life from and after conception. We need not resolve the difficult question of when life begins. When those trained in the respective disciplines of medicine, philosophy, and theology are unable to arrive at any consensus, the judiciary, at this point in the development of man's knowledge, is not in a position to speculate as to the answer.

. . . In view of all this, we do not agree that, by adopting one theory of life, Texas may override the rights of the pregnant woman that are at stake. We repeat, however, that the State does have an important and legitimate interest in preserving and protecting the health of the pregnant woman, whether she be a resident of the State or a nonresident who seeks medical consultation and treatment there, and that it has still *another* important and legitimate interest in protecting the potentiality of human life. These interests are separate and distinct. Each grows in substantiality as the woman approaches term and, at a point during pregnancy, each becomes "compelling."

With respect to the State's important and legitimate interest in the health of the mother, the "compelling" point, in the light of present medical knowledge, is at approximately the end of the first trimester. This is so because of the now established medical fact . . . that until the end of the first trimester mortality in abortion is less than mortality in normal childbirth. It follows that, from and after this point, a State may regulate the abortion procedure to the extent that the regulation reasonably relates to the preservation and protection of maternal health. Examples of permissible state regulation in this area are requirements as to the qualifications of the person who is to perform the abortion; as to the licensure of that person; as to the facility in which the procedure is to be performed, that is, whether it must be a hospital or may be a clinic or some other place of less-than-hospital status; as to the licensing of the facility; and the like.

This means, on the other hand, that, for the period of pregnancy prior to this "compelling" point, the attending physician, in consultation with his patient, is free to determine, without regulation by the State, that in his medical judgment the patient's pregnancy should be terminated. If that decision is reached, the judgment may be effectuated by an abortion free of interference by the State.

With respect to the State's important and legitimate interest in potential life, the "compelling" point is at viability. This is so because the fetus then presumably has the capability of meaningful life outside the mother's womb. State regulation protective of fetal life after viability thus has both logical and biological justifications. If the State is interested in protecting fetal life after viability, it may go so far as to proscribe abortion during that period except when it is necessary to preserve the life or health of the mother.

Measured against these standards, the Texas Penal Code, in restricting legal abortions to those "procured or attempted by medical advice for the purpose of saving the life of the mother," sweeps too broadly. The statute makes no distinction between abortions performed early in pregnancy and those performed later, and it limits to a single reason, "saving" the mother's life, the legal justification for the procedure. The statute, therefore, cannot survive the constitutional attack made upon it here.

*   *   *

Reversed.

Brown v. Board of Education of Topeka, Kansas (1954)

Brown v. Board of Education *(1954) was a momentous opinion, invalidating the system of segregation that had been established under* Plessy v. Ferguson *(1896). However, the constitutional pronouncement only marked the beginning of the struggle for racial equality, as federal courts got more and more deeply involved in trying to prod recalcitrant state and local governments into taking steps to end racial inequalities.*

The Brown *case involved appeals from several states. In each case, the plaintiffs had been denied access to public schools designated only for white children under a variety of state laws. They challenged the* Plessy v. Ferguson (1896) *"separate but equal" doctrine, contending that segregated schools were by their nature unequal.*

Chief Justice Warren first discussed the history of the Fourteenth Amendment's equal protection clause, finding it too inconclusive to be of assistance in determining how the Fourteenth Amendment should be applied to the question of public education.

CHIEF JUSTICE WARREN writing for the majority.

. . . The doctrine of "separate but equal" did not make its appearance in this Court until 1896, in the case of Plessy v. Ferguson, involving not education but transportation. American courts have since labored with the doctrine for over a half a century. In this Court, there have been six cases involving the "separate but equal" doctrine in the field of public education.

*   *   *

In the instant cases, [the question of the application of the separate but equal doctrine to public education] is directly presented. Here, . . . there are findings below that the Negro and white schools involved have been equalized, or are being equalized, with respect to buildings, curricula, qualifications and salaries of teachers, and other "tangible" factors. Our decision, therefore, cannot turn on merely a comparison of these tangible factors in the Negro and white schools involved in each of the cases. We must look instead to the effect of segregation itself on public education.

In approaching this problem, we cannot turn the clock back to 1868 when the [Fourteenth] Amendment was adopted, or even to 1896 when Plessy v. Ferguson was written. We must consider public education in the light of its full development and its present place in American life throughout the Nation. Only in this way can it be determined if segregation in public schools deprives these plaintiffs of the equal protection of the laws.

Today, education is perhaps the most important function of state and local governments. Compulsory school attendance laws and the great expenditures for education both demonstrate our recognition of the importance of education to our democratic society. It is required in the performance of our most basic responsibilities, even service in the armed forces. It is the very foundation of good citizenship. Today it is a principal instrument in awakening the child to cultural values, in preparing him for later professional training, and in helping him to adjust normally to his environment. In these days, it is doubtful that any child may reasonably be expected to succeed in life if he is denied the opportunity of an education. Such an opportunity, where the state has undertaken to provide it, is a right which must be made available to all on equal terms.

We come then to the question presented: Does segregation of children in public schools solely on the basis of race, even though the physical facilities and other "tangible" factors may be equal, deprive the children of the minority group of equal educational opportunities? We believe that it does.

In *Sweatt v. Painter*, in finding that a segregated law school for Negroes could not provide them equal educational opportunities, this Court relied in large part on "those qualities which are incapable of objective measurement but which make for greatness in a law school." In McLaurin v. Oklahoma State Regents, the Court, in requiring that a Negro admitted to a white graduate school be treated like all other students, again resorted to intangible considerations: ". . . his ability to study, to engage in discussions and exchange views with other students, and, in general, to learn his profession." Such considerations apply with added force to children in grade and high schools. To separate them from others of similar age and qualifications solely because of their race generates a feeling of inferiority as to their status in the community that may affect their hearts and minds in a way unlikely ever to be undone. The effect of this separation on their educational opportunities was well stated by a finding in the Kansas case by a court which nevertheless felt compelled to rule against the Negro plaintiffs:

"Segregation of white and colored children in public schools has a detrimental effect upon the colored children. The impact is greater when it has the sanction of the law; for the policy of separating the races is usually interpreted as denoting the inferiority of the Negro group. A sense of inferiority affects the motivation of a child to learn. Segregation with the sanction of law, therefore, has a tendency to [retard] the educational and mental development of Negro children and to deprive them of some of the benefits they would receive in a racial[ly] integrated school system." Whatever may have been the extent of psychological knowledge at the time of Plessy v. Ferguson, this finding is amply supported by modern authority. Any language in Plessy v. Ferguson contrary to this finding is rejected.

We conclude that in the field of public education the doctrine of "separate but equal" has no place. Separate educational facilities are inherently unequal. Therefore, we hold that the plaintiffs and others similarly situated for whom the actions have been brought are, by reason of the segregation complained of, deprived of the equal protection of the laws guaranteed by the Fourteenth Amendment. This disposition makes unnecessary any discussion whether such segregation also violates the Due Process Clause of the Fourteenth Amendment.

Because these are class actions, because of the wide applicability of this decision, and because of the great variety of local conditions, the formulation of decrees in these cases presents problems of considerable complexity. On reargument, the consideration of appropriate relief was necessarily subordinated to the primary question—the constitutionality of segregation in public education. We have now announced that such segregation is a denial of the equal protection of the laws.

United States v. Nixon (1974)

The Supreme Court has had few occasions to rule on the constitutional limits of executive authority. The Court is understandably reluctant to articulate the boundaries of presidential and legislative power, given the Court's own somewhat ambiguous institutional authority. In the case that follows, however, the Court looked at one of the ways in which the Constitution circumscribes the exercise of presidential prerogative.

United States v. Nixon (1974) involves claims to executive authority. President Richard Nixon was implicated in a conspiracy to cover up a burglary of the Democratic Party Headquarters at the Watergate Hotel in Washington, D.C., during the 1972 reelection campaign. The Special Prosecutor assigned to investigate the break-in and file appropriate criminal charges asked the trial court to order the President to disclose a number of documents and tapes related to the cover-up in order to determine the scope of the President's involvement. The President produced edited versions of some of the materials, but refused to comply with most of the trial court's order, asserting that he was entitled to withhold the information under a claim of "executive privilege."

CHIEF JUSTICE BURGER delivered the opinion of the Court.

In the District Court, the President's counsel argued that the court lacked jurisdiction to issue the subpoena because the matter was an intra-branch dispute between a subordinate and superior officer of the Executive Branch and hence not subject to judicial resolution. That argument has been renewed in this Court with emphasis on the contention that the dispute does not present a "case" or "controversy" which can be adjudicated in the federal courts. The President's counsel argues that the federal courts should not intrude into areas committed to the other branches of Government. He views the present dispute as essentially a "jurisdictional" dispute within the Executive Branch which he analogizes to a dispute between two congressional committees. Since the Executive Branch has exclusive authority and absolute discretion to decide whether to prosecute a case, it is contended that a President's decision is final in determining what evidence is to be used in a given criminal case.

. . . Although his counsel concedes the President has delegated certain specific powers to the Special Prosecutor, he has not "waived nor delegated to the Special Prosecutor the President's duty to claim privilege as to all materials which fall within the President's inherent authority to refuse to disclose to any executive officer." The Special Prosecutor's demand for the items therefore presents, in the view of the President's counsel, a political question since it involves a "textually demonstrable" grant of power under Art. II. . . .

The demands of and the resistance to the subpoena present an obvious controversy in the ordinary sense, but that alone is not sufficient to meet constitutional standards. In the constitutional sense, controversy means more than disagreement and conflict; rather it means the kind of controversy courts traditionally resolve. Here at issue is the production or non-production of specified evidence deemed by the Special Prosecutor to be relevant and admissible in a pending criminal case. It is sought by one official of the Government within the scope of his express authority; it is resisted by the Chief Executive on the ground of his duty to preserve the confidentiality of the communications of the President. Whatever the correct answer on the merits, these issues are "of a type which are traditionally justiciable."

*   *   *

. . . We turn to the claim that the subpoena should be quashed because it demands "confidential conversations between a President and his close advisors that it would be inconsistent with the public interest to produce." The first contention is a broad claim that the separation of powers doctrine precludes judicial review of a President's claim of privilege. The second contention is that if he does not prevail on the claim of absolute privilege, the court should hold as a matter of constitutional law that the privilege prevails over the subpoena. . . .

* * *

[The Court discussed its authority to interpret the Constitution, concluding that it had full power to adjudicate a claim of executive privilege.]

In support of his claim of absolute privilege, the President's counsel urges two grounds one of which is common to all governments and one of which is peculiar to our system of separation of powers. The first ground is the valid need for protection of communications between high government officials and those who advise and assist them in the performance of their manifold duties; the importance of this confidentiality is too plain to require further discussion. Human experience teaches that those who expect public dissemination of their remarks may well temper candor with a concern for appearances and for their own interests to the detriment of the decisionmaking process. Whatever the nature of the privilege of confidentiality of presidential communications in the exercise of Art. II powers the privilege can be said to derive from the supremacy of each branch within its own assigned area of constitutional duties. Certain powers and privileges flow from the nature of enumerated powers; the protection of the confidentiality of presidential communications has similar constitutional underpinnings.

The second ground asserted by the President's counsel in support of the claim of absolute privilege rests on the doctrine of separation of powers. Here it is argued that the independence of the Executive Branch within its own sphere, insulates a president from a judicial subpoena in an ongoing criminal prosecution, and thereby protects confidential presidential communications.

However, neither the doctrine of separation of powers, nor the need for confidentiality of high level communications, without more, can sustain an absolute, unqualified presidential privilege of immunity from judicial process under all circumstances. The President's need for complete candor and objectivity from advisers calls for great deference from the courts. However, when the privilege depends solely on the broad, undifferentiated claim of public interest in the confidentiality of such conversations, a confrontation with other values arises. Absent a claim of need to protect military, diplomatic or sensitive national security secrets, we find it difficult to accept the argument that even the very important interest in confidentiality of presidential communications is significantly diminished by production of such material for *in camera* inspection with all the protection that a district court will be obliged to provide.

The impediment that an absolute, unqualified privilege would place in the way of the primary constitutional duty of the judicial branch to do justice in criminal prosecutions would plainly conflict with the function of the courts under Art. III. In designing the structure of our Government and dividing and allocating the sovereign power among three coequal branches, the Framers of the Constitution sought to provide a comprehensive system, but the separate powers were not intended to operate with absolute independence. To read the Art. II powers of the President as providing an absolute privilege as against a subpoena essential to enforcement of criminal statutes on no more than a generalized claim of the public interest in confidentiality of nonmilitary and nondiplomatic discussions would upset the constitutional balance of "a workable government" and gravely impair the role of the court under Art. III.

Since we conclude that the legitimate needs of the judicial process may outweigh presidential privilege, it is necessary to resolve those competing interests in a manner that preserves the essential functions of each branch. The rights and indeed the duty to resolve that question does not free the judiciary from according high respect to the representations made on behalf of the President. The expectation of a President to the confidentiality of his conversations and correspondence, like the claim of confidentiality of judicial deliberations, for example, has all the values to which we accord deference for the privacy of all citizens and added to those values the necessity for protection of the public interest in his responsibilities against the inroads of such a privilege on the fair administration of criminal justice. The interest in preserving confidentiality is weighty indeed and entitled to great respect. However we cannot conclude that advisers will be moved to temper the candor of their remarks by the infrequent occasions of disclosure because of the possibility that such conversations will be called for in the context of a criminal prosecution.

On the other hand, the allowance of the privilege to withhold evidence that is demonstrably relevant in a criminal trial would cut deeply into the guarantee of due process of law and gravely impair the basic function of the courts. A President's acknowleged need for confidentiality in the communications of his office is general in nature, whereas the constitutional need for production of relevant evidence in a criminal proceeding is specific and central to the fair adjudication of a particular criminal case in the administration of justice. Without access to specific facts a criminal prosecution may be totally frustrated. The President's broad interest in confidentiality of communications will not be vitiated by disclosure of a limited number of conversations preliminarily shown to have some bearing on the pending criminal cases.

We conclude that when the ground for asserting privilege as to subpoenaed materials sought for use in a criminal trial is based only on the generalized interest in confidentiality, it cannot prevail over the fundamental demand of due process of law in the fair administration of criminal justice. The generalized assertion of privilege must yield to the demonstrated, specific need for evidence in a pending criminal trial.

* * *

In this case the President challenges a subpoena served on him as a third party requiring the production of materials for use in a criminal prosecution on the claim that he has a privilege against disclosure of confidential communications. He does not place his claim of privilege on the ground they are military or diplomatic secrets. As to these areas of Art. II duties the courts have traditionally shown the utmost deference to presidential responsibilities. No case of the Court, however, has extended this high degree of deference to a President's generalized interest in confidentiality. Nowhere in the Constitution, as we have noted earlier, is there any explicit reference to a privilege of confidentiality; yet to the extent this interest relates to the effective discharge of a President's powers, it is constitutionally based.

* * *

[*The Court distinguished this case from cases involving claims against the president while acting in an official capacity.*]

Mr. Chief Justice Marshall sitting as a trial judge in the *Burr* case was extraordinarily careful to point out that: "[I]n no case of this kind would a Court be required to proceed against the President as against an ordinary individual." Marshall's statement cannot be read to mean in any sense that a President is above the law, but relates to the singularly unique role under Art. II of a President's communications and activities, related to the performance of duties under that Article. Moreover, a President's communications and activities encompass a vastly wider range of sensitive material than would be true of any "ordinary individual." It is therefore necessary in the public interest to afford presidential confidentiality the greatest protection consistent with the fair administration of justice. The need for confidentiality even as to idle conversations with associates in which casual reference might be made concerning political leaders within the country or foreign statesmen is too obvious to call for further treatment. We have no doubt that the District Judge will at all times accord the presidential records that high degree of deference suggested in *United States v. Burr*, and will discharge his responsibility to see to it that until released to the Special Prosecutor no *in camera* [private] material is revealed to anyone. This burden applies with even greater force to excised material; once the decision is made to excise, the material is restored to its privileged status and should be returned under seal to its lawful custodian.

Affirmed.

United States v. Lopez (1995)

How far does Congress's authority extend with respect to the states? Since the 1930s, when a liberalization of Supreme Court doctrine cleared the way for an expansion of federal authority, Congress has relied on a loose interpretation of the Commerce Clause to justify extensive involvement in state and local affairs. (Congress can also shape what states do, for example, by placing conditions upon the receipt of federal funds). In 1990, Congress enacted the Gun-Free School Zones Act, making possession of a firearm in designated school zones a federal crime. When Alfonso Lopez, Jr., was convicted of violating the act, his lawyer challenged the constitutionality of the law, arguing that it was "invalid as beyond the power of Congress under the Commerce Clause." In a striking reversal of interpretation, the Supreme Court agreed and declared the law invalid, holding that banning guns in schools was too far removed from any effect on interstate commerce to warrant federal intervention. Critics of the decision argued that the Court's reasoning might invalidate a large body of federal crime and drug legislation that relies on the connection between regulated activity and interstate commerce. Supporters maintained that the decision marked a new era of judicial respect for federalism and state autonomy.

CHIEF JUSTICE REHNQUIST delivered the opinion of the Court.

In the Gun-Free School Zones Act of 1990, Congress made it a federal offense "for any individual knowingly to possess a firearm at a place that the individual knows, or has reasonable cause to believe, is a school zone." The Act neither regulates a commercial activity nor contains a requirement that the possession be connected in any way to interstate commerce. We hold that the Act exceeds the authority of "Congress to regulate Commerce . . . among the several States. . . ." (U.S. Constitution Art. I, 8, cl. 3).

On March 10, 1992, respondent, who was then a 12th-grade student, arrived at Edison High School in San Antonio, Texas, carrying a concealed .38 caliber handgun and five bullets. Acting upon an anonymous tip, school authorities confronted respondent, who admitted that he was carrying the weapon. He was arrested and charged under Texas law with firearm possession on school premises. The next day, the state charges were dismissed after federal agents charged respondent by complaint with violating the Gun-Free School Zones Act of 1990.

A federal grand jury indicted respondent on one count of knowing possession of a firearm at a school zone, in violation of 922(q) [the relevant section of the Act of 1990]. Respondent moved to dismiss his federal indictment on the ground that 922(q) "is unconstitutional as it is beyond the power of Congress to legislate control over our public schools." The District Court denied the motion, concluding that 922(q) "is a constitutional exercise of Congress' well-defined power to regulate activities in and affecting commerce, and the 'business' of elementary, middle and high schools . . . affects interstate commerce." Respondent waived his right to a jury trial. The District Court conducted a bench trial, found him guilty of violating 922(q), and sentenced him to six months' imprisonment and two years' supervised release.

On appeal, respondent challenged his conviction based on his claim that 922(q) exceeded Congress' power to legislate under the Commerce Clause. The Court of Appeals for the Fifth Circuit agreed and reversed respondent's conviction. It held that, in light of what it characterized as insufficient congressional findings and legislative history, "in the full reach of its terms, is invalid as beyond the power of Congress under the Commerce Clause." Because of the importance of the issue, we granted *certiorari* and we now affirm.

We start with first principles. The Constitution creates a Federal Government of enumerated powers. As James Madison wrote, "[t]he powers delegated by the proposed Constitution to the federal government are few and defined. Those which are to remain in the State governments are numerous and indefinite." (*The Federalist*, No. 45). This constitutionally mandated division of authority was adopted by the Framers to ensure protection of our fundamental liberties. Just as the separation and independence of the coordinate branches of the Federal Government serves to prevent the accumulation of excessive power in any one branch, a healthy balance of power between the States and the Federal Government will reduce the risk of tyranny and abuse from either front.

[For the next several pages Rehnquist reviews the evolution of interpretations of the Commerce Clause, starting with Gibbons v. Ogden *(1824). This case established the relatively narrow interpretation of the Commerce Clause in which the Court prevented* states *from interfering with interstate commerce. Very rarely did cases concern Congress's power. The 1887 Interstate Commerce Act and the 1890 Sherman Antitrust Act expanded Congress's power to regulate intrastate commerce "where the interstate and intrastate aspects of commerce were so mingled together that full regulation of interstate commerce required incidental regulation of intrastate commerce," arguing that the Commerce Clause authorized such regulation. Several New Deal era cases,* NLRB v. Jones & Laughlin Steel Corp. *(1937),* United States v. Darby *(1941), and* Wickard v. Filburn *(1942) broadened the interpretation of the Commerce Clause.]*

Jones & Laughlin Steel, *Darby*, and *Wickard* ushered in an era of Commerce Clause jurisprudence that greatly expanded the previously defined authority of Congress under that Clause. In part, this was a recognition of the great changes that had occurred in the way business was carried on in this country. Enterprises that had once been local or at most regional in nature had become national in scope. But the doctrinal change also reflected a view that earlier Commerce Clause cases artificially had constrained the authority of Congress to regulate interstate commerce.

But even these modern-era precedents which have expanded congressional power under the Commerce Clause confirm that this power is subject to outer limits. In *Jones & Laughlin Steel*, the Court warned that the scope of the interstate commerce power "must be considered in the light of our dual system of government and may not be extended so as to embrace effects upon interstate commerce so indirect and remote that to embrace them, in view of our complex society, would effectually obliterate the distinction between what is national and what is local and create a completely centralized government." Since that time, the Court has heeded that warning and undertaken to decide whether a rational basis existed for concluding that a regulated activity sufficiently affected interstate commerce.

* * *

Consistent with this structure, we have identified three broad categories of activity that Congress may regulate under its commerce power. First, Congress may regulate the use of the channels of interstate commerce. Second, Congress is empowered to regulate and protect the instrumentalities of interstate commerce, or persons or things in interstate commerce, even though the threat may come only from intrastate activities. Finally, Congress' commerce authority includes the power to regulate those activities having a substantial relation to interstate commerce, those activities that substantially affect interstate commerce.

Within this final category, admittedly, our case law has not been clear whether an activity must *affect* or *substantially affect* interstate commerce in order to be within Congress' power to regulate it under the Commerce Clause. We conclude, consistent with the great weight of our case law, that the proper test requires an analysis of whether the regulated activity *substantially affects* interstate commerce.

We now turn to consider the power of Congress, in the light of this framework, to enact 922(q) [The Gun-Free School Zones Act]. The first two categories of authority may be quickly disposed of: 922(q) is not a regulation of the use of the channels of interstate commerce, nor is it an attempt to prohibit the interstate transportation of a commodity through the channels of commerce; nor can 922(q) be justified as a regulation by which Congress has sought to protect an instrumentality of interstate commerce or a thing in interstate commerce. Thus, if 922(q) is to be sustained, it must be under the third category as a regulation of an activity that substantially affects interstate commerce.

First, we have upheld a wide variety of congressional Acts regulating intrastate economic activity where we have concluded that the activity substantially affected interstate commerce. Examples include the regulation of intrastate coal mining; intrastate extortionate credit transactions, restaurants utilizing substantial interstate supplies, inns and hotels catering to interstate guests, and production and consumption of home-grown wheat. These examples are by no means exhaustive, but the pattern is clear. Where economic activity substantially affects interstate commerce, legislation regulating that activity will be sustained.

Even *Wickard*, which is perhaps the most far reaching example of Commerce Clause authority over intrastate activity, involved economic activity in a way that the possession of a gun in a school zone does not. Roscoe Filburn operated a small farm in Ohio, on which, in the year involved, he raised 23 acres of wheat. It was his practice to sow winter wheat in the fall, and after harvesting it in July to sell a portion of the crop, to feed part of it to poultry and livestock on the farm, to use some in making flour for home consumption, and to keep the remainder for seeding future crops. The Secretary of Agriculture assessed a penalty against him under the Agricultural Adjustment Act of 1938 because he harvested about 12 acres more wheat than his allotment under the Act permitted. The Act was designed to regulate the volume of wheat moving in interstate and foreign commerce in order to avoid surpluses and shortages, and concomitant fluctuation in wheat prices, which had previously obtained. The Court said, in an opinion sustaining the application of the Act to Filburn's activity, "One of the primary purposes of the Act in question was to increase the market price of wheat and to that end to limit the volume thereof that could affect the market. It can hardly be denied that a factor of such volume and variability as home-consumed wheat would have a substantial influence on price and market conditions. This may arise because being in marketable condition such wheat overhangs the market and, if induced by rising prices, tends to flow into the market and check price increases. But if we assume that it is never marketed, it supplies a need of the man who grew it which would otherwise be reflected by purchases in the open market. Home-grown wheat in this sense competes with wheat in commerce" (317 U.S., at 128).

Section 922(q) is a criminal statute that by its terms has nothing to do with *commerce* or any sort of economic enterprise, however broadly one might define those terms. Section 922(q) is not an essential part of a larger regulation of economic activity, in which the regulatory scheme could be undercut unless the intra-state activity were regulated. It cannot, therefore, be sustained under our cases upholding regulations of activities that arise out of or are connected with a commercial transaction, which viewed in the aggregate, substantially affects interstate commerce.

Second, 922(q) contains no jurisdictional element which would ensure, through case-by-case inquiry, that the firearm possession in question affects interstate commerce. . . . 922(q) has no express jurisdictional element which might limit its reach to a discrete set of firearm possessions that additionally have an explicit connection with or effect on interstate commerce.

* * *

The Government's essential contention, in fine, is that we may determine here that 922(q) is valid because possession of a firearm in a local school zone does indeed substantially affect interstate commerce. The Government argues that possession of a firearm in a school zone may result in violent crime and that violent crime can be expected to affect the functioning of the national economy in two ways. First, the costs of violent crime are substantial, and, through the mechanism of insurance, those costs are spread throughout the population. Second, violent crime reduces the willingness of individuals to travel to areas within the country that are perceived to be unsafe. The Government also argues that the presence of guns in schools poses a substantial threat to the educational process by threatening the learning environment. A handicapped educational process, in turn, will result in a less productive citizenry. That, in turn, would have an adverse effect on the Nation's economic well-being. As a result, the Government argues that Congress could rationally have concluded that 922(q) substantially affects interstate commerce.

We pause to consider the implications of the Government's arguments. The Government admits, under its "costs of crime" reasoning, that Congress could regulate not only all violent crime, but all activities that might lead to violent crime, regardless of how tenuously they relate to interstate commerce. Similarly, under the Government's "national productivity" reasoning, Congress could regulate any activity that it found was related to the economic productivity of individual citizens: family law (including marriage, divorce, and child custody), for example. Under the theories that the Government presents in support of 922(q), it is difficult to perceive any limitation on federal power, even in areas such as criminal law enforcement or education where States historically have been sovereign. Thus, if we were to accept the Government's arguments, we are hard-pressed to posit any activity by an individual that Congress is without power to regulate.

Although Justice Breyer argues that acceptance of the Government's rationales would not authorize a general federal police power, he is unable to identify any activity that the States may regulate but Congress may not. Justice Breyer posits that there might be some limitations on Congress' commerce power such as family law or certain aspects of education. These suggested limitations, when viewed in light of the dissent's expansive analysis, are devoid of substance.

Justice Breyer focuses, for the most part, on the threat that firearm possession in and near schools poses to the educational process and the potential economic consequences flowing from that threat. Specifically, the dissent reasons that (1) gun-related violence is a serious problem;

(2) that problem, in turn, has an adverse effect on classroom learning; and (3) that adverse effect on classroom learning, in turn, represents a substantial threat to trade and commerce. This analysis would be equally applicable, if not more so, to subjects such as family law and direct regulation of education.

For instance, if Congress can, pursuant to its Commerce Clause power, regulate activities that adversely affect the learning environment, then, a fortiori, it also can regulate the educational process directly. Congress could determine that a school's curriculum has a "significant" effect on the extent of classroom learning. As a result, Congress could mandate a federal curriculum for local elementary and secondary schools because what is taught in local schools has a significant "effect on classroom learning," and that, in turn, has a substantial effect on interstate commerce.

Justice Breyer rejects our reading of precedent and argues that "Congress . . . could rationally conclude that schools fall on the commercial side of the line." Again, Justice Breyer's rationale lacks any real limits because, depending on the level of generality, any activity can be looked upon as commercial. Under the dissent's rationale, Congress could just as easily look at child rearing as "fall[ing] on the commercial side of the line" because it provides a "valuable service" namely, to equip [children] with the skills they need to survive in life and, more specifically, in the workplace. We do not doubt that Congress has authority under the Commerce Clause to regulate numerous commercial activities that substantially affect interstate commerce and also affect the educational process. That authority, though broad, does not include the authority to regulate each and every aspect of local schools.

Admittedly, a determination whether an intrastate activity is commercial or noncommercial may in some cases result in legal uncertainty. But, so long as Congress' authority is limited to those powers enumerated in the Constitution, and so long as those enumerated powers are interpreted as having judicially enforceable outer limits, congressional legislation under the Commerce Clause always will engender "legal uncertainty." As Chief Justice Marshall stated in *McCulloch v. Maryland*, (1819), "The [federal] government is acknowledged by all to be one of enumerated powers. The principle, that it can exercise only the powers granted to it . . . is now universally admitted. But the question respecting the extent of the powers actually granted, is perpetually arising, and will probably continue to arise, as long as our system shall exist." The Constitution mandates this uncertainty by withholding from Congress a plenary police power that would authorize enactment of every type of legislation. Congress has operated within this framework of legal uncertainty ever since this Court determined that it was the judiciary's duty "to say what the law is." Any possible benefit from eliminating this "legal uncertainty" would be at the expense of the Constitution's system of enumerated powers.

* * *

These are not precise formulations, and in the nature of things they cannot be. But we think they point the way to a correct decision of this case. The possession of a gun in a local school zone is in no sense an economic activity that might, through repetition elsewhere, substantially affect any sort of interstate commerce. Respondent was a local student at a local school; there is no indication that he had recently moved in interstate commerce, and there is no requirement that his possession of the firearm have any concrete tie to interstate commerce.

To uphold the Government's contentions here, we would have to pile inference upon inference in a manner that would bid fair to convert congressional authority under the Commerce Clause to a general police power of the sort retained by the States. Admittedly, some of our prior cases have taken long steps down that road, giving great deference to congressional action. The broad language in these opinions has suggested the possibility of additional expansion, but we decline here to proceed any further. To do so would require us to conclude that the Constitution's enumeration of powers does not presuppose something not enumerated, and that there never will be a distinction between what is truly national and what is truly local. This we are unwilling to do.

For the foregoing reasons the judgment of the Court of Appeals is Affirmed.

The Declaration of Independence

In Congress, July 4, 1776

When in the course of human events, it becomes necessary for one people to dissolve the political bands which have connected them with another, and to assume among the Powers of the earth, the separate and equal station to which the Laws of Nature and of Nature's God entitle them, a decent respect to the opinions of mankind requires that they should declare the causes which impel them to the separation.

We hold these truths to be self-evident, that all men are created equal, that they are endowed by their Creator with certain unalienable rights, that among these are Life, Liberty and the pursuit of Happiness. That to secure these rights, Governments are instituted among Men, deriving their just powers from the consent of the governed. That whenever any Form of Government becomes destructive of these ends, it is the Right of the People to alter or to abolish it, and to institute new Government, laying its foundation on such principles and organizing its powers in such form, as to them shall seem most likely to effect their Safety and Happiness. Prudence, indeed, will dictate that Governments long established should not be changed for light and transient causes; and accordingly all experience hath shown, that mankind are more disposed to suffer, while evils are sufferable, than to right themselves by abolishing the forms to which they are accustomed. But when a long train of abuses and usurpations, pursuing invariably the same Object evinces a design to reduce them under absolute Despotism, it is their right, it is their duty, to throw off such Government, and to provide new Guards for their future security.—Such has been the patient sufferance of these Colonies; and such is now the necessity which constrains them to alter their former Systems of Government. The history of the present King of Great Britain is a history of repeated injuries and usurpations, all having in direct object the establishment of an absolute Tyranny over these States. To prove this, let Facts be submitted to a candid world.

He has refused his Assent to Laws, the most wholesome and necessary for the public good.

He has forbidden his Governors to pass Laws of immediate and pressing importance, unless suspended in their operation till his Assent should be obtained; and when so suspended, he has utterly neglected to attend to them.

He has refused to pass other Laws for the accommodation of large districts of people, unless those people would relinquish the right of Representation in the Legislature, a right inestimable to them and formidable to tyrants only.

He has called together legislative bodies at places unusual, uncomfortable, and distant from the depository of their public Records, for the sole purpose of fatiguing them into compliance with his measures.

He has dissolved Representative Houses repeatedly, for opposing with manly firmness his invasions on the rights of the people.

He has refused for a long time, after such dissolutions, to cause others to be elected; whereby the Legislative powers, incapable of Annihilation, have returned to the People at large for their exercise; the State remaining in the mean time exposed to all the dangers of invasion from without, and convulsions within.

He has endeavoured to prevent the population of these States; for that purpose obstructing the Laws for Naturalization of Foreigners; refusing to pass others to encourage their migrations hither, and raising the conditions of new Appropriations of Lands.

He has obstructed the Administration of Justice, by refusing his Assent to Laws for establishing Judiciary Powers.

He has made Judges dependent on his Will alone, for the tenure of their offices, and the amount and payment of their salaries.

He has erected a multitude of New Offices, and sent hither swarms of Officers to harrass our People, and eat out their substance.

He has kept among us, in times of peace, Standing Armies without the Consent of our legislature.

He has affected to render the Military independent of and superior to the Civil Power.

He has combined with others to subject us to a jurisdiction foreign to our constitution, and unacknowledged by our laws; giving his Assent to their Acts of pretended Legislation:

For quartering large bodies of armed troops among us:

For protecting them, by a mock Trial, from Punishment for any Murders which they should commit on the Inhabitants of these States:

For cutting off our Trade with all parts of the world:

For imposing Taxes on us without our Consent:

For depriving us in many cases, of the benefits of Trial by jury:

For transporting us beyond Seas to be tried for pretended offences:

For abolishing the free System of English Laws in a neighbouring Province, establishing therein an Arbitrary government, and enlarging its Boundaries so as to render it at once an example and fit instrument for introducing the same absolute rule into these Colonies:

For taking away our Charters, abolishing our most valuable Laws, and altering fundamentally the Forms of our Governments:

For suspending our own Legislatures, and declaring themselves invested with Power to legislate for us in all cases whatsoever.

He has abdicated Government here, by declaring us out of his Protection and waging War against us.

He has plundered our seas, ravaged our Coasts, burnt our towns, and destroyed the lives of our people.

He is at this time transporting large armies of foreign mercenaries to compleat the works of death, desolation and tyranny, already begun with circumstances of Cruelty & perfidy scarcely paralleled in the most barbarous ages, and totally unworthy the Head of a civilized nation.

He has constrained our fellow Citizens taken Captive on the high Seas to bear Arms against their Country, to become the executioners of their friends and Brethren, or to fall themselves by their Hands.

He has excited domestic insurrections amongst us, and has endeavored to bring on the inhabitants of our frontiers, the merciless Indian Savages, whose known rule of warfare, is an undistinguished destruction of all ages, sexes, and conditions.

In every stage of these Oppressions we have Petitioned for Redress in the most humble terms: Our repeated Petitions have been answered only by repeated injury. A Prince, whose character is thus marked by every act which may define a Tyrant, is unfit to be the ruler of a free people.

Nor have we been wanting in attention to our British brethren. We have warned them from time to time of attempts by their legislature to extend an unwarrantable jurisdiction over us. We have reminded them of the circumstances of our emigration and settlement here. We have appealed to their native justice and magnanimity, and we have conjured them by the ties of our common kindred to disavow these usurpations, which, would inevitably interrupt our connections and correspondence. They too must have been deaf to the voice of justice and of consanguinity. We must, therefore, acquiesce in the necessity, which denounces our Separation, and hold them, as we hold the rest of mankind, Enemies in War, in Peace Friends.

WE, THEREFORE, the Representatives of the UNITED STATES OF AMERICA, in General Congress, Assembled, appealing to the Supreme Judge of the world for the rectitude of our intentions, do, in the Name, and by Authority of the good People of these Colonies, solemnly publish and declare, That these United Colonies are, and of Right ought to be FREE AND INDEPENDENT STATES; that they are Absolved from all Allegiance to the British Crown, and that all political connection between them and the State of Great Britain, is and ought to be totally dissolved; and that as Free and Independent States, they have full Power to levy War, conclude Peace, contract Alliances, establish Commerce, and to do all other

Acts and Things which Independent States may of right do. And for the support of this Declaration, with a firm reliance on the protection of Divine Providence, we mutually pledge to each other our Lives, our Fortunes and our sacred Honor.

The foregoing Declaration was, by order of Congress, engrossed, and signed by the following members:

John Hancock

NEW HAMPSHIRE
Josiah Bartlett
William Whipple
Matthew Thornton

MASSACHUSETTS BAY
Samuel Adams
John Adams
Robert Treat Paine
Elbridge Gerry

RHODE ISLAND
Stephen Hopkins
William Ellery

CONNECTICUT
Roger Sherman
Samuel Huntington
William Williams
Oliver Wolcott

NEW YORK
William Floyd
Philip Livingston
Francis Lewis
Lewis Morris

NEW JERSEY
Richard Stockton
John Witherspoon
Francis Hopkinson
John Hart
Abraham Clark

PENNSYLVANIA
Robert Morris
Benjamin Rush
Benjamin Franklin
John Morton
George Clymer
James Smith
George Taylor
James Wilson
George Ross

DELAWARE
Caesar Rodney
George Read
Thomas M'Kean

MARYLAND
Samuel Chase
William Paca

Thomas Stone
Charles Carroll,
  of Carrollton

VIRGINIA
George Wythe
Richard Henry Lee
Thomas Jefferson
Benjamin Harrison
Thomas Nelson, Jr.
Francis Lightfoot Lee
Carter Braxton

NORTH CAROLINA
William Hooper
Joseph Hewes
John Penn

SOUTH CAROLINA
Edward Rutledge
Thomas Heyward, Jr.
Thomas Lynch, Jr.
Arthur Middleton

GEORGIA
Button Gwinnett
Lyman Hall
George Walton

Resolved, That copies of the Declaration be sent to the several assemblies, conventions, and committees, or councils of safety, and to the several commanding officers of the continental troops; that it be proclaimed in each of the United States, at the head of the army.

The Constitution of the United States of America

Federalist Paper Number and Author

Annotated with references to the Federalist Papers; *bracketed material is by the editors of this volume.*

[PREAMBLE]

84 (Hamilton)

We the People of the United States, in Order to form a more perfect Union, establish Justice, insure domestic Tranquility, provide for the common defence, promote the general Welfare, and secure the Blessings of Liberty to ourselves and our Posterity, do ordain and establish this Constitution for the United States of America.

ARTICLE I

Section 1

[LEGISLATURE POWERS]

10, 45 (Madison)

All legislative Powers herein granted shall be vested in a Congress of the United States, which shall consist of a Senate and House of Representatives.

Section 2

[HOUSE OF REPRESENTATIVES, HOW CONSTITUTED, POWER OF IMPEACHMENT]

39 (Madison) 45 (Madison) 52–53, 57 (Madison)

The House of Representatives shall be composed of Members chosen every second Year by the People of the several States, and the Electors in each State shall have the Qualifications requisite for Electors of the most numerous Branch of the State Legislature.

52 (Madison), 60 (Hamilton)

No Person shall be a Representative who shall not have attained to the Age of twenty five Years, and been seven Years a Citizen of the United States, and who shall not, when elected, be an Inhabitant of that State in which he shall be chosen.

54 (Madison)

Representatives and *direct Taxes** shall be apportioned among

* [Modified by Sixteenth Amendment.]

the several States which may be included within this Union, according to their respective Numbers, *which shall be determined by adding to the whole Number of free Persons, including those bound to*
54
(Madison)
Service for a Term of Years, and excluding Indians not taxed, *three-fifths of all other Persons.** The actual Enumeration shall be made
58
(Madison)
within three Years after the first Meeting of the Congress of the United States, and within every subsequent Term of ten Years, in such Manner as they shall by Law direct. The Number of Representatives shall not exceed one for every thirty Thousand,
55–56
(Madison)
but each State shall have at Least one Representative; *and until such enumeration shall be made, the State of New Hampshire shall be entitled to chuse three, Massachusetts eight, Rhode Island and Providence Plantations one, Connecticut five, New-York six, New Jersey four, Pennsylvania eight, Delaware one, Maryland six, Virginia ten, North Carolina five, South Carolina five and Georgia three.†*

When vacancies happen in the Representation from any State, the Executive Authority thereof shall issue Writs of Election to fill such Vacancies.

79
(Hamilton)
The House of Representatives shall chuse their Speaker and other Officers; and shall have the sole Power of Impeachment.

Section 3

[THE SENATE, HOW CONSTITUTED, IMPEACHMENT TRIALS]

39, 45
(Madison),
60
(Hamilton),
The Senate of the United States shall be composed of two Senators from each State, *chosen by the Legislature thereof,‡* for six Years; and each Senator shall have one Vote.

62–63
(Madison)
59
(Hamilton)
Immediately after they shall be assembled in Consequence of the first Election, they shall be divided as equally as may be into three Classes. The Seats of the Senators of the first Class shall be vacated at the Expiration of the second Year, of the second Class at the Expiration of the fourth Year, and of the third Class at the Expiration of the sixth Year, so that one third may be chosen
68
(Hamilton)
every second Year: *and if Vacancies happen by Resignation, or otherwise, during the Recess of the Legislature of any State, the Executive thereof may make temporary Appointments until the next Meeting of the Legislature, which shall then fill such Vacancies.§*

62
(Madison),
64 (Jay)
No person shall be a Senator who shall not have attained to the Age of thirty Years, and been nine Years a Citizen of the

---

* [Modified by Fourteenth Amendment.]
† [Temporary provision.]
‡ [Modified by Seventeenth Amendment.]
§ [Modified by Seventeenth Amendment.]

United States, and who shall not, when elected, be an Inhabitant of that State for which he shall be chosen.

The Vice-President of the United States shall be President of the Senate, but shall have no Vote, unless they be equally divided.

39
(Madison),
65–67, 79
(Hamilton)
65
(Hamilton)
84
(Hamilton)

The Senate shall chuse their other Officers, and also a President pro tempore, in the Absence of the Vice-President, or when he shall exercise the Office of President of the United States.

The Senate shall have the sole Power to try all Impeachments. When sitting for that Purpose, they shall be on Oath or Affirmation. When the President of the United States is tried, the Chief Justice shall preside: And no Person shall be convicted without the Concurrence of two thirds of the Members present.

Judgment in Cases of Impeachment shall not extend further than to removal from Office, and disqualification to hold and enjoy any Office of honor, Trust or Profit under the United States: but the Party convicted shall nevertheless be liable and subject to Indictment, Trial, Judgment and Punishment, according to Law.

Section 4

[ELECTION OF SENATORS AND REPRESENTATIVES]

59–61
(Hamilton)

The Times, Places and Manner of holding Elections for Senators and Representatives, shall be prescribed in each State by the Legislature thereof; but the Congress may at any time by Law make or alter such Regulations, except as to the Place of Chusing Senators.

*The Congress shall assemble at least once in every Year, and such Meeting shall be on the first Monday in December, unless they shall by Law appoint a different Day.**

Section 5

[QUORUM, JOURNALS, MEETINGS, ADJOURNMENTS]

Each House shall be the Judge of the Elections, Returns and Qualifications of its own Members, and a Majority of each shall constitute a Quorum to do Business; but a smaller Number may adjourn from day to day, and may be authorized to compel the Attendance of absent Members, in such Manner, and under such Penalties as each House may provide.

Each House may determine the Rules of its Proceedings, pun-

* [Modified by Twentieth Amendment.]

ish its Members for disorderly Behavior, and, with the Concurrence of two-thirds, expel a Member.

Each House shall keep a Journal of its Proceedings, and from time to time publish the same, excepting such Parts as may in their Judgment require Secrecy; and the Yeas and Nays of the Members of either House on any question shall, at the Desire of one-fifth of those Present, be entered on the Journal.

Neither House, during the Session of Congress, shall, without the Consent of the other, adjourn for more than three days, nor to any other Place than that in which the two Houses shall be sitting.

Section 6

[COMPENSATION, PRIVILEGES, DISABILITIES]

The Senators and Representatives shall receive a Compensation for their Services, to be ascertained by Law, and paid out of the Treasury of the United States. They shall in all Cases, except Treason, Felony and Breach of the Peace, be privileged from Arrest during their Attendance at the Session of their respective Houses, and in going to and returning from the same; and for any Speech or Debate in either House, they shall not be questioned in any other Place.

55
(Madison),
76
(Hamilton)

No Senator or Representative shall, during the Time for which he was elected, be appointed to any civil Office under the authority of the United States, which shall have been created, or the Emoluments whereof shall have been increased during such time; and no Person holding any Office under the United States, shall be a Member of either House during his Continuance in Office.

Section 7

[PROCEDURE IN PASSING BILLS AND RESOLUTIONS]

66
(Hamilton)

All bills for raising Revenue shall originate in the House of Representatives; but the Senate may propose or concur with Amendments as on other Bills.

69, 73
(Hamilton)

Every Bill which shall have passed the House of Representatives and the Senate, shall, before it become a Law, be presented to the President of the United States; If he approve he shall sign it, but if not he shall return it, with his Objections to that House in which it shall have originated, who shall enter the Objections at large on their Journal, and proceed to reconsider it. If after such Reconsideration two-thirds of that House shall agree to pass the Bill, it shall be sent, together with the Objections, to the other House, by which it shall likewise be reconsidered, and if approved by two thirds of that House it shall become a Law. But in all such Cases the Votes of both Houses shall be determined by Yeas and Nays, and the Names of the Persons voting for and against the Bill shall be entered on the Journal of each House respectively. If any Bill shall not be returned by the President within ten Days (Sundays excepted) after it shall have been presented to him, the Same shall be a Law, in like Manner as if he had signed it, unless the Congress by their Adjournment prevent its Return, in which Case it shall not be a Law.

69, 73
(Hamilton)

Every Order, Resolution, or Vote to which the Concurrence of the Senate and House of Representatives may be necessary (except on a question of Adjournment) shall be presented to the President of the United States; and before the Same shall take Effect, shall be approved by him, or being disapproved by him, shall be repassed by two-thirds of the Senate and House of Representatives, according to the Rules and Limitations prescribed in the Case of a Bill.

Section 8

[POWERS OF CONGRESS]

The Congress shall have Power

30–36
(Hamilton),

41
(Madison)

To lay and collect Taxes, Duties, Imposts and Excises, to pay the Debts and provide for the common Defence and general Welfare of the United States; but all Duties, Imposts and Excises shall be uniform throughout the United States;

56
(Madison)

To borrow money on the Credit of the United States;

42, 45, 56
(Madison)

To regulate Commerce with foreign Nations, and among the several States, and with the Indian Tribes;

32
(Hamilton),

To establish an uniform Rule of Naturalization, and uniform Laws on the subject of Bankruptcies throughout the United States;

42
(Madison)
42
(Madison)

To coin Money, regulate the Value thereof, and of foreign Coin, and fix the Standard of Weights and Measures;

42
(Madison)

To provide for the Punishment of counterfeiting the Securities and current Coin of the United States;

To establish Post Offices and Post Roads;

42
(Madison)
43
(Madison)

To promote the Progress of Science and useful Arts, by securing for limited Times to Authors and Inventors the exclusive Right to their respective Writings and Discoveries;

81
(Hamilton)

To constitute Tribunals inferior to the supreme Court;

42
(Madison)

To define and Punish Piracies and Felonies committed on the high Seas, and Offenses against the Law of Nations;

41
(Madison)

To declare War, grant Letters of Marque and Reprisal, and make Rules concerning Captures on Land and Water;

23, 24, 26
(Hamilton),

To raise and support Armies, but no Appropriation of Money to that Use shall be for a longer Term than two Years;

41
(Madison)

To provide and maintain a Navy;

To make Rules for the Government and Regulation of the land and naval forces;

29
(Hamilton)

To provide for calling forth the Militia to execute the Laws of the Union, suppress Insurrections and repel Invasions;

29
(Hamilton),

56
(Madison)

To provide for organizing, arming, and disciplining the Militia, and for governing such Part of them as may be employed in the Service of the United States, reserving to the States respectively, the Appointment of the Officers, and the Authority of training the Militia according to the discipline prescribed by Congress;

32
(Hamilton),
43
(Madison)

43
(Madison)

To exercise exclusive Legislation in all Cases whatsoever, over such District (not exceeding ten Miles square) as may, by Cession of particular States, and the Acceptance of Congress, become the Seat of the Government of the United States, and to exercise like Authority over all Places purchased by the Consent of the Legislature of the State in which the Same shall be, for the Erection of Forts, Magazines, Arsenals, dock-Yards, and other needful Buildings;—And

29, 33
(Hamilton)

44
(Madison)

To make all Laws which shall be necessary and proper for carrying into Execution the foregoing Powers, and all other Powers vested by this Constitution in the Government of the United States, or in any Department or Officer thereof.

Section 9

[SOME RESTRICTIONS ON FEDERAL POWER]

42
(Madison)

*The Migration or Importation of such Persons as any of the States now existing shall think proper to admit, shall not be prohibited by the Congress prior to the Year one thousand eight hundred and eight, but a tax or duty may be imposed on such Importation, not exceeding ten dollars for each Person.**

83, 84
(Hamilton)

The privilege of the Writ of *Habeas Corpus* shall not be suspended, unless when in Cases of Rebellion or Invasion the public Safety may require it.

84
(Hamilton)

No Bill of Attainder or ex post facto Law shall be passed.

No Capitation, or other direct, Tax shall be laid, unless in Proportion to the Census or Enumeration herein before directed to be taken.†

* [Temporary provision.]
† [Modified by Sixteenth Amendment.]

No Tax or Duty shall be laid on Articles exported from any State.

32
(Hamilton)

No Preference shall be given by any Regulation of Commerce or Revenue to the Ports of one State over those of another: nor shall Vessels bound to, or from, one State, be obliged to enter, clear, or pay Duties in another.

No Money shall be drawn from the Treasury, but in Consequence of Appropriations made by Law; and a regular Statement and Account of the Receipts and Expenditures of all public Money shall be published from time to time.

39
(Madison),
84
(Hamilton)

No Title of Nobility shall be granted by the United States: And no Person holding any Office of Profit or Trust under them, shall, without the Consent of the Congress, accept of any present, Emolument, Office, or Title, of any kind whatever, from any King, Prince or foreign State.

Section 10

[RESTRICTIONS UPON POWERS OF STATES]

33
(Hamilton),
44
(Madison)

No State shall enter into any Treaty, Alliance, or Confederation; grant Letters of Marque and Reprisal; coin Money; emit Bills of Credit; make any Thing but gold and silver Coin a Tender in Payment of Debts; pass any Bill of Attainder, ex post facto Law, or Law impairing the Obligation of Contracts, or grant any Title of Nobility.

32
(Hamilton),

44
(Madison)

No State shall, without the Consent of the Congress, lay any Imposts or Duties on Imports or Exports, except what may be absolutely necessary for executing its inspection Laws: and the net Produce of all Duties and Imposts, laid by any State on Imports or Exports, shall be for the Use of the Treasury of the United States; and all such Laws shall be subject to the Revision and Controul of the Congress.

No State shall, without the Consent of Congress, lay any duty of Tonnage, keep Troops, or Ships of War in time of Peace, enter into any Agreement or Compact with another State, or with a foreign Power, or engage in War, unless actually invaded, or in such imminent Danger as will not admit of Delay.

ARTICLE II

Section 1

[EXECUTIVE POWER, ELECTION, QUALIFICATIONS OF THE PRESIDENT]

39
(Madison),
70, 71, 84
(Hamilton)

The executive Power shall be vested in a President of the United States of America. *He shall hold his Office during the Term* *of four years, and, together with the Vice-President, chosen for the same Term, be elected, as follows:**

69, 71
(Hamilton)
Each State shall appoint, in such Manner as the Legislature thereof may direct, a Number of Electors, equal to the whole Number of Senators and Representatives to which the State may
39, 45
(Madison),
be entitled in the Congress: but no Senator or Representative, or Person holding an Office of Trust or Profit under the United
68, 77
(Hamilton)
States, shall be appointed an Elector.

The electors shall meet in their respective States, and vote by ballot for two Persons, of whom one at least shall not be an Inhabitant of the same State with themselves. And they shall make a List of all the Persons voted for, and of the Number of Votes for each; which List they shall sign and certify, and transmit sealed to the Seat of the Government of the United States, directed to the President of the Senate. The
66
(Hamilton)
President of the Senate shall, in the Presence of the Senate and House of Representatives, open all the Certificates, and the Votes shall then be counted. The Person having the greatest Number of Votes shall be the President, if such Number be a Majority of the whole Number of Electors appointed; and if there be more than one who have such Majority, and have an equal Number of Votes, then the House of Representatives shall immediately chuse by Ballot one of them for President; and if no Person have a Majority, then from the five highest on the List the said House shall in like Manner chuse the President. But in chusing the President, the Votes shall be taken by States, the Representation from each State having one Vote; a quorum for this Purpose shall consist of a Member or Members from two-thirds of the States, and a Majority of all the States shall be necessary to a Choice. In every Case, after the Choice of the President, the Person having the greatest Number of Votes of the Electors shall be the Vice-President. But if there should remain two or more who have equal Votes, the Senate shall chuse from them by Ballot the Vice-President.†

The Congress may determine the Time of chusing the Electors, and the Day on which they shall give their Votes; which Day shall be the same throughout the United States.

No Person except a natural born Citizen, or a Citizen of the United States, at the time of the Adoption of this Constitution, shall be eligible to the Office of President; neither shall any Person be eligible to that Office who shall not have attained to the
64 (Jay)
Age of thirty-five Years, and been fourteen Years a Resident within the United States.

In Case of the Removal of the President from Office, or his Death, Resignation, or Inability to discharge the Powers and Du-

---

* [Number of terms limited to two by Twenty-second Amendment.]
† [Modified by Twelfth and Twentieth Amendment.]

ties of the said Office, the same shall devolve on the Vice-President, and the Congress may by Law provide for the Case of Removal, Death, Resignation or Inability, both of the President and Vice-President, declaring what Officer shall then act as President, and such Officer shall act accordingly, until the Disability be removed, or a President shall be elected.

73, 79
(Hamilton)

The President shall, at stated Times, receive for his Services, a Compensation, which shall neither be encreased nor diminished during the Period for which he shall have been elected, and he shall not receive within that Period any other Emolument from the United States, or any of them.

Before he enter on the Execution of his Office, he shall take the following Oath or Affirmation:—"I do solemnly swear (or affirm) that I will faithfully execute the Office of President of the United States, and will to the best of my Ability, preserve, protect and defend the Constitution of the United States."

Section 2

[POWERS OF THE PRESIDENT]

69, 74
(Hamilton)

The President shall be Commander in Chief of the Army and Navy of the United States, and of the Militia of the several States, when called into the actual Service of the United States; he may require the Opinion, in writing, of the principal Officer in each of the executive Departments, upon any Subject relating to the

74
(Hamilton)
69
(Hamilton)
74
(Hamilton)
42
(Madison)
64 (Jay),
66
(Hamilton)

42
(Madison),

66, 69,
76, 77
(Hamilton)

Duties of their respective Offices, and he shall have Power to Grant Reprieves and Pardons for Offenses against the United States, except in Cases of Impeachment.

He shall have Power, by and with the Advice and Consent of the Senate, to make Treaties, provided two thirds of the Senators present concur; and he shall nominate, and by and with the Advice and Consent of the Senate, shall appoint Ambassadors, other public Ministers and Consuls, Judges of the Supreme Court, and all other Officers of the United States, whose Appointments are not herein otherwise provided for, and which shall be established by Law: but the Congress may by Law vest the Appointment of such inferior Officers, as they think proper, in the President alone, in the Courts of Law, or in the Heads of Departments.

67, 76
(Hamilton)

The President shall have Power to fill up all Vacancies that may happen during the Recess of the Senate, by granting Commissions which shall expire at the End of their next Session.

Section 3

[POWERS AND DUTIES OF THE PRESIDENT]

77 (Hamilton) 69, 77 (Hamilton) 77 (Hamilton) 69, 77 (Hamilton) 42 (Madison), 69, 77 (Hamilton) 78 (Hamilton) He shall from time to time give to the Congress Information of the State of the Union, and recommend to their Consideration such Measures as he shall judge necessary and expedient; he may, on extraordinary Occasions, convene both Houses, or either of them, and in Case of Disagreement between them, with Respect to the Time of Adjournment, he may adjourn them to such Time as he shall think proper; he shall receive Ambassadors and other public Ministers; he shall take Care that the Laws be faithfully executed, and shall Commission all the Officers of the United States.

Section 4

[IMPEACHMENT]

39 (Madison), 69 (Hamilton) The President, Vice-President and all civil Officers of the United States, shall be removed from Office on Impeachment for, and Conviction of, Treason, Bribery, or other high Crimes and Misdemeanors.

ARTICLE III

Section 1

[JUDICIAL POWER, TENURE OR OFFICE]

81, 82 (Hamilton) 65 (Hamilton) 78, 79 (Hamilton) The judicial Power of the United States, shall be vested in one Supreme Court, and in such inferior Courts as the Congress may from time to time ordain and establish. The Judges, both of the supreme and inferior Courts, shall hold their Offices during good Behavior, and shall, at stated Times, receive for their Services a Compensation, which shall not be diminished during their Continuance in Office.

Section 2

[JURISDICTION]

80 (Hamilton) The judicial Power shall extend to all Cases, in Law and Equity, arising under this Constitution, the Laws of the United States, and Treaties made, or which shall be made, under their Authority;—to all Cases affecting Ambassadors, other public Ministers and Consuls;—to all Cases of admiralty and maritime Jurisdiction;—to Controversies to which the United States shall be a party;—to Controversies between two or more States;—*between a State and Citizens of another State*;—between Citizens of different States,—between Citizens of the same State claiming

Lands under Grants of different States, *and between a State*, or the Citizens thereof, *and foreign States, Citizens or Subjects.**

81
(Hamilton)

In all Cases affecting Ambassadors, other public Ministers and Consuls, and those in which a State shall be Party, the supreme Court shall have original Jurisdiction. In all the other Cases before mentioned, the Supreme Court shall have appellate Jurisdiction, both as to Law and Fact, with such Exceptions, and under such Regulations as the Congress shall make.

83, 84
(Hamilton)

The Trial of all Crimes, except in Cases of Impeachment, shall be by Jury; and such Trial shall be held in the State where the said Crimes shall have been committed; but when not committed within any State, the Trial shall be at such Place or Places as the Congress may by Law have directed.

Section 3

[TREASON, PROOF, AND PUNISHMENT]

43
(Madison),

98
(Hamilton)

Treason against the United States, shall consist only in levying War against them, or in adhering to their Enemies, giving them Aid and Comfort. No Person shall be convicted of Treason unless on the Testimony of two Witnesses to the same overt Act, or on Confession in open Court.

43
(Madison),
84
(Hamilton)

The Congress shall have Power to declare the Punishment of Treason, but no Attainder of Treason shall work Corruption of Blood, or Forfeiture except during the Life of the Person attained.

ARTICLE IV

Section 1

[FAITH AND CREDIT AMONG STATES]

42
(Madison)

Full Faith and Credit shall be given in each State to the public Acts, Records, and judicial Proceedings of every other State. And the Congress may by general Laws prescribe the Manner in which such Acts, Records and Proceedings shall be proved, and the Effect thereof.

Section 2

[PRIVILEGES AND IMMUNITIES, FUGITIVES]

80
(Hamilton)

The Citizens of each State shall be entitled to all Privileges and Immunities of Citizens in the several States.

A Person charged in any State with Treason, Felony, or other Crime, who shall flee from Justice, and be found in another State, shall on demand of the executive Authority of the State from

* [Modified by Eleventh Amendment.]

which he fled, be delivered up, to be removed to the State having Jurisdiction of the Crime.

*No Person held to Service or Labour in one State, under the Laws thereof, escaping into another, shall, in Consequence of any Law or Regulation therein, be discharged from such Service or Labour, but shall be delivered up on Claim of the Party to whom such Service or Labour may be due.**

Section 3

[ADMISSION OF NEW STATES]

43
(Madison)

New States may be admitted by the Congress into this Union; but no new States shall be formed or erected within the Jurisdiction of any other State; nor any State be formed by the Junction of two or more States, or Parts of States, without the Consent of the Legislatures of the States concerned as well as of the Congress.

43
(Madison)

The Congress shall have Power to dispose of and make all needful Rules and Regulations respecting the Territory or other Property belonging to the United States; and nothing in this Constitution shall be so construed as to Prejudice any Claims of the United States, or of any particular State.

Section 4

[GUARANTEE OF REPUBLICAN GOVERNMENT]

39, 43
(Madison)

The United States shall guarantee to every State in this Union a Republican Form of Government, and shall protect each of them against Invasion; and on Application of the Legislature, or of the Executive (when the Legislature cannot be convened) against domestic Violence.

ARTICLE V

[AMENDMENT OF THE CONSTITUTION]

39, 43
(Madison)
85
(Hamilton)

The Congress, whenever two-thirds of both Houses shall deem it necessary, shall propose Amendments to this Constitution, or, on the Application of the Legislatures of two-thirds of the several States, shall call a Convention for proposing Amendments, which, in either Case, shall be valid to all Intents and Purposes, as Part of this Constitution, when ratified by the Legislatures of three-fourths of the several States, or by Conventions in three-fourths thereof, as the one or the other Mode of Ratification may be proposed by the Congress; *Provided that no Amend-*

* [Repealed by the Thirteenth Amendment.]

ment which may be made prior to the Year One thousand eight hundred and eight shall in any Manner affect the first and fourth Clauses in the Ninth Section of the first Article;* and that no State, without its Consent, shall be deprived of its equal Suffrage in the Senate.

43
(Madison)

ARTICLE VI

[DEBTS, SUPREMACY, OATH]

43
(Madison)

All Debts contracted and Engagements entered into, before the Adoption of this Constitution, shall be as valid against the United States under this Constitution, as under the Confederation.

27, 33
(Hamilton),
39, 44
(Madison)

This Constitution, and the Laws of the United States which shall be made in Pursuance thereof; and all Treaties made, or which shall be made, under the Authority of the United States, shall be the supreme Law of the Land; and the Judges in every State shall be bound thereby, any Thing in the Constitution or Laws of any State to the Contrary notwithstanding.

27
(Hamilton),
44
(Madison)

The Senators and Representatives before mentioned, and the Members of the several State Legislatures, and all executive and judicial Officers, both of the United States and of the several States, shall be bound by Oath or Affirmation, to support this Constitution; but no religious Test shall ever be required as a Qualification to any Office or public Trust under the United States.

ARTICLE VII

[RATIFICATION AND ESTABLISHMENT]

39, 40, 43
(Madison)

The Ratification of the Conventions of nine States, shall be sufficient for the Establishment of this Constitution between the States so ratifying the Same.†

Done in Convention by the Unanimous Consent of the States present the Seventeenth Day of September in the Year of our Lord one thousand seven hundred and Eighty seven and of the Independence of the United States of America the Twelfth. *In Witness* whereof We have hereunto subscribed our Names,

G:⁰ WASHINGTON—
*Presidt, and Deputy
from Virginia*

* [Temporary provision.]
† [The Constitution was submitted on September 17, 1787, by the Constitutional Convention, was ratified by the conventions of several states at various dates up to May 29, 1790, and became effective on March 4, 1789.]

New Hampshire	JOHN LANGDON NICHOLAS GILMAN	Delaware	GEO READ GUNNING BEDFOR JUN JOHN DICKINSON RICHARD BASSETT JACO: BROOM
Massachusetts	NATHANIEL GORHAM RUFUS KING		
Connecticut	WM SAML JOHNSON ROGER SHERMAN	Maryland	JAMES MCHENRY DAN OF ST THOS. JENIFER DANL CARROLL
New York	ALEXANDER HAMILTON		
New Jersey	WIL: LIVINGSTON DAVID BREARLEY WM PATERSON JONA: DAYTON	Virginia	JOHN BLAIR— JAMES MADISON JR.
		North Carolina	WM BLOUNT RICHD DOBBS SPAIGHT HU WILLIAMSON
Pennsylvania	B FRANKLIN THOMAS MIFFLIN ROBT MORRIS GEO. CLYMER THOS. FITZSIMONS JARED INGERSOLL JAMES WILSON GOUV MORRIS	South Carolina	J. RUTLEDGE CHARLES COTESWORTH PINCKNEY CHARLES PINCKNEY PIERCE BUTLER
		Georgia	WILLIAM FEW ABR BALDWIN

Amendments to the Constitution

Proposed by Congress and Ratified
by the Legislatures of the Several States,
Pursuant to Article V of the Original Constitution.

Amendments I–X, known as the Bill of Rights, were proposed by Congress on September 25, 1789, and ratified on December 15, 1791. Federalist Papers comments, mainly in opposition to a Bill of Rights, can be found in #84 (Hamilton).

AMENDMENT I

[FREEDOM OF RELIGION, OF SPEECH, AND OF THE PRESS]
Congress shall make no law respecting an establishment of religion, or prohibiting the free exercise thereof; or abridging the freedom of speech, or of the press; or the right of the people peaceably to assemble, and to petition the Government for a redress of grievances.

AMENDMENT II

[RIGHT TO KEEP AND BEAR ARMS]
A well regulated Militia, being necessary to the security of a free State, the right of the people to keep and bear Arms, shall not be infringed.

AMENDMENT III

[QUARTERING OF SOLDIERS]
No Soldier shall, in time of peace be quartered in any house, without the consent of the Owner, nor in time of war, but in a manner to be prescribed by law.

AMENDMENT IV

[SECURITY FROM UNWARRANTABLE SEARCH AND SEIZURE]

The right of the people to be secure in their persons, houses, papers, and effects, against unreasonable searches and seizures, shall not be violated, and no Warrants shall issue, but upon probable cause, supported by Oath or affirmation, and particularly describing the place to be searched, and the persons or things to be seized.

AMENDMENT V

[RIGHTS OF ACCUSED PERSONS IN CRIMINAL PROCEEDINGS]

No person shall be held to answer for a capital, or otherwise infamous crime, unless on a presentment or indictment of a Grand Jury, except in cases arising in the land or naval forces, or in the Militia, when in actual service in time of War or public danger; nor shall any person be subject for the same offence to be twice put in jeopardy of life or limb; nor shall be compelled in any Criminal Case to be a witness against himself, nor be deprived of life, liberty, or property, without due process of law; nor shall private property be taken for public use, without just compensation.

AMENDMENT VI

[RIGHT TO SPEEDY TRIAL, WITNESSES, ETC.]

In all criminal prosecutions, the accused shall enjoy the right to a speedy and public trial, by an impartial jury of the State and district wherein the crime shall have been committed, which district shall have been previously ascertained by law, and to be informed of the nature and cause of the accusation; to be confronted with the witnesses against him; to have compulsory process for obtaining Witnesses in his favor, and to have the Assistance of Counsel for his defence.

AMENDMENT VII

[TRIAL BY JURY IN CIVIL CASES]

In suits at common law, where the value in controversy shall exceed twenty dollars, the right of trial by jury shall be preserved, and no fact tried by a jury shall be otherwise re-examined in any Court of the United States, than according to the rules of the common law.

AMENDMENT VIII

[BAILS, FINES, PUNISHMENTS]
Excessive bail shall not be required, nor excessive fines imposed, nor cruel and unusual punishments inflicted.

AMENDMENT IX

[RESERVATION OF RIGHTS OF PEOPLE]
The enumeration in the Constitution, of certain rights, shall not be construed to deny or disparage others retained by the people.

AMENDMENT X

[POWERS RESERVED TO STATES OR PEOPLE]
The powers not delegated to the United States by the Constitution, nor prohibited by it to the States, are reserved to the States respectively, or to the people.

AMENDMENT XI

[Proposed by Congress on March 4, 1794; declared ratified on January 8, 1798.]

[RESTRICTION OF JUDICIAL POWER]
The Judicial power of the United States shall not be construed to extend to any suit in law or equity, commenced or prosecuted against one of the United States by Citizens of another State, or by Citizens or Subjects of any foreign State.

AMENDMENT XII

[Proposed by Congress on December 9, 1803; declared ratified on September 25, 1804.]

[ELECTION OF PRESIDENT AND VICE-PRESIDENT]
The Electors shall meet in their respective states, and vote by ballot for President and Vice-President, one of whom, at least, shall not be an inhabitant of the same state with themselves; they shall name in their ballots the person voted for as President, and in distinct ballots the person voted for as Vice-President, and they shall make distinct lists of all persons voted for as President, and of all persons voted for as Vice-President, and of the number of votes for each, which lists they shall sign and certify, and transmit sealed to the seat of the government of the United States, directed to the President of the Senate;—The President of the Senate shall, in presence of the Senate and House of Representatives, open all the certificates and the votes shall then be counted;—The

person having the greatest number of votes for President, shall be the President, if such number be a majority of the whole number of Electors appointed; and if no person have such majority, then from the persons having the highest numbers not exceeding three on the list of those voted for as President, the House of Representatives shall choose immediately, by ballot, the President. But in choosing the President, the votes shall be taken by states, the representation from each state having one vote; a quorum for this purpose shall consist of a member or members from two-thirds of the states, and a majority of all the states shall be necessary to a choice. And if the House of Representatives shall not choose a President whenever the right of choice shall devolve upon them, before the fourth day of March next following, then the Vice-President shall act as President, as in the case of the death or other constitutional disability of the President. The person having the greatest number of votes as Vice-President, shall be the Vice-President, if such number be a majority of the whole number of Electors appointed, and if no person have a majority, then from the two highest numbers on the list, the Senate shall choose the Vice-President; a quorum for the purpose shall consist of two-thirds of the whole number of Senators, and a majority of the whole number shall be necessary to a choice. But no person constitutionally ineligible to the office of President shall be eligible to that of Vice-President of the United States.

AMENDMENT XIII

[Proposed by Congress on January 31, 1865; declared ratified on December 18, 1865.]

Section 1

[ABOLITION OF SLAVERY]

Neither slavery nor involuntary servitude, except as a punishment for crime whereof the party shall have been duly convicted, shall exist within the United States, or any place subject to their jurisdiction.

Section 2

[POWER TO ENFORCE THIS ARTICLE]

Congress shall have power to enforce this article by appropriate legislation.

AMENDMENT XIV

[Proposed by Congress on June 13, 1866, declared ratified on July 28, 1868.]

Section 1

[CITIZENSHIP RIGHTS NOT TO BE ABRIDGED BY STATES]

All persons born or naturalized in the United States, and subject to the jurisdiction thereof, are citizens of the United States and of the State wherein they reside. No state shall make or enforce any law which shall abridge the privileges or immunities of citizens of the United States; nor shall any State deprive any person of life, liberty, or property, without due process of law; nor deny to any person within its jurisdiction the equal protection of the laws.

Section 2

[APPORTIONMENT OF REPRESENTATIVES IN CONGRESS]

Representatives shall be apportioned among the several States according to their respective numbers, counting the whole number of persons in each State, excluding Indians not taxed. But when the right to vote at any election for the choice of electors for President and Vice-President of the United States, Representatives in Congress, the Executive and Judicial officers of a State, or the members of the Legislature thereof, is denied to any of the male inhabitants of such State, being twenty-one years of age, and citizens of the United States, or in any way abridged, except for participation in rebellion, or other crime, the basis of representation therein shall be reduced in the proportion which the number of such male citizens shall bear to the whole number of male citizens twenty-one years of age in such State.

Section 3

[PERSONS DISQUALIFIED FROM HOLDING OFFICE]

No person shall be a Senator or Representative in Congress, or elector of President and Vice-President, or hold any office, civil or military, under the United States, or under any State, who, having previously taken an oath, as a member of Congress, or as an officer of the United States, or as a member of any State legislature, or as an executive or judicial officer of any State, to support the Constitution of the United States, shall have engaged in insurrection or rebellion against the same, or given aid or comfort to the enemies thereof. But Congress may by a vote of two-thirds of each House, remove such disability.

Section 4

[WHAT PUBLIC DEBTS ARE VALID]

The validity of the public debt of the United States, authorized by law, including debts incurred for payment of pensions and bounties for services in suppressing insurrection or rebellion, shall not be questioned. But neither the United States nor any State shall assume or pay any debt or obligation incurred in aid of insurrection or rebellion against the United States, or any claim for the loss or emancipation of any slave; but all such debts, obligations and claims shall be held illegal and void.

Section 5

[POWER TO ENFORCE THIS ARTICLE]

The Congress shall have power to enforce, by appropriate legislation, the provisions of this article.

AMENDMENT XV

[Proposed by Congress on February 26, 1869; declared ratified on March 30, 1870.]

Section 1

[BLACK SUFFRAGE]

The right of citizens of the United States to vote shall not be denied or abridged by the United States or by any State on account of race, color, or previous condition of servitude.

Section 2

[POWER TO ENFORCE THIS ARTICLE]

The Congress shall have power to enforce this article by appropriate legislation.

AMENDMENT XVI

[Proposed by Congress on July 12, 1909; declared ratified on February 25, 1913.]

[AUTHORIZING INCOME TAXES]

The Congress shall have power to lay and collect taxes on incomes, from whatever source derived, without apportionment among the several States, and without regard to any census or enumeration.

Amendment XVII

[Proposed by Congress on May 13, 1912; declared ratified on May 31, 1913.]

[POPULAR ELECTION OF SENATORS]

The Senate of the United States shall be composed of two Senators from each State, elected by the people thereof, for six years; and each Senator shall have one vote. The electors in each State shall have the qualifications requisite for electors of the most numerous branch of the State Legislature.

When vacancies happen in the representation of any State in the Senate, the executive authority of such State shall issue writs of election to fill such vacancies: Provided, That the Legislature of any State may empower the executive thereof to make temporary appointments until the people fill the vacancies by election as the Legislature may direct.

This amendment shall not be so construed as to affect the election or term of any Senator chosen before it becomes valid as part of the Constitution.

Amendment XVIII

[Proposed by Congress December 18, 1917; declared ratified on January 29, 1919.]

Section 1

[NATIONAL LIQUOR PROHIBITION]

After one year from the ratification of this article, the manufacture, sale, or transportation of intoxicating liquors within, the importation thereof into, or the exportation thereof from the United States and all territory subject to the jurisdiction thereof for beverage purposes is hereby prohibited.

Section 2

[POWER TO ENFORCE THIS ARTICLE]

Congress and the several states shall have concurrent power to enforce this article by appropriate legislation.

Section 3

[RATIFICATION WITHIN SEVEN YEARS]

This article shall be inoperative unless it shall have been ratified as an amendment to the Constitution by the legislatures of the several states, as provided in the Constitution, within seven years from the date of the submission hereof to the states by Congress.*

* [Repealed by the Twenty-first Amendment.]

AMENDMENT XIX

[Proposed by Congress on June 4, 1919; declared ratified on August 26, 1920.]

[FEMALE SUFFRAGE]

The right of the citizens of the United States to vote shall not be denied or abridged by the United States or by any state on account of sex.

Congress shall have power, by appropriate legislation, to enforce this article by appropriate legislation.

AMENDMENT XX

[Proposed by Congress on March 2, 1932; declared ratified on February 6, 1933.]

Section 1

[TERMS OF OFFICE]

The terms of the President and Vice-President shall end at noon on the 20th day of January, and the terms of Senators and Representatives at noon on the 3rd day of January, of the years in which such terms would have ended if this article had not been ratified; and the terms of their successors shall then begin.

Section 2

[TIME OF CONVENING CONGRESS]

The Congress shall assemble at least once in every year, and such meeting shall begin at noon on the 3rd day of January, unless they shall by law appoint a different day.

Section 3

[DEATH OF PRESIDENT-ELECT]

If, at the time fixed for the beginning of the term of the President, the President-elect shall have died, the Vice-President-elect shall become President. If a President shall not have been chosen before the time fixed for the beginning of his term, or if the President-elect shall have failed to qualify, then the Vice-President-elect shall act as President until a President shall have qualified; and the Congress may by law provide for the case wherein neither a President-elect nor a Vice-President-elect shall have qualified, declaring who shall then act as President, or the manner in which one who is to act shall be selected, and such person shall act accordingly until a President or Vice-President shall have qualified.

AMENDMENTS TO THE CONSTITUTION **723**

Section 4

[ELECTION OF THE PRESIDENT]
The Congress may by law provide for the case of the death of any of the persons from whom the House of Representatives may choose a President whenever the right of choice shall have devolved upon them, and for the case of the death of any of the persons from whom the Senate may choose a Vice-President whenever the right of choice shall have devolved upon them.

Section 5

[AMENDMENT TAKES EFFECT]
Sections 1 and 2 shall take effect on the 15th day of October following ratification of this article.

Section 6

[RATIFICATION WITHIN SEVEN YEARS]
This article shall be inoperative unless it shall have been ratified as an amendment to the Constitution by the legislatures of three-fourths of the several States within seven years from the date of its submission.

AMENDMENT XXI

[Proposed by Congress on February 20, 1933; declared ratified on December 5, 1933.]

Section 1

[NATIONAL LIQUOR PROHIBITION REPEALED]
The eighteenth article of amendment to the Constitution of the United States is hereby repealed.

Section 2

[TRANSPORTATION OF LIQUOR INTO "DRY" STATES]
The transportation or importation into any State, Territory, or Possession of the United States for delivery or use therein of intoxicating liquors, in violation of the laws thereof, is hereby prohibited.

Section 3

[RATIFICATION WITHIN SEVEN YEARS]
The article shall be inoperative unless it shall have been ratified as an amendment to the Constitution by conventions in the several States, as provided in the Constitution, within seven years from the date of the submission hereof to the States by the Congress.

AMENDMENT XXII

[Proposed by Congress on March 21, 1947; declared ratified on February 26, 1951.]

Section 1

[TENURE OF PRESIDENT LIMITED]

No person shall be elected to the office of the President more than twice, and no person who has held the office of President or acted as President for more than two years of a term to which some other person was elected President shall be elected to the Office of the President more than once. But this Article shall not apply to any person holding the office of President when this Article was proposed by the Congress, and shall not prevent any person who may be holding the office of President, or acting as President, during the term within which this Article becomes operative from holding the office of President or acting as President during the remainder of such term.

Section 2

[RATIFICATION WITHIN SEVEN YEARS]

This Article shall be inoperative unless it shall have been ratified as an amendment to the Constitution by the legislatures of three-fourths of the several states within seven years from the date of its submission to the States by the Congress.

AMENDMENT XXIII

[Proposed by Congress on June 21, 1960; declared ratified on March 29, 1961.]

Section 1

[ELECTORAL COLLEGE VOTES FOR THE DISTRICT OF COLUMBIA]

The District constituting the seat of Government of the United States shall appoint in such manner as the Congress may direct:

A number of electors of President and Vice-President equal to the whole number of Senators and Representatives in Congress to which the District would be entitled if it were a State, but in no event more than the least populous State; they shall be in addition to those appointed by the States, but they shall be considered, for the purposes of the election of President and Vice-President, to be electors appointed by a State; and they shall meet in the District and perform such duties as provided by the twelfth article of amendment.

Section 2

[POWER TO ENFORCE THIS ARTICLE]

The Congress shall have power to enforce this article by appropriate legislation.

AMENDMENT XXIV

[Proposed by Congress on August 27, 1963; declared ratified on January 23, 1964.]

Section 1

[ANTI-POLL TAX]

The right of citizens of the United States to vote in any primary or other election for President or Vice-President, for electors for President or Vice-President, or for Senator or Representative in Congress, shall not be denied or abridged by the United States or any State by reason of failure to pay any poll tax or other tax.

Section 2

[POWER TO ENFORCE THIS ARTICLE]

The Congress shall have power to enforce this article by appropriate legislation.

AMENDMENT XXV

[Proposed by Congress on July 7, 1965; declared ratified on February 10, 1967.]

Section 1

[VICE-PRESIDENT TO BECOME PRESIDENT]

In case of the removal of the President from office or his death or resignation, the Vice-President shall become President.

Section 2

[CHOICE OF A NEW VICE-PRESIDENT]

Whenever there is a vacancy in the office of the Vice-President, the President shall nominate a Vice-President who shall take office upon confirmation by a majority vote of both houses of Congress.

Section 3

[PRESIDENT MAY DECLARE OWN DISABILITY]

Whenever the President transmits to the President pro tempore of the Senate and the Speaker of the House of Representatives his written declaration that he is unable to discharge the powers and duties of his office, and until he transmits to them a written declaration to the contrary, such powers and duties shall be discharged by the Vice-President as Acting President.

Section 4

[ALTERNATE PROCEDURES TO DECLARE AND TO END PRESIDENTIAL DISABILITY]

Whenever the Vice-President and a majority of either the principal officers of the executive departments or of such other body as Congress may by law provide, transmit to the President pro tempore of the Senate and the Speaker of the House of Representatives their written declaration that the President is unable to discharge the powers and duties of his office, the Vice-President shall immediately assume the powers and duties of the office as Acting President.

Thereafter, when the President transmits to the President pro tempore of the Senate and the Speaker of the House of Representatives his written declaration that no inability exists, he shall resume the powers and duties of his office unless the Vice-President and a majority of either the principal officers of the executive department or of such other body as Congress may by law provide, transmit within four days to the President pro tempore of the Senate and the Speaker of the House of Representatives their written declaration that the President is unable to discharge the powers and duties of his office. Thereupon Congress shall decide the issue, assembling within 48 hours for that purpose if not in session. If the Congress, within 21 days after receipt of the latter written declaration, or, if Congress is not in session, within 21 days after Congress is required to assemble, determines by two-thirds vote of both houses that the President is unable to discharge the powers and duties of his office, the Vice-President shall continue to discharge the same as Acting President; otherwise, the President shall resume the powers and duties of his office.

AMENDMENT XXVI

[Proposed by Congress on March 23, 1971; declared ratified on June 30, 1971.]

Section 1

[EIGHTEEN-YEAR-OLD SUFFRAGE]

The right of citizens of the United States, who are eighteen years of age or older, to vote shall not be denied or abridged by the United States or by any State on account of age.

Section 2

[power to enforce this article]
The Congress shall have power to enforce this article by appropriate legislation.

Amendment XXVII

[limiting congressional pay changes]
[Proposed by Congress on September 25, 1789; ratified on May 7, 1992.]

No law varying the compensation for the services of the Senators and Representatives shall take effect until an election of Representatives shall have intervened.

Acknowledgments

Aizenman, Nurith C. "The Case for More Regulation" from *The Washington Monthly*, October 1997, Vol. 9, Issue 10, pp. 16–21. Reprinted with permission from *The Washington Monthly*. Copyright by Washington Monthly Publishing, LLC, 1319 F St. NW, Suite 710, Washington, DC 20004.

Annas, George J. "Jumping Frogs, Endangered Toads, and California's Medical-Marijuana Law" from *The New England Journal of Medicine*, Vol. 353, Issue 21, pp. 2291–2296. Copyright © 2005 Massachusetts Medical Society. All rights reserved.

Beard, Charles A. Reprinted with the permission of Scribner, an imprint of Simon & Schuster Adult Publishing Group from *The Economic Interpretation of the Constitution of the United States* by Charles A. Beard. Copyright © 1935 by The Macmillan Company, Inc.; copyright © renewed 1963 by William Beard and Mrs. Miriam Beard Vagts. All rights reserved.

Brown, Robert E. *Charles Beard and the Constitution.* © 1956 Princeton University Press, 1984 renewed PUP. Reprinted by permission of Princeton University Press.

Burtless, Gary. "Growing American Inequality: Source and Remedies." From *Brookings Review* (Winter 1999). Reprinted with the permission of The Brookings Institution, Washington, DC.

Citizens Against Government Waste. "Introduction to *The Pig Book*." May 2004. Copyright © 2004 *Congressional Book Summary* by Citizens Against Government Waste.

Cohn, Jonathan. "Roll Out the Barrel: The Case Against the Case Against Pork." Reprinted with the permission of *The New Republic*, Copyright © 2002, The New Republic, LLC.

Cole, David and James X. Dempsey. Excerpt from the conclusion of *Terrorism and the Constitution: Sacrificing Civil Liberties in the Name of National Security*, 3rd Edition, 2006, pp. 239–50. © 2002, 2006 by the First Amendment Foundation. Reprinted with the permission of The New Press. www.thenewpress.com.

Cox, Meg E. "Access Denied" from the *Christian Century* Vol. 124: No. 12. Copyright © 2007 by the *Christian Century*. Reprinted by permission from the June 12, 2007, issue of the *Christian Century*.

Elazar, Daniel. "The Political Subcultures of the United States" from *American Mosaic: The Impact of Space, Time, and Culture on American Politics*, pp. 229–36, 239–46. Copyright © 1994 by Westview Press. Reprinted by permission of Westview Press, a member of Perseus Books Group.

Fiorina, Morris P. "The Decline of Collective Responsibility in American Politics." Reprinted by permission of *Daedalus*, Journal of the American Academy of Arts and Sciences, from the issue entitled "The End of Consensus?" (Summer 1980), Vol. 109, No. 3. "*What* Culture Wars?" in *The Wall Street Journal* (July 14, 2004). "Letter to the Editor," in *Commentary* (May 2006). Reprinted by permission of the author.

Friedman, Leon. "Overruling the Court." Reprinted with permission from Leon Friedman, *The American Prospect*, Vol. 12, No. 15: August 26, 2001. The American Prospect, 2000 L Street NW, Suite 717, Washington, DC 20036. All rights reserved.

Gallup, George H. "Polling the Public" from *A Guide to Public Opinion Polls*. © 1944

730 ACKNOWLEDGMENTS

Princeton University Press, 1948 revised 2d Edition, 1975 renewed. Reprinted by permission of Princeton University Press.

Goldston, David. Reprinted by permission from Macmillan Publishers Ltd.: "Party of One: Over a Pork Barrel" from *Nature*, Vol. 447, No. 7145, June 7, 2007. Copyright © 2007, Nature Publishing Group.

Hacker, Jacob. "Health Care for America" from Economic Policy Institute EPI Briefing Paper #180, January 11, 2007. Reprinted by permission.

Hartz, Louis. "The Concept of a Liberal Society" from *The Liberal Tradition in America: An Interpretation of American Political Thought Since the Revolution*, copyright © 1955 and renewed 1983 by Louis Hartz, reprinted by permission of Harcourt, Inc.

Hibbing, John and Elizabeth Theiss-Morse: "Too Much of a Good Thing: More Representative Is Not Necessarily Better." *Political Science & Politics* (March 1998). Reprinted with the permission of the authors.

Holt, Jim. "The Human Factor." Originally published in *The New York Times Magazine*, © Jim Holt 2004. Reprinted by permission of the author.

Huntington, Samuel P. Excerpted from *Who Are We? The Challenges to America's National Identity* by Samuel P. Huntington. Copyright © 2004 by Samuel P. Huntington. Used by permission of Simon & Schuster Adult Publishing Group.

John, David C. "Providing Social Security Benefits in the Future." From The Heritage Foundation, March 25, 2004. Reprinted with the permission of the publisher.

Jones, Charles. "Perspectives on the Presidency." From *The Presidency in a Separated System*. Reprinted with the permission of The Brookings Institution, Washington, DC.

Kammen, Michael. "Introduction" by Michael Kammen, from *The Origins of the American Constitution*, edited by Michael Kammen, copyright © 1986 by Michael Kammen. Used by permission of Viking Penguin, a division of Penguin Group (USA) Inc.

Keisling, Phil. "Election Fraud, American Style" from *The Washington Monthly*, Dec. 2006, Vol. 38, Issue 12, pp. 46–49. Reprinted with permission from *The Washington Monthly*. Copyright by Washington Monthly Publishing, LLC, 1319 F St. NW, Suite 710, Washington, DC 20004.

Key, V. O., Jr. Reprinted by permission of the publisher from *The Responsible Electorate: Rationality in Presidential Voting, 1936–1960* by V. O. Key, Jr., with the assistance of Milton C. Cummings, Jr., pp. 1–8, Cambridge, Mass.: The Belknap Press of Harvard University Press, Copyright © 1966 by the President and Fellows of Harvard College.

King, Martin L., Jr. "Letter from a Birmingham Jail." Reprinted by arrangement with the Estate of Martin Luther King, Jr., c/o Writers House as agent for the proprietor, New York, NY. Copyright 1963 Dr. Martin Luther King, Jr., Copyright renewed 1991 Coretta Scott King.

Krugman, Paul and Robin Wells. "The Health Care Crisis and What to Do About It" from the *New York Review of Books*, Vol. 53, Issue 5, March 23, 2006.

Light, Paul C. "Preparing Americans for Disaster." This article first appeared in *The Christian Science Monitor* (www.csmonitor.com), December 12, 2005. Reprinted by permission of the author.

Lindblom, Charles. "The Science of Muddling Through." *Public Administration Review*, Vol. 19, No. 2: 79–88. Reprinted with permission of the publisher, American Society for Public Administration c/o Sun Trust Bank.

Lomborg, Bjørn. "Global Warming—Are We Doing the Right Thing?" from *The Guardian*, August 14, 2001. Reprinted by permission of the author.

Lowi, Theodore. "American Business, Public Policy, Case Studies & Political Theory." *World Politics* 16:4 (1964): 677–715. © The Johns Hopkins University Press. Reprinted with permission of The Johns Hopkins University Press.

Lustick, Ian. "Trapped in the War on Terror" from *Middle East Policy*, Vol. 13, No. 4: 2–7.

Mayhew, David. Congress: *The Electoral Connection* (1974). Copyright © 1974 by Yale University Press. Reprinted with the permission of Yale University Press.

Menand, Louis. "Patriot Games: The New Nativism of Samuel P. Huntington." First published in *The New Yorker* May 17, 2004 © by Louis Menand, permission of The Wylie Agency. "The Unpolitical Animal: How Political Science Understands Voters." Copyright © Louis Menand. Granted with the permission of the author.

Morin, Richard. "Choice Words." Copyright © 1999, *The Washington Post*.

Nagourney, Adam. "Internet Injects Sweeping Change into U.S. Politics" from *The New York Times*, April 2, 2006. Copyright © 2006 The New York Times. All rights reserved. Used by permission and protected by the Copyright Laws of the United States. The printing, copying, redistribution, or retransmission of the Material without express written permission is prohibited.

Neustadt, Richard E. Excerpt pp. 26–43 from *Presidential Power* by Richard E. Neustadt. Copyright © 1986 by Macmillan Publishing Company. Reprinted by permission of Pearson Education, Inc.

O'Brien, David M. "The Court and American Life" from *Storm Center: The Supreme Court in American Politics*, Third Edition by David M. O'Brien. Copyright © 1993, 1990, 1986 by David M. O'Brien. Used by permission of W. W. Norton & Company, Inc.

Olson, Mancur. "The Logic of Collective Action" from *The Rise and Decline of Nations* (1982). Copyright © 1982 by Yale University Press. Reprinted with the permission of Yale University Press.

Parker, Richard. "Power to the Voters." *Harvard Journal of Law and Public Policy*. Vol. 24, No. 179 (2000). Reprinted by permission.

Perlmutter, David D. and Misti McDaniel. "The Ascent of Blogging" from *Nieman Reports*, Fall 2005, pp. 60–64.

Peterson, Paul. "The Price of Early Federalism." From *The Price of Federalism*. Copyright © 1995. Reprinted with the permission of publisher, The Brookings Institution.

Pfiffner, James P. "The First MBA President: George W. Bush as Public Administrator" from *Public Administration Review*, Vol. 67, Issue 1, Jan. 1, 2007. Copyright © 2007, Blackwell Publishing Ltd. Reprinted by permission of the publisher.

Pomper, Gerald. "Parliamentary Government in the United States." From *The State of the Parties*. Reprinted with the permission of the publisher, Rowman & Littlefield Publishers Inc.

Posner, Paul. "The Politics of Coercive Federalism in the Bush Era" from *Publius: Journal of Federalism*, Vol. 37, Issue 3 (2007), pp. 390–412. Reprinted by permission of Oxford University Press and the author.

Posner, Richard. "How Does National Security Shape Constitutional Rights?" from *Not a Suicide Pact: The Constitution in a Time of National Emergency*. Copyright © 2006 by Oxford University Press. Reprinted by permission of the author. "The Reorganized U.S. Intelligence System after One Year" from National Security Outlook, American Enterprise Institute Online, April 11, 2006. Reprinted with the permission of The American Enterprise Institute for Public Policy Research, Washington, DC.

Prior, Markus. "News vs. Entertainment: How Increasing Media Choice Widens Gaps in Political Knowledge and Turnout" from *American Journal of Political Science*, Vol. 49, Issue 3, July 2005. Copyright © 2005, Blackwell Publishers Ltd. Reprinted by permission of the publisher.

Rabe, Barry. "Environmental Policy and the Bush Era" from *Publius: Journal of Federalism*, Vol. 37, Issue 3 (2007), pp. 413–414, 422–431. Reprinted by permission of Oxford University Press.

Rauch, Jonathan. "In Defense of Prejudice." Copyright © 1995 by *Harper's Magazine*. All rights reserved. Reproduced from the May issue by special permission. "Objections to These Unions" © 2004 Jonathan Rauch. First published in *Reason*, (June 2004); this article is an excerpt from the author's book *Gay Marriage: Why It Is Good for Gays, Good for Straights and Good for America.* (Henry Holt and Co., 2004). "The Hyperpluralism Trap" © 1994

Jonathan Rauch. First published in *The New Republic* (June 1994). Reprinted with the permission of the author.

Rowe, Jonathan. "The GDP Myth: Why Growth Isn't Always a Good Thing" from *The Washington Monthly*, March 1999, Vol. 31, Issue 3, pp. 17–21. Reprinted with permission from *The Washington Monthly*. Copyright by Washington Monthly Publishing, LLC, 1319 F St. NW, Suite 710, Washington, DC 20004.

Scheufele, Dietram A. and David Tewksbury. "Framing, Agenda Setting, and Priming: The Evolution of Three Media Effects Models" from *Journal of Communication*, Vol. 57, Issue 1, March 2007. Copyright © 2007, Blackwell Publishing Ltd. Reprinted by permission of the publisher.

Scruton, Roger. "What Is Acceptable Risk?" *City Journal*, Vol. 11, No. 1 (Winter 01). Reprinted with the permission of the publisher, City Journal c/o Manhattan Institute.

Simendinger, Alexis. "Presidency—Politics Squared." Reprinted with permission from *National Journal*, June 2, 2007. Copyright 2007 by National Journal Group, Inc. All rights reserved.

Skocpol, Theda. Reprinted with permission from "Associations Without Members" by Theda Skocpol in *The American Prospect*, Volume 10, Number 45: July 1, 1999. The American Prospect, 2000 L Street NW, Suite 717, Washington, DC 20036. All rights reserved.

Smith, Rogers. "Beyond Tocqueville, Myrdal and Hartz: The Multiple Traditions in America" from *American Political Science Review*, Vol. 87, No. 3 (September 1993). Reprinted with the permission of Cambridge University Press.

Soros, George. "The Age of Open Society." From *The New Era*. Reprinted with the permission of the author.

Sundquist, James L. "Needed: A Political Theory for the New Era of Coalition Government in the United States" by James L. Sundquist from *Political Science Quarterly*. Reprinted by permission from *Political Science Quarterly* 103 (Winter 1988): 613–635.

Sutherland, Peter. "Reality Check." *Harvard International Review* (Winter 2000). Reprinted with permission of the publisher.

Teague, Peter. Reprinted with permission from Peter Teague, "Global Warming in an Age of Energy Anxiety," *The American Prospect Online*: June 26, 2007. The American Prospect, 2000 L Street NW, Suite 717, Washington, DC 20036. All rights reserved.

Tocqueville, Alexis de. "Political Associations in the United States." From *Democracy in America*, edited by J. P. Mayer and Max Lerner, translated by George Lawrence. English translation copyright © 1965 by Harper & Row, Publishers, Inc.

Truman, David B. "The Alleged Mischiefs of Faction" from *The Governmental Process* (Knopf, 1971). Reprinted with permission of Edwin M. Truman.

Turner, Grace-Marie. "Toward Free-Market Health Care," Heritage Lecture #1019, March 26, 2007. Published by the Heritage Foundation. Reprinted by permission.

Williams, Bob. "Election Fraud: Remains Commonplace." Reprinted with permission from *USA Today the Magazine*, November 2005. Copyright © 2005 by the Society for the Advancement of Education, Inc. All Rights Reserved.

Williams, David E. *2007 Congressional Pig Book® Summary*. Reprinted by permission of the author.

Wilson, James Q. "How Divided Are We?" © James Q. Wilson. Reprinted from *Commentary*, February 2006, by permission; all rights reserved. From *Bureaucracy: What Government Agencies Do & Why They Do It* by James Q. Wilson. Copyright © 1989 by Basic Books, Inc. Reprinted by permission of Basic Books, a member of Perseus Books Group.

Every effort has been made to contact the copyright holder of each of the selections. Rights holders of any selections not credited should contact Permissions Department, W. W. Norton & Company, Inc., 500 Fifth Avenue, New York, NY 10110, in order for a correction to be made in the next reprinting of our work.